R. Yates
DCS
Nov. 99

D1031840

THE LOEB CLASSICAL LIBRARY

FOUNDED BY JAMES LOEB

EDITED BY

G. P. GOOLD

PREVIOUS EDITORS

| T. E. PAGE | E. CAPPS |
| W. H. D. ROUSE | L. A. POST |

E. H. WARMINGTON

SELECT PAPYRI

II

LCL 282

SELECT PAPYRI

OFFICIAL DOCUMENTS

WITH AN ENGLISH TRANSLATION BY

A. S. HUNT

AND

C. C. EDGAR

HARVARD UNIVERSITY PRESS

CAMBRIDGE, MASSACHUSETTS

LONDON, ENGLAND

First published 1934
Reprinted 1956, 1963, 1977, 1995

ISBN 0-674-99312-8

Printed in Great Britain by St Edmundsbury Press Ltd,
Bury St Edmunds, Suffolk, on acid-free paper.
Bound by Hunter & Foulis Ltd, Edinburgh, Scotland.

CONTENTS

PREFACE

VOLUME I. of *Select Papyri* published in November 1932 consisted of documents dealing with private affairs ; the subject of its successor is public business, illustrated by documents emanating from or addressed to persons occupying official positions. As before, while endeavouring to tap new sources, we have necessarily included a number of texts figuring in other selections. Where English translations were already available these have again been freely utilized, though not without revision. The Explanatory Notes and Glossary of Technical Terms are reprinted with small alterations from Volume I. A selection from the new literary papyri is now in preparation and will follow in due course.

A. S. HUNT

February 1934

INTRODUCTION

THE papyri which are translated in this volume cover a span of nearly a thousand years, during which many changes took place in the government, institutions, customs, and religion of Egypt. It therefore seems desirable to give the reader to whom these matters are not familiar a brief sketch of some characteristic features of the different periods. Whoever wishes to study the subject more seriously will find in Bevan's *Ptolemaic Dynasty* and Milne's *Under Roman Rule* reliable summaries of the information yielded by the papyri and in Wilcken's *Grundzüge und Chrestomathie der Papyruskunde* a full and masterly survey of the whole material. The most that we can attempt here is to restate a few of the main facts, giving references to the texts which bear on them and confining ourselves to what seems useful for the understanding of the present selection.

Throughout the Ptolemaic period, which ended in 30 B.C., Egypt was an independent realm ; and for most of that period the kings, who resided in Alexandria, possessed territory or exercised suzerainty in various other parts of the Near East (see Nos. 267, 410). In Egypt itself the Ptolemies were not only absolute monarchs, but from about the middle of the 3rd century B.C. they assumed in their lifetime, along with their queens, the titles and honours of gods (*e.g.* Nos. 256, 272). They maintained an army and navy, held effective control over all departments of state, finance, justice, public works, etc., and kept the great native priesthood in strict subjection. Demands for redress, even on the part of humble villagers, were, at least in the earlier period, frequently addressed to the king (Nos. 268-270). Though as a rule these were dealt with by the local authorities, many petitions, as for instance No. 272, were actually examined and subscribed by the king himself and many judicial sentences were submitted to him for approval or modification. He promulgated financial and legal ordinances, the latter of which are referred to in No. 256, p. 195, and issued decrees on the most various subjects whether in the form of a letter or of an official edict. Nos. 207, 273, 411 afford examples of the questions about which he corresponded personally with his subordinates. Probably Philadelphus [a] took more interest in his work than most of his successors ; but whether the king himself was active or idle, the royal chancellery was always busy.

Apart from the palace secretaries, the most important official was the dioecetes, who is frequently mentioned in our texts (*e.g.* Nos. 409-411). He was the king's minister of finance, having as his chief duty the collection of revenue and possessing jurisdiction in matters affecting the Treasury. It was in his office that the regulations concerning the royal monopolies (see No. 203) were revised, and no doubt originally drafted, and it may be presumed that he took a large part in elaborating the details of taxation. The petition addressed to him by a citizen of Calynda, No. 267, shows that his influence was as

[a] 285-246 B.C.

powerful in the foreign cities under his master's suzerainty as in Egypt proper. His headquarters were in Alexandria and he had under him a certain number of sub-dioecetae (see No. 265), who probably had special districts allotted to them.

For purposes of administration the country was divided into districts called nomes, not unlike the modern *mudirias*. Each nome was governed by at least one official bearing the military title of strategus, and a group of nomes, at least in the later period, was probably placed under the authority of an epistrategus. The chief financial functionaries in the nomes were at first the so-called oeconomi (*e.g.* Nos. 203, 273), who were under the orders of the dioecetes and worked in close association with the district bankers appointed by the government; but after the 3rd century B.C. they become less prominent and are overshadowed by the strategus (*e.g.* No. 393). Other important officials were the nomarchs and toparchs, some of whose many functions are described in No. 203, and the royal scribes or secretaries, who assisted the oeconomus and the strategus. In the separate villages we find an epistates (*e.g.* No. 269), acting as head of the local police, a comarch (see No. 203), and a village scribe or secretary (Nos. 275, 276, 339).

The towns of Alexandria, Naucratis, and Ptolemais in Upper Egypt enjoyed an exceptional position, being organized more or less in the manner of autonomous Greek cities. For example, Alexandria had its own code of laws, of which excerpts are given in Nos. 201, 202, and the citizens were enrolled in tribes and demes, styling themselves, even when resident in other parts of Egypt, not Alexandrians, but members of such and such a deme (*e.g.* No. 253). But though these cities possessed a certain amount of self-administration and certain privileges, they were practically, like the rest of the country, in complete subjection to the king. Citizens of Alexandria could be called upon by him at any time to perform special services such as that of assize judges throughout the nomes in concert with his permanent officials (see No. 264).

The great bulk of the population was of course Egyptian. But, besides the inhabitants of the cities already mentioned, Greeks and Hellenized foreigners were settled in all parts of the interior, some as officials and soldiers in the king's service, others pursuing their private business. The soldiers of whom we hear most were cleruchs, men whom the king paid by grants of unoccupied land, a measure by which he not only increased the prosperity of the country but also held it in firmer domination; No. 412 is one of the many interesting documents on this subject. The Greeks who resided in the nomes kept up their own customs as far as possible, established gymnasia for the training of their youths, and held athletic and musical contests, such as the one referred to in No. 275. Jews are frequently mentioned, as for instance in No. 256, and it is not till the close of the Ptolemaic period that the papyri show any evidence of the prejudice against them which led to violent disturbances under Roman rule (Nos. 212, 298). No. 205 contains some regulations about the sale of slaves ; but in fact slaves did not form a large element in the population, manual labour being so cheap that there was no economic demand for them. Power and wealth were almost entirely in the hands of the Greek-speaking foreigners. The Egyptian masses, though nominally free, were exploited for the benefit of the Crown, overburdened with direct and indirect taxation, subject to compulsory labour, and forbidden to migrate at will from their domicile. Their discontent often culminated in a local revolt, such as the one spoken of in Nos. 417, 418. The class of natives which received most consideration was the priesthood, whose property and privileges were respected (see Nos. 210, 411) and whose gods were gradually adopted by the Greeks themselves. As time went on, the lower-class foreigners intermarried freely with the Egyptians, and a Greek or an Egyptian name occurring in a papyrus is not always a guarantee that the person who bore it was of pure Greek or pure Egyptian descent.

On the defeat of Antony and Cleopatra in 30 B.C. Egypt fell into the hands of Octavian, afterwards known as Augustus, and became a province of the Roman empire, or rather a preserve of the emperor, who was regarded by the Egyptians as the successor of the Pharaohs and Ptolemies. The Roman senate possessed no authority there, even of a nominal kind, and senators were jealously debarred from entering the country without express permission. The visit of Lucius Memmius recorded in No. 416 was merely a sign of the Romans' growing interest in Egypt; that of Germanicus, of which No. 211 is an interesting relic, infringed the imperial regulation and was viewed in Rome with disfavour and suspicion. The country was now governed by a praefect of equestrian rank appointed by the emperor and resident in Alexandria. Though matters of political importance, such as those dealt with in No. 212, and various other questions (*e.g.* No. 214) were decided in Rome, in practice it was the praefect rather than the distant emperor who took the place of the former king. The petitions which used to be addressed to the king were now presented to the praefect (see Section VII). He commanded the army, presided over the civil administration, and exercised jurisdiction, holding yearly assizes at certain towns. Examples of the cases which he decided, both legal and administrative, are given in Sections V. and VI. A high Roman official called the dicaeodotes or juridicus aided him in this branch of his work and also judged many cases separately (*e.g.* No. 263).

Though the powers of the great Ptolemaic dioecetes were taken over by the praefect, the title and no doubt many of the functions were given to a subordinate but important official (see No. 225) until some time in the 3rd century. The private revenue of the emperor, formerly that of the Ptolemies (see No. 367), was administered by the so-called idiologus, procurator of the privy purse, who was also high priest of all Egypt and exercised control over the temples and their property ; the interesting document No. 206 gives a picture of some of the affairs with which his department had to deal.

As in the Ptolemaic period, the unit of administration was still the nome, over which presided the strategus, assisted by the royal scribe, nomarchs, and other subordinates ; and in the villages the most active functionaries were still the village scribes, until in the 3rd century they were superseded by the comarchs. The nomes again were divided into three groups, each of which was governed by a

INTRODUCTION

Roman epistrategus appointed, like most of the higher officials, by the emperor ; a few records of his activities will be found in Sections V. and VI. The three Greek cities of Alexandria, Naucratis, and Ptolemais continued to enjoy their very limited autonomy, and a new city of similar standing, called Antinoopolis, was founded by the emperor Hadrian (see No. 288). The organization of magistracies, like that of Alexandria, in the nome-capitals brought them a step nearer self-government ; the names of the magistrates, gymnasiarch, exegetes, cosmetes, etc., occur continually in papyri of the Roman period ; and No. 241 contains an amusing account of the election of an unwilling nominee. In A.D. 202 the emperor Septimius Severus made a further innovation : in each nome-capital or metropolis, as well as in Alexandria from which this privilege had been hitherto withheld (see No. 212), he established a senate. The strategus was still governor of the nome, including the metropolis, but the senates now elected the municipal magistrates and also nominated many of the persons required for the performance of government duties, such as the decemprimi who supervised the collection of revenue and other public work throughout each nome (No. 225).

As regards the population, Romans had superseded Greeks as the upper class, though unlike the Greeks they had not imposed their language on the country. This privileged order included not only Romans by birth, who were comparatively few, but also natives of Egypt who had received the Roman citizenship, such as soldiers enrolled in a legion or honourably discharged from the auxiliary troops (No. 315). Next in standing came citizens of Alexandria and those Greeks throughout the country who were wholly or partially exempt from the poll-tax (see No. 314). Enrolment among the ephebi and membership of a gymnasium (see Nos. 299, 300) were the chief insignia of this class and the passport to a political career of a minor kind. Typically Hellenic were the honours bestowed upon successful athletes (Nos. 217, 306). As regards the lower orders, there was little change in their position ; they were no less oppressed and exploited by the Romans than they had been by the Ptolemies. Though predominantly Egyptian, they included more and more families of mixed nationality ; such names as Ptolemaeus son of Petosorapis (No. 316) or Tapesouris daughter of Isidora (No. 313) exemplify the fusion of the two races. In A.D. 212, by a decree of the emperor Marcus Aurelius Antoninus, known as Caracalla, the Roman citizenship was granted to all provincials of a certain standing, which in Egypt meant all persons exempt from payment of the full poll-tax, but not the subject masses whether they bore Egyptian or Greek names. The reader will notice how many individuals in the later documents call themselves Aurelius and Marcus Aurelius ; all these belong to the new class of Roman citizens, though they do not style themselves Romans.

The reforms of Diocletian at the end of the 3rd century introduced a new system of administration, and in the reign of Constantine the capital of the empire was transferred from Rome to Byzantium. Of this new system and of the changes which it underwent in the course of three hundred years we need only mention the few points that concern the texts selected for this volume. Egypt now formed part of the province of the praetorian praefect of the East, though not as a separate diocese until A.D. 381. The praefect of Egypt was deprived of his military command, but retained his former powers of administration and jurisdiction (*cf.* Nos. 227, 295). The country was divided into several large districts, which varied both in name and in extent at different periods (see Nos. 250, 333), and each of these was governed by a praeses who was subordinate to the praefect but transacted most of the business which the latter used to deal with in his former assizes. The Treasury was put under the charge of an official called the catholicus or rationalis (Nos. 227, 239, 294), who replaced the former dioecetes and idiologus and was independent of the praefect. In the reign of Justinian the main districts of Egypt became separate provinces, directly subject to the above-mentioned praetorian praefect. For instance Upper Egypt, called the Thebaid, was no longer under the control of a praefect in Alexandria, but was ruled by its own Dux et Augustalis, who exercised both military and civil powers, the praeses being subordinate to him. The important texts Nos. 218 and 363 belong to this phase of government, and No. 408 gives some idea of the pomp in which this great dignitary travelled.

Under the Byzantine system of government the strategus, so prominent in the former centuries, loses his importance and gradually disappears. His financial functions were taken over by the exactor, who was appointed for this service from among the members of the local senate, and the nome became the territory of what was formerly called its

INTRODUCTION

metropolis. No. 240 is an interesting record of the proceedings of a senate in the Byzantine period, showing how the district was administered through the senate, no longer taking orders from a strategus as in No. 226. The most important magistrates were now the logistes or curator, to whom was entrusted much of the administrative work formerly done by the strategus (Nos. 227, 333), and the defensor, to whom appeals for justice, as for instance No. 297, were now addressed. Another noticeable innovation is the division of the nome into numbered districts called pagi, each administered by a praepositus appointed by the senate. One notes the use of Latin alongside Greek in the official terminology of this period, as also in the minutes of legal proceedings (Nos. 250, 263).

The character of the population also changed. In Greek circles Hellenic culture gave way before Christianity ; ephebi and gymnasia were things of the past. Roman citizenship was granted to Egyptians and Graeco-Egyptians more and more freely, the Flavii becoming as common as the Aurelii, until finally the distinction between Romans and subjects vanished. But if the peasant masses were no longer stigmatized as a subject race, many of them were actually in stricter bondage than before. In the 4th and 5th centuries large tracts of land which formerly belonged to the state and to small owners had become the property of local magnates, and the peasants who had put themselves under their protection were reduced to the position of serfs tied to the soil ; see for instance Vol. I. No. 26. Many of these great land-owners held the office of pagarch, which in its later form was one of great

INTRODUCTION

authority and in particular gave them the right of collecting the public taxes in the districts which they ruled ; in No. 218 we have a striking example of the arrogance with which they sometimes exercised their powers.

The latest documents in this volume, Nos. 432-435, were written about seventy years after the Arab conquest, at a time when Greek was still in use as one of the official languages. Once more a ruling race was seated in Egypt ; but this time its claim to superiority was based not on nationality but on religion, and the cleavage between Moslem and Christian was more lasting than that between Greek and Egyptian in the Ptolemaic age or between Roman and non-Roman under the empire. Egypt was now administered by an Arab governor, who was appointed by the caliph and resided in the new city of Fustat at the south end of the modern Cairo. The Byzantine division of the country into provinces independent of each other had been swept away ; the municipalities had disappeared ; but the pagarchs, better suited to the actual conditions of the country, were still retained, and the pagarchy, like the nome of old, had become the unit of adminis-tration. The governor corresponded directly with the pagarchs ; for Basilius, whom he addresses in these letters as dioecetes or administrator, bears the title of pagarch in other documents. But whereas the Byzantine pagarchs acted almost as feudal lords, the tone and contents of these letters show how strictly their successors were controlled and called to account by the Arab government.

Conscription of labour for works of public utility was in Egypt an immemorial institution, to which

INTRODUCTION

there are many references in the papyri of all periods. No. 389 illustrates its most common object, the annual consolidation of the irrigation dykes. Apart from manual labour, we find in Ptolemaic papyri a few allusions to temporary duties imposed by the king and probably also by the governing bodies of the Greek cities. But it was not till the Roman period that the principle of compulsory service was adopted as the basis of an elaborate system. The tenure of various public offices became gradually an obligatory burden, from which only certain classes of people (see for example Nos. 217, 245, 285, 288) could claim exemption. In each town and village individuals who owned property of a certain value could be appointed to an office in correspondence with their means on the responsibility of the community or of the nominating functionaries. Nos. 342, 343 exemplify the procedure employed and the kind of work which they were called upon to perform ; but the mode of selection, nomination, and appointment varied from period to period. When the local senates were created, it was they who nominated the more important office-bearers not only in the towns but in the surrounding districts as well (Nos. 226, 237). In other cases we find a system of allotting certain duties to the inhabitants of each quarter of the town in rotation, the suitable persons being nominated by a local official (Nos. 290, 362). Even the magistracies themselves, such as the gymnasiarchship, became compulsory honours imposed upon such townsmen as were thought able to afford the expense involved ; No. 241 shows very clearly the reluctance with which they were sometimes undertaken. The main object of the system

INTRODUCTION

was to get public work done at private expense ; in effect it was a heavy tax on the moneyed classes and eventually brought them to ruin.

Another infliction which the inhabitants of Egypt had to endure was the custom of requisitioning food, labour, and means of transport on the occasion of visits from high officials or other great personages. No. 414 records a small contribution, only one of a hundred, to the larder of a travelling dioecetes. Distinguished tourists like the Roman senator in No. 416 were sumptuously entertained by the local officials, at the expense of the people. The coming of a king or emperor or praefect was awaited with apprehension ; in a letter not printed here the writer sends warning of the king's approach and suggests that the hay should be removed to a safer spot out of sight of the royal escort. The Byzantine account No. 408 gives some idea of what it cost to entertain the governor of the Thebaid for a fortnight. Lesser officials naturally followed the example of their superiors ; there are some references to their high-handed behaviour in No. 210 ; and even soldiers on their journeys (No. 221) were accustomed to help themselves to what they required.

Egypt's importance in the Graeco-Roman world was mainly due to the fertility of her soil, and agriculture has always been the chief employment of the population. In the Ptolemaic period probably the whole of the land belonged in theory to the king, and in any case the bulk of it was directly owned and managed by the Crown. The peasants who cultivated this Crown land held it on lease and paid rent in kind (No. 398), the leases being put up to auction from time to time. Their work was strictly

INTRODUCTION

superintended (see No. 204), and they were forbidden to leave their place of residence. In some cases they were forced to take up a lease if no bidders came forward, and they were of course subject to compulsory labour on the embankments and canals. On the other hand their position as revenue-producers gave them certain privileges (pp. 69, 73). Temple land (see No. 210) was exploited under state control in the same way, but the revenue was used for the maintenance of the temples. Again, large areas were allotted to cleruchs, chiefly military (see p. xii); though in course of time these holdings became hereditary, they were still in theory revocable by the king. But there was also a gradually increasing amount of what was practically private land, which could be bought and sold by individuals (*cf.* Vol. I. No. 27) and over which the Crown had no immediate rights.

In the Roman period state land, a large portion of which retained the name of Crown land (No. 236), was cultivated on the same system as before. The leases were put up to auction, as shown by No. 236, and seed was advanced to the cultivators as under the Ptolemies (No. 302). Another important category consisted of the imperial domains, comprising estates which had come into the private possession of the emperors by confiscation or inheritance; these were administered, under the same general system as the state land, by officials subordinate to the idiologus (No. 282). The Ptolemaic system of compelling cultivators to take up leases of unattractive areas was retained and elaborated. Private possession evolved in various ways, and more and more property passed into private hands.

INTRODUCTION

Cleruchs in the Ptolemaic sense no longer existed, but many of the old holdings were now private property, land of this kind being called catoecic or cleruchic and the owners, who enjoyed a privileged status (p. 341, note *a*), catoeci or cleruchs. A great deal of state land, especially if unremunerative, was sold to private individuals ; No. 355 is a good illustration of this kind of sale. Much of the privately owned land was burdened with a peculiar condition, alluded to in No. 284 : an adjoining parcel of state land was permanently attached to the property, and the owner was obliged to cultivate this parcel on the same terms as a state cultivator.

About agriculture in the Byzantine and Arabic periods the papyri in this volume have little to say, and only one matter need be mentioned. The petition No. 295, written in the first half of the 4th century, gives a picture of what was happening in many villages, especially in the Fayum : the peasants were deserting their homes, land was falling out of cultivation, and the government was finding increasing difficulty in administering its own property to advantage. Out of this state of things gradually emerged the great land-owners already spoken of, who swallowed up the small proprietors and absorbed the lands for which the government could no longer find cultivators.

The chief economic aim of the Ptolemies and of the emperors with regard to Egypt was to extract from it the greatest possible revenue. The many taxes and other forms of exaction which they employed for this purpose cannot be enumerated here ; a few, only a very few, are referred to in Sections XI.

INTRODUCTION

and XIII. ; but one or two features of the economic system may be noted.

In the Ptolemaic period the taxes, with the exception of those paid in corn, were as a rule farmed out to the highest bidder, who along with his sureties was responsible to the state for the amount which he had offered. This system was inherited by the Romans, as is shown for example by No. 420 ; but after a time they introduced a different method : instead of putting the taxes up to auction they appointed collectors for each village, the office being compulsory, under the general supervision of the strategus, and made them responsible for the amounts at which the yields of the taxes had been assessed (see No. 358). When the local senates were instituted, most of the supervision was entrusted to their nominees (p. 117, note *a*). In the later Byzantine period certain villages, as well as the great land-owners, obtained the right of collecting their own taxes and paying them to the Treasury (see No. 218), while those of the other villages were collected by the pagarchs.

As agriculture was the chief occupation of the country, so one great source of revenue was the rent of state lands, paid in kind by the peasants who cultivated them on lease, together with the taxes, likewise paid in kind, on other categories of land. Except in years of famine, there was a huge surplus of corn not required for use in the country. In Ptolemaic times this was presumably sold to exporters to the profit of the Crown. Under the empire it was dispatched every summer to Rome, and afterwards to Constantinople, to ensure a cheap supply of corn for the market and to provide a dole for the poor. The collection and transport of the grain form the subject of many papyri, of which a few specimens are included in the present selection. Nos. 343, 398, 400 illustrate the delivery of the corn dues at the local granaries ; No. 372 shows how it was carried to the nearest quays ; Nos. 365, 373, 423 deal with the transport by water to Alexandria ; and a letter printed in Vol. I. No. 113 alludes to the arrival of the grain fleet in Italy. Certain quantities were left in the state granaries to be distributed as seed for the next sowing and for other purposes (Nos. 302, 391). Besides the corn dues a further amount was acquired by the government through compulsory purchase at a price fixed by itself. It is supposed that in Ptolemaic times the provisions for the army (see No. 393) were bought up in this way. Under the Roman occupation the system of compulsory purchase for supplying the needs of the army, as exemplified by No. 387, was certainly employed for a long time, but it was gradually superseded by a direct exaction of corn, wine, and other necessaries, or of an equivalent sum of money. No. 426 and the Byzantine documents Nos. 388 and 396 are illustrations of the latter method.

Of the direct money-taxes the poll-tax was of outstanding importance. Our information on this subject belongs mainly to the Roman period, though the tax existed in some form under the Ptolemies and also under the Byzantine emperors, while after the Arab conquest it was exacted from non-Moslems only. In Roman times it was levied on all males of the subject population between the ages of 14 and 60. Greeks of a certain status were not liable to it, and exemption or partial exemption was also granted to a few privileged classes, such as owners of catoecic land and some of the Egyptian priests (Nos. 313, 338). The institution of the censuş had a close connexion with this tax. For taxes paid per head, such as the Ptolemaic salt-tax, registration of individuals was necessary and had long been customary, like the registration of taxable property illustrated by Nos. 321-323. But a new system of registration of individuals was introduced by the Romans, probably in the reign of Augustus : henceforward an exact census of the inhabitants of each house was taken every fourteen years, and in preparation for this all absentees were commanded to return to their own homes in order to register themselves there (see No. 220). Similarly at the census described in Luke, chapter 2, " all went to enrol themselves, every one to his own city." Examples of the declarations handed in on these occasions are given in Nos. 312 and 313. Notifications of birth and death from interested parties (Nos. 309, 310) formed useful supplements to the census lists. Again, the declarations handed in on behalf of youths who claimed to belong to the privileged classes, *e.g.* No. 314, had as their aim whole or partial exemption from the poll-tax.

Though the higher classes did not pay poll-tax, it must not be supposed that they were less heavily burdened, directly and indirectly, than the subject population. Every element in the community was taxed to the utmost. Toll was taken from property of all kinds, trades, traffic, imports. Even Roman citizens had their own special burdens, such as the five per cent tax on inheritances, corresponding to our death-duties (No. 326).

INTRODUCTION

Another important source of revenue, to which there are many references in the present selection, was the system of state monopolies. Those established in the early Ptolemaic age were very elaborate; in No. 203 we have a detailed description of one of the most lucrative. Among other monopolized commodities we may mention cloth, beer, paper, myrrh and perfumes, salt and natron. In some cases, as in that of oil, the production of the raw material as well as the sale of the monopolized article was strictly regulated, but naturally there were many differences in the regulations of the different monopolies. For instance sesame and croton were cultivated solely for making oil and the acreage to be assigned to these crops was determined by the requirements of the monopoly ; but as barley was grown for other purposes besides the manufacture of beer, the control in this case began at a later stage. When necessary, the monopolies were protected by heavy import taxes at the ports of entry ; thus the customs tax on imported oil was 50 per cent of its price in Egypt. (These customs dues are to be distinguished from the inland tolls mentioned in Nos. 381-383.) As in the case of Ptolemaic taxation the monopolies were operated to a large extent through contractors. Like the Crown peasants the employees of the monopolies enjoyed certain immunities (pp. 73-75), in order that the interests of the Crown might not suffer through their private troubles. In the Roman period we find no such elaborate system of monopolies, but the government was accustomed to obtain bids from would-be concessionaires for the sole right of carrying on certain trades, such as brick-making and perfumery, in

INTRODUCTION

certain localities and also for exclusive rights of fishing and fowling (Nos. 350, 351).

Many of the papyri included in this selection are of legal interest, but law in Egypt is too complicated a subject to be treated here. It must suffice to point out that some specimens of various steps in legal procedure, typical of Ptolemaic, Roman, and Byzantine Egypt, are given in Section VI. and that many of the petitions in Section VII. are really pre-liminaries to legal action. The laws applied by the tribunals varied in accordance with the nationality and domicile of the parties. No. 202 is an excerpt from the purely Greek laws of Alexandria, while Naucratis and Antinoopolis are known to have had similar codes of their own. Some articles of Roman law applicable to Romans in Egypt will be found in No. 206, and Nos. 213, 214 are legal pronouncements of the emperors. Native Egyptian law is referred to in No. 210, p. 73, and is adduced by an advocate, though without success, in No. 258.

Other interesting subjects to which there are scattered references in these texts, but to which we can only call attention are : the control exercised over the temples and priesthoods by the kings and afterwards by the emperors through a Roman high priest (Nos. 208, 210, 244, 338, 340, 405) ; the sale of priestly offices to the highest bidder (Nos. 210, 353, 425) ; the growth of Christianity (Nos. 318, 319) ; the organization of the Ptolemaic and Roman armies in Egypt ; the postal services (Nos. 366, 397) ; the land-registry (Nos. 219, 324, 325, 422). Lastly, it may be noted that most of these documents are written in a stereotyped style by official secretaries and professional scribes, and that only rarely, as in

INTRODUCTION

the letter of Ptolemy Philadelphus No. 207, can a personal touch be recognized. Nevertheless it is interesting to follow the development of official diction from the pure Greek of the 3rd century B.C. down to the empty verbosity of some of the Byzantine papyri. In some cases the influence of a Latin original is apparent, and the latest pieces are really Arabic in a Greek dress. Unfortunately, such distinctions are only faintly perceptible in a translation.

We should like once more to emphasize the fact that Greek papyrology is a comparatively new science, so that many points in the texts here printed are still obscure and many of the current interpretations are undergoing correction from time to time. To take an instance which has just arisen, it now appears that the explanation of ἀπόδος given on p. 273, note d, is erroneous and that the word really means, " give back to the petitioner."

EXPLANATORY NOTES

THE Egyptian civil year consisted originally of twelve 30-day months and five intercalary days. It was therefore about a quarter of a day shorter than the natural year. Thus at the beginning of the Ptolemaic period Thoth 1 fell on November 13 (Julian calendar) and at the beginning of the Roman period had moved back to August 30. But in the reign of Augustus the calendar was stabilized by the addition of a sixth intercalary day in every fourth year, so that thereafter the Egyptian months corresponded permanently with the Roman months as tabulated below. (It should be noted that the Egyptian leap-year immediately preceded the Roman leap-year.)

The Macedonian months, by which many papyri are dated, were originally lunar. In the earlier Ptolemaic period their relation to the Egyptian months is, except at certain intervals, somewhat obscure, but they seem to have gradually lost their lunar character, and before the end of the second century B.C. they were finally assimilated to the Egyptian months in the order shown.

Thoth 1	= Dius 1	= August 29 (or after a leap-year 30).
Phaophi 1	= Apellaeus 1	= September 28 (29).
Hathur 1	= Audnaeus 1	= October 28 (29).
Choiak 1	= Peritius 1	= November 27 (28).

EXPLANATORY NOTES

Tubi 1	= Dystrus 1	= December 27 (28).
Mecheir 1	= Xandicus 1	= January 26 (27).
Phamenoth 1	= Artemisius 1	= February 25 (26).
Pharmouthi 1	= Daesius 1	= March 27.
Pachon 1	= Panemus 1	= April 26.
Pauni 1	= Loius 1	= May 26.
Epeiph 1	= Gorpiaeus 1	= June 25.
Mesore 1	= Hyperberetaeus 1	= July 25.
Intercalary 1	= Intercalary 1	= August 24.

In the Imperial age various months received honorific titles, more or less ephemeral, such as Germaniceus, Domitianus. Where such names occur in the following texts their Egyptian equivalents are noted.

According to the Egyptian method of dating, the first year of a reign was the period between the accession and the following 1st of Thoth. In the fourth and third centuries B.C. the Greeks in Egypt used different starting-points in reckoning the years of the king, but after a time they adopted the Egyptian system together with the Egyptian calendar. The same system continued to be used under the Roman emperors. In the earlier Byzantine period the practice of dating by consulships became general; but from the time of Justinian onwards the consular date was either preceded or displaced by the year of the emperor, counted from the day of his accession to its recurrent anniversaries. Sometimes, too, an era is employed; and very often we find a reference to the indiction, which was a period of one year in a 15-year cycle originally introduced for fiscal purposes.

EXPLANATORY NOTES

Egyptian Money

In the earlier Ptolemaic papyri the unit by which
sums of money are generally reckoned is the silver
drachma (= 6 obols). But in the second and first
centuries B.C. it became more common to reckon
by copper drachmae. It is supposed that when the
copper standard was introduced one drachma of silver
was worth 60 of copper, but the ratio soon rose, and
at the end of the second century B.C. it was often as
high as 1 : 500. A tetradrachm = 4 drachmae, a mina
= 100 drachmae, and a talent = 6000 drachmae.

In Roman times, or rather after the reign of
Augustus, the ordinary unit of reckoning was a silver
drachma of 7 obols, though actually the lowest de-
nomination of silver issued by the Alexandrian mint
was the tetradrachm, which was nominally equal to
a Roman denarius. The purchasing power of this
drachma was much less than that of the Ptolemaic
and gradually diminished down to the time of
Diocletian. Though called silver, the coinage was
actually of very base alloy.

In the Byzantine texts the only stable unit is the
solidus, a gold coin weighing about $\frac{1}{72}$ of a Roman
pound. The inferior currency had depreciated to
such an extent that by the middle of the fourth
century a solidus was worth about 2000 myriads
of denarii, and by the end of the sixth about 7000
myriads. The purchasing power of a solidus was, at
a rough estimate, about twenty times that of a
Ptolemaic silver drachma.

EXPLANATORY NOTES

METHOD OF PUBLICATION AND LIST OF ABBREVIATIONS

The texts are printed in running form, though for convenience of reference the lines of the scribe are numbered according to the numbering of the *editio princeps*. Accents, punctuation, and marks of diaeresis are added in conformity with modern usage. Interpolations and corrections of the scribe are, as a rule, incorporated in the text and not specially marked or recorded. Faults of orthography and grammar, if likely to cause any difficulty, are corrected in the critical apparatus. Approved restorations and emended readings, most of which have been published or republished in Preisigke's *Berichtigungslisten*, are adopted without remark. Iota adscript has been printed where so written, otherwise iota subscript is employed. Square brackets [ ] indicate a lacuna, round brackets ( ) the resolution of a symbol or abbreviation, angular brackets ‹ › a mistaken omission in the original, braces { } a superfluous letter or letters, double square brackets ⟦ ⟧ a deletion. Dots placed within brackets represent approximately the number of letters lost or deleted ; dots outside brackets indicate mutilated or otherwise illegible letters. It has not been thought necessary, for the purpose of this edition, to follow the usual practice of placing dots under such letters as are doubtful ; but questionable readings, if of any importance, are duly noted.

In the Greek text (2nd hand), (3rd hand), etc., indicate that the following words were not written by the same hand as the preceding part of the document. The numbers in the critical notes refer to the lines of the text, and *l.* stands for *lege*. To prevent

xxxiv

EXPLANATORY NOTES

a possible misunderstanding it may be well to emphasize the fact that the translation gives the sense of the Greek as corrected in the critical apparatus. For instance, when a scribe, as often happens, misspells ἡμᾶς as ὑμᾶς, we reproduce his spelling in the text, correct it in the notes, and translate in accordance with the correction.

The abbreviated references used in the present volume are as follows :

Aegyptus = *Aegyptus, rivista italiana di Egittologia e di Papirologia.*

Annales = *Annales du Service des Antiquités de l' Égypte.*

Archiv = *Archiv für Papyrusforschung.*

B.G.U. = *Ägyptische Urkunden aus den Museen zu Berlin : Griechische Urkunden,* vols. i.-viii.

C.P.Herm. = *Corpus Papyrorum Hermopolitanorum (Studien zur Paläographie und Papyruskunde,* v.), by C. Wessely.

J.E.A. = *Journal of Egyptian Archaeology.*

O. Tait = *Greek Ostraca in the Bodleian Library and other Collections,* vol. i., by J. G. Tait.

P. Achmim = *Les Papyrus grecs d'Achmîm (Bulletin de l'Institut français d'Archéologie orientale,* xxxi.), by P. Collart.

P. Amh. = *The Amherst Papyri,* vols. i.-ii., by B. P. Grenfell and A. S. Hunt.

P. Bad. = *Veröffentlichungen aus den Badischen Papyrussammlungen,* Heft 4 : *Griechische Papyri,* by F. Bilabel.

P. Bour. = *Les Papyrus Bouriant,* by P. Collart.

P. Cairo Masp. = *Catalogue des antiquités égyptiennes du Musée du Caire : Papyrus grecs d'époque byzantine,* vols. i.-iii., by J. Maspero.

P. Cairo Zen. = *Catalogue des antiquités égyptiennes du Musée du Caire : Zenon Papyri,* vols. i.-iv., by C. C. Edgar.

P. Columbia 1 = *Tax Lists and Transportation Receipts from Theadelphia,* by W. L. Westermann and C. W. Keyes.

EXPLANATORY NOTES

P. Columbia Inventory 480 = *Upon Slavery in Ptolemaic Egypt*, by W. L. Westermann.

P. Eleph. = *Elephantine-Papyri* (*B.G.U.*, Sonderheft), by O. Rubensohn.

P. Enteuxeis = *Publications de la Société royale égyptienne de Papyrologie* : Ἐντεύξεις, by O. Guéraud.

P. Fay. = *Fayûm Towns and their Papyri*, by B. P. Grenfell and A. S. Hunt.

P. Freib. = *Mitteilungen aus der Freiburger Papyrussammlung*, by W. Aly, M. Gelzer, and J. Partsch.

P. Gen. = *Les Papyrus de Genève*, vol. i., by J. Nicole.

P. Giess. = *Griechische Papyri zu Giessen*, vol. i., by E. Kornemann, O. Eger, and P. M. Meyer.

P. Graux = *Papyrus Graux* (*Bulletin de l'Institut français d'Archéologie orientale*, vols. xxi. and xxvii.), by H. Henne.

P. Grenf. = *Greek Papyri*, series i. and ii., by B. P. Grenfell and A. S. Hunt.

P. Gurob = *Greek Papyri from Gurob*, by J. G. Smyly.

P. Hal. = *Dikaiomata*, etc., by the Graeca Halensis.

P. Hamb. = *Griechische Papyrusurkunden der Hamburger Bibliothek*, vol. i., by P. M. Meyer.

P. Hib. = *The Hibeh Papyri*, part i., by B. P. Grenfell and A. S. Hunt.

P. Lille = *Papyrus grecs de Lille*, vol. i., by P. Jouguet, P. Collart, J. Lesquier, and M. Xoual.

P. Lond. = *Greek Papyri in the British Museum*, vols. i.-v., by Sir F. G. Kenyon and H. I. Bell.

P. Lond. 1912 = *Jews and Christians in Egypt*, by H. I. Bell.

P. Oxy. = *The Oxyrhynchus Papyri*, vols. i.-xvii., by B. P. Grenfell and A. S. Hunt.

P. Par. = *Les Papyrus grecs du Musée du Louvre* (*Notices et Extraits*, vol. xviii. 2), by W. Brunet de Presle and E. Egger.

P. Petr. = *The Flinders Petrie Papyri*, parts i.-iii., by J. P. Mahaffy and J. G. Smyly.

P. Rein. = *Papyrus grecs et démotiques*, by Th. Reinach and others.

EXPLANATORY NOTES

P. Rev. Laws = *Revenue Laws of Ptolemy Philadelphus*, by B. P. Grenfell and J. P. Mahaffy.

P. Ryl. = *Catalogue of the Greek Papyri in the Rylands Library*, vol. i. by A. S. Hunt, and vol. ii. by J. de M. Johnson, V. Martin, and A. S. Hunt.

P.S.I. = *Papiri della Società italiana per la ricerca dei Papiri*, vols. i.-x., by G. Vitelli, Medea Norsa, and others.

P. Spec. Isag. = *Papyrorum scripturae graecae specimina isagogica*, by C. Wessely.

P. Strassb. = *Griechische Papyri der Universitätsbibliothek zu Strassburg*, vols. i.-ii., by F. Preisigke.

P. Tebt. = *The Tebtunis Papyri*, parts i.-iii., by B. P. Grenfell, A. S. Hunt, J. G. Smyly, and E. J. Goodspeed.

P. Thead. = *Papyrus de Théadelphie*, by P. Jouguet.

P. Tor. = *Papyri graeci regii Taurinensis Musei Aegyptii*, by A. Peyron.

Raccolta Lumbroso = *Raccolta di scritti in onore di Giacomo Lumbroso*.

Rec. Champ. = *Recueil d'études égyptologiques dédiées à la mémoire de Jean-François Champollion*.

Sitzungsber. Preuss. Ak. = *Sitzungsberichte der Preussischen Akademie*.

U.P.Z. = *Urkunden der Ptolemäerzeit (ältere Funde)*, vol. i., by U. Wilcken.

M. Chrest. = L. Mitteis, *Chrestomathie*.

W. Chrest. = U. Wilcken, *Chrestomathie*.

SELECT PAPYRI

I. CODES AND REGULATIONS

201. LEGAL RIGHTS OF CERTAIN CLASSES IN ALEXANDRIA

P. Hal. 1, ll. 124-165.   Middle of 3rd cent. B.C.

¹²⁴[Κα]τὰ δ[ὲ τῶ]ν ἀπεσταλμ[έ]νων ὑπ[ὸ τοῦ
βα]σιλέως δίκην μ[η-]¹²⁵θεὶς [εἰσαγέτ]ω μήτε
κ[α]τ' αὐτ[ῶν μή]τε κατὰ τ[ῶν] ¹²⁶ἐγγύ[ων, μη]δὲ
ὁ πράκτωρ μη[δ]ὲ οἱ [ὑπ]ηρέται παρα-¹²⁷λα[μβαν]έ-
τωσαν τούτ[ο]υς.

Κατὰ <τα>ὐτὰ δὲ καὶ ἐάν τ[ινες] ¹²⁸δίκας γράψων-
ται τ[ο]ῖ[ς] ἐν τ[ῆι ἀ]ποσκευῆι ἢ [[ἐν]] το[ῖς]
¹²⁹ἐγγύοις [. .] αὐτῶν περὶ ἐγκλη[μ]άτων γε-
γενημέ[νω]ν ¹³⁰ἐν [ν] ο[ῖ]ς ἐπεδήμουν χρόνοις οἱ
κ[α]ταλιπόντες α<ὐ>το[ύς], ¹³¹μὴ [ε]ἰσαγέσθωσαν,
ἐὰμ μὴ ὦσ[ι]ν ὄντες τῆς ἀποσ[κε]υ-¹³²ῆς τὸ δίκαιον
ε[ἰ]ληφότες π[α]ρά τινων περὶ ἐγκλ[η-]¹³³μάτων
γεγενημένων ἐν τ[οῖ]ς αὐτοῖς χρόνοις· κατ[ὰ δ]ὲ
¹³⁴τούτων εἰσαγέσθω.

Ἐὰν δέ [τ]ι[ν]ες φάσκωσιν εἶν[αι] ¹³⁵τῆς [ἀ]πο-
σκευῆς, οἱ δικασταὶ π[ερ]ὶ τούτου δ[ι]αγνωσκέ[τω-]
¹³⁶σαν [κ]αὶ ἐὰν γνω[σθ]ῶσιν [ὄ]ντες τῆς ἀποσκευῆς
καὶ τὲ ἐν-¹³⁷κλή[μ]ατα φαίνηται γ[ε]γενημένα

136. l. τά.

2

I. CODES AND REGULATIONS

201. LEGAL RIGHTS OF CERTAIN CLASSES IN ALEXANDRIA

Middle of 3rd cent. B.C.

No one shall bring into court a suit against persons who have been sent on service by the king, either against themselves or against their sureties, nor shall the collector of debts or his assistants arrest these.

Likewise if any persons bring suits against the dependants [a] (of the absentees) or against their sureties concerning matters of complaint which took place when those who left them behind were still at home, these suits shall not be brought into court, unless it happens that though classed as dependants they have themselves obtained legal satisfaction from others concerning matters of complaint which took place at the said time ; if the suit is against such persons, it shall be brought into court.

If any persons claim to belong to the class of dependants, the judges shall decide the point, and if they are recognized to belong to that class and if the matters of complaint are proved to have taken place

[a] Literally " those belonging to the baggage." The phrase usually denotes the wives and children of soldiers.

ἐπιδημού[ν]των τῶν ¹³⁸κατ[α]λιπόντων καὶ τὸ
[δ]ίκαι[ο]ν μὴ ὦσιν κατὰ τὰ γε-¹³⁹γραμμένα εἰλη-
φότες παρά τινων, αἱ μὲν δίκαι ὑπερ[βό]λι-¹⁴⁰μοι
ἔστωσαν ἕως ἂν οἱ καταλιπόντες α[ὐ]τοὺς παρα-
γ[έ-]¹⁴¹νωνται, τὰ δὲ ἐπιδέκατα ἢ ἐπιπεντεκαι-
δέκατα [κ]ομι-¹⁴²ζέσθωσαν οἱ θέντες.

"Οσοι δ' ἂν ἐνκαλῶσιν τοῖς ἐν τ[ῆι] ¹⁴³ἀποσκευῆι
οὖσιν ὡς ἠδικημέ[ν]οι ἐν οἷς χρόνοις ἀπ[εδ]ή-
¹⁴⁴μουν οἱ καταλιπόντες αὐτ[ο]ὺς [ἢ] οἱ ἐν τῆι
ἀποσκ[ευ-]¹⁴⁵ῆι ἑτέροις φάμενοι ἠδικῆσθα[ι] ἀφ'
οὗ χρόνου κατελ[ίπ]η-¹⁴⁶σαν, κρινέσθωσαν ἐπὶ τοῦ
ἀπο[δ]εδειγμένου κριτη[ρίου].

¹⁴⁷Ἐὰν δέ τινες γραψάμενοι δίκας ἀποστέλ-
λωνται ὑ[π]ὸ ¹⁴⁸τοῦ βασιλέως πρὸ τοῦ εἰσαχθῆνα[ι]
αὐτοῖς τὰς δίκας, τὰ μὲν ¹⁴⁹ἐπιδέκατα ἢ ἐπιπεντε-
καιδέκατα, ἐὰν βούλωνται, ἀναιρε[ί]σθω-¹⁵⁰σαν, αἱ
δὲ δίκαι ὑπερβόλιμοι ἔστ[ω]σαν [ἕ]ως [ἂ]ν παρα-
γέν[ω]νται· ¹⁵¹[μ]ὴ εἰσαγέ[σθω]σα[ν δὲ πρὶν ἢ πάλιν
τὰ ἐπιδέκατα] ¹⁵²ἢ ἐπιπεντε[καιδέκατα θῶσιν οἱ
ἂν ὦσιν κεκο-]¹⁵³μισμένοι.

Ἐ[ὰν δὲ οἱ] κα[τὰ τὴν χώραν γραψάμενοι
¹⁵⁴δίκ[ας] πρὸ τ[οῦ] ε[ἰσ]αχ[θῆ]ναι ἀ[πο]στ[έλ]-
λ[ων]ται ὑπ[ὸ] ¹⁵⁵τοῦ β[α]σιλέως, ὑπερ[β]όλιμοι
ἔστωσαν καὶ τούτ[ο]ις ¹⁵⁶κατὰ ταὐτὰ ἕως ἂν
ἐπανέλθωσιν.

Τῶν δὲ ¹⁵⁷{τῶν δὲ} ἐν τ[ῶι] στρατ[ι]ωτικῶ[ι]
τεταγμένων ὅσο[ι] ἂν ¹⁵⁸ἐν ['Αλ]εξα[ν]δρεία[ι] πεπο-
[λ]ιτογραφημένοι ¹⁵⁹ἐν[κα]λῶσ[ιν π]ερὶ σιτ[α]ρχιῶν
καὶ σιτομε[τ]ριῶν καὶ ¹⁶⁰πα[ρ]αγρα[φῶν] τῶ[ν ἐ]ξι-
τ[α]ρχίας ἢ σι[τ]ομετρίας ¹⁶¹γινομένω[ν, ἐ]ὰν καὶ

160. l. ἐ]κ σιταρχίας.

4

when those who left them behind were still at home and they have not obtained legal satisfaction from others as stated above, the suits shall be adjourned until those who left them behind return, but the depositors shall recover their cautions of one-tenth or one-fifteenth.[a]

All cases in which the dependants are accused by other persons of having wronged them after the departure of those who left them behind or in which the dependants accuse other persons, claiming to have been wronged by them after they had been left, shall be judged before the appointed court.

If any persons after bringing a suit are sent on service by the king before their suits have been brought into court, they shall, if they choose, take back their cautions of one-tenth or one-fifteenth, but the suits shall be adjourned until they return, and they shall not be brought into court before those who have recovered their cautions of one-tenth or one-fifteenth deposit them anew.

If persons residing in the country [b] bring a suit and are sent on service by the king before it has been brought into court, their suits shall be adjourned in like manner until they come back.

Of persons enrolled in the army all those who have been admitted to the citizenship in Alexandria and bring complaints concerning salaries and corn allowances and the amounts of money or corn credited to them, if their adversaries also are in the

---

[a] A certain percentage of the sum at issue was deposited by each party before the trial of the suit, to cover court expenses, the winner of the case being reimbursed by the loser.

[b] The " country " means Egypt apart from Alexandria.

5

SELECT PAPYRI

οἱ ἀντ[ίδ]ικοι ἐν τῶι [σ]τρατιω-¹⁶²τικῶι ὄντ[ες
π]ε, πολιτογ[ρ]αφημένοι ὦ[σ]ιν, λα[μ-]¹⁶³βαν[έτ]ωσαν
τὸ δ[ί]καιον [κ]αὶ ὑπεχέτω[σ]αν ἐν [τοῖς] ¹⁶⁴ξεν[ι]-
κοῖς δικαστη[ρί]οις καὶ αἱ π[ρ]άξεις ἔστω-¹⁶⁵σαν
κατὰ τὸ διάγραμμα.

202. PENALTIES FOR ASSAULT IN
ALEXANDRIAN LAW

P. Hal. 1, ll. 186-213.   Middle of 3rd cent. B.C.

¹⁸⁶[Σι]δήρου ἐπαντάσεως. ἐ[ὰν] ὁ ἐλε[ύθερος
τ]ῶι ἐλευθέρωι ἐπανατε[ί]νηται ¹⁸⁷σίδηρον ἢ χ[α]λ-
κὸ[ν] ἢ λίθον [ἢ . . . . . ἢ] ξύλον, ρ (δραχμὰς)
ἀποτεισάτω, ἐὰν ¹⁸⁸δίκηι ἡσσηθῆι. ἐὰν δὲ δ[οῦλος
ἢ ἡ] δούλη τούτων τι ποιήσηι ¹⁸⁹τῶι ἐλευθέρωι
ἢ τῆι ἐλευθέ[ραι, μασ]τιγούσθω μὴ ἔλασσον [ρ]
πληγῶν ¹⁹⁰ἢ τὴν ζημίαν διπλασία[ν ἀπο]τεισάτω
ὁ δεσπότης τοῦ [π]οιή-¹⁹¹σαντος [τ]ῶι παθόντι ἢ
⟨ἢ⟩ τῶ[ι ἐλευθέ]ρωι γέγραπται, ἐὰν δίκηι ¹⁹²νικηθῆι.

¹⁹³Μεθύοντος ἀδικιῶν. ὅταν τις τῶν εἰς τὸ
σῶ[μ]α ἀδικημάτ[ων] ¹⁹⁴μεθύων ἢ νύκτωρ ἢ ἐν
ἱερῶι ἢ ἐν ἀγορᾶι ἀδικήσηι, διπλασί[αν] ¹⁹⁵τὴν
ζημίαν ἀποτεισάτω τῆς γεγραμμένης.

¹⁹⁶Δούλωι ἐλεύθερον πατάξαντι. ἐὰν ὁ δοῦλος
ἢ ἡ δούλη πατάξη[ι τὸν ἐλεύ-]¹⁹⁷θερον ἢ τὴν
ἐλευθέραν, μαστιγούσθω μὴ ἔλασσον ρ πληγῶν ἢ
τὴ[ν ζημίαν] ¹⁹⁸διπλασίαν ἀποτεισάτω ὁ δεσπότης
ὑπὲρ το[ῦ] δούλου ἢ ἣν τὸν ἐλεύ[θερον] ¹⁹⁹γέγραπται
ἀποτεῖσαι, ἐὰν ὁμολογῆι. ἐὰν δὲ [ἀ]μφισβητῆι,

6

army and have been admitted to the citizenship, shall receive and give satisfaction in the courts for foreigners, and execution shall take place in conformity with the ordinance.[a]

[a] A code of regulations concerning legal procedure.

202. PENALTIES FOR ASSAULT IN ALEXANDRIAN LAW

Middle of 3rd cent. B.C.

Threatening with iron. If a freeman threatens a freeman with iron or copper or stone or . . . or wood, he shall forfeit a hundred drachmae, if he is worsted in the suit. But if a male slave or a female slave does any of these things to a freeman or a freewoman, they shall receive not less than a hundred stripes, or else the master of the offender, if he is defeated in the suit, shall forfeit to the injured party twice the amount of the penalty which is prescribed for a freeman.

Injuries done in drunkenness. Whoever commits a personal injury in drunkenness or by night or in a temple or in the market-place shall forfeit twice the amount of the prescribed penalty.

For a slave striking a freeman. If a male slave or a female slave strikes a freeman or a freewoman, they shall receive not less than a hundred stripes, or else the master, if he acknowledges the fact, shall pay on behalf of his slave twice the amount of the penalty which is prescribed for a freeman. But if he

7

γραφέσθ[ω μιᾶς πληγῆς] ²⁰⁰δίκην ρ (δραχμῶν),
ἐὰν δὲ ὄφληι, τριπλοῦν ἀτίμητον ἀποτεισάτω,
περ[ὶ δὲ] ²⁰¹πλειόνων πληγῶν τιμησάμενος δικασάσθω, ὅ τι δ᾽ ἂν τὸ δικαστ[ήριον τιμήσηι], ²⁰²τοῦτο
τριπλοῦν ἀποτεισάτω.

²⁰³Πληγῆς ἐλευθέροις. ἐὰν πατάξηι ὁ ἐλεύ-
θε[ρ]ος ἢ ἡ ἐλευθέρα τὸν [ἐλεύθερον] ²⁰⁴ἢ τὴν
ἐλευθέραν ἄρχων χειρῶν ἀδίκων, ρ (δραχμὰς)
ἀποτεισάτω ἀτιμήτ[ους, ἐὰν] ²⁰⁵δίκηι νι[κ]ηθῆι.
ἐὰν δὲ πλείονας πληγῆς μιᾶ[ς] πατάξηι, τιμη-
σάμ[ενος τὰς] ²⁰⁶πληγὰ[ς δι]κασάσθω, ὁπόσου
δ᾽ ἂν τιμήσηι τὸ δικαστήριον, τοῦτ[ο διπλοῦν]
²⁰⁷ἀποτεισ[άτ]ω. ἐὰν δέ τίς τινα τῶν ἀρχόντ[ων
π]ατάξηι τάσσοντ[α ὧν τῆι] ²⁰⁸ἀρχῆι γέ[γ]ραπται
τάσσειν, τριπλάσια τὰ ἐ[πι]τίμια ἀποτεισάτ[ω,
ἐὰν δίκηι] ²⁰⁹νικηθῆι.

²¹⁰῞Υβρεως. ἐάν τις καθυβρίσηι ἕτερος ἑτέρου
τ[ῶ]ν ἀγράφων, ὁ τα[λαιπωρού-]²¹¹μενος τιμησάμενος δικασάσθω, προσγρα[ψά]σθω δὲ ὀνομαστὶ
τ[ί ἂν φῆι] ²¹²ὑβρισθ[ῆ]ναι καὶ τὸν χρόνον ἐν ὧι
ὑβρίσθη. ὁ δ[ὲ] ὀφλὼν διπλοῦν ἀπ[οτεισάτω] ²¹³ὃ
ἂν τὸ δικαστήριον τιμήσηι.

disputes it, the plaintiff shall indict him, claiming for one blow a hundred drachmae, and if the master is condemned, he shall forfeit three times that amount without assessment ; and for a greater number of blows the plaintiff shall himself assess the injury when he brings the suit, and whatever assessment is fixed by the court, the master shall forfeit three times that amount.

Blows between freemen. If a freeman or a freewoman, making an unjust attack, strikes a freeman or a freewoman, they shall forfeit a hundred drachmae without assessment, if they are defeated in the suit. But if they strike more than one blow, the plaintiff in bringing the suit shall himself assess the damage caused by the blows, and whatever assessment is fixed by the court, the accused shall forfeit twice that amount. And if anyone strikes one of the magistrates while executing the administrative duties prescribed to the magistracy, he shall pay the penalties trebled, if he is defeated in the suit.

Outrage. If any person commits against another an outrage not provided for in the code, the injured party shall himself assess the damage in bringing his suit, but he shall further state specifically in what manner he claims to have been outraged and the date on which he was outraged. And the offender if condemned shall pay twice the amount of the assessment fixed by the court.

SELECT PAPYRI

203. THE OIL MONOPOLY OF PTOLEMY PHILADELPHUS

From Rev. Laws, cols. 38-56.   259 B.C.

(Col. 38) ¹("Ετους) κζ μηνὸς Λωίου ῑ, ²διωρθωσά-
μεθα ἐν τοῖς ⟦παρὰ⟧ ³Ἀπολλωνίου τοῦ διοικητοῦ.

(Col. 39) ¹ - - - τοῦ] ²μὲν [σησάμου τ]ὴν ἀρ[τ]άβ[ην
τὴν τριακο]νταχοί-³νικον κα[θαρὸν] εἰς ὅλμον
(δραχμῶν) [η, τοῦ δὲ κ]ρότωνος ⁴τὴν ἀρτάβην τὴν
τριακον[ταχοίνικ]ον καθαρὸν ⁵εἰς ὅλμον (δραχμῶν)
δ, κνήκου καθα[ρὸν εἰς ὅλ]μον τὴν ⁶ἀρτάβην (δραχμῆς) α (δυοβόλων), κολοκύνθ{ιν}ου τὴν ἀρτάβην
(τετρωβόλου), ⁷τοῦ {ἐκ τοῦ} λίνου σπέρματος (τριωβόλου).

⁸Ἐὰν δ[ὲ] μὴ βούληται ὁ γεωργὸς δ[ιδό]ναι
καθαρὸν ⁹εἰς ὅλμον, παραμετρείτω ἀπὸ τῆ[ς] ἅλω
καθάρας ¹⁰κοσκίνωι καὶ προσμετρείτω εἰ[ς τ]ὴν
ἀποκάθαρσιν ¹¹εἰς ὅλμον τοῦ μὲν σησάμου ταῖς
[ἑκα]τὸν ἀρ(τάβας) ζ, ¹²καὶ τοῦ κρότωνος τὸ ἴσον,
τῆς [δὲ κνήκ]ου ἀρ(τάβας) η.

ᵃ Monopolies were a conspicuous feature in the fiscal
policy of the Ptolemies, and of these the oil monopoly was
one of the most important. The government exercised strict
control over every stage of the industry, from the sowing of
the crops to the retailing of the finished product. It determined the acreage which was to be sown each year in each
nome, chiefly on Crown land leased to native cultivators.
Its agents, in conjunction with the contractors or lessees of
the monopoly, superintended the sowing and harvesting, and
bought up the crop at fixed prices. The manufacture of the
oil was carried on in State factories under the supervision of
the local authorities. For the sale of the oil, agreements
were made by the officials and contractors with the retailers
in the towns and villages, who each undertook to dispose of

10

203. THE OIL MONOPOLY OF PTOLEMY PHILADELPHUS [a]

259 B.C.

Year 27, Loius 10. Corrected in the office of Apollonius the dioecetes. [b]

[The persons authorized shall buy the produce from the cultivators at the following rates :] for each artaba of sesame containing thirty choenices, prepared for grinding, 8 drachmae, for each artaba of croton [c] containing thirty choenices, prepared for grinding, 4 drachmae, for each artaba of cnecus, [d] prepared for grinding, 1 drachma 2 obols, for each artaba of colocynth 4 obols, of linseed 3 obols.

If the cultivator does not wish to deliver his produce purified for grinding, he shall measure it out from the threshing-floor after cleaning it with a sieve, and against the further purification for grinding he shall add in the case of sesame 7 artabae to every 100, in the case of croton the same, and in the case of cnecus 8 artabae.

a certain quantity. It was sold to the consumers at fixed prices subject to revision. No private manufacture was permitted, though certain privileges were granted to the temples. Heavy penalties were prescribed against all persons, whether officials, contractors, or private individuals, who infringed any of the regulations. It will be observed that olive oil is not included in the monopoly, the reason probably being that at the date of the present code it had not begun to be manufactured in Egypt. The kinds of oil chiefly used at this time were sesame and castor oil, the former for human consumption, and the latter, mainly at least, for lamps.

[b] The minister of finance ; see Vol. I. p. 269, note a.
[c] Castor-oil plant.   [d] Safflower.

¹³Λαμβανέτωσαν δὲ παρὰ τῶ[ν γεω]ργῶν ¹⁴εἰς
τὰς δύο δραχμὰς τὰς λογ[ευο]μένας ¹⁵ἀπὸ τοῦ
σησάμου καὶ τὴν (δραχμὴν) α [τοῦ κ]ρότωνος
¹⁶σήσαμον καὶ κρότωνα τιμῆς τ[ῆς ἐν] τῶι ¹⁷δια-
γράμματι γεγραμμένης, ἀργύριον ¹⁸δὲ μὴ πρασσέσθωσαν.

¹⁹Ἄλλωι δὲ μηθενὶ ἐξουσίαν ἐχέτωσαν οἱ γεωρ-
γ[οὶ] ²⁰πωλεῖν μ[ήτε σή]σαμον μήτε κρότω[να].

(Col. 40) - - - ²- - - κ[αὶ ἀπο-]³σφρ[ά]γισμα
διδότ[ωσαν τῶι κ]ωμάρχηι ὧ[ν] ⁴παρ' ἑκάστ[ου]
γεω[ργοῦ ἔλαβο]ν. ἐὰν δὲ μὴ δῶσι ⁵τὸ ἀποσφρά-
γισμα, μὴ προιέσθω ὁ κωμάρχης ⁶ἐκ τῆς κώμης·
εἰ δὲ μή, ἀποτινέτω ⁷εἰς τὸ βασιλικὸν (δραχμὰς) Ἀ
καὶ ὅ τι ἂν ἡ ὠνὴ διὰ ταῦ-⁸τα καταβλαβῇ πεν-
[τ]απλοῦν.

⁹Πωλήσουσι δὲ τὸ ἔλαι[ον] ἐν τῆι χώραι τοῦ [μ]ὲν
¹⁰σησαμίνου καὶ τοῦ κν[η]κίνου πρὸς χαλκὸν ¹¹τὸμ
μετρητὴν τὸν [δωδε]κάχουν (δραχμῶν) μη, ¹²τοῦ δὲ
κίκιος καὶ κολοκ[υντίνο]υ καὶ ἐπελλυχνίου ¹³τὸμ
μετρητὴν δραχμῶν λ (altered to τό τε σησάμινον
καὶ τὸ κν[ή]κινον καὶ τοῦ κίκιος καὶ τοῦ κολοκυντίνου καὶ ἐπελλυχνίου πρὸς χαλκὸν τὸμ μετρητὴν
τὸν [δωδε]κάχουν δραχμῶν μη, τὴν δὲ κοτύλην
(δυοβόλων).)

¹⁴Ἐν Ἀλεξανδρείαι δὲ κ[αὶ] τῆι Λιβύηι πάσηι
¹⁵τοῦ σησ[α]μίνου τὸμ με[τρη]τὴν (δραχμῶν) μη
καὶ τοῦ ¹⁶κ[ί]κιος τὸμ μ[ετ]ρητὴν [(δραχμῶν)]
μη (altered to τοῦ σησ[α]μίνου καὶ τοῦ κίκι[ος]
τὸμ με[τρη]τὴν (δραχμῶν) μη, τὴν δὲ κοτύλην
(δυοβόλων)). καὶ πα[ρέ]ξουσιν ¹⁷ἱ[κανὸ]ν τοῖς [βου]-
λομένοις ὠνεῖσθαι π[ω]λο[ῦ]ντες ¹⁸δ[ιὰ χώ]ρας ἐν
[π]άσαις ταῖς πόλεσιν [καὶ κώ]μαις ¹⁹[. . . . .]σ . μ[. .

12

203. CODES AND REGULATIONS

They shall receive from the cultivators for the tax of two drachmae levied on sesame and the tax of one drachma on croton payment in sesame and croton at the price prescribed in the tariff, and shall not exact payment in silver.

The cultivators shall not be allowed to sell either sesame or croton to any other person.[a]

. . ., and they[b] shall give to the comarch a sealed receipt for what they received from each cultivator. If they fail to give the sealed receipt, the comarch shall not allow the produce to leave the village; otherwise he shall forfeit 1000 drachmae to the Crown, and five times the amount of whatever loss is incurred by the contract through his action.

They shall sell the oil in the country at the rate of 48 drachmae in copper for a metretes of sesame oil or cnecus oil containing 12 choes, and at the rate of 30 drachmae for a metretes of castor oil, colocynth oil, or lamp oil. (*Altered to* . . . both sesame and cnecus oil and castor oil, colocynth oil and lamp oil at the rate of 48 drachmae in copper for a metretes of 12 choes, and 2 obols for a cotyla.)

In Alexandria and the whole of Libya they shall sell it at the rate of 48 drachmae for a metretes of sesame oil and 48 drachmae for a metretes of castor oil. (*Altered to* . . . 48 drachmae for a metretes of sesame oil or castor oil, and 2 obols for a cotyla.) And they shall provide an amount sufficient for the demands of purchasers, selling it throughout the country in all the cities and towns by . . . measures

[a] Other than the authorized buyers.
[b] The buyers.

μ]έτ[ρ]οις τοῖς ἐξετα[σθεῖσιν] ὑπὸ [20][τοῦ οἰκονόμου
καὶ τοῦ ἀν]τιγραφέω[ς].

(Col. 41) - - - [3]᾿Αποδειξάτωσαν δὲ τὸν σπόρον τῶι
διοικοῦντι [4]τὴν ὠνὴν μετὰ τοῦ οἰκονόμου καὶ τοῦ
ἀντιγραφέως, [5]ἐὰν δὲ γεωμετρήσαντες μὴ εὕρωσιν
τὸ πλῆθος [6]τῶν ἀρουρῶν κατεσπαρμένον, ἀποτινέτωσαν [7]ὅ τε νομάρχ[η]ς καὶ ὁ τοπάρχης καὶ ὁ
οἰκονόμος [8]καὶ ὁ ἀντιγραφεὺς ἕκαστος τῶν α[ἰ]τίων
εἰς μὲν [9]τὸ βασιλικὸν (τάλαντα) β καὶ τοῖς τὴν ὠνὴν
ἔχουσι [10]τοῦ τε σησάμ[ου ὃ ἔ]δει λαβεῖν αὐτοὺς
τῆς ἀρ(τάβης) (δραχμὰς) β [11]τοῦ δὲ κρότω[νος] τῆς
ἀρ(τάβης) (δραχμὴν) α καὶ τὸ ἐπιγένημα [12]τοῦ
ἐλαίου κα[ὶ] τοῦ κίκιος· εἰσπραξάτω δὲ παρ᾿
αὐ-[13]τῶν ὁ ἐπὶ τῆς διο[ι]κήσεως τετεγμένος.

[14]῾Ο δὲ οἰκονόμος [πρ]ότερον ἢ τὴν ὥραν καθ-
ήκειν [15]τοῦ σ[π]είρεσθαι τὸ σήσαμον καὶ τὸν κρότωνα
[16]δότω τῶι προεστηκότι τοῦ νομοῦ νομάρχηι [17]ἢ
τοπάρχηι, ἐὰμ βούληται, εἰ[ς] τὸν σπ[ό]ρον τοῦ μὲν
σησάμου [18][τῆς ἀρού]ρα[ς] (δραχμὰς) δ, τοῦ δὲ
κρότ[ω]νο[ς] τῆς ἀρού[ρας (δραχμὰς)] β, κ[ο]μ[ι]-
ζέσθω δὲ ἀπὸ τῆς ἅλω ἀντὶ τοῦ (Col. 42) [- - -

[3]῞Οταν δὲ [ὥρ]α ἦι συνάγειν τ[ὸ] σήσ[α]μον καὶ
τὸν [4]κρότ[ω]να καὶ κνῆκον, ἐπαγγελλέτωσαν [5]οἱ
μὲν γεωργοὶ τῶι νομάρχηι καὶ τῶι τοπάρχηι, [6]οὗ
δὲ μὴ εἰσὶ νομάρχαι ἢ τοπάρχαι, τῶι οἰκο-[7]νόμωι,
οὗτοι δὲ παρακαλείτωσαν τὸν τὴν [8]ὠνὴ[ν] ἔχοντα,
ὁ δὲ τὴν ὠνὴν διοικῶν ἐπελ-[9]θὼν μετὰ τούτων ἐπὶ
τὰς ἀρούρας συντι-[10]μησ[άτ]ω.

[11]Οἱ δὲ [λαοὶ] καὶ οἱ λοιποὶ γεωργοὶ τιμάσθωσαν
[12]τὰ α[ὐτῶ]ν γενήματα ἕκαστα κατὰ γένος [13]πρότ-
[ερο]ν ⟨ἢ συν⟩κομίζειν, καὶ συγγραφὴν ποιείσθω-

(Col. 41) 13. *l.* τεταγμένος.

14

which have been tested by the oeconomus and the controller.

They shall exhibit the land sown to the director of the contract [a] with the oeconomus and the controller, and if after measuring it they find that the right number of arurae has not been sown, the nomarch and the toparch and the oeconomus and the controller shall, each who is responsible, forfeit to the Crown 2 talents, and to the holders of the contract for each artaba of sesame which they ought to have received 2 drachmae, and for each artaba of croton 1 drachma, together with the profit which would have been made on the sesame oil and the castor oil.[b] The dioecetes shall exact the payment from them.

Before the season arrives for sowing the sesame and the croton, the oeconomus shall give to the nomarch or toparch who is in charge in the nome, if he so desires, for the sowing of each arura of sesame 4 drachmae, and for each arura of croton 2 drachmae, and he shall receive from the threshing-floor in return for these payments . . .

When it is time to harvest the sesame and the croton and cnecus, the cultivators shall give notice to the nomarch and the toparch, or, where there are no nomarchs or toparchs, to the oeconomus, and these officials shall summon the holder of the contract, and the director of the contract shall visit the acreage with them and make an assessment.

The native peasants and the other cultivators shall assess their own crops severally by kind before they harvest them, and they shall make a duplicate sealed

[a] The contractors are variously designated as directors, holders, purchasers, etc., of the contract, but these distinctions are largely verbal.　　　　　　[b] See p. 19, note a.

15

σαν [14]πρὸς τ[ὸν] τὴν ὠνὴν ἔχοντα τῆς τιμήσεως
[15]διπλ[ῆν] ἐ]σφραγισμένην, [γ]ραφέτωσαν δὲ οἱ
[16][λ]αοὶ [τὸ]ν σπόρον [π]ὅσον ἔκ[α]στος κατέσ{σ}-
πα[ρκε]ν [17]κατ[ὰ] γένος μεθ' ὅρκου κ[αὶ] πό[σο]υ
ἔκαστος [τι-][18]μᾶτα[ι] καὶ σφραγιζ[έσθω]σαν τὴν
συνγραφήν, [19]συνεπ[ισ]φραγιζέσ[θ]ω δὲ καὶ ὁ [π]αρὰ
τοῦ νομάρ-[20][χου συν]αποσταλεὶς ἢ τοπ[άρχου].

(Col. 43) - - - [3]Δότω δὲ ὁ νομάρχης ἢ ὁ προ-
εστηκὼς τοῦ νο-[4]μοῦ τῶν ἀρ[ο]υρῶν τὸν σπόρον
κατὰ γεωργὸν πρό-[5]τερον ἢ συνκομίζεσθαι τὸν
καρπὸν ἡμέραις ἑξή-[6]κοντα. ἐὰν δὲ μὴ δῶι ἢ μὴ
παράσχηται τοὺς [7]γεωργοὺς ἐσπαρκότας τὸ πλῆθος
τὸ διαγραφέν, [8]ἀποτινέτω τῶι τὴν ὠνὴν πριαμένωι
καὶ τὰ ἐπί-[9]τιμα τὰ γεγραμμένα, αὐτὸς δὲ πρασ-
σέτω [π]αρὰ [10][τ]ῶν γεωργῶν τῶν ἠπειθηκότων.

[11][Ὅσ]οι δ' ἀτελεῖς εἰσιν κατὰ τὴν χώραν ἢ ἐν
δ[ωρεᾶ]ι [12][ἢ] ἐν συντάξει ἔχουσι[ν] κώμας καὶ
γῆν, παρ[αμε-][13]τ]ρείτωσαν πᾶν τὸ γενόμενον αὐτοῖς
σήσα[μο]ν [14][κ]αὶ τὸν κρότωνα καὶ τὰ λοιπὰ φορτία
τὰ συ[γκ]ύ-[15]ρ[ο]ντα εἰς τὴν ἐλαϊκήν, ὑπολιπόμενοι
εἰς σπ[έρ]μα [16]τὸ ἱκανόν, τιμὴν κομιζόμενοι πρὸς
χαλκ[ὸ]ν [17]τοῦ μὲν ση[σ]άμου τῆς ἀρ(τάβης)
(δραχμὰς) ϛ, τοῦ δὲ κρότωνος [18]τὴν ἀρ(τάβην)
(δραχμὰς) γ (δυοβόλους), τῆ[ς] δὲ κν[ή]κου τὴν
ἀρ(τάβην) (δραχμὴν) α.

(Col. 44) - - - [1]ἐργα[στήριον] εἶναι καὶ χαρ[ά]ξαν-
[τες] ἐπισημα-[2]νάσθωσαν.

[3]Ὅσαι δ' ἐν δωρεᾶι κῶμαί εἰσιν, ἐν ταύταις δὲ
[4]ἐλαιουργῖον μηθὲν καθιστάτωσαν.

[5]Παραθέσθωσαν δὲ ἐν ἑκάστωι ἐργαστηρίωι [6]καὶ
σήσαμον καὶ κρότωνα καὶ κνῆκον τὴν ἱκα-[7]νήν.

16

agreement [a] with the contractor concerning the assessment, and every peasant shall write down on oath the amount of land which he has sown with each kind of seed, and the amount of his assessment, and shall seal the agreement, and the delegate sent by the nomarch or toparch shall also seal it.

The nomarch or the official in charge in the nome shall report the number of arurae sown, cultivator by cultivator, sixty days before the crop is harvested. If he fails to report or to show that the cultivators have sown the amount of land appointed, he shall forfeit to the purchaser of the contract the prescribed penalty, and shall himself exact payment from the disobedient cultivators.

All persons throughout the country who are exempt from taxation or hold villages and land in gift or as a subsidy shall measure out all the sesame and croton grown by them, and the other kinds of produce included in the oil monopoly, leaving themselves a sufficient quantity for seed, and shall receive the value in copper at the rate of 6 drachmae for an artaba of sesame, 3 drachmae 2 obols for an artaba of croton, and 1 drachma for an artaba of cnecus.[b]

. . . to be a factory, and they [c] shall signify their approval by stamping it.

In none of the villages which are held in gift shall they set up any oil factory.

They shall deposit in each factory an adequate amount of sesame and croton and cnecus.

[a] The inner copy being sealed and the outer left open.
[b] These privileged persons were exempt from the tax mentioned in col. 39, but on the other hand they received a smaller price for their produce.
[c] The oeconomus and the controller.

SELECT PAPYRI

[8]Τοὺς δὲ ἐλαιουργοὺς τοὺς ἐν ἑκάστωι νομῶι
[9]καταταχθέντας μὴ ἐπιτρεπ[έ]τωσαν εἰς [10]ἄλλον
νομὸν μεταπορεύεσθα[ι. ἐὰ]ν δέ τινες [11]μετέλθω-
σιν, ἀγώγιμοι ἔστ[ωσα]ν τῶι τε διοι-[12]κοῦντι τὴν
ὠνὴν καὶ τῶι οἰκο[νό]μωι καὶ τῶι [13]ἀντιγραφεῖ.
[14]Μὴ ὑποδεχέσθω ⟦σα[ν]⟧ δὲ τοὺς ἐ[λ]αιουργοὺς
[15]μηθείς. ἐ[ὰ]ν δέ τις εἰδὼς ὑποδέξηται ἢ ἐπι-
[16]σταλέν[το]ς αὐτῶι μὴ ἀναγάγῃ, ἀποτινέτω
[17]ἑ[κ]άστου [ἐλ]αιουργοῦ (δραχμὰς) Γ καὶ ὁ ἐλαιουργὸς ἀγώγι-[18]μος ἔ[στω].

(Col. 45) - - - [2][τ]οῦ ἐλαίου μεριζέτω [. . . .] καὶ
ἀπ[ὸ τοῦ] ⟨ἐπι›γε-[3]νήματος τοῦ ⟦πωλουμένου⟧
κατεργαζομένου ἐλαίου το[ἱ]ς ἐλ[α]ιουργοῖς [4]τοῦ
μετρητοῦ τοῦ δωδεκαχοῦ (δραχμὰς) ⟦γ⟧ β (τριώβολον). τούτου δὲ [5]λαμβανέτω ὁ μὲν ἐλαιουργὸς
καὶ οἱ κοπεῖς (δραχμὴν) ⟦β⟧ α (τετρώβολον) [6]καὶ
οἱ τὴν ὠνὴν ἠγορακότες {(δραχμὴν)} ⟦α⟧ πεντώβολον.

[7]Ἐὰν δὲ ὁ οἰκονόμος ἢ ὁ παρ' αὐτοῦ καθεστηκὼς
[8]μὴ ἀποδιδῶι τοῖς ἐλαιουργοῖς τὸ κάτεργον ἢ τὸ
[9]μεμερισμένον αὐτοῖς ἀπὸ τῆς πράσεως, ἀπο-
[10]τινέτω εἰς μὲν τὸ βα[σιλι]κὸν (δραχμὰς) Γ καὶ
τοῖς ἐλαιουργοῖς [11]τὸμ μισθὸν καὶ ὅ τι ἂ[ν ἡ
ὠ]νὴ διὰ τούτους καταβλα-[12]βῇι διπλοῦν.

[13]Ἐὰν δὲ τὰ ἐλαιουργ[ῖ]α μὴ καταστήσωνται
καθό-[14]τι γέγραπται ἢ τὰ φορ[τ]ία τὰ ἱκανὸν μὴ
παρά-[15][θ]ωνται καὶ διὰ ταῦτα [ἡ] ὠνὴ καταβλαβῇι,
ἀποτι-[16][ν]έτω ὅ τε οἰκονόμος κ[αὶ ὁ] ἀντιγραφεὺς
τὴν ἔγδει-[17][αν] τὴν γενομένην [καὶ] τοῖς τὴν ὠνὴν
πριαμένοις [18][τὸ βλ]άβ[ος δι]πλοῦν.

[19][Χορηγείτωσαν] δὲ [ὁ οἰ]κονόμος κ[α]ὶ [ὁ ἀ]ντι-

(Col. 45) 14. l. ἱκανά.

18

203. CODES AND REGULATIONS

They shall not allow the oil-makers appointed in each nome to migrate to another nome. Any oil-maker who goes elsewhere shall be subject to arrest by the director of the contract and the oeconomus and the controller.

No one shall harbour oil-makers (from another nome). If anyone does so knowingly or fails to bring them back when ordered, he shall forfeit for each oil-maker 3000 drachmae, and the oil-maker shall be liable to arrest.

. . . and from the surplus [a] of the oil that is manu-factured he shall distribute to the oil-makers for every metretes containing 12 choes 2 drachmae 3 obols. Of this sum the oil-maker and the pounders shall re-ceive 1 drachma 4 obols, and the purchasers of the contract 5 obols.

If the oeconomus or his representative fails to pay the oil-makers their wages or their share in the profits from the sale, he shall forfeit to the Crown 3000 drachmae, and to the oil-makers their pay, and twice the amount of any loss incurred by the contract on account of the workmen.

If they fail to set up oil factories in accordance with these regulations, or to deposit a sufficient quantity of produce, and in consequence the contract incurs a loss, the oeconomus and the controller shall forfeit the amount of the deficit thus caused, and shall pay to the purchasers of the contract twice the amount of their loss.

The oeconomus and the controller shall provide the

[a] When sufficient oil had been sold to defray all the expenses of manufacture, the remainder was called the ἐπιγένημα or surplus. Of the profits derived from this a small portion was reserved for the contractors and workmen and the rest was taken by the Crown.

γ[ρ]αφε[ὺς ²⁰ἐν ἑκάστωι ἐργ]ασ[τ]ηρ[ίωι τὴν κατα-
σκευήν]. (Col. 46) - - - ²εἰς τ[ὸ κά]τεργον κατ[ιὼ]ν
μηθὲν ἐπικωλυ[σάτω] κα-³ταβλάπτων τὴν ὠνήν.
⁴ʼἘὰν δὲ μὴ χορηγῆι ἢ καταβλάψηι τι τὴν ὠνήν,
κρινέσ-⁵θω ἐπὶ τοῦ τεταγμένου ἐπὶ τῆς διοικήσεως,
καὶ ἐὰν κατα-⁶ληφθῆι, ἀποτεινέτω ἀργυρίου (τάλαντα) β καὶ τὸ βλά-⁷βος διπλοῦν.

⁸Οἱ δὲ τὴν ὠνὴν ἔχοντες καὶ ὁ ἀντιγραφεὺς ὁ
κατασ-⁹τα[θε]ὶς ὑπὸ τοῦ οἰκονόμου καὶ τοῦ ἀντι-
γραφέ[ω]ς κυ-¹⁰ρι[εύσου]σιν τῶν ⟦γεωργῶν⟧ ἐλαιουργῶν πάντων τῶν ἐν τ[ῶι ν]ομῶι ¹¹κ[αὶ τῶ]ν ἐργα-
στηρίων καὶ τῆς κατασκευῆς, [καὶ π]α-¹²ρα[σφρα]-
γιζέσθωσαν τὰ ὄργανα τὸν ἀργὸν το[ῦ χρό]νο[υ].

¹³Ἐπ[αν]αγκαζέτωσαν δὲ τοὺς ἐλαιουργοὺς [καθʼ]
ἡ-¹⁴μέ[ραν ἐρ]γάζεσθαι καὶ συμπαρέστωσαν, κατ-
[εργα]α-¹⁵ζέ[σθ]ωσαν δὲ μὴ ἔλασσον τὴν ἡμέραν
τοῦ [μ]ὲν ¹⁶ση[σ]άμου κατʼ ἕκαστον ὅλμον ἀρτάβης
⟦καὶ τρ[ί]του⟧, ¹⁷το[ῦ] δὲ κρότων[ος] ἀρ(ταβῶν) δ,
τῆς δὲ κνήκου ἀρ(τάβης), ¹⁸ἀπ[ο]διδότωσα[ν δὲ]
τ[. . . . .] τοῦ μὲν σησάμου ¹⁹[τῶν] δ [ἀρ(ταβῶν)]
δραχμὰς ., τοῦ δὲ κρότ]ωνος τῶν [.] ἀρ(ταβῶν)
²⁰(δραχμὰς) δ, [τῆ]ς δὲ κνήκ[ου τῶν . ἀρ(ταβῶν)
δραχμ]ὰς η.

(Col. 47) ¹[Σύντ]αξιν δὲ πρὸ[ς τοὺς ἐλ]αιουργοὺ[ς
περὶ τῆ]ς ῥύσεως ²τοῦ ἐλαίου μὴ ποιείσθω μήτε
ὁ οἰκονόμος μήτε ὁ πρα-³γματευόμενος τὴν ὠνὴν
παρευρέσει μηδεμιᾶι, ⁴μηδὲ τὰ ὄργανα τὰ ἐν τοῖς
ἐργαστηρίοις τὸν ἀργὸν ⁵τοῦ χρόνου ἀσφράγιστα
ἀπολειπέτωσαν. ἐὰν δὲ συν-⁶τά[ξ]ωνται πρός τινας
τῶν ἐλαιουργῶν ἢ ἀσφράγιστα ⁷τὰ ὄργανα ἀπο-
λείπω[σ]ιν, ἀποτ⟦ε⟧ινέτω[σ]αν εἰς μὲν ⁸τὸ βασι-

(Col. 46) 16. For καθʼ ἕκαστον.

plant in every factory. . . . when he comes down to pay wages, he shall not obstruct the work in any way to the damage of the contract.

If he fails to provide plant or causes any damage to the contract, he shall be judged before the dioecetes, and if he is found guilty, he shall forfeit 2 talents of silver and twice the amount of the damage.

The contractors and the checking clerk appointed by the oeconomus and controller shall have authority over all the oil-makers in the nome and over the factories and the plant, and shall seal up the implements during the time when there is no work.

They shall compel the oil-makers to work every day and shall stay beside them, and they shall each day make into oil not less than 1 artaba of sesame at each mortar, and 4 artabae of croton, and 1 of cnecus, and they shall pay as wages for crushing 4 artabae of sesame . . . drachmae, and for . . . artabae of croton 4 drachmae, and for . . . artabae of cnecus 8 drachmae.

Neither the oeconomus nor the manager of the contract shall make an arrangement with the oil-makers concerning the flow of the oil[a] on any pretext, nor shall they leave the implements in the factories unsealed during the time when there is no work. If they arrange with any of the oil-makers or leave the implements unsealed, each of the guilty

[a] The meaning seems to be that the output was not to be manipulated by private arrangement, to the possible disadvantage of the Crown.

λικὸν ἕκαστος τῶν αἰτίων ἀργυρίου (τάλαντον) α
⁹καὶ ἐάν τινα ἡ ὠνὴ ἔγδε[ια]ν ποιῇ.

¹⁰ᶜΟ δὲ παρὰ τοῦ οἰκονόμ[ου κ]αὶ τοῦ ἀντιγραφέως καθεσ-¹¹τηκὼς ἀναγραψάσθω τ[ὰ ὀ]νόματα
τῶν καπήλων ¹²τῶν ἐν ἑκάστηι πόλει ὄ[ντ]ων καὶ
τῶν μεταβόλων ¹³καὶ συνταξάσθω πρὸ[ς α]ὐτοὺς
μετὰ τῶν τὴν ὠνὴν ¹⁴πραγματευομένων π[όσο]ν
δεῖ ἔλαιον καὶ κίκι λαμβάνον-¹⁵τες καθ' ἡμέραν
πωλεῖν, ἐν Ἀλεξανδρείαι δὲ συντασσέσθωσαν
¹⁶πρὸς τοὺς παλινπρατ[ο]ῦντας, καὶ συγγραψά-
σθωσαν ¹⁷[πρὸς] ἕκα[σ]τ[ο]ν συνγρα[φ]ήν, πρὸς μὲν
τοὺς ἐν τῆι χώ[ραι ¹⁸κατὰ μῆνα, πρὸς δὲ το]ὺς
ἐ[ν Ἀ]λεξα[νδρείαι - - -

(Col. 48) - - - ³῞Οσον δ' ἂν συνγράψωνται οἱ
κάπηλοι καὶ οἱ μετάβολοι ⁴οἳ ἐν ἑκάστηι κώμηι
διαθήσεσθαι ἔλαιον καὶ κίκι, παρακομι-⁵ζέτωσαν ὅ
τε οἰκονό<μο>ς καὶ ὁ ἀντιγραφεὺς πρότερον ἢ
τὸν μῆνα ⁶ἐπιστῆναι τὸ πλῆθ[ος] εἰς ἑκάστην κώμην
ἑκάστου γένους ⁷καὶ μετρείτωσαν τοῖ[ς] καπήλοις
καὶ τοῖς μεταβόλοις κατὰ ⁸π[ε]νθήμερον καὶ κομι-
ζέσθωσαν τὰς τιμάς, ἐὰμ μὲν ⁹δ[υν]ατὸν ἦι, αὐθήμερον, εἰ δ<ὲ μ>ή, μὴ ἐξελθου[σ]ῶν τῶν πέντε
¹⁰ἡ[μερῶ]ν καὶ καταβαλλέτωσαν ἐπὶ τὴν [βα]σιλικὴν
¹¹τ[ρά]πεζαν, τὸ δὲ ἀνήλωμα τὸ εἰς τὴν [πα]ρα-
κομιδὴν ¹²δ[ι]δότωσαν ἀπὸ τῆς ὠνῆς.

¹³Τὴν δὲ σύνταξιν ἣν ἂν ποιήσωνται πρὸς
[ἕ]καστον ἐπι-¹⁴κ[η]ρυσσέτωσαν πρότερον ἢ τὸν
μ[ῆ]να· ἐπιστῆναι ἔμ-¹⁵προσθεν ἡμέραις δέκα καὶ
γράψαντες ἐκτιθέτωσαν ¹⁶τὸ εὕρισκον ἐφ' ἡμέρας
δέκα ἔν τε τῆι μητροπόλει καὶ ¹⁷ἐν τῆι κ[ώμ]ηι
κ[α]ὶ τοῦ κυρωθέντες συγγραφὴν ποιείσθω-¹⁸σαν.

(Col. 49) ⁵- - - μήτε ὅ]λμους ἐκ[. . . . .]

parties shall forfeit 1 talent of silver to the Crown and make good any deficit incurred by the contract.

The agent appointed by the oeconomus and the controller shall register the names of the dealers in each city and of the retailers, and together with the managers of the contract arrange with them how much oil and castor oil they are to take and sell from day to day ; and in Alexandria they shall arrange with the traders ; and they shall make a written agreement with each of them, with those in the country every month, with those in Alexandria . . .

Whatever quantity of oil and castor oil the dealers and retailers in each village agree to dispose of, the oeconomus and the controller shall convey the full quantity of each kind to each village before the beginning of the month, and they shall measure it out to the dealers and retailers every five days, and shall receive the price, if possible, on the same day, but if not, before the expiry of the five days, and shall pay it into the royal bank, debiting the contract with the cost of transport.

The quantity which they arrange for in each case shall be put up to auction [a] ten days before the beginning of the month, and they shall publish in writing the latest bid for ten days both in the metropolis and in the village, and shall make an agreement for the finally approved sum.

. . . nor shall they take away (?) mortars or

---

[a] That is, to middlemen who distributed the oil to the retailers and made themselves responsible to the government for the price of the arranged quota.

(Col. 47) 14. *l.* λαμβάνοντας.   (Col. 48) 17. *l.* κυρωθέντος.

⁶μήτε ἱπωτ[ή]ρια μήτε ἄλλο μηθὲν τῶν τῆι ἐρ-
[γασίαι] ⁷ταύτηι συγκυρόντων παρευρέσει μηδεμιᾶι,
⁸εἰ δὲ μή, ἀποτινέτωσαν εἰς μὲν τὸ βασιλικὸν
(τάλαντα) ε ⁹καὶ τοῖς τὴν ὠνὴν πριαμένοις τὸ
βλάβος πενταπλοῦν. ¹⁰παρ' οἷς δὲ προυπάρχει
τούτων τι ἀπογραφέσθωσαν πρὸς ¹¹τὸν τὴν ὠνὴν
διοικοῦντα καὶ πρὸς τὸν παρὰ τοῦ οἰκονόμου ¹²καὶ
τοῦ ἀντιγραφέως ἐν ἡμέραις τριάκοντα καὶ ἐπι-
¹³δεικνύτωσαν τούς τε ὅλμ[ο]υς καὶ τὰ ἱπωτήρια,
¹⁴οἱ δὲ τὴν ὠνὴν ἔχοντες κα[ὶ ὁ] παρὰ τοῦ οἰκονόμου ¹⁵καὶ τοῦ ἀντιγραφέως μετε[νεγ]κάτωσαν
εἰς τὰ ¹⁶βασιλικὰ ἐλαιουργία.

Ἐὰν δ[έ τι]ς εὑρεθῆι σήσαμον ¹⁷ἢ κρότωνα ἢ
κνῆκον κατε[ργα]ζόμενος τρόπωι ¹⁸ὡιτινιοῦν ‹ἢ›
τὸ ἔλαιον ⟦καὶ⟧ τὸ σησάμιν[ον] ἢ τὸ κνήκινον {τ}ἢ
τὸ κίκ[ι] {ἢ} ἀλλοθέμ ποθεν ὠνού-¹⁹μενος καὶ μὴ
παρὰ τῶν τὴν ὠνὴν ἐχόντων, περὶ μὲν ²⁰αὐτοῦ ὁ
βασιλεὺς διαγνώσεται, ἀποτινέτω δὲ τοῖς ²¹τὴν
ὠνὴν ἔχουσι (δραχμὰς) Γ καὶ τοῦ ἐλαίου καὶ τῶν
φορτίων ²²στερέσθω· εἰσπρασσέσθω δὲ ὑπὸ τοῦ
οἰκονόμου καὶ τοῦ ²³[ἀν]τιγραφέως, ἐὰν δὲ ἄπρα-
κτος ἦι, παραδ[ότ]ω αὐτὸν (Col. 50) ¹εἰς [- - -

⁶- - - παρευρέσει] ²μηδεμιᾶι μηδ' εἰς Ἀλε[ξάν-
δρ]ειαν εἰσάγεσθαι ³ἔξω τ[ο]ῦ βασιλικοῦ. ἐὰν δέ τινες
εἰσάγωσι πλέον ⁹οὗ μέλλουσιν ἀνηλώσιν ἕκαστος
⟦τὴν⟧ κατὰ σῶμα ¹⁰ἡμερῶν τριῶν, τῶν τε φορτίων
σ⟦ε⟧τερέσθωσαν ¹¹καὶ τῶν πορείων καὶ προσαποτινέτωσαν καθ' ἕκα-¹²στον μετρητὴν (δραχμὰς) ρ
καὶ τοῦ πλείονος καὶ τοῦ ἐλάσ-¹³σονος κατὰ λόγον.

¹⁴Οἱ δὲ μάγειροι τὸ στέαρ καταχράσθωσαν καθ'
ἡ-¹⁵μέραν [ἐ]ναντίον τοῦ τὴν ἐλαϊκὴν ἔχοντος,
¹⁶αὐτὸ [δὲ] καθ' αὑτὸ μηδενὶ πωλείτωσαν παρ[ευ-]
24

presses or any other implement used in this industry on any pretext ; otherwise they shall forfeit to the Crown 5 talents, and to the purchasers of the contract five times the damage. Persons who already possess any of these implements shall make a declaration before the director of the contract and the agent of the oeconomus and controller within thirty days and shall exhibit their mortars and presses, and the holders of the contract and the agent of the oeconomus and controller shall transfer them to the royal factories.

If anyone is detected manufacturing oil from sesame or croton or cnecus in any manner whatsoever, or buying sesame oil or cnecus oil or castor oil from any quarter except from the contractors, the king shall decide his punishment, but he shall forfeit to the contractors 3000 drachmae and be deprived of the oil and the produce ; and payment of the penalty shall be exacted by the oeconomus and the controller, and if he is without means, he shall be committed . . .

. . . on any pretext, nor bring oil into Alexandria apart from the government supply. If any persons bring in more than they are likely to use for their own consumption in three days, they shall be deprived both of the goods and of the means of transport, and shall in addition forfeit 100 drachmae for each metretes, and for more or less in proportion.

The butchers shall use up the lard every day in the presence of the oil contractor, and shall not sell it separately to any person on any pretext nor melt

¹⁷ρέσει μη[δε]μιᾶι μηδὲ συντηκέτωσαν μηδὲ ἀπ[ο-]
¹⁸τιθέσθ[ω]σαν, εἰ δὲ μή, ἀποτινέτω ὅ τε ἀποδό-
μενος κ[αὶ ὁ πρι]άμενος ἕκαστος ¹⁹τῶι τ[ὴ]ν ἐλαϊκὴν
πριαμένωι καθ᾽ ἕκαστον ὧν ἂν πρίητα[ι] [[ἑκάστην
ἡμέραν]] (δραχμὰς) ν.

²⁰Οἱ δ᾽ ἐλα[ι]ουργοῦντες ἐν τοῖς ἱεροῖς τοῖς κατὰ
τὴ[ν] ²¹χώραν ἀπογραφέσθωσαν πρὸς τὸμ πραγμα-
τευόμ[ε]νον ²²τὴν ὠνὴν καὶ πρὸς τὸν παρὰ τοῦ
οἰκονόμου κα[ὶ] τοῦ ²³ἀντιγραφέως πόσα τε ἐλαι-
ουργῖα ὑπάρχει ἐν ἑκάστωι ²⁴ἱε[ρῶ]ι κα[ὶ] πόσο[ι]
ὄλμοι ἐν ἑκάσ[τ]ωι ἐργαστηρίωι (Col. 51) ¹[καὶ
ἱπωτ]ήρια, καὶ ἐπιδε[ικνύτωσαν τὰ ἐργαστ]ή[ρ]ια,
²[τοὺς δὲ ὄλμ]ους καὶ τὰ ἱπ[ωτήρια παρεχέ]τω-³[σαν
εἰς πα]ρασφραγισμόν - - - ⁷ἐὰ[ν δὲ μὴ] ἀπογρά-
[ψωνται μηδ᾽ ἐπ]ιδείξω[σι μηδὲ] ⁸παρά[σχων]ται εἰς
παρασφραγ[ι]ζμόν, ἀποτι[νέτ]ω-⁹σαν οἱ ἐπὶ τῶν
ἱερῶν τεταγμένοι εἰς μὲν τὸ βασι-¹⁰λικὸν ἕκαστος
τῶν αἰτίων (τάλαντα) γ καὶ τοῖς τὴν ¹¹ὠνὴν πριαμένοις ὅσου ἂν διατιμήσωνται τὸ βλάβος πενταπλοῦν. ὅταν ¹²δὲ βούλωνται κατεργάζεσθαι ἐν τοῖς
ἱεροῖς τὸ ἔλαι-¹³ον τὸ σησάμινον, παραλαμβανέτω-
σαν τὸν τὴν ὠνὴν ¹⁴πραγματευόμενον καὶ τὸν παρὰ
τοῦ οἰκονόμου καὶ ¹⁵τοῦ ἀντιγραφέως καὶ ἐναντίον
τούτων ἐλαιουρ-¹⁶γείτωσαν, κατεργαζέσθω[σα]ν δὲ
ἐν διμήνωι ὅσον ¹⁷ἀπεγράψαντο εἰς τὸν ἐνια[υτὸ]ν
ἀνηλωθήσε[σ]θαι. ¹⁸τὸ δ[ὲ κ]ίκι τὸ ἀνηλισκόμενο[ν
λ]αμβανέτωσ[α]ν παρὰ ¹⁹τῶν [τ]ὴν ὠνὴν ἐχόντων
τῆ[ς κ]αθισταμένη[ς τ]ιμῆς.

²⁰ᶜῬ δὲ οἰκονόμος καὶ ὁ ἀντιγραφεὺς τὸ ἀνήλωμ[α]
τὸ γινό-²¹μενον εἰς ἕκαστον ἱερὸν τ[ο]ῦ τε κίκιος
καὶ τοῦ ἐλαίου ²²ἀποστελ[λ]έτωσαν τὴν γρα[φ]ὴν
πρὸς τὸμ βασιλέα, ²³διδότωσαν δὲ καὶ τῶι ἐπὶ τῆς
26

it down nor store it up[a]; otherwise both the seller and the buyer shall each forfeit to the oil contractor for every piece that is bought 50 drachmae.

Those who make oil in the temples[b] throughout the country shall declare before the manager of the contract and the agent of the oeconomus and controller the number of the oil workshops in each temple and of the mortars and presses in each workshop, and shall exhibit the workshops, and deliver the mortars and presses to be sealed up. . . . If they fail to make the declaration or to exhibit the workshops or to deliver the implements to be sealed up, the persons in charge of the temples shall, each of them who is guilty, forfeit to the Crown 3 talents, and to the contractors five times the amount at which the latter estimate the damage. When they wish to manufacture sesame oil in the temples, they shall call in the manager of the contract and the agent of the oeconomus and controller and make the oil in their presence ; and they shall manufacture within two months the amount which they declared that they would consume in the year. But the castor oil which they use they shall obtain from the contractors at the fixed price.

The oeconomus and the controller shall write down the amounts of castor oil and sesame oil used by each temple and send the list to the king, and shall

---

[a] The object of this curious regulation was to protect the monopoly by making it illegal to sell lard as a substitute for oil.

[b] The temples, which formed little communities of priests and minor attendants, were allowed to make sesame oil under the supervision of the monopoly, but not more than was sufficient for their own needs.

διοικήσεως τετα-²⁴γμένωι.   μὴ ἐξέστω δὲ τοῦ
ἐλαίου τοῦ κατερ-²⁵γαζομέ[νο]υ εἰς τὰ ἱερὰ μηθενὶ
πωλεῖν, εἰ δὲ μή, στερέ- (Col. 52) ¹σ[θωσαν τοῦ
ἐλαίου κ]αὶ προσαποτινέτ[ωσαν τοῦ] ²μ[ετρητοῦ
(δραχμὰς) ρ καὶ το]ῦ πλείονος καὶ ἐλ[άσσονος]
³κ[ατὰ λόγον].

⁷- - - μὴ ἐξέστω] ⁸ἀνάγειν εἰς τὴν χώρ[αν ἐ]πὶ
πράσει μήτε ἐξ ᾽Αλεξαν-⁹δρείας μήτε ἐκ Πηλουσίου
μήτε ἄλλοθεν μηθαμόθεν.   ¹⁰ἐὰν δέ τινες ἀνάγωσιν,
τοῦ τε ἐλαίου στερέσθωσαν καὶ προσ-¹¹εισπρασ-
σέσθωσαν τοῦ με(τρητοῦ) (δραχμὰς) ρ καὶ τοῦ
πλείονος καὶ ¹²ἐλάσσονος κατὰ λόγον.

¹³᾽Εὰν δέ τινες εἰς τὴν ἰδίαν χρείαν ξενικὸν ἔλαιον
κομί-¹⁴ζωσιν, οἱ μὲν ἐξ ᾽Αλεξανδρείας ἄγοντες
ἀπογραφέσθω-¹⁵σαν ἐν ᾽Αλεξανδρείαι καὶ καταβαλλέτωσαν ⟦ἐκάσ⟧τοῦ μετ(ρητοῦ) (δραχμὰς) ιβ
¹⁶καὶ το[ῦ] ⟨πλείονος καὶ⟩ ἐλάσσονος κατ[ὰ] λόγον
καὶ σύμβολον λ[α]βόντες ¹⁷ἀναγ[έ]τωσαν.

¹⁸Οἱ δὲ ἐκ [Πη]λουσίου ἄγοντες καταβαλλέτω-
[σαν] τὸ τέλος ἐμ ¹⁹Πηλου[σίωι] καὶ σύμβολ[ον
λ]αμβανέτωσαν.

²⁰Οἱ δὲ λογ[εύο]ντες ἐν ᾽Αλε[ξ]ανδρείαι καὶ Πη-
λουσίω[ι] ²¹καταχ[ωρι]ζέτωσαν τὸ [τέ]λος εἰς ὃν ἂν
νομὸν ἄγω[σι τ]ὸ ²²ἔλαιον.

²³᾽Εὰν δέ τινες εἰς τὴν ἰδ[ίαν] χρείαν ἄγοντες τὰ
τέλη μὴ κα-²⁴ταβάλλωσιν ἢ τὸ σύμβολον μὴ
κομίζωσιν, τοῦ τε ἐλαίου ²⁵στερέσθωσαν καὶ
προσαποτινέτωσαν τοῦ με(τρητοῦ) (δραχμὰς) ρ.
ὅσοι δὲ τῶν ἐμπόρων ²⁶ἐκ Πηλουσίου ξενικὸν
ἔλαιον ἢ Σύρον παρακομίζ[ω]σιν εἰς [᾽Αλ]εξάν-
δ[ρ]ειαν, ἀτελεῖς ἔστωσαν, σύμβ[ο-²⁷λον δ]ὲ κομιζέ-
[τω]σ[αν] παρὰ [τ]οῦ ἐμ Π[η]λουσίωι καθεσ[τηκό]-

also give one to the dioecetes. It shall not be lawful to sell to any person any of the oil manufactured for the temples ; whoever does so shall be deprived of the oil, and shall in addition forfeit 100 drachmae for each metretes, and for more or less in proportion.

It shall not be lawful to bring [foreign oil] into the interior *a* for sale, either from Alexandria or Pelusium or any other place. Whoever does so shall be deprived of the oil, and shall in addition pay a fine of 100 drachmae for each metretes, and for more or less in proportion.

If any persons carry with them foreign oil for their personal use, those who bring it from Alexandria shall declare it in Alexandria, and shall pay down 12 drachmae for each metretes, and for more or less in proportion, and shall obtain a voucher before they bring it inland.

Those who bring it from Pelusium shall pay the tax in Pelusium and obtain a voucher.

The collectors in Alexandria and Pelusium shall place the tax to the credit of the nome to which the oil is brought.

If any persons bringing such oil for their personal use fail to pay the tax or to carry with them the voucher, they shall be deprived of the oil, and shall forfeit in addition 100 drachmae for each metretes. All merchants who carry foreign or Syrian oil from Pelusium across the country to Alexandria shall be exempt from the tax, but shall carry a voucher from the collector stationed at Pelusium and the

a Foreign oil could be imported to Alexandria and Pelusium on payment of a fifty per cent customs tax and disposed of there under stringent conditions. But it could not be taken into the interior as merchandise except in transit to Alexandria.

τος λ[ογ]εύτ[ου] καὶ τοῦ οἰκ[ο]νόμ[ου κα]θάπερ
[28][ἐν] τῶι νόμωι γέγ[ρα]πται, ὡσαύτ[ω]ς δὲ καὶ τοῦ
ἀπ[. . . . .]ε[. . .] εἰς ᾿Αλε]ξάνδρειαν
[29][. . .] καὶ το[ύ]του [σύμβο]λον κομιζ[έ]τωσαν
[π]αρὰ τ[οῦ . . . .]ν ἀπ[. . . . .]
ε[ὰ]ν δ[ὲ μὴ (Col. 53) [1][[[. . . . μέ]νου συμβ]] . . . .
μ]ένου συμβόλου τω[. . . . . τοῦ
ἐλαίου] [3]στερέσθωσαν.

(Col. 54) - - - [15]Παρα[κ]αταστήσουσι δὲ οἱ πριά-
μενοι τὴ[ν ὠ]νὴν [16]καὶ ἀν[τιγ]ραφεῖς ἐν ᾿Αλεξαν-
δρείαι καὶ Πηλουσίωι [τοῦ] ἐλαί-[17]ου τοῦ [ἐκ
Σ]υρίας ἀπο-σ[τ]ελλομένου εἰς Πηλο[ύσιον] καὶ
[18]᾿Αλεξά[νδρει]αν, καὶ πα[ρα]σφραγιζέσθωσαν τὰ
ἀ[ποδ]ό-[19]χια κα[ὶ τῶ]ι ἀνηλισκομ[έ]νωι παρακολου-
θείτω[σαν].

[20]῾Ο δὲ κα[τα]σταθεὶς ἀντι[γρα]φεὺς τῆς ὠνῆς
ὑπὸ τοῦ ο[ἰ]κονό-[21]μου διαλογιζέσθω π[ρὸς] τὸν
τὴν ὠνὴν ἔχοντα κ[α]τὰ [22]μῆνα ἐναντίον τοῦ
ἀντι[γρ]αφέως, γραφέτω δὲ ἐν τοῖς λόγοις [23]τά τε
φορτία ὅσα ἑκάστο[υ γ]ένους παρείληφεν καὶ ὅσα
(Col. 55) [1][κατεί]ργασται καὶ πέ[πρα]κε τιμῆς τῆς
ἐν τῶι διαγ]ράμματι γεγραμμένης [. . . . . . χωρὶς]
τοῦ ἀφαι-[2][ρετοῦ] τήν τε τιμὴν τῶ[ν παρειλημ-
μένων] τὴν ἐν [3][τῶι] διαγράμματι γεγρ[αμμένην
. . . . σ]ὺν τῶι [4][κερα]μίωι καὶ τοῖς λοιποῖ[ς
ἀνηλώμασι, τοῦ μὲν σ]ησάμου [5][τῆς] ἀρ(τάβης)
(δραχμῆι) α, τοῦ δὲ κρό[τωνος . , τῆς δὲ κν]ήκου
(δυοβόλοις), [6][τοῦ δὲ κολοκύντου ., τοῦ δὲ λίνου
σπέρματος ., [7]τοῦ δὲ σησαμίνου ἐλαίου τῶν .
ἀρ(ταβῶν) (δραχμαῖς) ., τοῦ δὲ κίκιος τῶν] [8]ε
[ἀρ(ταβῶν) (δραχμῆι)] α (ὀβολῶι), τοῦ δὲ κνηκ[ίνου
τῶν η ἀρ(ταβῶν) [(δρ .) .], τοῦ δὲ [9]ἐπ[ελλ]υχνίου

oeconomus, as is prescribed in the law ; likewise for oil which is brought from . . . to Alexandria they shall also carry a voucher from the . . . ; but if they transport it without (?) a voucher, they shall be deprived of the oil.

The contractors shall also appoint agents at Alexandria and Pelusium to check the oil which is dispatched from Syria to Pelusium and Alexandria, and these shall keep the store-houses under seal and check the oil as it is issued.

The checking clerk of the oil contract appointed by the oeconomus shall hold a balancing of accounts with the contractor every month in the presence of the controller, and he shall write in his books the amount which he has received of each kind of produce and the amount of oil which he has manufactured and sold at the price prescribed in the tariff, except the oil which is set apart, and the price of the produce received as prescribed in the tariff, together with the price of the jars and the other expenses, namely 1 drachma for each artaba of sesame, . . . for croton, 2 obols for cnecus, . . . for colocynth, . . . for linseed, and for each . . . artabae made into sesame oil . . . drachmae, for each 5 artabae made into castor oil 1 drachma 1 obol, for each 8 artabae made into cnecus oil . . ., for each 7 artabae

τῶν ζ ἀρ(ταβῶν) (δραχμῆι) α, κολοκυντίνου τῶν
ιβ ἀρ(ταβῶν) α (ὀβολῶι), ¹⁰καὶ τὸ συντεταγμένον
μερίζεσθαι ἀπὸ τοῦ ἐπιγενήματος ¹¹τῶι ἐλαιουργῶι
καὶ τῶι τὴν ὠνὴν διοικοῦντι καὶ ὅ τι ἂν εἰς ¹²τὴν
παρακομιδὴν τῶν φορτίων γένηται.
¹³Οἱ δὲ μισθοὶ τοῖς πραγματευομένοις τὴν ὠνὴν
διδόσθω-¹⁴σαν ἀπὸ τοῦ μεμερισμένου ἐκ τοῦ ἐπιγενήματος.
¹⁵Ἐν Ἀλ[εξ]ανδρείαι δὲ τό τε κάτεργον τοῦ
σησαμίνου ἐλαίου καὶ τὸ προπωλητικὸν ¹⁶καὶ οἱ
μ[ισ]θοὶ διδόσθωσαν καθότι ἂμ προκηρυχθῆι ἐπὶ
τῆ[ς] πράσεως.
¹⁷Ζήτησις. ¹⁸ἐὰν δὲ οἱ ἠγορακότες τὴν ὠ[νὴν]
ἢ οἱ ⟦ἐπὶ⟧ τούτ[οις]ων ὑπηρέται ¹⁹βο[ύλ]ωνται
ζητεῖν φάμε[νοι ἔλ]αιον παρά τ[ισι]ν ὑπάρχειν
²⁰κλ[όπ]ιμον ἢ ἐλαιουργῖ⟦ον⟧α, ζ[η]τείτωσαν π[αρ]-
όντος τοῦ ²¹π[αρὰ] τοῦ οἰκονόμου ⟦καὶ⟧ ἢ τοῦ
[παρὰ τ]οῦ [ἀντι]γραφέως. ἐ[ὰν δ]ὲ παρακλη-
²²θ[εὶς ὁ] παρὰ τοῦ οἰκονό<μο>υ ἢ τοῦ [ἀν]τι-
γραφέως μ[ὴ ἀ]κολουθήσηι ²³ἢ [μὴ] παραμείνηι
ἕως ἂν ἡ ζήτησις γένητα[ι, ἀ]ποτινέτωσαν ²⁴τ[οῖς]
τὴν ὠνὴν πριαμένοις τὴν διατίμησιν [ὅσο]υ ἂν
διατιμή-²⁵σωνται διπλῆν, ⟦μὴ⟧ καὶ ἐξέστω δὲ
τοῖς τὴν [ὠν]ὴν ἔχουσι ²⁶ζη[τεῖν ἐντὸς . ἡμ]ερῶν.
(Col. 56) - - - ⁷τὸν δὲ μὴ εὑρόντα [ἃ] ἔφη
ζητεῖν ἐξέστω [τ]ῶι ⁸ζητουμένωι ὀρκίσαι ἐν ἱερῶι
ἦ μὴν μηθενὸς ἄλλου ⁹ἕνεκεν τὴν ζήτησιν ποιεῖσθαι
ἀλλὰ τῶν προσ-¹⁰αγγελέντων καὶ συγκυρόντων εἰς
τὴν ὠνήν.
¹¹Ἐὰν δὲ μὴ ὁμόσηι αὐθήμερον ἢ τῆι ὑστεραίαι,
ἀπο-¹²τινέτω τῶι ἐξορκίζοντι τὸ τίμημα ὅσου ἐτι-
μή-¹³σατο ⟦ἐπὶ⟧ πρὶν τὴν ζήτησιν ποιεῖσθαι διπλοῦν.

made into lamp oil 1 drachma, for each 12 artabae made into colocynth oil 1 drachma 1 obol, and the amount out of the profits which is the appointed share of the oil-maker and the contractor, and the expenses, whatever they may be, of the transport of the produce.

The contractors shall receive their pay from the allotted portion of the profits.

In Alexandria the wages for making sesame oil and the brokerage and the contractors' pay shall be given in accordance with the proclamation made at the auction.

Search. If the contractors or their subordinates wish to make a search, stating that certain persons are in possession of contraband oil or of oil-presses, they shall hold a search in the presence of the agent of the oeconomus or the agent of the controller. If the agent of the oeconomus or controller when summoned fails to accompany them or to remain until the search is completed, they shall forfeit to the contractors twice the amount of the latter's valuation of the contraband, and the contractors shall be allowed to make the search within . . . days.

. . . If the searcher does not find what he professed to be looking for, the person whose property is searched shall have the right to make him swear an oath in a temple that he made the search for no other than its declared object and the interests of the oil contract.

If he fails to take the oath the same day or the day after, he shall forfeit to the person who exacts the oath twice the amount at which he valued the contraband before making the search.

SELECT PAPYRI

¹⁴Οἱ δὲ πριάμενοι τὴν [ὠ]νὴν ἐγγύους καταστή-
¹⁵σουσι τῶ[ν] ἐφεικόστων, καὶ διορθώσονται τὰ
[μ]ὲν λο-¹⁶γεύμα[τ]α καθ' ἡμέραν [ἐ]πὶ τὴν τρά-
πεζ[αν, τὴ]ν ¹⁷δ' ἀναφορ[ὰν τ]ὴν ἐπιβάλ[λ]ουσαν
τῶι μηνὶ ἐν τ[ῶι ἐχ]ο-¹⁸μένωι [πρὸ] τῆς διχο-
[μ]ηνίας.

(Col. 56) 15.=ἐπεικόστων.

204. EXTRACTS FROM THE INSTRUCTIONS OF A DIOECETES TO A SUBORDINATE

From P. Tebt. 703.   Late 3rd cent. B.C.

⁴⁰ʺΑμα δὲ ἐν τῶι ἐφο-⁴¹δεύειν πειρῶ πε[ριερ-
χ]όμενος ἕκαστον ⁴²παρακαλεῖν καὶ εὐθαρσεστέρους
παρα-⁴³σκευάζειν, καὶ τοῦτο μὴ μόνον λόγωι
⁴⁴γίνεσθαι ἀλλὰ καί, ἐάν τινες αὐτῶν ⁴⁵τοῖς κωμο-
γραμματεῦσι ἢ κωμάρχαις ⁴⁶ἐγκαλῶσι περί τινος
τῶν εἰς τὴν γεωρ-⁴⁷γίαν ἀνηκόντων, ἐπισκοπεῖν,
καὶ ἐφ' ὅ-⁴⁸σον ἂν ἐκποῆι εἰς ἐπίστασ[[ε]]ιν τὰ
τοιαῦ-⁴⁹τα ἀγέσθω. ὅταν δὲ διεξαχθῆ ὁ σπόρος,
⁵⁰οὐ χεῖρον ἂν γίνοιτο εἰ ἐπιμελῶς ἐφοδεύ-⁵¹οις·
οὕτως γὰρ τὴν [[τ]] ἀνατολὴν ἀκριβῶς ⁵²ἐπόψει,
καὶ τὰ μὴ καλῶς ἐσπαρμένα ⁵³ἢ τὸ ὅλον ἄσπορα
ῥαιδίως κατανοή-⁵⁴σεις, καὶ τοὺς ὠλιωρηκότας
εἴ[σει ἐκ] ⁵⁵τούτου καὶ σοὶ γνώριμον ἔσται [[.]] [εἴ
τινες] ⁵⁶τοῖς σπέρμασι εἰς ἄλλα κατα[κ]έ-⁵⁷χρην-

49. l. διεξαχθῇ.   54. ὠλιωρηκότας=ὠλιγωρηκότας.

^a The text from which these extracts are taken is probably
a copy of a standard series of instructions sent by the

The contractors shall present sureties for a sum exceeding their liabilities by one-twentieth, and the taxes [a] which they collect they shall pay into the bank from day to day, and the instalment for each month before the middle of the month following.

[a] It is not clear to what this refers. Perhaps, as Wilcken conjectures, a direct tax was levied on consumers in addition to the indirect exaction of the monopoly.

204. EXTRACTS FROM THE INSTRUCTIONS OF A DIOECETES TO A SUBORDINATE [a]

Late 3rd cent. B.C.

In your tours of inspection try in going from place to place to cheer everybody up and to put them in better heart ; and not only should you do this by words but also, if any of them [b] complain of the village scribes or the comarchs about any matter touching agricultural work, you should make inquiry and put a stop to such doings as far as possible.

When the sowing has been completed it would be no bad thing if you were to make a careful round of inspection ; for thus you will get an accurate view of the sprouting of the crops and will easily notice the lands which are badly sown or are not sown at all, and you will thus know those who have neglected their duty and will become aware if any have used the seed for other purposes. [c]

dioecetes, the Ptolemaic minister of finance, to each newly appointed oeconomus in the interior of Egypt.

[b] The persons meant are primarily the peasants who cultivated Crown land.

[c] For the inspection of oil-producing crops compare No. 203, pp. 15-17. The corn crops were no doubt supervised with equal care.

35

ται. ἵνα δὲ καὶ τ[οῖ]ς κατὰ τὴν δια-[58]γραφὴν τοῦ
σπόρου γένεσιν ὁ νομὸς [59]κατασπείρηται κείσθω
σοι ἐν τοῖς [60]ἀναγκαιοτάτοις· καὶ ἄν τινες ὦσι
[61]κατατεταμένο[ι] τοῖς ἐκφορίοις ἢ [62]καὶ παν-
τ[ελῶς ἀ]νειμένοι, μὴ ἀ-[63]νεπίσκεπτ[ον ἐά]σθω.
ἀναγραφὴν δὲ [64]ποίησαι καὶ τῶ[ν ἐν τ]ῆι γεωργίαι
ὑπαρ-[65]χόντων βασιλι[κῶν τ]ε καὶ ἰδιωτικῶν
[66]κτηνῶν, καὶ τὴν ἐνδεχομένην ἐπιμέ-[67]λειαν
ποίησαι ὅπως ἡ ἐκ τῶν βασιλι-[68]κῶν ἐπ[ιγο]νή,
ὅταν εἰς τὸ χορτ[ο]φαγεῖν [69]ἔλθηι, π[αρ]αδίδωτ[αι]
εἰς τὰ μ[οσχο]τρο-[70]φῖα. - - - [80]ἐπιμελὲς [81]δέ σοι
ἔστω καὶ ἵνα αἱ διαγεγραμμέ-[82]ναι ἀγοραὶ κατ-
άγ[ωντ]αι εἰς Ἀλεξάν-[83]δρειαν ὧν σοι καὶ [τ]ὴν
γραφὴν ἐπιστέλ-[84]λομε[ν ἀπ]οστέλλων κα[ὶ] κατὰ
τοὺς [85]καιρο[ύς, μὴ μ]όνον ἀριθμὸν ἔχουσαι [86]ἀλλὰ
κα[ὶ δ]ε[δο]κιμασμέναι καὶ ἐπι-[87]τήδε<ι>οι πρὸς
τὰς χρείας. ἐπιπορεύ-[88]ου δὲ καὶ ἐπὶ τὰ ὑφαντεῖα
ἐν οἷς τὰ ὀ-[89]θόνια ὑφαίνετα[ι] καὶ τὴν πλείστην
[90]σπουδὴν ποιοῦ ἵν[α πλεῖσ]τα τῶν ἱσ-[91]τέων
ἐνεργὰ ἦι, συντελούντων [92]κ[α]ὶ τῶν ὑφαντῶν τὴν
διαγεγραμ-[93]μένην τῶι νομῶι ποικιλίαν. ἐὰν δέ
[94]τινες πρὸς τὰς συντεταγμένας [95]ἐκτομὰς ὀφείλωσι,
πρασσέσθωσαν [96]καθ' ἔκαστον γένος τὰς ἐκ τοῦ
δια- [97]γράμμα[τ]ος τιμάς. ὅπως δὲ καὶ τὰ ὀθόνια
[98]χρηστὰ ἦι κ[αὶ τ]ὰς ἁ[ρ]πεδόνας ἔχωσι κατὰ
τὸ [99]διάγραμμα [μὴ πα]ρέργως φρό[ντι]ζε. - - -
[165]οὔσης δὲ καὶ τῆς κατὰ τ[ὸ] ἐννόμιον προσόδου
[166]ἐν ταῖς πρώταις, μάλι[σ]τ' ἂν εἰς ἐπίδοσιν ἔλθο[ι]
[167]εἰ τὴν ἀναγραφὴν ἀπὸ τοῦ βελτίστου [ποιή-]
[168]σα<ι>σθε. εὐφυέστατος δὲ ὁ καιρός ἐστιν τῶι

---

[a] A regulation of the crops to be sown in each nome on
Crown land.

204. CODES AND REGULATIONS

You must regard it as one of your most indispensable duties to see that the nome be sown with the kinds of crops prescribed by the sowing-schedule.[a] And if there be any who are hard pressed by their rents or are completely exhausted, you must not leave it unexamined.

Make a list of the cattle employed in cultivation,[b] both the royal and the private, and take the utmost care that the progeny of the royal cattle, when old enough to eat hay, be consigned to the calf-byres. . . .

Take care also that the prescribed supplies of corn, of which I send you a list, are brought down to Alexandria punctually, not only correct in amount but also tested and fit for use.[c]

Visit also the weaving-establishments in which the linen is woven,[d] and do your utmost to have the largest possible number of looms in operation, the weavers supplying the full amount of embroidered stuffs prescribed for the nome. If any of them are in arrears with the pieces ordered, let the prices fixed by the ordinance for each kind of stuff be exacted from them. Take especial care, too, that the linen is good and has the prescribed number of weft-threads. . . .

Since the revenue from the pasturage dues, too, is one of the most important, it will most readily be increased if you carry out the registration (of cattle) in the best possible way.[e] The most favourable

[b] With a view to distributing the cattle to the best advantage during the seasons of ploughing, harvesting, and transport.

[c] Compare No. 365.

[d] Weaving was one of the government monopolies.

[e] The tax was payable at the rate of so much for each sheep, goat, etc. A registration was therefore necessary; compare No. 321.

πε-[169]ρὶ τ[αῦ]τ' ὄντι περὶ τὸμ Μεσορὴ μῆνα· ἐγ
γὰρ τού-[170]τω[ι] τῆ[ς πάσης] χώρας ἐπεχομένης
ὑπὸ τῶν [171]ὑδάτω[ν] σ[υ]μβαίνει τοὺς κτηνοτρό-
φ[ο]υς εἰς [172]τοὺς ὑψηλοτάτους τόπους ἀποστεῖλ[αι
τὴν] [173]λε[ί]αν, οὐκ ἐχόντων ἐξουσίαν εἰς ἄλ[λους
τό-][174]πους διαρίπτειν. μελέτω δέ σοι καὶ [ἴ]να
τὰ [ὤ-][175]νια μὴ πλείονος πώληται τῶν διαγε-
γραμ-[176][μ]ένων τιμῶν· ὅσα δ' ἂν ἦι τιμὰς οὐχ
ἐστη-[177][κ]υίας ἔχοντα, ἐπὶ δὲ τοῖς ἐργαζομένοις
[178][ἐσ]τὶν τ[ά]σσειν ἃς ἂν βο[ύ]λωνται, ἐξεταζέσ-
[179][θ]ω καὶ τοῦτο μὴ παρέργως, καὶ τὸ σύμ-
[180]μετρον ἐπιγένημα ⟦τα⟧ τάξας τῶν πω-[181][λ]ου-
μένων φορτίων συνανάγκα[ι]ζε τοὺς [182]. [.] . .
κου[. .] . ς τὰς διαθέσεις ποιεῖσθα[ι].

205. FRAGMENT OF AN ORDINANCE CONCERNING SLAVES

P. Columb. Inventory 480.   About 198–197 B.C.

[1]Ἐκ τοῦ διαγράμματος τοῦ τ[ῶ]ν ἀνδραπό[δ]ω[ν].
[2]Ὁ πραγματευόμενος τὴν ὠνὴν τῶν ἀνδραπόδων
[3]καὶ ὁ ἀντιγραφεὺς πράξονται τῶν σωμάτων [4]ὧν ἂν
αἱ ὠναὶ ἐπὶ τῶν ἀγορανόμων καταγράφωνται [5]τῆς
τιμῆς ἧς ἂν καταγράφωνται πρὸς ἀργύριον [6]παρὰ
τοῦ ἀποδ[ο]μένου σὺν τῆι ἑ[κα]τοστῆ[ι] πρ[ό-]
[7]τερον λογευομένηι εἰς τὴν Δικαιάρχου δωρεὰν [8]τῆς
μνᾶς (δραχμὰς) θ (δυοβόλους) (ἥμισυ) καὶ παρὰ τοῦ
ἀ[γορ]άσαντος (δραχμὰς) η (δυοβόλους) [(ἥμισυ)],
[9]ὥστε γίνεσθαι τῆς μνᾶς (δραχμὰς) ιζ (πεντώβολον),
38

season for one so engaged is about the month of
Mesore ; for the whole country in this month being
covered with water, it happens that cattle-breeders
send their flocks to the highest places, being unable
to scatter them on other places.

See to it, too, that the goods for sale be not sold
at prices higher than those prescribed.[a] Make also
a careful investigation of those goods which have no
fixed prices and on which the dealers may put what
prices they like ; and after having put a fair surplus[b]
on the wares being sold, make the . . . dispose of them.

[a] See for instance the prices prescribed for oil in No. 203.
[b] That is, a fair addition to the cost of production.

205. FRAGMENT OF AN ORDINANCE
CONCERNING SLAVES

About 198–197 B.C.

From the ordinance concerning slaves.

The farmer of the tax on slaves and the controller
shall exact in the case of those whose sales are recorded before the agoranomi, upon the price at which
they are recorded to have been made, the following
sums in silver : from the vendor, including the one
per cent tax formerly collected for the grant to
Dicaearchus,[a] 9 drachmae 2½ obols per mina, and
from the purchaser 8 drachmae 2½ obols, making a
total of 17 drachmae 5 obols per mina, and for the city

[a] An Aetolian mercenary of infamous character, who took
service in Egypt under Ptolemy Epiphanes, and was re-
warded with a grant out of public funds, consisting of the
proceeds of certain small taxes.

[καὶ] τῆι πόλει προ-¹⁰πωλητικὸν παρὰ τοῦ ἀπο-
δομέν[ο]υ τοῦ σώματο[ς] (δραχμὰς) δ (ὀβολόν).

¹¹Ἐὰν δέ τις ἀγοράσηι ἐφ᾽ ὧι τὰ τέλη πάντα
καταβ[α]λεῖ, ¹²πράξονται τῆι μνᾶι (δραχμὰς) κ
(ὀβολὸν) καὶ τῆι πόλ[ει] τοῦ σ[ώ]ματο[ς] (δραχμὰς)
δ [(ὀβολόν)].

¹³Ἐὰν δέ τις ἐξ ὑπερβολῆς ἢ ἀνθυπερβο[λῆ]ς
κατάσχ[ηι], ¹⁴προσκαταβαλεῖ τῆι πόλει ἄλλο προ-
πρατι[κ]όν.

¹⁵Τῶν δὲ πωλουμένων διὰ ξενικῶν πράκτορ[ος]
¹⁶τάξο[ν]ται οἱ ἀγοράσαντες τῆς μ[νᾶς] (δραχμὰς)
ιθ καὶ ¹⁷κηρ[ύκειον ἑ]κατοστὴν (δραχμὴν) α καὶ εἰς
[τὴν] δωρεὰν ¹⁸γραφῖ[ο]ν τοῦ σώματος (δραχμὴν) α.

¹⁹Τῶν δὲ πρὸς βασιλικὰ πωλουμένων π[ρα]χθή-
σοντα[ι] οἱ ²⁰ἀγοράσ[α]ντες τῆς μνᾶς (δραχμὰς) ιϛ
(πεντώβολον) κα[ὶ κ]ηρύκειον ἑ-²¹κατοστὴν (δραχμὴν) α καὶ γραφῖον εἰς τὴν Δικαιάρχ[ο]υ ²²δωρεὰν
τοῦ σώματος (δραχμὴν) α.

²³[Τ]ῶν δὲ ὑποχρέων σωμάτων ὅσα ἂν ἐλεύ[θε]ρα
ὄντα ἑαυ-²⁴[τὰ ὑποθῆι (?) πρὸς] τὸ χρέος πράξονται
τὸν δα[ν]είζον-²⁵[τα τῆς μνᾶς] (δραχμὰς) ε (ὀβολὸν)
καὶ τὸν δανειζόμε[νο]ν (δραχμὰς) ε (ὀβολόν), ²⁶[ὥστ᾽
εἶναι τῆι] μνᾶι (δραχμὰς) ι (διωβόλους), καὶ γραφῖον
τοῦ σ[ώ]ματ[ο]ς (δραχμὴν) α.

²⁷[᾽Εὰν δὲ καὶ (?) πωλῆτ]αι πρὸς τὸ χρέος πρ[ά-
ξ]ονται τὸν ²⁸[ἀγοράσαντα (?) τῆς] μνᾶς (δραχμὰς)] .

16. τάξο[ν]ται E.-H.: [π]ράξο[ν]ται Ed.   23-24. Or
ἑαυ[τὰ παράσχηι Schönbauer.   27-28. Suppl. E.-H.
Or [ἐὰν δὲ κρατῆτ]αι ... [δανειστὴν Schönbauer.

---

[a] In such cases the purchaser would no doubt pay a
correspondingly smaller sum for the slave.

[b] A still higher offer in reply to an overbid at a public
auction.

a brokerage fee from the vendor of 4 drachmae 1 obol per head.

If anyone purchases with the stipulation that he shall pay all the taxes,[a] they shall exact 20 drachmae 1 obol per mina, and for the city 4 drachmae 1 obol per head.

If anyone obtains possession through an overbid or a counterbid,[b] he shall pay to the city an additional brokerage fee.

Upon those sold through the collector of foreign debts[c] the purchasers shall pay 19 drachmae per mina, and a one per cent crier's fee of 1 drachma per mina, and to the account of the grant a clerical fee of 1 drachma per head.

Upon those sold in consequence of debts to the Crown the purchasers shall be charged 16 drachmae 5 obols per mina, and a one per cent crier's fee of 1 drachma per mina, and a clerical fee to the account of the grant to Dicaearchus of 1 drachma per head.

Upon debtors who being still freemen mortgage (?) their persons against the debt [d] there shall be exacted from the lender 5 drachmae 1 obol per mina and from the borrower 5 drachmae 1 obol, making 10 drachmae 2 obols on the mina, and a clerical fee of 1 drachma per head.

And if they are sold (?) to meet the debt, there shall be exacted from the purchaser . . . drachmae

[c] The meaning of this term is obscure. One possible explanation is that it refers to debts owed by strangers, *i.e.* persons whose permanent domicile was in a different locality.

[d] The interpretation is disputed. According to Schön-bauer " For mortgaged slaves, who being free from other claims can be offered as security for the debt, etc.," and in the next sentence " If they are seized to meet the debt, there shall be exacted from the lender, etc."

41

(πεντώβολον) κα[ὶ] ἑκατ[οσ]τὴν [(δραχμὴν) α καὶ
²⁹γραφῖον τοῦ σώματος (δραχμὴκ) α (?)].

206. EXTRACTS FROM THE GNOMON OF
THE IDIOLOGUS

B.G.U. vol. v.   2nd cent. A.D.

(Preamble) ¹Το[ῦ γ]νώμον[ος] ὃν ὁ θεὸς Σεβαστὸς τῇ τοῦ ἰδίου λόγου ²ἐπιτροπῇ [παρ]εστήσατο
καὶ τῶν ὑπὸ χεῖρα αὐτῷ ³π[ρ]οσγεγονότ[ω]ν ἤτοι
ὑπὸ αὐτοκρατόρων ἢ συνκλή-⁴[το]υ ἢ τῶν [κατ]ὰ
καιρὸν ἐπάρχων ἢ ἰδίων λόγων τὰ ⁵ἐν μέ[σ]ῳ
[κεφ]άλαια συντεμὼν ὑπέταξ[ά] σοι, ὅπως τῇ
⁶τ[ῆς] ἀναγραφῆς ὀλιγομερίᾳ τὴν μνήμην ἐπι-
στή-⁷[σας] εὐχερ[ῶς] τῶν πραγμάτων περικ[ρ]ατῇς.
²⁶ε. Τ[ὰ] ὑπὸ Ἀλεξανδρέων οἷς οὐ προσήκει
διατασσόμενα χωρεῖ ²⁷τοῖς κατὰ νόμους [[αυ]]
κληρονομεῖν αὐτοὺς δυναμένοις, ἐάν-²⁸περ ὦσι καὶ
ἐπιδικάζονται.
²⁹ϛ. Ἀλεξανδρεῖ οὐκ ἐξὸν διατάξαι γυναικὶ
γενεᾶς αὐτῷ ἐξ αὐ-³⁰τῆς μὴ οὔσης πλέον τετάρτου
μέρους ἧς ἔχει περιουσίας, ³¹τέκνων δὲ αὐτῷ ἐξ
αὐτῆς ὄντων οὐ πλείονος ἐξὸν ³²μερίζειν τῇ γυναικὶ
ἢ ὅσων ἐὰν ἑκάστῳ τῶν υἱῶν διατάξῃ.
³³ζ. Δ[ι]αθῆκαι ὅσαι μὴ κατὰ δημοσίους χρημα-
τισμοὺς γείνων-³⁴ται ἄκυροί εἰσι.

28. l. ἐπιδικάζωνται.   31-32. πλείονος, ὅσων for the more
natural πλεῖον, ὅσον.

ᵃ " Gnomon " was the Greek name for this list of rules.
The present text shows the form which it had reached in the
time of Antoninus Pius. It should be noted that the directions were originally drawn up in Latin.

5 obols, and a one per cent tax of 1 drachma per mina, and a clerical fee of 1 drachma per head (?).

206. EXTRACTS FROM THE GNOMON OF THE IDIOLOGUS

2nd cent. A.D.

(Preamble) Of the list of directions *a* which the deified Augustus delivered to the administration of the *idios logos*,*b* with the additions made to it from time to time either by emperors or senate or the praefects or idiologi of the day, I *c* have appended for you a summary of the articles in common use, in order that applying your memory to the simplified form of exposition you may easily master the questions.

5. Property bequeathed by Alexandrians to persons not qualified is given to those who can legally inherit from them, if such there be and if they claim it at law.

6. An Alexandrian may not bequeath to his wife, if he has no offspring by her, more than a fourth part of his estate ; and if he has children by her, he may not allot to his wife a larger share than what he bequeaths to each of his sons.

7. All wills which are not in the form of public instruments are invalid.

b In Ptolemaic times the " private account " of the kings, in Roman times that of the emperors. The administrator of it, who was sometimes called the idiologus, was appointed directly by the emperor and, apart from the praefect, was the chief financial authority in Egypt.

c The summary may perhaps have been drawn up by order of the idiologus of the time as a circular for the instruction of his subordinates.

³⁵η. Ἐὰν Ῥωμαϊκῇ δια⟦κ⟧θήκῃ προσκαίηται ὅτι ὅσα δὲ ἐὰν διατά-³⁶ξω κατὰ πινακίδας Ἑλληνικὰς κύρια ἔστω, οὐ παραδεκτέα ³⁷[ἐ]στίν, οὐ γὰρ ἔ[ξ]εστιν Ῥωμαίῳ διαθήκην Ἑλληνικὴν γράψαι.

⁵¹ιϛ. Ὅσα ἀπελευθέροις Ῥωμαί[οις]ων διατάσσεται ἐπὶ τῷ καὶ εἰς ἐγγόνους ⁵²αὐτῶν ἐλθεῖν, ἐὰν ἀποδειχθῇ τὰ ἔγγονα μηδέπω γε[γο]νότα ὅτε ⁵³ἡ διάταξις ἐγράφετο, ἐγλιπόντων τῶν λαβόντων ἀνα[λ]αμβάνεται.

⁵⁴ιζ. Τὰ καταλειπόμενα εἰς θυσίας κατοιχομένων, ὅταν μη[κ]έτι ὦσιν ⁵⁵οἱ ἐπιμεληθησόμενοι τού-⟦του⟧ ⟨των⟩, ἀναλαμβάνεται.

⁵⁶ιη. Τὰς κατὰ πίστιν γεινομένας κληρονομίας ὑπὸ Ἑλλήνων εἰς Ῥω-⁵⁷μαί[ων]ους ἢ ὑπὸ Ῥωμαίων εἰς Ἕλληνας ὁ θεὸς Οὐεσπασιανὸς [ἀ]νέλαβεν, ⁵⁸οἱ μέντοι τὰς πίστεις ἐξωμολογησά[ντες]μενοι τὸ ἥμισ[υ ε]ἰλήφασι.

⁵⁹ιθ. Τὰ διατασσόμενα ἀπελευθέροις οὐδέπω ἐσχηκό[σι ν]ομίμην ⁶⁰ἀπελευθέρωσιν ἀναλαμβάνεται. νομίμη δέ ἐστιν [ἀ]πελευθέρω-⁶¹σις ἐὰν ὁ ἀπελευθερούμενος ὑπὲρ τριάκοντα [ἔ]τ[η] ἦν γε[γ]ονώς.

⁶²κ. Δούλῳ ἐν δεσμοῖς γενομένῳ καὶ ὕστερον ἀπελευθερωθέντι ἢ καὶ ⁶³μηδέπω τριάκοντα ἐτῶν γενομένῳ τὰ διατασσόμενα ἀναλαμβ(άνεται).

⁶⁴κα. Ὁ ἐλευθερωθεὶς ἐντὸς τριάκοντα ἐτῶν καὶ οὐἱ⟨ν⟩δίκταν λαμβάνων ⁶⁵δι' ἔπαρχος ἴσος ἐστὶν τῷ μετὰ τρι[ά]κοντα ἔτη ἐλευθερωθέντι.

⁶⁶κβ. Τῶν τελευτώντων Λατίνων τὰ ὑπάρχοντα δίδοται τοῖς πάτρω-⁶⁷σι καὶ υἱοῖς αὐτῶν καὶ θυγατράσι καὶ κλη[ρ]ονόμοις, τὰ δὲ διατασσό-

35. l. προσκέηται.   58. l. ἐξομολογησάμενοι.   61. ἦν for ᾖ, a not infrequent vulgarism.   65. l. ἐπάρχου.

8. If to a Roman will is added a clause saying, " whatever bequests I make in Greek codicils shall be valid," it is not admissible, for a Roman is not permitted to write a Greek will.

16. All property which is bequeathed to freedmen of Romans with the stipulation that it is to descend to their offspring is confiscated on the decease of the recipients if it be proved that no offspring had yet been born when the bequest was written.

17. Property left to provide sacrifices to the departed is confiscated when there are no longer any persons to take charge of these.

18. Inheritances left in trust by Greeks to Romans or by Romans to Greeks were confiscated by the deified Vespasianus ; nevertheless those acknowledging their trust have received the half.

19. Bequests made to freedmen who have not yet acquired legal emancipation are confiscated. It is legal emancipation if the person freed is over thirty years old.

20. Bequests made to one who as a slave was put in chains [a] and was afterwards freed or who was freed when not yet thirty years old are confiscated.

21. One who was freed under thirty years of age by receiving manumission through the praefect counts as one who was freed when over thirty.

22. The property of deceased Latins [b] is given to their patrons and to the sons and daughters and heirs

[a] That is, a slave guilty of misconduct.
[b] Latins = *Latini Iuniani*, persons freed by the *lex Iunia Norbana*, who lived as freedmen but died in the status of slaves. The " patrons " are their former masters.

⁶⁸μενα ὑπὸ μηδέπω ἐσχηκότων νομίμ[η]ν ἐλευθερείαν Ῥωμαιος ⁶⁹ἀναλαμβάνεται.

⁷⁰κγ. Οὐκ ἐξὸν Ῥωμαίοις ἀδελφὰς γῆμαι οὐδὲ τηθίδας, ἀδελφῶν ⁷¹θυγατέρας συνκεχώρηται. Παρδαλᾶς μέντοι ἀδελφῶν συν-⁷²ελθόντων τὰ ὑπάρχοντα ἀνέλαβεν.

⁷³κδ. Τὴν διδομένην προ{ο}οῖκα ὑπὸ γυναικὸς Ῥωμαίας ὑπὲρ πεν-⁷⁴τήκοντα ἔτη γεγονυ[ί]ας ἀνδρὶ Ῥωμαίῳ ἐντὸς ἑξήκοντα ⁷⁵ἐτῶν γεγονότι μετὰ θάνατον ὁ φίσκος ἀναλαμβάνει.

⁷⁶κε. Ὁμοίως καὶ τὴν διδομένην ὑπὸ γυναικὸς ἐντὸς ν̄ ἐτῶν ⁷⁷οὔσης ἀνδρὶ ὑπὲρ ἑξήκοντα ἔτη γεγονότι ἀναλαμβάνεται.

⁷⁸κϛ. Κἂν Λατείνα ὑπὲρ πεντήκοντα ἔτη δῷ τι ὑπὲρ ξ̄ ἔτη, ὁμοίω{ς} ἀναλαμβ(άνει).

⁷⁹κζ. Ὅσα Ῥωμαῖο{ι}ς ἑξηκονταετὴς ἄτεκνος ἀγύναιος ὢν κληρονο-⁸⁰μεῖ, ἀναλαμβάνεται. ἐὰν δὲ ἔχῃ γυναῖκαν τέκνα δὲ μὴ καὶ ἑαυ-⁸¹τὸν προσαγγείλῃ, τὸ ἥμισυ αὐτῷ συνχωρεῖται.

⁸²κη. Γυνὴ ἐὰν ⟨ᾖ⟩ ἐτῶν ν̄, οὐ κληρονομεῖ, ἐ[ὰ]ν δὲ ἡττόνων καὶ ἔχῃ τέ-⁸³κνα γ̄, κληρονομεῖ, ἀπελευθερικὴ δέ, ἐὰν ἔχῃ τέκνα τέσσαρα.

⁸⁴κθ. Ῥωμαία ἐνγενὴς ἔχου[σ]α οὐσίαν σηστερτίων κ̄, μέχρι ἄγαμός ⁸⁵ἐστιν, δίδωσι κατ' ἔτος ἑκατοστήν, καὶ ἀπελευθερικὴ δὲ ἔχου-⁸⁶σα σηστερτίων κ̄ τὸ αὐτὸ δίδωσι ἕως ἂν γαμήσῃ.

⁸⁷λ. Αἱ καταλειπόμεναι κληρονομεῖαι γυναιξὶ

---

68. l. Ῥωμαίαν.   77. l. ἀναλαμβάνει.

ᵃ An idiologus.

of these ; and bequests made by those who have not yet acquired legal Roman freedom are confiscated.

23. Romans are not permitted to marry their sisters or their aunts, but marriage with their brother's daughters has been conceded. Pardalas [a] indeed, when a brother married a sister, confiscated the property.

24. The dowry brought by a Roman woman over fifty years of age to a Roman husband under sixty years of age is after death confiscated by the Treasury.[b]

25. That likewise is confiscated which is brought by a woman under fifty years of age to a husband over sixty.

26. And if a Latin [c] woman over fifty brings any property to a husband over sixty, it is likewise confiscated.

27. Whatever property a Roman sixty years old, who has neither child nor wife, inherits, is confiscated. If he has a wife but no children and declares his position, he is allowed to take the half.

28. If a woman is fifty years old, she does not inherit ; if she is less and has three children, she inherits, but in the case of a freedwoman, if she has four children.

29. A freeborn Roman woman having a property of 20,000 sestertii pays one-hundredth yearly so long as she is unmarried, and a freedwoman possessing 20,000 sestertii pays the same until she marries.

30. Inheritances left to Roman women possessing

[b] Such a marriage was in Roman law called *impar matrimonium*, and on the death of either party the dowry fell not to the survivor, but to the Treasury.

[c] See note b, p. 45.

Ῥωμαίαις ἐχού-[88]σαις οὐσίας σηστερτίων ν̄ ἀγά-
μοις κ[α]ὶ ἀτέκνοις ἀναλαμβάνεται.

[89]λ̄α. Ῥωμαίᾳ ἐξὸν ἀνδρὶ [κ]αταλείπειν τὸ
δέκατον ὧν κέκτητ[αι], [90]ἐὰν δὲ πλείονα, ἀναλαμ-
βάνε[ται].

[91]λ̄β. Ῥωμαῖοι{ς} ὑπὲρ ἑκατὸν σηστέρτια ἔχοντες ἄγαμοι καὶ [92]ἄτεκνοι οὐ κληρονομοῦσι, οἱ δὲ
ἔλαττον ἔχοντες κληρονο[ν]μοῦσι.

[93]λ̄γ. Ῥωμαίᾳ οὐκ ἐξὸν ὑπὲρ τὴν καλουμένην
κουηεμπτίωνα δια-[94]τάσσειν· ἀνελήμφθη δὲ καὶ
ληγᾶτον καταλειφθὲν ὑπὸ Ῥωμαί-[95]ας ἀφήλικι
Ῥωμαίᾳ.

[96]λ̄δ. Τοῖς ἐν στρατείᾳ καὶ ἀπὸ στρατείας οὖσι
συνκεχώρηται διατίθεσθα[ι] [97]καὶ κατὰ Ῥωμαϊκὰς
καὶ Ἑλληνικὰς διαθήκας καὶ χρῆσθαι οἷς βού-
[98]λωνται ὀνόμασι, ἕκαστον δὲ τῷ ὁμοφύλῳ κατα-
λείπειν καὶ οἷς ἔξ[εσ]τιν.

[99]λ̄ε. Τοὺς στρατευομένους καὶ ἀδιαθέτους τελευ-
τῶντας ἐξὸν τέκνοι[ς] [100]καὶ συγγενέσει κληρονομεῖν, ὅταν τοῦ αὐτοῦ γένους ὦσι οἱ μετερχ[όμε]νοι.

[138]ν̄γ. Αἱ ἀγόμεναι ὑπὸ μισσικίων [γυν]αῖκες
Αἰγύπτιαι, ἐὰν χρηματίσωσι ὡς Ῥω-[139]μαῖα⟨ι⟩,
τῷ τῆς ἀκαταλληλία[ς κρ]ατεῖται.

[140]ν̄δ. Θυγατρὶ μ[ι]σσικίου Ῥωμαίᾳ γεν[ομ]ένῃ
Οὖρσος οὐκ [ἐπέτρε]ψε [141]κληρον[ομ]ῆσαι τὴν
μητέραν Αἰγ[υπ]τίαν οὖσαν.

88. l. ἀναλαμβάνονται.   100. l. συγγενέσι.   139.
l. κρατοῦνται.

---

[a] Marriage by mock sale. Roman women sometimes
underwent a fictitious marriage of this kind in order to
acquire the right to bequeath by will.

50,000 sestertii, if unmarried and childless, are confiscated.

31. A Roman woman is permitted to leave to her husband the tenth part of what she possesses ; anything more is confiscated.

32. Romans possessing more than 100,000 sestertii, if unmarried and childless, do not inherit, but those who have less inherit..

33. A Roman woman is not permitted to bequeath outside of the so-called *coemptio.*[a] A legacy left by a Roman woman to a Roman girl who was a minor was confiscated.

34. Soldiers in service and after leaving service have been allowed to dispose of their property both by Roman and by Greek wills and to use what words [b] they choose ; but in every case they must leave it to fellow-nationals and to those to whom it is permissible.

35. Children and kinsmen of soldiers who die intestate are permitted to inherit from them, if the claimants are of the same nationality.

53. Egyptian women married to discharged soldiers are, if they formally style themselves Romans, subject to the article on nonconformity to status.

54. A discharged soldier's daughter who became a Roman was not allowed by Ursus [c] to inherit from her mother who was an Egyptian.

[b] This is supposed to mean that they were not restricted to the *certa et solemnia verba* of Roman usage. But it may be that ὀνόμασι here simply means " names," for provincial soldiers were accustomed to take Roman names.

[c] Praefect of Egypt about A.D. 84–85.

¹⁴²νε. Ἐὰν Αἰγύπτ[ιο]ς λαθὼν στρατεύσητα[ι ἐ]ν
λεγ‹ε›ῶνι, ἀπολυθ[εὶς εἰ]ς τὸ ¹⁴³Αἰγύπτιο[ν] τάγμα
ἀποκαθίστατ[αι]. ὁμοίως δὲ καὶ οἱ ἐκ [τοῦ] ἐρε-
¹⁴⁴τικοῦ ἀπ[ολ]υθέντες ἀποκαθίστανται πλὴν μόνων
τῶ[ν] ἐκ ¹⁴⁵Μησινῶν [σ]τόλου.

¹⁴⁶νϛ. Οἱ στρατευ[όμ]ενοι καὶ μὴ νομίμην [ἔ]χ[ον-
τ]ες ἀπόλυσιν, ἐ[ὰν χ]ρ[η]-¹⁴⁷ματίσωσ[ι] ὡς Ῥω-
μαῖοι, τεταρτολο[γ]οῦνται.

¹⁵⁰νη. Οἱ μὴ ἀπογεγραμμένοι ταῖς [κατ'] οἰκίαν
ἀπογ[ρα]φα[ῖ]ς ἑ]αυτούς ¹⁵¹τε κα[ὶ] οὓς [δ]εῖ τε-
ταρτολογοῦνται, [κα]ὶ ἐὰν δυσὶν ἀπογρ[αφ]α[ῖ]ς μ]ὴ
¹⁵²ἀπογραψάμενοι εἰσδοθῶσιν, [δὶς] τέταρτ[ο]ν
⟦ἀναλ[α]⟧ [κατακ]ρίνονται.

¹⁵³νθ. Ῥωμαῖοι κ[α]ὶ Ἀλεξανδρεῖς μὴ ἀπ[ογρ]α-
ψάμενοι οὓς δεῖ, ἐά[ν τ]ε ἕνα ¹⁵⁴ἐάν τε πλεί[ο]υς,
ἓν τέταρτον κατ[ακρ]ίνοντα[ι].

¹⁵⁵ξ. Οἱ μὴ ἀπογραψάμενοι ἀνδράπο[δα μ]όνων
τῶν ἀνδ[ρα]πόδω[ν] στέρωνται.

¹⁵⁶ξα. Τῶν ἀναπογ[ρ]άφων δούλων ἢ ἐπ[ιγον]ἡ
δίδοται τοῖς δ[ε]σπότ[αι]ς, ἐάν-¹⁵⁷περ μηδένα πόρον
ἔχωσι ἢ ⟦μὴ⟧ μ[όν]ους τοὺς δούλου[ς].

¹⁵⁸ξβ. Οἱ ἐν στρατε[ί]ᾳ ὄντες ἀναπόγραφ[οι ο]ὐ
κρατοῦνται, γυναῖκ[ε]ς δὲ ¹⁵⁹αὐτῶν κ[αὶ] τέκνα
εὐθύνοντ[αι].

¹⁶⁰ξγ. Οἱ εὐθυνόμενοι ὡς μὴ ἀπογρα[ψά]μενοι
τῇ προτέρᾳ ἀπογ[ρα]φῇ, ¹⁶¹ἐὰν ἡ προσθήκη μέχρι
γ ἐτῶν [ᾖ], συγγνωμονοῦνται.

143. Or Αἰγυπτίω[ν].   145. l. Μισηνῶν.   155. l.
στέρονται.   156. ἐπ[ιγον]ή doubtful.

---

^a If not a Roman citizen, an Egyptian was not permitted
to join a legion.

^b If honourably discharged, they were entitled to the
Roman citizenship.

55. If an Egyptian serves in a legion without being detected,[a] he returns after his discharge to the Egyptian status. Discharged oarsmen return likewise, except only those belonging to the fleet of Misenum.

56. Soldiers who have not received a legal discharge, if they style themselves Romans,[b] are fined a quarter of their property.

58. Persons who in the household censuses have not registered themselves and those whom they ought are fined a quarter of their property, and if they are reported not to have registered on two occasions,[c] they are sentenced to the same fine doubled.

59. Romans and Alexandrians who have not registered those whom they ought, whether one person or more, are sentenced to a fine of one quarter.

60. Those who have failed to register slaves suffer confiscation of the slaves only.

61. The offspring (?) of unregistered slaves is given to the masters, if they have no means of support except only the slaves.

62. Soldiers in active service are not held responsible if unregistered, but their wives and children are called to account.

63. Persons called to account for not having registered at the last census are excused if the additional subject for registration was under three years old.[d]

---

[c] A general census, house by house, was taken every fourteen years for purposes of taxation.

[d] That is, they were not punished for failing to declare an infant under three.

¹⁶²ξ̄δ̄. Τὰ περὶ τῶν χωρὶς ἀποστόλου ἐκπλεόντων νῦν ἡγεμονικῆς δια-¹⁶³γνώσεως [ἐ]γένετο.

¹⁶⁴ξ̄ε̄. Δοῦλοι κατ' ἄγνοιαν τοῦ δεσπότου ἐξαχθέντες ἐπράθησαν.

¹⁶⁵ξ̄ϛ̄. Οἱ ἐξ[ὸ]ν ἐκπλεῖν ἀναπόστολοι πλέοντες τριτολογο[ῦντ]αι, ἐὰν δὲ δούλους ¹⁶⁶ἰδίο[υς] ἐξάγωσιν ἀναποστόλους, ἐξ ὅλων ἀναλαμβάν[οντα]ι.

¹⁶⁷ξ̄ζ̄. Οἱ Αἰγυ[πτ]ίων δούλων οἰκογενεῖς τάσσοντες ἢ πωλοῦντες [ἀ]πὸ οἰκογενείας ὑπὲρ ¹⁶⁸τοῦ [ἐκ]πλεῖν αὐτοὺς ὅτε μὲν ἐξ ὅλων ὅτε δὲ ἐξ ἡμίσου[ς ὅτ]ε δὲ ἐκ τετάρτ[ο]υ ἀνε-¹⁶⁹λήμ[φ]θησαν, κατὰ τῶν συνγνόντων ἐ[π]ίτειμα ὡρίσθ[η]· τ[ῶ]ν μέντοι οἰκογε-¹⁷⁰νῶ[ν], κἂν [μ]ὴ Αἰγυπτίων μητέρων ὦσιν, τὸ μητρικὸν [γ]ένος οὐκ ἐξετάζεται.

¹⁷¹ξ̄η̄. Ῥωμ[αῖ]ο[ς] ἐκπ]λεύσας μὴ πλήρη τὰ πρὸς ἔκπλουν γράμματα [ἐσχ]ηκὼς κατεκρίθ[η] (τάλαντ . .)[.].

¹⁷²ξ̄θ̄. Αἰγυ[πτ]ία διὰ Πηλουσίου δούλους ἐκπέμψασα σὺν υἱ[ο]ῖ[ς . . . .]υμέν[ο]ις κατεκρί[θη] (τάλαντον) α (δραχμὰς) ˏΓ.

64. Cases of persons departing by sea without a pass are now under the jurisdiction of the praefect.

65. Slaves exported owing to their master's ignorance (of the rules) were sold.

66. Persons permitted to depart by sea who sail without a pass are fined a third of their property, and if they export slaves of their own without a pass, they suffer confiscation of the whole.

67. Persons who by registration or sale alter the status of house-born slaves of Egyptian origin with a view to their departing by sea have suffered confiscation sometimes of their whole property, sometimes of the half, sometimes of the quarter, and penalties have been ordained against those accessory. But the house-born slaves' maternal descent is not investigated, even if their mothers are not Egyptian.[a]

68. A Roman who departed by sea without having received his departure papers in full was sentenced to a fine of . . . talents.

69. An Egyptian woman who sent out slaves by way of Pelusium along with her sons and . . . was sentenced to a fine of one talent 3000 drachmae.

[a] That is, a house-born slave, οἰκογενής, is presumed to be of Egyptian descent, and a claim that the mother was not Egyptian will not even be examined.

II. EDICTS AND ORDERS

207. LETTER OF PTOLEMY PHILADELPHUS

P. Hal. 1, ll. 166-185.   Middle of 3rd cent. B.C.

¹⁶⁶Βασιλεὺς Πτολεμαῖος Ἀντιόχωι χαίρειν. περὶ
τῆς ¹⁶⁷σταθμοδοσίας τῶν στρατιωτῶν ἀκούομεν
πλείω τινὰ ¹⁶⁸βίαν γίνεσθαι τὰς καταλύσεις παρὰ
τῶν οἰκονόμων ¹⁶⁹οὐ λαμβανόντων, ἀλλ' αὐτῶν
εἰς τὰς οἰκίας εἰσπηδώντων ¹⁷⁰τοὺς ἀνθρώπους
ἐγβάλλοντας βίαι ἐνοικῖν. σύνταξον οὖν ¹⁷¹ὅπω[ς]
τοῦ [λ]οιποῦ μὴ γίνηται τοῦτο· ἀλλὰ μάλιστα μὲν
αὐτοὶ ¹⁷²στε[γ]ανομείσθωσαν, εἰ δὲ ἄρα δεῖ αὐτοῖς
σταθμοὺς ¹⁷³δίδο[σθα]ι π[α]ρὰ τῶν οἰκονόμων,
διδότωσαν α[ὐ]τοῖς ¹⁷⁴τοὺς ἀναγκαίους. καὶ ὅταν
ἀπολύωνται ἐκ τῶν [στ]αθμῶν, ¹⁷⁵ἀναποιή[σ]αντες
ἀφιέτωσα[ν] τοὺς σταθμοὺς καὶ μὴ ¹⁷⁶καταλ[ι]-
πέτωσαν ἕως ἂν πά[λ]ιν παραγένωνται, καθάπερ
¹⁷⁷νῦν ἀ[κο]ύο[με]ν γίνεσθαι, ὅτ[αν] ἀποπορεύων-
ται, ἀπ[ο-]¹⁷⁸μισθοῦν αὐτοὺς καὶ ἀποσφρα[γισα]-
μένους τὰ οἰκήματα ¹⁷⁹ἀποτρ[έ]χειν. μάλιστα δὲ
π[ρονό]ησον Ἀρσινόης τῆς ¹⁸⁰κατὰ Ἀ[π]όλλωνος
πόλιν ὅπω[ς, ἐὰ]ν παραγένωνται ¹⁸¹στρατ[ιώ]ται,
μηθεὶς ἐπιστα[θ]μεύσηι, ἀλλὰ καὶ ἐν Ἀπόλλ-¹⁸²ωνος
π[ό]λει διατρίβωσιν. [ἐ]ὰν δέ τι ἀναγκαῖον ἦι

172. στε[γ]ανομείσθωσαν Schubart : στεγνοποιείσθωσαν Edd.

54

II. EDICTS AND ORDERS

207. LETTER OF PTOLEMY PHILADELPHUS

Middle of 3rd cent. B.C.

King Ptolemy to Antiochus [a] greeting. About the billeting of the soldiers, we hear that some undue violence is used, as they do not receive lodgings from the oeconomi, but themselves break into the houses and ejecting the inhabitants occupy them by force. Give orders therefore that in future this is not to be done ; if possible, let them provide accommodation for themselves, but if indeed it is necessary that quarters should be given to them by the oeconomi, let these give them what they strictly require. And when they depart from their quarters, let them give them up after putting them in order and not leave them as theirs until they return, as we hear that they now do ; for it seems that when they go away they let them to others or seal up the rooms before leaving. Be particularly careful about Arsinoe near Apollonopolis,[b] to see that, if soldiers come, none of them shall be billeted there, but that they shall reside in Apollonopolis. But if they have

[a] Perhaps the military secretary of the district.
[b] The modern Edfu in Upper Egypt.

176. καταλ[ι]πέτωσαν suggested by Schubart : καταχ[ρ]ή-στωσαν Edd.

¹⁸³ἐν Ἀρσιν[ό]ηι καταμένειν, ἑ[αυ]τοῖς οἰκίδια ἀνα-
πλασσέτωσαν, ¹⁸⁴καθάπερ καὶ οἱ πρότερ[ον παρ]α-
γενόμενοι ἐποίησαν. ¹⁸⁵ἔρρωσο.

183. Suppl. E.-H.: καταμέν[ουσιν αὐ]τοῖς Schubart.

208. DECREE OF PTOLEMY PHILOPATOR

B.G.U. 1211.   3rd cent. B.C.

¹Βασ[ιλ]έως προστάξαντο[ς]. ²τοὺς κατὰ τὴν
χώραν τελοῦντα[ς] ³τῶι Διονύσωι καταπλεῖν εἰς
Ἀλε[ξ]άν-⁴δρειαν, τοὺς μὲν ἕως Ναυκράτε[ως]
ἀ-⁵φ᾽ ἧς ἡμέρας τὸ πρόσταγμα ἔκκειται ⁶ἐν ἡμέραις
ι, τοὺς δὲ ἐπάνω Ναυκράτε-⁷ως ἐν ἡμέραι<ς> κ,
καὶ ἀπογράφεσθ[αι] πρὸς ⁸Ἀριστόβουλον εἰς τὸ
καταλογεῖον [ἀ]φ᾽ ἧ[ς] ⁹ἂν ἡμέρας παραγένωνται ἐν
ἡμ[έρ]αις ¹⁰τρ[ι]σίν, διασαφεῖν δὲ εὐθέως καὶ π[αρὰ
τί-]¹¹νων παρειλήφασι τὰ ἱερὰ ἕως γενε[ῶν
τρι-]¹²ῶν καὶ διδόναι τὸν ἱερὸν λόγον ἐ[σφ]ραγισ-
[μένον] ¹³ἐπιγράψαντα [[τὸ ὄνομα]] ἕκαστ[ον] τὸ
αὐ[το]ῦ ¹⁴ὄνομα.

209. ROYAL DECREE

B.G.U. 1730.   50 B.C. (?)

¹Βασιλέως καὶ βασιλίσσης προσταξάντων. ²μη-
δένα τῶν ὑπὲρ Μέμφιν νομῶν ³ἀγοράζοντα πυρὸν

2. Or ⟨ἐκ⟩ τῶν (Wilcken).

---

^a Cleopatra VII. and Ptolemy XIV.; or perhaps

any urgent reason for staying in Arsinoe, let them erect for themselves mud huts, as did those who came formerly.   Goodbye.

208. DECREE OF PTOLEMY PHILOPATOR

3rd cent. B.C.

By decree of the king.   Persons who perform the rites of Dionysus [a] in the interior shall sail down to Alexandria, those between here and Naucratis within 10 days from the day on which the decree is published and those beyond Naucratis within 20 days, and shall register themselves before Aristobulus at the registration-office within three days from the day on which they arrive, and shall declare forthwith from what persons they have received the transmission of the sacred rites for three generations back and shall hand in the sacred book [b] sealed up, inscribing thereon each his own name.

[a] Ptolemy Philopator is known to have been particularly devoted to this cult.
[b] Concerning the mysteries of Dionysus.

209. ROYAL DECREE

50 B.C. (?)

By decree of the king and queen.[a]   No one purchasing wheat or pulse from the nomes above

Ptolemy Auletes and Cleopatra Tryphaena, in which case the date would be 70 B.C.

ἢ ὄσπριον κατά-[4]γειν εἰς τὴν κάτω χώραν, ἀλλὰ
μη-[5]δ᾽ εἰς τὴν Θηβαΐδα ἀνάγειν παρευ-[6]ρέσει μηδεμιᾶι, πάντας δ᾽ ἀνυφοράτους [7]ὄντας εἰς Ἀλεξάνδρειαν παρακο[μ]ίζειν, [8]ἢ ὁ φωραθεὶς θανάτωι
ἔνοχος ἔσται. [9]μηνύειν δὲ τὸν βουλόμενον περὶ
[10]τῶν παρὰ ταῦτα ποιησόντων [11]τοῖς κατὰ νομὸν
στρατηγοῖς, ἐφ᾽ ᾧ [12]μήμψεται τῆς τοῦ ἐνσχεθη-
[13]σομένου οὐσίας τὸ τρίτον μέρος, [14]ἐὰν δὲ δοῦλος
ᾖ, ἐλεύθερός τ᾽ ἔσται [15]καὶ προσλήμψεται τὸ ἔκτον.
[16](ἔτους) γ Φαῶφι κγ̄.

(2nd hand) [17ε]Ὧρος τοπογραμματεὺς . . . δι᾽ Ὀνίου
γρα(μματέως) [18]ἐκτέθεικα ἐν ἀντί[γραφον τοῦ πρ]ο-
κε[ι-][19]μένου προστάγματος. [20](ἔτους) γ Ἀθὺρ . ε.

12. l. λήμψεται.   18. Wilcken proposes ἐναντί[ον τοῦ
προεκ]κε[ι]μένου.

210. ROYAL INDULGENCES

From P. Teb. 5.   118 B.C.

[1][Βασιλεὺς] Πτολεμαῖος καὶ βασίλισσα Κλεοπάτρα ἡ ἀδελφὴι [2][καὶ βασίλισσ]α Κλεοπάτρα ἡ
γυνὴ [ἀ]φιᾶσει τοὺς ὑ[πὸ] τὴ[ν[3] βασιλήαν π]άντας
ἀγνοημάτων, ἁμαρτημ[άτ]ων, [ἐ]ν-[4][κλημάτων,
‹καταγνωσμάτων›], αἰτ[ι]ῶν πασῶν τῶν ἕως θ
τοῦ Φα[ρμοῦ(θι) τοῦ] νβ (ἔτους) [5][π]λὴν τ[ῶν
φόν]ους ἑκουσίοις καὶ ἱεροσυλίαις ἐνεχομ[ένων].

[6]Προστετά[χα]σι δὲ καὶ τοὺς ἀνακεχωρηκότας

1-7. The restorations are from another copy.   5. l. φόνοις.

[a] Ptolemy Euergetes II.   The indulgences appear to have
been proclaimed on the conclusion of a long strife between
the supporters of the king and the faction of his sister

Memphis [a] shall carry it down to the low country [b] or yet carry it up to the Thebaid on any pretext, though all may transport it to Alexandria free of question, on pain of being liable to death if detected.[c] Whoever wishes shall inform the strategus of his nome about contraventions of this order, on the understanding that he shall receive the third part of the property of the person found guilty, or, if he be a slave, shall be freed and in addition receive the sixth part.   Year 3, Phaophi 23.

(Docketed) I, Horus, district scribe, acting through Onias, scribe, have posted up one copy of the foregoing decree.   Year 3, Hathur [.]5.

[a] That is, the nomes of Middle, but not Upper, Egypt.
[b] The Delta, not including Alexandria.
[c] The persons aimed at in this decree are probably Alexandrian traders commissioned to purchase supplies for the city (Wilcken).

210. ROYAL INDULGENCES

118 B.C.

King Ptolemy [a] and Queen Cleopatra the sister [b] and Queen Cleopatra the wife [c] proclaim an amnesty to all their subjects for errors, crimes, accusations, condemnations, and offences of all kinds up to the 9th of Pharmouthi of the 52nd year, except to persons guilty of wilful murder or sacrilege.

And they have decreed that persons who have gone

Cleopatra. Some of them refer to acts committed during the troubles, while others are simply provisions against common abuses.
[b] Cleopatra II., sister and former wife of Euergetes.
[c] Cleopatra III., niece and wife of Euergetes.

δ[ιὰ τὸ ἐνέχεσθαι 'λ]ήαις καὶ ἑτέρα‹ι›s αἰτίαις
καταπορευομένους εἰς [τὰς ἰδίας ἐρ-⁸γ]άσεσθαι
π[ρ]ὸς αἷς καὶ πρότερον ἦσαν ἐργασία[ις καὶ . . .
. . . . ⁹τὰ] ἔτι ὑπάρ[χοντα ἄπρατα ἀπὸ τῶν
διατα[. . . . .]

¹⁰['Ἀφιᾶσι] δὲ π[ά]ν[τας] τῶ[ν ὀφ]ειλ[ο]μένων
τ[ῶι βα(σιλικῶι) εἰς τοὺς ¹¹αὐτο]ὺς χρόνους πρός τε
τὴν σιτικὴν μί(σθωσιν) κα[ὶ ἀργυ(ρικὴν) π]ρ(όσ-
οδον) πλὴν ¹²τῶν μεμισθωμένων εἰς τὸ πατρικὸν
[ὑπὲ]ρ ὧν δ[ι]εγγυή(ημα) ¹³ὑπάρχει. - - -

³⁶Προστετάχα[σι] δὲ κ[αὶ] τοὺ[ς] κεκληρουχη-
μένους πάντας καὶ τοὺς ³⁷τὴν ἱερὰν γῆν καὶ τὴν
ἄλλην τὴν ἐν ἀφέσει γῆν ἐχόντων ³⁸[π]άντας καὶ
τοὺς ἐπιβεβηκότας ἐπὶ τὴν βα(σιλικὴν) καὶ τοὺς
ἄλλους ³⁹[τ]οὺς τὴν πλείωι γῆν ἔχοντας τῆς καθ-
ηκούσης ἀποβάν-⁴⁰τας ὧν ἔχουσι πλει‹όν›ων ἁπάντων καὶ προσαγγείλαν-⁴¹τας ἑα[υ]τοὺς καὶ παρα-
δόντ[ας] ἐνιαυτοῦ ἐκφόριον ἀπολύ-⁴²εσθαι τῶν ἕως
τοῦ να (ἔτους) χρόνων κ[αὶ ἀπὸ τοῦ νβ (ἔτους)]
⁴³κρατεῖν κυ[ρ]ίως.

⁴⁴[Τοὺς δὲ ἐπιλέ]κ[τους] καὶ μαχ(ίμους) ⟦καὶ⟧
(δεκαρούρους) καὶ (ἑπταρούρους) κ[αὶ τοὺς το]ύ-
⁴⁵[τ]ων ἡ[γου]μέν[ο]υς καὶ τοὺς ἄλλους τοὺς φερο-
μ[ένους ἐν τῆι συντ]ά(ξει) ⁴⁶[καὶ τοὺς] να[υκ]ληρο-
μαχ(ίμους) καὶ τοὺς ἐκ τοῦ πολ[. . . . .
⁴⁷κρατεῖ]ν ὧν κατεσχήκασι κλή(ρων) ἕως τοῦ [νβ
(ἔτους) ἀκατηγο-⁴⁸ρήτου]ς καὶ ἀνεπιλήπτους ὄντας.

⁴⁹['Ἀφει]άσει δὲ πάν[τ]ας καὶ τοῦ ὀφειλομένου
λειτουργ[ι]κοῦ [- - -].

⁵⁰[Προσ]τετάχασι δὲ κ[αὶ τὴν ἱερ]ὰν γῆν καὶ τ[ὰς
ἄ]λλας ἱερ[ὰς προσόδους ⁵¹τ]ὰς ὑπαρχούσας τοῖς

37. *l.* ἔχοντας.

into hiding because they were guilty of robbery or other offences shall return to their own homes and resume their former occupations and shall [recover] the property which is still unsold out of the . . .

And they remit to all persons the arrears for the said period in respect both of rents in corn and of money taxes, except to hereditary lessees [a] for whom security has been given. . . .

And they have decreed that all recipients of grants of land and all holders of temple land and of other liberated [b] land, both those who have encroached on Crown land and all others who hold more than their proper portion, shall, on giving up all the excess and declaring themselves and paying a year's rent, be released from responsibility for the period up to the 51st year and have legal possession of the land from the 52nd year.

And that men of the native guard, and native soldiers who own ten or seven arurae, and their leaders, and all others placed in that class, and the native marines, and those of the . . . shall keep the holdings of which they have entered into possession up to the 52nd year, and shall not be subject to accusation or interference.

And they remit to everyone the arrears of the corvée-tax.[c]

And they have decreed that the temple land and the other sacred revenues which belong to the

---

[a] The leases being for an indefinite period and descending from father to son.

[b] Apparently land released from the direct control of the Crown, but it is not clear whether the term denotes all such land or a particular category of it.

[c] A tax paid in lieu of personal service on public works.

ἱεροῖς [[. .]] μένιν [κυρί]ως, λ[ήμψε]σθαι δὲ ⁵²[κα]ὶ
τὰς ἀπομοίρας ἃς ἐλάμβαν[ο]ν ἔκ τε τ[ῶν κ]τημ-
μάτων καὶ τῶν ⁵³[π]αραδεί(σων) καὶ τῶν ἄλλων.

Ὡσαύτως δὲ καὶ τὰ ὑποκείμενα χρήματα ⁵⁴ἦι ἃ
ἐκ τοῦ βα(σιλικοῦ) εἰς τὰς συν[τ]ά[ξις] τῶν ἱερ[ῶ]ν
καὶ τᾶλλα τὰ συνκεκρε‹ι›μένα ⁵⁵[ἕ]ως [το]ῦ να
(ἔτους) ἀπ[ο]διδόναι εὐτάκτως ‹ὡς› ἐ[π]ὶ τῶν
ἄλλων {ων} καὶ μηιθεν[ὶ ⁵⁶ἐ]ξεῖν[αι] λαμβάνειν τι ἐκ
τούτων.

⁵⁷Μ[η]θ[ένα δὲ] παραιρεῖσθαι μηθὲν τῶν ἀν-
ιερωμένων τοῖς θεοῖς [μ]ετὰ βί[α]ς ⁵⁸μηιδὲ [πειθ]-
ανάγκην [π]ροσάγειν τοῖς προεστηκόσι τῶν ἱερῶν
προσόδω[ν], ⁵⁹ἤιτοι κώ(μας) ἦι γᾶς ἦι ἄλλας ἱερὰς
πρ(οσόδους), μη[δὲ] κ[οι]νωνι(κὰ) μηδὲ στεφά(νους)
μηδὲ τὰ ἀρτα(βίεια) ⁶⁰λαμβάνειν ἐκ τῶν ἀνιερω-
μένων τοῖς θεο[ῖς μηδ]ὲ τὰς ἱερὰς (ἀρούρας)
σκε[π]άζειν ⁶¹παρε[υ]ρ[έ]σι.μηδεμιᾶ, ἐὰν δὲ διὰ τῶν
ἱερέ[ων αὐτῶν δ]ιοικεῖσθαι.

⁶²Ἀφείᾶσ[ι] δὲ καὶ τοὺς ἐπιστάτας τῶν ἱερῶν καὶ
τοὺς ἀρχιερεῖς καὶ ἱερ[εῖς τῶν] ⁶³ὀφε[ι]λομένων
πρός τε τὰ ἐπιστατικὰ καὶ τὰς προστιμή[σεις τῶν]
⁶⁴ὀθονίων ἕως τοῦ ν (ἔτους).

⁶⁵Ὁμοίως δὲ καὶ τοὺς ἔχοντας ἐκ τοῖς ἱεροῖς
γέρ[α κα]ὶ προφητεία{ι}ς καὶ γρ(αμματείας) κ[αὶ
ἄλ]λας ⁶⁶λει(τουργίας) τῶν ὀφειλομένων ἐν αὐτοῖς

65. l. ἐν.

---

[a] That is, as in the case of other government subsidies.
[b] A euphemism for torture.
[c] An offering to the king, exacted on special occasions, as
for instance on taking up an appointment.
[d] A tax on arable land, paid in corn.

temples shall remain assured to them, and that the temples shall receive the tithes which they used to receive from vineyards and orchards and other land.

And in like manner that the appointed sums or what they received from the Treasury as subsidies for the temples and the other sums awarded to them up to the 51st year shall be paid regularly as in other cases,[a] and no one shall be allowed to appropriate any part of these grants.

Nor shall anyone take away by force anything of what has been dedicated to the gods, nor apply forcible persuasion [b] to the superintendents of the sacred revenues, whether the things in question be villages or lands or other sacred revenues, nor collect the tax on associations or the crown-tax [c] or the artaba-tax [d] from property dedicated to the god, nor assume protection of the temple lands on any pretext, but leave them to be administered by the priests themselves.

And they remit to the overseers of the temples and the chief priests and priests their arrears in respect both of the tax for overseers and of the values of linen cloths [e] up to the 50th year.

They likewise remit to holders of honourable offices and prophetships and secretaryships and other functions [f] in the temples the arrears owed by them

---

[e] Weaving was under the control of a government monopoly, and as certain fabrics were chiefly or exclusively manufactured in the temples, the priests were bound by contract to deliver specified quantities of these or pay the value in money.

[f] These priestly offices, which were more or less lucrative, were bought from the Crown. The reason why certain of the proceeds had been claimed by the Crown is not clear, but probably had some connexion with the late troubles.

πρὸς τὰς ἐπὶ ἐνίοις καιροῖς ἀπητημέν[α]ς [καρ-]
[67]πείας ἕως τοῦ ν (ἔτους).

[68]Ὁμοίως δὲ καὶ τοὺς πλείονας καρπεία{ι}ς ἐξ-
ενηνεγμένους ἕως τοῦ αὐτ[οῦ χ]ρόνου τῶν ἐπιτίμων.

[70]Ὡσαύτως δὲ κ[αὶ] τοὺς ἐν τοῖς ἐλάσσοσιν
ἱεροῖς καὶ Ἰσιείοις καὶ ἰβίω(ν) τρ(οφαῖς) κ[αὶ
ἱ]ερακεί(οις) [71]καὶ Ἀνουβιείοις [καὶ] τοῖς ἄλλοις
τοῖς παραπλήσιον τῶν παραπλ[η]σίων [72]πρ[.]τους
ἕως τοῦ [α]ὐτοῦ χρόνου. - - - -

[77][Προστε]τάχασι δὲ καὶ τὰ εἰς τὴν ταφὴν τοῦ
Ἄπιος καὶ Μνήσιος ζητεῖν ἐκ τοῦ βα(σιλικοῦ)
[78][ὥ]ς καὶ ἐπὶ τῶν ἀποτεθεωμένων. ὡσαύτως δὲ
καὶ τῶν ἄλλων ἱερῶν [79]ζώ<ω>ν τὰ ὑποκείμενα.

[80]Τὰς ἠγορασμένας προφητείας καὶ γέρα καὶ
γρ(αμματείας) εἰς τὰ ἱερὰ ἐκ τῶν ἱερῶν προσόδων
[ὧ]ν [81]τ[ὰ]ς τιμὰς τεταγμέναι εἰσὶ μένειν τοῖς ἱεροῖς
κυρίως, ταύτας δὲ [μ]ὴ ἐξ[εῖ]ναι [82][τοῖ]ς ἱερεῦσι
{μὴ} παραχωρῖν τοῖς ἄλλοις.

[83]Πρ[ο]στετάχισ<ι>ν δὲ ἐκ τῶν ὑπαρχόντων ἀσύ-
λων τόπων μ[η]θένα [ἐξάγειν] [84]μήιτε ἀποβιάζεσθαι
παρευρέσι μηιδεμιᾷ.

[85]Καὶ [ἐ]πὶ προσπείπτει τοὺς πρὸς ταῖς σιτο-
λο(γίαις) καὶ ἀντιγρ(αφείαις) μίζοσι μέ[τ]ροις [πα]ρὰ
τὰ εὖσ<ταθμα> [86]ἐν ἑκάστωι νομῶι ἀποδεδει[γ-
μέ]να χα(λκᾶ) . . . μέτροις παραλα . . μενου-
[   ] . . . . ε . [στα]θμ[ᾶσ]θαι τῶν [87]εἰς τὸ
βα(σιλικὸν) καθηκόντων [κ]αὶ κατὰ τοῦτο τοὺς
γεω(ργοὺς) μὴ τ[. .]ς χ . . [. . . .]ας α[ἰτ]εῖσθαι

---

77. l. Μνήσιος.   79. The first twelve words of l. 80
written after ὑποκείμενα, then deleted and rewritten in a new
line.   81. l. τεταγμένοι.   83. l. προστετάχασιν.
85. l. ἐπεί.

in respect of the emoluments demanded on certain occasions up to the 50th year.

Likewise to those who have obtained more than their due emoluments up to the said period they remit the penalties.

Likewise to office-bearers in the lesser temples, both Isis-shrines and feeding-places of ibises and hawk-shrines and Anubis-shrines and other similar places, they grant similar remissions up to the same period. . . .

And they have decreed that the expenses for the burial of Apis and Mnevis [a] are to be demanded from the Crown, as in the case of the deified personages.[b] Likewise the normal expenses for the other sacred animals.[c]

The prophetships and honourable offices and secretaryships which have been bought for the temples out of the temple revenues, and of which the prices have been paid, shall remain assured to the temples, but these offices the priests are not permitted to make over to other persons.

And they have decreed that no one is to be taken away or forcibly ejected from the existing sanctuaries on any pretext.

And since it is reported that the corn-collectors and the checking clerks use larger measures than the correct bronze measures appointed in each nome . . . in estimating dues to the Crown and in consequence the cultivators are made to pay more . . . ,

[a] The sacred bulls of Memphis and Heliopolis.
[b] That is, the kings and other members of the royal family who received deification.
[c] Compare No. 410.

[88][π]ροστετάχασι ⟦καὶ⟧ τοὺς στ[ρ]α(τηγοὺς) καὶ
τοὺς ἐπὶ τῶν προ(σόδων) καὶ τοὺς βα(σιλικοὺς)
γρ(αμματεῖς) τὰς στάθμας τῶν μ[έ]τρων [89][ἀ]πὸ
τοῦ βελτίστου ποιεῖσθαι παρόντων τῶν κατὰ τ[ὰ]ς
προ(σόδους) τῶν [.] . ( ) καὶ τῶν [ἱ]ε[ρ]έων
[90]καὶ τῶν κληρούχων καὶ τῶν ἄλλων τῶν τὴν ἐν
ἀφέσει ⟨γῆ⟩ν ἐχόντων . . . . . χα(λκ) [91]καὶ
μὴι πλεῖον ἔχειν τῶν εἰς τὰ παραπτώματα ἐ[π]ι-
κεχωρημένω[ν] . . . . ι . . [92][. .] β, τοὺς δὲ παρὰ
ταῦτα ποιοῦντας θαν[άτωι ζ]ημιοῦσθαι.

[93]Προστετάχασι δὲ καὶ τοὺς γεω(ργοῦντας)
κα[[ι]]τὰ τὴν χώραν γ[ῆν ἀ]μπελῖτιν [ἢι] παρα-
δείσους [94]ἃς ἂν καταφυτ[ε]ύσωσι ἐν τῆι κατα-
κεκλ[υσ]μένηι καὶ κεχερ[σ]ωμένη{ς} [95]ἀπὸ τοῦ νγ
(ἔτους) ἕως τοῦ νζ (ἔτους) ἀτελεῖς ἀφεῖναι ἀφ᾽ οὗ
ἂν α[ὐ]τὰς καταφυτεύσωσι ἐφ᾽ ἔτηι ε, [96]κ[α]ὶ ἀπ[ὸ]
το[ῦ] ς (ἔτους) εἰς ἄλλα τρία ἔλασσον τοῦ καθήκοντος πράσσειν τῶι τετάρτωι [97]ἔτ[ε]ι, ἀπὸ δὲ
τοῦ θ (ἔτους) πάντας τελεῖν καθὰ καὶ οἱ ἄλλοι
[οἱ] τὴν [φό]ριμον κεκτημένοι, τοῖς [98]δ᾽ ἐν τῆι
Ἀλεξα(νδρέων) χώρα πρὸς τοῖς ἐπὶ τῆ[ς] χώ(ρας)
προσδοῦναι ἄ[λλ]α (ἔτη) γ.

[99]Προστετάχασι δὲ καὶ τοὺς ἠγορα{σ}κότας ἐκ
τοῦ βα(σιλικοῦ) οἰκ[ία]ς ἢι ἀμπελῶνας ἢι παρα-
δείσ[ο]υς [100]ἢι ἄλλα σταθα ἢι πλοῖα ἢι ἄλλο τι
καθ᾽ ὁ{υ}ντινοῦν τρόπον μ[έν]ειν κυρίως, καὶ τὰς
[101]ο[ἰ]κίας μὴ ἐπισταθμεύεσθαι. - - -

[147]Προστετάχασι δὲ καὶ τοὺς κυρίους τῶν [148]κατ-
ε[σπ]ασμένων καὶ ἐμπεπυρισμένων [149]οἰκιῶν ἐὰν
⟨ἂν⟩οικοδομεῖν ἐπὶ {τῶν} τὰ ὑποκείμενα [150]μέτρα.

95. For ἐπ᾽ ἔτη.

they have decreed that the strategi and the overseers of the revenues and the royal scribes shall test the measures in the most thorough manner in the presence of those concerned in the revenues of . . . and the priests and the cleruchs and the other owners of liberated land . . . and the measures must not exceed (the government standard) by more than the 2 . . . allowed for errors. Those who disobey these orders are punishable with death.

And they have decreed that cultivators of vineland or orchards in the interior, if they plant them between the 53rd and 57th years in the land which has become flooded or dry, shall be left untaxed for five years from the time of planting them, and from the sixth year for three years more they shall be required to pay less than the regular amount, payment being made in the fourth year, but from the ninth year onwards they shall all pay the same taxes as the other owners of productive land ; and that cultivators in the territory of Alexandria shall be allowed an extra three years' grace.

And they have decreed that those who have bought from the Crown [a] houses or vineyards or orchards or other . . . or boats or anything else in any manner whatsoever shall have their possession confirmed, and the houses shall not be requisitioned for billets. . . .

And they have decreed that owners of houses which have been pulled down or burnt [b] shall be allowed to rebuild them according to the prescribed measurements.

[a] This paragraph is perhaps intended to regularize the position of those who had made purchases from the rival government of the queen.

[b] That is, in the late civil war.

[151]Ἐπιχωρῆσαι δὲ καὶ τοῖς ἰδίᾳ ε[. . . . .
. .]ν [152]κωμῶν τ[ὸ]ν αὐτὸν τρόπον ἕ[ως . . . .]
τὰς ἰδίας [153]καὶ τὰ ἱερὰ ἀνοικοδομεῖν ἕως ὕψους
π(ηχῶν) ι πλὴν τῶν [154]ἐκ Πανῶν πόλεως.

[155]Μηθένα δὲ λογεύειν μηθὲν παρὰ τῶν γεω(ρ-
γῶν) [156]καὶ τῶν ὑποτελῶν καὶ τῶν ἐπιπεπλε-
[157]γμένων ταῖς προσόδοις καὶ μελεισσουργῶν [158]καὶ
τῶν ἄλλων ὥστε τοῖς στρατηγοῖς [159]καὶ ἐπι-
στάταις τῶν φυ(λακιτῶν) ἢ ἀρχιφυ(λακίταις) ἢ
οἰκο(νόμοις) ἢ τοῖς [160]παρ' αὐτῶν ἢ τοῖς ἄλλοις
τοῖς πρὸς ταῖς [161]πραγματεία<ι>ς καθ' ὁντινοῦν
τρόπον.

[162]Μηδὲ τοὺς στρα(τηγοὺς) {καὶ} μηδὲ τοὺς ἐπὶ
χρειῶν τετα-[163]γμένους ⟦καὶ τοὺς κειμένην βα(σιλικὴν) γῆν⟧ καὶ τοὺς [164]τούτοις ὑποτεταγμένους καὶ
τοὺς ἄλλους [165]πάντας τὴν ἐν ἀρετῆι κειμένην
βα(σιλικὴν) γῆν [166]παραιρεῖσθαι τῶν γεω(ργῶν)
μηδὲ ἐπὶ ἐγλογῆι [167]γεωργεῖν.

[168]Ἀνεπιστάθμους [δ'] εἶν[αι] καὶ τοὺς στρα-
τευ-[169]ομένους Ἕλληνας [καὶ τοὺ]ς ἱερεῖς καὶ
τοὺς [170]γεω(ργοῦντας) βα(σιλικὴν) γῆν καὶ τοὺς
[. . . . . .]ς καὶ τοὺς ποκόφους [171]καὶ τανυ-
φά[ντας πάντ]ας καὶ τοὺς ὑοφορβοὺς [172]καὶ χηνο-
βο(σκοὺς) κ[αὶ . . . .]ς καὶ ἐλαιουργοὺς καὶ [173]κικιουργοὺς καὶ με[λισσουργο]ὺς καὶ
ζυτοποιοὺς [174]τοὺς τελοῦντας τὰ καθή(κοντα) εἰς
τὸ βασ(ιλικὸν) ἕκαστων αὐ(τῶν) [175]οἰκίας μιᾶς ἐν
ἧ αὐτὸς καταγείνεται, [176]τῶν δ' ἄλλων τῶν δοσίμων
μὴ πλεῖον ἐπι-[177]σταθμεύεσθαι τοῦ ἡμίσους.

170. l. ποκύφους.　　　　174. l. ἕκαστον.

---

[a] This town was presumably excepted because of the part
it had played in the revolt.

And that persons who have private property (?) in villages shall likewise be allowed to rebuild the private houses to the height of . . . and the temples to the height of 10 cubits, except the inhabitants of Panopolis.[a]

No one is to collect anything in any manner whatsoever from the cultivators and those who work for state interests [b] and those connected with the revenues and bee-keepers and other such persons for the benefit of the strategi or superintendents of the police or chief policemen or oeconomi or their agents or the other officials.

Neither strategi nor holders of official positions nor their subordinates nor any other persons whatever shall take Crown land of good quality from the cultivators by fraud or select it for themselves to cultivate.[c]

Greeks serving in the army and priests and cultivators of Crown land and . . . and all wool-weavers and cloth-makers and swineherds and gooseherds and . . . and makers of oil and castor oil and bee-keepers and brewers,[d] who pay to the Crown the sums due from them, shall not have anyone quartered in the individual houses in which they severally live, and of their other houses which may be used for quarters not more than one-half shall be thus occupied.

[b] The word ὑποτελεῖς, difficult to translate, denotes mainly contractors and employees responsible for the working of the royal monopolies.

[c] Officials on receiving their appointments might be required to cultivate a certain amount of unproductive land at a fixed rent (cf. No. 339).

[d] The people mentioned were employed in industries wholly or partially controlled by the government and were therefore specially favoured.

[178]Προστετάχασι δὲ μηδὲ τοὺς στρα(τηγοὺς) καὶ τοὺς [179]ἄλλους τοὺς πρὸς ταῖς πραγματείαις ἕλκειν [180]τινὰς τῶν κατοικούντων ἐν τῆι χώρᾳ [181]εἰς λειτουργίας ἰδίας μηδὲ κτήνηι αὐτῶν [182]ἐγγαρεύειν ἐπί τι τῶν ἰδίων μηδὲ [183]ἐπιρίπτειν μόσχους μηδὲ ἱερεῖα τρέφειν [184]μηδὲ χῆνας μηδὲ ὄρνιθας μηδὲ οἰνικὰ [185]ἢ σιτικὰ γενή(ματα) ἐπιρίπτειν τιμῆς μηδ' εἰς [186]ἀν{ν}ανεώσεις μηδὲ συναναγκάζειν ἔργα [187]δωρεὰν συντελεῖν παρευρέσει μηδεμιᾷ.

[188]Ἀφιᾶσει δὲ καὶ τοὺς κατὰ τὴν χώραν φυ(λα)κίτας) τῶν [189]παραγραφομένων πρὸς τὰς βα(σιλικὰς) ἐπισκοπείας καὶ [190]πρὸς ἃ καταπρόεινται γενή(ματα) καὶ τῶν παρα-[191]δεδομένων αὐτοῖς πρὸς ὀφει(λήματα) καὶ πρὸς ἄλλας [192]αἰτίας καὶ διαπεπρακότων ἕως τοῦ ν (ἔτους).

[193]Ἀπολῦσαι δὲ καὶ τοὺς μὴ παραδεδωκότας εἰς τὸ βασ(ιλικὸν) [194]τιμῆς τὰ ἐκ τῆς κληρουχικῆς καὶ τῆς ἱερᾶς [195]καὶ τῆς ἄλλης ἐλαικὰ φορτί‹α ἕ›ως τοῦ αὐτοῦ χρόνου, καὶ [196]τοὺς μὴ παρεστακότας τὰ{ι} πορεῖα πρὸς τὴν [197]σύνκλητον τῶν ἐξακολοθούντων.

Ὡσαύτως [198]δὲ καὶ τοὺς μὴ παραγεωχότας ἐπὶ τὰ χώματα [199]τὴν καλαμείαν καὶ τὰς κουφεία[ς].

[200]Ὁμοίως δὲ καὶ τοὺς βα(σιλικοὺς) γεω(ργοὺς) καὶ τοὺ[ς] ἱερεῖς] καὶ τοὺς ‹ἄλλους› [201]τοὺς τὴν ἐν ἀφέσει γῆν ἔχ[οντας καὶ] μὴ [202]καταπεφ‹υτ›ευκότας τὰς καθη[κούσας φυ(τείας)] [203]ἕως τοῦ να (ἔτους) τῶν ἐξακολουθούντων προστίμων, [204]τὴν δὲ φυτείαν ποιεῖσθαι ἀπὸ τοῦ νβ (ἔτους).

182. l. ἀγγαρεύειν: so in l. 252. 192. l. διαπεπτωκότων?

And they have decreed that the strategi and the other officials shall not impress any of the inhabitants of the country for private services, nor requisition their cattle for any purpose of their own, nor force them to feed calves or pigs, nor force them to provide geese or fowls or wine or corn at a price or on the occasion of renewals,[a] nor compel them to work without payment on any pretext whatever.

And they remit to the policemen throughout the country the penalties entered against them in connexion with the government inspections and in respect of the produce which they have allowed to be lost, and also the sums which have been delivered to them for arrears or for other reasons and which have disappeared, up to the 50th year.

And (they have decreed) that those who have failed to deliver to the Crown at a price the oil-yielding produce from cleruchic or temple or other land up to the said period and those who have failed to provide transport for the assembly [b] are released from the consequent penalties.

Likewise those who have failed to provide reeds and light material for the embankments.

Likewise the cultivators of Crown land and the priests and other persons owning liberated land, who have failed to plant the proper number of trees up to the 51st year, are released from the consequent penalties, but they shall plant them from the 52nd year onwards.

[a] The meaning is doubtful; perhaps a reference to the gifts expected from a minor official when his appointment was renewed.
[b] It is not known what assembly is referred to.

²⁰⁵Καὶ τοὺς κεκοφότας τῶν ἰδίων ξύλα παρὰ ⟨τὰ⟩ ἐκ⟨κ⟩είμενα ²⁰⁶προστάγματα.

²⁰⁷Προστετάχασι δὲ καὶ περὶ τῶν κρινομένων Α[ἰ]γυπτίων ²⁰⁸πρὸς Ἕλληνας καὶ περὶ τῶν Ἑλλήνων τῶν [π]ρὸς τοὺς ²⁰⁹Αἰγυπτίους ἢ Αἰγυ(πτίων) πρὸς Ἕλληνας γενῶν πάντων ²¹⁰πλὴν τῶν γεω(ργούντων) βα(σιλικὴν) γῆν καὶ τῶν ὑποτελῶν καὶ τῶν ²¹¹ἄλλων τῶν ἐπιπεπλεγμένων ταῖς προσόδοις τοὺς ²¹²μὲν καθ' Ἑλληνικὰ σύμβολα συνηλλαχότας ²¹³Ἕλλησιν Αἰγυπτίους ὑπέχειν καὶ λαμβάνειν ²¹⁴τὸ δίκαιον ἐπὶ τῶν χρηματιστῶν, ὅσοι δὲ Ἕλληνες ²¹⁵ὄντες συνγραφόμενοι κατ' Αἰγύ(πτια) συναλλάγματα ²¹⁶ὑπέχειν τὸ δίκαιον ἐπὶ τῶν λαοκριτῶν κατὰ τοὺς ²¹⁷τῆς χώρας νόμους, τὰς δὲ τῶν Αἰγυ(πτίων) πρὸς τοὺς ²¹⁸αὐτοὺς ⟨Αἰ⟩γυ(πτίους) κρίσεις μὴ ἐπισπᾶσθαι τοὺς χρημα(τιστὰς) ²¹⁹ἀλλ' ἐὰν ⟦κριν⟧ διεξάγεσθαι ἐπὶ τῶν λαοκριτῶν κατὰ .τοὺς ²²⁰τῆς χώρας νόμους.

²²¹Προστετάχασι δὲ καὶ τοὺς τῶν ξενικῶν ²²²πράκτορας μὴ παραλαμβάνειν τοὺς βα(σιλικοὺς) γεω(ργοὺς) ²²³μηδὲ τοὺς ὑποτελεῖς μηδὲ τοὺς ἄλλους ²²⁴τοὺ⟨ς⟩ κωλυομένους διὰ τῶν προεκκειμένων ²²⁵προσταγμάτων εἰς προβολὴν τέσθαι ²²⁶⟦μη⟧ παρευρέσει μηδεμιᾷ⟦ν⟧, τὰς δὲ ²²⁷πράξεις τῶν ἐν αὐτοῖς γενέσθαι ²²⁸ἐκ τῶν ἄλλων ὑπαρχόντων τῶν μὴ ²²⁹ἀνειργο{υ}μένων δι⟨ὰ⟩ τοῦ προστάγματος ²³⁰τούτου.

²³¹Προστετάχασι δὲ καὶ τῶν βα(σιλικῶν) γεω(ργῶν) μὴ πωλεῖν ²³²ἕως οἰκίας μιᾶς ἐν ᾗ τὴν γεωρ-⟦γικα⟧²³³γικὴν κατασκευὴν ἀπερίδεσθαι ⟦τὰ⟧ ²³⁴μηδὲ τὰ κτήνηι μηδὲ τὰ ἄλλα τὰ πρὸς τὴν ²³⁵γεωργίαν σκεύηι μήτε προσ[άγειν] ²³⁶πρὸς ἱερευ-

210. EDICTS AND ORDERS

Also those who have cut down wood on their own property in contravention of the published decrees.

And they have decreed as follows concerning cases of Egyptians sued by Greeks and Greeks sued by Egyptians and Egyptians by Egyptians, including all classes except the cultivators of Crown land and those who work for state interests and all others connected with the revenues : Egyptians who have made an agreement with Greeks in Greek contracts shall give and receive satisfaction before the chrematistae ; but all Greeks who make agreements (with Egyptians) in Egyptian contracts shall give satisfaction before the native judges in accordance with the national laws ; and suits of Egyptians against Egyptians shall not be taken into their own hands by the chrematistae, but they shall allow them to be decided before the native judges in accordance with the national laws.

And they have decreed that collectors of foreign [a] debts shall not on any pretext whatever attach the persons of the cultivators of Crown land or those who work for state interests or the others whom the previously issued decrees forbid to be brought up for accusation, but the exaction of their debts shall be made from their property in so far as it is not exempted by the present decree.

And they have decreed that in the case of cultivators of Crown land the collectors shall not sell up one house at least, in which their agricultural gear shall be stored, or their cattle or other equipment necessary for agriculture, nor shall they apply these

[a] See p. 41, note c.

---

209. *l.* Αἰγυπτίους for Ἕλληνας.   225. *l.* θέσθαι.

τικὴν μηδὲ πρὸς ἄλλην [237]παρευρέσει μηδεμιᾷ, τὸν αὐτὸν δὲ [238]τρόπον μηδὲ λινυφαντεία μηδὲ τῶν [239]λινύφων καὶ βυσσουργῶν καὶ ἐριουφαντ[ῶν] [240]μηδὲ τῶν ἄλλων τῶν παραπλησ[ίω]ν [241]παρευρέσει μηδεμιᾷ μηδ' ἄλλους [242]κτᾶσθαι μηδὲ χρῆσθαι τοῖς τε λινυ-[243]φαντικοῖς καὶ βυσσουργικοῖς ἐργαλείοις [244]πλὴν αὐτῶν τῶν ὑποτελῶν κ[αὶ] τῶν [245]βυσσουργῶν, τούτους δὲ χρῆσθαι ἐν αὐτοῖς [246]τοῖς ἱεροῖς πρὸς τὴν συντέλειαν τῶν βα(σιλέων) [247]καὶ τὸν στολισμὸν τῶν ἄλλων θεῶν.

[248]Μηδὲ τοὺς ἐπὶ πραγμάτων τεταγμένους [249]καὶ τοὺς ἄλλους ἐπιρίπτειν τοῖς λινύφοις [250]καὶ βυσσουργοῖς καὶ πελπούφοις ἔργα δωρεὰν [251]μηδὲ μισθῶν ὑφειμένων.

[252]Προστετάχασι δὲ μηθένα ἐγγαρεύειν [253]πλοῖα κατὰ μηδεμίαν παρεύρεσι‹ν› [254]εἰς τὰς ἰδίας χρείας.

[255]Μηδὲ τοὺς στρα(τηγοὺς) μηδὲ τοὺς ἄλλο‹υ›ς τοὺς [256]πρὸς χρείαις πάντας τῶν τε βασιλικῶν [257]καὶ πολιτικῶν καὶ ἱερευτικῶν ἀπαγόμενον [258]μηθένα πρὸς ἴδιον ὀφείλημα ἢ ἀδίκημα [259]μηδὲ ἰδίας ἔκθρας ἕνεκεν μηδ' ἐν τα[ῖς] [260]οἰκίαις ἢ ἐν ἄλλοις τόποις συνέχειν ἐν εἱ[ρκτῆι] [261]παρευρέσει μηδεμιᾷ, ἐὰν δ' ἔν τισειν [262]ἐνκαλῶσειν ἀνάγειν ἐπὶ τὰ ἀποδεδειγμέ[να] [263]ἐν ἑκάστοις ἀρχεῖα καὶ λαμβάνειν καὶ ὑπέχειν τὸ δίκαιον [264]κατὰ τὰ προστάγματα καὶ τὰ διαγράμματα.

246. Or perhaps τῶν βα(σιλικῶν).   250. l. πεπλύφοις.
259. l. ἔχθρας.

---

[a] See p. 63, note *e*, and p. 69, note *d*.   Byssus was a fine linen.

to the cultivation of temple land or any other land on any pretext whatever. And in the same way they shall not sell any factories either of linen-weavers or byssus-makers or wool-weavers [a] or other similar craftsmen on any pretext whatever, nor shall the implements for linen-weaving and byssus-manufacture be acquired or used by any other persons than those who work for the monopoly and the byssus-makers, who alone shall use them in the temples themselves for the contribution due to the sovereigns and the vestments of the other gods. [b]

And that no one holding an official position nor any other person shall impose labour upon the linen-weavers and byssus-makers and robe-weavers gratis or at reduced wages.

And they have decreed that no one [c] shall requisition boats for his own use on any pretext whatever.

And that neither the strategi nor other persons who are in charge of royal or civic or sacred interests shall arrest anyone for a private debt or injury or because of a private quarrel and keep him imprisoned in their houses or other places on any pretext whatever ; but if they accuse anyone, they shall bring him before the magistrates appointed in each nome and shall receive or give satisfaction in accordance with the decrees and regulations.

[b] The sovereigns being counted as gods themselves. Wilcken suggests that " the other " was added by an obsequious copyist.

[c] That is, no official in virtue of his position.

211. TWO EDICTS OF GERMANICUS

Sitzungsber. Preuss. Ak. 1911, p. 796.   A.D. 19.

¹[Γερμανικὸς Καῖσαρ Σεβαστοῦ ²υἱὸς θεοῦ
Σεβαστοῦ υἱωνὸς ³ἀνθύπατος λέγει· εἰς τὴν ἐμὴν
⁴παρουσίαν νῦν ἤδη ἀκούων] ⁵ἀ[γγα]ρ[είας . . . .
. . . πλοίων] ⁶καὶ κτηνῶν γείνεσθαι καὶ ⁷ἐπὶ σκη-
νώσεις καταλαμβά-⁸νεσθαι ξενίας πρὸς βίαν καὶ
⁹καταπλήσσεσθαι τοὺς ἰδιώτας, ¹⁰ἀνανκαῖον ἡγησάμην δη-¹¹λῶσαι ὅτι οὔτε πλοῖον ὑπό τινος ¹²ἢ
ὑποζύγιον κατέχεσθαι βού-¹³λομαι, εἰ μὴ κατὰ τὴν
Βαιβίου ¹⁴τοῦ ἐμοῦ φίλου καὶ γραμματέως ¹⁵προσ-
ταγήν, οὔτε ξενίας καταλαμ-¹⁶βάνεσθαι. ἐὰν γὰρ
δέῃ, αὐτὸς Βαίβιος ¹⁷ἐκ τοῦ ἴσου καὶ δικαίου τὰς
ξενίας ¹⁸διαδώσει· καὶ ὑπὲρ τῶν ἀγγαρευ-¹⁹ομένων
δὲ πλοίων ἢ ζευγῶν ²⁰ἀποδίδοσθαι τοὺς μισθοὺς
κατὰ ²¹τὴν ἐμὴν διαγραφὴν κελεύωι. ²²τοὺς δὲ
ἀντιλέγοντας ἐπὶ τὸν ²³γραμματέα μου ἀνάγεσθαι
βού-²⁴λομ[αι, ὃ]ς ἢ αὐτὸς κωλύσει ἀδι-²⁵κεῖσθαι
τοὺς ἰδιώτας ⟨ἢ⟩ ἐμοὶ ἀναν-²⁶γελεῖ. τὰ δὲ διὰ τῆς
πόλεως διατρέ-²⁷χοντα ὑποζύγια τοὺς ἀπαντῶν-
²⁸τας πρὸς βίαν περιαιρεῖσθαι κωλύω. ²⁹τοῦτο γὰρ
ἤδη ὁμολογουμένης ³⁰λῃστείας ἐστὶν ἔργον.

³¹Γερμανικὸς Καῖσαρ Σεβασ[τ]οῦ υἱὸς ³²θεοῦ
Σεβαστοῦ υἱωνὸς ἀνθύπατος ³³λέγει· τὴν μὲν
εὔνοιαν ὑμῶν, ³⁴ἣν ἀεὶ ἐπιδείκνυσθε ὅταν με εἴ-
³⁵δητε, ἀποδέχομαι, τὰς δὲ ἐπιφθόνου[ς] ³⁶ἐμοὶ καὶ
ἰσοθέους ἐκφωνήσεις ³⁷ὑμῶν ἐξ [ἅ]παντος παραιτοῦμαι. ³⁸πρέπουσι γὰρ μόνῳ τῶι σωτῆρι ³⁹ὄντως

3-4. Restored by Zucker *exempli gratia.*

211. TWO EDICTS OF GERMANICUS [a]

A.D. 19.

Proclamation of Germanicus Caesar, son of Augustus and grandson of the deified Augustus,[b] proconsul. [Being informed that in view of my visit] requisitions of boats and animals are being made and that quarters for lodging are being occupied by force and private persons intimidated, I have thought it necessary to declare that I wish neither boat nor beast of burden to be seized by anyone except on the order of Baebius my friend and secretary, nor quarters to be occupied. For if it be necessary, Baebius himself will allot the quarters fairly and justly ; and for boats or animals which we requisition I command that hire be paid in accordance with my schedule. Those who disobey I desire to be brought before my secretary, who will either himself prevent private persons from being wronged or will report the case to me. And I forbid beasts of burden to be forcibly appropriated by those who meet them traversing the city ; for this is nothing but an act of open robbery.

Proclamation of Germanicus Caesar, son of Augustus and grandson of the deified Augustus, proconsul. Your goodwill, which you display on all occasions when you see me, I welcome, but your acclamations, which for me are invidious and such as are addressed to gods, I altogether deprecate. For they are appropriate only to him who is actually the

[a] For the visit of Germanicus to Egypt see Tacitus, *Annals*, ii. 59.

[b] That is, son (by adoption) of Tiberius, who was himself the adopted son of the Emperor Augustus.

καὶ εὐεργέτῃ τοῦ σύνπαντος ⁴⁰τῶν ἀνθρώπων
γένους, τῷ ἐμῷ ⁴¹πατρὶ καὶ τῇ μητρὶ αὐτοῦ, ἐμῇ
δὲ ⁴²μάμμῃ. τὰ δὲ ἡμέτερα ε . . . .
⁴³ἐστὶν τῆς ἐκείνων θειότητος, ὡς ⁴⁴ἐάμ μοι μὴ
πεισθῆτε, ἀνανκᾶτέ με ⁴⁵μὴ πολλάκις ὑμεῖν
ἐνφανίζεσθαι.

212. LETTER OF CLAUDIUS TO THE ALEXANDRIANS

P. Lond. 1912.   A.D. 41.

¹Λούκιος Αἰμίλλιος ῾Ρῆκτος λέγει· ²ἐπειδὴ τῇ
ἀναγνώσει τῆς ἱεροτάτης ³καὶ εὐεργετικωτάτης ἰς
τὴν πόλιν ⁴ἐπιστολῆς πᾶσα ἡ πόλεις παρατυχεῖν
⁵οὐκ ἠδυνήθη{ν} διὰ τὸ πλῆθος αὐτῆς, ⁶ἀνανκαῖον
ἡγησάμην ἐκθεῖναι ⁷τὴν ἐπιστολὴν ἵνα κατ' ἄνδρα
ἕκαστον ⁸ἀναγεινόσκων αὐτὴν τήν τε μεγαλιότητα
⁹τοῦ θεοῦ ἡμῶν Καίσαρος θαυμάσητε ¹⁰καὶ τῇ πρὸς
τὴν πόλιν [[ὁμοία]] εὐνοίᾳ ¹¹χάριν ἔχητε. (ἔτους) β
Τιβερίου Κλαυδίου ¹²Καίσαρος Σεβαστοῦ Γερμανικοῦ Αὐτοκράτορος, ¹³μηνὸς Νέου Σεβαστο(ῦ) ιδ.

¹⁴Τιβέριος Κλαύδιος Καῖσαρ Σεβαστὸς Γερμανι-
κὸς Αὐτοκράτωρ ἀρχιερεὺς ¹⁵μέγειστος δημαρχι-
κῆς ἐξουσίας ὕπατος ἀποδεδιγμένος ᾿Αλεξανδρέων
¹⁶τῇ πόλει χαίρειν. Τιβέριος Κλαύδιος Βάρβιλλος,
᾿Απολλώνις ᾿Αρτεμιδώρου, ¹⁷Χαιρήμων Λεονίδου,
Μάρκος ᾿Ιούλιος ᾿Ασκληπιάδης, Γάιος ᾿Ιούλιος
Διονύσιο(ς), ¹⁸Τιβέριος Κλαύδιος Φανίας, Πασίων
Ποτάμωνος, Διονύσιος Σαββίωνος, ¹⁹Τιβέριος
Κλαύδις ‹᾿Αρχίβιος›, ᾿Απολλώνις ᾿Αρίστονος,
78

saviour and benefactor of the whole human race, my father, and to his mother, my grandmother. But our position is . . . their divinity, so that unless you comply with my request, you will compel me to appear in public but seldom.

212. LETTER OF CLAUDIUS TO THE ALEXANDRIANS

A.D. 41.

Proclamation by Lucius Aemilius Rectus.[a] Seeing that all the populace, owing to its numbers, was unable to be present at the reading of the most sacred and most beneficent letter to the city, I have deemed it necessary to display the letter publicly in order that reading it one by one you may admire the majesty of our god Caesar and feel gratitude for his goodwill towards the city. Year 2 of Tiberius Claudius Caesar Augustus Germanicus Imperator, the 14th of Neus Sebastus.[b]

Tiberius Claudius Caesar Augustus Germanicus Imperator, Pontifex Maximus, holder of the Tribunician Power, consul designate, to the city of Alexandria greeting. Tiberius Claudius Barbillus, Apollonius son of Artemidorus, Chaeremon son of Leonidas, Marcus Julius Asclepiades, Gaius Julius Dionysius, Tiberius Claudius Phanias, Pasion son of Potamon, Dionysius son of Sabbion, Tiberius Claudius Archibius, Apollonius son of Ariston, Gaius

---

[a] The praefect.　　　　　　[b] =the Egyptian Hathur.

---

2. l. ἱερωτάτης.　　　8. l. ἀναγινώσκοντες.　　　17. l. Λεωνίδου.　　　19. l. Ἀρίστωνος.

SELECT PAPYRI

Γάιος Ἰούλιος Ἀπολλώνιος, Ἑρμαῖσκος [20]Ἀπολλωνίου, ὑ πρέσβεις ὑμῶν, ἀναδόντες μοι· τὸ ψήφισμα πολλὰ περὶ [21]τῆς πόλεως διεξῆλθον, ὑπαγόμενοί μοι δῆλον πρὸς τὴν εἰς ἡμᾶς [22]εὔνοιαν, ἣν ἐκ πολλῶν χρόνων, εὖ εἴστε, παρ᾽ ἐμοὶ τεταμιευμένην {ε . } [23]εἴχεται, φύσει μὲν εὐσεβεῖς περὶ τοὺς Σεβαστοὺς ὑπάρχοντες, ὡς [24]ἐκ πολλῶν μοι γέγονε γνόριμον, ἐξερέτως δὲ περὶ τὸν ἐμὸν [25]οἶκον καὶ σπουδάσαντες καὶ σπουδασθέντος, ὧν εἵνα τὸ τελευ-[26]ταῖον εἴπωι παρεὶς τὰ ἄλλα μέγειστός ἐστιν μάρτυς οὑμὸς ἀδελφὸς [27]Γερμανικὸς Καῖσαρ γνησιωτέραις ὑμᾶς φωναῖς προσαγορεύσας· [28]διόπερ ἡδέως προσεδεξάμην τὰς δοθείσας ὑφ᾽ ἡμῶν μοι τιμὰς [29]καίπερ οὐκ ὢν πρὸς τὰ τοιαῦτα ῥ{ρ}άιδιος. καὶ πρῶτα μὲν Σεβαστὴν [30]ὑμεῖν ἄγειν ἐπιτρέπωι τὴν ἐμὴν γενεθλείαν ὃν τρόπον αὐτοὶ προ-[31]εῖρησθαι, τάς τε ἑκα{τας}σταχοῦ τῶν ἀνδριάντων ἀναστάσεις [32]ἐμοῦ τε καὶ τοῦ γένους μου ποιήσασθε συνχωρῶι· ἐγὼ ὁρῶι γὰρ [33]<ὅτι> πάντη μνημεῖα τῆς ἡμετέρας εὐσεβείας εἰς τὸν ἐμὸν οἶκον [34]ὑδρόσασθαι <ἐ>σπουδάσαται. τῶν δὲ δυοῖν χρυ{σῶ}ν ἀνδριάντων [35]ὁ μὲν Κλαυδιανῆς Εἰρήνης Σεβαστῆς γενό[με]νος, ὥσπερ ὑπέθετο [36]καὶ προσελειπάρη-[σ]εν ὁ ἐμοὶ τιμ[ι]ώτατος Βάρβιλλος ἀρνουμένου [37]μου διὰ τὸ φορτικότε[ρο]ς δ[οκ]εῖ[ν], ἐπεὶ Ρώμης ἀνατεθήσεται, (Col. 3) [38]ὁ δὲ ἕτερος ὃν τρόπον ὑμεῖς ἀξιοῦτε πομπεύσει ταῖς ἐπωνύμαις [39]ἡμέραις παρ᾽ ὑμῖν· συνπομπευέτωι δὲ ⟦καὶ αὐ⟧ αὐτῶι καὶ

20. *l. οἱ.*   21. *l. με* for *μοι?* Schubart proposes *ζῆλον* for *δῆλον.* Bell corrects *ἡμᾶς* to *ὑμᾶς,* another possibility.   23. *l. εἴχετε.*   24. *l. γνώριμον, ἐξαιρέτως.*   25. *l. σπουδασθέντες.*   28. *l. ὑμῶν.*   29. *l. πρῶτα.*   30. *l. προῄρησθε.*   32. *l. ποιήσασθαι.*   33. *l. ὑμετέρας.*

80

212. EDICTS AND ORDERS

Julius Apollonius, Hermaiscus son of Apollonius, your ambassadors, having delivered to me the decree, discoursed at length concerning the city, directing my attention to your goodwill towards us, which from long ago, you may be sure, had been stored up to your advantage in my memory ; for you are by nature reverent towards the Augusti, as I know from many proofs, and in particular have taken a warm interest in my house, warmly reciprocated, of which fact (to mention the last instance, passing over the others) the supreme witness is my brother Germanicus addressing you in words more clearly stamped as his own.[a] Wherefore I gladly accepted the honours given to me by you, though I have no weakness for such things. And first I permit you to keep my birthday as a *dies Augustus* as you have yourselves proposed, and I agree to the erection in their several places of the statues of myself and my family ; for I see that you were anxious to establish on every side memorials of your reverence for my house. Of the two golden statues the one made to represent the Pax Augusta Claudiana,[b] as my most honoured Barbillus suggested and entreated when I wished to refuse for fear of being thought too offensive, shall be erected at Rome, and the other according to your request shall be carried in procession on name-days in your city ; and it shall be accompanied by a throne, adorned with whatever

[a] Germanicus spoke to them, and in Greek ; Claudius wrote to them, and in Latin, which had to be translated.

[b] A personification of the peace established by the Emperor.

---

34. *l.* ἱδρύσασθαι ἐσπουδάσατε. 37. *l.* φορτικώτε[ρο]s,
ἐπί. 38. *l.* ἐπωνύμαις.

δίφρος ⁴⁰ῷ βούλεσθαι κόσμωι ἠσκημένος. εὐῆθες
δ' ἴσ{σ}ως τοσαύτας ⁴¹προσ[ι]έμενον τειμὰς ἀρ-
νήσασθαι φυλὴν Κλαυδιανὰν καταδῖξαι ⁴²ἄλση τε
κατὰ νόμον παρεῖναι τῆς Αἰγύπ<τ>ου· διόπερ καὶ
ταῦτά [ἡμῖν] ⁴³θ' ὑμεῖν ἐπιτρέπωι, εἰ δὲ βούλεσθαι
καὶ Οὐειτρασίου Πωλείωνος ⁴⁴τοῦ ἐμοῦ ἐπιτρόπου
τοὺς ἐφίππους ἀνδριάντας ἀναστήσατε. τῶν δὲ
⁴⁵τετραπώλων ἀναστάσε[ι]ς <ἃς περὶ τὰς εἰσ>βολὰς
τῆς χώρας ἀφιδρῦσέ μοι βούλεσθαι ⁴⁶συνχωρῶι τὸ
μὲν περὶ τὴν Ταπόσιριν καλουμένην τῆς Λιβύης,
⁴⁷τὸ δὲ περὶ Φάρον τῆς Ἀλεξανδρείας, τρίτον δὲ
περὶ Πηλούσιον ⁴⁸τῆς Αἰγύπ<τ>ου στῆσαι. ἀρχι-
ιερέα δ' ἐμὸν καὶ ναῶν κατασκευὰς ⁴⁹παρετοῦμε,
οὔτε φορτικὸς τοῖς κατ' ἐμαυτὸν ἀνθρόποις ⁵⁰βουλό-
μενος εἶναι τὰ ἱερὰ δὲ καὶ τὰ τοιαῦτα μόνοις τοῖς
θεοῖς ⁵¹ἐξέρετα ὑπὸ τοῦ παντὸς αἰῶνος ἀποδεδόσθαι
κρίν[ω]ν. ⁵²περὶ δὲ τῶν αἰτημάτων ἃ παρ' ἐμοῦ
λαβεῖν ἐσπουδάκα-⁵³τε οὕτως γεινώσκωι· ἅπασι
τοῖς ἐφηβευκώσει ἄχρει τῆς ⁵⁴ἐμῆς ἡγεμονείας
βαί[βον]βαιον διαφυλάσσωι τὴν Ἀλεξανδρέων ⁵⁵πο-
λειτείαν ἐπὶ τοῖς τῆς πόλεως τειμείοις καὶ φιλαν-
θρόποις ⁵⁶πᾶσει πλὴν εἰ μή τινες ὑπῆλθον ὑμᾶς ὡς
ἐγ δούλων ⁵⁷γ[ε]γονότες ἐφηβεῦσαι, καὶ τὰ ἄλλα δὲ
οὐχ ἧσσον εἶναι βούλομε ⁵⁸βέβαια πανθ' ὅσα ὑμεῖν
ἐχαρίσθη ὑπό τε τῶν πρὸ ἐμοῦ ἡγεμόνων ⁵⁹καὶ τῶν
βασιλέων καὶ τῶν ἐπάρχων, ὡς καὶ [ὁ] θεὸς
Σεβαστὸς ἐβεβαίωσε. (Col. 4) ⁶⁰τοὺς δὲ νεοκό-

40. l. βούλεσθε: so in ll. 43, 45.　　45. l. ἀφιδρῦσαι.
49. l. παραιτοῦμαι, ἀνθρώποις.　　51. l. ἐξαίρετα.　　53. l.
ἐφηβευκόσι.　　54. l. βέβαιον.　　55. l. φιλανθρώποις.
57. l. βούλομαι.

trappings you choose. It would perhaps be foolish, while accepting such great honours, to refuse the institution of a Claudian tribe [a] and the establishment of groves after the manner of Egypt; wherefore I grant you these requests as well, and if you wish you may also erect the equestrian statues given by Vitrasius Pollio my procurator. As for the erection of those in four-horse chariots which you wish to set up to me at the entrances into the country, I consent to let one be placed at Taposiris, the Libyan town of that name, another at Pharos in Alexandria, and a third at Pelusium in Egypt.[b] But I deprecate the appointment of a high-priest to me and the building of temples, for I do not wish to be offensive to my contemporaries, and my opinion is that temples and such forms of honour have by all ages been granted as a prerogative to the gods alone.

Concerning the requests which you have been anxious to obtain from me, I decide as follows. All those who have become ephebi [c] up to the time of my principate I confirm and maintain in possession of the Alexandrian citizenship with all the privileges and indulgences enjoyed by the city, excepting such as by beguiling you have contrived to become ephebi though born of servile mothers; and it is equally my will that all the other favours shall be confirmed which were granted to you by former princes and kings and praefects, as the deified Augustus also confirmed them. It is my will that the *neocori* [d] of

---

[a] As one of the civic bodies at Alexandria.

[b] Libya and Alexandria being distinguished from Egypt proper.

[c] The ephebi were youths qualified by descent to receive the citizenship.

[d] Temple overseers, usually appointed for a limited period.

ρους τοῦ ἐν Ἀλεξανδρείᾳ ναοῦ ὅς ἐστιν τοῦ θεοῦ
[61]Σεβαστοῦ κληροτοὺς εἶναι βούλομε καθὰ καὶ ὑ ἐν
Κανόπωι [62]τοῦ αὐτοῦ θεοῦ Σεβαστοῦ κληροῦνται.
ὑπὲρ δὲ τοῦ τὰς πολει-[63]τεικὰς ἀρχὰς τριετῖς εἶναι
καὶ πάν‹υ› ἐμοὶ 〚υ〛 καλῶς βεβουλεῦσθαι [64]δοκεῖ-
ται, ὑ γὰρ ‹ἄρ›χοντες φώβωι τοῦ δώσειν εὐθύνας
ὧν κακῶς [65]ἦρξαν μετριώτεροι ἡμεῖν προσενεκ-
θήσονται τὸν ἐν ταῖς [66]ἀρχαῖς χρόνον. περὶ δὲ τῆς
βουλῆς ὅ τι μέν ποτε σύνηθες [67]ὑμεῖν ἐπὶ τῶν
ἀρχαίων βασιλέων οὐκ ἔχωι λέγειν, ὅτι δὲ ἐπὶ τῶν
[68]πρὸ ἐμοῦ Σεβαστῶν οὐκ εἴχεται σαφῶς οἴδατε.
καινοῦ δὴ [69]πράγματος νῦν πρότων καταβαλλομένου
ὅπερ ἄδηλον εἰ συνοί-[70]σει τῇ πόλει καὶ τοῖς ἐμοῖς
πράγμασει ἔγραψα Αἰμιλλίωι Ῥήκτωι [71]διασκέ-
ψασθαι καὶ δηλῶσέ μοι εἴ ται καὶ συνείστασθαι τὴν
ἀρχὴν δεῖ, [72]τόν τε τρόπον, εἴπερ ἄρα συνάγειν δέυ,
καθ' ὃν γενήσεται τοῦτο. [73]τῆς δὲ πρὸς Ἰουδαίους
ταραχῆς καὶ στάσεως μᾶλλον δ' εἰ χρὴ τὸ ἀληθὲς
[74]εἰπεῖν τοῦ πολέμου πότεροι μὲν αἴτιοι κατέστησαν
καίπερ [75]ἐξ ἀντικαταστάσεως πολλὰ τῶν ἡμετέρων
πρεσβέων [76]φιλοτειμηθέντων καὶ μάλιστα Διονυσίου
τοῦ Θέων[ο]ς ὅμως [77]οὐκ ἐβουλήθην ἀκριβῶς
ἐξελέγξαι, ταμιευόμενος ἐμαυτῶι [78]κατὰ τῶν πάλειν
ἀρξαμένων ὀργὴν ἀμεταμέλητον· [79]ἁπλῶς δὲ προσ-
αγορεύωι ὅτι ἂν μὴ καταπαύσηται τὴν ὀλέ-
[80]θριον ὀργὴν ταύτην κατ' ἀλλήλων αὐθάδιον
ἐγβιασθήσομαι [81]δῖξαι ὗόν ἐστιν ἡγεμὼν φιλάν-

---

61. *l.* κληρωτούς, βούλομαι, οἱ, Κανώπωι.   64. *l.* δοκεῖτε,
οἱ, φόβωι.   65. *l.* προσενεχθήσονται.   68. *l.* εἴχετε.
69. *l.* πρῶτον.   71. *l.* δηλῶσαι, τε.   72. *l.* δέοι.
79. *l.* καταπαύσητε.   81. *l.* οἶον, φιλάνθρωπος.

the temple of the deified Augustus in Alexandria shall be chosen by lot in the same way as those of the said deified Augustus in Canopus are chosen by lot. With regard to the civic magistracies being made triennial your proposal seems to me to be very good ; for through fear of being called to account for any abuse of power your magistrates will behave with greater circumspection during their term of office. Concerning the senate, what your custom may have been under the ancient kings [a] I have no means of saying, but that you had no senate under the former Augusti you are well aware. As this is the first broaching of a novel project, whose utility to the city and to my government is not evident, I have written to Aemilius Rectus to hold an inquiry and inform me whether in the first place it is right that a senate should be constituted and, if it should be right to create one, in what manner this is to be done.

As for the question which party was responsible for the riots and feud (or rather, if the truth must be told, the war) with the Jews, although in confrontation with their opponents your ambassadors, and particularly Dionysius son of Theon, contended with great zeal, nevertheless I was unwilling to make a strict inquiry, though guarding within me a store of immutable indignation against whichever party renews the conflict ; and I tell you once for all that unless you put a stop to this ruinous and obstinate enmity against each other, I shall be driven to show what a benevolent prince can be when turned to

[a] The sentence indicates that the Alexandrians had claimed to have possessed a senate under the Ptolemies, or at least under the earlier ones.

θροπος εἰς ὀργὴν δικαίαν μεταβεβλη-⁸²μένος. διόπερ
ἔτι καὶ νῦν διαμαρτύρομε εἶνα Ἀλεξανδρεῖς μὲν
⁸³πραέως καὶ φιλανθρόπως προσφέροντε Ἰουδαί-
ο<ι>ς τοῖς ⁸⁴τὴν αὐτὴν πόλειν ἐκ πολλῶν χρόνων
οἰκοῦσει (Col. 5) ⁸⁵καὶ μηδὲν τῶν πρὸς θρησκείαν
αὐτοῖς νενομισμένων ⁸⁶τοῦ θεοῦ λοιμένωνται ἀλλὰ
ἐῶσιν αὐτοὺς τοῖς ἔθεσιν ⁸⁷χρῆσθαι ὗς καὶ ἐπὶ τοῦ
θεοῦ Σεβαστοῦ, ἅπερ καὶ ἐγὼι ⁸⁸διακούσας ἀμφοτέρων ἐβεβαίωσα· καὶ Ἰουδέοις δὲ ⁸⁹ἄντικρυς
κελεύωι μηδὲν πλήωι ὧν πρότερον ⁹⁰ἔσχον περιερ-
γάζεσθαι μηδὲ ὥσπερ ἐν δυσεὶ πόλεσειν κα-⁹¹τοι-
κοῦντας δύο πρεσβείας ἐκπέμπειν τοῦ λοιποῦ, ⁹²ὢ
μὴ πρότερόν ποτε ἐπράκθη, μηδὲ ἐπισπαίειν
⁹³γυμνασιαρχικοῖς ἢ κοσμητικοῖς ἀγῶσει, ⁹⁴καρ-
πουμένους μὲν τὰ οἰκῖα ἀπολα<ύ>οντας δὲ ⁹⁵ἐν ἀλ-
λοτρίᾳ πόλει περιουσίας ἀπθόνων ἀγαθῶν, ⁹⁶μηδὲ
ἐπάγεσθαι ἢ προσείεσθαι ἀπὸ Συρίας ἢ Αἰγύπ<τ>ου
⁹⁷καταπλέοντας Ἰουδαίους, ἐξ οὗ μείζονας ὑπονοίας
⁹⁸ἀνανκασθήσομε λαμβάνειν· εἰ δὲ μή, πάντα
⁹⁹τρόπον αὐτοὺς ἐπεξελεύσομαι καθάπερ κοινήν
¹⁰⁰τεινα τῆς οἰκουμένης νόσον ἐξεγείροντας. ἐὰν
¹⁰¹τούτων ἀποστάντες ἀμφότεροι μετὰ πραότητος
¹⁰²καὶ φιλανθροπείας τῆς πρὸς ἀλλήλους ζῆν ἐθελή-
σητε, ¹⁰³καὶ ἐγὼι πρόνοιαν τῆς πόλεως ποήσομαι
τὴν ἀνατάτωι ¹⁰⁴καθάπερ ἐκ προγόνων οἰκίας ὑμῖν
ὑπαρχούσης. ¹⁰⁵Βαρβίλλωι τῶι ἐμῶι ἑτέρωι
μαρτυρῶι ἀεὶ πρόνοια[ν] ¹⁰⁶ἡμῶν παρ' ἐμοὶ ποιου-
μένωι, ὃς καὶ νῦν πάσηι φιλο-¹⁰⁷τειμείᾳ περὶ τὼν

82. l. διαμαρτύρομαι.   83. l. φιλανθρώπως προσφέρωνται.
86. l. λυμαίνωνται.   87. l. οἷς.   88. l. Ἰουδαίοις.
89. l. πλείω.   92. l. ὅ, ἐπράχθη, ἐπεισπαίειν.   95. l.
ἀφθόνων.   98. l. ἀναγκασθήσομαι.   103. l. ἀνωτάτω.

righteous indignation. Wherefore once again I conjure you that on the one hand the Alexandrians show themselves forbearing and kindly towards the Jews who for many years have dwelt in the same city, and dishonour none of the rites observed by them in the worship of their god, but allow them to observe their customs as in the time of the deified Augustus, which customs I also, after hearing both sides, have sanctioned ; and on the other hand I explicitly order the Jews not to agitate for more privileges than they formerly possessed, and not in future to send out a separate embassy as if they lived in a separate city, a thing unprecedented, and not to force their way into gymnasiarchic or cosmetic games,[a] while enjoying their own privileges and sharing a great abundance of advantages in a city not their own, and not to bring in or admit Jews who come down the river from Syria or Egypt, a proceeding which will compel me to conceive serious suspicions ; otherwise I will by all means take vengeance on them as fomenters of what is a general plague infecting the whole world.   If desisting from these courses you consent to live with mutual forbearance and kindliness, I on my side will exercise a solicitude of very long standing for the city, as one which is bound to us by traditional friendship.   I bear witness to my friend Barbillus of the solicitude which he has always shown for you in my presence and of the extreme zeal with which he has now advocated

[a] Games presided over by the civic magistrates called gymnasiarchs and cosmetae, in which the Jews were not entitled to take part, as they did not possess the coveted citizenship.

---

104. *l.* οἰκείας ἡμῖν.   105. *l.* ἑταίρωι : so in l. 108.
106. *l.* ὑμῶν.   107. *l.* τὸν ἀγῶνα, κέχρ[ηται].

ἀγῶνα τὸν ὑπὲρ ὑμῶν κέχρ[ητε], [108]καὶ Τιβερίωι
Κλαυδίωι Ἀρχιβίωι τῶι ἐμῶι ἐτέ[ρωι]. [109]ἔρ-
ρωσθαι.

109. l. ἔρρωσθε.

213. LETTER OF HADRIAN

B.G.U. 140.   A.D. 119.

[1]Ἀν[τί]γρα(φον) ἐπιστ[ολ(ῆς) τοῦ κυρίου με]θηρ-
μ[ην]ευ-[2]μένης [. . . . .]ω [ἢ [3](ἔτους)] γ̄
Τραϊ[α]νο[ῦ Ἀδριανοῦ Σεβαστο]ῦ, [4][Που]πλίου
Α[ἰ]λίου τὸ γ̄ καὶ Ῥου]στικοῦ [5][ὑπά]τοις, προε[τέθη
ἐν Ἀλεξανδρείᾳ(?) ἐν τῇ] παρεμβολ(ῇ) [6]τῆ[ς] χει-
μασία[ς λεγιῶνο(ς) τρίτης] Κυ[ρ]ηναϊκῆς [7]κ[αὶ]
λεγιῶνο(ς) [β̄] κ[αὶ εἰκο]στ[ῆ]ς Δηϊοτεριανῆς [8]πρίδιε
νό[ν]ας Ἀουγο[ύσ]τας, ὅ ἐστιν Μεσορὴ [9]ῑᾱ, ἐν
πρινκε[π]ίοι[ς].

[10]Ἐπί[σ]ταμαι, Ῥάμμιέ μου, τ[ο]ύτους ο[ὓ]ς οἱ
[11]γονεῖς αὐτῶν τῷ τῆς στρατείας ἀνεί-[12]λαντο
χρόνῳ τὴν πρὸς τὰ πατρικὰ [13][ὑ]π[ά]ρχοντα πρόσοδον κεκωλῦσθαι, [14]κ[αὶ τ]οῦτο οὐκ ἐδόκει σκληρὸν
ε[ἶ]ναι [15][τοῦ]ναντίον αὐτῶν τῆς στρατιω[τι]κῆς
[16][διδα]χῆς πεποιηκότων. ἥδιστα δὲ [17]αὐτὸς προ-
είεναι τὰς ἀφορμὰς δι' ὧν [18]τὸ αὐστηρότερον ὑπὸ
τῶν πρὸ ἐμοῦ [19]αὐτοκρατόρων σταθὲν φιλαν-
θρωπό-[20]τερ[ο]ν ἑρμηνεύω. ὅνπερ τοιγαροῦν [21]τ[ρό]-
π]ον οὔκ εἰσιν νόμιμοι κληρο-[22][νόμ]οι τῶν ἑαυτῶν
πατέρων οἱ τῷ [23][τ]ῆς στρατείας χρόνῳ ἀναλημφθέν-
[24]τες, ὅμως κατοχὴ[ν] ὑ[πα]ρχόντων [25]ἐξ ἐκείνου
τοῦ μέ[ρ]ους τοῦ διατάγμα-[26]τος οὗ καὶ τοῖς πρὸς
[γ]ένους συνγενέσι [27]δίδοται αἰτεῖσθαι δύνασθαι

your cause, and likewise to my friend Tiberius
Claudius Archibius. Farewell.

213. LETTER OF HADRIAN

A.D. 119.

Copy of a letter of the emperor, translated . . .,
which was publicly displayed in the 3rd year of
Trajanus Hadrianus Augustus, in the consulship of
Publius Aelius for the 3rd time and of Rusticus, at
Alexandria (?) in the winter camp of legion iii
Cyrenaica and legion xxii Deioteriana, on the 4th of
August which is the 11th of Mesore, at headquarters.

I know, my dear Rammius,[a] that persons whom
their parents in the period of their military service
acknowledged as their issue have been debarred from
succeeding to their fathers' property, and this measure
did not appear to be harsh as their action was contrary to military discipline.[b] But for my own part I
have much pleasure in enunciating a principle which
allows me to interpret more liberally the rather strict
rule established by the emperors before me. For
although those who were thus acknowledged in the
period of military service are not legitimate heirs of
their fathers, nevertheless I decide that they also are
able to claim possession of the property through that
clause of the edict which gives this right to kinsmen

---

[a] The praefect.
[b] Soldiers were forbidden to marry, and their children
were illegitimate.

---

4. *l.* Πουπλίῳ, etc.   17. *l.* προίεμαι.

καὶ αὐτοὺς ²⁸κρε[ίν]ω. ταύτην μου τὴν δωρεὰν
²⁹καὶ τοῖς στρατιώταις ἐμοῦ καὶ τοῖς οὐε-³⁰τρανοῖς
εὔγνωστόν σε ποιῆσαι δεή-³¹σει, οὐχ ἕνεκα τοῦ
δοκεῖν με αὐτοῖς ³²ἐνλογεῖν, ἀλλὰ ἵνα τούτῳ
χρῶνται, ³³ἐὰν ἀγνοῶσι.

214. RESCRIPT OF SEVERUS AND CARACALLA

B.G.U. 267.   A.D. 199.

¹[Αὐτοκ]ρ[άτωρ] Καῖσαρ ²[Λούκιος Σεπτίμιος
Σεουῆρ]ος Περ[τ]ίναξ [Σε]βαστὸς ³[᾽Αραβικὸς
᾽Αδιαβη]νικὸς ⁴[Παρθικὸς Μέγιστος] καὶ Αὐτο-
κρά[τωρ] Καῖσαρ ⁵[Μάρκος Αὐρήλιος ᾽Αντω-
νεῖνος Σεβαστὸς ⁶᾽Ιουλιανῇ Σω[σθ]ενιανοῦ διὰ
Σωσθένους ⁷ἀνδρός. [μ]ακρᾶς νομῆς παραγρα-
φὴ{ς} ⁸τοῖς δικαία[ν] αἰτ[ί]αν ἐσχηκόσι καὶ ἄνευ
⁹τινὸς ἀμφισβητήσεως ἐν τῇ νομῇ ¹⁰γενομ[έν]οις πρὸς
μὲν τοὺς ἐν ἀλλο-¹¹τρίᾳ πόλει διατρείβοντας ἐτῶν
εἴκοσι ¹²ἀριθμῷ βεβαιοῦται, τοὺς δὲ ἐπὶ τῆς ¹³αὐτῆς
ἐτῶν δέκα. προετέθη ἐν ᾽Α¹⁴λεξανδρείᾳ η (ἔτους)
Τῦβι γ.

215. EXTRACTS FROM A LETTER OF CARACALLA

P. Giess. 40, col. 2, ll. 16-29.   A.D. 215.

¹⁶Αἰ[γύπτι]οι πάντες οἵ εἰσιν ἐν ᾽Αλεξανδρείᾳ,
καὶ μάλιστα ἄ[γ]ροικοι, οἵτινες πεφε[ύγασιν] ¹⁷ἄλ-

by birth. This bounty of mine it will be your duty
to make well known both to my soldiers and to the
veterans, not to enable me to take credit in their eyes,
but in order that they may use this privilege, should
they be ignorant of it.

214. RESCRIPT OF SEVERUS AND CARACALLA

A.D. 199.

The Emperor Caesar Lucius Septimius Severus
Pertinax Augustus Arabicus Adiabenicus Parthicus
Maximus and the Emperor Caesar Marcus Aurelius
Antoninus Augustus to Juliana daughter of Sos-
thenianus, through her husband Sosthenes. A plea
of long possession, made by those who have had
rightful grounds for entering thereon and remained
in possession without any dispute, is established
against claimants who live in a different city, by the
lapse of twenty years, and against those in the same
city, by the lapse of ten years.[a] Displayed publicly
in Alexandria on Tubi 3 of year 8.

[a] See No. 261.

215. EXTRACTS FROM A LETTER OF CARACALLA

A.D. 215.

All Egyptians in Alexandria, especially countryfolk, who have fled from other parts and can easily be

[λοθεν κ]αὶ εὐμαρῶς ἐ[ὐ]ρίσ[κε]σθαι δύναντα[ι],
πάντη πάντως ἐγβλήσιμοί εἰσιν, ο[ὐχ]ὶ [18]μ[έν]τοι
γε χοιρέμπο[ρ]οι καὶ ναῦται ποτά[μ]ιοι ἐκεῖνοί τε
οἵτινες κάλαμον πρ[ὸ]ς τὸ [19]ὑποκαίειν τὰ βαλα[νεῖ]α
καταφέρουσι. τοὺς δὲ ἄλλους ἔγβ[α]λλε, οἵτινες
τῷ πλήθε[ι] τῷ [20]ἰδίῳ κα[ὶ οὐ]χὶ χρήσει ταράσσουσι
τὴν πόλιν. Σαραπείοις καὶ ἑτέραις τισὶν ἑορ-
[21]τασί[μοις ἡ]μέραις εἰωθέναι κατάγειν θυσίας
εἵνεκεν ταύρους καὶ ἄλλα τινὰ [22]ἔνψ[υ]χα ἢ καὶ
ἄλλαις ἡ[μ]έραις Αἰγυπτίους μανθάνω· διὰ τοῦτο
οὔκ εἰσι κωλυτέοι. [23]ἐ[κεῖνοι] κωλ[ύ]εσθαι ὀφε[ί]-
λουσι οἵτινες φεύγουσι τὰς χώρας τὰς ἰδίας ἵνα
μὴ [24]ἔρ[γον] ἄγροικον ποιῶσι, οὐχὶ μέντοι ⟨οἵτινες⟩
τὴν πόλ[ι]ν τὴν Ἀλεξανδρέων τὴν λαμπρο-[25]τάτ[ην]
{ην} ἰδεῖν θέλον[τ]ες εἰς αὐτὴν συνέρχονται ἢ
πολειτικωτέρας ζωῆς ἕνε-[26]κεν [ἢ πρ]αγματείας
προ[σ]καίρου ἐνθάδε κ[α]τέρχονται. μεθ' ἕτερα·
ἐπιγεινώσκε-[27]σθαι γὰ[ρ] εἰς τοὺς λ[ι]νούφ[ο]υς οἱ
ἀληθινοὶ Αἰγύπτιοι δύναντ[α]ι εὐμαρῶς φωνῇ, ἢ
[28]ἄλλων [δηλ]οῖ ⟨αὐτοὺς⟩ ἔχειν ὄψεις τε καὶ σχῆμα·
ἔτι τε καὶ ζω[ῇ] δεικνύει ἐναντία ἤθη [29]ἀπὸ ἀνα-
στροφῆς [πο]λειτικῆς εἶναι ἀγροίκους Α[ἰ]γυπτίους.

28. ζω[ῇ] E.-H. : ζω[ή] Ed.

detected, are by all manner of means to be expelled,[a] with the exception, however, of pig-dealers and river boatmen and the men who bring down reeds for heating the baths. But expel all the others, as by the numbers of their kind and their uselessness they are disturbing the city. I am informed that at the festival of Sarapis and on certain other festal days Egyptians are accustomed to bring down bulls and other animals for sacrifice, or even on other days ; they are not to be prohibited for this. The persons who ought to be prohibited are those who flee from their own districts to escape rustic toil, not those, however, who congregate here with the object of viewing the glorious city of Alexandria or come down for the sake of enjoying a more civilized life or for incidental business.

A further extract : For genuine Egyptians can easily be recognized among the linen-weavers by their speech, which proves them to have assumed the appearance and dress of another class ; moreover in their mode of life their far from civilized manners reveal them to be Egyptian countryfolk.

[a] The present text partly confirms and partly corrects the statement of Dio Cassius that Caracalla, after the massacre of the Alexandrians which his soldiers had perpetrated by his command, drove all strangers out of the city except the merchants. What he actually did was to expel the Egyptian refugees who had no business there.

SELECT PAPYRI

216. EDICT OF SEVERUS ALEXANDER CONCERNING THE *AURUM CORONARIUM*

P. Fay. 20.   A.D. 222.

[The papyrus, which probably dates from the early
4th century, contains little more than the second
half of a very corrupt copy of the edict; and the
text which we print is not an exact transcript, but
a reconstruction in modern form made by the original
editors and other scholars.]

(Col. 1) ¹[Αὐτοκράτωρ Καῖσαρ θεοῦ Μεγάλου
Ἀντωνίνου Εὐσεβοῦς υἱὸς θεοῦ ²Σεπτιμίου Σεουήρου Εὐσεβοῦς υἱωνὸς Μάρκος Αὐρήλιος Σεουηρο]ς
³[Ἀλέξανδρος Εὐσε]βὴς Εὐτυχ[ὴ]ς Σεβαστὸς [ἀρχ-
ιερεὺς μέγιστος δ]ημαρ-⁴[χικῆς ἐξουσίας ὕ]πατος
[πα]τὴρ πατρίδο[ς λέγει· - - - (Col. 2) ¹ὅ[πω]ς μὴ
διὰ τὸ τῆς χαρᾶς τῆ[ς] ἑαυτῶν δήλωσιν ποιήσασθαι
ἐπ[ε]τινὴν (?) ἐπ᾽ ἐμοὶ παρελθόντι ἐπὶ τὴν ἀρχὴν
²εἰστε[λ]εῖν βιασθεῖεν μείζω ἢ δύνανται. ὅθεν μοι
παρέστη τὸ βούλευμα τοῦτο οὐδὲ ἀποδέοντι παρα-
δειγμάτων, ³ἐν οἷς Τραϊανόν τε καὶ Μάρκον τοὺς
ἐμαυτοῦ προγόνους, Αὐτοκράτορας δὲ μάλιστα δὴ
θαυμάσαι ἀξίους ⁴γεγενημένους, μιμεῖσθαι ἔμελ-
λον, ὧν καὶ πρὸς τἆλλα τὴν προαίρεσιν ζηλοῦν
ἐγὼ γνώμην ποιοῦμαι, ⁵ὡς εἴ γε μὴ τὸ τῆς π[α]ρὰ
τοὺς καιροὺς δημοσίας ἀπορίας ἐμποδὼν ἦν, πολὺ
ἂν φανερωτέραν τὴν ἐμαυτοῦ ⁶μεγαλοψυχίαν ἐπι-
δεικ[ν]ύμενος οὐδ᾽ ἂν ἐμέλλησα καὶ εἴ τι ἐκ τοῦ
παρελθόντος χρόνου ἐκ τῆς τοιουτοτρό-⁷που συντελείας κατιὸν ὠφείλετο, καὶ ὅπόσα πρὸς τὴν
Καίσαρος προσηγορίαν ἐπὶ τῷ τῶν [σ]τεφάνων

216. EDICT OF SEVERUS ALEXANDER CONCERNING THE *AURUM CORONARIUM* [a]

A.D. 222.

Proclamation of the Emperor Caesar, son of the deified Magnus Antoninus Pius, grandson of the deified Septimius Severus Pius, Marcus Aurelius Alexander Pius Felix Augustus, Pontifex Maximus, holder of the Tribunician Power, consul, father of his country.

. . . lest for the purpose of making an annual (?) manifestation of their joy at my accession to empire they should be compelled to contribute more than they are able. Wherefore I have formed this design, not wanting in precedents, among which I sought to follow the example of Trajan and Marcus, my own ancestors and emperors who have made themselves specially worthy of admiration, whose policy in other matters also I am resolved to emulate, so that, if the poverty of the government in these times had not prevented me, I should have offered a much more conspicuous proof of my magnanimity, and should not have hesitated to remit likewise whatever arrears were still owing from the past for contributions of this sort and whatever sums had been already voted under the title of crowns for my pro-

[a] Properly a tribute of gold on the accession of an Emperor, but under Elagabalus, the predecessor of Severus Alexander, it had developed into an annual impost.

(Col. 1) 1-4. Restored by Wilcken. (Col. 2) 1.
ἐπ[ε]τινήν (?) E.-H.

ὀνόματι [8]ἐψηφισμένα πρότερον καὶ ἔτι ψηφισθησό-
μενα κατὰ τὴν αὐτὴν αἰτίαν ὑπὸ τῶν πόλεων εἴη,
καὶ ταῦτα [9]ἀνεῖναι. ἀλλὰ ταῦτα μὲν οὐκ οἴομαι,
δι᾽ ἃ μικρὸν ἔμπροσθεν εἶπον· ταῦτα δὲ μόνα
ἐπα . . φ . . . ιν τὰς πόλεις, [10]ὡς ἐκ τῶν παρόντων ὁρῶ, δυναμένας οὐ παρεῖδον. διόπερ ἴστωσαν
ἅπαντες ἐν ταῖς πόλεσιν ἁπάσαις [11]ταῖς τε κατ᾽
Ἰταλίαν κα[ὶ] ταῖς ἐν τοῖς ἄλλοις ἔθνεσιν τὰ καὶ
ἐπὶ τῇ προφάσει τῆς ἐμαυτοῦ ἀρχῆς τῆς Αὐτοκράτορος, [12]ἐφ᾽ ἣν καὶ βουλομένων καὶ εὐχομένων
ἁπάντων παρῆλθον, ἀντὶ τῶν χρυσῶν στεφάνων
χρήματα ανδ . . . η-[13]θέντα ἀνεῖναι αὐταῖς, ταῦτα
δὲ οὐ διὰ περιουσίαν πλούτου ποιοῦντα ἀλλὰ διὰ
τὴν ἐμαυτοῦ προαίρεσιν, δι᾽ ἣ-[14]ς ἀεὶ [ἐ]πεὶ
Καῖσάρ εἰμι καὶ περικέκμηκα τὸ κλῖνον ἀναλήμ-
ψασθαι οὐχ<ὶ φ>όρων ζητήσεσιν ἀλλὰ σωφρο[σύνη]
[15]μόνον, οὐ πρὸς τὸ ἴδιον γινομένων ἀναλωμάτων.
οὐδὲ γὰρ τοῦτό μοι σπουδαιότε[ρο]ν ἐξ ἁπάντω[ν
κρατεῖν] [16]χρημάτων, πλὴν μᾶλλον φιλανθρωπίᾳ
τε καὶ εὐεργεσίαις συναύξειν ταύτην τὴν ἀρχήν,
ἵνα μου [17]καὶ τοῖς ἡγεμόσιν τοῖς κατ᾽ ἐπιτροπείας
παρ᾽ ἐμοῦ ἀπεσταλμένοις, οὓς ἐγὼ εἰς τὸ ἀκρι-
βέστατον δοκιμάσας [18]καὶ προελόμενος [ἀ]πέστειλα,
κἀκείνοις συμβούλευμα εἴη ὡς μετριωτάτους παρέχειν αὐτούς. μᾶλλον [19]γὰρ δὴ καὶ μᾶλλον [ο]ἱ τῶν
ἐθνῶν ἡγεμόνες καταμάθοιεν ἂν μεθ᾽ ὅσης αὐτοὺς
προθυμίας φείδεσθαι καὶ [20]προορᾶσθαι τῶν ἐθνῶν
οἷς ἐφεστήκασι προσήκει, ὁπότε καὶ τὸν Αὐτοκράτορα ὁρᾶν παρείη αὐτοῖς [21]μετὰ τοσαύτης

14. οὐχ ὅρων Edd.: οὐ χορῶν_(=χωρῶν) Wilcken: οὐ φόρων
Wilamowitz. 16. μου: redundant, perhaps corrupt (? ὁμοῦ).

clamation as Caesar [a] or should still be voted for the same reason by the cities. But though I fear that I cannot remit these for the reason which I have stated a little above, yet I have not failed to observe that these, as far as I can see under present circumstances, are all that the cities can afford to pay. Therefore let all persons in all the cities both in Italy and in other countries know that I remit to them the sums due in place of golden crowns on the occasion of my accession to the empire, to which I have attained in accordance with the wishes and prayers of all, and that I do this not owing to a superfluity of wealth but to my personal policy, in pursuance of which I have always striven since I became Caesar to restore our declining fortunes, not by extortion of taxes [b] but by economy only, avoiding expenditure on private ends. For it was not my aim to amass money by every means, but rather by liberality and kindnesses to increase the welfare of this empire, in order that my governors whom I have sent abroad to occupy charges, and whom I tested and selected with the utmost care before dispatching, should likewise make it their purpose to behave with the utmost moderation. For the governors of the provinces will learn more and more how zealously it behoves them to spare and be considerate for the peoples over whom they have been placed, when they are able to see the emperor

[a] In contrast with his proclamation as emperor.
[b] Or, according to another reading, "by acquisitions of territory."

97

κοσμιότητος καὶ σωφροσύνης καὶ ἐγκρατείας τὰ
τῆς βασιλείας διοικοῦντα. τούτου τοῦ ἐμοῦ ²²δόγ-
ματος ἀντίγραφα τοῖς καθ᾽ ἑκάστην πόλιν ἄρ-
χουσιν γενέσθω ἐπιμελὲς εἰς τὸ δημόσιον μάλιστα
ἑστάν[αι] ²³σύνοπτα τοῖς ἀναγιγνώσκουσιν.
²⁴(ἔτους) α Παῦνι λ.

217. RESCRIPT OF GALLIENUS

C. P. Herm. 119, verso iii, ll. 8-16.   A.D. 267.

⁸Αὐτοκράτωρ Καῖσαρ Πούβλιος [Λ]ι[κίν]νιος
Γαλλιηνὸς Εὐσεβὴς Εὐτυχ[ὴ]ς Σεβαστὸς ⁹Αὐρηλίῳ
Πλουτίωνι χαίρειν. καλῶς καὶ προσηκόντως
¹⁰αὐτὸ ἐποίησας πρὸ[ς τ]ὴν ὀρφανίαν ἐπιμεληθεὶς
τοῦ πα[ιδὸ]ς καὶ ὑπὲρ αὐ-¹¹τοῦ ἐπιστε[ίλ]ας μοι.
κα[λε]ῖ δὲ καὶ ἡ το[ῦ δι]καίου τάξις ὡς καὶ τὰ ἐκ
τῆς παρὰ σοῦ δεήσεως ¹²ἑτοίμως [δ]ιδ[ό]ναι χάριν.
γεγενημένος γὰρ ἐκ γονέων μὲν Ἀσκληπιάδου
¹³παιδὸ[ς τ]ε Νείλου ἀ[νδρ]ῶν εὐδοκίμων κατὰ τὴν
ἄθλησ[ιν] γενομένων, πῶς ¹⁴[ο]ὐ κ[όσ]μος ἦν καὶ
πα[ῖδα ε]ὐχερῶς τυχεῖν; ἀφείσθω τοίνυν Αἴλιος
Ἀσκληπιάδης ¹⁵[ὁ] καὶ [Νεῖ]λος χρειῶν [κα]ὶ
ἀρχῶν καὶ [λε]ιτουργιῶν ἁπασῶ[ν, ἵν]α διὰ τὴν
[τῶν προγόνων] ¹⁶ἀρετὴν ἀπολαύσῃ τῆς ἐμῆς
φιλανθρωπίας.

15. χρειῶν Hunt, Örtel : πορειῶν Ed.

also conducting the business of his realm with so much propriety and moderation and self-restraint. Let the magistrates in each city see to it that copies of this my edict are set up in public in full view of those who wish to read. Year 1, Pauni 30.

217. RESCRIPT OF GALLIENUS

A.D. 267.

The Emperor Caesar Publius Licinius Gallienus Pius Felix Augustus to Aurelius Plution [a] greeting. You did well and properly, in view of his orphanhood, to take thought for the boy and write to me concerning him. The duty of justice as well as the matter of your request urges me to grant the favour readily. For was it not fitting that he should obtain it with ease, a boy of such descent, whose parents were Asclepiades and a daughter of Nilus,[b] men once famous in athletics ? Therefore let Aelius Asclepiades also called Nilus be exempted from all services and offices and public duties, in order that for the sake of his ancestors' prowess he may enjoy my benevolence.

[a] A procurator.
[b] The Greek text is suspect, but in any case it is probable that Asclepiades and Nilus were the father and grandfather of the boy.

SELECT PAPYRI

218. RESCRIPT OF JUSTINIAN

P. Cairo Masp. 67024.   About A.D. 551.

¹[Προ]σελθὼν ἡμῖν ἐδίδα[ξεν] {ἡμῖν} ὁρμᾶσθαι
μὲν ἐκ τῆσδε ²[τῆ]ς κώμης τῆς Θηβαίων χώρα[ς]
{διδάσκων}, τὸν πατέρα δ[ὲ ³τὸ]ν οἰκ[εῖον τὸ]ν ἐν
αὐτῇ κε[κτημ]ένον πρῶτον γενόμενο[ν ⁴καὶ] τὰς
ὑπὲρ τοῦ παντὸς χωρίου συντελείας ἀναλεγόμενον
⁵[ἐπὶ] τ[οὺς] τῆς ἐπιχωρίου τάξεως ταύτας κατα-
τιθέναι, ἐπειδὴ δὲ ⁶παρὰ τῶν κατὰ καιρὸν ἀρχόντων
οὐ τὰς τυχούσας ἀδικίας ⁷ὑπέμεινον, τῷ θείῳ ἡμῶν
οἴκῳ σφᾶς αὐτοὺς ἐπιδοῦναι καὶ ὑπὸ τὴν προσ-
⁸τασίαν αὐτοῦ γενέσθαι {τὴν αὐτοῦ}, Θεοδόσιον δὲ
τὸν μεγαλοπρεπέ(στατον) τῆς ἀπουσίας ⁹δραξάμενον
τοῦ πατρὸς τοῦ δεομένου τοὺς μὲν τῆς κώμης ¹⁰ἀνα-
λέξασθαι φόρους, οὐδὲν δὲ καταθεῖναι παντελῶς
¹¹[ἐπ]ὶ τὸν δημόσιον λόγον, ὥστε τοὺς τῆς ἐπιχωρίου τάξεως ¹²πάλιν ἐκ δευτέρου τοὺς ἱκέτας τὰς
ἐπικειμένας αὐτοῖς ¹³συντελείας εἰσπρᾶξαι, περί τε
τούτου θείας ἡμῶν ἤδη ¹⁴πορίσασθαι συλλαβὰς πρὸς
τὴν σὴν ἐνδοξ(ότητα) γεγραμμένας, ¹⁵ἀλλὰ τὴν
ἐκείνου περιδρομὴν πλέον τῶν ἡμετέρων ¹⁶ἰσχῦσαι
κελεύσεων, ὥστε τῷ δεομένῳ δευτέρας ἀφορμῆς
¹⁷ὁδοῦ καὶ μείζονος καταστῆναι τὸ πρᾶγμα τριβῆς.
θεσπίζομεν ¹⁸τοίνυν τὴν ἐνδοξ(ότητα) τὴν σὴν νῦν
γοῦν ταῖς δεδομέναις ¹⁹περὶ τούτου τῷ ἱκέτῃ θείαις
συλλαβαῖς πέρας ἐπιθεῖναι τὸ ²⁰προσῆκον καὶ μὴ
χρόνους ἐκ χρόνων αὐτὸν ἤτοι τὴν ²¹κατ' αὐτὸν
κώμην τῶν ἐποφειλομένων αὐτοῖς ἀπο-²²στερεῖσθαι,

The text is one of three slightly different versions of the
original.   2. διδάσκων as if preceded by προσῆλθεν
(so in the 3rd version).   3. *l.* τῶν . . . -ένων.

100

218. RESCRIPT OF JUSTINIAN

About A.D. 551.

(Dioscorus) [a] has approached us and informed us
that he comes from this village [b] in the Thebaid and
that his own father, being the chief of the proprietors
there, used to collect the contributions for the whole
place and deliver them to the agents of the local
officium [c] ; that on being subjected to some flagrant
injustices by the governors of the day they betook
themselves to our divine house and had recourse to its
protection, and that the most magnificent Theodosius,
taking advantage of the absence of the petitioner's
father, collected the taxes of the village, but paid
nothing whatever into the public account, so that the
agents of the local *officium* exacted a second time over
from the suppliants the contributions imposed upon
them ; and that concerning this matter they previously obtained from us a divine letter addressed to
your excellency,[d] but the intrigues of that person
were of more avail than our orders, so that the petitioner had the trouble of undertaking a second
journey [e] and of a prolonged delay. We therefore
decree that now at least your excellency shall give
proper effect to the divine letter about this question
which has been given to the suppliant and that he
or rather his village shall not be deprived year after

[a] A lawyer, poet of a sort, and a leading personage in
the little town of Aphrodito in Upper Egypt. A very large
portion of our Byzantine papyri comes from his archive.
[b] Aphrodito.
[c] The bureau of the *praeses*, the civil administrator.
[d] The rescript is addressed to the Dux or military commander and governor of the Thebaid. [e] To Constantinople.

101

ὡς μὴ κατὰ τὴν πρόφασιν ταύτην ἀτονίαν ²³αὐτοῖς
ὀλίγον ὕστερον περὶ τὴν τῶν δημοσίων φόρων
²⁴γενέσθαι καταβολήν. ἐπειδὴ δέ φησίν τινας τῶν
κατὰ ταύτην ²⁵[κεκτημ]ένων τὴν κώμην πράγματα
τοῦ δεομένου καὶ τῶν ²⁶ἀδελφῶν τῶν αὐτοῦ παρὰ
τὸν τοῦ [δικα]ίου λ[ό]γον ἀφελέσθ[αι], ²⁷⟦ἀφορμὴ
τῆς τοῦ εἰρημέ(νου) δημοσίου δευτέρας⟧ {εἰσ-
πράξεως} θεσπίζομεν τὴν ἐνδοξ(ότητα) τὴν σὴν ²⁸[καὶ
τὰ περὶ] τούτου[{ς}] σκοποῦσαν, εἰ οὕτως ἔχοντα
εὕροις, ²⁹τὸ ἱκανὸν τῷ τε δεομένῳ καὶ τοῖς ἀδελφοῖς τοῖς αὐτοῦ [κατὰ τὸν] ³⁰νόμον γενέσθαι παρα-
σκευάσαι. πρὸς τούτοις ἐδίδαξαν ἡμᾶς ³¹Ἰουλιανὸν
παγάρχην τῆς Ἀνταιοπολιτῶν βουληθῆναι τὴν κατ'
αὐτοὺς ³²κώμην ὑπὸ τὴν οἰκείαν παγαρχίαν ποιήσασθαι, καὶ ταῦτα μηδέ-³³ποτε τελεσάντων ὑπὸ
παγαρχίαν αὐτῶν ἀλλὰ κατὰ τὸ τῶν ³⁴αὐτοπράκτων
σχῆμα δι' ἑαυτῶν τοὺς δημοσίους φόρους ἐπὶ
⟦τοὺς⟧ ³⁵τὴν ἐπιχώριον τάξιν κατατιθέντων, ἐπειδὴ
δὲ οὐκ ἠνέσχο[ν-]³⁶το τούτου τοῦ μέρους, ἐπελθεῖν
αὐτοῖς καὶ πραγμάτων ἁρπαγὴν ³⁷ἁμαρτῆσαι καὶ
τοσαύτην ἁπλῶς τὴν ἀτοπίαν γενέσθαι τὴν ³⁸αὐτοῦ
αὐτοῖς τε καὶ τῇ αὐτ[ῶν κώμῃ] ὥστε καὶ ὑπὸ τὴν
παγαρχίαν ποιήσασθαι, πρᾶγμα πάσης ³⁹ἀτοπίας
ἐπέκεινα. θεσπίζομεν τοίνυν τὴν ἐνδοξ(ότητα) τὴν
σὴν ⁴⁰ἐξετάσαι τὰ περὶ τούτου μεθ' ὅσης νόμος
ἀκριβείας προστατεῖ ⁴¹καί, εἰ ταῖς ἀληθείαις μηδέ-
ποτε τοὺς τὴν αὐτὴν κώμην οἰκοῦντ[ας] ⁴²ὑπὸ
παγαρχίαν τελέσαντας εὕροις, ἀποστῆσαι μὲν τὸν
προειρημ(ένον) ⁴³⟨Ἰουλιανὸν⟩ τῆς πρὸς αὐτοὺς
μετουσίας, θεραπεῦσαι δὲ παρα-⁴⁴σκευάσαι τοῖς
δεομένοις τὰς ἀπηνηνεγμένας παρ' αὐτ[οῦ] ⁴⁵βλαβὰς

30. Or ἐδίδαξεν as in the 3rd version.

year of what is due to them, so that they shall not on this account be shortly reduced to exhaustion over the payment of the public taxes. And whereas he says that some of the proprietors in that village have robbed the petitioner and his brothers of certain property contrary to principles of justice, we decree that your excellency shall examine this case also and, if you find that it is so, shall cause satisfaction to be given to the petitioner and his brothers according to the law. Further, they have informed us that Julianus, pagarch of the Antaeopolite nome, wished to place their village under his own pagarchy, in spite of the fact that they have never been subject to a pagarchy for taxation, *a* but following the system of self-exaction used to pay the public taxes directly to the local *officium* ; and that when they would not accept this position, he attacked them and was guilty of seizing their property, and shortly, such was the enormity of his conduct to them and their village, that he did indeed place them under his pagarchy, an act of extreme enormity. We therefore decree that your excellency shall examine this case with as much strictness as the law rules, and that, if you find that in truth the inhabitants of the said village have never been subject to a pagarchy for taxation, you shall stop the aforesaid Julianus from meddling with them and cause him to make good to the petitioners the harm which he has inflicted on them according

---

a At this late period the pagarchs (see Glossary) had the right of collecting the taxes in their own districts, but certain villages such as Aphrodito were granted the privilege of collecting their own taxes and paying them directly to the local branch of the Treasury.

---

44. *l.* ἀπενηνεγμένας.

αὐτοῖς καθὰ τοῖς περὶ τούτου νόμοις δοκεῖ. ἄξει
[δὲ] ⁴⁶καὶ τοὺς ἄλλους ἡ σὴ ἐνδοξ(ότης), ὅσοι τῆς τε
σῆς τάξεως καὶ παγανῶν τοῖς δεομένοις ἐπί τ[ε]
⁴⁷χρήμασιν καὶ ἐγκλήμασιν ὑπεύθυνοι φάνειεν
⁴⁸τυγχάνειν, καὶ τά τ' ἐς χρήματα βλέποντα θερα-
πεῦσαι τοῖς ⁴⁹δεομένοις κατὰ τὸν νόμον, ὑπέρ τε
τῶν ἐγκλημάτων ⁵⁰νομίμοις ποιναῖς ὑποθεῖναι φρον-
τιεῖ {η} τοὺς μὲν ταῦτα ⁵¹ἡμαρτηκότας, ὥστε τὸ
ἱκανὸν ἐφ' ἑκατέρῳ, τοῖς τε δεομένοις ⁵²καὶ τῷ
νόμῳ, γενέσθαι ╇, τῶν κατὰ συναρπαγὴν οἷον εἰκὸς
συλλαβῶν ⁵³ποριζομένων παρὰ τὰ παρ' ἡμῶν νῦν
θεσπισθέντα {θεσπίζομεν} οὐδεμίαν ⁵⁴δυναμένων
ἔχειν ἰσχύν, {ταῦτα} ⁵⁵<παραφυλαττούσης ταῦτα
τῆς τε σῆς <ἐνδοξότητος> ⁵⁶καὶ τοῦ κατὰ καιρὸν τὴν
αὐτὴν ἀρχὴν παραλημψομένου καὶ ⁵⁷τῆς πειθομένης
ὑμῖν τάξεως, ποινῆς τριῶν χρυσίου λιτρῶν ⁵⁸ἐπι-
κειμένης κατὰ τῶν ταῦτα παραβαίνειν τολμώντων
⁵⁹ἢ παραβαίνεσθαι συγχωρούντων. ╇ >

54-59. Not in our text, but restored from the 3rd version.

219. EDICT OF METTIUS RUFUS

P. Oxy. 237, col. 8, ll. 27-43.   A.D. 89.

²⁷Μάρκος Μέττι-²⁸ος Ῥοῦφος ἔπαρχος Αἰγύπτου
λέγει· Κλαύδιος Ἄρειος ὁ τοῦ Ὀξυρυγχείτου
στρατηγὸς [ἐ]δήλωσέν μοι μήτε τὰ ἰ[δι]ωτικὰ
μ[ήτε τὰ δημ]όσια ²⁹πράγματα τὴν καθήκουσαν
λαμβάνειν διοίκησιν διὰ τὸ ἐκ πολλῶν χρόνων μὴ
καθ' ὃν ἔδει τρόπον ᾠκονομῆσθαι τὰ ἐν τῇ τῶν
ἐν-³⁰κτήσεων βιβλιοθήκῃ δια[σ]τρώματα, καίτοι
104

to the provisions of the laws on that subject. And all other persons belonging to your *officium* or to the civilian class who appear to be answerable to the petitioners in regard to money or accusations your excellency shall force to make good to the petitioners their losses with regard to money according to the law, and concerning the accusations you will take care to subject the guilty persons to the legal penalties so that satisfaction shall be given on both heads, to the petitioners and to the law ; and letters which, as is probable, were obtained by rapacity can possess no force against what we have now decreed, and your excellency and whoever shall in time succeed you in your post and the *officium* which serves you shall observe these orders closely, a penalty of three pounds of gold being imposed upon those who venture to transgress them or allow them to be transgressed.

219. EDICT OF METTIUS RUFUS

A.D. 89.

Proclamation of Marcus Mettius Rufus, praefect of Egypt. Claudius Arius the strategus of the Oxyrhynchite nome has informed me that neither private nor public business is receiving proper treatment owing to the fact that for many years the abstracts in the property record-office have not been kept in the manner required, although the praefects before

SELECT PAPYRI

πολλάκις κριθὲν ὑπὸ τῶν πρὸ ἐμοῦ ἐπάρχων τῆς
δεούσης αὐτὰ τυχεῖν ἐπανορθώ-³¹σεως· ὅπερ οὐ
καλῶς ἐνδέχεται, εἰ μὴ ἄνωθεν γένοιτο ἀντίγραφα.
κελεύω οὖν πάντας τοὺς κτήτορας ἐντὸς μηνῶν
ἓξ ἀπογρά-³²ψασθαι τὴν ἰδίαν κτῆσιν εἰς τὴν τῶν
ἐνκτήσεων βιβλιοθήκην καὶ τοὺς δανειστὰς ἃς
ἐὰν ἔχωσι ὑποθήκας καὶ τοὺς ἄλλους ³³ὅσα ἐὰν
ἔχωσι δίκαια. τὴν δὲ ἀπογραφὴν ποιείσθωσαν
δηλοῦντες πόθεν ἕκαστος τῶν ὑπαρχόντων κατα-
βέβηκεν εἰς αὐτοὺς ³⁴ἢ κτῆσεις. παρατιθέτωσαν
δὲ καὶ αἱ γυναῖκες ταῖς ὑποστάσεσι τῶν ἀνδρῶν,
ἐὰν κατά τινα ἐπιχώριον νόμον κρατεῖται τὰ
ὑπάρ-³⁵χοντα, ὁμοίως δὲ καὶ τὰ τέκνα ταῖς τῶν
γονέων, οἷς ἡ μὲν χρῆσεις διὰ δημοσίων τετήρηται
χρηματισμῶν, ἡ δὲ κτῆ-³⁶σις μετὰ θάνατον τοῖς
τέκνοις κεκράτηται, ἵνα οἱ συναλλάσσοντες μὴ
κατ᾽ ἄγνοιαν ἐνεδρεύονται. παραγγέλλω δὲ καὶ
τοῖς συναλλα-³⁷γματογράφοις καὶ τοῖς μνήμοσι
μηδὲν δίχα ἐπιστάλματος τοῦ βιβλιοφυλακ[ίου
τελειῶσαι, γνοῦσιν ὡς οὐκ ὄφελος τὸ] τοιοῦτο,
ἀλλὰ καὶ ³⁸αὐτοὶ ὡς παρὰ τὰ προστεταγμένα
ποιήσοντες δίκην ὑπομενοῦσι τὴν προσήκουσαν.
ἐὰν δ᾽ εἰσὶν ἐν τῇ βιβλιοθήκῃ τῶν ἐπά-³⁹νω χρόνων
ἀπογραφαί, μετὰ πάσης ἀκρειβείας φυλασσέσθω-
σαν, ὁμοίως δὲ καὶ τὰ διαστρώματα, ἵν᾽ εἴ τις
γένοιτο ζήτησις εἰς ⁴⁰ὕστερον περὶ τῶν μὴ δεόντως
ἀπογραψαμένων ἐξ ἐκείνων ἐλεγχθῶσι. [ἵνα] δ᾽
[ο]ὖν β[εβ]αία τε καὶ εἰς ἅπαν διαμένῃ τῶν δια-

36. l. ἐνεδρεύωνται.

---

[a] General registrations of property in land were ordered
by the praefects from time to time owing to special circumstances, such as a failure to keep the records in good order.

me have often ordered that they should undergo the necessary revision, which is not really practicable unless copies are made from the beginning. Therefore I command all owners to register their property at the property record-office within six months, and all lenders the mortgages which they hold, and all other persons the claims which they possess.[a] In making the return they shall declare the source from which in each case the possession of the property devolved upon them. Wives also, if on the strength of some native law they have a lien on the property, shall add an annotation[b] to the property-statements of their husbands, and likewise children to those of their parents, if the enjoyment of the property has been secured to the latter by public instruments and the possession of it after their death has been settled on their children, in order that those who make agreements with them may not be defrauded through ignorance. I also command the scribes and recorders of contracts not to execute any deed without authorization of the record-office, being warned that such a transaction has no validity and that they themselves will suffer the due penalty for disregarding orders. If the record-office contains any property-returns of earlier date, let them be preserved with the utmost care, and likewise the abstracts of them, in order that if afterwards an inquiry should be held concerning persons who have made false returns, they may be convicted thereby. In order then that the use of the abstracts may become secure and

[a] New acquisitions and changes in ownership were notified to the record-office as they took place.

[b] Referring to the marriage contracts establishing their eventual claim ; and in the case of the children, to the testamentary contracts of the parents.

σ-⁴¹τρωμάτων ἢ χρήσεις πρὸς τὸ μὴ πάλιν ἀπογραφῆς δεηθῆναι, παραγγέλλω τοῖς β[ι]βλιοφύλαξι διὰ
πενταετίας ἐπανανεοῦσθαι ⁴²τὰ διαστρώματα μετα-
φερομένης εἰς τὰ καινοποιούμενα τῆς τελευταίας
ἑκάστου ὀνόματος ὑποστάσεως κατὰ κώμην καὶ
κα-⁴³τ’ εἶδος. (ἔτους) θ Δομειτιανο[ῦ], μηνὸς
Δομιτ{τ}ιανοῦ δ.

220. EDICT OF VIBIUS MAXIMUS

P. Lond. 904, ll. 18-38.   A.D. 104.

¹⁸Γ[άιος Οὐί]βιο[ς Μάξιμος ἔπα]ρχ[ος] ¹⁹Αἰγύπ-
τ[ου λέγει]· ²⁰τῆς κατ’ οἰ[κίαν ἀπογραφῆς ἐ]ν-
εστώ[σης] ²¹ἀναγκαῖον [ἐστιν πᾶσιν τοῖ]ς καθ’
ἥ[ντινα] ²²δήποτε αἰτ[ίαν ἀποδημοῦσιν ἀπὸ τῶν]
²³νομῶν προσα[γγέλλε]σθαι ἐπα[νελ-]²⁴θεῖν εἰς τὰ
ἑαυ[τῶν ἐ]φέστια, ἵν[α] ²⁵καὶ τὴν συνήθη [οἰ]κο-
νομίαν τῆ[ς ἀπο-]²⁶γραφῆς πληρώσωσιν καὶ τῇ
προσ[ηκού-]²⁷σῃ αὐτοῖς γεωργίαι προσκαρτερή-
σω[σιν]. ²⁸εἰδὼς μέντο[ι ὅ]τι ἐνίων τῶν [ἀπὸ]
²⁹τῆς χώρας ἡ πόλις ἡμῶν ἔχει χρε[ίαν], ³⁰βούλο-
μ[αι] πάντα[ς τ]οὺς εὔ[λ]ογον δο[κοῦν-]³¹τα[ς]
ἔχειν τοῦ ἐνθάδε ἐπιμένιν [αἰ-]³²τίαν ἀπογράφε-
σ[θ]αι παρὰ Βουλ . . . [. . .] ³³Φήστῳ ἐπάρχῳ[ι]
εἴλης, ὃν ἐπὶ το[ύτῳ] ³⁴ἔταξα, οὗ καὶ τὰς [ὑ]πο-
γραφὰς οἱ ἀποδ[εί-]³⁵ξαντες ἀναγκ[αίαν α]ὑτῶν
τὴν παρου[σίαν] ³⁶λήμψοντα[ι κατὰ τ]οῦ[τ]ο τὸ
παράγγελμ[α] ³⁷ἐντὸς [τῆς τριακάδος τοῦ ἐν-]
εσ[τ]ῶτος μη-³⁸νὸς Ἐ[πείφ - - -

permanent, so that another registration shall not be required, I command the keepers of the record-office to revise the abstracts every five years, transferring to the new lists the last statement of property of each person arranged under villages and kinds. The 9th year of Domitian, Domitianus [a] 4.

[a] The month Domitianus = the Egyptian Phaophi, corresponding to October.

220. EDICT OF VIBIUS MAXIMUS

A.D. 104.

Proclamation of Gaius Vibius Maximus, praefect of Egypt. The house-to-house census [a] having started, it is essential that all persons who for any reason whatsoever are absent from their nomes be summoned to return to their own hearths, in order that they may perform the customary business of registration and apply themselves to the cultivation which concerns them. Knowing, however, that some of the people from the country are needed by our city, I desire all those who think they have a satisfactory reason for remaining here [b] to register themselves before . . . Festus, *praefectus alae*, whom I have appointed for this purpose, from whom those who have shown their presence to be necessary shall receive signed permits in accordance with this edict up to the 30th of the present month Epeiph. . . .

[a] See Nos. 312, 313.   [b] In Alexandria.

SELECT PAPYRI

221. EDICT OF PETRONIUS MAMERTINUS

P.S.I. 446.   A.D. 133–137.

¹Μάρκος Πετρώνιος Μαμερτῖνος ²ἔπαρχος Αἰγύπτου λέγει· ³ἐπέγνων πολλοὺς τῶν στρατ[ι]ω-
τῶν ἄνευ διπλῆς ⁴διὰ τῆς χώρας πορευομένους
πλοῖα καὶ κτήνη καὶ ⁵ἀνθρώπους αἰτεῖν παρὰ τὸ
προσῆκον, τὰ μὲν αὐ-⁶τοὺς π[ρ]ὸς βίαν ἀποσπῶν-
τας, τὰ δὲ καὶ κατὰ χάριν ⁷ἢ θαράπειαν π[α]ρὰ
τῶν στρατηγῶν λαμβάνοντας, ⁸ἐξ οὗ τοῖς μὲν
ἰδιώταις ὕβρις τε καὶ ἐπηρείας γείνε-⁹σθαι, τὸ δὲ
στρατ[ι]ωτικὸν ἐπὶ πλεονεξίᾳ καὶ ἀδικίᾳ ¹⁰δια-
βάλ[λ]εσθαι συνβέβηκε. παραγγέλλω δὴ τοῖς στρα-
¹¹τηγοῖς καὶ βασιλικοῖς ἁπαξαπλῶς μηδενὶ παρ-
έ-¹²χιν ἄν[ε]υ διπλῆς μηθὲ ἓν τῶν ἰς παραπομπὴν
¹³διδο[μέ]νων μήτε πλέοντι μήτε πεζῇ βαδί[ζον-]
¹⁴τι, ὡς [ἐμ]οῦ κο[λ]άσοντος ἐρρωμένως ἐάν τις
ἁλῷ ¹⁵μετὰ τ[οῦτο] τὸ διάταγμα λαμβάνων ἢ
διδούς ¹⁶τι τῶν [προειρη]μένων. ¹⁷[(ἔτους) . .]
Ἀδριανοῦ Καίσαρος τοῦ κυρίου, Θ[ὼ]θ ή.

7. *l.* θεράπειαν.   10. διαβάλ[λ]εσθαι revised reading.
12. *l.* μηδὲ ἕν, or μηθέν.

222. EDICT OF MANTENNIUS SABINUS

B.G.U. 646.   A.D. 193.

¹Μαντέ[ν]νιος Σαβεῖνος στρ(ατηγοῖς) (Ἑπτὰ)
Νομ(ῶν) ²καὶ Ἀρσι(νοΐτου) χαίρειν. τοῦ πεμ-
φ<θ>έντος εἰς ³τὴν λαμπρ[ο]τάτην Ἀλεξάνδρειαν
⁴διατάγματος ὑπ' ἐμοῦ ἀντίγρ(αφον) ὑπο-⁵ταγῆναι

110

221. EDICT OF PETRONIUS MAMERTINUS

A.D. 133–137.

Proclamation of Marcus Petronius Mamertinus, praefect of Egypt. I am informed that without having a warrant many of the soldiers when travelling through the country requisition boats and animals and persons improperly, in some cases seizing them by force, in others obtaining them from the strategi through favour or obsequiousness, the result of which is that private persons are subjected to insults and abuses and the army is reproached for greed and injustice. I therefore command the strategi and royal scribes never in any case to furnish to any person without a warrant, whether travelling by river or by land, any contribution for the journey, understanding that I will vigorously punish anyone who after this edict is discovered receiving or giving any of the aforesaid things. The . . year of Hadrianus Caesar the lord, Thoth 8.

222. EDICT OF MANTENNIUS SABINUS

A.D. 193.

Mantennius Sabinus to the strategi of the Heptanomia [a] and of the Arsinoite nome greeting. I have ordered a copy of the edict sent by me to the most illustrious Alexandria to be appended, in order

[a] The district of Middle Egypt.

111

ἐκέλευσα, ἵνα πάντες ἰδί-⁶ητα[ι] καὶ ταῖς ἴσαις
ἡμέραις ἑορτά-⁷σητ[α]ι. ἐρρῶσθε ὑμᾶς βούλομαι.
⁸(ἔτους) α [Αὐτο]κράτορος Καίσαρος Πουβλίου
⁹Ἐλ[ουί]ου Περτίνακος Σεβαστοῦ Φα-¹⁰με[ν]ὼθ ῑ.
Ἀ(ντίγραφον) διατάγματος.   ¹¹Ἑορ[τ]άζοντας
ἡμᾶς ἐπεὶ τῇ εὐ-¹²τυχ[ε]στάτῃ βασιλίᾳ τοῦ κυρίου
¹³ἡμῶν Αὐτοκράτορος Πουβλίου ¹⁴Ἀ[λουί]ου Περ-
τίν[ακ]ος τοῦ Σεβ[αστο]ῦ ¹⁵[πρώτ]ου τῆς ἱ[ε]ρ[ᾶς]
συνκ[λ]ήτ[ου] ¹⁶π[ατρ]ὸς πατρίτος καὶ Πουβλίου
¹⁷Ἐλουίο]υ [Π]ερτίνακος τοῦ ὑέος ¹⁸[αὐτοῦ] καὶ
Φ[λ]αυίας Τιττιανῆς ¹⁹[Σεβασ]τῆς [ἀ]κόλουθόν ἐστιν,
²⁰[ὦ ἄνδρ]ες Ἀλεξανδρεῖς, πανδημεὶ ²¹[θ]ύο[ν]τας
καὶ εὐχομένους ὑπέρ τε ²²τοῦ διηνεκοῦς αὐτο-
κρατοῦς ²³κ[αὶ το]ῦ σύνπαντος οἴκου στεφα-²⁴[νο-
φ]ορῆσαι ἡμέρας πεντεκαίδε-²⁵[κα ἀ]ρξαμένους ἀπὸ
τῆς σήμ[ερο]ν.

5. *l.* εἰδείητε.	6. *l.* ἑορτάσητε.	7. *l.* ἐρρῶσθαι.
11. *l.* ὑμᾶς ἐπί.	14. *l.* Ἐ[λουίο]υ.	16. *l.* πατρίδος.

223. CIRCULAR FIXING THE PRICE OF MYRRH

P. Tebt. 35.   111 B.C.

¹Ἀπολλώνιος [τ]οῖς ἐν τῆι Πολέμωνος μερίδος
²ἐπιστάταις καὶ τοῖς ἄλλοις τοῖς ἐπὶ χρειῶν τετα-
³γμένοις χαίρειν. τῆς ἀναδεδομένης κατὰ κώμην
⁴ζμύρνης μηδένα πλεῖον πράσσει{σι}ν τῆς ⁵μνᾶς
ἀργυ(ρίου) (δραχμῶν) μ, ἐν χα(λκῶι) (ταλάντων)
γ Β, καὶ τούτοις κατα-⁶γωγίμου τῶι (ταλάντωι)
(δραχμῶν) σ, ταῦτα δὲ διαγρ(άφειν) ἕως γ ⁷τοῦ

1. *l.* μερίδι.

that you should all be informed and that you may hold festival for the like number of days. I wish you good health. The 1st year of the Emperor Caesar Publius Helvius Pertinax Augustus, Phamenoth 10.

Copy of the edict. It is fitting that you, O Alexandrians, holding festival for the most fortunate accession of our lord the Emperor Publius Helvius Pertinax the Augustus, head of the sacred senate, father of his country, and of Publius Helvius Pertinax his son, and of Flavia Titiana Augusta,[a] should in full assembly make sacrifices and prayers on behalf of his lasting empire and of all his house and wear garlands for fifteen days beginning from to-day.

[a] Wife of Pertinax.

223. CIRCULAR FIXING THE PRICE OF MYRRH

111 B.C.

Apollonius to the epistatae [a] in the division of Polemon and to the other officials greeting. For the myrrh [b] distributed in the villages no one shall exact more than 40 drachmae of silver for a mina-weight, or in copper 3 talents 2000 drachmae [c] with a charge of 200 drachmae on the talent for carriage [d]; which sum shall be paid not later than the 3rd of Phar-

[a] The village overseers.
[b] Perfumes and spices were the object of a government monopoly.
[c] That is, 40 silver drachmae = 20,000 copper drachmae, the ratio between the copper and the silver drachma being at this period 1 : 500.
[d] To cover the cost of transporting the unwieldy copper money to Alexandria.

113

SELECT PAPYRI

Φαρμοῦθι τῶι ἀπεσταλμένωι τούτωι χάριν ⁸πράκ-
τορι. τὸ δ᾽ ὑποκείμενον πρόγραμμα ἐκτεθῆι-⁹τωι
καὶ διὰ τῆς τοῦ κωμογραμματέως ¹⁰γνώμης, ὃς
κ[α]ὶ μεθ᾽ ὑμῶν ὑπὸ τὴν ἐντο-¹¹λὴν {ε} ὑπογράφει.
ἧι ὅ τι {ο} παρὰ ταῦτα ποι-¹²ῶν ἑ[α]υτὸν [[ε.]] αἰτιάσεται. πεπόμφαμεν ¹³δὲ τούτων χάριν καὶ τοὺς
μαχαιροφόρους. ¹⁴ἔρρωσθε. (ἔτους) ϛ Φαρμοῦθι β.

¹⁵Τοὺς ἐπ . . (   ) παρὰ τῶν κατὰ κώμην
ἐπιστατῶν ¹⁶καὶ τῶν ἄλλων ζμύρναν μὴ πλεῖον
διαγράφειν ¹⁷τῆς μνᾶς ἀργυ(ρίου) (δραχμῶν) μ, ἐν
χα(λκῶι) (ταλάντων) γ (δραχμῶν) ᾽Β, καὶ ¹⁸κατ-
αγώγιον τῶι (ταλάντωι) (δραχμῶν) σ, ἧι ὅ τι παρὰ
¹⁹ταῦτα ποιῶν ἑαυτὸν αἰτιάσεται.

7. *l.* τούτων.

224. CIRCULAR OF A PRAEFECT

P. Oxy. 1408, ll. 11-21.   A.D. 210-214.

¹¹[Βαίβιος] Ἰουγκῖνος στρατηγοῖς Ἑπτὰ νομῶν
καὶ Ἀρσινοΐτου χαίρειν. ¹²[ἐ]γὼ μὲν ὑμεῖν καὶ δι᾽
ἑτέρ[ων] μου γραμμάτων προστάξας πεφροντισ-
μ[έ]ν[ως ¹³τὴ]ν τῶν λῃστῶν ἀναζήτησ[ιν] ποιήσασθαι, κίνδυνον ὑμεῖν ἐπαρτήσας εἰ ἀμ[ε-¹⁴λε]ῖτε, καὶ
νῦν δὲ διατάγματ[ι β]εβαιῶσαί μου τὴν γνώμην
ἠθέλησα, ἵνα πά[ν-¹⁵τε]ς εἰδῶσιν οἱ κατὰ τὴν
Αἴγυπτον οὐκ ἐκ παρέργου τιθέμενον τοῦτο τὸ
¹⁶[χρέ]ος, ἀλλ[ὰ] καὶ τοῖ[ς] συλλημψομένοις ὑμῖν
γέρα προτιθέντα, κίνδυνον [δὲ ¹⁷τοῖς ἀπει]θεῖν
προαιρουμένο[ι]ς ἐπανατεινόμενον. ὅπερ διάταγμα
βού[λομαι ¹⁸ἔν τε ταῖς μη]τροπόλεσι καὶ τοῖς

12. [ἐ]γώ Wilcken : [ἔ]χω Edd.

114

mouthi to the collector sent for the purpose. Let the subjoined notice be posted up with the concurrence of the village secretary, who shall sign his name below the order along with you. Whoever contravenes these instructions will render himself liable to accusation. We have therefore also sent the sword-bearers.[a] Goodbye. Year 6, Pharmouthi 2.

Purchasers of myrrh from the epistatae in the several villages and from the other officials shall not pay more than 40 drachmae of silver for the mina-weight, or in copper 3 talents 2000 drachmae with a charge of 200 drachmae on the talent for carriage, and whoever contravenes these instructions shall render himself liable to accusation.

[a] Armed attendants, whose services might be required.

224. CIRCULAR OF A PRAEFECT

A.D. 210–214.

Baebius Juncinus to the strategi of the Hepta-nomia and the Arsinoite nome greeting. I have already ordered you in a previous letter to search out robbers with all care, warning you of the peril of neglect, and now I wish to confirm my resolve by an edict,[a] in order that all inhabitants of Egypt may know that I am not treating this duty as an affair of secondary importance, but offer rewards to those of you who co-operate, and threaten with peril those who choose to disobey. This edict I desire to be publicly displayed in both the capitals and the most

[a] A copy of the edict followed the present copy of the circular, but only the beginning of it is preserved.

ἐπισημοτάτοις τῶν νομῶν ⟨τόποις⟩ προτεθῆν[αι,
¹⁹ζημίας ὑμῖν ἐπικ]ειμένης μετὰ κινδύνου εἴ τις
κακουργὸς λαθὼν β[ιάζε-²⁰σθαι δύναται]. ἐρρῶσθαι ὑμᾶς βούλομαι. ²¹[(ἔτους) . .] Φαῶφι κη.

225. CIRCULARS OF A STRATEGUS AND DIOECETES

P. Oxy. 1409.   A.D. 278.

¹Αὐρήλιος Ἁρποκρατίων στρατηγὸς Ὀξ[υρυγ-
χίτο]υ δεκαπρώτ[οις τοῦ νομοῦ χαίρειν]. ²τῆς
γραφείσης ἐπιστολῆς εἰς κοινὸν ἡμῖν στρατη[γοῖς
καὶ δε]καπρώτοις τῆς ['Επτανομίας καὶ Ἀρσινο]-
ΐτ[ο]υ ³ὑπὸ Οὐλπίου Αὐρηλίου τοῦ κρατ[ίσ]του
διοικητοῦ περ[ὶ τῆς τῶν] χωμάτων ἀπερ[γασίας καὶ
τῆς τῶν διωρύχω]ν ἀνα-⁴καθάρσεως ἀντίγραφον
ἐπιστέλλεται ὑμῖν, φίλτ[ατοι, ἵνα εἰ]δῆτε καὶ τοῖς
γρ[αφεῖσιν ἀκολουθῆτε. ὃς δ'] ἂν πρό-⁵τερος ὑμῶν
κομίσηται τόδε τ[ὸ] ἐπίσταλμα τοῖς [λοι]π[οῖς]
μεταδότω. ἐρρῶ[σθαι ὑμᾶς εὔχομαι, φίλτ]ατοι.
⁶(ἔτους) γ τοῦ κυρίου ἡμῶν Μάρκου Αὐρηλίου
Πρόβου Σεβαστοῦ Φαρμοῦθι [.].

⁷Οὔλπιος Αὐρήλιος στρατηγοῖς κ[αὶ] δεκαπρώτοις
'Επτανομίας καὶ Ἀρσινοΐτου [χαίρειν. τοῦ καιροῦ
τῆς τῶν] ⁸χωμάτων ἀπεργασίας καὶ τῆ[ς] τῶν
διωρύχων ἀνακαθάρσεως ἐνεστη[κότος παραγγέλ-
λειν ὑμῖν ἀναγ-]⁹καῖον ἡγησάμην διὰ τῶνδε τῶν
γραμμάτων ὡς χρὴ σύμπαντας τοὺς γε[ωργοὺς
. . . .] ¹⁰ταῦτα ἀπ-
εργάζεσθαι ἤδη μετὰ πάσης προθυμίας ἐπὶ τὰ

conspicuous places of the nomes, penalties and peril awaiting you if in the future any evil-doer is able to use violence without being detected. I wish you good health. The . . year, Phaophi 28.

225. CIRCULARS OF A STRATEGUS AND DIOECETES

A.D. 278.

Aurelius Harpocration, strategus of the Oxyrhynchite nome, to the *decemprimi* [a] of the nome greeting. A copy of the circular letter addressed to us, the strategi and *decemprimi* of the Heptanomia [b] and the Arsinoite nome, by his excellency the dioecetes, Ulpius Aurelius, concerning the consolidation of the dykes and the cleansing of the canals is sent to you, dear friends, in order that you may know and follow his instructions. Whoever of you first receives this order should transmit it to the others. I pray for your health, dear friends. The 3rd year of our lord Marcus Aurelius Probus Augustus, Pharmouthi [.].

Ulpius Aurelius to the strategi and *decemprimi* of the Heptanomia and the Arsinoite nome greeting. The season for the consolidation of the dykes and the cleansing of the canals having arrived, I thought it necessary to instruct you by this letter that all the cultivators and . . . ought now to carry out these operations with all zeal on the . . . belonging to them,

[a] Members of the local senates elected to supervise the collection of the corn dues and for other complementary services.

[b] See No. 222, p. 111, note *a*.

διαφέροντα αὐτοῖς π . [. . . . . .] πρὸ[ς τὸ
δ]η[μοσίᾳ τε] [11]πᾶσιν καὶ ἰδίᾳ ἑκάστῳ σύμφερον·
τὴν γὰρ ἀπὸ τῶν ἔργων τούτων γεινομένη ὠφ[ε-
λί]αν πάντας ε[ἰδέναι πέ-][12]πεισμαι. ὅθεν διὰ
φροντίδος ὑμῖν τοῖς στρατηγοῖς καὶ τοῖς δεκαπρώτοις γενέ[σθω ἐπ]εῖξαι μὲν ἅπαν[τας ἀντι-][13]λαβέ-
σθαι τῆς ἀναγκαιοτάτης ταύτης ἐργασίας, αἱρεθῆναι
δὲ τοὺς εἰωθότας εἰ[ς] τοῦτο χειροτονεῖσθα[ι ἐπι-
μελη-][14]τὰς ἐξ ἀρχόντων ἢ καὶ ἰδιωτῶν τοὺς
ἀναγκάσοντας ἑκάστους τὰ προσήκοντα ἔργα
αὐτοῖς σώμ[ασιν ἀπο-][15]πληρῶσαι κατὰ τὸν δοθέντα
ὅρον ἐν τῇ τοῦ ἀποτάκτου συστάσει ἄνευ τιν[ὸ]ς
ἀπεχθείας ἢ χάριτο[ς, ὥστε ἐπε-][16]νεχθῆναι εἰς τὸ
τεταγμένον ὕψος τε καὶ πλάτος τὰ χώματα καὶ τοὺς
διακόπους ἀποφραγῆναι πρὸ[ς τὸ δύνα-][17]σθαι ἀντ-
έχειν τῇ ἐσομένῃ εὐτυχῶς πλημύρᾳ τοῦ ἱερωτάτου
Νείλου, τάς τε διώρυχας ἀνα[καθαρη-][18]ναι μέχρι
τῶν καλουμένων γνωμόνων καὶ τοῦ συνήθους
διαστήματος, ἵν[α ε]ὐμαρῶς [τὴν] ἐσομέν[ην τῶν]
[19]ὑδάτων εἴσροιαν ὑποδέχοιντο πρὸς ἀρδείαν τῶν
ἐδαφῶν, τούτου κοινωφ[ελ]οῦς τυγχ[άνοντος], μη-
δ[ένα δὲ] [20]ἀντὶ τῶν ἔργων ἀργύριον τὸ παράπαν πράττεσθαι. ἐὰν γὰρ τοιοῦτο ἐπιχειρ[ῆσ]αι
τολμήσ[σ]ῃ ἢ τῶν πρ[οστετα-][21]γμένων ἀμελήσῃ,
ἴστω ὅτι ὡς λυμαινόμενος τοῖς ἐπὶ τῇ σωτηρίᾳ
συνπά[ση]ς τῆς Αἰγύπτου προηρ[ημέ-][22]νοις οὐ
μόνον περὶ χρημάτων ἀλλὰ καὶ περὶ αὐτῆς τῆς
ψυχῆς τὸν ἀγῶνα ἕξε[ι. ἐ]ρρῶσθαι ὑμᾶς εὔχομαι.
(ἔτους) γ [. . . . . .] (2nd hand) [23]Αὐρήλιο[ς
Σ]ιλβανὸς ὑπηρέτης ἐπήνεγκα (ἔτους) γ Φαρμοῦθι ς.

with a view both to the public good and to their own private advantage. For I am persuaded that everyone is aware of the benefit resulting from these works. Therefore let it be the care of you, the strategi and *decemprimi*, both to urge all to take in hand this most necessary labour and to see that the overseers usually elected for the purpose are chosen from magistrates or even private individuals, their task being to compel everyone to perform his proper work in person, according to the rule given in the constitution of the appointment, without enmity or favour, so that the dykes are brought up to the prescribed height and breadth and the breaches filled in, to enable them to withstand the flood of the most sacred Nile auspiciously approaching, and that the canals are cleansed to the depth of the so-called standards and the usual width, in order that they may easily absorb the coming influx of water for the irrigation of the fields, this being a matter of public utility, and that in no case is money exacted from any person instead of work. If anyone dares to attempt such a thing or disregards these orders, let him know that by impairing measures designed for the welfare of the whole of Egypt he will put to stake not only his property but his very life. I pray for your health. The 3rd year, . . .

(Subscribed) Presented by Aurelius Silvanus, assistant, in the 3rd year, Pharmouthi 6.

SELECT PAPYRI

226. CIRCULAR CONCERNING THE APPOINT-
MENT OF FINANCIAL SUPERINTENDENTS

P. Oxy. 58.   A.D. 288.

¹[Σ]ερβαῖος Ἀφρικανὸς στρατηγοῖς ἐπι-²στρατη-
γίας ῾Επτὰ νομῶν καὶ Ἀρσινοΐτου ³χαίρειν. ⁴ἀπ'
αὐτῶν τῶν <λ>όγων ἐφάνη ὡς ⁵πολλοὶ βουλόμενοι
τὰς ταμιακὰς οὐσί-⁶ας κατεστείειν ὀνόματα ἑαυτοῖς
ἐξευ-⁷ρόντες, οἱ μὲν χειριστῶν, οἱ δὲ γραμ-⁸ματέων,
οἱ δὲ φροντιστῶν, ὄφελος ⁹μὲν οὐδὲν περιποιοῦσιν
τῷ ταμείῳ, ¹⁰τὰ δὲ περιγεινόμενα κατεστείουσιν·
¹¹δι' ὅπερ ἐδέησεν ἐπισταλῆναι ὑμεῖν ¹²ἵνα ἑκάστης
οὐσίας ἕνα τινὰ φρον-¹³τιστὴν ἀξι[ό]χρεων κινδύνῳ
ἑκάστης ¹⁴βουλῆς αἱρεθῆναι ποιήσητε, τὰ δὲ
¹⁵λοιπὰ ὀνόματα παύσηται, δυναμένου ¹⁶τοῦ αἱρου-
μένου φροντιστοῦ δύο ¹⁷ἢ τό γε πλεῖστον τρεῖς
προσαιρε[ῖ]ν ¹⁸τοὺς ἐξυπηρετησομένους αὐτῷ ¹⁹πρὸς
τὴν φροντίδα. οὕτω[ς αὖ]τά τε ²⁰τὰ μάταια ἀναλώματα π[α]ύσεται ²¹καὶ αἱ ταμιακαὶ οὐσίαι τῆς
προσηκού-²²σης ἐπιμελείας τεύξονται. δηλα-²³δὴ
δὲ τοιούτους αἱρεθῆναι ποιήσε{ι}-²⁴τε τοὺ<ς> τοῖς
φρον[τι]σταῖς ὑπηρετη-²⁵σομένους οἳ καὶ βασάνοις
ὑποκείσον-²⁶ται. ἔρρωσθε. ²⁷(ἔτους) ε (ἔτους) καὶ δ
(ἔτους) Θὼθ ιϛ.

6. l. κατεσθίειν.   10. l. κατεσθίουσιν.

ᵃ Probably the epistrategus of the district.
ᵇ About the beginning of the third cent. A.D., senates,

226. EDICTS AND ORDERS

226. CIRCULAR CONCERNING THE APPOINT-
MENT OF FINANCIAL SUPERINTENDENTS

A.D. 288.

Serbaeus Africanus [a] to the strategi of the epistrategia of Heptanomia and the Arsinoite nome greeting. It is apparent from the accounts alone that a number of persons wishing to batten on the estates of the Treasury have devised titles for themselves, such as administrators, secretaries, or superintendents, whereby they procure no advantage for the Treasury, but eat up the profits. It has therefore become necessary to send you instructions to cause a single superintendent of good standing to be elected for each estate on the responsibility of the senate [b] concerned, and to put an end to the other offices, though the superintendent elected shall have power to choose two or at most three other persons to assist him in the superintendence. By this means the wasteful expenses will also be put an end to, and the estates of the Treasury will receive proper attention. You will of course make sure that only such persons are appointed to assist the superintendents as will be able to stand the test. Goodbye. The 5th which is also the 4th year,[c] Thoth 16.

βουλαί, were instituted in the capital towns of the nomes and took over much of the responsibility formerly entrusted to government officials. See Nos. 237 and 240.
   [c] 5th of Diocletian and 4th of Maximian.

SELECT PAPYRI

227. LETTER OF A PRAEFECT

P. Oxy. 2106.　　　　　　　　　　　Early 4th cent. A.D.

¹[. . . . .]ι . [. . . . . 'Οξυρυγχ(ι-
τῶν)] ἄ[ρχο]υσι καὶ βουλῇ καὶ [λο]γιστῇ 'Οξυρυγ-
χ(ίτου) χαίρειν. ²ἡ θεία καὶ [σεβασμία τύχη τ]ῶν
δεσποτῶν ἡμῶν Αὐτοκρα-³τόρων τε κα[ὶ Καισάρων
προσ]έταξεν γραμμάτων θείων πρός ⁴με ἀπο-
σταλέ[ντων χρυσὸν] ἀπὸ τῆς ἐπαρχίου συνωνηθῆ-
⁵ναι. φροντὶς ὑμῖ[ν ἔστω], τοῦ πράγματος ὑπέρ-
θεσιν ⁶οὐδεμίαν ἐπιδεχομένου, προστέτακται γὰρ
εἴσω δ ⁷τοῦ Θωθ μη(νὸς) ὁ πᾶς χρυσὸς ἐν Νικο-
μηδίᾳ παρα-⁸δοθῆναι, ἐντὸς ἡμερῶν λ, τοῦτ' ἔστιν
εἴσω τῆς ⁹ε'' τοῦ Μεσορή, καὶ ἐν τούτῳ τὴν
κατοσίωσιν τὴν ¹⁰ἡμετέραν ἐνδικνυμένοι⟨ς⟩, λη''
μόνας λί(τρας) ἀπαιτῆσαι ¹¹παρ' ἑκάστου κατὰ
δύναμιν καὶ ἀγαγεῖν εἰς τὴν λαμ-¹²πρὰν 'Αλεξ-
ανδρέων πόλιν, δηλαδὴ ταύτας κομιζόν-¹³των σοῦ
τε τοῦ λογιστοῦ καὶ ἑνὸς ἐξ ὑμῶν τοῦ τὴν ¹⁴πρώτην
τάξιν ἐν τῇ ἀρχῇ ἐπέχοντος, συμβαλ-¹⁵λομένων
ὑμεῖν ἐν τῇ εἰσφορᾷ ταύτῃ τῶν τε ¹⁶τὴν τ[. .] .-
[ο]υσαν ὕλην πραγματευομένων καὶ τῶν ¹⁷δυν[α]-
τ[ωτ]άτων ὄντων, οὐκ ἐν[ο]χλουμένων δὲ ¹⁸τῶν
ξέν[ων] εἰ μὴ ἄρα τὸ ἐφέστ[ιον] αὐτόθι κατ-
¹⁹εστήσαντο καὶ μηδέπω ἐπολιτεύσαντο εὔπο-²⁰ροί
τε ὄντ[ε]ς τυγχάνουσιν, δέκα μυριάδων δη-²¹λαδὴ
ὑπὲ[ρ] ἑκάστης λίτρας ἀριθμουμένων τοῖς ²²παρ-
έχου[σ]ιν ὑπὸ τοῦ ἱερωτάτου ταμειείου. καὶ ἵνα
²³ἐπὶ τῶν τόπων τὸ τίμημα τούτων ἐξ ἑτοίμου
²⁴τούτοις καταβληθείη ἐπέστειλα τῷ κυρίῳ μου

　　9. l. καθοσίωσιν.　　　10. l. ὑμετέραν.　　　16. τ[. .] or
π[. .].
122

227. EDICTS AND ORDERS

227. LETTER OF A PRAEFECT

Early 4th cent. A.D.

. . . to the magistrates and senate of Oxyrhynchus and the logistes [a] of the Oxyrhynchite nome greeting. The godlike and august fortune of our masters the Emperors and Caesars has commanded by a divine letter sent to me the purchase of gold from the province. Make it your care, as the matter brooks no delay, for the command is that all the gold is to be delivered at Nicomedia by the 4th of Thoth, to collect within 30 days, that is, by the 5th of Mesore, herein again displaying your devotion, 38 pounds only, from each according to his means, and bring them to the illustrious city of Alexandria ; let them be conveyed by you the logistes and one of your number who holds the first place in the magistracy, and let assistance be given you in this contribution by those who deal with the . . . material and those who are best able, but strangers are not to be importuned unless they have established their homes here and have not yet been senators and happen to be well-to-do. Ten myriads [b] for each pound shall be paid to the contributors by the sacred Treasury. And in order that the price may be paid to them on the spot in ready money, I have sent word to my lord and brother the

[a] An official who in the Byzantine period performed some of the duties previously entrusted to the strategus.
[b] That is, 100,000 denarii, the nominal value of a pound's weight of gold in the depreciated currency of the day. The contributors were required to furnish a certain quantity of gold and were repaid in debased silver on the government's own terms.

²⁵καὶ ἀδελφῷ τῷ διασημοτάτῳ καθολικῷ ὡς ἂν
αὐτὸς ²⁶προστάξιεν τοῖς ἐπιτρόποις τοῦτο ποιῆσαι.
²⁷ἐρρῶσθαι ὑμᾶς εὔχομαι. μεθ᾽ ἃ Ῥωμαικά.

228. CIRCULAR FROM AN OFFICIAL IN ANTIOCH

W. Chrest. 469.   A.D. 380–390.

¹Γάιος Οὐαλέριος Εὐσέβι[ο]ς ²ῥιπαρίοις κατὰ
πόλιν ἀπὸ Θηβαΐδος ἕως Ἀντιοχίας. ³τοὺς νεολέκ-
τους τοὺς ἀποστελλομένους ἐκ τῆς Αἰγ[υ]πτιακῆς
⁴διοικήσεως παρὰ τῶν τὴν εἴσπραξιν π[ο]ιο[υ-
μ]έ[ν]ων ⁵ὑποδεξάμενοι κατὰ διαδοχὴν εἰς τὴν
Ἀντιοχέων ἰδίῳ κινδύνῳ ⁶παραπέμψατε ἐκεῖνο
γινώσκοντες ὡς, εἴ τις διαφύγοι ⁷τούτων, οὐκ
ἀτιμώρητος ἀπελεύσεται ἐκεῖνος οὗ παρὰ ⁸τὴν
ἀμέλειαν φαίνεται ἀποδράς, ἀναγκ[α]σθή[σ]εται δὲ
⁹αὐτόν τε ἐκεῖνον ἢ ἀντ᾽ ἐκείνου ἕτερον παραστῆσαι
¹⁰μετὰ τοῦ καὶ δίκην τὴν ὑπὲρ τῆς ἀμελίας
ὑποσχεῖν.

ᵃ Perhaps, as suggested by Wilcken, the Eusebius known
from the letters of Libanius, in any case a very high official.
   ᵇ A certain class of police officers. The name suggests

229. ORDER OF A STRATEGUS

P. Tebt. 288.   A.D. 226.

¹[Αὐρ]ήλιος Σερηνίσκος ὁ καὶ Ἑρμησίας [στ]ρα-
(τηγὸς) Ἀρσι(νοΐτου) Θε(μίστου) [καὶ] Πολ(έ-

most eminent catholicus [a] to give orders himself to the overseers to do this. I pray for your health. Followed by Latin.[b]

[a] Head of the Treasury in Alexandria.
[b] The papyrus, which is only a copy, omits the Latin subscription of the original.

228. CIRCULAR FROM AN OFFICIAL IN ANTIOCH

A.D. 380–390.

Gaius Valerius Eusebius [a] to the *riparii* [b] in the respective cities from the Thebaid to Antioch. Take over from those who are conducting the levy the new recruits now being sent from the Egyptian diocese,[c] and passing them on from one to another send them forward at your own peril to the city of Antioch, understanding that if any of them should desert, the person through whose negligence he is proved to have escaped shall not get off unpunished, but shall be compelled to produce either the deserter himself or another man in his place and at the same time be brought to justice for his negligence.

that they had originally some functions in connexion with the river-banks.
[c] A province of the Byzantine empire. Egypt became a separate diocese about A.D. 381.

229. ORDER OF A STRATEGUS

A.D. 226.

Aurelius Sereniscus also called Hermesias, strategus of the divisions of Themistes and Polemon in the

μωνος) μερίδος· ²παραγ‹γ›έλλεται τοῖς πράκ-
[τ]ορσι τοῦ ε (ἔτους) τῶν [γε]ωργ(ῶν) ³καὶ κληρούχων ἐπακολουθῆσαι τῇ γεινομένῃ ἐπ᾽ ἀ-⁴[γ]αθοῖς
ἀναμετρήσει τοῦ σπόρου καὶ ἀναγράψασθαι ⁵πᾶσαν
τὴν ἐσπαρμένην γῆν ἔν τε πυρῷ καὶ ἄλλοις
⁶γ[ένεσ]ι καὶ τὰ [ὀνό]ματα τῶν κατὰ φύσιν ‹γε›-
γεωργη-⁷κ[ότ]ων δημοσίων γεωργῶν καὶ κληρ[ο]ύ-
⁸χων πρὸς τὸ μηδὲν ἐπὶ ‹περι›γραφῇ τοῦ ἱερωτάτου ⁹ταμείου γενέσθαι ὑπὸ τῶν λαογράφων ¹⁰ἢ
πραγματικῶν, ὡς τοῦ κινδύνου καὶ ὑμεῖν ¹¹[αὐ]τοῖς
ἅμα ἐκείνοις διοίσοντος ἐάν τι φανῇ ¹²[κε]κακουρ-
γημέ[νο]ν ἢ οὐ δεόντως πεπρ[α]γ-¹³μένον, μηδε-
μειᾶς προφάσεως ὑμεῖν ¹⁴ὑπολειπομένης ἐπὶ τῆς
ἀπαιτήσεως ¹⁵ἕνεκεν γνωρισμοῦ· καὶ τῆς μέντοι
γει-¹⁶[ν]ομένης ὑφ᾽ ὑμῶν ἀναγραφὴν τὴν ¹⁷ἴσην
ἐπίδοτε. ¹⁸(ἔτους) ε Αὐ[τοκρά]τορος Καίσαρος
Μάρκου ¹⁹[Αὐ]ρηλί[ου] Σεουήρ[ου] Ἀλε]ξάνδρου
Εὐσεβοῦς ²⁰Εὐτυχοῦς Σεβαστοῦ Μεχεὶρ θ.

16. l. ἀναγραφῆς.

230. ORDER OF A STRATEGUS

P. Oxy. 1411.   A.D. 260.

¹Αὐρήλιος Πτολεμαῖος ὁ καὶ Νεμεσιανὸς ²στρατη-
γὸς Ὀξυρυγχείτου. τῶν δημοσίων εἰς ³ἓν συν-
αχθέντων καὶ αἰτιασαμένων ⁴τοὺς τῶν κολλυβισ-
τικῶν τραπεζῶν ⁵τραπεζείτας ὡς ταύτας ἀπο-
κλεισάν-⁶τ[ω]ν τῷ μὴ βούλεσθαι προσ{σ}ίεσθαι ⁷τὸ
θεῖον τῶν Σεβαστῶν νόμισμα, ἀ[νάγ-]⁸κη γεγέ-
νηται παραγγέλματι π[αραγ-]⁹γελῆναι πᾶσει τοῖς
τὰς τραπέζας κεκτ[ημέ-]¹⁰ν[οι]ς ταύτας ἀνοῖξαι

Arsinoite nome. An order is hereby given to the collectors of revenues from the cultivators and cleruchs for the 5th year to follow the auspiciously proceeding survey of the sowings and make a list of all the land that has been sown both with wheat and with other crops and of the names of the public cultivators and cleruchs who have sown each kind, so that nothing be done to defraud the most sacred Treasury by the laographi [a] or finance officials, since you yourselves will share the risk with them if any villainy or irregularity be brought to light, no pretext with regard to the collection being left to you touching the identification (of the crops) ; and moreover send in a duplicate of the survey-list which you make. The 5th year of the Emperor Caesar Marcus Aurelius Severus Alexander Pius Felix Augustus, Mecheir 9.

[a] Officials who made up the lists of individuals liable to the poll-tax.

230. ORDER OF A STRATEGUS

A.D. 260.

From Aurelius Ptolemaeus also called Nemesianus, strategus of the Oxyrhynchite nome. Since the officials have assembled and accused the bankers of the banks of exchange of having closed these through their unwillingness to accept the divine coin [a] of the Emperors, it has become necessary that an injunction should be issued to all the owners of the banks to open

[a] Probably the silver coinage of Alexandria, which by this time had become extremely debased.

5. *l.* ἀποκλείσαντας.

καὶ πᾶν [[πλ]] νόμι-[11]σ[μ]α προσίεσθαι πλὴν
μάλισ[τα] [12]παρατύπου καὶ κιβδήλου καὶ κατα-
κ[ερμα-][13]τίζειν, οὐ μόνοις δὲ αὐτοῖς ἀλλὰ [τοῖς]
[14]καθ᾽ ὄντινα δὴ τρόπον τὰς συνα[λλα-][15]γὰς
ποιουμένοις, γεινώσκουσι[ν] [16]ὡς, εἰ μὴ πειθαρ-
χήσιαν τῇδε τ[ῇ παρ-][17]αγγελίᾳ, πειραθήσονται
ὧν τὸ [μέ-][18]γεθος τῆς ἡγεμονίας καὶ ἔτι ἄνω[θεν]
[19]ἐπ᾽ αὐτοῖς [[το με]]γε[[θος]]νέσθαι προ[οσ-][20]έταξεν.
ἐσημειωσάμην. ἔτου[ς πρώ-][21]το[υ] ῾Αθὺρ[[ι]] ὀγδόη
κ[[ει]]αὶ εἰκάς.

10. πᾶν corr. from πλην.

231. OFFICIAL ORDER

B.G.U. 325.   3rd cent. A.D.

[1]Κώμης Σοκνοπ[αίου Νήσ]ου. [πα]ραγγέλλεται
τοῖς ὑπ[ο-][2]γεγραμμένοις λῃστοπιασταῖ[ς συνε]λ-
θεῖν τοῖς τῆς κώμης [3]δημοσίοις καὶ ἀναζητῆσαι
τοὺ[ς ἐπ]ιζητουμένους κακούργους. [4]ἐὰν δὲ ἀμε-
λήσωσι, δ[ε]δ[ε]μένοι πεμφθήσον[τ]αι ἐπὶ τὸν λαμ-
πρότ(ατον) [5]ἡμῶν ἡγεμόνα.
[6]Εἰσὶ δέ· ῾Σελεουᾶς Πακύσεως προν . . . . ( ),
Παέμμις μηχανάριος, [8]Εἰεὺς ᾽Αλατούλεως, Σωτᾶς
᾽Ωρίωνος, [9]Οὐτιψῆμις ᾽Ιαμοῦς.

232. ORDER FOR ARREST

P. Oxy. 65.   3rd or early 4th cent. A.D.

[1]Π(αρὰ) τοῦ στατίζοντος β(ενε)φ(ικιαρίου) [2]κωμ-
άρχαις κώμης Τερύθεως. παράδοτε τῷ ἀποσταλέν-
128

these and to accept and change all coin except what is clearly spurious and counterfeit, and not to them only, but to all who engage in business transactions of any kind whatever, understanding that if they disobey this injunction they will experience the penalties which in former years his highness the praefect ordained for their case. Signed by me. The 1st year, Hathur 28.

231. OFFICIAL ORDER

3rd cent. A.D.

Village of Socnopaei Nesus. An order is given to the under-mentioned thief-catchers to join with the village officials and hunt out the malefactors who are wanted. If they neglect this, they shall be sent in bonds to appear before our most illustrious praefect.

Their names are : Seleouas son of Pakusis, . . .; Paemmis, mechanician ; Eieus son of Alatoulis ; Sotas son of Horion ; Outipsemis son of Iames.

232. ORDER FOR ARREST

3rd or early 4th cent. A.D.

From the *beneficiarius* on duty to the comarchs of the village of Teruthis. Deliver up to the officer

τι ὑπηρέτ[ῃ] ³Παχοῦμιν Παχούμις ὃν κατεσχήκατε
σήμερον καὶ κατηνέγκατε ἐν τῇ κώμῃ ⁴ὑμῶν
πολίτην ὄντα. εἰ δὲ ἔχετε εὐλογίαν τινὰ πρὸς
αὐτόν, ⁵ἀνέρχεσθε ἅμα αὐτῷ καὶ λέγετε. ἀλλ' ὅρα
μὴ κατάσχητε τὸν ὑπη-⁶ρέτη‹ν›. σεση(μείωμαι).

sent by me Pachoumis son of Pachoumis whom you have to-day arrested and brought to your village though he is a citizen. If you have any plausible complaint against him,[a] come up with him and state it. But see that you do not detain the officer. Signed.

[a] Or, as formerly interpreted, "anything to say in his favour."

III. PUBLIC ANNOUNCEMENTS

233. ANNOUNCEMENT OF A GOVERNMENT AUCTION

P. Eleph. 14.   About 223 B.C.

¹Ἐπὶ τοῖσδε πωλοῦμεν ἐφ᾽ οἷς [ ] οἱ [κ]υρω-
θέντ[ε]ς διορθώσονται ²εἰς τὸ βα(σιλικὸν) κατ᾽
ἐ[ν]ιαυτὸν τῶν μὲν ἀμπελώνων τοὺς καθήκον-³τας
ἀργυρικοὺς φόρους καὶ τὴν γενομένην ἀπόμοιραν
τῆι ⁴Φιλαδ[έλφωι, τῆς] δὲ γῆς τὰ ἐπιγεγραμμένα
σιτικὰ ἐκφόρια καὶ εἴ ⁵[τι ἄλλο καθήκει] πρὸς [τὴν]
γῆν δίδοσθαι. τάξονται δὲ τὰς τιμὰς ⁶[τῶν μὲν (?)]
ἀνηκόν]των εἰς τ[ὸ βα]σιλικὸν ἐπὶ τὴν βα(σιλικὴν)
τρά(πεζαν), τῶν δὲ εἰς τ[.] ⁷τῶν [. . . . .] ι
τρα(πεζίτηι) ἐν (ἔτεσι) γ, τῶν μὲν γερῶν τῆς πάσης
[τι-]⁸μῆς τὸ δ μέρος χρυ(σίου) ἢ [ἀ]ργυρίου τοῦ
καινοῦ νομ[ί]σματος, ⁹τὸ δὲ [λο]ιπὸν χα(λκοῦ) καὶ
τὴν εἰθισμένην ἀλλαγὴν ὡς τῆι μν(ᾶι) ι (δυοβόλους)

1. Possibly ἐφ᾽ οἷς [ὑπόκ(ειται)]; or there may have been a
blank space after οἷς.   3. *l.* γινομένην.   6-7. τῶν δὲ
εἰς τ[ι] τῶν [ἱερῶν τῶι ἰδί]ωι τρα(πεζίτηι)?   9. (δυοβόλους)
(ἡμιωβέλιον) Wilcken: ιϛ ὀ[β(ολούς)] Ed.

ᵃ A tax of one-sixth, or in some cases one-tenth, of the
produce of vineyards and orchards, formerly paid to the
temples, was appropriated by Ptolemy II. and applied

132

III. PUBLIC ANNOUNCEMENTS

233. ANNOUNCEMENT OF A GOVERNMENT AUCTION

About 223 B.C.

We offer (the properties) for sale on the following terms. The successful bidders shall pay annually to the Crown in the case of the vineyards the proper money taxes and the *apomoira* due to (Arsinoe) Philadelphus,[a] and for the arable land the rents in kind which have been imposed upon it and whatever other payment is required in respect of such land.[b] They shall pay the price of that which concerns (?) the Crown to the royal bank, and of that which concerns any of the temples (?) to its own banker (?), in 3 years, the 4th part of the whole price of the priestly offices [c] in gold or silver of the new coinage and the remainder in copper with the customary agio at the rate of 10 drachmae $2\frac{1}{2}$ obols on the mina,[d] and the price of the

---

[a] nominally to the maintenance of the cult of the deified Arsinoe II.

[b] In the case of arable land the purchasers did not acquire freehold possession, but an unlimited lease descending from father to son.

[c] See p. 63, note *f*. Some such offices with their emoluments were among the properties put up to auction.

[d] The copper being taken at a discount of $10\frac{5}{12}$ per cent on its nominal value.

(ἡμιωβέλιον), [10]τῶν δ' ἄλ[λω]ν ἐνγαίων χα(λκοῦ)
καὶ τὴν εἰθισμένην ἀλλαγήν, πρ[οσ-][11]διορθώσονται
δὲ καταγώγιον τῆι μν(ᾶι) (τριώβολον) καὶ τὴν
καθήκου-[12]σαν (ἐξηκοστὴν) καὶ κηρύκειον τοῦ παντὸς (χιλι)οστήν. ὁ δὲ πριάμενος τῶν [13]μὲν γε[ρ]ῶν
λήψεται τὰς γινομένας καρπείας ἅμα τῶι [14]τὴν [ἀ
ἀν]αφ[ο]ρὰν διαγραφῆναι τῶι βα[σιλικῶι], τῆς δὲ
γῆς κυρι-[15]εύσει καὶ τῶν καρπῶν, ἐὰν ἦι ὑπὸ τῶν
κυρίων κατεσπαρμένη, [16]ἐὰν δὲ ἦ μεμισθωμένη,
διορθώσονται οἱ γεγεωργηκότες τὸ [17]{τὸ} ἐκ[φόριο]ν
[τῶι] ἀγοράσαντι ἐκ τῶν πρὸς τοὺς γεωρ-[18]γοὺς
συν[γ]ρ[α]φῶν. [τῆς] δ[ὲ τιμ]ῆς τάξονται παραχρῆμα [19]τὸ δ μέρος, τὸ δὲ λοιπὸν ἐν (ἔτεσι) γ ἀπὸ
τοῦ εκ (ἔτους) τασσόμε-[20]νοι κατ' ἐνιαυτὸν τοῦ
Ἐπεὶφ καὶ Μεσορὴ τὸ ἐπιβάλλον [21]σωμάτ[ιο]ν, ἔκ
τε κτηνῶν καὶ σκευῶν παραχρῆμα τὴν [22]π . [.] . .
. . . . στην καὶ τὴν ἐννενηκοσ[τή]ν. κυριεύσου-
σιν δὲ [23]καθὰ καὶ οἱ πρῶτον κύριοι ἐκέκτηντο.
ἐξέσται δὲ τῶι βου-[24]λομένωι ὑπερβάλλειν, ἕως ἔτι
ἐν τοῖς κύκλοις εἰσὶν ὅσοι ἂν [25]βούλη[τ]αι, ὅταν δὲ
ἀπὸ τῆς πράσεως γένωνται τοῖς ἐπι-[26]δεκ[ά]τοις,
μέχρι τοῦ τὴν ᾱ ἀναφορὰν διαγραφῆναι· τὰ δὲ
[27]πωλούμενα ἄπρατα ἐν ταῖς κα<τὰ> τὸ διάγραμμα
ἡ(μέραις) ϛ (?).

22. στην . . . . . ἐννενηκοσ[τή]ν P. Meyer: καὶ τήν E.-H.
27. Or ἡ(μέραι)ς, as suggested by Wilcken.

other landed property in copper with the customary agio, and they shall pay in addition for the cost of carriage (of the copper) three obols per mina and the proper $\frac{1}{90}$th [a] and as crier's fee on the whole purchase $\frac{1}{1000}$th. The purchaser shall receive the due revenues of the priestly offices as soon as the first instalment has been paid to the Crown, and he shall be owner of the land and of its produce, if it has been sown by the former owners, and if it has been leased, those who have cultivated it shall pay the rent to the purchaser in accordance with the contracts made with the cultivators. The purchasers shall pay the 4th part of the price immediately and the remainder in 3 years beginning from year 25, paying annually in Epeiph and Mesore the amount which falls due, and on cattle and implements they shall pay immediately the taxes of . . . and $\frac{1}{90}$th. They shall own the properties in the same way as those who formerly possessed them. Whoever wishes shall be permitted to raise the bid, by as much as he pleases while the auction-ring is still open, but only by ten per cent after the auction is ended and until the 1st instalment has been paid; and (if there is no purchaser) the objects offered shall be classed as unsold after the 6 (?) days prescribed by the ordinance.

[a] It is not known what this charge was for.

234. OFFER OF A REWARD FOR RECOVERY OF AN ESCAPED SLAVE

P. Par. 10 (= U.P.Z. 121).　　　　　　　156 B.C.

¹Τοῦ κε Ἐπεὶφ ιϛ. Ἀριστογένου τοῦ Χρυσίππου
²Ἀλαβανδέως πρεσβευτοῦ παῖς ἀνακεχώ-³ρηκεν
(2nd hand) ἐν Ἀλεξανδρείᾳ, (1st hand) ὧι ὄνομα
Ἕρμων, ὃς καὶ Νεῖλος ⁴καλεῖται, τὸ γένος Σύρος
ἀπὸ Βαμβύκης, ⁵ὡς ἐτῶν ιη, μεγέθει μέσος, ἀ-
γένειος, ⁶εὔκνημος, κοιλογένειος, ⁷φακὸς παρὰ ῥῖνα
⁷ἐξ ἀριστερῶν, οὐλὴ ὑπὲρ χαλινὸν ἐξ ἀριστερῶν,
⁸ἐστιγμένος τὸν δεξιὸν καρπὸν γράμμασι ⁹βαρβαρι-
κοῖς δυσίν, ἔχων χρυσίου ἐπισήμου ¹⁰μναϊεῖα γ,
πίνας ι, κρίκον σιδηροῦν ¹¹ἐν ὧι λήκυθος καὶ
ξύστραι, καὶ περὶ τὸ σῶμα ¹²χλαμύδα καὶ περίζωμα.
τοῦτον ὃς ἂν ἀνα-¹³γάγῃ λήψεται χαλκοῦ (τάλαντα)
β (2nd hand) γ, (1st hand) ἐφ᾽ ἱεροῦ δείξας
(τάλαντον) α (2nd hand) β, (1st hand) παρ᾽ ἀνδρὶ
ἀξιοχρείωι καὶ δωσιδίκωι (τάλαντα) γ (2nd hand) ε.
(1st hand) ¹⁵μηνύειν δὲ τὸν βουλόμενον τοῖς παρὰ
τοῦ ¹⁶στρατηγοῦ. ¹⁷ἔστιν δὲ καὶ ὁ συναποδεδρακὼς
αὐτῶι ¹⁸Βίων δοῦλος Καλλικράτου τῶν περὶ αὐλὴν
¹⁹ἀρχυπηρετῶν, μεγέθει βραχύς, πλατὺς ²⁰ἀπὸ τῶν
ὤμων, κατάκνημος, χαροπός, ²¹ὃς καὶ ἔχων ἀνα-
κεχώρηκεν ἱμάτιον καὶ ²²ἱματίδιον παιδαρίου καὶ
σεβίτιον γυναι-²³κεῖον ἄξιον (ταλάντων) ϛ καὶ χαλκοῦ

ᵃ A town in Caria.

ᵇ The native name for Hierapolis.

ᶜ Wilcken has shown that these marks were a symbol of
consecration to the Syrian gods of Bambyce, Hadad and
Atargatis, and suggests that the two barbaric letters may
have been the first Aramaic letters of their names.

234. OFFER OF A REWARD FOR RECOVERY OF AN ESCAPED SLAVE

156 B.C.

The 25th year, Epeiph 16. A slave of Aristogenes son of Chrysippus, of Alabanda,[a] ambassador, has escaped in Alexandria, by name Hermon also called Nilus, by birth a Syrian from Bambyce,[b] about 18 years old, of medium stature, beardless, with good legs, a dimple on the chin, a mole by the left side of the nose, a scar above the left corner of the mouth, tattooed on the right wrist with two barbaric letters.[c] He has taken with him 3 octadrachms of coined gold, 10 pearls, an iron ring on which an oil-flask and strigils are represented,[d] and is wearing a cloak and a loincloth. Whoever brings back this slave shall receive 3 talents [e] of copper; if he points him out in a temple, 2 talents; if in the house of a substantial and actionable man, 5 talents. Whoever wishes to give information shall do so to the agents of the strategus.

There is also another who has escaped with him, Bion, a slave of Callicrates, one of the chief stewards at court, short of stature, broad at the shoulders, stout-legged, bright-eyed, who has gone off with an outer garment and a slave's wrap and a woman's dress (?) [f] worth 6 talents 5000 drachmae of copper.

---

[d] According to Letronne and Wilcken, a neck-band on which the oil-flask and strigils, symbols of a bath-attendant, were worked.

[e] The original text has "2 talents," "1 talent," and "3 talents," but apparently the reward was raised, for above these figures a scribe has written 3, 2, and 5.

[f] Or perhaps a toilet box.

[.] Ἐ. [24]τοῦτον ὃς ἂν ἀναγ‹άγ›η λήψεται ὅσα καὶ
ὑπὲρ τοῦ [25]προγεγραμμένου. μηνύειν δὲ καὶ ὑπὲρ
[26]τούτου τοῖς παρὰ τοῦ στρατηγοῦ.

235. DRAFT OF A PROCLAMATION OF NERO'S ACCESSION

P. Oxy. 1021.   A.D. 54.

[1]Ὁ μὲν ὀφειλόμενος [2]τοῖς προγόνοις καὶ ἐν-
[3]φανὴς θεὸς Καῖσαρ εἰς [4]αὐτοὺς κεχώρηκε, [5]ὁ δὲ
τῆς οἰκουμένης [6]καὶ προσδοκηθεὶς καὶ ἐλπισ-[7]θεὶς
Αὐτοκράτωρ ἀποδέ-[8]δεικται, ἀγαθὸς [9]δαίμων δὲ
τῆς [10]οὐκουμένης [ἀρ]χὴ ὢν [11]⟦μεγισ⟧τε πάντων
[12]ἀγαθῶν Νέρων [13]Καῖσαρ ἀποδέδεικται. [14]διὸ
πάντες ὀφείλομεν [15]στεφανηφοροῦντας [16]καὶ βουθυ-
τοῦντας [17]θεοῖς πᾶσι εἰδέναι [18]χάριτας. (ἔτους) α
Νέρωνος [19]Κλαυδίου Καίσαρος Σεβαστοῦ Γερμανικοῦ [20]μη(νὸς) Νέ(ου) Σεβα(στοῦ) κα.

10. l. οἰκουμένης.   10-11. Reading doubtful.   15-16.
l. -ες καὶ -ες.

236. INVITATION TO LEASE GOVERNMENT LANDS

B.G.U. 656.   2nd cent. A.D.

[1]Οἱ βουλόμενοι μισθώσασθαι [2]ἐκ τῆς o͞z κλη-
(ρουχίας) Ἰμούθου Φάσει [3]Πατσόντεως βασιλ(ικῆς)

[a] In Roman times simply a division of the land of a

138

Whoever brings back this slave shall receive the same rewards as for the above-mentioned. Information about this one also is to be given to the agents of the strategus.

235. DRAFT OF A PROCLAMATION OF NERO'S ACCESSION

A.D. 54.

The Caesar who was owed to his ancestors, god manifest, has gone to join them, and the Emperor whom the world expected and hoped for has been proclaimed, the good genius of the world and source of all blessings, Nero Caesar, has been proclaimed.[a] Therefore ought we all wearing garlands and with sacrifices of oxen to give thanks to all the gods. The 1st year of Nero Claudius Caesar Augustus Germanicus, the 21st of the month Neus Sebastus.[b]

[a] Perhaps an alternative version of the preceding clause, and not the final form of the proclamation.
[b] = Hathur 21 or November 17. This was thirty-five days after the death of Claudius.

236. INVITATION TO LEASE GOVERNMENT LANDS

2nd cent. A.D.

Persons wishing to lease the following lands, from the 77th cleruchy[a] of Imouthes son of Phasis at

village. The present cleruchy was called after Imouthes, who may have been a former holder of the land.

ἐν τόπῳ Πετσενώσει ⁴λεγομένου (ἀρούρας) θ, καὶ
⁵Πτολεμαΐδος ἱερᾶς ἀπὸ (ἀρουρῶν) ζ (ἀρούρας) ε,
⁶ὁμοίως βασιλ(ικῆς) (ἀρούρας) ε, καὶ ⁷Κερκεσούχων
προσχ( ) (ἀρούρας) ε σὺν ϛ (ἀρούραις) ⁸προσερχέ-
στωσαν τοῖς πρὸς τούτοις ⁹ἔρεσειν διδόντες.

4. l. λεγομένῳ.　　8. l. προσερχέσθωσαν.　　9. l. αἵρεσιν.

237. NOTICE OF A SPECIAL MEETING
OF A SENATE

P. Oxy. 1412.　　　　　　　　　　About A.D. 284.

¹Αὐ[ρ]ή[λι]ος Ε[ὐδ]αίμων ὁ καὶ Ἑλλάδιος γ[ε]νό-
μενος εὐθ[η-]²νάρχης κοσμητὴς ἐξηγητὴς ὑπο-
μνηματογράφος ³βουλευτὴς τῆ[ς] λαμπροτάτης
πόλεως τῶν Ἀλεξανδρέων, ⁴γ[υ]μνασ[ι]αρχήσας
βουλ[ε]υτὴς ἔναρχος πρύτανις τῆς ⁵λαμπρᾶς κ[αὶ]
λαμπροτάτη[ς Ὀ]ξυρυγχιτῶν πόλεως. ⁶τὰ τῆς
ἀνακ[ο]μιδῆς τῆς εὐθενείας τῶν [γ]ενναιοτάτων
⁷στρα[τ]ιωτῶν οὐδὲ βραχεῖαν ἀνάθεσ[ι]ν ἐπιδέ-
χεται, καὶ διὰ τοῦτο, ⁸καὶ γραμμάτων ἡμᾶς εἰς
τοῦτο κατεπειγόντων τοῦ κρα-⁹τίστου διοικητοῦ
Αὐρηλίου Π[ρ]ωτέα ἔτι [δ]ὲ κ[α]ὶ τ[οῦ] κρατίστου
¹⁰Ἀμμ[ω]νίου, καὶ τῶν πλοίων ἤδη τῶν ὑπ[ο]δεχο-
μένων ¹¹τὰ εἴδη ἐφορμούντων, ἐδέησεν εἰς ἐπιμελῆ
τόπον δ[η-]¹²μοσίαν συναγαγεῖν πρόσκλητον βου-
λήν, ἵνα προτεθείση[ς] ¹³σκέψεως περὶ μόνου τούτου τοῦ κεφαλαί[ο]υ τέλεσιν τὴν ¹⁴ταχίστην λάβῃ
τὰ λειτουργήματα.　ἵν[α οὖν π]άντες ἑκόντες
¹⁵[ὦσι ?] βουλευταὶ τοῦτο γνόν[τε]ς ἐν τῇ σήμερο[ν
ἥτ]ις ἐστ[ὶ]ν ιε, ¹⁶[τὰ γρά]μμ[α]τα δημοσίᾳ πρό-
140

Patsontis 9 arurae of Crown land in the place called Petsenosis, at Ptolemais 5 out of 7 arurae of temple land, likewise 5 arurae of Crown land, at Kerkesoucha 5 arurae . . . with 6 arurae, shall address themselves to the officials appointed for this duty, submitting their offers.

237. NOTICE OF A SPECIAL MEETING OF A SENATE

About A.D. 284.

Aurelius Eudaemon also called Helladius, formerly eutheniarch, cosmetes, exegetes, hypomnematographus, senator of the most illustrious city of Alexandria, ex-gymnasiarch, senator, prytanis in office of the illustrious and most illustrious city of Oxyrhynchus. The question of the transport of provisions for the most noble soldiers does not admit even a brief delay, and for this reason, and since letters from his excellency the dioecetes Aurelius Proteas,[a] as well as from his excellency Ammonius,[b] are urging us to see to this, and the boats to receive the supplies are already at the quay, it has become necessary to call an extraordinary general meeting of the senate at a suitable place, in order that a discussion may be held on this single subject and the obligatory services performed as quickly as possible. Accordingly in order that all, being informed of this, may willingly do their duty as senators to-day, which is the 15th, the letters

[a] Known to have been in office in the 2nd year of Carinus (283-284).

[b] Identified as the ἐπείκτης δημοσίου σίτου, collector of government corn.

141

κειτ[α]ι. καλῶς δ[ὲ] ἔχειν ἐνόμισα [17][γινώσκει ?]ν
ὑμᾶς δι[ὰ το]ῦδε τοῦ προ[γ]ράμματος συντετα-
[18][χέναι ἡμᾶς] ὑμῖν συνε[ιδό]σιν πρὸς τὰ κελευσθέντα ὀξέως [19][συναχ]θῆναι, ο[ὐ]δενὸς ἄ[λλο]υ
ἐν τῇ παρούσῃ συνόδῳ μένον-[20][τος, ψ]ηφίσασθαί
τε τὰς [τ]ῶν λ[ιτ]ουργῶν χειρο[τ]ο[ν]ίας. [21][(ἔτους)
β ?, ιε].

238. DRAFT OF A PROCLAMATION TO THE EPHEBI

P. Oxy. 42.   A.D. 323.

[1]Διοσκουρίδης λογιστὴς Ὀξυρυγχίτου. [2]τῶν
ἐφήβων σύμβλημα εἶναι αὔριον κδ´ [3]καὶ τὸ ἔθος
ὁμοῦ τε καὶ ἡ πανήγυρις προάγουσα [4][σ]ημαίνει
[ὅτ]ι προθυμότατα τοὺς ἐφήβους [5][τ]ὰ γυμνι[κὰ]
ἐπιδείκνυσθαι προσήκει ⟦πρὸς [6][τ]έ[ρ]ψιν⟧ δι[π]λῇ
τῶν θεατῶν συνπαρεσο-[7][μέ]νω[ν [τῇ] ἑορτῇ] τέρψει.
[8][ἐπὶ τῆς ὑπατείας ?] τῶν δεσποτῶν ἡμῶν Λικινίου
Σεβαστοῦ τὸ ϛ´ καὶ [9][Λικινίου τοῦ ἐπ]ιφ<αν>ε-
στάτου Καίσαρ[ο]ς τὸ β´, τοῖς ἀποδειχθησομένοις
ὑπάτοις τὸ γ̄, [10]Τῦβι κγ´.

8. [μετὰ τὴν ὑπατίαν] Seeck, but see E. H. Kase, *A Papyrus
Roll in the Princetown Collection*, pp. 32 ff.

are publicly exhibited. I have thought it right that you should know by this proclamation that I have instructed you, on being informed of the facts, to assemble promptly in view of the orders, there being no other subject to deal with at the present meeting, and elect by vote those who are to serve. The 2nd (?) year, (month) 15.

238. DRAFT OF A PROCLAMATION TO THE EPHEBI

A.D. 323.

Dioscorides, logistes of the Oxyrhynchite nome. The contest of the ephebi will take place to-morrow, the 24th. Tradition, no less than the distinguished character of the festival, requires that the ephebi should display their athletic attainments with the utmost ardour, to the redoubled enjoyment of the spectators who will be present. In the consulship of our masters Licinius Augustus for the 6th time and Licinius the most eminent Caesar for the 2nd time, in their 3rd year of office,[a] Tubi 23.

[a] The translation assumes that the said consulship began in A.D. 321 and continued for several years. The consuls appointed by Constantine were not recognized in Egypt at this time.

IV. REPORTS OF MEETINGS

239. REPORT OF A PUBLIC MEETING

P. Oxy. 41.   About A.D. 300.

¹[- - -]αριας πανηγύρεως οὔσης ²[. . . . .
. . . . τοῖς Ῥωμαίοις] εἰς [ἐ]ῶνα τὸ κράτος ³τ[ῶ]ν Ῥωμαίων, Ἄγουστοι κύριοι, εὐτύχη
[ἡγεμ]ών, εὐτυχῶ[ς] τῷ καθολικῷ. ⁴Ὠκαιαναὶ
πρύτανι, Ὠκααναὶ δόξα πόλεω[ς], Ὠκααναὶ Διό[σ-
κ]ορε πρωτοπολῖτα, ⁵ἐπὶ σοῦ τὰ ἀγαθὰ καὶ
πλέον γίνεται, ἀρχηγαὶ τῶν ἀγαθῶν, ισιην φιλῖ σε
καὶ ἀναβαίνι, ⁶εὐτυχῶς τῷ φιλοπολίτῃ, εὐτυχῶς
τῷ φιλομετρίῳ, ἀρχηγὲ τῶν ἀγαθῶν, κτίστα τῆς
⁷π[όλεως . . . .] . . . . Ὠκααναὶ . . . ου [. . .]
ψηφισθήτω ὁ πρύ(τανις) ἐν τυαύτῃ [ἡμέρ]ᾳ, ⁸πολ-
λῶν ψηφισμάτων ἄξιος, πολλῶν ἀγαθῶν ἀπο-
λαύομεν διὰ σαί, πρύτανι. ⁹δέησιν τῷ καθολικῷ
περὶ τοῦ πρυτάνεως εὐτυχῶς τῷ καθολικῷ δεόμεθα, ¹⁰καθολικέ, τὸν πρύτανιν τῇ πόλι, εὐερ-
[γέτ]α κα[θολι]καί, τὸν κτίστην τῇ πόλι, ¹¹Ἄγου-
στοι κύριοι εἰς τὸν ἐῶνα· δέησ[ιν] τῷ [καθολι]κῷ

---

2. *l.* αἰῶνα, so in 11 and 21.   3. *l.* Αὔγουστοι, so in 11,
20, 29.   *l.* εὐτύχει, so in 13, 14, 21.   4. *l.* Ὠκεανέ, so
throughout.   5. *l.* ἀρχηγέ.   7. *l.* τοιαύτῃ, so
in 15.   8. *l.* διὰ σέ.   10. *l.* καθολικέ, so throughout.

IV. REPORTS OF MEETINGS

239. REPORT OF A PUBLIC MEETING

About A.D. 300.

. . . when the assembly had met, (the people cried)
" . . . the Roman power for ever ! lords Augusti !
good fortune O governor,[a] good fortune to the
catholicus ! Bravo president, bravo the city's boast,
bravo Dioscorus chief of the citizens ! under you our
blessings still increase, source of our blessings, . . .
loves you and rises, good luck to the patriot ! good
luck to the lover of equity ! source of our blessings,
founder of the city, . . . bravo . . . let the president
receive the vote on this great day, many votes does he
deserve, for many are the blessings we enjoy through
you, O president ! This petition we make to the
catholicus about the president, with good wishes to
the catholicus, asking for the city's president, beneficent catholicus, for the city's founder, lords Augusti
for ever, this petition to the catholicus about the

[a] The meeting was held on the occasion of a visit paid to
Oxyrhynchus by the praeses, the civil governor of the district
in the Byzantine period, and the catholicus, the head of the
Treasury in Alexandria. It was largely a demonstration in
honour of the prytanis, the president of the senate ; but
the particular object of the acclamations and entreaties is
not clear.

περὶ τοῦ πρυτάνεως, ¹²τὸν ἄρχοντα τοῖς μετρίοις,
ἰσάρχο[ντ]α [τοῖς . . . . .]ς, τὸν ἄρχοντα τῇ πόλι,
τὸν ¹³κηδεμόνα τῇ πόλι, τὸν φιλομέτριον [τῇ
π]όλ[ι], τὸ[ν] κτίστην τῇ πόλι, εὐτύχη ¹⁴ἡγεμών,
εὐτύχη καθολικαί, εὐεργ[έ]τα ἡγεμών, εὐεργέτα
καθολικαί, δεόμεθα, ¹⁵καθολικαί, περὶ τοῦ πρυ-
τάνεως· ψ[ηφισ]θήτω ὁ πρύτανις, ψηφισθήτω ἐν
τυαύ-¹⁶τῃ ἡμέρα. τοῦτο πρῶτον καὶ ἀναγκαῖον. ὁ
πρύ(τανις) εἶπ(εν)· τὴν μὲν παρ' ὑμῶν ¹⁷τιμὴν
ἀσπάζομαι καί γε ἐπὶ τούτῳ σφόδρα χαίρω· τὰς
δὲ τοιαύτα[ς] ¹⁸μαρτυρίας ἀξιῶ εἰς καιρὸν ἔννομον
ὑπερτεθῆναι, ἐν ᾧ καὶ ὑμῖς ¹⁹βεβαίως παρέχεται
καὶ ἐγὼ ἀ[σφ]αλῶς λαμβάνω. ὁ δῆμος ἐβόησεν·
²⁰πολλῶν ψηφισμάτων ἄξιος, τὸ νοκ[. . .]αν εἰς
τὸ μέσον, Ἄγουστοι κύριοι, ²¹πασεινῖκαι (?) τοῖς
Ῥωμαίοις, εἰς ἐῶνα τὸ κράτος τῶν Ῥωμαίων.
εὐτύχη ἡγεμώ[ν], ²²σωτὴρ μετρίων, καθολικαί,
δεόμεθα, καθολικ[αί], τὸν πρύτανιν τῇ πόλι, τὸν
φ[ιλο-] ²³μέτριον τῇ πόλι, τὸν κτίστην τῇ πόλι·
δεόμ[ε]θα, καθολικαί, σῶσον πόλιν ²⁴τοῖς κυρίοις,
εὐεργέτα καθολικαί, τὸν ε[ὔφρο]να τῇ πόλι, τὸν
φιλοπολίτην τῇ πό[λ]ι. ²⁵Ἀριστίων σύνδικος εἶ-
π(εν)· τὴν ἀπ[αίτησιν ὑμῶν] παραθησόμεθα τῇ
κρατίσ[τ]ῃ β[ο]υλῇ. ²⁶ὁ δῆμος· δεόμεθα, καθολικαί, τὸ[ν κ]ηδε[μό]να τ[ῇ πό]λι, τὸν κτίστην ²⁷τῇ
πόλι, στρατηγὲ πισταί, εἰρήνη πόλεως. [Ὠ]κααναὶ
Διοσκουρίδη, πρωτοπολῖτα, ²⁸Ὠκααναὶ Σεύθη,
πρωτοπολῖτα, ἰσάρχων, ἰσ[ο]πολῖτ<α>, ²⁹ἁγνοὶ
πιστοὶ σύνδικοι, ἁγνοὶ πιστοὶ στρατ[ηγο]ί, ἱς ὥρας
πᾶσι τοῖς ³⁰τὴν πόλιν φιλοῦσιν, Ἄγουστοι κύριοι
εἰς τὸ[ν α]ἰῶνα.

president, for the honest man's magistrate, the . . . equitable magistrate, the city's magistrate, the city's patron, the city's lover of justice, the city's founder. Good fortune O governor, good fortune O catholicus, beneficent governor, beneficent catholicus ! We beseech you, catholicus, concerning the president; let the president receive the vote, let him receive the vote on this great day. This is the first and urgent duty." The president said : " I welcome, and with much gratification, the honour which you do me, but I beg that such demonstrations be reserved for a legitimate occasion when you can make them with authoritative force and I can accept them with assurance." The people cried : " Many votes does he deserve, the . . . to the fore, lords Augusti, all-victorious for the Romans, the Roman power for ever ! Good fortune O governor, protector of honest men, O catholicus ! We ask, catholicus, for the city's president, the city's lover of justice, the city's founder ! We beseech you, catholicus, preserve the city for our lords, beneficent catholicus, we beseech you for the city's well-wisher, the city's patriot ! " Aristion the counsellor said : " We will lay your request before their excellencies the senate." The people : "We ask, catholicus, for the city's patron, the city's founder, O trusty strategus, O peace of the city ! Bravo Dioscorides, chief of the citizens, bravo Seuthes, chief of the citizens, equitable magistrate, equitable citizen ! True and trusty counsellors, true and trusty strategi ! Long life to all who love the city ! Long live the lords Augusti ! "

---

18. ᾧ corr. from τούτῳ. corr. from παρέχοντες. E.-H.: πασεινι καί Edd.

19. παρέχεται (l. παρέχετε) 21. πασεινῖκαι (for πασινῖκαι) (?) 27. l. πιστέ.

SELECT PAPYRI

240. PROCEEDINGS OF A SENATE

P. Oxy. 2110.   A.D. 370.

¹Ὑ[πα]τίας τῶν δεσποτῶν ἡμῶν Οὐαλεντινιανοῦ
καὶ Οὐάλεντος αἰωνίων Αὐγούστων τὸ γ, Φαῶθι
θ, ²βουλῆς οὔσης, πρυτανίας Κλαυδίου Ἑρμείου
Γελασίου γυμ(νασιαρχήσαντος) βουλευτοῦ, μετὰ
τὰς εὐφημίας ³καὶ παρελθόντος εἰς μέσον Θέωνος
Ἀμμωνίου βουλευτοῦ διὰ Μακροβίου υἱοῦ καὶ
καταθεμένου οὕτως· οἴδατε καὶ ὑμῖς, συνβουλευταί,
⁴ὅ[τι] ἐπὶ τῆς μελλο‹ύ›σης κήρας εἰμὶ καὶ ἐν τοῖς
εἰκοσιτέσσαρές εἰμι τοῖς διατυπωθεῖσιν ὑπὸ τοῦ
κυρίου τοῦ λαμ(προτάτου) Τατιανοῦ εἰς τὰς παγ-
αρχίας καὶ κονδου-⁵κτορίας, καὶ ἴσως κατ᾽ ἄγνοιαν
ὁ πρόεδρος ἐχιροτόνησέν με εἰς ἐπιμέλειαν τῆς
στρατιωτικῆς ἐρεᾶς ἐσθῆτος τῆς ιδ (ἔτους) ἰνδικ(τίονος), μάλιστα νῦν ⁶ἱπποτ[ρ]όφου τυγχάνοντός μου,
καὶ διὰ τοῦτο παρατίθημι ἐν ὑμῖν ὡς οὐ χρὴ
λύεσθαι τὰ διατυπωθέντα· οἱ βουλευταὶ ἐφώνησαν·
κύριον τὸ κατὰ κήραν· ⁷οὐ [χ]ρὴ παραλύεσθαι τὰ
καλῶς διατυπωθέντα.   Πτολεμῖνος λογιστεύσας
εἶπ(εν)· βέβαια καὶ ἀσάλευτα χρὴ εἶναι τὰ διατυπωθέντα ὑπὸ τοῦ κυρίου ⁸λαμ(προτάτου) Τατιανοῦ ἐκ
συναινέσεως παντὸς τοῦ βουλευτηρίου, ὥστε μὴ
λειτουργεῖν τοὺς εἰκοσιτέσσαρας εἰς μηδ᾽ ὁτιοῦν
λειτούργημα ἀλλὰ ⁹ἔχειν ἐπὶ ταῖς βαρυτέραις

1. l. Φαῶφι.   4. l. εἰκοσιτέσσαρσίν εἰμι.

ᵃ He was on the official list of persons designated for the
more important services, and he complains that the prytanis,
the president of the senate, has nominated him for an
additional, though lesser duty. His fellow members shout
in sympathy; then, rising one by one, they maintain that

240. PROCEEDINGS OF A SENATE

A.D. 370.

In the 3rd consulship of our masters Valentinian and Valens, eternal Augusti, Phaophi 9, at a meeting of the senate, in the prytany of Claudius Hermeias son of Gelasius, ex-gymnasiarch and senator, after the plaudits Theon son of Ammonius, senator, represented by his son Macrobius, came forward and made the following statement : " Fellow councillors you know as well as I that my name is on the tablet about to come into force [a] and that I am one of the twenty-four ordained by our lord the most illustrious Tatianus [b] for the pagarchies and contractorships.[c] Perhaps in ignorance the president has appointed me to the administration of the soldiers' woollen clothing for the 14th indiction, at the very time when I have horses to keep ; wherefore I put it to you that the ordinances ought not to be infringed." The senators cried : " What is on the tablet is valid ; what has been rightly ordained must not be infringed." Ptoleminus, ex-logistes, said : " What has been ordained by our lord the most illustrious Tatianus with the approval of the whole senate must stand fast and unshaken, whence it follows that the twenty-four are not to serve in any other service whatever but

his nomination by the praefect for the heavier services exempts him from the minor ones and that the president's action was *ultra vires*. In the end the president announces that he will cancel the offensive appointment.

[b] The praefect of Egypt.

[c] The pagarchy, which in later times developed into an important office, was at present the administration of a small district. The contractorships probably included the postal service, but nothing definite is known about them.

λειτουργείαις, οὐ μόνον ἐπὶ τῆς πρυτανίας ταύτης
ἀλλὰ ἐπὶ τῶν μελλόντων πρυτανεύειν. εἰ δὲ βού-
λεταί [[σ]] τις [10][λ]ε[ιτουργ]εῖν εἰς ἕτερον λειτούργημα,
οὐ κινδύνῳ τοῦ βουλευτηρίου λειτουργεῖ, καὶ οὐκ
ὀφείλει Μακρόβιος ἐνοχλεῖσθαι. Γερόντιος ἐξακτο-
[11][ρεύσας εἶπ(εν)·] τὰ καλῶς διατυπωθέντα καὶ μετὰ
τοῦ νομίμου γενόμενα ὑπὸ τοῦ κυρίου μου Τατιανοῦ
καὶ ἀνενεχθέντα πρὸς τοὺς [12]δεσ[πότας ἡ]μῶν καὶ
πρὸς τοὺς κυρίους μου τοὺς λαμ(προτάτους) ἐπ-
άρχους τοῦ ἱεροῦ πραιτωρίου καὶ ἐκῖθεν τὸ κῦρος
ἔχει{ν}, ὅθεν οὐ προσῆκον [13]ἐστιν Μακ[ρό]β[ιο]ν
ὀχλεῖσθαι ὑπό τε τοῦ πρυτάνεως οὐδ' ὑπὸ τοῦ
μελλοπρυτάνεως εἰς ἑτέρας ἐπιμελείας. Σαρμάτης
λογιστεύσας εἶπ(εν)· [14]ἴσως κατ' ἄγνοιαν ὁ ἀδελφὸς
ἡμῶν Ἑρμείας ὁ πρόεδρος ὑ[π]έλαβεν Μακρόβιον
ὄντα ἐκ τῶν κδ τῶν διατυπωθέντων ὑπὸ τοῦ κυρίου
μου [15][Τα]τιανοῦ, οὗ[τος] δὲ οὐκ ὀφίλει ἐνοχλεῖσθαι
προφάσει ἐπιμελεία{ι}ς. εἰ δὲ βουληθείη τις ἐκ
τῶν κδ ἀμβιτεύειν, οἶδεν τὸν ἑαυτοῦ κίνδυνον.
[16][. .]μο . . [. .] . [. . . . .]ς εἶπ(εν)· οὐκ ὀφίλει
τις ἐκ τῶν εἰκοσιτεσσάρων τῶν διατυπωθέντων ἐκ
τῆς καθαρότητος τοῦ κυρίου μου Τατιανοῦ [17][. . .
. . . . .] μ [. . . . .]. . . αλ . . . προ-
έδρων, Μακρόβιος δὲ νῦν οὐκ ὀφίλει ἐνοχλεῖσθαι εἰς
τὴν ἐπιμέλειαν τῆς στρατιωτικῆς ἐρεᾶς [18][ἐσθῆτος
ο]ὐδ' εἰς ἕτερόν τι, ἀλλ' ἀρκεῖσθαι αὐτὸν ταῖς
βαρυτάταις λειτουργείαις. Ἀμμωνιανὸς ἐξακτο-
ρεύσας εἶπ(εν)· τὰ καλῶς διατυπωθέντα [19][κα]ὶ
μετὰ . . . . ειας καὶ ἀρέ-
σαντα το[ῖς] δ[εσ]πότα[ι]ς τῆς οἰκουμένης καὶ τοῖς
κυρίοις μου τοῖς λαμπροτάτοις ἐπάρχοις οὐ χρὴ
[20]παραλύεσθαι οὔτε ὑπὸ τοῦ νῦν πρυτάνεως οὔτε

keep to the heavier liturgies, not only in this but in future prytanies. If, however, anyone wishes to serve in another service, he does not do so on the responsibility of the senate, and Macrobius ought not to be burdened." Gerontius, ex-exactor, said : " What has been rightly ordained and legally done by my lord Tatianus and referred to our sovereigns and to my lords the most illustrious praefects of the sacred praetorium has its validity from them, and hence it is not proper for Macrobius to be burdened by either the prytanis or the future prytanis with other administrations." Sarmates, ex-logistes, said : " Perhaps it was in ignorance that our brother Hermeias the president impressed Macrobius who is one of the 24 ordained by my lord Tatianus, and he ought not to be burdened on the score of an administration. But if any one of the 24 should wish to be ostentatious, he knows his own responsibility." . . . said : " One of the twenty-four ordained by the rectitude of my lord Tatianus ought not to [suffer through the fault of ?] presidents, and Macrobius ought not now to be burdened with the administration of the soldiers' woollen clothing nor anything else, but should confine himself to the heavy liturgies." Ammonianus, exexactor, said : " What has been rightly and . . . ordained and approved by the masters of the world and by my lords the most illustrious praefects should not be infringed either by the present prytanis or by

ὑπὸ [μελλόντ]ων πρυτάνεων, ὅθεν οὐκ ὀφίλει
Μακρόβιος ἐνοχλεῖσθαι εἰς ἑτέρας λειτουρ-[21]γείας.
Οὐαλέριος Εὐδαίμονος γυμ(νασιαρχήσας) εἶπ(εν)·
οὐκ ἔστιν ἀκό[λουθον ἡμ]ῖν ἔτι πρᾶξαί τι ἐκτὸς τῶν
δια[τυ]πωθέντων ὑπὸ τοῦ κυ[ρίου] μο[υ] Τατιανοῦ,
[22][ὅ]θεν οὐκ ὀφίλει Μακρόβιος οὔτ' ἕτερός τις {τ}
ἐκ [τῶν κδ ?] ἐπιβουλεύεσθαι εἰς τὸ παράπαν ἀλλὰ
τούτους φυλάττεσθαι τῇ [κα]λῶς γενομένῃ [23]διοι-
κήσι. Μακρόβιος ῥιπάριος εἶπ(εν)· εἷς ὢν ἐκ τῶν
κδ Μακρόβιος οὐκ ὀφίλει εἰς ἕτερον [24]λειτούργημα
ἐνοχλεῖσθαι. Ἀχιλλεὺς Ποσὶ ῥιπάριος εἶπ(εν)· χάριν
τότε πάντες [25]ὡμολογήσαμεν ἐπὶ τῇ καλῶς γενομένῃ διοικήσι ὑπὸ τοῦ κυρίου τοῦ λαμ(προτάτου)
Τατιανοῦ· [26]οὐκ ὀφίλει Μακρόβιος τοίνυν ἐνοχλεῖσθαι εἰς τὴν ἐπιμέλειαν τῆς στρατιωτικῆς [27]ἐρεᾶς
ἐσθῆτος οὐδὲ εἰς ἕτερόν τι λειτούργημα, διὰ τὸ ἕνα
αὐτὸν εἶναι τῶν κδ. [28]Ζωΐλος Διονυσίου γυμ(νασιαρχήσας) εἶπ(εν)· κἀγὼ σύνψηφός εἰμι ἐπὶ τοῖς
κατατεθεῖσιν [29]ὑπὸ τῆς κοινότητος ὥστε μὴ ἐνοχλεῖσθαι τοὺς κδ τούτους οὔτε ὑπὸ <τοῦ νῦν πρυτάνεως οὔτε ὑπὸ ?> τῶν [30]μελλόντων πρυτανεύειν·
ὅθεν οὐκ ὀφίλει Μακρόβιος ἐνοχλεῖσθαι μάλ{λ}ιστα
[31]εἷς ὢν τῶν κδ. Θέων Εὐσεβίου πρυτανεύσας
εἶπ(εν)· ὁ ἀδελφὸς ἡμῶν ὁ πρόεδρος [32]ἴσως κατ'
ἄγνοιαν μὴ γινώσκων Θέωνα διὰ Μακροβίου υἱοῦ
ὄντα ἐκ τῶν κδ ἀνδρῶν [33]τῶν διατυπωθέντων εἰς
τὰς βαρυτέρας λειτουργείας ὑπέβαλεν αὐτὸν εἰς τὴν
[34]ἐσθῆτα, ὅθεν {δ'} ὀνε[ι]δίζομεν ὡς οὐ προσήκει
αὐτὸν ἐνοχλεῖσθαι προφάσι ἐπιμελείας [35]τῆς αὐτῆς
ἐρεᾶς ἐσθῆτος. Εὐλόγιος Πτολεμαίου γυμ(νασιαρχήσας) εἶπ(εν)· Θέων Ἀμμωνίου διὰ [36]Μακροβίου
υἱοῦ εἷς ὢν τῶν διατυπωθέντων κδ εἰς τὰς βαρυ-

future prytaneis, hence Macrobius ought not to be burdened with other liturgies." Valerius son of Eudaemon, ex-gymnasiarch, said : " It is not seemly for us to do anything beyond what has been ordained by my lord Tatianus, hence neither Macrobius nor any other of the 24 (?) ought to be subject to intrigue in any way, but they ought to be protected by the disposition which has been rightly made." Macrobius, police-officer, said : " Being one of the 24 Macrobius ought not to be burdened with another service." Achilles son of Posi, police-officer, said : " We all returned thanks at the time for the disposition rightly made by my lord the most illustrious Tatianus ; Macrobius accordingly ought not to be burdened with the administration of the soldiers' woollen clothing, nor any other service, because he is one of the 24." Zoilus son of Dionysius, ex-gymnasiarch, said : "I too am in agreement with the view which has been generally expressed that these 24 should not be burdened either by (the present prytanis or by) future prytaneis ; Macrobius therefore ought not to be burdened, especially as he is one of the 24." Theon son of Eusebius, ex-prytanis, said : " Perhaps in ignorance our brother the president, being unaware that Theon represented by his son Macrobius is one of the 24 persons ordained for the heavier liturgies, imposed upon him the clothing ; we therefore object that it is not right that he should be burdened on the score of the administration of the said woollen clothing." Eulogius son of Ptolemaeus, ex-gymnasiarch, said : " Theon son of Ammonius, represented by his son Macrobius, being one of the 24 ordained for the

τάτας λειτουργείας {καὶ} ³⁷οὐκ ὀφίλει ὄχλησίν τινα
παθεῖν προφάσι ἑτέρων λειτουργιῶν. ὁ πρύτανις
εἶπ(εν)· ³⁸ὅσα κοινῇ τε καὶ καθ' ἓν προηνέγκεσθαι
ἔχει ἡ πίστις τῶν ὑπομνημάτων, καὶ οὐκ ³⁹ἐν-
οχληθήσεται Μακρόβιος εἰς τὴν ἐπιμέλειαν τῆς
στρατιωτικῆς ἐρεᾶς ἐσθῆτος ⁴⁰τῆς ιδ (ἔτους) ἰν-
δικ(τίονος). (2nd hand) ⁴¹Αὐρήλιο[ς Ἰσ]ίδωρος
σκρίβας ἐξεδόμην τὰ ὑπομνήματα.

38. *l.* προηνέγκεσθε.

241. MINUTES OF A PUBLIC SESSION
BEFORE A STRATEGUS

P. Ryl. 77, ll. 32-47.   A.D. 192.

³²Ἀντίγραφον ὑπομνήματος· με[. . . . . δη]μό-
σια πρὸς τῷ β[ήματι] παρόντων τῶ[ν ἐνάρ]χων
Δίου γυμ[ν]ασιάρχου Διονυσίου ³³[το]ῦ καὶ [.] .
νθεου ἐξηγητοῦ, Ὀλυμ[πιο]δώρου προδίκου, Ἀπολ-
[λων]ί[ο]υ Ἡρακλαπόλλων[ος γυ]μνασιαρχ(ήσαντος)
καὶ Ἀχιλ[λέως] Κορνηλίου, τῶν π[αρ]εστώτων ἀπὸ
τῆς πόλεως ἐπιφωνη-³⁴[σ]άντων· στεφέσθω Ἀχιλλεὺς κοσμητείαν· μιμοῦ τὸν πα[τ]έρα τὸν φιλότιμον
τὸν [γ]έροντα φῶτα, Ἀχιλλε[ὺ]ς εἶπεν· πειθόμενος
τῇ ἐμαυτοῦ πατρίδι ἐπιδέχομαι στεφα-³⁵[νη]φόρον
ἐξηγητείαν ἐπὶ τῷ ἐτήσια εἰσφέρειν με τάλαντα δύο
καὶ ἀπαλλαγῆναι ἐπιτηρήσεως διαμισθουμένης γῆς.
Ὀλυμπιόδωρος εἶπ(εν)· ἡ τύχη τοῦ κυρίου ἡμῶν
³⁶Αὐ[το]κράτορος ἀφθόνως ἀρχὰ[ς] παρέχει καὶ τῆς

ᵃ Achilles had been nominated for the office of cosmetes,
and the matter was referred to the strategus sitting in public

heaviest liturgies, ought not to suffer any burden on
the score of other liturgies." The prytanis said :
" The opinions which you have advanced collectively
and individually are in the safe keeping of the minutes,
and Macrobius shall not be burdened with the administration of the soldiers' woollen clothing for the 14th
indiction." (Signed) I, Aurelius Isidorus, scribe,
drew up the minutes.

241. MINUTES OF A PUBLIC SESSION
BEFORE A STRATEGUS

A.D. 192.

Copy of minutes. . . ., there being present at the
tribunal from the magistrates in office Dius, gymnasiarch, and Dionysius also called . . ., exegetes,
Olympiodorus, advocate, Apollonius son of Heracla-
pollon, ex-gymnasiarch, and Achilles son of Cornelius,
the townsmen standing by cried out, " Let Achilles
be crowned as cosmetes ; imitate your father, the
man of public spirit, the old champion," whereupon
Achilles said : " In compliance with the wish of my
native city I offer to undertake the office of a crowned
exegetes on the condition that I contribute an annual
sum of two talents and am freed from the superintendence of land under lease." [a] Olympiodorus said :
" The fortune of our lord the Emperor provides offices
abundantly and augments the prosperity of the city ;

audience. As a means of escaping this burdensome duty
Achilles offers to undertake, on certain conditions, the office
of exegetes, which was superior in rank but, according to him,
less expensive. All these offices were very costly for the
occupants.

πόλ(εως) αὐξάνε[ι] τὰ πράγματα, τί τ᾽ οὐκ ἤμελλεν
ἐπὶ τῇ ἐπαφροδείτῳ ἡγεμονίᾳ Λαρκίου Μέμορος;
εἰ μὲν οὖν ὁ Ἀχιλλεὺς [37]βούλεται στεφανωθῆναι
ἐξηγητείαν, εἰσενεγκάτω τὸ ἰσητήριον ἐντεῦθεν, εἰ
δὲ μή, ⟨οὐχ⟩ ἧττον ἑαυτὸν ἐχειροτόνησεν εἰς τὴν
κατεπείγουσαν ἀρχὴν κοσμητεί-[38]αν. Ἀχιλλεὺς
εἶπ(εν)· ἐγὼ ἀνεδεξάμην ἐξηγητείαν ἐπὶ τῷ κατ᾽
ἔτος δύο τάλαντα εἰσφέρειν, οὐ γὰρ δύναμαι κοσμητείαν. Ὀλυμπιόδωρος εἶπ(εν)· ἀναδεξάμενος [39]τὴν
μείζονα ἀρχὴν οὐκ ὀφείλει τὴν ἐλάττον᾽ ἀποφεύγειν.
Ἀμμωνίων Διοσκόρου ὑποτυχὼν εἶπ(εν)· πάσης τῆς
ἐνεστώσης ἔτυψέ με ὁ Ἀχιλλεὺς καὶ αὐτὰ ταῦτα
[40]ἀσφαλίσομαι διὰ τῶν σῶν ὑπομνημάτων ὅτι καὶ
ἐντυγχάνω τῷ λαμπροτάτῳ ἡγεμόνι περὶ τῆς
ὕβρεως. Ἀχιλλεὺς εἶπ(εν)· οὔτε ἔτυψα αὐτὸν οὔτε
ὕβρισα. [41]Σαραπίων ὁ καὶ Ἀπολλώνιος στρα-
(τηγὸς) εἶπ(εν)· ἃ μὲν εἰρήκατε γέγραπται, μετα-
πεμφθήσονται δὲ καὶ οἱ κοσμηταὶ ἵνα ἐπὶ παροῦσι
αὐτοῖς αὐτὰ ταῦτα εἴπητε. μετ᾽ ὀλίγον [42]πρὸς τῷ
Καισαρείῳ Διογένης καὶ Διόσκορος καὶ ⟨οἱ⟩ σὺν
αὐτοῖς κοσμηταὶ προελθόντες παρόντος τοῦ Ἀχιλλέως διὰ τοῦ ἑνὸς αὐτῶν, Διογένης εἶπ(εν)· ἐμά-
θομεν τὸν Ἀχιλ-[43]λέα προβαλόμενον ἑαυτὸν εἰς ἐξ-
ηγ(ητείαν) ἀπόντων ἡμῶν, τοῦτο δὲ οὐκ ἐξῆν, ὁ
γὰρ θειότατος Ἀντωνῖνος διὰ ⟨δια⟩τάγματος ἐκέλευσεν μὴ συγχωρῖσθαι ἄνευ τριῶν ἐπιλόγ-[44]χων
εἰς ἐξηγ(ητείαν)· πολλῶν οὖν ἐπιλόγχων ⟨ὄντων⟩
ὀφείλει εἰς τὴν κατεπείγο[υσα]ν ἀρχὴν παραβαίνειν,

37. l. εἰσιτήριον.

---

[a] Implying that Achilles had no intention of doing so and
that his proposal to undertake the superior office of exegetes
was a mere pretence.

how could it be otherwise under the charming prae-fecture of Larcius Memor ? If then Achilles wishes to be crowned as exegetes, let him forthwith pay the initial contribution [a] ; if he does not, he has none the less nominated himself for the office immediately required, that of cosmetes." Achilles said : " I en-gaged to undertake the office of exegetes on the condition that I should contribute two talents yearly ; for I am not able to support the office of cosmetes." Olympiodorus said : " After engaging to undertake the greater office he ought not to evade the lesser." Ammonion son of Dioscorus, interrupting, said : " All through this day Achilles struck me, and I will certify these very facts by means of your minutes, because I am petitioning the most illustrious praefect con-cerning the insult." Achilles said : " I neither struck him nor insulted him." Sarapion also called Apollonius, strategus, said : " What you have said has been recorded, but the cosmetae shall also be summoned in order that you may repeat the same statements in their presence." After a while Diogenes and Dioscorus and their fellow cosmetae came forward at the Caesareum [b] in the presence of Achilles, making one of them their spokesman ; and he, Diogenes, said : " We have learned that in our absence Achilles proposed himself for the office of exegetes. But this was not permissible ; for the most divine Antoninus ordained by edict that no one may become an exegetes without three designated successors [c] ; so, as there are many designated suc-cessors, he ought to pass on to the office immediately

---

[b] The temple of the Caesars ; compare No. 242, p. 163.
[c] A waiting list of three persons who would succeed to the office in turn.

ὡς ἀναγνώσομαί σοι τὸ διάταγμα. καὶ ἀναγνόντος
ἀντίγρα(φον) διατάγματος [45]Μάρκου Αὐρηλίου
Ἀντωνίνου Καίσαρος Ἀσπιδᾶς πατὴρ Ἑρμᾶ
κοσμητ[ε]ύ(σαντος) παρὼν εἶπ(εν)· ἰδίῳ κινδύνῳ
στέφω τὸν Ἀχιλλέα τὴν κοσμητείαν. Ὀλυμπιόδωρος εἶπ(εν)· [46]ἔχομεν δὴ φωνὴν τοῦ Ἀσπιδᾶ ὅτι
ἰδίῳ κινδύνῳ αὐτὸν στέφει. κα[ὶ] ὀφείλει στεφῆναι,
ἤδη γὰρ ἡ ἀρχὴ ἀδιάπτωτός ἐστιν τῇ πόλ(ει). ὁ
στρα(τηγὸς) εἶπ(εν) τὰ εἰρημένα ὑπομνηματισθῆ-
[47]ναι.

required ; in proof of which I will read you the edict."
When he had read a copy of the edict of Marcus
Aurelius Antoninus Caesar, Aspidas father of Hermas
the ex-cosmetes, being present, said : " On my personal responsibility [a] I crown Achilles for the office
of cosmetes." Olympiodorus said : " We have now
the declaration of Aspidas that he crowns him on his
own responsibility ; and he ought to be crowned, for
the office is now safeguarded for the city." The
strategus ordered the statements to be entered on
the minutes.

[a] That is, he guaranteed the expenses of the office.

V. OFFICIAL ACTS AND INQUIRIES

242. EXTRACTS FROM THE JOURNAL OF A STRATEGUS

From P. Par. 69 (= W. Chrest. 41). A.D. 242.

(Col. 2) ¹['Υπομνημ]ατισμοὶ Α[ὐ]ρ[ηλίου Λεοντᾶ
στρατηγοῦ ²'Ομβίτ]ου 'Ελεφαν[τίνης. ³(ἔτους) ι]β
Αὐτοκράτορος Κα[ίσαρος Μάρκου ⁴Αὐρη]λίου Σεουήρου 'Αλεξάνδρ[ου Εὐσεβοῦς ⁵Εὐτυ]χοῦς Σεβαστοῦ.
⁶[Θὼθ ᾱ. ὁ] στρατηγὸς ὑπὸ νύκτα [. . . . .
⁷ἐ]ν τῷ γυμνασίῳ ἅμα Αὐρη[λίῳ . . . .
⁸ἔ]στεψεν εἰς γυμνασιαρχ[ίαν Αὐρήλιον ⁹Π]ελαιᾶν
'Αρπαήσιος 'Ιέρα[κος (?) καὶ ἔθυ-¹⁰σ]εν ἔν τε τῷ
Καισαρείῳ κα[ὶ ἐν τῷ γυ-]¹¹μνασίῳ, ἔνθα σπονδά[ς
τε καὶ ¹²δε]ήσεις ποιησάμενος ἀπ[εδήμησεν ¹³εἰ]ς
τὸν ἕτερον νομὸν 'Ομβ[ίτην, ἔνθα τῶν ¹⁴συ]νηθῶν
ἱερουργιῶν Δι[. . . . . . ¹⁵γε]νομένων καὶ τῇ ἀγο-
[μένῃ κωμα-¹⁶σ]ίᾳ τοῦ αὐτοῦ παρέτυχεν. (2nd hand)
160

V. OFFICIAL ACTS AND INQUIRIES

242. EXTRACTS FROM THE JOURNAL OF A STRATEGUS

A.D. 242.

Acts of Aurelius Leontas, strategus of the Ombite nome *a* and of Elephantine.*b* The 12th year of the Emperor Caesar Marcus Aurelius Severus Alexander Pius Felix Augustus. Thoth 1. The strategus towards nightfall . . . in the gymnasium along with Aurelius . . . crowned as gymnasiarch Aurelius Pelaias son of Harpaesis son of Hierax (?) and sacrificed in the Caesareum and the gymnasium. Having there made both libations and prayers he departed to the other nome, the Ombite, where after the traditional rites of . . . had been performed he attended the procession held in honour of the said

a In Upper Egypt, the capital of the nome being Ombos, the present Kom Ombo.
b The island town opposite Aswan. In other documents the title is given more fully as "strategus of the Ombite nome and the nome round Elephantine."

ἀ[νέγνων. (3rd hand) ¹⁷Αὐρ]ήλιος Διονυσόδωρος
ὑπ(ηρέτης) προθεὶ[ς δημοσίᾳ κατεχώρισα. ¹⁸(ἔτους)
ι]β Θὼθ β.

(Col. 4) ¹['Υπομ]νημα[τ]ισμοὶ Α[ὐρηλίου Λεοντᾶ
στρατηγοῦ 'Ομβίτου ²'Ελεφαντίνης. ³ἔτου]ς ιβ
Αὐτοκράτορος Καίσ[αρος Μάρκου Αὐρηλίου Σεουήρου ⁴'Αλε]ξάνδρου Εὐσεβοῦς Εὐτυχ[οῦς Σεβαστοῦ. ⁵. . . ὁ] στρατηγὸς περὶ ἑσπέρα[ν
ἐπεδήμησεν. (2nd hand) ἀνέγνων. (1st hand)
⁶. . . ὁ] στρατηγὸς πρὸς τῷ λογιστ[ηρίῳ τοῖς
διαφέρουσι σχο-⁷λ]άσας τὴν τῶν ὠνίων ἀγορ[ὰν
ἐπεσκέψατο. (2nd hand) ἀνέγνων. (1st hand)
⁸. .] ὁ στρατηγὸς πρὸς τῷ λογιστη[ρίῳ τοῖς
διαφέ]ρουσι ἐσχό-⁹λασεν. (2nd hand) [ἀνέγνων.
(1st hand) ¹⁰. .] ὁ στρατηγὸς πρὸς τῷ λογιστ[ηρίῳ τοῖς] ¹¹διαφέρουσι ἐσχόλασεν. (2nd hand)
ἀνέγ[νων. (1st hand) ¹² . .] ὁ στρατηγὸς πρὸς
τῷ λογιστη[ρίῳ . . . . .] ¹³ποιησάμενος περὶ
δείλην ὀ[ψίαν?] ¹⁴παρέτυχεν κωμασίᾳ ἐξ ἔθ[ους
ἀγομέ-]¹⁵νη "Ισιδος θεᾶς μεγίστης. (2nd hand)
ἀ[νέγνων. (1st hand) ¹⁶. .] ὁ στρατηγὸς πρὸς
τῷ Καισα[ρείῳ τοῖς] ¹⁷διαφέρουσι σχολάσας ἐγέ-
ν[ετο πρὸς τῷ ¹⁸λο]γιστηρίῳ δημοσίοις π[ράγμασι
. . . . . . (2nd hand) ἀνέγνων. - - - (1st hand)
²²[. .] ὁ στρα[τηγὸς πρὸς τῷ λογιστηρίῳ διά-
κρισιν πρα-]²³κτόρων ποιησάμεν[ος ἀπεδήμησεν
εἰς τὸν] ²⁴ἕτερον νομὸν 'Ομβίτην. (2nd hand)
ἀ[νέγνων]. (3rd hand) ²⁵Αὐρήλιος Διονυσόδωρος
ὑπ(ηρέτης) προθ[εὶς δημοσίᾳ κατεχώρισα. . . .]

13. ὀ[ψίαν?] E.-H.

god. (Signed) Read. (Subscribed) Registered by me, Aurelius Dionysodorus, assistant, after being publicly displayed.[a]

Acts of Aurelius Leontas, strategus of the Ombite nome and of Elephantine. The 12th year of the Emperor Caesar Marcus Aurelius Severus Alexander Pius Felix Augustus. [Date.] The strategus returned home about evening. (Signed) Read. [Date.] The strategus after working at the office on matters of business inspected the market of salable goods. (Signed) Read. [Date.] The strategus worked at the office on matters of business. (Signed) Read. [Date.] The strategus worked at the office on matters of business. (Signed) Read. [Date.] The strategus, after making . . . at the office, late in the evening attended the procession held according to custom in honour of Isis the most great goddess. (Signed) Read. [Date.] The strategus after working at the Caesareum on matters of business sat at the office attending to public affairs. (Signed) Read. . . . [Date.] The strategus after holding an examination of the tax-collectors at the office departed to the other nome, the Ombite. (Signed) Read. (Subscribed) Registered by me, Aurelius Dionysodorus, assistant, after being publicly displayed.

[a] The acts of the strategi were first posted up in public and then filed, one copy being kept in the local archives and another sent to the central archives in Alexandria, where anyone who required could consult them. Acts of other officials were similarly accessible to the public.

SELECT PAPYRI

243. AN OFFICIAL DISCUSSION

P.S.I. 1100.   A.D. 161.

¹['Ἐξ] ὑπομνηματισμῶν Οὐη[δ]ίου Φα[ύ]στου
τ[οῦ] κρατίστου ἐπιστρατ[ήγου. ²με]θ' ἔτερα·
Φαῦστος σκεψάμενος μετὰ τῶν συνεδρευόντων
Ἁρποκρα-³[τίω]νι στρατηγῶι Θεμίστου καὶ Πολέμωνος μερίδω(ν) εἶπεν· κατὰ τὰ ὑπ' ἐμο[ῦ ⁴ἐξ]ετα-
σθέντα καὶ τὰ ὑπὸ τοῦ λαμπροτάτου ἡγεμόνος
κελευσθέντα δεή-⁵[σι] ἀφικέσθαι πρὸς τὴν αὐτοῦ
διάγνωσιν, ὧι δηλόσω πάντα τὰ ἐπ' ἐμοῦ πε-
⁶[πρα]γμένα. ἔσοντε δὲ ἐφ' ἱκανῷ κατελευσόμενοι
πρὸς τὴν διάγνωσιν ὅ τ[ε] 'νομοφύλαξ Διὸς καὶ
οἱ συνπαραλαβόντες τὸν Ἁρφαῆσιν Δημήτριος καὶ
Ἐπίμ[α-]⁸χος, ἔτι δὲ καὶ οἱ παλαιστροφύλακες
Ἡρακλείδης καὶ Μύσθης. Διὸς ν[ο-]⁹μοφύλαξ
εἶπεν· καὶ Ἑρμείας καὶ Διὸς μαχεροφόροι συν-
παρέλαβαν ἡμεῖν τὸ[ν] ¹⁰ᶜἉρπαῆσι(ν). Φαῦστος
ἐκέλευσεν αὐτοὺς κληθῆναι, καὶ μὴ ὑπακουσάν-
των ¹¹Φαῦστος εἶπεν· ἐὰν μὴ παρατύχωσιν, τὸ
ἀκόλουθον ἔσται, δώσι δὲ καὶ Ἄρειος ¹²ὁ γρα(μ-
ματεὺς) Ἁρποκρατίωνος τοῦ στρατηγοῦ ἱκανὸν
μέχρις ἂν εὑρεθῆ [[ὁ]] Ἁρποκρᾶς ¹³ὁ ὑπηρέτης·
κἀκεῖνος γὰρ ἀναγκαῖός ἐστιν. Ἁρποκρατίων
στρατηγὸς ¹⁴εἶπεν· ϙβ' πυροῦ ἐν θησαυροῖς ἔχω
καὶ κριθῆς ιθ∠' καὶ φακοῦ πα καὶ ¹⁵πρὸς καὶ
ἄλλα γένηι, ἡ δὲ ἐκμέτρησις τούτων ἐμοὶ διαφέρει.
καὶ ὑφορόμ[α]ι ¹⁶μὴ ἐπὶ πιριγραφῇ τῇ ἐμῇ ταῦτα
βασταχθῆ καὶ παραπόληται τῷ ταμί[ῳ]. ¹⁷Φαῦσ-

5. l. δηλώσω; so in 24 and 25.   6. l. ἔσονται.   9. l.
μαχαιροφόροι.   15. l. γένη, ὑφορῶμαι.   16. l. περιγραφῇ.

ᵃ Harpaesis had been arrested for some unspecified offence.

243. AN OFFICIAL DISCUSSION

A.D. 161.

From the minutes of his excellency the epistrategus Vedius Faustus. Extract :—Faustus after holding an inquiry along with the council of Harpocration, strategus of the divisions of Themistes and Polemon, said : " According to my investigations and the orders of the most illustrious praefect it will be necessary to go and ask his decision ; and I will let him know all the results of the meeting held by me. The following persons shall be prepared to go down under caution for his decision [a] : Dius the nomophylax, Demetrius and Epimachus who assisted him to take Harpaesis into custody, and also the keepers of the palaestra Heraclides and Mysthes." Dius, nomophylax, said : " Hermias and Dius, sword-bearers, also assisted us to take Harpaesis into custody." Faustus ordered them to be called ; when they failed to answer, he said : " If they do not present themselves, the appropriate action will be taken. Arius also, the secretary of Harpocration the strategus, will give caution for the appearance of Harpocras the assistant ; for he too is required." Harpocration, strategus, said : " I have in granaries 92 artabae of wheat, 19½ of barley, 81 of lentils, and other produce besides. The measuring-out of these is my concern, and I am uneasy lest with the object of defrauding me they be carried away and lost to the treasury." Faustus

The praefect wished to examine the persons responsible for the arrest, and the object of the discussion was to decide what persons should go down to Alexandria to see him. Apparently the strategus was expected to accompany them, but he succeeds in evading the mission by pleading that he has pressing business at home.

τος ἐπύθετο ὑπὸ τίνος βασταχθ[ῇ]; ἀπεκρίνατο·
ὑπὸ τῶν σιτ[ο-]¹⁸λόγων καὶ τῶν ἄλλων. ἐὰν οὖν
σο[ι] δοκ[ῇι], κατάστησόν τινας ἐπακολουθ[οῦν-]
¹⁹τας. Φαῦστος εἶπεν· [. . .] . . [. . . . .]χρ.
. . α . επραξ . . περὶ τούτων. ²⁰ἀπεκρίνατο·
οὐκ ἀναπαύσ[ομαι πράττων (?) κ]ατ[ὰ] καιρὸν
τοῦτον ἄχρ[ι] ²¹ταῦτα διοικηθῇ. Φαῦστος ἐπύ-
θετο· πόσου χρόνου δεῖ εἰς τὴν ἐκ-²²μέτρησιν;
ἀπεκρίνατο· ὁ μὲν λαμπρότατος ἡγεμὼν ἐκέλευσεν ²³ἐν λ ἡμέραις γενέσθαι, π[ρ]ὸς δὲ κ[αὶ]
ἄλλων χρέα ἔστε. Φαυσ-²⁴τος εἶπεν· ὡς προεῖπον,
πάντα ταῦτα δηλόσω τῷ λαμπροτάτῳ ²⁵ἡγεμόνι·
καὶ τοῦτο ὁμοίως δηλόσω, ὃ πάρεστι, ἀναγκαιο-
τάτην εἶναι ²⁶τὴν ἐκμέτρησιν, ἵν' ὃ ἐὰν αὐτῷ δόξῃ
κελεύσῃ γενέσθαι. Ἁρπο-²⁷κρατίων στρατηγὸς
εἶπεν· ἐν τοσούτῳ οὖν κελεύεις με μένιν; ²⁸Φαῦσ-
τος εἶπεν· περίμειν⟦ον⟧ε οἷα δεῖ πράττων· γράψω
γὰρ αὐτῷ ²⁹ἵν', ἐὰν θέλῃ εὐθύς σε ἥκειν, δηλώσι
μοι. ³⁰(ἔτους) β̄ Ἀντωνίνου καὶ Οὐήρου τῶν
κυρίων Σεβαστῶν μηνὸ⟨ς⟩ Ἁδριανοῦ κ̄η̄.

23. l. χρεία ἔσται.   25. ὅπαρ (for ὅπερ) ἐστί Edd.
28. l. περίμενε.   29. δηλώσι (= δηλώσει) for δηλώσῃ.

244. EXTRACT FROM THE ACTS OF
A CHIEF PRIEST

B.G.U. 347.   A.D. 171.

¹Ἐξ ὑπομνηματισμ[ῶν] Οὐλπίου [Σε]ρη[ν]ιανοῦ
τοῦ κρα-²τίστου ἀρχιερέως. (ἔτους) ια Αὐρηλίου
Ἀντωνείνου ³Καίσαρος τοῦ κυρίου Τῦβ[ι] κ̄η̄. ἐν

asked : " Carried away by whom ? " He replied :
" By the sitologi and the others. If therefore you
think good, appoint some persons to keep check."
Faustus said : " . . . about this." He replied :
" I will not cease to exert myself (?) at this season
until the business is settled." Faustus asked :
" How much time is needed for the measuring-
out ? " He replied : " The most illustrious praefect
ordered it to be done in 30 days, but we shall need
more than that." Faustus said : " As I said before,
I will explain all the matter to the most illustrious
praefect ; this circumstance too I will explain to him
likewise, that the measuring-out is most urgent, in
order that he may command what he thinks best to
be done." Harpocration, strategus, said : " Meanwhile then you order me to remain ? " Faustus said:
" Wait and continue to do what is necessary ; for
I will write to him to let me know if he wishes you
to come at once." The 2nd year of Antoninus
and Verus the lords Augusti, 28th of the month
Hadrianus.[a]

[a] = Choiak.

244. EXTRACT FROM THE ACTS OF A CHIEF PRIEST

A.D. 171.

From the minutes of his excellency Ulpius
Serenianus, chief priest. The 11th year of Aurelius
Antoninus Caesar the lord, Tubi 28. At Memphis.

Μέμφει. ἠσπάσατο ⁴τὸν λαμπρότατον ἡγ[ε]μόνα
καὶ μετὰ τα[ῦτ]α πρὸς τῷ ⁵'Απείῳ Πανεφρέμ-
μ[[εως]]ει [Σ]τοτοήτιος ἀνθ' οὗ Σατα-⁶βοῦτος
π[ρεσ]βυτέρο[υ] ἱε[ρέ]ως πρ[ο]σαγαγόντ[ος] υἱὸν
⁷[ἑαυτ]οῦ Πανεφρέμμ[ι]ν κα[ὶ ἀξ]ιώσαντος ἐπι-
τρα-⁸πῆναι περιτεμεῖν αὐτὸν ἀ[ν]αδόντ[ο]ς [τ]ε τὴν
περὶ αὐ-⁹τ[ο]ῦ γραφεῖσαν ἐπι[στο]λὴν ὑ[πὸ Σα]ρα-
πί[ωνο]ς στρατηγοῦ ¹⁰'Αρσ[ι]νοείτου 'Ηρακ[λεί]-
δο[υ μερί]δος δ[ι]ὰ 'Αλεξάνδρου ¹¹γυμνασιαρχή-
[σαντο]ς, [κ]εχ[ρ]ονι[σ]μένην [ε]ἰς τὸ διε-¹²ληλυθὸς
ι (ἔτος) Φαῶφι ε̄, Σερηνια[νὸ]ς ἐπύθετο ¹³τῶν
παρόν[τ]ων κορυφα[ί]ων καὶ ὑ[ποκορυ]φαίων καὶ
¹⁴ἱερογραμματέων εἰ [σ]ημ[εῖο]ν ἔχοι ὁ [παῖ]ς.
εἰπόντων ¹⁵ἄσημον αὐτὸν εἶναι [Οὔλπιος] Σερην[ι]-
α[νὸ]ς ἀρχιερεὺς ¹⁶καὶ ἐπὶ τῶν ἱερῶν [σημειω-
σά]μενος τὴν ἐπιστ[ο]λὴν ¹⁷ἐκέλευσεν τὸν παῖ[δα
περιτ]μηθῆναι [κατὰ] τὸ ἔθος. ἀνέγνω(ν).

4. l. Πανεφρέμμιος.

245. DECISION OF A PRAEFECT

P. Oxy. 40.   2nd cent. A.D.

¹'Αντίγραφον ὑπομνηματισμοῦ Οὐα[λερίου Εὐ-
δαί-]²μονος τοῦ ἡγεμονεύσαντος (ἔτους) [. 'Αντωνίνου ³Κα]ίσαρος τοῦ κυρίου Φαμενὼθ ι[. ἐπε]ρχο-
⁴μένου Ψάσνιος. προσελθ[ό]ντ[ος Ψάσνι]ος ⁵καὶ
εἰπόντος· ἰατρὸς ὑπάρχων τὴ[ν τέ]χνην ⁶τούτους
αὐτοὺς οἵτινές με εἰς λειτου[ρ]γ[ί]αν ⁷δεδώκασι
ἐθεράπευσα, Εὐδαίμων εἶπεν· τά-⁸χα κακῶς αὐτοὺς
ἐθεράπευσας. δίδαξον τ[ὸ κατα-]⁹τήκον, εἰ ἰατρὸς
168

He saluted the most illustrious praefect,[a] and after that, as he held audience at the temple of Apis, Panephremmis son of Stotoetis also called Satabous, elder priest, brought forward his son Panephremmis and asked permission to circumcise him,[b] presenting the letter written about him by Sarapion, strategus of the division of Heraclides in the Arsinoite nome, through Alexander, ex-gymnasiarch, dated Phaophi 6 of the past 10th year.[c] Serenianus inquired of the coryphaei and sub-coryphaei and sacred scribes who were present whether the boy had any blemish. When they replied that he was without blemish, Ulpius Serenianus, chief priest and superintendent of the temples, signed the letter and ordered the boy to be circumcised according to custom. Read by me.

[a] The praefect was evidently holding an assize at Memphis.
[b] Boys intended for the priesthood were required to be circumcised, and permission had to be obtained from the chief priest, a Roman official.
[c] Applications were first examined by the strategus, who if he found no impediment gave the parents a letter to the chief priest. Compare No. 338.

245. DECISION OF A PRAEFECT

2nd cent. A.D.

Copy of a minute of Valerius Eudaemon, then praefect, dated year . . . of Antoninus Caesar the lord, Phamenoth 1[.]. Claim of Psasnis. Psasnis appeared and said : " I am a doctor by profession and I have treated these very persons who have nominated me for a public service." Eudaemon said : " Perhaps you treated them unskilfully. If you are a doctor officially practising mummification, tell me

εἶ δημοσ[ιεύ]ων ἐπὶ ταρι[χείᾳ], ¹⁰καὶ ἕξεις τὴν
ἀλειτουργησίαν.

9. Or δημόεσ[ιος τ]ῶν.

246. INQUIRY CONCERNING AN
IRREGULAR APPOINTMENT

B.G.U. 15, col. i.   A.D. 194.

¹Ἐξ ὑπομνηματισμῶν Ἰουλίου Κουιντιανοῦ τοῦ
κρατίστου ²ἐπιστρατηγοῦ. ἔτους δευτέρου Λουκίου
³Σεπτιμίου Σεουήρου Περτείνακος Σεβαστοῦ Μεσορὴ β. μεθ' (ἕτερα)· ⁴κληθέντος Πεκύσις Ἀπύγχεως καὶ ὑπακούσαντος Διάδελ-⁵φος ῥήτωρ εἶπεν·
ἐάν σοι δοκῇ, κάλεσον τὸν τῆς Νείλου ⁶πόλεως
κωμογραμματέα, ᾧ ὁ ἡμέτερος ἐνκαλεῖ. κλη-
⁷θέντος καὶ μὴ ὑπακούσαντος Ἀρτεμίδωρος στρατηγὸς εἶπ[ε]ν· ⁸κωμογραμματέα οὐκ ἔχι ἡ Νείλου
πόλις, ἀλλὰ πρεσβυτέρους ⁹διαδεχομένους. Διά-
δελφος ῥήτωρ εἶπεν· κεκέλευσται ὑπὸ ¹⁰τῶν κατὰ
καιρὸν ἡγεμόνων ἕκαστον ἰς τὴν ἑαυτοῦ κώ-¹¹μην
καὶ μὴ ἀπ' ἄλλης κώμης εἰς ἄλλην μεταφαίρεσθαι.
¹²ὅτι νῦν κωμογραμματεὺς ἐπηρεάζει τῷ συνηγο-
ρου-¹³μ[έ]νῳ, ἀνέδωκεν αὐτὸν πράκτορα ἀργυρικῶν τῆς ἰδίας ¹⁴κώμης εἰς ἄλλην λειτουργείαν.
ἀξιοῖ ἀναγεινώσκων τὰ κε-¹⁵κελευσμένα μὴ ἀφ-
έλκεσθαι ἀπὸ τῆς ἰδίας εἰς ἀλλοτρίαν. ¹⁶Κοιν-
τιανὸς εἶπεν· στρατηγὸς διαλήμψεται, ὃ τῶν ἐμῶν
¹⁷μερῶν καταλάβηται, ἐπ' ἐμὲ ἀναπέμψιν.

11. l. μεταφέρεσθαι.

ᵃ A village in the Fayum.
ᵇ The meaning probably is that a man already under-

the solvent,[a] and you shall have immunity from service."

[a] The solvent used in mummification. The praefect put this question as a test to see whether the applicant knew the rudiments of his profession.

246. INQUIRY CONCERNING AN IRREGULAR APPOINTMENT

A.D. 194.

From the minutes of his excellency Julius Quintianus the epistrategus. The second year of Lucius Septimius Severus Pertinax Augustus, Mesore 2. Extract :—Pekusis son of Apunchis having been summoned and having appeared, Diadelphus, advocate, said : " If it seem good to you, summon the village scribe of Nilopolis [a] whom my client accuses." When he had been summoned and failed to appear, Artemidorus, strategus, said : " Nilopolis has no village scribe, but only elders who are acting as deputies." Diadelphus, advocate, said : " Orders have been given by successive praefects that every individual is to be restricted to service in his own village and not transferred from one village to another.[b] Now because the village scribe has a spite against my client, he has nominated him, though collector of money taxes in his own village, for another service (elsewhere). He begs you, and he is ready to read the orders, not to let him be removed from his own village to a strange one." Quintianus said : " The strategus will decide, referring to me any question which he finds to be my concern."

taking a public service in his own village was not to be appointed to another service in another village.

VI. JUDICIAL BUSINESS

247. A SUMMONS

P. Hib. 30, ll. 13-26.   Before 270 B.C.

¹³[. . . . . τῶν Ἀλε]ξάνδρο[υ]
δεκα-¹⁴[νικὸς Πε]ρδίκκαι Μακεδό[ν]ι τῶν Ἀλεξάν-
δρ[ο]υ ¹⁵[. . . . .]ι ὅτι ὀφείλων μοι κατὰ συν-
γραφὴν ¹⁶[(δραχμὰς) . . ὧ]ν ἔγγυός ἐστιν Ἀντίγονος
Λιμναίου ¹⁷[ταύτας] ἀπαιτούμενος ὑπό μου πολλάκις οὐκ ἀ-¹⁸[ποδίδ]ωις οὔτε τῶι πράκτορι ἠβού-
λου ἐξομο-¹⁹[λογήσ]ασθαι, διὸ δικάζομαί σοι τοῦ
ἀρχαίου ²⁰[καὶ τόκο]υ (δραχμῶν) Ἀν. τίμημα τῆς
δίκης (δραχμαὶ) Ἀν. ²¹[κλήτορες] Καφύσιος
Κῶιος τῶν Ἀλεξάνδρου ἰδιώ-²²[της, ...]λαος
Μένωνος Θρᾶιξ τῆς ἐπιγονῆς. ²³[ἔτους . . ἐφ'
ἱε]ρέως Φιλίσκου τοῦ Σπουδαίου μηνὸς ²⁴[. . . .
. . .]ου ιδ. ἡ δίκη σοι ἀναγραφήσετ[α]ι ἐν ²⁵[τῶι
ἐν Ἡρ]ακλέους πόλει δικαστηρίωι [ἐ]νώπιον ²⁶[. . .
. . . . . ἔ]κπλωι. (2nd hand) δι' Ἐπιμένους.

21. Or .]καφύσιος Edd.

VI. JUDICIAL BUSINESS

247. A SUMMONS

Before 270 B.C.

. . ., decurion of the troop of Alexander, to Perdiccas, Macedonian, . . . of the troop of Alexander, (notifying you) that you owe me by a contract . . . drachmae, for which Antigonus son of Limnaeus is surety, and that though frequently asked by me for this sum you still fail to repay it and refused to acknowledge the debt to the collector, wherefore I am taking legal proceedings against you for principal and interest amounting to 1050 drachmae; the assessment of damages is 1050 drachmae. Witnesses of the summons: Caphysius (?), Coan, private of the troop of Alexander, and . . . laus son of Menon, Thracian of the Epigone. The . . . year, in the priesthood of Philiscus son of Spoudaeus, the 14th of the month. . . . The case will be presented against you in writing in the court at Heracleopolis in your presence . . . (Signed) Through Epimenes.

SELECT PAPYRI

248. REQUEST TO SERVE A SUMMONS

P. Tebt. 303.   A.D. 180.

¹Θέωνι τῷ καὶ Σκυ[. . . . . . στρα(τηγῷ)]
²’Αρσι(νοΐτου) Θεμίστου κα[ὶ Πολ(έμωνος) με-]
ρίδ(ων)] ³παρὰ Κρονίωνος Πακήβκ[εως καὶ Μά-]
ρωνος] ⁴Κρονίωνος καὶ Μάρωνος Μ[άρωνος καὶ]
Πα-]⁵νήσεως Μαρσισούχ[ου] καὶ Παν[ήσεως ’Ον-]
⁶νώφρεως καὶ Πανήσεως [. . . . .] ⁷τῶν ϛ
δι’ αὐτῶν ἱερέων ἀπολυσίμων ⁸ἱεροῦ λογίμου τοῦ
ὄντος ἐν κώμῃ ⁹Τεπτύνει τῆς Πολέμωνο[ς] μερίδος.
¹⁰ἔχοντες πρὸς Κρονίωνα Σαβείνου ¹¹περὶ ὧν εἰς
ἡμᾶς διεπράξατο ἀτοπη-¹²μάτων ἃ καὶ ἐπὶ τοῦ
ῥητοῦ δηλώσω-¹³μεν, ἀξιοῦμεν δι’ ἑνὸς τῶν
περὶ σὲ ¹⁴ὑπηρετῶν παραγγεῖλα[ι] αὐτῷ ὅπως
¹⁵παρατύχῃ εἰς τὸν ἐπ’ ἀγαθῶι γινόμε-¹⁶νον δια-
λογισμὸν ὑπὸ τοῦ λαμπροτά-¹⁷του ἡγεμόνος
Πακτουμ[η]ίου Μ[άγνου]. ¹⁸Κρονίων Πακήβκεως
ἐπιδέδω[κα]. (2nd hand) ¹⁹Μάρων Κρονίωνος
συνεπ[ιδέ-]²⁰δ[ωκα. Μάρ]ων Μάρωνος συ[νεπιδέ-
²¹δωκα. Π]ανῆσις Μαρσισ[ούχου ²²συνεπιδέδω]κα.
Παν[ῆσις ²³’Οννώφρεως συ]νεπι[δέδωκα. - - -

12. l. δηλώσομεν.   17. l. ἡγεμόνος.

249. ENGAGEMENT TO APPEAR IN COURT

P. Hamb. i. 4.   A.D. 87.

¹’Αντίγραφον χειρογραφίας. Νεμεσίωνι β(ασι-
λικῷ) γρ(αμματεῖ) ‘Ηρακλ(είδου) μ(ερίδος) ²Λούκιος
174

248. REQUEST TO SERVE A SUMMONS

A.D. 180.

To Theon also called Scy[. . . . . . .], strategus of the divisions of Themistes and Polemon in the Arsinoite nome, from Cronion son of Pakebkis, Maron son of Cronion, Maron son of Maron, Panesis son of Marsisouchus, Panesis son of Onnophris, and Panesis son of . . ., all six in their own right exempted [a] priests of the famous temple at the village of Tebtunis in the division of Polemon. Having a case against Cronion son of Sabinus concerning the offences which he committed against us, which we will specify at the appointed time, we beg that notice be given him through one of your attendants to appear at the assize [b] to be auspiciously held by the most illustrious praefect Pactumeius Magnus. I, Cronion son of Pakebkis, have presented this. I, Maron son of Cronion, have joined in presenting it. I, Maron son of Maron, have joined in presenting it. I, Panesis son of Marsisouchus, have joined in presenting it. I, Panesis son of Onnophris, have joined in presenting it. . . .

[a] Exempt from ordinary taxes and especially the poll-tax.
[b] The praefect held a yearly assize in certain central towns (*cf.* p. 169, note *a*).

249. ENGAGEMENT TO APPEAR IN COURT

A.D. 87.

Copy of bond. To Nemesion, royal scribe of the division of Heraclides, from Lucius Vettius Epaphro-

Οὐέττιος Ἐπαφρόδιτος. ὀμνύο ³Αὐτοκράτορα
Καίσαρα Δομετιανὸν Σεβαστὸν ⁴Γερμανικὸν εἰ μὴν
ἔως τῆς κγ τοῦ Φαρμοῦθ(ι) ⁵μηνὸς τοῦ ἐνεστῶτος
ϛ′ (ἔτους) Αὐτοκράτορος ⁶Καίσαρος Δομετιανοῦ
Σεβαστοῦ Γερμανικοῦ ⁷καταντήσιν εἰς Ἀλεξάν-
δριαν καὶ προσ-⁸καρτερήσιν τῷ ἱερωτάτῳ τοῦ
κρατίστου ⁹ἡγεμόνος Γαΐου Σεπτιμίου Οὐεγέθου
¹⁰βήματι μέχρι οὗ ἐκβιβάσω ἃ ἔχει πρός με
¹¹Μάρκος Ἀντώνιος Τιτουλήειος στρατιώτης ¹²ἀκο-
λούθως τῇ παρακομισθίσῃ Κλαυδίωι ¹³Χάρητι
στρατηγήσαντι ἐπιστολῇ, εἰ ἔνοχος ¹⁴εἴην τῷ ὅρκῳ.
ἔγραψεν ὑπὲρ αὐτοῦ φαμένου ¹⁵μὴ εἰδέναι γρά[μ-
μα]τα Ἰσίδωρος νομογράφος. ¹⁶Ἐπαφρόδιτος
(ἐτῶν) λε οὐ(λὴ) δακ(τύλῳ) μικ(ρῷ) χιρὸ(ς) δεξι(ᾶς)
¹⁷διὰ Τεβούλου ὑπηρέτου. ¹⁸(ἔτους) ϛ Αὐτοκράτορος Καίσαρος Δομετιανοῦ Σεβαστοῦ ¹⁹Γερμανι-
κοῦ Φαρμοῦθ(ι) γ.

2. *l.* ὀμνύω.   4. *l.* ἦ.   9. *l.* Οὐεγέτου.   13. *l.* ἦ.

250. REPORT OF LEGAL PROCEEDINGS
PER LIBELLUM

P. Oxy. 1877.   About A.D. 488.

²- - - *ex o].ffic(io)*. ἐπιδ(έδωκε) Παμούθιος ὁ
βοηθὸς τῶν κομμέν[των - - - βιβλί-³ον τῇ ὑμε-
τ]έρᾳ ἐξουσίᾳ ὅπερ ἔχω μετὰ χεῖρας καὶ ἀνα-

―――――――
ᵃ That is, by means of a petition recited in the court of the
authority addressed, in this case the *praeses* of the province,
176

ditus. I swear by the Emperor Caesar Domitianus Augustus Germanicus that I will present myself in Alexandria not later than the 23rd of the month Pharmouthi of the current 6th year of the Emperor Caesar Domitianus Augustus Germanicus and will attend the most sacred court of his excellency the praefect Gaius Septimius Vegetus until I have contested the case which Marcus Antonius Tituleius, soldier, is bringing against me, in conformity with the order delivered to Claudius Chares, late strategus, otherwise may I incur the consequences of the oath. Isidorus, public scribe, has written for him, as he professes to be illiterate. (Identification) Epaphroditus, aged 35 years, with a scar on the small finger of the right hand, described by Tebulus, assistant.[a] The 6th year of the Emperor Caesar Domitianus Augustus Germanicus, Pharmouthi 3.

[a] A minor functionary, who wrote this description at the foot of the original bond in place of a signature.

250. REPORT OF LEGAL PROCEEDINGS *PER LIBELLUM* [a]

About A.D. 488.

. . . From the *officium* [b] : " Pamouthius, the assistant in the secretariat, has presented to your excellency a *libellus* which I have in my hands and will read, if

who after hearing it made a pronouncement directing what action should be taken. Nos. 251 and 252 illustrate further stages in cases thus initiated. The whole procedure is typically Byzantine.

[b] The bureau of the *praeses*, at this time the civil governor.

γιγνώσκω, εἰ προστάξει σου τὸ μέγεθος. ⁴. . . . .
Apio Th]eodosius Ioha(n)nes viri sp(ectabilis)
com(es) sacro consist(orii) et praesis pruvinc(iae)
Arc(a)d(iae). ἀνάγν[ωθι. et recitavit. πρὸς τὴν
ὑμετέραν ⁵ἐξουσίαν π]αρὰ Πα[μου]θίου βοηθοῦ
κομμέντων. οἱ ἑξῆς ὑποτεταγμένοι ὁρμώμενοι
[ἀπὸ - - - ὑπεύθυνοί ⁶μοι καθε]στήκασιν κατὰ
διαφόρους τρόπους, καὶ οὗτοι πολλάκις παρ' ἐμοῦ
ὑπομνησθέντε[ς - - - εὐγνωμοσύνην πρὸς ⁷ἐμὲ
θέσ]θαι οὐκ ἠνέσχοντο τοῦ συ[ν]χωρεῖν. παρακαλῶ τὴν ὑμετέραν μεγαλοπρέπειαν πρ[οστάξαι
- - - ⁸. . .] συνελαύνεσθαι πρὸς εὐγνωμοσύνην,
[καὶ] ἐγὼ τούτου τυχὼν χάριτας ὁμολογήσω τῇ
ὑμ[ετέρᾳ μεγαλοπρεπείᾳ - - - ⁹. . . ., μ]εγαλο-
πρεπέστατε κόμες καὶ ἡγε[μὼν] κύριε. εἰσὶν δὲ
Φὶβ καὶ Λισαβὲτ [- - - ¹⁰(2nd hand) . . . .]
Φοιβάμμων πρεσβ(ύτερος) καὶ Κόλλουθος. Παμούθιος βοηθὸς κομμέντ[ων ἐπιδέδωκα (?) ¹¹(1st
hand) . . . . . .] Apio Theodosius I[oha]nnes viri
sp(ectabilis) com(es) sacri consist(orii) et praesis
provinc(iae) Arc(a)d(iae). - - - ¹²ο[. .] ἡ τάξις
ὑπομνήσει ἢ πρὸ δίκης τὰς τοῦ χρησαμένου ˙τῇ
διδασκαλίᾳ . [- - - ἢ ἀντιλέγον-]¹³τας δικάσασθαι
βιβλίον ἐπιστελλομένους. ¹⁴edantur.

Verso : +διφθ(έρα) τῶν ῥιπαρ(ίων) τῆς Ὀξυρυγ-
χ(ιτῶν).

4. l. vir (so in l. 11), sacri, provinc(iae).

your lordship so directs." . . . Apio Theodosius
Johannes, the illustrious count of the sacred consistory [a] and *praeses* of the province of Arcadia [b] :
" Read." And he read : " To your excellency from
Pamouthius, assistant in the secretariat. The underwritten persons, of . . ., became liable to me in
various ways, and these persons, although often
called upon by me [to discharge their obligations and
treat me honestly], would not comply. I request
your magnificence to direct . . . that they be compelled to honest treatment ; and I, having received
this favour, shall acknowledge [the utmost] gratitude
to your magnificence, most magnificent count and
lord *praeses*. They are : Phib and Elizabeth, . . .
Phoebammon, priest, and Colluthus. I, Pamouthius,
assistant in the secretariat, presented this." . . .
Apio Theodosius Johannes, illustrious count of the
sacred consistory and *praeses* of the province of
Arcadia : " . . . the *officium* will call upon them
either to [discharge their debt to] the petitioner
before the case is taken or, if they contest it, to
become parties to a suit, submitting a *libellus*." Let
a summons be served. (Endorsed) Document of the
riparii of Oxyrhynchus. [c]

[a] A Byzantine dignity. The consistory was the emperor's
council.
[b] The province or eparchy of Arcadia, corresponding to
the modern Middle Egypt.
[c] The police officers by whom notice of the sentence was to
be given to the debtors. See No. 228, note b.

251. ABANDONMENT OF LEGAL
PROCEEDINGS

P. Oxy. 1880.   A.D. 427.

¹Με[τ]ὰ τὴν ὑ[π]ατίαν τῶν δεσποτῶν ἡμῶν
Θεοδοσίου τὸ ιβ καὶ ²Οὐ[α]λεντινι[α]νοῦ τὸ β τῶν
[α]ἰ[ω]νίων 'Αγούστων Φαμενὼθ α. ³τῇ τάξει
το[ῦ π]ρίνκιπος τῆς ἐξουσίας τοῦ κυρίου μου τοῦ
μεγαλοπρεπεστάτου ⁴ἄρχοντος τ[ῆ]ς χώρας Φλαουίου Δημητριανοῦ [Μαξί]μου, ἑπομένου ⁵Παύλου
σιγγουλαρίου, Αὐρήλιος Κῦρος υἱὸς Λεωντίου
πρ[α]γμ[α]τε[υ]τῆς ἀπὸ τῆς ⁶μεγ[α]λ[οπ]όλεως
'Αλεξ[α]νδρίας τανῦν χρηματιζώμενο[ς] ἐνταῦθα
⁷τῇ λαμπρᾷ ['Ο]ξυρυγχιτῶν [π]όλει. προσελθὼν
τῇ αὐτῇ ἐξουσίᾳ διὰ ⁸[λι]βέλλου δόσεως ἤτοι
ἐντυχίας ᾐτιασάμην Νηστόριον υἱὸν ⁹Ν[η]στω-
ρί[ο]υ καὶ αὐτὼν 'Αλεξανρδέα πραγματευτὴν περὶ
χρέους ¹⁰καὶ παραστ[α]θέντα καὶ τὼ εἰκανόν μοι
πεποιηκότα κατὰ τοῦτο ¹¹ἐντε[ῦθ]εν οὐδένα λόγον
ἔχω πρ[ὸ]ς ἑ[α]υτὸν οὔτε ἐνκαλῶ οὔτε ¹²ἐνκαλέσω
ταύτης ἕνεκα τῆς προφάσεως, δι' ἧς ὁ[μ]ολογῶ
¹³ἐπομνύμενος θεῶν τῶν παντωκράτωρα καὶ τὴν
εὐσέβιαν ¹⁴τῶν τὰ πάντα νικώντων δεσποτῶν
ἡμῶν Θεοδοσίου καὶ Οὐ-¹⁵αλεντινιανοῦ τῶν αἰωνίων 'Αγούστων ἐνμενὶν με ¹⁶πᾶσι τοῖς ἐνγεγραμ-
μένοις καὶ κατὰ μηδὲν παραβῆναι, ¹⁷καὶ πρὸς
ἀσφάλιαν ταύτην πεποίημε τὴν διάλυσιν ἁπλῆν
¹⁸[γρ]αφῖσαν καὶ ἐπερ(ωτηθεὶς) ὡμολόγησα. (2nd
hand) Αὐρήλιος Κῦρος Λεον-¹⁹[τίου . . . .
. . . . πεπ]οίημα[ι] τὴν διάλυσιν καὶ ὤ-
²⁰[μοσα τὸν θεῖον ὅρκον καὶ ποιήσομαι ὡς πρόκειται.

251. ABANDONMENT OF LEGAL PROCEEDINGS

A.D. 427.

The year after the consulship of our masters Theodosius for the 12th time and Valentinianus for the 2nd time, the eternal Augusti, Phamenoth 1. To the *officium* of the *princeps* [a] of his eminence my lord the most magnificent governor of the province, Flavius Demetrianus Maximus, with the co-operation of Paul the *singularis*,[b] from Aurelius Cyrus son of Leontius, trader, of the great city Alexandria, now doing business here in the illustrious city of Oxyrhynchus. I approached his said eminence by presenting a *libellus* or petition in which I accused Nestorius son of Nestorius, himself an Alexandrian and a trader, concerning a debt ; and since he has been brought forward and has given me satisfaction, I accordingly have henceforth no claim against him, nor do I nor will I accuse him on this account, and I hereby agree, swearing by God the Almighty and the piety of our all-conquering masters Theodosius and Valentinianus the eternal Augusti, to abide by all that is herein written and in no wise to transgress it ; and for security I have made this acquittance, written in a single copy, and in answer to the formal question I gave my consent. (Signed) I, Aurelius Cyrus son of Leontius . . ., have made the acquittance and swore the divine oath, and I will do as aforesaid.

[a] The head of the bureau of the *praeses*.
[b] Orderly attached to the staff of the governor.

---

5. *l.* Λεοντίου.   6. *l.* χρηματιζόμενος.   9. *l.* αὐτόν.
10. *l.* τό, τοῦτο.   11. *l.* [α]ὐτόν.   13. *l.* θεὸν τὸν
παντοκράτορα.   17. *l.* πεποίημαι.

SELECT PAPYRI

Verso: διάλυσις Κύρου πραγματευτοῦ Ἀλεξ-
ανδρέως πρὸς Νη[στώριον.

252. COUNTERPLEA

P. Oxy. 1881.   A.D. 427.

¹Μετὰ τὴν ὑπατίαν τῶν δεσποτῶν ἡμῶν Θεο-
δοσίο[υ] τὸ ιβʹ καὶ Οὐαλεντινιανοῦ τὸ βʹ ²τῶν
αἰωνίων Αὐγούστων Φαμενὼθ ιζ. ³τῇ τάξι τοῦ
πρίγκιπος τῆς ἐξουσίας τοῦ κυρίου μου τοῦ λαμπροτάτου ἡγεμόνος ⁴ἐπαρχίας Ἀρκαδίας ἑπομένων
Πτολεμαίου καὶ Παύλου σιγγυλαρίων ⁵καὶ ἐκ-
βιβαστῶν παρὰ Αὐρηλίων Παϋσιρίου καὶ Ὡρίωνος
υἱῶν Ὡρονα....., ⁶τοῦ αὐτοῦ Ὡρίωνος
ποιουμένου τὸν λόγον ὑπὲρ Ὀννωφρίο[υ] Ὀν-
νωφρ[ί]ου ⁷κατὰ τὴν δοθεῖσαν αὐτῷ ἔγγραφον ἐν-
τολήν, ἀμφοτέρων ἀπὸ κώμης ⁸Σενοκώμεως τοῦ
Ὀξυρυγχίτου νομοῦ. Κύρου ἀπὸ τῆς μεγαλο-
πόλεως ⁹πραγματευτοῦ διὰ λιβέλλου δόσεως προσελθόντος τῇ αὐτῇ ἐξουσίᾳ τοῦ αὐτοῦ ¹⁰κυρίου
μου τοῦ λαμπροτάτου ἡγεμόνος Φλαουίου Δημητριανοῦ Μαξίμου καὶ αἰτιασαμένων ¹¹ἡμᾶς περὶ
χρέους καὶ τῆς ἀποφάσεως ἐμφανισθείσης ἡμῖν
τῆς βουλομένης ¹²ἢ διαλύσασθαι ἢ δικάσασθαι,
ἐπεριζόμενοι τοίνυν τοῖς ἡμετέροις δικαίοις ¹³εἰς
τὴν δέ[ουσ]αν ἀντίρρησιν ἐληλύθαμεν, ἐπικαλού-
μενοι τὴν ἐν τῷ ἀχράντῳ σου ¹⁴δικαστηρίῳ{ν}
διάγνωσιν, εἰς περέωσιν τῶν ἀποφανθέντων.
¹⁵κ[α]τὰ τοῦτο ὁμολογοῦμεν ἐξ ἀλλ⟨ηλ⟩εγγύης

10. l. αἰτιασαμένου.   12. l. ἐπερειδόμενοι.   14. l.
περαίωσιν.

182

(Endorsed)   Acquittance from Cyrus, trader of Alexandria, to Nestorius.

252. COUNTERPLEA

A.D. 427.

The year after the consulship of our masters Theodosius for the 12th time and Valentinianus for the 2nd time, the eternal Augusti, Phamenoth 17.   To the *officium* of the *princeps* of his eminence my lord the most illustrious *praeses* of the eparchy of Arcadia, with the co-operation of Ptolemaeus and Paul, *singulares* and *exsecutores*,[a] from Aurelius Pausirius and Aurelius Horion, sons of Horona . . ., the said Horion speaking on behalf of Onnophrius son of Onnophrius in accordance with the written instructions given to him, both of the village of Senokomis in the Oxyrhynchite nome.   Cyrus, of the great city, trader, having by presentation of a *libellus* appealed to his said eminence, my lord the most illustrious *praeses*, Flavius Demetrianus Maximus, and accused us concerning a debt, and the decision having been notified to us, desiring us either to arrange terms or to come into court, we accordingly relying on our rights have proceeded to the proper counterplea,[b] invoking the judgement of your immaculate court, in performance of the decision.   Accordingly we agree on our mutual

---

[a] Officials who served the summons and saw to the execution of the judgement.

[b] An ἀντίρρησις was properly a counter-statement denying the plaintiff's claims, but in this late document the word is used of a mere declaration that the defendant would contest the case.

ἐπομνύμενοι θεὸν τὸν παντοκράτορα ¹⁶καὶ τὴν
εὐσέβι[α]ν τῶν τὰ πάντα νικώντων δεσποτῶν
ἡμῶν Φλαουίων ¹⁷[Θ]εοδοσίου καὶ Οὐαλεντινιαν[ο]ῦ
τῶν αἰωνίων Αὐγούστων ἐπὶ τῷ ἡμᾶς ἐντεῦθεν
¹⁸ἤδη ἀναπλε[ῦ]σαι εἰς τὴν τάξιν ὅπου δ' ἂν διάγει
τὸ δικαστήριον καὶ δικάσασθαι πρὸς τὸν ¹⁹[προ-
κεί]μενον ἀντίδικον καὶ μὴ ἀπολιφθῆναι ἄχρι πέρατος τύχῃ τὰ τῆς ὑποθέσεως ²⁰[ε]ἰς [τὸ] ἐν μηδε[ν]ὶ
ἡμᾶς μεμφθῆναι. κυρία ἡ ἀ[ντί]ρρησις ἁπλῆ
γρ[α]φεῖσα καὶ ἐπερ(ωτηθεὶς) ὡμολόγησα. (2nd
hand) ²¹Αὐρήλιοι Παυσίριος καὶ Ὡρίων υἱοὶ
Ὥρονα . . [. .] ἀ[π]ὸ κ[ώ]μης Σεν[οκώμε]ως πεποιήμεθα τὴν ²²ἀντίρ‹ρ›ησιν καὶ ὠμόσαμεν τὸ[ν]
θεῖον ὅρκον κα[ὶ] ποιησόμεθα ὡς πρόκειται.
Αὐρήλιος Ἡρακλᾶς ²³Γαϊανοῦ ἔγραψα ὑπὲρ αὐτῶν
γράμματα μ[ὴ εἰ]δότων. (1st hand?) ²⁴di emu
. . . . meu.

Verso: ²⁵ἀντίρρησις Παυσιρίου καὶ Ὡρίωνος
ἀδελφ(οῦ) ἀπὸ Σενοκώμεως.

18. l. διάγῃ.

253. DEPOSITION OF A WITNESS

Annales xx. p. 184.   245 b.c.

¹Μαρτυρεῖ Ἀντιπάτρωι Εὐφρόνιος Ἀπολλωνίδου
Ἀμμωνιεὺς ὡς (ἐτῶν) λε εὐμεγέθης εὔρωστος
κλαστὸς μελίχρους ὀρθόγωνος οὐλὴ ὀφρύων δεξιᾶι(?).
οἰκῶ ἐμ Φιλαδελφείαι τοῦ Ἀρσινοΐτου. ²τοῦ δὲ β
(ἔτους) μηνὸς Πανήμου, ὄντος μου καὶ Νίκωνος καὶ
ἄλλων τινῶν ἐν τῶι Εὐδόξου κουρείωι, παραγενό-

security, swearing by God Almighty and the piety of our all-conquering masters Flavius Theodosius and Flavius Valentinianus the eternal Augusti, that we will forthwith make the voyage to the *officium* wherever the court is held, and will plead our cause against our aforesaid adversary and not abandon it until the case has been brought to a conclusion, so that we may be free from any blame. This counter-plea, of which there is a single copy, is valid, and in answer to the formal question I gave my consent. (Signed) We, Aurelius Pausirius and Aurelius Horion, sons of Horona . . ., of Senokomis, have made this counterplea and sworn the divine oath and will act as aforesaid. I, Aurelius Heraclas son of Gaianus, wrote on their behalf, as they are illiterate. (Subscribed) Executed by me, . . . (Endorsed) Counterplea of Pausirius and his brother Horion, of Senokomis.

253. DEPOSITION OF A WITNESS

245 B.C.

Witness given for Antipater by Euphronius son of Apollonides, of the Ammoniean deme,[a] aged about 35 years, tall, robust, curly-haired, fair-skinned, square-shouldered, with a scar on the right of the eyebrows (?). I live at Philadelphia in the Arsinoite nome. In the month Panemus of the 2nd year, while I and Nicon and some others were in the barber's shop of Eudoxus, Antipater and Simon,[b] for whom

[a] Of Alexandria.
[b] In this case a woman's name.

185

μενος ³'Αντίπατρος καὶ Σῖμον, οἷς μαρτυρῶ, εἰς τὸ
κουρεῖον τοῦτο ἠξίουν Νίκωνα ἀποδοῦναι αὐτοῖς
τὸν υἱὸν αὐτῶν Θεο-⁴δόσιον· Νίκων δὲ ὁ κρινόμενος
πρὸς 'Αντίπατρον οὐκ ἔφατο εἰληφέναι τὸ παιδάριον
παρ' αὐτῶν οὐδὲ ἔχειν αὐτὸ ⁵παρευρέσει οὐδεμιᾶι.

Verso: ⁶Εὐφρονίου. (Docket on left) (ἔτους) β
Γορπιείου κ͞ϛ. φέρει ⁷'Αντιπάτρωι πρὸς ἀντίδικον
⁸Νίκωνα.

254. DEPOSITION OF WITNESSES

Aegyptus xii. pp. 129-130.   A.D. 153.

¹[Οἱ σφραγίσα]ντες ὀμόσαντες τὴν Αὐτοκράτορος
Καίσαρος {Καίσαρος} Τίτου Αἰλίου 'Αδριανοῦ
'Αντω[νείνου Σεβαστοῦ Εὐσεβοῦς τύχην ²καλῆ]
π[ίσ]τει μαρτυρεῖν τὰ ὑπογεγραμμένα ῥήματα·
παρόντες ἐν κώμῃ Φιλαδελφείᾳ τοῦ ['Αρσινοείτου
νομοῦ τῆς 'Ηρακλείδου ³μερ]ίδος πρὸς τῷ Καισαρείῳ οὕτως ψε ἐθεασάμεθα Γάιον Μηούιον 'Απελλᾶν
οὐετρανὸν εἴ[λης 'Απριανῆς δερόμενον] τοῦ στρατηγοῦ 'Ιέρακος κελεύοντος ⁴[ὑπὸ] φυλάκων δύο
ῥάβδοις καὶ κόμμασι· διὸ καλῇ πίστει μαρτυροῦμεν
θεωρήσασθ[αι αὐτὸν δερόμενον ἐν κώμῃ ⁵Φιλ-
αδελ]φ[ε]ίᾳ. ἔτει ιϛ 'Αντωνείνου Καίσαρος τοῦ
κυρίου Μεχεὶρ ιζ. Below, part of the same text,
the deposition having been written as a duplicate
deed.

Verso:]α . . . [. . . . .] Διόδωρος ἐσφ[ρά]-

1. [Οἱ σφρ.] Wilcken: [Σφρ.] Ed.   3. γε E.-H.: {ε}
Ed.: {τ} Wilcken.   4-5. Restoration doubtful.

I testify, came into that shop and asked Nicon to give them back their son Theodosius, and Nicon who is being sued by Antipater denied that he had taken the boy from them or was keeping him on any pretext. (Endorsed) (Testimony of) Euphronius. (Docketed Year 2, Gorpieius 26. Bears witness for Antipater in his case against Nicon.

254. DEPOSITION OF WITNESSES

A.D. 153.

The sealers (declare), having sworn by the fortune of the Emperor Caesar Titus Aelius Hadrianus Antoninus Augustus Pius that they give the following testimony in good faith. Being present in the village of Philadelphia in the division of Heraclides in the Arsinoite nome at the Caesareum [a] we in this way beheld Gaius Maevius Apellas, veteran of the *ala Apriana*,[b] being flogged at the order of the strategus Hierax by two guards with rods and scourgings.[c] Wherefore we in good faith testify that we beheld him being scourged in the village of Philadelphia. The 16th year of Antoninus Caesar the lord, Mecheir 17. (Endorsed) I, . . . Diodorus, have sealed. I, Publius

[a] Temple of the Caesars; compare No. 242, p. 163.
[b] An auxiliary division, stationed in Egypt.
[c] A Roman citizen, as the veteran was, could not be legally scourged if he appealed to the name of the Emperor.

187

γισα. Πούπλις Κορνήλις Ἀμμ[-] ἐσφράγισα.
[Πόπ]λιος Μηούιος ἐσφράγισα. Μάρκος Ἀντώνιος
Διογένη[ς] ἐσφράγισα. Μάρκος Ἀντώνιος ἐσφρά-
γισα. [Κ]ορνήλ[ιος - - - ἐσφράγισα].

255. BAIL FOR FIVE WEAVERS

P. Ryl. 94.   A.D. 14–37.

¹Ἡρακλῆς Πετεσούχ(ου) ἡγούμενος γερδίων ²Εὐ-
ημερήας καὶ Ἀφροδ(ίσιος) Ἀσκληπιάδου ³γραμ-
ματεὺς τῶν αὐτῶν γερδίων ⁴Ἥρωνι χιριστῇ Σώτου
ἐξηγητοῦ χα(ίρειν). ⁵ὁμο{υ}λογοῦ[μ]εν ἐνγεγυῆ-
σ{σ}θαι ⁶παρὰ σοῦ Ἀφ[ε]ῦν Ἀφεῦτος καὶ Ἁρπα-
⁷γάθην Ὀρσε[ν]ούφιον καὶ Ἡρᾶν Ὀρσεν(ούφιος)
⁸καὶ Μέλαν[α Ἑ]ργέως καὶ Ἡρακλῆν ⁹Ἀπολ-
λωνί‹ου›, τοὺς πέντε γερδίους ¹⁰τῶν ἀπὸ τῆς αὐτῆς
Εὐημερήας, ¹¹καὶ ἐπάνανκον παραστῆσι‹ν› σοι
αὐτοὺ‹ς› ¹²ὁπηνίκα ἐὰν ἐρῇ ἐκδικοῦντες τὰ διὰ
¹³τοῦ ὑπομνήματος Πανινούτιος τοῦ ¹⁴Ἀφροδισίου
ἐρι(ουργοῦ ?). Ἀφροδ(ίσιος) ὁ προγεγραμμέ-¹⁵νος
ἔγραψα ὑπὲρ αὐτο‹ῦ› Ἡρακλήου διὰ ¹⁶τ[ὸ] μὴ
εἰδέναι αὐτὸν γράμματα. (ἔτους) ¹⁷[. . Τιβε]-
ρί[ο]υ Καίσαρος Σεβαστοῦ ¹⁸Ἐπεὶφ ιη.

7. l. Ὀρσε[ν]ούφιος.   12. l. αἱρῇ, ἐκδικοῦντας.

Cornelius Amm . . ., have sealed. I, Publius Maevius, have sealed. I, Marcus Antonius Diogenes,
have sealed. I, Marcus Antonius, have sealed. I,
Cornelius . . ., have sealed.[a]

[a] The name of another witness is lost, for as this deposition
is drawn up in accordance with Roman usage, seven witnesses
were required. Each has signed his own name.

255. BAIL FOR FIVE WEAVERS

A.D. 14–37.

Heracles son of Petesouchus, head of the weavers
of Euhemeria,[a] and Aphrodisius son of Asclepiades,
secretary of the same weavers, to Heron, agent of
Sotas, exegetes, greeting. We acknowledge that
we have received from you on bail Apheus son of
Apheus, Harpagathes son of Orsenouphis, Heras son
of Orsenouphis, Melas son of Hergeus, and Heracles
son of Apollonius, all five weavers of the said Euhemeria, and that it is incumbent on us to produce
them to you whenever you choose, to answer the
claims stated in the petition of Paninoutis son of
Aphrodisius, wool-worker. I, the aforesaid Aphrodisius, have written for Heracles, because he is
illiterate. The . .th year of Tiberius Caesar Augustus, Epeiph 18.

[a] A village in the Fayum.

SELECT PAPYRI

256. JUDGEMENT OF THE PTOLEMAIC
COURT OF TEN

P. Gurob 2.   226 b.c. (?)

¹Βασιλεύοντος [Πτο]λεμαίου τοῦ Πτολεμαίου καὶ
Ἀρσινόης θεῶν Ἀδελφῶν ²ἔτους κβ, ἐ[φ' ἱερέως]
τοῦ ὄντος ἐν Ἀλεξανδρείαι Ἀλεξάνδρου καὶ θεῶν
Ἀδελφῶν ³καὶ Εὐερ[γετ]ῶν, κανηφόρου Ἀρσινόης
Φιλαδέλφου τῆς οὔσης ἐν Ἀλεξανδρείαι, ⁴μηνὸς
Δύστρου κβ, ἐγ Κροκοδίλων πόλει τοῦ Ἀρσινοΐτου
νομοῦ, ἐπὶ προ[έδρου] ⁵Ζηνοθέμιδος δικασταὶ Διο-
μήδης, Πολυκλῆς, Ἄνδρων, Θεοφάνης, Μαιάνδριος,
⁶Σώνικος, Διοτρέφης. καθίσαντος ἡμᾶς Πολυ-
δεύκου τοῦ εἰσαγωγέως κατὰ τὸ ⁷παρὰ Ἀριστο-
μάχου τοῦ πρὸς τῆι στρατηγίαι τοῦ Ἀρσινοΐτου
νομ[οῦ τετ]αγμένου ⁸γραφὲν αὐτῶι πρόσταγμα, οὗ
ἐστιν ἀντίγραφον τόδε· " Πολυδ[εύκει χαίρειν].
⁹ἠξίωκεν τὸν βασιλέα διὰ τῆς ἐντεύξεως ἡ Ἡράκλεια καθίσ[αι . . . . -]¹⁰σαντας πάντας δικαστὰς πλὴν ὧν ἂν ἑκάτερος ἐξαναστήσηι
κατὰ τὸ διάγραμ-¹¹μα. (ἔτους) κα Δύστρου ι̅ϛ̅
Παχὼν ι̅θ̅," τάδε ἔγνωμεν πε[ρὶ τῆς δίκης] ἧς
ἐγράψατο ¹²Δωσίθεος Ἡρακλείαι κατὰ τὸ ἔγκλημα
τόδε· " Δωσί[θεος . . . . .]ίου Ἰουδαῖος ¹³τῆς
ἐπιγονῆς Ἡρακλείαι Διοσδότου Ἰουδαίαι καθ[ὰ
. . . .] ¹⁴σαυτὴν ὑπηγόρευσας (?), ὅτι [τοῦ κα (ἔτους) μηνὸς] Περιτίου κβ,

13. Διοσδότου very doubtful.   14. ὑπηγόρευσας (?)
E.-H. : κατηγορησας Ed.

ᵃ A special local court of ten judges chosen by lot. The
scope of its jurisdiction is not known, but it was evidently
used only by foreign residents in the interior.

190

256. JUDGEMENT OF THE PTOLEMAIC COURT OF TEN [a]

226 B.C. (?)

In the 22nd year [b] of the reign of Ptolemy, son of Ptolemy and Arsinoe, gods Adelphi, the priest of Alexander and the gods Adelphi and the gods Euergetae and the canephorus of Arsinoe Philadelphus being those officiating in Alexandria,[c] the 22nd of the month Dystrus, at Crocodilopolis in the Arsinoite nome, under the presidency of Zenothemis, the judges being Diomedes, Polycles, Andron, Theophanes, Maeandrius, Sonicus, Diotrephes.[d] Polydeuces, the clerk of the court, having constituted us in accordance with the order sent to him by Aristomachus, appointed strategus of the Arsinoite nome, of which this is a copy :

" To Polydeuces greeting. Heracleia has requested the king in her petition to form a court of all the judges . . . except such as either party may challenge in accordance with the regulations. Year 21, Dystros 16, Pachon 19 "

we have given judgement as below in the action brought by Dositheus against Heracleia according to the following indictment :

" Dositheus son of . . ., Jew of the Epigone, to Heracleia daughter of Diodotus, Jewess, as you in your . . . of yourself declared (?). (I state) that on

[b] In another copy of the document the year is given as the 21st, which accords better with the other dates.
[c] The scribe did not know or did not trouble to write the names of the eponymous priest and priestess.
[d] Probably two of the judges had been challenged and withdrawn.

SELECT PAPYRI

εἰσιόντος ἐμοῦ ¹⁵τε καὶ ἄλλων ἐν τῆι Ἀπίωνος
[. . . . . ἀ]πὸ τῆς λεγομένης ¹⁶Πασύτιος οἰκίας, ἥ ἐστιν ἐγ Κροκοδίλων
[πόλει τοῦ Ἀρσιν]οΐ[του] ν[ομοῦ] ¹⁷ἀπέναντι τῆς
λεγομένης Πασύτιος οἰκίας τοῦ μ[. . . . .,
παρα]γενομένη εἰς τὸν ¹⁸τόπον τοῦτον μετὰ Καλ-
λίππου τοῦ . . . . . . αν . . . ου ἐλοι-
δόρησας ¹⁹φαμένη με εἰρηκέναι πρός τινας δι[ότι
- - -] ²⁰γυναῖκα, ἐμοῦ δέ σε ἀντιλοιδοροῦντος
οὕτως ἔπτυσας [- - -] ²¹καὶ λαβομέ[νη μ]ου τῆς
ἀναβολῆς τοῦ ἱματίου - - - ²⁶διὸ δικάζομαί σοι
κατα- ²⁷[. . . . . ὕ]βριν (δραχμῶν) σ.
τίμημα τῆς δίκης (δραχμαὶ) [. .]. ὑβρισ[μένος δὲ]
καὶ ²⁸τὸ ἀν[. . . . . . .]αι διὰ τοῦ ἐγκλήματο[ς]
τοῦδε εν[. . . .]τομαι. (ἔτους) κα, [ἐφ' ²⁹ἱερέως
Γαλέσ]του τοῦ Φιλιστίωνος Ἀλεξάνδρου καὶ θεῶν
Ἀδελφῶν καὶ [θεῶν ³⁰Εὐεργετῶν, καν]ηφόρου
Ἀρσινόης Φιλαδέλφου Βερενίκης τῆς Σωσιπόλ[ιος]
³¹μηνὸς [. . . . .]ϛ̄. ἡ δὲ δίκη σοι γραφήσε-
ται ἐν τῶι δικαστηρίωι τῶι ὄντι ἐν ³²τῶι ⟦δικα-
στηρίωι⟧ Ἀρσινοΐτηι νομῶι οὗ εἰσαγωγεὺς Πολυδε[ύ]κης (ἔτους) κα μη-³³νὸς Περιτίου [. .], καὶ
τὸ ἔγκλημα ἔχεις κληθεῖσα ἐνωπία· κλήτορες
. . . .] ³⁴φάνης Νικίου Θρᾶιξ τῶν ἐπέργων,
Ζώπυρος Συμμάχου Πέρσης ³⁵τῆς ἐπιγονῆς."
τούτου δὲ τοῦ ἐγκλήματος ὄντος καὶ Δωσιθέου
³⁶μὲν ⟦αὐτοῦ⟧ οὐ παρόντος καὶ οὔτε τὸν γραπτὸν
λόγον θεμένου οὔτε ³⁷[βου]λομένου κ[ατηγο]ρεῖν,
Ἡρακλείας δὲ παρούσης μετὰ κυρίου Ἀρισ-³⁸τίδου
τοῦ Πρωτέου Ἀθηναίου τῆς ἐπιγονῆς καὶ ἅμα

28. ἐν[επισκήπ]τομαι Ed., but εν doubtful.   37.
[βου]λομένου κ[ατηγ]ορεῖν E.-H. : [. .]γομένου τ[. . .]ορην Ed.
192

Peritius 22 of year 21, as I with other persons was
entering the . . . of Apion . . . from the so-called
house of Pasutis which is in Crocodilopolis in the
Arsinoite nome opposite the so-called house of
Pasutis *a* the . . ., you came to that place with
Callippus the . . . and abused me saying that I
had told certain persons that . . ., and on my
abusing you in return you thereupon spat on me
and seizing the loop of my mantle . . . Wherefore I bring an action of assault against you for
200 drachmae, the assessment of damages being
. . drachmae. And as the assaulted party I by this
indictment . . . The 21st year, the priest of Alexander and the gods Adelphi and the gods Euergetae
being Galestes son of Philistion, the canephorus of
Arsinoe Philadelphus being Berenice daughter of
Sosipolis, the [.]6th of the month . . . The case will
be presented against you in the court sitting in the
Arsinoite nome, of which Polydeuces is the clerk, on
Peritius . . of the 21st year, and you have received
the indictment and have been personally summoned,
the witnesses of the summons being . . . phanes son
of Nicias, Thracian, official employee, Zopyrus son
of Symmachus, Persian of the Epigone."

Whereas this was the indictment, and Dositheus
neither appeared in person nor put in a written statement nor was willing to plead his case ; and whereas
Heracleia appeared with her guardian Aristides son
of Proteas, Athenian of the Epigone, and put in both

a Perhaps the scribe has repeated these words by mistake
and the text should run " opposite the . . . ".

τε ³⁹γραπτὸν λόγον θεμένης καὶ τὰ δικαιώματα
βουλομένης τε ἀπο-⁴⁰λογεῖσθαι τὴν δίκην, ἐπειδὴ
καὶ τὸ διάγραμμα, ὃ καὶ παρέδοτο ⁴¹ἐν τοῖς δικαιώ-
μασιν ἡ Ἡράκλεια, συντάσσει καὶ δικάζειν [. . . .
. . . . . -] ⁴²κῶς, ὅσα μὲν ἐν τοῖς βασιλέως Πτολεμαίου διαγράμμασιν εἴδη ⁴³γεγραμμένα ἢ ἐμφα-
νίζηι τις ἡμῖν, κατὰ τὰ διαγράμματα, ὅσα τε ⁴⁴μὴ
ἔστιν ἐν τοῖς διαγράμμασιν ἀλλ' ἐν τοῖς πολιτικοῖς
νόμοις, κα-⁴⁵τὰ τοὺς νόμους, τὰ δ' ἄλλα γνώμηι
τῆι δικαιοτάτηι [. . . . . . . ⁴⁶. .] συντάσσει, ἐὰν
δὲ ἀμφοτέρων τῶν ἀντιδίκων [κληθέν-⁴⁷των ἐν τῶι
δικαστ]ηρίωι ἑκάτερος οὖν αὐτῶν μὴ βούληι[ται
γραπ-⁴⁸τὸν λόγον θέσθαι] ἢ κατηγορεῖν ἢ ἀποδέ-
χ[ε]σθαι ἡσσ{θ}ᾶσθαι [. . . . . . . .⁴⁹. . .
κρινέ]τωσαν ἀδικῆσαι, ἀπεδικάσαμεν τὴ[ν δίκην.

48. ἢ κατηγορεῖν ἡσσ{θ}ᾶσθαι E.-H. : . . . . . . ορην, ἢ συ-
θασθαι (for συνίστασθαι) Ed.

257. MINUTES OF LEGAL PROCEEDINGS
BEFORE A STRATEGUS

P. Oxy. 37.   A.D. 49.

(Col. 1) ¹'Εξ ὑπομ[ν]ηματισμῶν Τι[βερίο]υ
Κλαυδ[ίο]υ Πασίωνος στρατη(γοῦ). ²(ἔτους) ἐνά-
τ[ο]υ Τιβερίου Κλαυδίου Καίσαρος Σεβαστοῦ
Γερμανικοῦ ³Αὐτοκ[ρά]τορος Φαρμοῦθι γ̄, ἐπὶ
τοῦ βήματος. ⁴[Π]εσοῦρι[ς] πρὸς Σαραεῦν. Ἀρι-
στοκλῆς ῥήτωρ ⁵ὑπὲρ Πεσούριος· Πεσοῦρις, ὑπὲρ
οὗ λέγωι, ζ (ἔτους) ⁶Τιβερίου Κλαυδίου Καίσαρος
194

a written statement and justificatory documents, and was also willing to defend her case ; and whereas the code of regulations which was handed in by Heracleia among the justificatory documents directs us to give judgement in a . . . manner on all points which any person knows or shows us to have been dealt with in the regulations of King Ptolemy, in accordance with the regulations, and on all points which are not dealt with in the regulations, but in the civic laws,[a] in accordance with the laws, and on all other points to follow the most equitable view ; but when both parties have been summoned before the court and one of them is unwilling to put in a written statement or plead his case or acknowledge defeat (?) . . . he shall be judged guilty of injustice ; we have dismissed the case.

[a] The special laws of a Greek city ; see for instance Nos. 201 and 202.

257. MINUTES OF LEGAL PROCEEDINGS BEFORE A STRATEGUS

A.D. 49.

From the minutes of Tiberius Claudius Pasion, strategus.[a] The 9th year of Tiberius Claudius Caesar Augustus Germanicus Imperator, Pharmouthi 3, at the court. Pesouris *versus* Saraeus. Aristocles, advocate for Pesouris, said : " Pesouris, for whom I appear, in the 7th year of Tiberius Claudius Caesar

[a] The strategi and epistrategi in Roman times had no jurisdiction in their own right, but they were often delegated to try cases by the praefect, who was the supreme judge.

τοῦ κυρίου ἀνεῖλεν ⁷ἀπὸ κοπρίας ἀρρενικὸν σωμάτιον ὄνομα Ἡρα-⁸κ[λᾶν]. τοῦτο ἐνεχείρισεν τῆι
ἀντιδίκωι· ἐγένε-⁹το ἐνθάδε ἡ τροφεῖτις εἰς υἱὸν
τοῦ Πεσούριος. ¹⁰τοῦ πρώτου ἐνιαυτοῦ ἀπέλαβεν
τὰ τροφεῖα. ¹¹ἐνέστη ἡ προθεσμία τοῦ δευτέρου
ἐνιαυτοῦ ¹²κα[ὶ] πάλιν ἀπέλαβεν. ὅτι δὲ ταῦτα
ἀληθῆι λέγωι, ¹³ἔστιν γράμματα αὐτῆς δι᾽ ὧν
ὁμολογεῖ εἰλη-¹⁴φέναι. λειμανχουμέν[ο]υ τοῦ σω-
ματ[ί]ου ἀπέ-¹⁵σπασεν ὁ Πεσοῦρις. μετ[ὰ] ταῦτα
καιρὸν εὑροῦσ[α] ¹⁶εἰσεπήδησεν εἰς τὴν τοῦ ἡμετέρου [ο]ἰκίαν ¹⁷καὶ τὸ σωμάτιον ἀφήρπασεν, καὶ
βούλεται ὀν[ό-]¹⁸ματι ἐλευθέρου τὸ σωμάτιον ἀπ-
ενέγκασ-¹⁹θαι. ἔχω[ι] πρῶτον γράμμα τῆς τρο-
φείτιδος, ²⁰ἔχωι δεύτερο[ν] τῶν τροφείων τὴν
[ἀ]ποχή[ν]. ²¹ἀξιῶι ταῦ[τα] φυλαχθῆ[ν]αι. Σα[ρα]-
εῦς· ²²ἀπεγαλάκ[τισά] μου τὸ [π]αιδίον, κα[ὶ] τούτων ²³σωμάτιόν μοι ἐνεχειρίσθη. ἔλαβ[ον] παρ᾽
αὐ-²⁴τῶν τοὺ[ς] πάντας ὀκτὼι στατῆρας. μετὰ
²⁵ταῦτα [ἐτελεύ]τησεν τ[ὸ σ]ωμάτιο[ν . στα-]²⁶τήρων
π[ερ]ιόντων. νῦν βούλον[ται τὸ] (Col. 2) ¹ἰ̓[δι]όν
μου τέκνον ἀποσπάσαι. Θέων· ²γράμματα τοῦ
σωματίου ἔχομεν. ³ὁ στρατηγός· ἐπεὶ ἐκ τῆς
ὄψεως φαίνεται τῆς ⁴Σαραεῦτος εἶναι τὸ παιδίον,
ἐὰν χιρογραφήσηι ⁵αὐτῆι τε καὶ ὁ ἀνὴρ αὐτῆς
ἐκεῖνο τὸ ἐνχει-⁶ρισθὲν αὐτῆι σωμάτιον ὑπὸ τοῦ
Πεσούριος ⁷τετελευτηκέναι, φαίνεταί κατὰ τὰ ὑπὸ
⁸τοῦ κυρίου ἡγεμόνος κριθέντα ἀποδοῦσαν ⁹αὐτὴν
ὃ εἴληφεν ἀργύριον ἔχειν τὸ [ἴδιο]ν ¹⁰τέκνον.

the lord picked up from a rubbish-heap a male foundling called Heraclas. This he entrusted to the defendant, and the nurse's contract which was made here referred to it as a son of Pesouris. She received her wages for the first year. The pay-day for the second year came round and again she received them. To show that these statements are true, we have her receipts in which she acknowledges payment. As the foundling was being starved, Pesouris took it away. Subsequently, seizing an opportunity, she burst into the house of my client and carried the foundling off; and she seeks to obtain possession of the foundling as being her free-born child. I have here, first, the written contract for nursing, I have, secondly, the receipt for the wages. I demand that these be recognized." Saraeus : " I weaned my own child and the foundling of these persons was entrusted to me. I received from them the whole eight staters. Subsequently the foundling died, [.] staters being still unearned.[a] Now they seek to take away my own child." Theon [b] : " We have the papers relating to the foundling." The strategus : " Since from its looks the child appears to be the son of Saraeus, if she and her husband will sign a sworn declaration that the foundling entrusted to her by Pesouris has died, I give judgement in accordance with the decision of our lord the praefect that on paying back the money which she has received she shall have her own child."

[a] As the child died before the end of the second year, some of the wages paid in advance were not actually earned.
[b] Perhaps the advocate of Saraeus.

SELECT PAPYRI

258. MINUTES OF LEGAL PROCEEDINGS BEFORE A PRAEFECT

Oxy. 237, col. vii. 19-29.   A.D. 133.

¹⁹Ἐξ ὑπομνη-²⁰ματισμῶν Φλαουίου Τειτιανοῦ
τοῦ ἡγεμονεύσαντος. (ἔτους) ιβ θεοῦ Ἁδριανοῦ
Παῦνι η̄, ἐπὶ τοῦ ἐν τῇ ἀγορᾷ βήματος. Ἀντωνίου
²¹τοῦ Ἀπολλωνίου προσελθόντος λέγοντός τε διὰ
Ἰσιδώρου νεωτέρου ῥήτορος Σεμπρώνιον πενθερὸν
ἑαυτο[ῦ] ἐκ μη[τ]ρὸς ἀφορ-²²μῆς εἰς διαμάχην
ἐλθ[όν]τα ἄκουσαν τὴν θυγατέρα ἀπεσπακέναι,
νοσησάσης δὲ ἐκείνης ὑπὸ λοίπης τὸν ἐπιστράτηγον
Βάσσον ²³μεταπαθῶς ἀναστραφ[έν]τα ἀποφαίνεται
ὅτι οὐ δεῖ αὐτὸν κωλύεσθαι εἰ συνοικεῖν ἀλλήλοις
θέλοιεν, ἀλλὰ μηδὲν ἠνυκέναι· ²⁴τὸν γὰρ Σεμπρώνιον ἀποσι[ω]πήσαντα τοῦτο καὶ τῷ ἡγεμόνι
περὶ βίας ἐντυχόντα ἐπιστολὴν παρακεκομικέναι
ἵνα οἱ ἀντίδι-²⁵κοι ἐκπεμφθῶσι· αἰτεῖσθαι οὖν ἐὰν
δοκῇ μὴ ἀποζευχθῆναι γυναικὸς οἰκείως πρὸς
αὐτὸν ἐχούσης. Δίδυμος ῥήτωρ ἀπεκρεί-²⁶νατο
μὴ χωρὶς λόγου τὸν Σεμπρώνιον κεκεινῆσθαι· τοῦ
γὰρ Ἀντων[ί]ου προσενεγκαμένου θυγατρομειξίας
ἐγκαλεῖν, μὴ ἐνέγκαν-²⁷τος τὴν ὕβριν τῇ κατὰ τοὺς
νόμους συνκεχωρημένῃ ἐξουσίᾳ κεχρῆσθαι, ἡτιᾶ-
σθαι δ' αὐτὸν καὶ περὶ [. . . . . .]πες ἐ[ν-
κ]λημάτων. ²⁸Προβατιανὸς ὑπὲρ Ἀντωνίου προσ-
έθηκεν, ἐὰν ἀπερίλυτος ἦν ὁ γάμος, τὸν πατέρα
μήτε τῆς προικὸς μηδὲ τῆς παιδὸς τῆς ἐκδεδο-

22. *l.* λύπης.   23. *l.* ἀποφαίνεσθαι.   28. For
μηδὲ *l.* μήτε.

198

258. MINUTES OF LEGAL PROCEEDINGS
BEFORE A PRAEFECT

A.D. 133.

From the minutes of Flavius Titianus, sometime praefect. The 12th year of the deified [a] Hadrianus, Pauni 8, at the court in the market-place. Antonius son of Apollonius appeared and stated through his advocate, Isidorus the younger, that his father-in-law Sempronius at the instigation of his mother had made a quarrel with him and taken away his daughter [b] against her will, and that when the latter fell ill through grief the epistrategus Bassus, being moved to sympathy, declared that if they wished to live together Antonius ought not to be prevented, but all to no effect. For Sempronius ignoring this declaration presented to the praefect a complaint of violence and had brought back an order that the rival parties were to be sent up for trial. Antonius therefore claimed, if it pleased the praefect, that he should not be separated from a wife affectionately disposed towards him. The advocate Didymus replied that Sempronius had had good reason for having been provoked. For it was because Antonius had threatened to charge him with incest that he, refusing to bear the insult, had used the power granted him by the laws [c] and had also brought . . . accusations against the other. Probatianus on behalf of Antonius added that if the marriage had not been annulled the father had no power either over the dowry or over

---

[a] " Deified " was of course not part of the original dating.

[b] Daughter of Sempronius and wife of Antonius.

[c] That is, by Egyptian law, which gave the father this authority over a married daughter.

199

²⁹μένης ἐξουσίαν ἔχειν. Τειτιανός· διαφέρει παρὰ
τίνι βούλεται εἶναι ἡ γεγαμημένη. ἀνέγνων.
σεσημ(είωμαι).

ᵃ Official signature of the praefect.

259. JUDGEMENT OF A PRAEFECT

P. Ryl. 75, ll. 1-12.   A.D. 150

¹Ἐξ ὑπομνημ[α]τισμῶν Μου[να]τίου. ²(ἔτους) ιγ
θεοῦ Αἰλίο[υ] Ἀντωνίνου Φ[αρ]μοῦθι κβ. ³προσ-
αχθέντων Γλύκωνος Διονυσίου ⁴καὶ Ἀπολλωνίου
Γλύκωνος μεθ' ἕτερα ⁵Ἀρχ[έλ]αος ῥήτωρ εἶπεν·
ἄπορός ἐστιν ⁶ὁ Γλύκων καὶ ἐξίσταται. Μ[ο]υνά-
τιος ⁷εἶπεν· ζητηθήσεται ὁ πόρος αὐτο[ῦ], ἤδη
⁸μέντοι τύπος ἐστὶν καθ' ὃν ἔκρεινα ⁹πολλάκις καὶ
τοῦτο δίκαιον εἶναί ¹⁰μοι φαίνεται ἐπὶ τῶν ἐ[κ]ξ-
ιστανο⟦με⟧-¹¹μένων ὥστε, εἴ τι ἐπὶ περιγρ[α]φῇ
¹²τῶν δανιστῶν ἐποίησαν, ἄκοιρον εἶναι.

12. l. ἄκυρον.

260. PETITION FOR RELIEF FROM A GUAR-
DIANSHIP, AND MINUTES OF PROCEED-
INGS

J.E.A. xviii. p. 70.   A.D. 173 (?).

¹[Ἀντίγρα]φον [ἀνα]φ[ορ]είου. ²Ἰουλίωι Λου-
κούλλωι τῷ κρατίστῳ ἐπιστρατήγῳ ³[π]αρὰ Γαΐου

the daughter whom he had given away. Titianus said : " The decisive question is with whom the married woman wishes to live." Read over and signed by me.[a]

259. JUDGEMENT OF A PRAEFECT

A.D. 150

From the minutes of Munatius.[a] The 13th year of the deified Aelius Antoninus, Pharmouthi 22. Glycon son of Dionysius and Apollonius son of Glycon having been brought in, during the course of the proceedings Archelaus, advocate, said : " Glycon is without means and resigns his property." Munatius said : " His means shall be inquired into ; there is however a principle according to which I have often given judgement and which seems to me to be equitable in cases of persons resigning their property, namely that, if they have done anything to defraud their creditors, the resignation shall not be valid."

[a] L. Munatius Felix, who was praefect about A.D. 150.

260. PETITION FOR RELIEF FROM A GUAR- DIANSHIP, AND MINUTES OF PROCEED- INGS

A.D. 173 (?).

Copy of application. To his excellency the epi-strategus Julius Lucullus from Gaius Apollinarius

SELECT PAPYRI

Ἀπολιναρίου Νίγερος Ἀντινοέως Ὀσοραντινοείου
τ[ο]ῦ καὶ Ἑρμα[ιέ]ως. Μάρκος Ἀνθέστιος ⁴Γέ-
μελλος οὐετρανὸς τελευτῶν δι' ἧς ἔθετο διαθήκης
ἠθέλησεν κληρονό[μο]ν ἑαυτοῦ γενέσθαι τὴν θυ-
⁵γατέρα Οὐαλερίαν Τερτίαν τὴν καὶ Θαισάριον
ἀφήλικα τῶν ἀπολιφθέντων ὑπὸ αὐτοῦ ἐν νομῷ
Ἀρσι-⁶νοείτῃ, ἧς τῆς ὀρφανείας κατέλιψεν ἐπιτρόπους μὲν ἐμὲ τὸν Ἀπολινάριον Νίγερα καὶ
Οὐαλέριον Ἰκόμωνα, ἐπακολουθήτριαν δὲ τὴν τῆς
παιδὸς μάμμην Οὐαλερίαν Σεμπρονίλλαν. κεκε-
λευσμένου ⁸οὖν, κύριε, ὑπό τε Ἐρεννίου Φιλώτα
τοῦ ἐπιστρατηγήσαντος καὶ Ἀντω[ν]ίου Μάκρωνος
ὁμοίως ⁹περὶ τοῦ Ἀντινοέα μηδενὸς ἄλλου ἐπι-
τροπεύειν ἢ μόνου τοῦ ἐν τῇ νομαρχίᾳ Ἀ[ν]τι-
νοέως, οὐ δυνάμε-¹⁰νος οὖν οὐδὲ αὐτὸς ὑπακούειν
ταύτῃ τῇ ἐνχειρισθείσῃ μοι ἐπιτροπῇ ἀξιῶ, ὑποτάξαι
σοι τῷ κυρίῳ ¹¹μου ἀντίγραφ[ον] τῶν ἐφ' ὁμοίων,
ἀπαλλαγῆναι τούτου κατὰ τὰ κελευσθέντα καὶ τὸ
δόξαν σοι κελεῦσαι ¹²γενέσθαι, ἵνα ὦ [β]εβοηθη-
μένος. διευτύχει.

Ἐστι δὲ ἀντίγραφον. (ἔτους) ιᾱ Αὐτοκράτορος
Καίσαρος ¹³Τίτου Αἰλίου [Ἁδρι]ανοῦ Ἀντωνίνου
Σεβαστοῦ Εὐσεβοῦς Μεσορὴ ξ̄. κληθέντος ἐκ
βιβλιδ<ί>ου Εὐδαίμονος ¹⁴ᶜἙρμαίου, προσελθόντος
Διονυσίου καὶ ἀναγνωσθέντος τοῦ ἐπιδοθέντο[ς]
ὑπὸ αὐτοῦ βιβλιδίου, Φιλώ-¹⁵τας εἶπεν· πόθεν ἦν
[ὁ] καταλιπὼν Εὐδαίμονα ἐπί[τ]ροπον; Ἀπολλώνιος νεώτερος εἶπεν· Ῥωμαῖος ¹⁶[ὢν κατῴκησ]εν
ἐν [Ἰ]βιῶνι Παννυκτέρει. Φιλώτας εἶπεν· τοῦτο
δικαίως ἀ[π]έλεγεν εἰ <μὴ> Ἀντινοεὺς ἦν ¹⁷[ὁ

3. l. Ὀσειραντινοείου.   10. l. ὑποτάξας.   16. ⟨μή⟩ E.-H.
202

Niger, Antinoite, of the Osirantinoean tribe and the Hermaean deme.[a] Marcus Anthestius Gemellus, veteran, expressed in the will which he drew up his dying wish that his daughter Valeria Tertia also called Thaisarion, a minor, should be heir of the property left by him in the Arsinoite nome. As guardians of her orphan state he appointed me, Apollinarius Niger, and Valerius Comon, and as associate the girl's grandmother, Valeria Sempronilla. Now as it has been enjoined, my lord, by Herennius Philotas the former epistrategus and by Antonius Macron likewise that an Antinoite shall not act as guardian for any person except only an Antinoite belonging to the nomarchy,[b] and as I myself am therefore unable to accept this guardianship which has been entrusted to me, I have subjoined for you, my lord, a copy of the decisions in such cases and beg that I be relieved of this task in accordance with these injunctions and that you order your decision to be carried out, so that I may gain relief. Farewell.

The copy is : The 11th year of the Emperor Caesar Titus Aelius Hadrianus Antoninus Augustus Pius, Mesore 6. Eudaemon son of Hermaeus having been summoned in consequence of a petition, and Dionysius having come forward and the petition presented by him having been read, Philotas said : " What by origin was the person who appointed Eudaemon a guardian ? " Apollonius the younger said : " He was a Roman residing at Ibion Panukteris." [c] Philotas said : " He did right to refuse this duty if the person

---

[a] Antinoe or Antinoopolis was instituted by Hadrian as a true Greek city and the citizens were divided into tribes and demes.

[b] Under the administration of the nomarch of Antinoopolis.   [c] A village in the Hermopolite nome.

καταστήσα]ς αὐτὸν ἐ[πίτ]ρ[ο]πον, ἄλλῳ γὰρ οὐδενὶ
ἀγώγιμός ἐστιν ἐπιτ[ρο]πεύει<ν> αὐτοῦ τῶν κτη-
μάτων ¹⁸[ἢ Ἀντινοεῖ] τῶν ἐν τῇ νομαρχίᾳ. Ἀπολλώνιος εἶπεν· ἀποδίξομεν αὐτοὺς ἀντιλαβομένους
¹⁹[τῆς ἐπιτροπῆς] καὶ πάντα πεποιηκότας ὡς ἐπιτρόπους. Φιλώτας εἶπεν· ὅτι μ[ὲ]ν οὐκ ὀφε<ί>λι
ὁ Εὐδαί-²⁰[μων ἐπιτροπ]εύειν εἰ μὴ μόνου Ἀντινοέως κέκριται. εἰ δὲ ἀντελάβετο αὐτῇ[ς] τῆς
ἐπιτροπῆς, ²¹[καὶ κριτὴν κ]αὶ λογοθέτας δώσωι.
Ἀπολλώνιος ὁ νεώτερος εἶπεν· Εὐδαί[μω]ν Ἑρ-
μ[αίο]ν οὐκ ἀντελάβετο ²²[. . . . . a]ὐτοῦ
ἀντελάβετο. Φιλώτας εἶπεν· Ἀντινοεύς ἐστιν;
Ἀντινοεύς ἐστιν; ἀπεκρίνατο· ναί, ²³[καὶ αἰτεῖ
εὐ]εργεσίαν τὴν ἀπὸ σοῦ. Φιλώτας εἶπεν· δώσω
κριτὴν καὶ λογοθέτην τὸν αὐτὸν ὃς ἐξετά-²⁴[σει εἰ
ἀντ]ελάβετο τῆς ἐπιτροπῆς καὶ τοὺς λόγους ἐξετά-
σει καὶ ἐπαναγκάσει τὸ φανὲν παρὰ τοῖς ἐπι-²⁵[. . .
. . δο]ῦναι] τῶι κ[ατ]ασταθησομένωι ἐπιτρόπῳ. ὁ
δὲ τῆς Ἑρμοῦ πόλεως ἐξηγητὴς προνοήσει ²⁶[ἐπί-
τροπ]ον κατασταθῆναι. Θρακίδας εἶπεν· ἵνα μὴ
δοκῶμεν σεσιωπηκέναι ἀσφαλιζόμεθα ²⁷[. . . . .
. . .]α ἥμισυ τάλαντα ὀφείλειν τῇ ὀρφάνῃ. Φιλώτας εἶπεν· ἃ εἶπας γέγραπται. Διόσκορος ²⁸[εἶπεν·
ἀξιο]ῦμεν τὸν κατασταθησό[μενο]ν ἐπίτροπον ἐπὶ
τοῖς α[ὐ]τοῖς δικαίοις κατασταθῆναι ²⁹[ἐφ' οἷς
Εὐ]δαίμων κατὰ τὰς διαθήκα[ς] κατεστάθη. Φιλώτας εἶπεν· ἐπὶ τοῖς αὐτοῖς κατασταθῆναι. ³⁰[Διόσ-
κορος ε]ἶπεν· ε[ἴ σο]ι δοκεῖ, δὸς ἡμεῖν τὸν λογοθέτην. Φιλώτας εἶπεν· Ἑρμίαν τὸν ἀγορανομήσαντα
³¹[καὶ κοσμη]τε(ύσαντα).

18. [ἢ Ἀντινοεῖ] E.-H.: [οὐχ ὑπαρχόν-]των Ed.   21. [καὶ

who appointed him guardian was not an Antinoite, for he is not obliged to act as guardian of the property of any person other than an Antinoite belonging to the nomarchy." Apollonius said : " We will prove that they undertook the guardianship and have done all the work of guardians." Philotas said : " It has been decided that Eudaemon is not bound to act as guardian except only for an Antinoite. But, if he undertook the actual guardianship, I will provide a judge and auditors." Apollonius the younger said : " Eudaemon son of Hermaeus did not undertake it, his . . . undertook it." Philotas said : " Is he an Antinoite ? Is he an Antinoite ? " He replied : " Yes, and he asks your clemency." Philotas said : " I will provide a judge and auditor in one, who shall investigate whether he undertook the guardianship and examine the accounts and compel the . . . to deliver whatever is found in their possession to him who is to be appointed guardian. And the exegetes of Hermopolis shall see to the appointment of a guardian." Thracidas said : " Lest we be thought to have suppressed the fact, we certify that we owe . . . and a half talents to the orphan girl." Philotas said : " Your statement has been taken down." Dioscorus said : " We ask that the prospective guardian be appointed with the same rights as those with which Eudaemon was appointed by the will." Philotas said : " He shall be appointed with the same rights." Dioscorus said : "If you please, give us the auditor." Philotas said : " I give you Hermias the ex-agoranomus and ex-cosmetes."

E.-H. : [τόν Ed.
ἐπι[τηδείοις καί] Ed.

24-25. ἐπι-[. . . . . δοῦναι] E.-H. :
30. ε[ἰ σο]ι Wilcken : ἐ[μο]ί Ed.

SELECT PAPYRI

Καὶ ἄλλου. ᾿Αντώνιος Μάκρων ᾿Αφροδισίῳ
ἐνάρχωι ἐξηγητῇ ᾿Αντινό<ο>υ πόλεως ³²[χα(ίρειν).
περὶ τῶν] ὀ[ρ]φάνων ᾿Αντινοέων περὶ ὧν γράφεις,
τῶν μὲν ἐνθάδε πραγμάτων αὐτοῖς ἐπιτρόπους
³³[ἀξιοχρέους κ]αὶ ἐπιτηδείους κατάστησον, τῶν δὲ
ἐν ἄλλοις νομοῖς ἐπίστειλον τοῖς στρατηγοῖς ἵνα
³⁴[. . . . .]ω καὶ αὐταὶ ἐπι[τη]δείους
καὶ ἀξιοχρέους ἕλωνται. (ἔτους) κβ Αὐτοκράτορος
Καίσαρος Τραϊανοῦ ³⁵[᾿Αδριανοῦ Σεβασ]τοῦ Φαμενὼ[θ] θ.

᾿Αντίγρ(αφον) ὑπογραφῇ[ς]. παραγγείλῃ τοῖς
οἰκείοις τῆς ³⁶[ὀρφάνης ἢ ἐν]έτυχέ μοι τὴν ἀξίωσίν
σου δοκιμα[σθ]ῆν<αι>. ἡ ἔγβασις τῆς διαλήμψεως
ἐὰν ³⁷[. . . . .]ῃ τὴν ἐπιτροπήν, οὐκ
ἀγνοεῖς ὅτι δὴ καὶ εἰς τὸ παρεληλυθὸς τῷ σῷ
κιν-³⁸[δύνῳ ἐξε]χώρησας. (ἔτους) ιγ Παῦνι β.
ἀπόδος.

32. Suppl. E.-H., following Wilcken: [. . . . τῶν δή] Ed.
34. l. αὐτοί? 35. l. παραγγεῖλαι? 36. δοκιμα[σθ]-
ῆν<αι> E.-H. : δοκιμα[στ]ήν Ed. 38. ἐξε]χώρησας E.-H. :
ἀνε]χώρησας Ed.

261. MINUTES OF PROCEEDINGS BEFORE
A PRAEFECT

P. Strassb. 22, ll. 10-24. A.D. 207.

¹⁰Σουβατιανοῦ ᾿Ακύλα ἡγεμονεύσαντος ¹¹(ἔτους)
ιε″ Φαμενὼθ ιζ. κληθέν[τ]ων Σαβείνου ¹²καὶ
Μαξίμου Διονυσίου καὶ ὑπακο[υ]σάντων, ¹³μεθ᾽
ἕτερα ᾿Ακύλας εἶπεν· τί ἀποκρείνῃ ¹⁴πρὸς τὸν

(Copy) of another. Antonius Macron to Aphrodisius, officiating exegetes of Antinoopolis, greeting. With regard to the Antinoite orphans about whom you write, for their property there appoint as their guardians reputable and suitable persons, but for their property in other nomes write to the strategi to choose suitable and reputable persons . . . The 22nd year of the Emperor Caesar Trajanus Hadrianus Augustus, Phamenoth 9.

Copy of the subscription. Announce to the relatives of the orphan who petitioned me that your request has been approved. If the outcome of the judgement . . . the guardianship, you are aware that as regards the past you have withdrawn at your own risk.[a]   Year 13, Pauni 2.   Deliver.[b]

[a] That is, he was still responsible for his conduct of the guardianship in the past.
[b] To the official who posted up such petitions with the answers given to them.

261. MINUTES OF PROCEEDINGS BEFORE A PRAEFECT

A.D. 207.

Before the former [a] praefect Subatianus Aquila, on Phamenoth 17 of the 15th year.   Sabinus and Maximus Dionysius having been called and having answered the summons, in the course of the proceedings Aquila said : " What reply do you make

[a] The present copy was made in the time of a later praefect. In the original minutes the heading would be " Before the praefect Subatianus Aquila."

χρόνον [τ]ῆς νο[μ]ῆς, ὥς φησι[ν] με-[15]τὰ τὴν ὠνὴν
τῆς Παϋσοράπιος ἐτῶ[ν] σχε-[16]δὸν δεκατεσσάρων,
καὶ τὴν ἐν τούτῳ σιωπήν; [17]᾿Ασκληπιάδης ῥήτωρ
εἶπεν· γέγονεν. ᾿Ακύ-[18]λας εἶπεν· διατάξεις εἰσὶν
τῶν κυρίων περὶ [19]τῶν ἐν τοῖς ἔθνεσιν οἰκούντων,
ἂν ἀλλα-[20]χόσε νομὴ παρακολουθήσῃ ἔχοντός τινος
[21]ἀφορμὴν κἂν βραχεῖαν δικαίαν κατοχῆς, [22]σιω-
πήσαντος τοῦ νομίζοντος αὐτῷ διαφέρειν [23]καὶ
ἀνασχομένου ὑπὲρ δεκαετίαν, ἔχειν τ[ὸ] βέ-[24]βαιον
τοὺς κατασχόντας.

15. l. Ταϋσοράπιος.

262. MINUTES OF LEGAL PROCEEDINGS BEFORE AN EPISTRATEGUS

P. Thead. 15.   A.D. 280–281.

[1]῎Ετους ς τοῦ κ[υρί]ου ἡμῶν Μάρκ[ο]υ Αὐρη-
λίο[υ Π]ρόβου Σεβα[στο]ῦ, ἐν τῷ ᾿Αρσι-][2]νοΐτῃ,
πρὸ βήματος. [3]᾿Ισίδωρος ἀπὸ [συν]ηγοριῶν εἶπ(εν)·
῎Αρτεμις ἐπιτυγχάνει δύο μηνῶν κα[θεστ]υίη καὶ
[4]οἱ παῖδες οἱ ἀφήλικες προσεδρεύουσίν σου τῷ
δικαστηρίῳ· προ[σ]εδρεύου-[5]σιν δὲ ἐκ κελεύσεως
τοῦ διασημοτάτο[υ] ἡγεμόνος ἀναπέμψαντος [6]τὸ
πρᾶγμα ἐπὶ σέ, ἵνα τὴν βίαν κωλύσῃς· τὴν δὲ βίαν
πολλάκις παρεθέ-[7]μεθα διὰ τῶν σῶν ὑπομνημάτων.
Συρίων γὰρ μετὰ τὸν θάνατον [8]τοῦ πατρὸς τῶν

3. συνηγορ{ι}ῶν Ed.   κα[θεστ]υίη (l. -υῖα) for -εστῶσα E.-H.

---

[a] See No. 293.

with regard to the period of possession, which is alleged to have been nearly fourteen years from the date of the sale made by Tausorapis, and with regard to your silence during this time?" Asclepiades, advocate, said: "We admit the fact." Aquila said: "There are rescripts of our emperors[a] concerning parties who live in the provinces, to the effect that if the possession is transferred elsewhere by someone who has rightful, even if transitory, grounds for entering into it, should the party who considers himself to be the owner remain silent and make no objection for more than ten years, the claim of the holders shall be confirmed."

[a] See No. 214. The translation follows the view of Kreller that the rescripts refer to the possession of movables, such as slaves, and not, as formerly supposed, to the occupation of immovable property.

262. MINUTES OF LEGAL PROCEEDINGS BEFORE AN EPISTRATEGUS

A.D. 280–281.

The 6th year of our lord Marcus Aurelius Probus Augustus, in the Arsinoite nome, at the court. Isidorus, advocate, said: "Artemis has appeared before you two months ago, and her sons, who are minors, are attending your court. This they do in consequence of the command of the most eminent praefect who has referred the case to you,[a] in order that you may put a stop to an act of violence which we have several times placed on record in your minutes. For Syrion after the death of the boys' father cast a

209

παίδων ἐποφθαλμιάσας τοῖς θρέμμασιν τοῖς ὑπὸ
[9]τοῦ πατρὸς αὐτῶν καταλιφθεῖσιν, ποιμὴν γὰρ
ἐτύγχανεν, ἐξήκον-[10]τα ὄντα τὸν ἀριθμὸν ἥρπασεν,
καὶ σὺ ἀγανακτ[ή]σας ἐκέλευσας [11]αὐτῷ τῷ Συρίωνι
παραστῆσαι τοὺς ποιμένας μεθ᾽ [ὧ]ν ἐποίμαινεν ὁ
τῶν [12]παίδων πατὴρ καὶ Αὐνῆν καὶ τὸν ἀδελφὸν
αὐτοῦ, [ἵνα] οὕτως μηδεμιᾶς [13]ἀμφισβητήσεως
οὔσης ἀποκατασταθῇ τοῖς παιδίοις τὰ πρόβατα.
ἀλλ᾽ ὅρα τί [14]διαπράττεται ὁ Συρίων· ἀντιπράττει
τοῖς ὑπὸ σοῦ κελευσθεῖσιν καὶ [15]τοῖς ὑπὸ τῆς
ἡγεμονίας· καὶ διὰ τοῦτο καὶ νῦν μαρτυρόμεθα
ὅπως ἤδη ποτὲ κε⟦λε⟧-[16]λεύσῃς αὐτὸν ἀχθῆναι καὶ
ἀποδοῦναι τοῖς παιδίοις ἃ ἥρπασεν. ὁ ἐπί-[17]τροπος
εἶπ(εν)· ἐπειδὴ Συρίων εἰς τὰ ἀναγκαιότερα τὰ τῷ
ταμιείῳ διαφέ-[18]ροντα ἀπέσταλται, ὅσον οὐδέπω
ἐπανελθὼν ἀποκριθήσεται πρὸς τὰ [19]ἐπιφέροντα
αὐτῷ. Ἰσίδωρος ἀπὸ συνηγοριῶν εἶπ(εν)· ἐὰν οὖν
φυγοδικήσῃ; [20]Αὐρήλιος Ἡρακλείδη[ς] ὁ κρά(τιστος) ἐπιστρά(τηγος) εἶπ(εν)· ἐντευχθεὶς ὅρον δώσω.

12-13. [ἵνα] . . . ἀποκατασταθῇ E.-H.: [καὶ] . . . ἀποκατα-
σταθη Ed.   20. ὁ κρά(τιστος) ἐπιστρά(τηγος) as suggested
in P. Ryl. 114. 35, note.

263. MINUTES OF A TRIAL BEFORE THE JURIDICUS

P. Bour. 20.   After A.D. 350.

[1]- - -]o v(iris) c(larissimis) co(n)s(ulibu)s die
Idus Novembr(es) Ἀθὺρ [2]ιζ. [praesentibus] H[o]ro
et Nonna et Dionu[s]io Gennadius d(ixit)· ὑπὲρ

210

covetous eye on the animals left by their father, who
was a shepherd, and seized them to the number of
sixty ; and you, struck with indignation, commanded
Syrion to produce the shepherds with whom the boys'
father associated, both Aunes and his brother, in order
that thus, if the facts were not disputed, the sheep
should be restored to the children. But see how
Syrion is behaving : he resists your commands and
those of the praefect ; and therefore we now again
call upon you to command at once that he be brought
before you and made to surrender what he stole to
the children." The representative (of Syrion) said :
" Syrion has been dispatched on pressing business
affecting the Treasury, but the moment he returns
he will reply to the charges against him." Isidorus,
advocate, said : " What if he should flee from
justice ? " His excellency the epistrategus, Aurelius
Heraclides, said : " If you apply to me, I will fix a
limit."

263. MINUTES OF A TRIAL BEFORE THE JURIDICUS

After A.D. 350.

In the consulship of . . . and . . . the most illustrious, November 13, Hathur 17. Horus and Nonna
and Dionysius being present, Gennadius said : " I

Εὐ[σ]τοργίου κατ' ἐντολὴν δοθεῖσαν Ὤρῳ καὶ
ἀναγνώσομαί σοι τὴν ἐντολὴν τὴν δοθεῖσαν ³[Ὤρῳ
ὑπὲρ Εὐ]στοργίου, ἥτις ἐν τοῖς ὑπομνήμασιν τοῖς
πραχθεῖσιν κατ' ἐντολὴν ἐπὶ τῆς σῆς καθοσιώσεως
ἀνελήμφθη. ⁴[Fl(avius) Gennadius v(ir) p(erfectissimus) j]uridic(us) Alex(andreae) d(ixit)· ἀνάγνωθι.
Gennadius d(ixit)· ἀναγνώσομαι, et rec(itavit)· Sergio
et Nigriniani v(iris) c(larissimis) co(n)s(ulibu)s die Φαῶφι
ιθ ecc(aetera). O(rator) adjecit· ⁵[τοιαύτη μέν ἐστι]ν ἡ
ἐντολή· ἀξιοῦμεν δὲ τὴν παροῦσαν ἢ ἀπ[ο]στῆναι τοῦ
μέρου[ς] τοῦ διαφέροντος τῇ βοηθου[μένῃ], τετάρτου μὲν αὐλυδρίου, ἡμίσεως δὲ ⁶[τοῦ ἄρτου, τετάρ]-
του δὲ δωρεᾶς καὶ ἀποθήκης, ἢ τὴν ἀποκατά-
στασιν ἡμῖν ποιήσασθαι τούτων ἢ τὸ ἄξιον στεγα-
νόμιον ὅπερ ἂν παράσχοιεν ἕτερος, ⁷[ἀρχιτέκτονός?
τι]νος ἐπιθεοροῦντος περὶ τοῦ αὐλυδρίου τὸ παραρτίδιον ὅπερ καὶ [ἐ]κοῦσα ἀποδώσει⟨ν⟩ συνέστηκεν. Nonna d(ixit)· εἰς τὸ μέρος Εὐστοργίου
⁸[. . . . .]υδισι ἐδώκα[μεν] τὸ τέταρτον. ⁹[Fl(avius) Gennad]ius v(ir) p(erfectissimus)
ju[ridic(us) Alex(andreae) d(ixit)· ἀκό]λου[θόν] ἐστιν
ἀ[ρχιτ]έκτον[α ἐ]πὶ τῶ[ν] τόπων γενόμε[ν]ον
δοκ[ιμ]άσαντα ὁρίσαι πόσον ὀφείλι ¹⁰[. . . . . ὑπὲρ
τοῦ τετάρτου τ]οῦ τε αὐλυδρίου καὶ τ[ῆς] ἀποθήκης Εὐστοργί[ῳ] Νόννα στεγανόμιο[ν . . . . .]

4. l. Nigriniano.   7. l. ἐπιθεωροῦντος.

ᵃ Eustorgion is the plaintiff who is suing her sister
Nonna for her share of the property which was left to them
and to their two brothers Philadelphus and Dionysius in
equal parts.   It will be noticed that in the text of the papyrus
the dates and headings are in Latin, which at this period
was the official language for the minutes of proceedings
before the higher courts, while the speeches are reproduced

appear on behalf of Eustorgion [a] in virtue of a mandate given to Horus, and I will read you the mandate given to Horus on Eustorgion's behalf, which has been recorded in the minutes of proceedings conducted by mandate before your worship." His eminence Flavius Gennadius, juridicus [b] of Alexandria, said : " Read it." Gennadius said : " I will read it," and he read out : " In the consulship of Sergius and Nigrinianus the most illustrious, Phaophi 19, etc." The advocate continued : " Such is the mandate, and we demand that the woman now present shall either abandon the portion which belongs to my client, namely a fourth of the cottage, a half loaf,[c] a fourth of the donation [d] and of the storehouse, or make delivery of them to us or else pay the proper rent which another person would pay, letting an architect scrutinize with regard to the cottage the subsidiary bread allowance [e] which she of her own accord has agreed to give." Nonna said : " For the portion of Eustorgion we have already given the quarter . . ." His eminence Flavius Gennadius, juridicus of Alexandria, said : " It is right that an architect shall go to the place and after examination determine the amount which Nonna ought to pay to Eustorgion as rent for the fourth part of the cottage and the storehouse and

in Greek, in which they were no doubt delivered. Compare No. 250.

[b] The juridicus or δικαιοδότης was a judge, usually a Roman knight, appointed by the Emperor and subordinate only to the praefect, to whom he acted as assistant.

[c] Apparently the four heirs were to receive between them two loaves daily.

[d] The nature of this " donation " is not clear.

[e] The meaning of the Greek word παραρτίδιον is obscure. The translation assumes it to be a payment in bread as rent for the cottage.

. . τηθη[να]ι καὶ τοῦτο Νόννα‹ν› [11]["Ωρῳ τ]ῷ
ταύτης [ἐκδίκῳ πορ]ίσαι διὰ τὸ μάλειστα καὶ
[Νόν]ναν τούτῳ τῷ λόγῳ συνδεδραμηκέναι καὶ
[ὑπισ]χνῖσθαι ὅσον ἐὰν ἕτερος μέλλοι [12][. . . . . .]-
ρέσειν τ[οσοῦτον ἔν]δον οἰκοῦσαν παρασχ[εῖ]ν,
προνοουμένης εἰς τοῦτο τῆς τάξεως. [Genna]dius
d(ixit)· ταῦτα μὲν π[ε]ρὶ τοῦ αὐλυδρίου [13][καὶ
περ]ὶ τῆς ἀπο[θήκης εἶπ]εν ἡ σὴ καθ[ο]σίωσις εἰ[ς
τὸ πρό]σωπον Νόννης· ἀξ[ιούμ]εν δὲ καὶ [[τὸ]] περὶ
τοῦ ἡμί[σεως] τοῦ ἄρτου καὶ τοῦ τετάρτου τῆς
δωρεᾶς [14][ἀποδοῦν]αι αὐτ[ὰ Νόνναν τῷ] ἐντολι-
καρί[ῳ] τῆς συνη[γορο]υμένης, ἅπαξ ἐντολῆς παρα-
σχεθείσης. [15][Fl(avius) Gennadi]us v(ir) p(erfectissimus) juri[dic(us) Alex(andreae) d(ixit)·] τί ‹φη›σιν καὶ
περὶ τούτων [Νό]ννα; Nonna d(ixit)· ἐπὶ ἀντίδικον
λαμβάνιν ‹ἐ›ξουσίαν. Gennadius d(ixit)· ἐπειδὴ
ἀμφιβάλλι [16][. . . . .
ἐντ]ολὴ δὲ ἀνεγνώσθη καὶ γ[ρα]μματεῖον αὐτῆς
ἔχομεν ὁμολογούσης αὐτῇ φυλάττιν [τ]αῦτα [[τα]],
κατὰ τὴν ἐντολὴν ἀποδότω. [17][Fl(avius) Gennad]ius
v(ir) p(erfectissimus) ju[ridic(us) Alex(andreae) d(ixit)·
γρα]μματεῖ[ο]ν ὅ φῃς ἔχε[ι]ν ἀνάγνωθι. et rec(itavit)·
Αὐρηλία [Ν]όννα θυγά[τηρ] Ἡλί‹του› δίκαι[ο]ν
παίδων ἔχουσα Αὐρη[λί]α [18][Εὐστοργίῳ ἀδελφῇ μου]
συν[πα]ρόντος καὶ το[ῦ] ἀν[δρός] σου Αὐρηλίου
Φ‹ιλ›έου Ἀπολλωνίου χαίρειν. ὁμολογοῦμ[εν]
μεμισθῶσθαι καὶ παρειληφέναι παρὰ σοῦ [19][μ]έρος
τέταρτον ecc(aetera). O(rator) Gennadius d(ixit)·
ὡμο[λόγ]ηται καὶ τὸ ἀρτίδιον δι[α]φέρειν ἐκείνῃ,
λέγω δὴ τὸ ἥμισυ καὶ τὸ τέταρτον τῆς δωρεᾶς,
[20]καὶ ἀξιοῦμεν αὐτὴν ἀπολύειν ταῦτα αὐτὰ τὰ
ἀρτίδι[α] τῷ μέρι τῷ ἡμετέρῳ. C[ur]us d(ixit)·

that Nonna shall furnish this amount to Horus the other's representative, especially as she has concurred in this proposal and promises, so long as she lives therein, to pay as much as another person would be expected to do, the execution of this measure being seen to by my office." Gennadius said : " With regard to the cottage and the storehouse such is your worship's decision, pronounced in the presence of Nonna. With regard again to the half loaf and the quarter of the donation we demand that Nonna shall render them to the mandatory of the plaintiff, the mandate having been given once for all." His eminence Flavius Gennadius, juridicus of Alexandria, said : " What says Nonna to this again ? " Nonna said : " That I seek authorization to deal with my opponent (?)." Gennadius said : " Since she is in doubt . . ., and whereas the mandate has been read out and we possess a document in which she acknowledges that she is keeping these things for Eustorgion, let her give them up in accordance with the mandate." His eminence Flavius Gennadius, juridicus of Alexandria, said : " Read the document which you say you possess " ; and he read out : " Aurelia Nonna daughter of Elitas, possessing the *jus liberorum,*[a] to Aurelia Eustorgion my sister, accompanied by your husband Aurelius Phileas son of Apollonius, greeting. I acknowledge that I have leased and taken over from you a fourth part etc." The advocate Gennadius said : " This is an acknowledgement that the bread also belongs to Eustorgion, that is to say, the half loaf and the quarter of the donation, and we demand that she shall deliver these same allowances to our side." Cyrus said : " She acknowledges that

[a] See No. 305.

215

ὁμολογεῖ καὶ Εὐστόργιον ἔχειν ἥμισυ μέρος ἄρτου,
²¹ὁμολογεῖ δὲ καὶ τῆς δωρεᾶς μέρος τέταρτον, καὶ
ἀξιοῖ τὸ δικαστήριον ὁρίσαι τίνι δέοι παρασχεθῆ-
ναι [ἐ]ξ ὀνόματος ἐκείνου. ²²Fl(avius) Gennadius
v(ir) p(erfectissimus) juridic(us) Alex(andreae) d(ixit)·
ἀκόλουθόν ἐστιν κατὰ τὴν παρασχεθεῖσαν ἐντολὴν
ὑπὸ Εὐστοργίου Ὥρῳ καὶ ἀφ' ὧν ἡ ²³ἀνάγνωσις
τῆς συνταχθείσης ὑπὸ Νόννης ὁμολογίας ἐδίδαξεν
καὶ τὸ ἥμισυ μέρος [τ]οῦ ἄρτου καὶ τῆς ²⁴δωρεᾶς
τὸ τέταρτον τῷ ἐκδίκῳ Εὐστοργίου Ὥρῳ παρὰ
Νόννας ἀποκατασταθῆναι. Gennadius d(ixit)· ταῦτα
μὲν ἡ σὴ ²⁵καθοσίωσις ἀπεφήνατο, οἷς καὶ τὸ
ἔργον προσενεχθῆναι ἀξιοῦμεν διὰ τῆς τάξεως.
ἐπειδὴ δὲ καὶ Διονύσιος ἕστηκεν, ἀξιοῦμεν ²⁶αὐτὴν
εἰπεῖν τί βούλεται καὶ περὶ τούτου. Curus
d(ixit)· Διονύσιος μὲν καὶ ἀδελφός ἐστιν· διὰ
δὲ τὸ μὴ ἔχειν παρακολουθήσεις ²⁷κουράτωρ
αὐτῷ κατεστάθη, ὁ δὲ ἀδελφὸς Φιλάδελφος ὃς
καὶ ἐν τῇ Αἰγύπτῳ ἐστὶν καὶ οὐ μετὰ πολὺ ἥξει·
τέως δὲ ὁ παῖς καὶ ²⁸συν[ο]ικῖ τῇ ἀδελ[φῇ] καὶ
τὸν ἄρτον κομίζε[ται] καὶ οὐδεὶς φθόνος ἐστίν.
²⁹Fl(avius) Gennadius v(ir) p(erfectissimus) juridic(us)
Alex(andreae) d(ixit)· τοῦτο δῖξον. Curus d(ixit)· κουρά-
[το]ρα ἔχει ὃς καὶ ἄπεστιν· ὁ δὲ ἀντίδικος ὑπανα-
πίσας τοῦτον ³⁰κατέσχεν βουλόμενος πάλιν ἑτέραν
περιγραφὴν ἐργέσασθαι κατὰ τῆς βοηθο[υ]μένης.
³¹Fl(avius) Gennadius v(ir) p(erfectissimus) juridic(us)
Alex(andreae) d(ixit)· ἐπειδὴ κουράτορος ἐμνημό-
νευσας, ἀνάγνωθι ὅπως κουράτωρ ³²γεγένηται
Φιλάδελφος Διονυσίου τοῦ παρόντος. Curus d(ixit)·

30. l. ἐργάσασθαι.

Eustorgion is entitled to a half loaf, likewise a quarter share of the donation, and she asks the court to decide to whom they ought to be delivered in the name of that person." His eminence Flavius Gennadius, juridicus of Alexandria, said : " It is right that, in accordance with the mandate given by Eustorgion to Horus and in consequence of what we have learned from the recital of the agreement made by Nonna, both the half loaf and the quarter of the donation shall be handed over by Nonna to Horus the representative of Eustorgion." Gennadius said : " Such is the decision pronounced by your worship, and we ask that effect be given to it by your office. But since Dionysius also has come forward,[a] we ask her to say what her intentions are about him." Cyrus said : " Dionysius again is her brother ; but as he is unfit for business, a guardian has been appointed for him in the person of his brother Philadelphus who is in Egypt [b] and will be here before long ; meanwhile the boy lives with his sister and receives his bread without any grudging." His eminence Flavius Gennadius, juridicus of Alexandria, said : " Prove this." Cyrus said : " He has a guardian, who however is absent, and our opponent has suborned this boy and taken control of him with the intention of practising one more fraud against my client." His eminence Flavius Gennadius, juridicus of Alexandria, said : " Since you have spoken of a guardian, read the document showing how Philadelphus has become guardian of Dionysius here present." Cyrus said : " The guardian is

[a] The case of Eustorgion *versus* Nonna having been settled, the younger brother Dionysius is now brought forward as a second claimant against Nonna, and the advocate Gennadius pleads for him also.

[b] That is, in Egypt proper, not in Alexandria.

ἐν τῇ Αἰγύπτῳ ἐστὶν ὁ κουράτωρ, ἡ δὲ ἀδελφὴ
[33]χορηγεῖ μέρος τοῦ ἄρτου τῷ ἀδελφῷ καὶ οὐ
κωλύει εἰσιόντα αὐτὸν καὶ οἰκοῦντα ἐν τῇ αὐλῇ.
[34]Fl(avius) Gennadius v(ir) p(erfectissimus) juridic(us)
Alex(andreae) d(ixit)· ὁ κουράτωρ ἀπαντήσας οὐ
κωλυθήσεται τούτοις χρήσασθαι [35]τοῖς λόγοις
οἷσπερ καὶ σὺ νῦν λέγεις, εἴ γε ἀληθῆ ἐστιν τὰ
παρὰ σοῦ εἰρημένα. Curus d(ixit)· [36]ἵνα μ[ὴ] ὁ παῖς
ὑπαναπισθεὶς ὑπὸ τοῦ ἀντιδίκου δοκοίη περι-
γραφήν τινα ὑπομένειν—τοῦτο γὰρ σπουδάζει—
μηδεμίαν [37]καινοτομίαν γίγνεσθαι ἀπόντος τ[οῦ]
κουράτορος· ἕτοιμος γάρ ἐστιν ἡ ἀδελφὴ χορηγήσιν
Διονυσίῳ καὶ τὸ [38]μέρος τοῦ ἄρτου καὶ τὸ στεγα-
νόμιον τὸ ἐπιβάλλον. [39]Fl(avius) Gennadius v(ir)
p(erfectissimus) jurid(icus) Alex(andreae) d(ixit)· τέως
καθ' ἃ ἐπηγγίλατο Νόννα σπουδασάτω τὴν χορη-
γίαν τοῦ τε ἡμίσεως ἄρτου, [40]ἔτι γε μὴν καὶ τοῦ
στεγανομίου Διονυσίῳ ἀμέμπτως παρέχ[ειν]· εἰ
γὰρ κἂν πρό[ς] τι βραχὺ τῆς χορηγίας [41]τούτων
παραμελήσειεν, δυνήσεται πρόσοδον ποιησάμενος
τῷ δικαστηρίῳ Διονύσιος τῆς ὀφι-[42]λομένης αὐτῷ
ἐπικουρίας τυχ[[ε]]ῖν. Gennadius d(ixit)· πόται
προσάγι ὅν φησιν; ἡμῖς γὰρ οὐδὲ εἴσμεν [43]ὅλως
τοιοῦτόν τι πεπραγμένον ὁποῖον διατίνεται, κουράτορα ἐσχηκέναι τὸν καὶ ἐρρωμένον [44]τὴν διάνο[ι]αν
καὶ ἑστῶτα καὶ ἀπαίτησιν ποιούμ[ε]νον τῶν αὐτῷ
διαφερόντων. Curus d(ixit)· ἐπειδὴ ἐν τῷ [45]Ἀρ-
[σ]ιν[οε]ίτ[ῃ] ἐστὶν ἴσω τεσσεράκοντα ἡμερῶν
προσάγομεν ἐκῖνον. [46]Fl(avius) Gennadius v(ir)
p(erfectissimus) juridic(us) Alex(andreae) d(ixit)·
εἰ μὴ ἴσω τῶν τεσσεράκοντα ἡμερῶν τὸν λεγό-
με[ν]ον εἶναι κουράτορα Διονυσίου [47]προσαγάγοι

218

in Egypt, and the sister supplies to her brother his portion of bread and does not prevent him from entering and living in the cottage." His eminence Flavius Gennadius, juridicus of Alexandria, said : " When the guardian appears, he will be free to use the pleas which you now make, provided that what you have said is true." Cyrus said : " Lest we should find that the boy, suborned by our opponent, is being used for some fraud—for that is our opponent's aim—let no new step be taken in the absence of the guardian ; for his sister is prepared to give Dionysius both his share of bread and his due portion of the rent." His eminence Flavius Gennadius, juridicus of Alexandria, said : " For the present let Nonna in accordance with her promise exert herself to furnish to Dionysius without fault both the half loaf and besides that the rent ; for if she should be even a little negligent in doing this, Dionysius shall be empowered to make an appeal to the court and obtain the relief to which he is entitled." Gennadius said : " When will he produce the person he speaks of ? For we have no knowledge at all of any such thing as he asserts having taken place, of a guardian having been given to one who is sound of mind and has come forward claiming the property which belongs to him." Cyrus said : " Seeing that he is in the Arsinoite nome, we will produce him within forty days." His eminence Flavius Gennadius, juridicus of Alexandria, said : " If within forty days Nonna should not produce to the court the person said to be the guardian of Diony-

---

42. *l.* πότε.   προσάγι ὅν E.-H. : προσάγιον Ed.

Νόννα τῷ δικαστηρίῳ ἢ αὐτὸς δι᾽ ἑαυτοῦ παρὼν
ἐπιδίξ[[ε]]ιεν ἑαυτὸν κουράτορα σὺν νόμῳ ⁴⁸αὐτοῦ
γεγε[ν]ῆσθαι ἐντευχθείη τε τὸ δικαστήριον αὖθεις
ὑπὸ Διονυσίου, τότε προ[σ]ταχθήσεται καὶ ἡ νομὴ
⁴⁹ὑπὸ Νόν[ν]ας τοῦ ἡμίσεως τοῦ ἄρτου καὶ τοῦ
τετάρτου τῆς δωρεᾶς, ἔτι γε μὴν καὶ τοῦ τετάρτου
μέρους ⁵⁰τοῦ τε αὐλυδρίου καὶ τῆς ἀποθήκης Διονυσίῳ ἀποκατασταθῆναι. ⁵¹Exemplum.

264. ORDER FOR EXECUTION OF A JUDGEMENT

P. Tor. 13 (= U.P.Z. 118).   136 (or 83) B.C.

¹Τῶι ἐν Μέμφει ξενικῶν πράκτορι. τῆς γεγενη-
μένης ὑπογραφῆς ὑπόκειται ²τὸ ἀντίγ[ρα]φον. ἐπι-
τε[λε]σθήτω οὖν καθὼς συνκέκριται. ³(ἔτους) λδ
Τῦβι ιε.

⁴Ἔτους λδ Τῦβι ε̄ ἐν Μέμφει τοῦ Μεμφίτου.
χρηματισταὶ τῶν τὰς βασιλικὰς Ἀλέξανδρος
⁵Ἀλεξάνδρου Φιλομητόρειος, Ἡρακλείδης Ἡρακλείδου Θεσμοφόριος, Σωγένης Σωγένους ⁶Κοινεὺς
[ο]ἱ τὰ βασιλικὰ καὶ προσοδικὰ καὶ ἰδιωτικὰ κρί-
νοντες. ⁷καταστάντος Χονούφιος τοῦ Πετήσιος,
τοῦ δὲ προσκεκλημένου Ψινταέους οὐχ ὑπακούσαντος, ⁸διὰ πλείον[ων] ὁ Χονοῦφις <ἐξ ἧς ἐ>δε-
δώκει ἐντεύξεως ἐσήμανεν δεδανεικέναι τῶι εὐθυνο-

ᵃ See p. 41, note c.
ᵇ Assize judges officiating in boards of three.

sius or he himself appear of his own accord and
prove that he has been legally constituted the boy's
guardian, and if the court should again be appealed
to by Dionysius, then an order will be made that the
possession now held by Nonna of his half loaf and his
quarter of the donation and also his quarter share of
the cottage and storehouse is to be handed over to
Dionysius." Copy.

264. ORDER FOR EXECUTION OF A JUDGEMENT

136 (or 83) B.C.

To the collector of foreign debts [a] in Memphis.
Appended is a copy of the decision which has been
given. Let the judgement be executed accordingly.
Year 34, Tubi 15.

Year 34, Tubi 5, at Memphis in the Memphite
nome. Chrematistae [b] in the service of the king [c] :
Alexander son of Alexander, of the Philometorean
deme,[d] Heraclides son of Heraclides, of the Thesmo-
phorian deme, Sogenes son of Sogenes, of the
Coinean deme, judges of Crown and fiscal and private
cases. Chonouphis son of Petesis having appeared
and Psintaes having failed to answer the summons,
Chonouphis referring to the petition which he had
presented explained at length that he had lent to the

[c] Understanding λειτουργίας as the substantive to be
supplied with τὰς βασιλικάς.
[d] A deme of Alexandria. The two following demes have
not been identified, but they certainly belonged to a Greek
city in Egypt.

[9]μένωι [κατ]ὰ συγγραφὴν τροφῖτιν τὴν ἀναγραφεῖ-
σαν διὰ τοῦ γραφίου ἀργυ(ρίου) (δραχμὰς) φ ἐπὶ
τῆι ἐξονομαζο-[10]μένηι Θα[υ]ῆτι τῆι καὶ Ἀσκλη-
πιάδι εἰς τὸ χορηγεῖν ταύτηι καθ᾽ ἔτος ὀλυρῶν
(ἀρτάβας) ξ καὶ ἀργ(υρίου) (δραχμὰς) οβ [11][συ]νευ-
δοκησάσης τῆς τε τοῦ Ψινταέους γυναικὸς Θαυῆτος
καὶ τοῦ ἀμφοτέρων υἱοῦ Ζμανρέους, [12]προσδια-
σταλ[έ]ντος τὰ ὑπάρχοντα αὐτῶν ὑποκεῖσθαι πρὸς
τὸ δίκαιον τῆς συγγραφῆς ⟨- - -⟩, διά τε τοῦτο
καὶ [13]ἠξιώκει ἐ[κ]τεῖσαι αὐ[τ]ὸν τὰς προκειμένας
ἀργυ(ρίου) (δραχμὰς) φ καὶ ἐτῶν δ τὰς συναγομένας ὀλυ(ρῶν) (ἀρτάβας) σμ [14]ὡς τῆς (ἀρτάβης)
ἀ[ρ]γυ(ρίου) (δραχμὰς) β ⟨- - -⟩ τὰς δὲ πάσας
ἀργυ(ρίου) (δραχμὰς) Ἀσξη, βλαβέων δὲ καὶ
δαπανημάτων χα(λκοῦ) (τάλαντα) ε, καὶ ἐὰν [15]μὴ
ἀπαντήσῃ ἐπὶ τὸ κριτήριον, ἐπισταλῆναι τῶι τῶν
ξενικῶν πράκτορι συντελεῖν αὐτῶι [16]τὴν πρᾶξ[ιν]
τῶν προκειμένων κεφαλαίων. τὰ μὲν τῆς ἐνκλή-
σεως εἰς ἐπίγνωσιν ἦκτο [17]τῶι Ψινταεῖ ἕνεκα τοῦ
κεκομίσθαι τὸ ἀντίγραφον τῆς ἐντεύξεως ἐνωπίωι
διὰ τοῦ [18]ἀπὸ τοῦ κ[ριτ]ηρίου ὑπη[ρέτ]ου, τῶν δὲ
κατ᾽ αὐτοὺς προτεθέντων καὶ ἄλλοτε μὲν καὶ τῆι
β [19]τοῦ προ[κειμέ]νου μην[ὸς] καὶ μηδ᾽ ο[ὕ]τως
ὑπακούσαντος τοῦ Ψινταέους, προσεκέκλητο [20]καὶ
διὰ προ[γράμ]ματ[ος . . .] . . ρε . εν[. .] παρα-

---

20. προ[γράμ]ματ[ος restored by Gradenwitz.

[a] A contract made by a husband for the maintenance of
his wife.   In the present case it is probable that Chonouphis
was the father of Thaues.

[b] Wilcken argues with some force that this Thaues was
the elder wife and Thaues called Asclepias the younger wife
of Psintaes, although there is no other trace of polygamy
among the Egyptians of this period.   But various views are

defendant according to a contract of aliment [a] registered by the record-office 500 drachmae of silver in
favour of the woman therein named, Thaues also called
Asclepias, to enable him to furnish to her yearly 60
artabae of olyra and 72 drachmae of silver, to which
deed both Thaues [b] the wife of Psintaes and Zmanres
their common son had given their approval, a stipulation having been added that their property [c] should
be pledged for the rights of the contract; ⟨- - -⟩ and
he had therefore demanded that Psintaes should
forfeit to him the aforesaid 500 drachmae of silver
and the 4 years' total of 240 artabae of olyra at 2
drachmae of silver the artaba ⟨and the 4 years' total
of 288 drachmae of silver⟩, making in all 1268
drachmae of silver, and for damages and expenses
5 talents of copper, and that if the defendant did not
appear in court an order should be sent to the collector of foreign debts to carry out for the plaintiff
the exaction of the aforesaid sums. Whereas the
terms of the complaint had been brought to the knowledge of Psintaes, inasmuch as he had personally
received a copy of the petition through the assistant
of the court, and whereas, although their case was
posted up for hearing both before and on the 2nd of
the aforesaid month and nevertheless Psintaes did not
appear, a further summons had been issued by proclamation to the effect that he should present himself

held about the relationship of the parties mentioned in the
text.

[c] In alimentary contracts the property of the husband was
assigned as security to the wife for the payment of the aliment, and a legal expectancy to it was given to the children,
so that it could not be disposed of arbitrarily (cf. No. 219).
It is therefore doubtful whether " their property " means
this family property or some separate property of Thaues
and Zmanres.

γίνεσθαι αὐτὸν ἐπὶ τὸ κριτήριον τῆι ²¹ἐνεστώση[ι ἢ]
συνχωρηθήσεσ‹θ›αι τ[ῶι] Χονούφει τ[ὸ] ἀξίωμα,
κατακολουθήσαντες τοῖς ²²προδιειλ[εγμέν]οις καὶ
κ[αλῶ]ς ἔχειν ἡγ[ού]μενοι τὴν ἁρμόζουσαν τοῖς ἐν-
εστηκόσι ἐπακο-²³λου[θῆσαι οἰκο]νομίαν, σ[υ]νεκρί-
ναμ[ε]ν ἐπικεχωρῆσθαι τῶι ἐντετευχότι τὸ ἀξίωμα
καὶ ²⁴γρ[αφῆναι τῶι ση]μαινομέ[νωι] πράκτορι
συντελεῖν αὐτῶι τὴν πρᾶξιν τῶν κατε . . μένων
κεφαλαίων ²⁵[καὶ ὧν? ὑπ]ερβάλλει. ²⁶δι' εἰσαγω-
(γέως) Ἀρτεμιδώρου . . . . (2nd
hand) Ἀρ[τε]μίδωρος· ²⁷ἀνέγνωσται.

Verso : Τῶι ἐν Μέμφει ξενικῶν πράκτορι.

before the court on the present day, otherwise the claim of Chonouphis would be conceded, we therefore, guided by the previous examination and thinking it right that a settlement should ensue in conformity with the circumstances, have given judgement that the petitioner's claim is granted and that an order shall be written to the collector mentioned to carry out for him the exaction of the . . . sums and of the additional items (?). (Subscribed) Drawn up by the clerk of the court, Artemidorus . . . (Signed) Artemidorus. Has been read over. (Addressed) To the collector of foreign debts at Memphis.

VII. PETITIONS AND APPLICATIONS

265. PETITION TO A SUB-DIOECETES

P. Cairo Zen. 59236.   254 or 253 b.c.

¹Διοτίμωι διοικητῆι χαίρειν Νεοπτόλεμος Μακεδὼν τῶν ἐν Φιλαδελφείαι κληρούχων. ἀδικεῖταί
μου ὁ πατὴρ Στρά-²τιππος ὑπὸ Θεοκλέους τοῦ
οἰκονομήσαντος τὸν Ἀφροδιτοπολίτην νομὸν καὶ
Πετοσίριος τοῦ βασιλικοῦ γραμματέως. ἐπιγραφὴν γὰρ ³ποιούμενοι τοῖς ἀμπελῶσι ἐκ τριῶν
ἐτῶν τὰ γενήματα λαμβάνοντες τὸ τρίτον μέρος
ἐπέγραφον, τῶι δὲ πατρὶ ἐκ δύο ἐτῶν ⁴τὴν ἐπιγραφὴν πεποίηνται φάμενοι νεόφυτον εἶναι. δέομαι
οὖν σου, εἴ σοι δοκεῖ, ἐπισκέψασθαι περὶ τούτων,
κἂν ἦι ταῦτα ἀληθῆ, ⁵ἐπειδὴ καὶ τοῖς λοιποῖς ἐκ
τριῶν ἐτῶν πεποίηνταὶ τὴν ἐπιγραφήν, δοῦναί μοι
πρόσταγμα πρὸς [[αὐτοὺς]] Ἑρμόλαον καὶ Πετο-
σῖριν ὅπως ἂν ἐκ τριῶν ἐτῶν ⁶τὴν ἐπιγραφὴν καὶ
τῶι πατρὶ ποιήσωνται, εἴτε βούλονται ἀπὸ τοῦ
ἐνάτου καὶ εἰκοστοῦ ἔτους τὴν ἀρχὴν ποιούμενοι,

ᵃ Not the great dioecetes in Alexandria, but one of the
sub-dioecetae subordinate to him.

VII. PETITIONS AND APPLICATIONS

265. PETITION TO A SUB-DIOECETES

254 or 253 B.C.

To Diotimus, dioecetes,[a] greeting from Neoptolemus, Macedonian, one of the cleruchs at Philadelphia. My father Stratippus is being wronged by Theocles the former oeconomus of the Aphroditopolite nome and Petosiris the royal scribe. For in calculating the tax to be paid on the vineyards they used to take the produce of the last three years and make the third part of this the basis for the tax, but in the case of my father they have calculated the tax on the average of the last two years, saying that his vineyard was lately planted.[b] I beg you therefore, if you think fit, to inquire into this and, if my statement be correct, since they have calculated the tax for all the others on the average of three years, to give me an order to Hermolaus[c] and Petosiris to calculate the tax for my father also on the average of three years, beginning either from the twenty-ninth year or from the thirtieth year, just as they

[b] Their contention being that to include a year in which it was not fully productive would not give a fair average.

[c] The present oeconomus.

εἴτε ἀπὸ τοῦ τρια-⁷κοστοῦ ἔτους, ἤδη γὰρ οἰνοποιή-
καμεν ἐξ αὐτοῦ ἔτη τέσσαρα, καὶ προσδέξασθαι
αὐτῶι τὸ πεπτωκὸς ἐπὶ τράπεζαν ἀργύριον παρὰ
⁸τῶν οἰνοκαπήλων οἴνου οὗ ἔλαβον ἐκ τοῦ ἀμπελῶνος, ὅπως ἂν διὰ σὲ τοῦ δικαίου τύχηι. ⁹εὐτύχει.

Verso: ¹⁰Νεοπτόλεμος Διοτίμωι ἔντευξιν περὶ
ἀμπελῶνος.

266. PETITION OF A LENTIL-COOK

P.S.I. 402.   Middle of 3rd cent. B.C.

¹Φιλίσκωι χαίρειν Ἀρεντώτης φακηψὸς ²Φιλ-
αδελφείας. δίδωμι κατὰ μῆνα (ἀρταβῶν) λε ³καὶ
ἀνδρίζομαι ἵνα ἀναπληρῶ τοὺς φόρους κατὰ ⁴μῆνα,
ἵνα μηθέν μοι ἐγκαλῇς. ὁ λαὸς οὖν ὁ ἐν τῆι ⁵πόλι
⟦πόλις⟧ τὰς κολυκύνθας ὀπτῶσιν. διὰ ταύτην ⁶οὖν
τὴν αἰτίαν οὐθεὶς παρ' ἐμοῦ φακῆν ἀγοράζι ⁷ἐν τῶι
νῦν καιρῶι. δέομαι οὖν σου καὶ ἱκετεύω, ⁸εἴ σοι
δοκεῖ, γενέσθαι μοι, ὥσπερ καὶ ἐν Κροκοδίλων
πόλι ⁹πεποιήκασι, βραδῦναι τῶι βασιλεῖ τοὺς
φόρους ¹⁰ἀναπληροῦν. καὶ γὰρ τὸ πρωὶ εὐθέως
παρακάθην-¹¹ται τῆι φακῆι πωλοῦντες τὰς κολυκύνθας καὶ οὐκ ἐῶσι ¹²πωλῖν τὴν [φακ]ῆν.

choose, for we have now made wine from the vineyard
for four years, and to credit him with the money paid
into the bank by the wine-dealers for the wine which
they received from the vineyard, in order that he may
obtain justice at your hands. Farewell. (Endorsed)
Petition from Neoptolemus to Diotimus about a
vineyard.

266. PETITION OF A LENTIL-COOK

Middle of 3rd cent. B.C.

To Philiscus [a] greeting from Harentotes, lentil-
cook of Philadelphia. I give the product of 35
artabae a month [b] and I do my best to pay the tax
every month in order that you may have no complaint
against me. Now the folk in the town are roasting
pumpkins. For that reason then nobody buys lentils
from me at the present time. I beg and beseech you
then, if you think fit, to be allowed more time, just
as has been done in Crocodilopolis, for paying the
tax to the king. For in the morning they straightway
sit down beside the lentils selling their pumpkins and
give me no chance to sell my lentils.

[a] Probably the oeconomus in Crocodilopolis.
[b] The meaning may be that he had contracted to deliver
to the government the price of 35 artabae of roasted lentils,
being supplied by it with that amount of the raw beans.

SELECT PAPYRI

267. DRAFT OF A PETITION TO THE DIOECETES

P. Cairo Zen. 59341 (a), ll. 7-36.   247 B.C.

⁷Ἀπολλωνίωι διοικητῆι χαίρειν Θεόπροπος ⁸θεω-
ρὸς ἀπὸ Καλύνδων. τοῦ η καὶ λ (ἔτους) ⁹ὁ γεωργός
μου Θήρων ἐπρίατο παρὰ ¹⁰τῆς πόλεως παρασχεῖν
οἶνον τῆι γινομένηι ¹¹πανηγύρει ἐγ Κυπράνδοις κατ'
ἐνιαυτόν, ¹²ὑπὲρ οὗ ἐγὼ παρέσχον τὸν οἶνον μετρη-
¹³τὰς πδ τὸμ μετρητὴν ἀνὰ (δραχμὰς) ι, ¹⁴ὃ γίνονται (δραχμαὶ) ων, ⟦δανεισά-¹⁵μενος τόκων ἐννόμων
διὰ τὸ τὸν Θήρωνα ¹⁶μὴ ἔχειν ἀνηλῶσαι, δι' ἐμοῦ
δὲ ἠγορακότα⟧. ¹⁷καὶ εἰς τοῦτο ἀποδεδωκότων μοι
τῶν ταμιῶν Διοφάντου καὶ Ἀκρισίου ¹⁸⟦ἀποδεδω-
κότων μοι⟧ (δραχμὰς) χ, τὸ δὲ λοιπὸν ⟦(δραχμὰς)
σν⟧ ¹⁹οὐκ ἀποδιδόντων (δραχμὰς) σν διὰ τὸ μὴ
πεσεῖν πάσας τὰς συμβολάς, κατέστησα τοὺς
ταμίας ⟦Διο⟧ ²⁰ἐπί τε τὸν στρατηγὸν Μότην καὶ
τὸν οἰκονόμον ²¹Διόδοτον ἀπαιτῶν τὰς σν (δραχμὰς)
⟦καὶ τὸν τόκον⟧. ²²οἱ δὲ ταμίαι Διόφαντος καὶ
Ἀκρίσιος ἠξίουν ²³ψήφισμα αὐτοῖς γραφῆναι
φάμενοι ⟦μὴ κύριοι⟧ οὐκ εἶναι κύριοι ἄνευ φηφί-
σματο[ς] ἀποδιδόντες, οἱ δὲ πρυτάνεις ²⁴καὶ ὁ
γραμματεὺς παρήλκυσαν καὶ οὐκ ἔγραψαν ²⁵τὸ
ψήφισμα ἕως ὅτου προχειρισθεὶς ὑπὸ τῆς πόλεως
θεωρὸς ²⁶μετὰ Διοφάντου ἑνὸς τῶν ταμιῶν παρ-
εγενή-²⁷θην ἐνταῦθα πρὸς τὸν βασιλέα. εἰ οὖν σοι
²⁸δοκεῖ, καλῶς ποιήσεις γράψας πρός τε τὴν πόλιν

16. δε interpolated.

ᵃ A city in Caria.

267. DRAFT OF A PETITION TO THE DIOECETES

247 B.C.

To Apollonius the dioecetes greeting from Theopropus, sacred envoy from Calynda.[a] In the 38th year my farmer Theron purchased from the city a concession to provide wine for the festival which is held yearly at Cypranda, and I provided the wine on his behalf, amounting to 84 metretae at 10 drachmae the metretes, which makes 840 dr., [borrowing at the legal interest, as Theron had no money to spend and had made the purchase through me].[b] And as the treasurers Diophantus and Acrisius had paid me 600 dr. towards this sum, but were withholding the balance of 250[c] dr. because the subscriptions had not all come in, I brought them before the strategus Motes and the oeconomus Diodotus,[d] demanding the 250 dr. [and the interest]. The treasurers Diophantus and Acrisius asked that a decree should be drawn up for their instruction, saying that they had no authority to pay without a decree. But the prytaneis and the secretary procrastinated and had not proposed the decree up to the time when, having been appointed by the city as sacred envoy along with Diophantus, one of the treasurers, I came here to salute the king.[e] If therefore you approve, kindly write to our city and to the strategus and the oecono-

---

[b] The bracketed passages have been deleted by the writer on second thoughts.   [c] A mistake for 240.

[d] These were royal officials appointed from Alexandria with some authority over the civic administration.

[e] Probably on the occasion of the festival called τὰ Πτολεμαίεια, held every four years in honour of the royal house.

²⁹ἡμῶν καὶ τὸν στρατηγὸν ⟦Μο⟧ καὶ τὸν οἰκονόμον
³⁰ἀποδοθῆναί μοι τὰς σν (δραχμὰς) ⟦καὶ τὸν τόκον
³¹ὅσος ἂν γένηται ἀφ' οὗ εἰσανήλωκα εἰς τὸν οἶνον
³²τῆι πόλει αὐτὸς παρ' ἑτέρων δανεισάμενος ³³καὶ
τόκους φέρων ἔτι καὶ νῦν, [ἐπειδ]ὴ καὶ πρότερον
ἑτέρο[ις . . . .] . . σιν ἐ[. . . . .]. το ἀποδ[οῦναι]
διὰ τὸ μὴ ἐ[κπο]ιῆσαι ἐκ τῶν σ[υμβ]ολῶν τὴν
ἀ[πόδ]οσιν γενέσθαι,⟧ [ἵνα] μὴ ἀδικηθῶ, ³⁴ἀλλὰ καὶ
ἐγὼ ὦ ⟦.⟧ τῆς παρὰ σοῦ φιλανθρωπίας ³⁵τετευχώς.
³⁶εὐτύχει.

33. e.g. ἑτέρο[ις ἀπαιτ]οῦσιν ἐ[ψηφίζ]ετο.

268. PETITION TO THE KING

P. Enteuxeis 26.   220 B.C.

¹Βασιλεῖ Πτολεμαίωι χαίρειν Κτησικλῆς. ἀδικοῦμαι ὑπὸ Διονυσίου καὶ Νίκης τῆς θυγατρός
μου. ²ἐμοῦ γὰρ ἐκθρέψαντος τὴν ἐμαυτοῦ θυγα-
τέ[ρα] καὶ παιδεύσαντος καὶ ε[ἰς ἡ]λικίαν ἀγαγόν-
³τος, ἀκληρήσαντος δέ μου κατὰ τὸ ἴδιον σῶμ[α]
καὶ τοῖς ὀφθαλμοῖς ἀδυνατοῦντος, οὐχ οἷα ⁴μοι ἦν
ἐπαρκεῖν τῶν ἀναγκαίων οὐδέν· ἐμοῦ δὲ βουλομένου
[π]αρ' αὐτῆς τὸ δίκαιον ⁵λαβεῖν ἐν Ἀλεξανδρείαι,
κατεδεήθη μου καὶ τοῦ ιη (ἔτους) ἐχειρογράφησέ
μοι ὅρκον βασιλικὸν ⁶ἐπὶ τοῦ Ἀρσινόης ἀκτίας
ἱεροῦ δώσειν μοι καθ' ἕκαστον μῆνα δραχ[μὰ]ς
εἴκοσι ἐργαζομένη{ι} ⁷αὐτή{ι} τῶι ἰδίωι σώματι· ἐὰν
δὲ μὴ ποιῆι ἢ πα[ρ]αβαίνη[ι] τι τ[ῶν κατὰ τὴν]
χειρογραφίαν, ⁸ἀπο[τεῖσα]ί μοι αὐτὴν (δραχμὰς) φ

6-7. ἐργαζομένη{ι} αὐτή{ι} E.-H. : ἐργαζομένη αὐτῆι Ed.

mus to let the 250 dr. be paid to me ⟦with the interest, whatever it may amount to from the time when I spent money on the wine for the city, as I myself borrowed from others and am still paying interest, seeing that before now it has been decided by decree to reimburse other such claimants (?) when the amount payable could not be obtained from the subscriptions⟧, in order that I may not be wronged, but may have personal experience of your benevolence.   Farewell.

268. PETITION TO THE KING

220 B.C.

To King Ptolemy [a] greeting from Ctesicles.   I am being wronged by Dionysius and my daughter Nice. For though I had nurtured her, being my own daughter, and educated her and brought her up to womanhood, when I was stricken with bodily infirmity and my eyesight enfeebled she would not furnish me with any of the necessaries of life.   And when I wished to obtain justice from her in Alexandria, she begged my pardon and in year 18 she gave me in the temple of Arsinoe Actia [b] a written oath by the king that she would pay me twenty drachmae every month by means of her own bodily labour ; if she failed to do so or transgressed any of the terms of her bond, she was to forfeit to me 500 drachmae on pain of incurring the consequences of

[a] Ptolemy Philopator.
[b] Arsinoe Philadelphus, the deified wife of Ptolemy II. The epithet Actia suggests that the temple was situated on the sea-shore.

ἢ τῶι ὅρκωι ἔνοχον εἶναι. [νῦν δὲ φθαρεῖσα ὑπὸ
Διονυσ]ίου ὄντος ⁹κιναί[δο]υ οὐ π[οιεῖ] μοι τῶν
κατὰ τὴν χειρογραφ[ί]αν οὐδ[ἐν] καταφρονοῦ[σά
μου τοῦ τε γ]ή-¹⁰ρως κ[αὶ τ]ῆς ὑπ[αρ]χούσης μοι
ἀκληρίας. δέομαι οὖν [σου], βασιλεῦ, [μ]ὴ πε[ρι-
ιδεῖν με ὑ]πὸ τῆς ¹¹θυγ[ατρὸ]ς ἀδικού[μ]ενον καὶ
Διονυσίου τοῦ φθε[ί]ραντος [αὐ]τὴν κινα[ί]δ[ου,
ἀλλὰ προστάξ]αι ¹²Διοφά[νει] τῶι [στρατ]ηγῶι
ἀνακαλεσάμενον αὐτοὺς διακ[ο]ῦσαι [ἡμῶν καὶ ἐὰν
ἦι ἀληθῆ ?] ¹³τῶι μ[ὲν] φθε[ίρ]α[ν]τι αὐτὴν χρῆσα-
σθαι Διοφάν[η]ν ὡς ἂν α[ὐτῶι φαίνηται, Νίκην δὲ]
¹⁴τὴν θ[υγατέρ]α μου ἐπαναγκάσαι τὰ δίκαιά [μ]οι
ποιεῖν κ[. . . . . τούτων γὰρ γενο-]¹⁵μέ-
νω[ν οὐ]κ ἀδικηθήσομαι, ἀλλὰ ἐπὶ σέ, βασιλε[ῦ],
καταφυ[γὼν τοῦ δικαίου τεύξομαι]. (2nd hand)
¹⁶συναπεστάλη Εὐφορ[. .] . . . . . . [

Verso : ¹⁷(ἔτους) α Γορπιαίου λ Τῦβι ιγ̄. ¹⁸Κτησι-
κλῆς πρὸς Διονύσιον καὶ ¹⁹Νίκην τὴν θυγατέρα
περὶ χειρογρ(αφίας).

9. μου διὰ τοῦ γ]ήρως Ed.

269. PETITION TO THE KING

P. Enteuxeis 82 (= P. Magd. 33).   220 B.C.

¹Βασιλεῖ Πτολεμαίωι χαίρειν Φιλίστα Λυσίου
τῶν κατοικουσῶν [ἐ]ν Τρικωμίαι. ἀδικοῦμαι ὑπὸ
Πε-²τεχῶντος. λουομένης γάρ μου ἐν τῶι βαλα-
νείωι τῶι ἐν τῆι προειρ[η]μένηι κώμηι (ἔτους) α
Τῦβι ζ, πα-³ραχέων ἐν τῶι γυναικείωι [θό]λωι,
ἐγβεβηκυίας μου ὥστε ζμήσασθ[αι], εἰσενέγκας
234

the oath. Now, however, corrupted by Dionysius, who is a comedian, she is not keeping any of her engagements to me, in contempt of my old age and my present infirmity. I beg you therefore, O king, not to suffer me to be wronged by my daughter and Dionysius the comedian who has corrupted her, but to order Diophanes the strategus [a] to summon them and hear our case ; and if my words are true, let Diophanes deal with her corrupter as seems good to him and compel my daughter Nice to yield me my rights. . . . For by this means I shall no longer be wronged, but having sought your protection, O king, I shall obtain justice. (Docketed) We have delegated [b] . . . (Endorsed) Year 1, Gorpiaeus 30 Tubi 13. Ctesicles against Dionysius and Nice his daughter concerning a written oath.

[a] Diophanes was strategus of the Arsinoite nome, stationed at Crocodilopolis where the complainant probably resided.

[b] It is not clearly known what the person delegated by the strategus was required to do.

269. PETITION TO THE KING

220 b.c.

To King Ptolemy [a] greeting from Philista daughter of Lysias resident in Tricomia.[b] I am wronged by Petechon. For as I was bathing in the baths of the aforesaid village on Tubi 7 of year 1, and had stepped out to soap myself, he being bathman in the women's

[a] Ptolemy Philopator, as in Nos. 268 and 270. Petitions of this nature addressed to the king were in most cases not actually submitted to him, but dealt with by the local strategus.   [b] A village in the Fayum.

θερμοῦ τὰς ἀρυταί-⁴νας κα{σ}τεσκέδασεν μου
κ[. . .] καὶ κατέκαυσεν τήν τε κοιλίαν καὶ τὸν
ἀριστερὸν μηρὸν ἕως τοῦ γόνατος ⁵ὥστε καὶ
κινδυνεύειν με· [ὃν κ]αὶ εὑροῦσα παρέδωκα Νεχθοσίρι τῶι ἀρχιφυλακίτηι τῆς κώμης, παρόν-⁶τος
Σίμωνος τοῦ ἐπιστάτου. δέομαι οὖν σου, βασιλεῦ,
εἴ σοι δοκεῖ, ἱκέτις ἐπὶ σὲ καταπεφευγυῖα, μὴ
περι-⁷ιδεῖν με οὕτως ἠνομημένην χειρόβιον οὖσαν,
ἀλλὰ προστάξαι Διοφ[ά]νει τῶι στρατηγῶι γράψαι
Σίμωνι ⁸τῶι ἐπιστάτηι καὶ Νεχθοσίρι τῶι φυλα-
κίτηι ἀναγαγεῖν ἐφ᾽ αὑτὸν τὸν Πετεχῶντ[α ὅ]πως
Διοφάνης ἐπισκέψηται περὶ ⁹τούτων, ἵν᾽ ἐπὶ σὲ
καταφυγοῦσα, βασιλεῦ, τὸν πάντων κοινὸν εὐ[ερ]-
γέτην τοῦ δικαίου τύχω. ¹⁰εὐτύχει. (2nd hand)
¹¹Σίμωνι. ἀπόστειλον τὸν ἐνκαλούμενον. (ἔτους)
α Γ[ορπι]αίου κ̄η̄ Τῦβι ῑβ̄.

Verso : ¹²(ἔτους) α Γορπιαίου κ̄η̄ Τῦβι ῑβ̄. ¹³Φι-
λίστα πρὸς Πετεχῶντα ¹⁴παραχύτην περὶ τοῦ κατα-
¹⁵κεκαῦσθαι.

4. Or μ[ίαν]?

270. PETITION TO THE KING

P. Enteuxeis 48.   217 B.C.

¹Βασιλεῖ Πτολεμαίωι χαίρειν Πίστος Λεοντομένους Πέρσης τῆς ἐπιγονῆς. ἀδικοῦμαι ὑπὸ
Ἀριστοκράτου ²Θραικὸς (ἑκατονταρούρου) τῆς ᾱ
ἱπ(παρχίας) τῶν κατοικούντων ἐν Αὐτοδί[κηι].
τοῦ γὰρ γ (ἔτους) μηνὸς Αὐδναίου η̄ ἐμοῦ ἐμαυτο[ν
ἐγμισθώ-]³σαντος αὐτῶι κατὰ συγ[γρ]αφὴν [τὴν

2. Suppl. Wilcken.   3, 4. Suppl. E.-H.

rotunda and having brought in the jugs of hot water emptied one (?) over me and scalded my belly and my left thigh down to the knee, so that my life was in danger. On finding him I gave him into the custody of Nechthosiris the chief policeman of the village in the presence of Simon the epistates. I beg you therefore, O king, if it please you, as a suppliant who has sought your protection, not to suffer me, who am a working woman, to be thus lawlessly treated, but to order Diophanes the strategus to write to Simon the epistates and Nechthosiris the policeman that they are to bring Petechon before him in order that Diophanes may inquire into the case, hoping that having sought the protection of you, O king, the common benefactor of all, I may obtain justice. Farewell. (Docketed) To Simon. Send the accused. Year 1, Gorpiaeus 28 Tubi 12.

(Endorsed) Year 1, Gorpiaeus 28 Tubi 12. Philista against Petechon, bathman, about having been scalded.

270. PETITION TO THE KING

217 B.C.

To King Ptolemy greeting from Pistus son of Leontomenes, Persian of the Epigone. I am being wronged by Aristocrates, Thracian, holder of 100 arurae, of the 1st hipparchy,[a] resident in Autodice.[b] For in year 3, on the 8th of the month Audnaeus, I hired myself out to him in accordance with a

---

[a] Regiment of cavalry.
[b] A village in the Fayum.

κειμένην πα]ρὰ Πτολεμαίωι, ἐφ᾿ ὧι ἀκολουθήσω
αὐτῶι ἐν τῆι στρατεί[αι τὰς] ⁴χρείας αὐτῶι παρ-
εχόμε[νο]ς ἕω[ς τοῦ με αὐτὸν κατ]αστῆσαι εἰς
Αὐτοδίκην, λαμβάνων παρ᾿ αὐτοῦ μισθοῦ κατὰ
μῆν[α] ⁵τὸ συγχωρηθὲν πρὸς ἀλλήλους, ἐμ[οῦ δ᾿
αὐτῶι] τὰς χρείας παρεσχημένου καὶ ἀνεγκλήτου
γεγονότος καὶ κατε-⁶στηκότος μου αὐτὸν εἰς
Αὐτοδίκην [ὥσπερ καὶ ἡ] συγγραφὴ διαγ[ορεύει],
προσοφείλων μοι Ἀριστοκράτης ἀπὸ τῶν μισθῶ[ν
⁷ι δραχμ]άς, ἀπαιτούμενος ὑπό μου οὐκ [ἀποδίδω]σι
καταφρο[νῶν μου] τῆς ἀσθενείας, ἀλλὰ οἷός ἐστιν
ἐπιπλέκειν με. δέομαι οὖν σου, βασιλεῦ, ⁸προστάξαι
Διοφάνει τῶι στρατηγῶι γ[ράψαι Πυθι]άδει τ[ῶι
ἐπισ]τάτηι ἀποστεῖλαι Ἀριστοκράτην ἐπ᾿ αὐτὸν
⁹καί, ἐὰν ᾖ ἃ γράφω ἀληθῆ, ἐπαν[α]γκά[σαι αὐτὸν
ἀ]ποδοῦν[αί μ]οι τὰς ι (δραχμὰς) καὶ ἄρασθαί μοι
τὴν συγγραφήν, ὅπως ¹⁰μὴ ἐπιπλεκῶ ὑπ᾿ αὐτοῦ,
ἵνα διὰ σέ, βασιλ[εῦ], τύχω τῆς βοηθείας. ¹¹εὐ-
τύχει. (2nd hand) ¹²Πυθιάδει. ἐπι(σκεψάμενος)
φ(ρό)ν(τισον) ὅπ(ως) τ[ῶν δικαίω]ν [τύχηι]. (ἔτους)
δ Δαισίου κζ Ἀθὺρ κθ.

Verso : ¹³(ἔτους) δ Δαισίου κζ Ἀθὺρ κθ. ¹⁴Πίσ-
τος Λεοντομένους Πέρσης ¹⁵πρ(ὸς) Ἀριστοκράτην
(ἑκατοντάρουρον) περὶ (δραχμῶν) ι ¹⁶καὶ συγ-
γρ(αφῆς).

7. διὰ] τῆς Ed.

238

contract deposited with Ptolemaeus, on the condition that I should accompany him on the campaign [a] and give him my services until I brought him back to Autodice, receiving from him a monthly wage of the amount agreed upon between ourselves ; and though I have given him my services and behaved irreproachably and brought him back to Autodice as the contract orders, Aristocrates in spite of my demand will not pay me 10 drachmae which he owes me from my wages, despising my feebleness, but intends to trick me. I beg you therefore, O king, to order Diophanes the strategus to write to Pythiades the epistates to send Aristocrates to appear before him, and if my words are true, let Diophanes compel him to pay me the 10 drachmae and carry out the contract with me, in order that I may not be tricked by him, that so, O king, I may receive your help. Farewell. (Docketed) To Pythiades. Examine the case and take care that he receives justice. Year 4, Daesius 27 Hathur 29. (Endorsed) Year 4, Daesius 27 Hathur 29. Pistus son of Leontomenes, Persian, against Aristocrates, holder of 100 arurae, concerning 10 drachmae and a contract.

---

[a] A war was at this time in progress between Ptolemy Philopator and Antiochus III. for the possession of Coele-Syria.

SELECT PAPYRI

271. PETITION CONCERNING A DOWRY

P. Tebt. 776.   Early 2nd cent. B.C.

¹Πτολεμαίωι οἰκονόμωι ²παρὰ Σενήσεως τῆς
Μενε-³λάου τῶν κατ[οι]κουσῶν ἐν Ὀξυ-⁴ρύγχοις
τῆ[ς Πολέ]μωνος μερίδος. ⁵συνούσης μ[ο]υ Διδύ-
μωι ⁶Πετειμ[ο]ύθου τῶν ἐκ τῆς αὐτῆς ⁷κώμης
[κα]τὰ συγγραφὴν Αἰγυ-⁸πτίαν τ[ροφ]ῖτιν ἀργυρίου
⁹χρυσῶν [.]α κατὰ τοὺς τῆς ¹⁰χώρας νό[μο]υς, καὶ
πρὸς ταῦτα ¹¹καὶ τὴ[ν τρο]φήν μου ὑπο-¹²κει-
μ[ένω]ν τῶν ὑπαρχόντων ¹³αὐτ[ῶι πά]ντων, ἐν οἷς
καὶ οἰκίας ¹⁴ἐν τῆι προγεγραμμένηι κώμηι, ¹⁵ὁ
ἐγκαλούμενος βουλόμενός με ¹⁶ἀποστερέσαι ἕως
μὲν προσ-¹⁷πορευόμενος ἑνὶ καὶ ἑκάστωι ¹⁸τῶν ἐκ
τῆς αὐτῆς κώμης ¹⁹ἠβούλετο αὐτὴν ἐξαλλοτριῶσαι,
²⁰τούτων δὲ οὐχ ὑπομενόντων ²¹ἕνεκα τοῦ μὴ
συνεπικελεύ-²²ειν ἐμέ, μετὰ ταῦτα ἐξείργασται
²³τοῦ δοῦναι ἐν διεγγυήματι ²⁴ὑπὲρ Ἡρακλείδου
τελώνου ²⁵εἰς τὸ βασιλικόν, καὶ κατὰ τοῦτο ²⁶οἴεται
ἐκκλ{.}είειν με τῶν δικαίων. ²⁷διὸ ἀξιῶ σε δεομένη
γυνὴ οὖσα ²⁸καὶ ἀβοήθητον μὴ ὑπεριδεῖν με
²⁹ἀποστερηθεῖσαν τῶν ὑποκειμένων ³⁰πρὸς τὴν
φερνὴν διὰ τὴν τοῦ ³¹ἐγκαλουμένου ῥαδιουργίαν
ἀλλ᾽, ἐὰν ³²φαίνηται, συντάξαι γράψαι Πτ[ολε-]
³³μαίωι τῶι ἐπιμελητῆι μὴ π[ροσ-]³⁴δέχεσθαι τὴν
Διδύμου τοῦ [δη -]³⁵λουμένου οἰκίαν ἐν διεγγυή-
[ματι].   ³⁶τούτου δὲ γενομέ[νου τε]ύξο[μαι τῆς]
³⁷παρὰ σοῦ βοηθείας. ³⁸[εὐτύχει.]

28. l. ἀβοήθητος.

271. PETITION CONCERNING A DOWRY

Early 2nd cent. B.C.

To Ptolemaeus, oeconomus, from Senesis daughter of Menelaus, inhabitant of Oxyrhyncha [a] in the division of Polemon. I lived with Didymus son of Peteimouthes, an inhabitant of the said village, on the terms of an Egyptian alimentary silver contract [b] for [.]1 gold pieces [c] in accordance with the laws of the country, and for this sum and for my maintenance all his property, including a house in the aforesaid village, was pledged. Wishing to deprive me of this the accused, approaching the inhabitants of the said village one by one, for a time desired to alienate it ; but as they did not venture because I did not concur, he has subsequently contrived so as to give it to the Treasury in surety for Heraclides, tax-farmer, and thus thinks to exclude me from my rights. I therefore, being a defenceless woman, beg and request you not to suffer me to be deprived of what is pledged for my dowry through the misbehaviour of the accused, but, if it be your pleasure, to order a letter to be written to Ptolemaeus the epimeletes forbidding him to accept in surety the house of the said Didymus. If this is done, I shall receive your succour. Farewell.

[a] A Fayum village, not the great Oxyrhynchus.
[b] See No. 264.
[c] This sum, either 11 or 21 gold pieces (= 220 or 420 silver drachmae), though a receipt was given for it, was not actually paid over, but represented the penalty which the husband was obliged to pay to his wife if he divorced her.

272. PETITION OF PTOLEMAEUS THE
RECLUSE ON BEHALF OF HIS BROTHER

P. Lond. 23 (= U.P.Z. 14), ll. 5-35.   158 B.C.

⁵Βασιλεῖ Πτολεμαίωι καὶ βασιλίσ<σ>ηι Κλεο-
πάτραι τῇ ἀδελφῇ θεοῖς Φιλομήτορσι χαίρειν
⁶Πτολεμαῖος Γλαυκίου Μακεδὼν τῆς ἐπιγονῆς τῶν
ἐκ τοῦ Ἡρακλεοπολίτου. ⁷τοῦ προιρημένου μου
πατρὸς Γλαυκίου ὄντος μὲν τῶν ἐν τῶι Ἡρακλεο-
⁸πολίτηι συνγενῶν κατοίκων, τούτου δὲ μεταλ-
λάξαντος τὸν βίον ⁹ἐν [[τῇ]] τοῖς τῆς ταραχῆ<ς>
χρόνοις καὶ ἀπολελοιπότος ἐμέ τε καὶ Ἀπολλώνιον
¹⁰τὸν νεότερόν μου ἀδελφόν, συνβάντος δὲ γεγονέναι με ἐν κατοχῇ ¹¹ἐν τῷ πρὸς Μέμφει μεγάλῳ
Σαραπιείωι ἔτη ιε̄, προσδεομένου ¹²δέ μου τοῦ
περιποιῆσαι τῷ σημαινωμένωι ἀδελφῶι στρατείαν
¹³διὰ τὸ ἄτεκνόν με εἶναι, δι᾽ ἧς καὶ αὐτός τε ἐν
κατοχῇ ὢν ἔξω τε ¹⁴αὐτοῦ διευσχημονεῖν καὶ
βοήθειαν ἔχειν, δέομαι ὑμῶν ¹⁵τῶν μεγίστων θεῶν
Φιλομητόρων ἐμβλεύσαντας ¹⁶εἰς τὰ προγεγραμμένα ἔτηι, καθότι οὐθαμόθεν ἔχω τὰ ἐπιτήδηαι
¹⁷πλὴν τοῦ τὴν ἐφ᾽ ὑμᾶς καταφυγὴν τοὺς θεοὺς
μεγίστους ¹⁸καὶ ἀντιλήμπτορας ποιησάμενον τυχεῖν
με τῆς δηλουμένης ¹⁹εἰς τὸν ἀδελφὸν στρατείας,

7. l. προειρημένου.   10. l. νεώτερον.   12. l.
σημαινομένωι.   14. l. δέομαι.   15. l. ἐμβλέψαντας.
16. l. οὐδαμόθεν, ἐπιτήδεια.

ᵃ Ptolemy VII., called Philometor.
ᵇ Sister and wife of the king.
ᶜ See Vol. I. Nos. 98-100.

272. PETITION OF PTOLEMAEUS THE RECLUSE ON BEHALF OF HIS BROTHER

158 B.C.

To King Ptolemy [a] and Queen Cleopatra the sister,[b] gods Philometores, greeting from Ptolemaeus [c] son of Glaucias, Macedonian of the Epigone, of the Heracleopolite nome. As my aforesaid father Glaucias, who belonged to the cleruchs called cousins [d] in the Heracleopolite nome, departed this life at the time of the disturbances [e] and has left behind him both me and my younger brother Apollonius, and as it has happened that I have been in detention [f] in the great Serapeum by Memphis for 15 years and I require, seeing that I am childless, to procure for my said brother a military post, which will enable me too, who am in detention, to live here [g] decently and receive succour, I beseech you, the most great gods Philometores, to take note of the above-mentioned years and, inasmuch as I have no means of gaining the necessaries of life except by seeking refuge with you, the most great gods and protectors, and obtaining the said military post for my brother, to let me

[d] Perhaps a title given by the king to a certain class among the cleruchs.

[e] Probably a rising of the natives. The death of Glaucias took place in 164 B.C.

[f] Imposed on him by the will of the god. A person on whom such an injunction was laid, though not in physical detention, felt himself religiously bound to remain within the precincts of the temple.

[g] Perhaps, as Wilcken suggests, δι᾽ should be supplied before αὐτοῦ in l. 14, or τε corrected to δι᾽. The meaning would then be " through him," *i.e.* Apollonius.

ἐὰν φαίνηται, μερίσαι κἀμοὶ ἧς ἔχετε ²⁰πρὸς
πάντας τοὺς τοιούτους θεοσεβοῦ⟦α⟧ς ἀντιλήμψεως
⟨καὶ προστάξαι⟩ ²¹γραφῆηι οἷ⟨ς⟩ καθήκει προσ-
λαβέσθαι τὸν προωνομασμένον μου ²²ἀδελφὸν
²³Ἀπολλώνιον εἰς τὴν Δεξειλάου σημέαν, ²⁴ἧ τὸ
εταγμένον ἔχει ἐν Μέμφει, καὶ ²⁵ἐκθεῖναι αὐτῶι
ὅσον καὶ ⟦οἱ ἐκειν⟧ αὐτοὶ ²⁶λαμβάνουσιν μετρή-
ματα καὶ ὀψόνι-²⁷α, ὅπως διευσχημονῶν δύνωμαι
²⁸ἐπιτελεῖν τὰς θυσίας ὑπέρ τε ὑμῶν ²⁹καὶ τῶν
τέκνων, ὅπως κυριεύητε ³⁰πάσης χώρας ἧς ὁ ἥλιος
ἐφορᾶι τὸν ³¹ἅπαντα χρόνον. τούτου δὲ γενομένου ³²ἔσομαι δι' ὑμᾶς ἐσχηκὼς τὸν βίον ³³τὸ[ν]
ἀέναον χρόνον. ³⁴εὐτυχεῖτε.

Subscription : ³⁵Ποιῆσαι, ἀνενεκεῖν δὲ πόσον ἔσται.

21. l. γραφῆναι.   26. l. ὀψώνια.   35. l. ἀνενεγκεῖν.

273. PETITION TO THE KING AND QUEEN

P. Amh. 33.   About 157 B.C.

¹Βασιλεῖ Πτολεμαίωι καὶ βασ[ιλί]σσηι Κλεο-
π[άτρ]αι τῆι ἀδελφῆι ²θεοῖς Φιλομήτορσι χαίρ[ειν]
³Μαρεπάθις Σισούχου καὶ Π[α]τκῶς Ὀννώφ[ριος
καὶ Τ]εσενοῦφις ⁴Μαρρέως καὶ Φατρῆς Θο[το]ῆτος
καὶ Ἁρπ[. . . . . Ἀμα]ράντου ⁵βασιλικοὶ γεωργοὶ
τῶν [ἀπὸ τ]ῆς Σοκνοπ[αίου Ν]ήσου τῆς ⁶Ἡρα-
κλείδο[υ] μερίδος τ[οῦ] Ἀρσινοΐτου νο[μοῦ]. ἐν-
εστηκυίας ⁷ἡμῖν καταστάσεως ἐπὶ [Ζω]πύρου τοῦ
ἐπι[μ]ελητοῦ καὶ Πετε-⁸αρψενήσιος τοῦ βασιλικοῦ
γ[ρα]μματέως, συ[ν]εδρευόντων ⁹καὶ τῶν ἐν τῶι
προειρημένωι νομῶι τὰ βασιλικὰ καὶ προσο-¹⁰δικὰ

too partake, if it seem good to you, of the pious ^a protection which you afford to all men in such case and to let an order be written to the proper authorities to enrol my above-named brother in the company of Dexilaus which is garrisoned in Memphis and assign him the same pay as his fellows receive in corn and money, that so being decently circumstanced I may be able to perform sacrifices on behalf of you and your children, to the end that you may be lords of every land on which the sun looks down for all time. If this be done, I shall have my livelihood secured by your help in perpetuity. Farewell. (Subscribed) Let it be done, but report how much the cost will be.^b

^a The original of which the present text is a copy may have had θεοσεβεῖς in l. 20 (Wilcken), in which case the meaning would be " to god-fearing persons like myself."
^b A copy of the king's subscription.

273. PETITION TO THE KING AND QUEEN

About 157 B.C.

To King Ptolemy and Queen Cleopatra the sister, gods Philometores, greeting from Marepathis son of Sisouchus, Patkos son of Onnophris, Tesenouphis son of Marres, Phatres son of Thotoes, and Harp . . . son of Amarantus, cultivators of Crown land, of Socnopaei Nesus in the division of Heraclides in the Arsinoite nome. A trial is due to take place before Zopyrus the epimeletes and Peteharpsenesis the royal scribe, assisted by the chrematistae who judge cases concerning the Crown and the revenues and private

245

καὶ ἰδιωτικὰ κριν[όν]των χρημat[ισ]τῶν ὧν εἰσ-
αγω-[11]γεὺς Δέξιος, πρὸς Τεσενοῦφιν τὸν κωμ-
αρχήσαντα τὴν [12]προειρημένην κώμην ἀφ' ὧν
ἐπιδ[ε]δώκειμεν αὐτοῖς [13]ἐνφανισμῶν περί τινων
ἀδικημάτω[ν] καὶ παραλογειῶν [14]σίτου τε καὶ
χαλκοῦ καὶ ἤδη τῶν καθ' ἡμᾶς εἰσαγομένων
[15]πυνθανόμεθα τὸν ἐνκαλούμενον Τεσενοῦφιν μετὰ
συνηγό-[16]ρων συνκαθίστασθαι, προστεταχότων τῶν
προγόνων [17]ὑμῶν διὰ τοῦ ὑποκειμένου προστάγ-
ματ[ο]ς τοὺς προσπο-[18]ρευομένους συνηγόρους πρὸς
τὰς προσοδικὰς κρίσεις [19]ἐπὶ βλάβῃ τῶν προσόδων
πρᾶξαι εἰς τὸ β[α]σιλικὸν διπλοῦν [20]τὸ ἐπιδέκατον
καὶ τούτοις μηκέτι ἐξεῖνα[ι] συνηγορᾶσαι. [21]δεό-
μεθ' ὑμῶν τῶν μεγίστων θεῶν, εἰ ὑμῖν δοκεῖ,
[22]ἀποστεῖλαι ἡμῶν τὴν ἔντευξιν ἐπὶ τοὺς αὐτοὺς
χρημα-[23]τιστὰς ὅπως ἐπὶ τῆς διαλογῆς τῶν ἐν-
τ[εύ]ξεων συντά-[24]ξωσιν τῶι Τεσενοῦφει μὴ μετὰ
συνηγόρου συνκαθίστασθαι. [25]τούτου γὰρ γενομένου οὐθὲν τῶν ὑμῖν συμφερόντων [26]διαπεσεῖται.
[27]εὐτυχεῖτε.

[28]Βασιλεὺς Πτολεμαῖος Ἀπολλωνίωι χαίρειν.
ἐπειδή τινες [29]τῶν ὑπογεγραμμένων συνηγόρων
προσπορεύονται πρὸς τὰς [30]προσοδικὰς κρίσεις
καταβλάπτοντες τὰς προσόδους, σύνταξον [31]ὅπως
πραχθῶσι εἰς τὸ βασιλικὸν οἱ συνηγορήσαντες
διπλοῦν [32]τὸ ἐπιδέκατον καὶ τούτ[οι]ς μηκέτι
ἐξέστω συνηγορᾶσαι περὶ μη-[33]θενὸς πράγματος.
ἐὰν δέ τις τῶν καταβλαπτόντων τὰς προσόδους
[34]ἐλεγχθῆι συνηγορήσας περὶ πράγματός τινος,
αὐτόν τε [35]πρὸς ἡμᾶς μετὰ φυλακῆς ἀποστείλατε

12. *l.* ἐπεδεδώκειμεν.   20. *l.* συνηγορῆσαι ; so in 32.

affairs in the aforesaid nome and whose clerk is Dexius, between us and Tesenouphis the ex-comarch of the aforesaid village, on the ground of the written declarations which we had submitted to them, concerning certain misdeeds and peculations both of corn and money. Just as our case is being brought into court we hear that the defendant Tesenouphis is appearing with advocates to help him, although your ancestors have ordained by the decree appended that advocates who take up fiscal cases to the detriment of the revenues shall be made to pay to the Crown the ten per cent caution-money [a] doubled and shall not be allowed to act as advocates any longer. We beseech you, the most great gods, if it please you, to send our petition to the said chrematistae in order that when the examination of petitions is held they may forbid Tesenouphis to appear in court with an advocate. For this measure will prevent your interests from suffering any harm. Farewell.

King Ptolemy to Apollonius [b] greeting. Seeing that certain of the advocates named below are taking up fiscal cases to the injury of the revenues, give orders that those who have acted as advocates be made to pay to the Crown the ten per cent caution-money doubled and forbid them to act any longer as advocates in any case. If any one of those who are injuring the revenues is convicted of having acted as advocate in any case, send him to us under arrest

---

[a] See No. 201, note a, p. 5.
[b] The letter quoted is from Ptolemy Philadelphus to Apollonius the dioecetes (see No. 267) and dates from 259 B.C.

---

35. ἐπιστείλατε Edd., but the normal ἀποστείλατε seems justified by the facsimile.

καὶ τὰ ὑπάρχοντα αὐτοῦ ³⁶καταχωρίσατε εἰς τὸ
βασιλικόν. ³⁷(ἔτους) κζ Γορπιαίου ιε.

274. PETITION FROM THE PRIESTS OF SOCNOPAEUS TO THE STRATEGUS

P. Amh. 35.   132 B.C.

¹ʼΑπολλωνίωι τῶν πρώτων φίλων ²καὶ στρατηγῶι
καὶ ἐπὶ τῶν προσόδων ³παρὰ τῶν ἱερέων τοῦ
Σοκνοπαίου ⁴θεοῦ μεγάλου καὶ ῎Ισιος Σνεφορ-
σήτος ⁵θεᾶς μεγίστης καὶ τῶν συννάων ⁶θεῶν καὶ
βασιλικῶν γεωργῶν ⁷τῶν ἐκ τῆς Σοκνοπαίου
Νήσου. ⁸τῆι ιη τοῦ ᾽Επεὶφ τοῦ λη (ἔτους) καιρο-
⁹τηρήσας ἡμᾶς ἀσχολουμένους ἐν ¹⁰Κροκοδίλων
πόλει Πετεσοῦχος ¹¹ὁ λεσῶνις τοῦ Σοκν[ο]παίου
θεοῦ μεγάλ[ο]υ ¹²καταβὰς εἰς Διονυσιάδα καὶ παρα-
¹³λογισάμενος τοὺς παρʼ ἡμῶν γεωργοὺς ¹⁴Τεῶν
καὶ Στοτοῆτιν ὡς ἀπεσταλ-¹⁵μένος ὑφʼ ἡμῶν ἐπὶ
τὴν παράλημ-¹⁶ψιν τῶν ἐκφορίων ἧς γεωργοῦσι
ἱερᾶς ¹⁷γῆς Σοκνοπαίου θεοῦ μεγάλου βιασά-
¹⁸μενος αὐτοὺς ἐπὶ τῆς ἅλω μετε-¹⁹νήνοχεν πυροῦ
(ἀρτάβας) σκ[ε] ἐπὶ τὴν τ[ο]ῦ ²⁰Πααλᾶτος οἰκίαν.
ὑπὲρ ὧν ἐντυχόντες ²¹σοι ἐπὶ τοῦ Πρεμὶτ τῆι κβ
τοῦ αὐτοῦ ²²μηνὸς καὶ προσκαλεσάμενος τὸν
²³Πααλᾶσιν κατεγγεγυήκας τὸν ²⁴πυρὸν τοῦ Σοκνοπαίου θεοῦ μεγάλου, ²⁵ὑπὲρ ὧν κεχειρογράφηκεν
τὸν βασι-²⁶λικὸν ὅρκον Πετεσοῦχος ὁ λεσῶνις ὑπὲρ
τοῦ ²⁷μὴ ἐφάψεσθαι τῶν ἐκφορίων τῆς γῆς ²⁸κατὰ
μηδένα τρόπον ἐν τῆι γεγονυίᾳ ²⁹ἡμῶν πρὸς αὐτὸν

ᵃ That is, of the king.

and confiscate his property to the Crown.   Year 27,
Gorpiaeus 15.

274. PETITION FROM THE PRIESTS OF
SOCNOPAEUS TO THE STRATEGUS

132 B.C.

To Apollonius, one of the first friends [a] and strategus
and superintendent of the revenues, from the priests
of the great god Socnopaeus [b] and the most great goddess Isis Snephorses and the associated gods, being
also cultivators of Crown land, residing at Socnopaei
Nesus.   On the 18th of Epeiph of the 38th year
Petesouchus the chief priest of the great god Socnopaeus, having waited for a favourable opportunity
when we had business at Crocodilopolis, went down
to Dionysias [c] and imposed upon the cultivators employed by us, Teos and Stotoetis, by pretending to
have been sent by us to collect the rents of the temple
land of the great god Socnopaeus which they cultivate,
and overpowering them at the threshing-floor he
carried off 225 artabae of wheat to the house of
Paalas.   Concerning this we addressed a complaint
to you at the Premit [d] on the 22nd of the same month,
and you summoned Paalas and laid an embargo on
the wheat of the great god Socnopaeus, for the reason
that Petesouchus the chief priest, in the compact
which he made with us on assuming office in the 38th
year, has signed an undertaking under the royal oath

[b] One of the crocodile gods of the Fayum.   The village of
Socnopaei Nesus was called after him; see No. 282, note a.

[c] Another village in the Fayum.

[d] Probably an official place of business in Crocodilopolis.

249

συναλλάξει τῆς ³⁰λεσωνείας τοῦ λη (ἔτους) καὶ
παραβεβη-³¹κότος τὰ τῆς χειρογραφίας. ἐπεὶ οὖν
³²σέσωσαι ἐν τῆι ἀρρωστίαι ὑπὸ τοῦ ³³Σοκνοπαῖτος
θεοῦ μεγάλου καὶ Ἴσιος Σνε-³⁴φορσῆτος θεᾶς
μεγίστης καὶ τῶν συννάων ³⁵θεῶν, ἀξιοῦμεν ἐὰν
φαίνηται συν-³⁶τάξαι καταχωρίσαι ἡμῶν τὸ ὑπόμνημα ³⁷παρὰ σοὶ ἐν χρηματισμῷ πρὸς τὴν ἐσο-
μέ-³⁸νην ἡμῖν πρὸς τὸν Πετεσοῦχον τὸν λεσῶνιν
³⁹κατάστασιν, ὅπως μὴ ἐξῆι αὐτῶι ἐφάπτεσθαι
⁴⁰τοῦ πυροῦ, καὶ γράψαι Ἀπολλωνίωι τῶι ἐπιστάτει
καταστῆ-⁴¹σαι αὐτὸν ἐπὶ σὲ πρὸς τὴν τούτων
διεξαγωγήν, ⟦τούτου ⁴²γενομένου τευξόμεθ' ἀντι-
λήψεως⟧ ἵν' ἐὰν ἦι ταῦθ' οὕτως ⁴³ἔχοντα, ἡμεῖς μὲν
κομισώμεθα τὰς σκε (ἀρτάβας) (πυροῦ) εἰς τὸν
τοῦ ⁴⁴θεοῦ λόγον, περὶ δὲ ἧς πεποίηται βίας καὶ
χειρογρ(αφίας) διαλαβεῖν ⁴⁵περὶ αὐτοῦ ⁴⁶μισοπονή-
⁴⁷ρως πρὸς ⁴⁸ἐπίστα(σιν) ἑτ<έρ>ων, ⁴⁹ὅπως δυνώ-
⁵⁰μεθα ἐπι-⁵¹τελεῖν ⁵²τὰ νομιζό-⁵³μενα τοῖς θεοῖς
ὑπέρ ⁵⁴τε τοῦ βα(σιλέως) καὶ ⁵⁵τῶν βα(σιλι)κῶν
τέκνων ⁵⁶τυχόντες ⁵⁷τῆς παρὰ σ[ο]ῦ ⁵⁸ἀντιλήψεως.
⁵⁹εὐτύχει. ⁶⁰(ἔτους) λη ⁶¹Ἐπεὶφ κβ.

48. ἑτ<έρ>ων E.-H. : ε . . ν Edd.

275. PETITION TO THE VILLAGE SCRIBE

B.G.U. 1256.   2nd cent. B.C.

¹Πετεαρποχράτηι κωμογραμμα-²τεῖ Φιλαδελφείας
³παρὰ Ἕρμωνος τοῦ Θεοκρίτου ⁴Μακεδόνος τῶν
Πρωτογένου ⁵καὶ Πρωτογένου τοῦ υἱοῦ ⁶τῆς ζ
ἱπ(παρχίας) (ὀγδοηκονταρούρου). ἐπεὶ ἐν τῶι ⁷προ-

that he would not lay hands on the rents of the land in any manner and he has violated his written oath. Since therefore you have been saved when in sickness by the great god Socnopaeus and the most great goddess Isis Snephorses and the associated gods, we entreat you, if it please you, to give instructions that our petition shall be registered and filed in your office in view of the coming audience for our suit against Petesouchus the chief priest, in order that he may not be able to lay hands on the wheat, and also to write to Apollonius the epistates to produce him in your court for the deciding of this case, in order that, if our statements are found to be correct, we may recover the 225 artabae of wheat and place them to the account of the god, and for the violence and perjury of which he is guilty you may pass judgement on him with righteous zeal as a deterrent to others, enabling us to make the customary sacrifices to the gods on behalf of the king and of the royal children, if we obtain your support. Farewell. Year 38, Epeiph 22.

275. PETITION TO THE VILLAGE SCRIBE

2nd cent B.C.

To Peteharpochrates, village scribe of Philadelphia, from Hermon son of Theocritus, Macedonian, of the troop of Protogenes and his son Protogenes, of the 7th hipparchy,[a] holder of 80 arurae. Whereas, al-

---

[a] Cavalry regiment.

τεθέντι ἀγῶνι ἠλκυσμέ-⁸νων τινῶν λαμπαδαρχῶν
⁹τῆι ι̅ϛ̅ τοῦ Θωὺθ τ[οῦ] λε (ἔτους) ¹⁰τῆι δὲ ι̅θ̅ τοῦ
αὐτοῦ μηνὸς ¹¹ἤλκυσμαι λαμπαδάρχης ¹²ἀνδρῶν οὐ
καθηκόντως ¹³χάριν τοῦ μὴ ἔχειν με μηδε-¹⁴μίαν
ἀφορμὴν μηδὲ περίστα-¹⁵σιν πρὸς τὸ χορηγῆσαι τὰ
τῆς ¹⁶λαμπαδαρχίας ἀλλὰ διαζῶν-¹⁷τος ἐξ ὀλίων ἃ
καὶ μόλις ¹⁸αὐταρκεῖται ἐμοί τε καὶ ¹⁹τῆι γυναικὶ
καὶ τοῖς τέκνοις, ²⁰οὕς τε ἠλκύκησαν πρὸ ἐμοῦ
²¹λαμπαδάρχας ἐν τῶι αὐτῶι ²²ἀγῶνι κατασυν-
εργοῦντες ²³καὶ καταχαριζόμενοι [ἀ]πολέ-²⁴λυκαν,
ἀξιῶ μὴ ὑπὲρ-²⁵ιδεῖν με ἀγνωμονούμενον ²⁶ἀλλὰ
ἐπανενέγκαι ἐπί τε τὸν ²⁷γυμνασίαρχον καὶ [ἐ]πὶ
τοὺς ²⁸ἐκ τοῦ ἐν τῆι Φιλαδελφείαι ²⁹γυμνασίου
νεανίσκους, ³⁰ὅπως ἀπολυθῶ τῆς λαμπα-³¹δαρχίας,
εἰ δὲ μή γε, ὑπο-³²τάξαι μου τὸ ὑπόμνημα ³³ὧι
καθήκει, ἵνα μὴ ἐ[. . . .]ν ³⁴[- - -

---

17. l. ὀλίγων.   20. ἠλκύκησαν = εἰλκύκεισαν.

---

[a] Persons who presided over and defrayed the cost of the
torch-races.

276. PETITION TO THE VILLAGE SCRIBE

P. Tebt. 39.   114 B.C.

¹Μεγχεῖ κωμογραμματεῖ Κερκεοσίρεως ²παρ᾽
Ἀπολλοδώρου ἐξειληφότος τὴν ³διάθεσιν καὶ τὸ
τέλος τοῦ ἐλαίου τῆς αὐτῆς ⁴τὸ δ (ἔτος). τυγχάνωι
καὶ πρότερον ⁵ἐπιδεδωκὼς Πολέμωνι τῶι τῆς
⁶κώμης ἐπιστάτει περὶ τοῦ προσπεσόν-⁷τος μοι τῆι
κζ τοῦ Φαῶφι εἶναι ἐν τῆι ⁸Σισόιτος τοῦ Σεναπύγ-
χιος οἰκίαι τῆι ⁹οὔσηι ἐν τῶι αὐτόθι Θοηριείωι
252

though certain persons had been impressed on the 16th of Thoth of the 35th year as lampadarchs [a] at the advertised games, I have been impressed as lampadarch of the foot-race for men on the 19th of the same month, improperly because I have no means or substance to provide the requirements of the lampadarchy but am existing on a small income which is barely sufficient for myself and my wife and children, and whereas they have released those whom they had impressed before me as lampadarchs at the said games, conspiring with them and favouring them, I request you not to allow me to be unfairly treated but to refer my case to the gymnasiarch and to the juniors [b] belonging to the gymnasium at Philadelphia, in order that I may be released from the lampadarchy, or, failing that, to forward my petition to the proper official, in order that I may not . . .

[b] A special class of young men trained, perhaps for military service, in the gymnasium.

276. PETITION TO THE VILLAGE SCRIBE

114 B.C.

To Menches, village scribe of Kerkeosiris,[a] from Apollodorus, contractor for the retailing of oil and the tax upon oil [b] at the said village for the 4th year. I have already reported to Polemon the epistates of the village about my having heard on the 27th of Phaophi that there was some contraband oil in the house of Sisois son of Senapunchis which is in the

[a] A village in the Fayum.   [b] See No. 203, p. 35, note a.

ἐλαϊκὸν [10]ἐπίτιμον. εὐθέως παραλαβὼν [11]Τρύχαμ-
βον τὸν παρὰ τοῦ οἰκονόμου [12]ἀπεσταλμένον ἐπὶ
τὴν διαγραφὴν [13]δι[ὰ τὸ μ]ὴ βούλεσθαί σε καὶ τοὺς
ἐπὶ πρα-[14]γμάτων συνεκαλουθεῖν ἐπὶ τὴν σημαινο-
[15]μένην οἰκίαν καὶ ἐπελθὼν οὕτως, ὁ προ-[16]γεγραμ-
μένος καὶ ἡ τού[το]υ γυνὴ Ταϋσῖρις [17]ἐμπλεκέντες
μοι καὶ δόντες πληγὰς [18]πλείους ἐγβιασάμενοι
ἀπέ[κλει]σαν [19]τήν τε τοῦ ἱεροῦ κ[αὶ τ]ῆς οἰ-
κ[ία]ς [20]θύραν. ὅθεν τῆι δ [τοῦ] Ἀθὺρ [ἐμ]πε-
[21]σόντος μου τῶι Σισόιτ[ι] παρὰ τὸ αὐτόθι [22]Διὸς
ἱερὸν καὶ βουλομένου ἀγωγὴν [23]ποιήσασθαι, Ἰνεί-
λοτος μαχαιροφόρου [24]παρόντος καὶ Τρυχάμβου,
ἐπεκχυ-[25]θέντες ἡμῖν Παυσῖρις ὁ τούτου ἀδελφὸς
[26]σακκοφόρος καὶ Βελλῆς καὶ Δημᾶς [27]καὶ Μάρων
Τακοννῶτος σὺν ἄλλοις [28]ὧν τὰ ὀνόματα ἀγνοῶι
καὶ ἡμῶν [29]ἐγκρατεῖς γενόμενοι ἐμβαλόντες [30]ἡμῖν
πληγὰς πλείους αἷς εἴχοσαν [31]κράνοις καὶ ἐτραυ-
μάτισαν τὴν γυναῖ-[32]κά μου εἰς τὴν δεξιὰν χεῖρα
κἀμὲ [33]ὁμοίως, ὥστ᾽ ἂν βλάβος γεγονέναι τῆι
[34]ὠνῆι εἰς χα(λκοῦ) (τάλαντα) ι. ἐπιδίδωμί σοι
[35]τὸ προσάγγελμα ὅπ[ω]ς συντάξῃς [36]οἷς καθήκει
ἵν᾽ εἰσπ[ρ]αχθέντες - - -

14. l. συνακολουθεῖν.

277. PETITION TO THE STRATEGUS

P. Rein. 18. 108 B.C.

[1]Ἀσκληπιάδει συγγενεῖ καὶ στρατηγῶι [2]παρὰ
Διονυσ[ί]ου τοῦ Κεφαλᾶ βασιλικοῦ γεωργοῦ [3]τῶν
254

temple of Thoeris [a] here. I immediately took Try-chambus the agent of the oeconomus who had been sent for the payment, since you and the other officials were unwilling to accompany me, to the house mentioned and made a descent upon it with him, when the aforesaid Sisois and his wife Tausiris set upon me and after giving me many blows drove us out and shut the door of the temple and of the house. Wherefore on encountering Sisois on the 4th of Hathur beside the temple of Zeus here I wished to arrest him, Ineilos the sword-bearer and Try-chambus being present. But Pausiris the brother of Sisois, a porter, and Belles and Demas and Maron son of Takonnos, with others whose names I do not know, hurled themselves upon us and overpowered us, showering blows upon us with the cudgels which they carried, and they wounded my wife on the right hand and myself also. The consequent loss to my contract amounts to 10 talents of copper. I accordingly present to you this statement in order that you may instruct the proper officials to exact from them (this sum) . . .

[a] An Egyptian goddess having the form of a hippo-potamus.

277. PETITION TO THE STRATEGUS

108 B.C.

To Asclepiades, king's cousin [a] and strategus, from Dionysius son of Cephalas, cultivator of Crown land,

[a] An honorary title.

ἐκ κώμ[η]ς Τήνεως τῆς καὶ Ἀκώρεως ⁴τοῦ Μω-
χίτου. διὰ τὰς ἐπὶ τοῦ πράγματος ὑπο-⁵δειχθη-
σομέ[ν]ας αἰτίας γραψαμένου ἐμοῦ τε ⁶καὶ τῆς
μη[τρ]ός μου Σεναβολλοῦτος Ἀδμή-⁷τωι τῶι καὶ
Χεσθώτηι τῶν ἐκ τῆς αὐτῆς ⁸κώμης συ[γγρ]αφὴν
δανείου διὰ τοῦ μνημο-⁹νείου πυρῶν (ἀρταβῶν) ρν
ἐν τῶι θ (ἔτει), οὐ μόνον ¹⁰δ', ἀλλὰ καὶ ἐθέμην
αὐτῶι ἐν πίστει καθ' ὧν ¹¹ἔχω ψιλῶν τό[π]ων
συγγραφὴν ὑποθήκης, ¹²ὁ ἐγκαλούμενος ἐγκρατὴς
γενόμενος ¹³τῶν συναλλάξ[ε]ων οὐθὲν τῶν δια-
σταθέντων ¹⁴μοι πρὸς αὐτ[ὸ]ν ἐπὶ τέλος ἤγαγεν, ὧν
¹⁵χάριν οὐκ ὀλί[γα] μοι βλάβη δι' αὐτὸν παρ-
η-¹⁶κολούθησεν· [καὶ] νῦν δ' ἐπ' ἀδίκου στάσεως
¹⁷ἱστάμενος, συνορῶν με περὶ τὴν κατα-¹⁸σπορὰν
ἧς γεω[ρ]γῶ γῆς κατασχολούμενον, ¹⁹καταδρομάς
μ[ο]υ ποιούμενος οὐκ ἐᾷ πρὸς ²⁰τῆι γεωργίᾳ γίνεσθαι, παρὰ τὰ περὶ ἡμῶν ²¹τῶν γεωργῶν δ[ιὰ]
πλειόνων προστετα-²²γμένα· ὅθεν τῆ[ς γ]ῆς ἐκ-
φ[υγεῖ]ν κινδυνευ-²³ο[ύ]σης ἠνάγκ[α]σμαι, ἐπ[ὶ] τοῦ
παρόντος ²⁴οὐ δυνάμενος πρὸς αὐτὸν περὶ τῶν συν-
²⁵αλλαγμάτων δ[ι]αδικεῖν, τὴν ἐπὶ σὲ κατα-²⁶φυγὴν
ποιήσασθαι. ἀξιῶ, ἐὰν φαίνηται, ²⁷συντάξαι πρὸ
[π]άντων μὲν γράψαι τῶι τῆς ²⁸Ἀκώρεως ἐπισ-
στ[άτ]ει μὴ ἐπιτρέπειν τῶι ²⁹ἐγκαλουμένωι μήτ'
ἐμὲ μ[ή]τε τὴν ³⁰μητέρα μου π[α]ρενοχλεῖν, δοῦναι
³¹δέ μοι τὰς πίστεις δι' ἐγγράπτων, μέχρι τοῦ
³²ἀπὸ τῆς κατασπορᾶς γενομένον με ³³συστήσασθαι
α[ὐ]τῶι τὸν περὶ ἑκάστων ³⁴λόγον. τούτου δὲ
γενομένου οὐθὲν τῶν τῶι ³⁵βασιλεῖ χρησί[μ]ων
διαπεσεῖται, ἐγώ τ' ἔ-³⁶σομαι ἀντειλ[ημ]μένος.
³⁷εὐτύχει. (2nd hand) ³⁸Βίαντι. ε[ἰ ἔσ]τι βασιλι-
κὸς ³⁹γεωργός, [πρ]ονοηθῆναι ὡς ⁴⁰ἀπερίσπ[αστο]ς

of the village of Tenis also called Akoris in the Mochite district.[a] For reasons which will be indicated in the course of the affair I and my mother Senabollous made with Admetus also called Chesthotes, of the same village, a contract of loan through the record-office for 150 artabae of wheat in the 9th year ; not only so, but I also made with him for guarantee a contract of mortgage on the unoccupied sites which I possess. Having obtained these agreements the accused performed none of the things about which we had come to terms, whereby he has caused me no slight damage; and now on wrongful grounds, seeing me busily engaged in sowing the land which I cultivate, he persecutes me and does not allow me to attend to the cultivation in spite of the decrees repeatedly issued about us cultivators ; wherefore as the land threatens to get out of hand, being unable at present to go to law with him about the agreements, I have been compelled to seek your protection. I request you, if you approve, to give orders first of all for a letter to be written to the epistates of Akoris not to allow the accused to molest either me or my mother, and to give me a safe-conduct in writing, until I have finished the sowing and can settle accounts with him on every point. By this means none of the king's interests will suffer, while I myself shall obtain relief. Farewell. (Below, the order of the strategus.) To Bias. If he is a cultivator of Crown land, see to it that he

---

[a] In Middle Egypt.

κατασταθήσεται ⁴¹μέχρι [ἂν ἀπὸ] τοῦ σπόρου ⁴²γένη-
ται. (ἔτους) ι Θωὺθ κδ.
Verso : Βίαντι. (To left) Διονυσίου.

278. COMPLAINT OF ROBBERY

P. Ryl. 125.   A.D. 28–29.

¹Σεραπίωνι ἐπιστάτῃ φυλακειτῶν ²παρὰ Ὀρ-
σενούφιος τοῦ Ἁρπαήσιος ³ἡγ[ο]υμένου κώμης Εὐ-
ημερίας ⁴τῆς Θεμίστου μερίδος. τῷ Μεσορὴ ⁵μηνὶ
τοῦ διελη(λυθότος) ιδ (ἔτους) Τιβερίου Καίσαρος
⁶Σεβαστοῦ ποιουμέ[ν]ου μου κα-⁷τασπασμὸν τειχα-
ρίων παλαιῶ(ν) ⁸ἐν τοῖς οἰκοπέδο[ι]ς μου διὰ Πε-
⁹τεσούχου τοῦ Πετεσούχου οἰκοδόμ(ου) ¹⁰καὶ ἐμοῦ
χωρισθέντος εἰς ἀπο-¹¹δημίαν βιωτ[ι]κῶν χάριν
¹²εὗρεν ὁ Πετεσοῦχος ἐν τῷ κατασ-¹³πασμῷ τὰ
ὑπὸ τῆς μητρός ¹⁴μου ἀποτεθειμένα ἐν πυξι-
¹⁵δίωι ἔτι ἀπὸ τοῦ ις (ἔτους) Καίσαρος ¹⁶ἐνωτίων
χρυσὸ(ν) ζεῦγο(ς) (τεταρτῶν) δ καὶ ¹⁷μηνίσκο(ν)
χρυσο(ῦν) (τεταρτῶν) γ καὶ ψελίω(ν) ¹⁸ἀργυρῶν
ζεῦγο(ς) ὁλκῆ(ς) ἀσήμο(υ) (δραχμῶν) ιβ ¹⁹καὶ ὁρ-
μίσκον ἐν ᾧ ἀργυρᾶ ἄξιο(ν) (δραχμῶν) π ²⁰καὶ
ἀργυ(ρίου) (δραχμὰς) ξ, καὶ διαπλανήσας ²¹τοὺ[ς
ὑπ]ουργοῦντας καὶ τοὺς ἐμοὺς ²²ἀπηνέγκατο παρ᾽
ἑατὸν διὰ τῆς ²³ἑατοῦ θυγατρὸς παρθένου· ²⁴ἐκ-
κενώσας τὰ προκείμενα ²⁵ἔριψεν ἐν τῇ οἰκίᾳ μου
τὴν ²⁶πυξίδα κενήν, ὃς καὶ ὡμολ[ό-]²⁷γησεν τὴν
πυξίδα ὡς προ-²⁸φέρεται κενήν. διὸ ἀξιῶ, ²⁹ἐὰν

16. l. χρυσῶν.   22. l. ἑαυτόν.   23. l. ἑαυτοῦ.

remains undisturbed until he finishes the sowing.
Year 10, Thoth 24. (Addressed) To Bias. (Docket)
From Dionysius.

278. COMPLAINT OF ROBBERY

A.D. 28–29.

To Serapion, chief of police, from Orsenouphis son
of Harpaesis, notable of the village of Euhemeria [a]
in the division of Themistes. In the month Mesore
of the past 14th year of Tiberius Caesar Augustus
I was having some old walls on my premises demolished by the mason Petesouchus son of Petesouchus, and while I was absent from home to gain my
living, Petesouchus in the process of demolition discovered a hoard which had been secreted by my
mother in a little box as long ago as the 16th year of
Caesar,[b] consisting of a pair of gold earrings weighing
4 quarters, a gold crescent weighing 3 quarters, a pair
of silver armlets of the weight of 12 drachmae of
uncoined metal, a necklace with silver ornaments
worth 80 drachmae, and 60 silver drachmae. Divert-
ing the attention of his assistants and my people he
had them conveyed to his own home by his maiden
daughter, and after emptying out the aforesaid
objects he threw away the box empty in my house,
and he even admitted finding the box, though he
pretends that it was empty. Wherefore I request,

[a] See No. 255, note a.   [b] That is, Augustus.

φαίνηται, ἀχθῆναι τὸν ³⁰ἐνκαλούμενο(ν) ἐπὶ σὲ
πρὸς τὴν ³¹ἐσομένη(ν) ἐπέξοδ(ον). ³²εὐτύχ(ει).
³³Ὀρσενοῦφ(ις) (ἐτῶν) ν οὐ(λὴ) πήχ(ει) ἀρισ(τερῷ).

279. PETITION TO THE EXEGETES OF ALEXANDRIA

P. Ryl. 119.   A.D. 54–67.

¹Τιβερίωι Κλαυδίωι Κρονίωι ἐξηγητῆι τῆς πόλεως Ἀλεξανδ(ρέων) ²παρὰ Δημητρίου τοῦ Ἀρι-
στομένου τῶν ἐκ τ[ο]ῦ ὑπὲρ Μέμφιν ³ʿΕρμοπο-
λείτου. τυγχάνωι κεκριμένος ὑπὸ τοῦ κρατίστου
⁴ἡγεμόνος Γαΐου Καικίνα Τούσκου τῶι ιβ (ἔτει)
θεοῦ ⁵Κλαυδίου Καίσαρος Σεβαστοῦ Γερμανικοῦ
Αὐτοκράτορος, ⁶ἡνίκα ἦν δικαιοδότης, σὺν τοῖς
πατραδέλφ[ο]ις μου Διονυσίωι ⁷καὶ Δημητρίωι
πρεσβυτέρωι ἀμφοτέροις Δημητρίου ὑπέρ τε ⁸ἡμῶν
καὶ τῆς τοῦ Διονυσίου θυγατρὸς Φιλωτέρας πρὸς
⁹δανειστὴν ἡμῶν Μουσαῖον ʿΕρμοφίλου γυμνασί-
αρχον ¹⁰περὶ λογοθεσίας ἧς ἔχει ἡμῶν ὑποθήκης
ἀρουρῶν ¹¹ὀγδοήκοντα τριῶν τετάρτου καὶ περὶ
ὧν ἀπηνέγκατο ¹²ἐκ τούτων πλειόνων ἐκφορίων
ὑπὲρ τὸ διπλοῦν τοῦ ¹³κεφαλαίου, μετὰ τὰ ἐν
κ[α]τενγυήσει γεν[ό]μενα ἄλλα ¹⁴ἐκφόρια (δραχμὰς)

ᵃ A civic magistrate who appears to have had certain
judicial powers not only in Alexandria, but also in the
country towns.   ᵇ See No. 263.

ᶜ Some time previously the plaintiffs had borrowed from
Musaeus 4800 drachmae on the security of 83¾ arurae of
and.   What then happened is not clear, but when litigation

if you approve, that the accused be brought before you for the consequent punishment.   Farewell.

Orsenouphis, aged 50, scar on left forearm.[a]

[a] Added by the scribe for the purpose of identification.

279. PETITION TO THE EXEGETES OF ALEXANDRIA

A.D. 54–67.

To Tiberius Claudius Cronius, exegetes of Alexandria,[a] from Demetrius son of Aristomenes, of the Hermopolite nome above Memphis.   It happens that I, with my paternal uncles Dionysius and the elder Demetrius, both sons of Demetrius, in the 12th year of the deified Claudius Caesar Augustus Germanicus Imperator had a case judged by his excellency the praefect Gaius Caecina Tuscus when he was juridicus,[b] in which we and Dionysius's daughter Philotera were suing our creditor Musaeus son of Hermophilus, gymnasiarch, for an audit of the mortgage which he holds against us of eighty-three and a quarter arurae, and for the numerous rents therefrom which he had appropriated to the amount of more than double the capital sum, apart from the further sum of 5000 drachmae in rents on which an embargo had been laid.[c]   He de-began, Musaeus was occupying the land and had been receiving the revenues from it, though after the opening of the case an embargo had been laid on future revenues.   In the case tried by Tuscus the plaintiffs, on grounds about which we have no definite information, were claiming (1) restitution of the mortgaged land, *i.e.* the 83¾ arurae, and (2) the revenues which Musaeus had appropriated since his occupation of it.

Ἐ · ἐδικαίωσεν ἀποδοῦναι ἡμᾶς τὸ κεφά-[15]λαιον
καὶ ἀνακομίσασθαι τὴν ὑποθήκην ἀπολυθῆ-[16]ναί
τε τὸν Μουσαῖον ὧν ἔφθη λαβεῖν ἐκφορίων.
προσ-[17]ελθόντων δὲ ἡμῶν ἀκολ{λ}ούθως τοῖς αὐτοῦ
ὑπομνη-[18]ματισμοῖς τῶι Μουσαίωι δοῦναι ἡμεῖν
μέρος τῆς [19]ὑποθήκης εἰς πρᾶσιν ὥστε ἀποδοθῆναι
αὐτῶι τὸ κε-[20]φάλαιον, μηδενὸς πόρου ἡμεῖν
ὑπάρχοντος πλὴν τῆς [21]ὑποθήκης, οὐκ ἐπένευσεν
ἐξόφθαλμος αὐτῆς κα-[22]θεστὼς διὰ τὸ πλῆθος τῶν
κατ᾽ ἔτος γενημάτων, δεκαρ-[23]τάβου πυροῦ ὄντος
κατ᾽ ἔτος τοῦ ἐκφορίου, ἀλλὰ καὶ τὰ πα-[24]ρὰ
γεωργοῖς ἐν κατεγγυήσει ἀπὸ ἐπιστολῆς αὐτοῦ
[25]Τούσκου γενόμενα ἐκφόρια ι (ἔτους) καὶ ια
(ἔτους) ἀνήρπα-[26]σεν καὶ μέχρι νῦν καρπίζεται τὴν
αὐτὴν ὑποθήκην [27]ἀφ᾽ ἧς ἀπηνέγκατο εἰς λόγον
ἀργυ(ρίου) (ταλάντων) ε ἀντὶ κεφαλαίου [28](δραχμῶν) Δω. κατὰ πᾶν οὖν συνηρπασμένοι ὑπὸ
τούτου καθ᾽ οὗ [29]καὶ πλείστας ἐντυχίας καὶ ἐπι-
δόσεις ἀναφορῶν ἐποιη-[30]σάμεθα, καὶ ἐν οὐδενὶ
ἡγήσατο καθὸ ὑπερισχύων ἡ-[31]μᾶς ἐπὶ τῶν τόπων,
μεταδόντες αὐτῶι καὶ τοῖς αὐτοῦ [32]υἱοῖς Ἑρμο-
φίλωι καὶ Κάστορι διαστολικὸν ὑπόμνημα κατελ-
[33]θεῖν εἰ[ς] τὸν διαλογισμόν, οἱ δὲ υἱοὶ παρηγησά-
μενοι οὐ πα-[34]ρεγένοντο. ὧν χάριν ἀξιοῦμεν περὶ
πάντων τούτων [35]διαλαβεῖν ὅπως τύχωμεν τῶν
παρὰ σοῦ δικαίων καὶ [36]ὦμεν εὐεργετημένοι.

[37]Ἑρμοπολ(ῖται) Δημήτριος Ἀριστομένους καὶ
Φιλωτέρα{ς} [38]Διονυσίου ὑπὲρ ἧς ἀνὴρ συνεστά[θη]
Εὔδημος [39]Μετόκου πρὸς Μουσαῖον Ἑρμ[ο]-
φίλ[ο]υ δανι[σ]τὴν καὶ [40]τοὺς αὐτοῦ υἱοὺς Ἑρ-
μόφιλ(ον) καὶ Κάστορα περὶ ἀνοκο-[41]μιδῆς ὑπο-

40. l. ἀνακομιδῆς.

cided that we should repay the capital sum and recover the security and that Musaeus should receive
a discharge for the rents which he had already
obtained. In conformity with his recorded judgement we proposed to Musaeus that he should give
us part of the security to sell so that we should
be able to repay him the capital sum, as we had
no means other than the security, but he refused,
having grown covetous of it owing to the amount
of its yearly produce, the rent being at the rate of
ten artabae of wheat per year. Not only that but
he seized the rents of the 10th and 11th years which
were lying with the cultivators under embargo in
consequence of a letter from Tuscus, and he continues
up till now to enjoy the said security, by which he
has profited to the extent of 5 talents in return for
a capital sum of 4800 drachmae. We have therefore
been robbed on every side by this man, against whom
we made petitions and presented reports many in
number, which he scorned in virtue of his superior
local power, and we served a summons upon him
and his sons Hermophilus and Castor to go down to
the assize, but his sons made light of it and did not
appear; wherefore we request you to give a decision
on all these points, allowing us to obtain justice at
your hands and to experience your benevolence.

Demetrius son of Aristomenes and Philotera
daughter of Dionysius, on behalf of whom her husband Eudemus son of Metocus has been appointed
a representative, citizens of Hermopolis, *versus*
Musaeus son of Hermophilus, their creditor, and his
sons Hermophilus and Castor *re* the restitution of the

θήκη(ς) (ἀρουρῶν) πγδ´ καὶ καρπῶν αὐτῶν πλει-
⁴²ό[ν]ων κεφαλαίων (ταλάντων) ε.

280. PETITION TO THE STRATEGUS
ABOUT AN OIL-FACTORY

P. Spec. Isag. pl. xi. No. 21
    (= W. Chrest. 176).   A.D. reign of Nero.

¹Φιλοξένωι κοσμητεύσαντι στρατηγῶι ²·³Ἀρσι-
νοΐτου Θεμίστου μερίδος ³παρὰ Ἑρ[ι]έως τοῦ
Σαταβοῦτος τῶν ἀπὸ τῆς Σο-⁴κνεπαίου Νήσου.
ἐμισθωσάμην ἔτι ἀπ[ὸ τοῦ] ⁵ιγ (ἔτους) θεοῦ
Κλαυδίου ἐκ τῆς πρότερον Ναρκίσσου ⁶οὐσίας
ἐλαιουργῖον ἐπὶ φόρωι (δραχμαῖς) σ καὶ ἐλαίου
⁷χόεσι τρισί. ἔκτοτε δὲ τῶν προεστώτω[ν] ⁸μὴ
δόντων εἰς τὸ ὄργανον μήτε χοινικίδε[ς] ⁹μήτε τὰ
ἄλλα ἃ ἔδει, αὐτὸς ἠναγκάσθην ἐκ ¹⁰τοῦ ἰδίου ἀγο-
ράσας ἐξαρτίσαι καὶ μηχανὴ[ν] ¹¹ὁμοίως καὶ θυΐας
καὶ τὰ ἄλλα τὰ ἐνχρήζοντα ¹²πάλιν ἐκ τοῦ ἰδίου,
μηδεμίαν μου ἐπιστρ[ο-¹³]φὴν ποιησαμένων αὐτῶν.
ἐπεὶ οὖν καὶ αὐ-¹⁴τὸ τὸ ἐλαιουργῖον συνεχυτρώθη
καὶ ἠναγ-¹⁵κάσθην δοκοὺς καὶ ἐρείσματα παρα-
τιθένα[ι]¹⁶καὶ διετίαι ἀναγκάζομαι ἔξω τοῦ ἐλαιουρ-
γίου ¹⁷ὧν τοὺς φόρους ἐξ [οἴ]κόθεν διαγράφειν,
ἀξιῶ ¹⁸οὐκέτι εὔ[τον]ῶν ὑπομέν[ειν] τὰς ζημίας
¹⁹ἐπαναγκάσαι τοὺς πρ[ο]εστῶτας ἀπαρενόχλη-
²⁰τόν με ποιῆσαι ὑπὲρ τ[ῶ]ν φόρων.

        3. l. Σοκνοπαίου.   8. l. χοινικίδα[ς].

security of 83¼ arurae and of the numerous revenues from them amounting to 5 talents.

280. PETITION TO THE STRATEGUS ABOUT AN OIL-FACTORY

A.D. reign of Nero.

To Philoxenus, ex-cosmetes, strategus of the division of Themistes in the Arsinoite nome, from Herieus son of Satabous, of Socnopaei Nesus. As long ago as the 13th year of the deified Claudius I leased from the former estate of Narcissus [a] an oil-factory at a rent of 200 drachmae and three choes of oil. But as afterwards the superintendents of the estate did not give me either iron sockets or the other things which were needed for the oil-press, I was compelled to supply them by purchase at my own expense, likewise a lever and mortars and the other necessaries, all at my own expense, for they paid no attention to me. Since therefore the factory itself was in a state of collapse and I was compelled to put in beams and props and for two years have been compelled, though not using the factory, to pay the rent from my own resources, I request you, as I am no longer able to support the losses, to constrain the superintendents to leave me free from molestation about the rent.

[a] The well-known favourite of the Emperor Claudius. After his fall, and at the date of the petition, the estate had been added to the Imperial domains.

281. DRAFT OF A PETITION TO THE PRAEFECT

P. Graux 2.   A.D. 55–59.

¹Τιβερίωι Κλαυδίωι Βαλβίλλωι ²παρὰ Νεμε-
σίωνος πράκτορος λαογραφ(ίας) Φειλ(αδελφείας)
καὶ Χαριδήμου πράκτορος λαογρ(αφίας) Βακχ(ιά-
δος) καὶ ³Σαμβᾶτος πράκτορος λαογρ(αφίας) Νέσ-
το(υ) ἐποικί(ου) καὶ Πανεφρέμμιος πράκτορος
Σοκνοπαίο(υ) Νή(σου) καὶ Ἰσχυ-⁴ρίωνος πράκτορος
λαογρ(αφίας) Φειλοπάτορας καὶ Πτολεμαίου πράκτορος λαογρ(αφίας) Ἱερᾶς Νήσου, τῶν ἐξ πρακτό-
⁵ρων ⟦λαογραφίας τινῶν⟧ τῶν προκειμένων κωμῶν
τῆς ⁶Ἡρακλείδου μερίδος τοῦ Ἀρσινοείτου νομοῦ.
⁷ἀπὸ τῶν ἔμπροσθεν πολυανδρούντων ⁸ἐν ταῖς
προκειμέναις κώμαις νυνεὶ κα-⁹τήντησαν εἰς ὀλί-
γους διὰ τὸ τοὺς μὲν ¹⁰ἀνακεχωρηκέναι ἀπόρους,
τοὺς δὲ τετε-¹¹λευτηκέ[ναι] μὴ ἔχοντας ἀγχιστεῖς,
καὶ διὰ ¹²τοῦτο κ[ιν]δυνεύειν ἡμᾶς δι᾽ ἀσθένειαν
¹³προλιπε[ῖν] τὴν πρακτορείαν· ὧν χάριν ¹⁴ἐπὶ σὲ
κατ[α]ντήσαντες ⟦πρὸς τὸ μὴ προλι-¹⁵πεῖν τὴν
[π]ρακτορείαν⟧ ἀξιοῦμέν σε τὸν ¹⁶πάντων σωτῆρα
καὶ εὐεργέτην, ἐὰν φαί-¹⁷νηται, γράψαι τῶι τοῦ
νομοῦ στρατηγῶι ¹⁸Ἀσινιανῶι ἀπαρανοχλήτους
ἡμᾶς φυλάξαι ¹⁹[κα]ὶ ἐπισχεῖν μέχρι τῆς σῆς
διαγνώσε-²⁰ως ἐπὶ διαλογισμοῦ τοῦ νομοῦ ἄνω, ἵν᾽
ὦμεν εὐεργετ(ημένοι). ²¹διευτύχει.

2-6. The titles have been interpolated after the names and
λαογραφιας τινων altered to των προκειμενων.   l. Φιλ(αδελφείας) and in l. 4 Φιλοπάτορος.   18. l. ἀπαρενοχλήτους.

281. DRAFT OF A PETITION TO THE PRAEFECT

A.D. 55–59.

To Tiberius Claudius Balbillus from Nemesion, collector of poll-tax for Philadelphia, and Charidemus, collector of poll-tax for Bacchias, and Sambas, collector of poll-tax for the hamlet of Nestus, and Panephremmis, collector for Socnopaei Nesus, and Ischyrion, collector of poll-tax for Philopator, and Ptolemaeus, collector of poll-tax for Hiera Nesus, all six collectors for the aforesaid villages in the division of Heraclides in the Arsinoite nome. The once numerous inhabitants of the aforesaid villages have now been reduced to a few,[a] because some have fled for lack of means and others have died without leaving heirs-at-law, and for this reason we are in danger owing to impoverishment of having to abandon the collectorship ; wherefore resorting to you ⟦in order not to have to abandon it⟧ [b] we request you, who are the saviour and benefactor of all, to write, if it please you, to Asinianus the strategus of the nome to keep us free from molestation and await your decision at the assize of the nome up here,[c] in order that we may enjoy your beneficence.   Farewell.

[a] The text shows, though perhaps the writers exaggerated, that even at this early period the oppressive Roman rule was leading to depopulation.   Three centuries later the villages on the edge of the Fayum were almost entirely empty.   *Cf.* No. 295.
[b] The bracketed words have been deleted as superfluous.
[c] Memphis was the usual seat of the assize for Middle Egypt, though one was occasionally held at Arsinoe in the Fayum.

SELECT PAPYRI

282. COMPLAINT AGAINST THE SUPER-INTENDENT OF A CUSTOM-HOUSE

P. Amh. 77, ll. 1-33.   A.D. 139.

¹Ἰουλίῳ Πετρωνιανῷ τῶι κρατ[ί]στῳ ἐπιστρατήγῳ ²παρὰ Παβοῦτ[ο]ς τοῦ Στοτοήτεως τοῦ
Πανομιέως ³ἱερέως ἀπὸ κώμης [Σ]οκνοπαίου Νήσου
τῆς ⁴ʽΗρακλείδου μερίδος [τοῦ ʼΑ]ρσ[ι]νοΐτου
νομοῦ ʼΑραβο-⁵τοξότου πύλη[ς] τῆς αὐτῆς Σοκνοπαίου Νήσου. ⁶[.] . [. . . .]ν κατηγορ . [. .,
ἀ]λλὰ ὁρῶν τὸν φίσκον ⁷περιγραφόμενον ὑπὸ
Πολυδεύκους τετραετεῖ ⁸ἤδη χρόνωι παρὰ τὰ
ἀπειρημένα ἐπιτηροῦν-⁹τος τὴν προκειμένην πύλην
καὶ ὑπὸ ¹⁰[ʼΑρπαγ]άθ[ου το]ῦ Ερο[. .]τακος ἐπ-
έδωκα ¹¹τ[ο]ῖς τῆς [νομαρχίας ἐπι]τηρητα[ῖ]ς
ἀντί[γρα-]¹²φον ὧν εἶχ[ο]ν τοῦ ʼΑρπαγάθου ἰδι[ο-
γ]ράφ{ι}ων ¹³ἀναγραφίων τῶν διὰ τῆς πύλης εἰσαχ-
θέντων ¹⁴[κ]αὶ ἐξαχθ[έντων, ἀ]ξιῶν τὴν ἐξέτασιν
αὐ[τ]ῶν ¹⁵γ[ε]νέσ[θαι εἰς] τὸ ἐπ[ιγ]νῶναι εἰ προσ-
ετέ[θη] ¹⁶αὐτῶν τὰ τέλη τῷ κυριακῶι λόγωι. καὶ
¹⁷ἐπιγνοὺς ὁ Πολυδε[ύκ]ης ἐπελθών μοι ¹⁸μεθ'
ἑτέρων, ὧν τὰ ὀνόματα ἀγνοῶι, πλείσ[τ]α[ι]ς
¹⁹πληγαῖς με ἠκίσατο, καὶ μὴ ἀρκεσθε[ὶ]ς ²⁰ἐπ-
ή[ν]εγκέ μοι ʽΗρα[κλ]ᾶν τινα μαχαιρο-²¹φόρων
οὐσιακῶν καὶ ἀμφότεροι βίᾳ ²²βασ[τ]άξαντές με
εἰσήνεγκαν εἰς τὸ λογ[ι]στήριον ²³τοῦ ἐπιτρόπου
τῶν οὐσιῶν καὶ ἐποίησάν με ²⁴ . [.]κ[.] . αιον ὄντα
μαστιγοῦσθαι εἰς τὸ ἀναδῶ-²⁵[ναί] με α[ὐτοῖς]
τὸ τοῦ [ʼΑρπ]αγάθου ἀναγράφιον, ὅπερ ²⁶φανερὸν

ᵃ This village lay on the north bank of Lake Moeris, on
the edge of the desert, and a good deal of commerce with the
Oases passed through the toll-gate.

282. COMPLAINT AGAINST THE SUPER-INTENDENT OF A CUSTOM-HOUSE

A.D. 139.

To his excellency the epistrategus Julius Petronianus from Pabous son of Stotoetis son of Panomieus, priest, of the village of Socnopaei Nesus *a* in the division of Heraclides in the Arsinoite nome, Arab archer *b* at the custom-house of the said Socnopaei Nesus. Not because I sought an occasion of accusation (?), but because I saw the Treasury being defrauded by Polydeuces, who contrary to the prohibition has now for four years been in charge of the aforesaid custom-house, and by Harpagathes son of Ero . . ., I presented to the overseers of the nomarchy a copy of the returns which I possessed in Harpagathes' own hand of the imports and exports passing through the custom-house, requesting that an examination of them should be made in order to determine whether the taxes upon them had been added to the Treasury account. Polydeuces having discovered this attacked me with other persons whose names I do not know and belaboured me with many blows, and not satisfied with this set upon me Heraclas, one of the sword-bearers attached to the domains,*c* and the two of them taking me up by force carried me to the counting-house of the superintendent of the domains and caused me . . . to be scourged in order to make me give up to them the register of Harpagathes, an act

---

b Name of a class of watchmen, perhaps used for service on the desert edge.

c Private property of the Emperors, under a special administration.

τοῦτο ἐγένετ[ο] τοῖς τε τῆς νομαρχίας ἐπιτηρη-
²⁷τ[αῖς] καὶ τῷ ἐ[πὶ] τῶν τόπων τότε ὄντι βεφιν[ι]-
καρίωι ²⁸[. . . . . . ὅθεν] κατὰ τὸ ἀνα[γ]καῖ[ον
ἐπιδίδ]ωμι ²⁹καὶ ἀξι[ῶ, ἐὰ]ν δ[ό]ξῃ σοι, [πέ]μψαι
[πρὸς σ]ὲ καὶ ³⁰τὸν Πολυδεύκην καὶ τὸν Ἁρπα-
[γάθην τὸ]ν ³¹κράτιστον τοῦ κακοῦ καὶ προσεπί-
τροπο[ν], ἵνα ³²δυνηθῶ τὴν ἀπόδιξιν ἐπ᾽ αὐτοὺς
π[ο]ιησ[ά]μενο(ς) ³³τυχεῖν καὶ τῆς ἀπὸ σοῦ εὐεργεσίας. διευτύχει.

283. PETITION TO THE PRAEFECT FROM A PHYSICIAN

P. Fay. 106, ll. 6-25.   About A.D. 140.

⁶Γαΐωι ᾽Αουιδίωι ῾Ηλιοδώρωι ἐ[πάρχ(ῳ) Αἰ-
γ(ύπτου)] ᾽παρὰ Μάρ‹κου› Οὐαλερ[ί]ου Γεμέλλου
[ἰατροῦ]. ⁸παρὰ τὰ ἀπηγορευμένα ἀχθ[εὶς εἰς ἐπι-]
⁹τήρησιν γε[ν]ημα[τ]ογραφουμ[ένων] ¹⁰ὑπαρχόντ[ων
πε]ρὶ κώμα[ς Βακχ(ιάδα)] ¹¹καὶ ῾Ηφαιστιάδα τῆς
῾Ηρακλ[είδου] ¹²μερίδος τοῦ ᾽Αρσινοΐτου τ[ετραε-]
¹³τεῖ ἤδη χρόνωι ἐν τῇ χρ[είαι] ¹⁴πονούμενος ἐξεσ-
θένησα [ὅλως ?], ¹⁵κύριε, ὅθεν ἀξιῶ σαὶ τὸν σω[τῆρα]
¹⁶ἐλεῆσαί με καὶ κελεῦσαι ἤ[δη με] ¹⁷ἀπολυθῆναι
τῆς χρείας, ὅπ[ως δυ-]¹⁸νηθῶ ἐμαυτὸν ἀνακτήσα-
[σθαι ἀ-]¹⁹πὸ τῶν καμάτων, οὐδὲν δ[ὲ ἦτ-]²⁰τον καὶ
ὁμοιώμ[ατα] ὑποτάξα[ς δι᾽ ὧν] ²¹τέλεον ἀπολύονται
τῶν [λειτουρ-]²²γιῶν οἱ τὴν ἰατρικὴν ἐπιστή[μην]
²³μεταχειριζόμενοι, μάλ[ι]στα [δὲ οἱ δε-]²⁴δοκιμασ-
μένοι ὥσπερ κἀγ[ώ, ἵν᾽] ²⁵ὦ εὐεργετημένος. δι-
ευτύ[χει].

15. l. σέ.   19-20. Suppl. E.-H.

which became known both to the overseers of the
nomarchy and to the *beneficiarius* then in the district.
I am therefore compelled to present this petition,
requesting you, if you think fit, to send for Polydeuces
and Harpagathes, the chief cause and prime mover
in the mischief, in order that I may present the
proofs against them and enjoy your beneficence.
Farewell.

---

27. *l.* βενεφικιαρίωι.   31. κράτιστον and προσεπίτροπον
doubtful.

283. PETITION TO THE PRAEFECT FROM A PHYSICIAN

About A.D. 140.

To Gaius Avidius Heliodorus, praefect of Egypt,
from Marcus Valerius Gemellus, physician. Contrary to the prohibition I have been impressed as a
superintendent of sequestrated property within the
villages of Bacchias and Hephaestias in the division
of Heraclides in the Arsinoite nome, and through
labouring on this task for the last four years I have
become quite impoverished, my lord; wherefore I
entreat you, my preserver, to have pity on me and
order me now to be released from my task, in order
that I may be able to recover from the effects of my
labours, having at the same time appended precedents
by which complete exemption from compulsory services is granted to persons practising the profession
of medicine,[a] especially to those who have been approved like myself, that so I may experience your
benevolence. Farewell.

[a] Compare No. 245.

284. PETITION OF A WOMAN CONCERNING EXEMPTION FROM THE COMPULSORY CULTIVATION OF STATE LAND

B.G.U. 648.   A.D. 164 or 196.

- - -¹τῶι κρ[α]τίσ[τ]ωι ²παρὰ Ταμύσθας Κεν-
θυ[ο]ύφ[εως . . . . -]³κους ἀπ[ὸ κ]ώμης
Θερενο[ύθεως τοῦ Πρ]ο-⁴σωπείτου νομοῦ. τ[οῦ]
πα[τρ]ό[ς μου], κ[ύρ]ιε, ⁵τελευτήσαντος καὶ κατ[α]-
λιπόντ[ο]ς μοι τὸ ⁶ἐπιβάλλον αὐτῷ μέρ[ος] οἰκο-
πέδων καὶ ⁷φοινικῶνος ἐν Σκίθι πατρικῶν αὐτοῦ
⁸ὄντων, ὁ τούτου ἀδελφὸς Πανετβῆς καὶ ⁹Θαῆσις
Πατερμούθεως ἀνεψιά μου βι-¹⁰αίως ἀντι[λ]αμ-
βάνονται τ[ο]ῦ πατρικοῦ ¹¹μου μέρους προφάσει
γεωργίας βασιλικῆς ¹²γῆς, εἰς ἢν γυνὴ οὖσα οὐκ
ὀφείλω καθέλ-¹³κεσθαι κατὰ τὰ ὑπὸ τῶν ἡγεμόνων
καὶ ¹⁴ἐπιτρόπων περὶ τούτου διατεταγμένα, ¹⁵ἐπεὶ
καὶ ἄτεκν[ός] εἰμι καὶ οὐδὲ ἐμαυτῆι ¹⁶ἀπαρκεῖν
δύναμαι. ἀξιῶ οὖν, κύριε, ¹⁷ἐάν σου τῇ τύχῃ δόξῃ,
κελεῦσαι γραφῆναι ¹⁸τῷ τοῦ νομοῦ στρατηγῷ
ἐπαναγκάσαι αὐ-¹⁹τοὺς τὸ πατρικόν μοι μέρος
ἀποκαταστῆ-²⁰σαι, τὴν δὲ γεωργίαν ὑπό τε τοῦ
Πανε-²¹τβήους καὶ τῶν τῆς Θαήσιος τέκνων γεί-
²²νεσθαι, ἵν᾽ ὦ εὐεργετημ(ένη). (2nd hand) διευ-
(τύ)χει. (3rd hand) ²³Ταμύσθα ἐπιδέδωκα. Διονύσιος ἔγρα-²⁴ψ[α] ὑπὲρ αὐτῆς γράμματα μὴ ἰδυίης.
(2nd hand) ²⁵(ἔτους) ε″ Θὼθ ιγ. (4th hand)
²⁶[ἔ]ντ[υχε] τῷ στρ[α]τηγῷ, ὃς τὰ ἑαυτῷ προσήκοντα [πο]ιήσ[ει]. (5th hand) ἀ[πό]δος.

ᵃ Probably the dioecetes.
ᵇ A village on the western edge of the Delta.

284. PETITION OF A WOMAN CONCERNING EXEMPTION FROM THE COMPULSORY CULTIVATION OF STATE LAND

A.D. 164 or 196.

To his excellency [a] . . . from Tamystha daughter of Kenthnouphis . . ., of the village of Terenouthis [b] in the Prosopite nome. My father having died, my lord, and left me the portion falling to him of house sites and of a palm-grove at Skithis, inherited by him from his father, his brother Panetbes and my cousin Thaesis daughter of Patermouthis are appropriating by force the portion which I inherited from my father, on the plea that this involves the cultivation of state land,[c] a burden which I being a woman ought not to be forced to undertake in virtue of the edicts of praefects and procurators on this subject, seeing that I am both childless and unable to provide even for myself. I ask you therefore, my lord, if it please your fortune, to command instructions to be written to the strategus of the nome to compel them to restore my patrimony and to assign the cultivation to Panetbes and the children of Thaesis, that so I may enjoy your beneficence. Farewell. (Signed) I, Tamystha, have presented the petition. I, Dionysius, wrote for her, as she is illiterate. (Dated) Year 5, Thoth 13. (Subscribed) Submit your case to the strategus, who will do what is in his competence. (Order to the clerk) Deliver.[d]

[c] Owners of private land were required to undertake the cultivation of a certain amount of state land, but exemption was granted to women, or perhaps only to childless women.

[d] To the proper authority, in order that the petition with the answer should be posted up in public.

SELECT PAPYRI

285. PETITION OF A VETERAN FOR A TERM OF EXEMPTION FROM COMPULSORY OFFICES

B.G.U. 180.   A.D. 172.

- - - ¹παρὰ [Γα]ΐου Ἰ[ου]λ[ίου Ἀπολ]ινα[ρίο]υ
οὐ[ε-]²τρανοῦ γε[ο]υχ[ο]ῦ[ντος ἐν] κώμῃ Κα[ρα-]
³νίδι. [δ]ιατέτακ[ται, κ]ύριε, τοῦ‹ς› οὐετρα-⁴νοὺς
ἔχειν μετὰ τ[ὴν ἀπό]λυσιν πεντ[α-]⁵ετῆ χρό[ν]ον
ἀναπ[αύσε]ως. παρὰ δὴ ταύ-⁶την τὴν [δι]άτ[α]ξιν
ἐ[γὼ] ἐπηρεάσθην ⁷μ[ε]τὰ διετίαν τῆς [ἀπο]λύσεως
κα[ὶ] ⁸ἀ[ν]εδόθην κατ᾽ ἐπή[ρια]ν εἰς λειτουργίαν ⁹καὶ
μέχρι τοῦ δεῦρο [κ]ατὰ τὸ ἑξῆς ¹⁰ἐν λειτουργίᾳ
εἰμ[ὶ] ἀδιαλεί[πτ]ως. ¹¹τοῦ τοιούτου παντ[ὶ] ἀπ-
ηγορευ-¹²μένου [ἐ]πὶ τῶν ἐν[χ]ωρίων πολλῷ ¹³πλεῖον
ἐπ᾽ ἐμοῦ συντηρεῖσθαι ¹⁴ὀφείλι τοῦ ὑπηρετήσαντος
τὸν ¹⁵τοσοῦ[το]ν τῆς στρατείας χρόνον. ¹⁶διόπερ
προσφεύγειν σοι ἠναγκήσ-¹⁷θην δικαίαν δέ[ησ]ιν
ποιούμενος ¹⁸καὶ ἀξιῶ συντηρῆσαί μοι τὸν τῆς
¹⁹ἀναπαύσεως ἴσον χρόνον κατὰ ‹τὰ› ²⁰περὶ τούτου
διατεταγμένα, ἵνα δυνηθῶ ²¹κά{α}γὼ τ[ὴ]ν ἐπιμέλειαν τῶν ἰδίων ²²ποιεῖσθαι, ἄ[ν]θρ[ω]πος πρεσβύ-
[τη]ς καὶ ²³μόνος τυγχ[άν]ων, [κ]αὶ τῇ τύχῃ σου
²⁴εἰς ἀεὶ εὐχαριστῶ. διευτύχει. (2nd hand) ²⁵Γάιος
Ἰούλιος Ἀπολινάριος ἐπιδέδω{κ}-²⁶κα. (3rd hand)
²⁷(ἔτους) ιβ″ Μεχεὶρ κθ. (4th hand) ²⁸τῷ σ[τρα-
τη]γ[ῷ] ἔντυχ[ε] καὶ τὰ ²⁹πρ[οσήκο]ντα ποιήσει.
(5th hand) ³⁰ἀ[πόδος].

16. l. ἠναγκάσθην.

285. PETITION OF A VETERAN FOR A TERM OF EXEMPTION FROM COMPULSORY OFFICES

A.D. 172.

. . . from Gaius Julius Apollinarius, veteran owning land in the village of Karanis.[a] It has been decreed, my lord, that after their discharge veterans should have a five-year period of repose. In spite of this regulation I was molested two years after my discharge and arbitrarily nominated for a public duty, and from then till now I have been on duty without a break. Such a prolonged burden being universally forbidden in the case of natives, much more ought the rule to be observed in the case of myself who have served such a long time in the army. Wherefore I have been compelled to have recourse to you with a righteous request, and I ask you to secure for me an equivalent period of repose in accordance with the decree on this subject, in order that I may be able to attend to my own property, being an elderly and lonely man, and may be grateful to your fortune for ever. Farewell. (Signed) Presented by me, Gaius Julius Apollinarius. (Dated) Year 12, Mecheir 29. (Subscribed) Submit your case to the strategus, and he will do what is within his competence. (Order to the clerk) Deliver.[b]

[a] In the Fayum.
[b] See No. 284, note d.

286. COMPLAINT AGAINST TAX-COLLECTORS

B.G.U. 515.   A.D. 193.

¹'Αμμωνί[ῳ] Πατέρνῳ (ἐκατοντάρ)χ(η) ²παρὰ
Σύρου Σ[υ]ρίωνος ἐπικαλου-³μένου Πετεκᾶ ἀπὸ τῆς
μητροπό-⁴λεως. ἐγὼ καὶ ὁ ἀδελφός μου ⁵ὅσα
ὠφείλαμεν σιτικὰ δημό-⁶σια μεμετρήκαμεν τῷ
Παῦνι ⁷[μη]νί, ὡσαύτως καὶ τὰ ὑπὲρ λο-⁸γίας
[ἐ]πιβληθέντα ἡ[μ]εῖν ἐν ⁹κώμῃ Καρανίδι πυ[ροῦ]
ἀρτά-¹⁰βας ἐννέα ἀπὸ ἀρταβῶν δέκα. ¹¹ἕνεκα οὖν
τῆς λοιπῆς ἀρτάβης ¹²μιᾶς, ἐμοῦ ἐν ἀγρῷ ὄντος,
ἐπε[ι-]¹³σῆλθαν τῇ ο[ἰ]κίᾳ μου οἱ πρά-¹⁴κτορες
τῶ[ν σ]ιτικῶν Πετε-¹⁵ῆσι[ο]s Τκελὼ καὶ Σαραπίων
Μά-¹⁶ρωνος καὶ ὁ τούτων γραμμα-¹⁷τεὺς Πτολεμαῖος σὺν καὶ ὑπη-¹⁸[ρ]έ[τ]ῃ 'Αμμων[ί]ῳ [κ]αὶ
ἀφήρπα-¹⁹σα[ν] ἀπὸ τῆς [μη]τρός μου ἱμά-²⁰[τιο]ν
καὶ . . .[. . . .]σμασιν αὐτὴν ²¹[. . .]έβαλον. [διὸ
ἐκ τ]ούτου τε κλει-²²[νήρου]s α[ὐτῆς γ]ενομένης,
²³[. . . . . μ]ὴ δυν[αμέ]νης τῷ ²⁴[. . . .]ν, ἀξιῶ
[ἀχθῆναι] αὐ-²⁵[το]ὺς ἐπὶ σέ, ὅπως τῶν ἀπὸ ²⁶[σ]οῦ
δικαίων τύχω. διευτύχει. ²⁷εἰκ(όνικα)· (ἐτῶν) μζ
οὐλ(ὴ) γόνατι δεξιῷ ²⁸φα(μένου) (?) μὴ εἰδ(έναι)
γρ(άμματα). ²⁹(ἔτους) λγ Αὐρηλίου Κομμόδου
³⁰Καίσαρος τοῦ κυρίου μηνὸς ³¹Παῦνι η.

287. COMPLAINT OF ASSAULT

P. Ryl. 116.   A.D. 194.

¹'Αντίγραφον ἐγκλήματος Σαπρίωνος. ²ʿΗρα-
κλείδῃ στρατ(ηγῷ) ʿΕρμοπ(ολίτου) ³παρὰ Σαπρίω-

286. COMPLAINT AGAINST TAX-COLLECTORS

A.D. 193.

To Ammonius Paternus, centurion, from Syrus son of Syrion surnamed Petekas, of the metropolis.[a] I and my brother have delivered in the month of Pauni all the government corn-dues which we owed, and likewise for the contributions imposed upon us in the village of Karanis nine artabae out of ten. Now on account of the remaining one artaba the collectors of corn-dues Peteesis son of Tkelo and Sarapion son of Maron and their scribe Ptolemaeus together with their assistant Ammonius made a descent on my house while I was in the fields and tore a mantle off my mother's back and cast her . . . Wherefore, as in consequence of this she has taken to her bed and cannot . . . because of . . ., I request that they be brought before you, in order that I may obtain justice at your hands. Farewell. I (the amanuensis) have given his description, as he says he is illiterate : 47 years of age, scar on the right knee. Year 33 of Aurelius Commodus Caesar the lord, Pauni 8.

[a] Arsinoe, the metropolis of the nome.

---

28. φα(μένου) (?) E.-H.: ιτ ( ) Wilcken.

287. COMPLAINT OF ASSAULT

A.D. 194.

Copy of a complaint by Saprion. To Heraclides, strategus of the Hermopolite nome, from Saprion also

νος τοῦ καὶ Ἑρμαίου υἱοῦ Σαραπίω-⁴νος κοσμη-
τ(εύσαντος) καὶ γυμνασιαρχήσαντος Ἑρμοῦ πό-
⁵λεως τῆς μεγάλης. κοινολογουμένου μου ⁶τῇ
μητρὶ Εὐδαιμονίδι Εὐδαίμονος πρεσβυτέ-⁷ρου Σωτᾶ
περὶ τῶν καταλειφθέντων μοι ὑ-⁸πὸ τοῦ πατρός
μου Σαραπίωνος ἀκολούθως ⁹ᾗ ἔθετο διαθήκῃ καὶ
θλειβομένη τῇ συνει-¹⁰δήσει περὶ ὧν ἐνοσφίσατο
ἔν τε ἐνδομε-¹¹νείᾳ καὶ ἀποθέτοις καὶ ἄλλοις
πλείστοις οὐκ ὀ-¹²λίγοις οὖσι ἐπῆλθέ μοι μετὰ
Σερήνου τοῦ καὶ ¹³Τιβερείνου γυμνασιαρχήσαντος
ἀνδρὸς ¹⁴τῆς ἀδελφῆς, καὶ οὐ μόνον ἐξύβρισαν ἀλ-
¹⁵λὰ καὶ τὴν ἐσθῆτά μου περιέσχισαν βου-¹⁶λόμενοι
ἀποστερέσαι τῶν ἐμῶν. ὅθεν ¹⁷ἐπιδίδωμι τόδε τὸ
βιβλείδιον ἀξιῶν εἶναι ¹⁸ἐν καταχωρισμῷ πρὸς
μαρτυρίαν ἄχρις ¹⁹τῆς κατ' αὐτῶν προ‹σ›-
ελεύσεως, λόγου μοι ²⁰φυλασσομένου περὶ ὧν ἔχω
δικαίων ²¹πάντων. (ἔτους) β Αὐτοκράτορος
Καίσαρος ²²Λουκί[ο]υ Σεπτιμίου Σευήρου Περτίνακος ²³Σεβαστοῦ Παχὼν κ. Σαπρίων ὁ καὶ
Ἑρ-²⁴μαῖο[ς] ἐπιδέδωκα.

288. COMPLAINT ABOUT THE IMPOSITION
OF A LITURGY

B.G.U. 1022.   A.D. 196.

¹Τῆι κρατίστηι βουλῆι Ἀντινοέων ²Νέων Ἑλ-
λήνων ³παρὰ Λουκίου Οὐαλερίου Λουκρη-⁴τιανοῦ
Ματιδείου τοῦ καὶ Πλωτινί-⁵ου καὶ Λ[ουκίο]υ
Λογγείνου Ἐρεννίου ⁶Παυλεινίου τοῦ καὶ Μεγα-
λεισίου. οὐκ ἀ-⁷[γ]νοεῖτε, ἄνδρες κράτιστοι, ὅτι

called Hermaeus son of Sarapion, ex-cosmetes and ex-gymnasiarch of Hermopolis Magna. As I was conferring with my mother Eudaemonis daughter of Eudaemon elder son of Sotas about the property left me by my father Sarapion according to the will which he made, she, oppressed by consciousness of what she had appropriated both of furniture and stores and other things very far from few, assaulted me with the aid of Serenus also called Tiberinus, ex-gymnasiarch and husband of her sister, and they not only abused me but tore my garments, wishing to deprive me of my own property. Wherefore I present this petition, requesting that it be filed as evidence until I proceed against them, without prejudice to any of my rights. The 2nd year of the Emperor Caesar Lucius Septimius Severus Pertinax Augustus, Pachon 20. I, Saprion also called Hermaeus, have presented this petition.

288. COMPLAINT ABOUT THE IMPOSITION OF A LITURGY

A.D. 196.

To their excellencies the senate of the citizens of Antinoe, Neo-Hellenes, from Lucius Valerius Lucretianus, of the Matidian tribe and the Plotinian deme,[a] and Lucius Longinus Herennius, of the Paulinian tribe and the Megalisian deme.[a] You are not un-

---

[a] Of Antinoe, which was organized as a Greek city. The population, which was collected from various districts and included many persons not of pure Greek descent, received the appellation of Neo-Hellenes or " new Greeks."

πασῶν ⁸[λει]τουργιῶ[ν] ἀφ{θ}είθημεν τῶν ἀλλαχοῦ
⁹[κατ]ὰ διάταξιν θεοῦ Ἀδριανοῦ ⟨κτίστου⟩ καὶ
οἰκιστοῦ ¹⁰[τ]ῆς ἡμετέρα[ς πό]λ[ε]ως. ἐπεὶ οὖν
γενόμε-¹¹[νο]ι [ε]ἰς Φειλα[δ]έλφιαν κ[ώ]μην τοῦ
Ἀρσινο-¹²[εί]τ[ο]υ τῆς [Ἡρα]κλείδου μερίδος, ἔνθα
γεου-¹³[χο]ῦμεν, ἐπ[ὶ τῆς] διορθ[ώσ]εως δη-
μ[οσ]ίων ¹⁴[ὀφει]λημάτων ὁ τῆς προκ[ει]μένης
κώμης ¹⁵[κωμ]ογραμματεὺς Ἀφροδᾶς Θέωνος κατ'
ἐπή-¹⁶[ρια]ν ἐπέδωκεν ἡμᾶς ἐπὶ τῆς καταγωγῆς
¹⁷τοῦ σείτου παρὰ τὰ διατεταγμένα, κατὰ τὸ
ἀναγ-¹⁸[καῖο]ν, κύριοι, [τ]ὴν πρόσοδο[ν] πρὸς ὑμᾶς
ποι-¹⁹[οῦ]μεν ἀξιοῦντες, ἐὰν ὑμῖν δόξῃ, ἀνε-
²⁰νεγκεῖν τῷ κρατίστῳ ἐπιστρατήγῳ ²¹Καλπουρ-
νίωι Κονκέσσῳ περὶ τούτου, ὅπως ²²κατὰ τὰ ὑπάρχοντα ἡμῖν δίκαια κελεύσαι ²³ἑτέρ[ο]υς ἀνθ' ἡμῶν
κατασταθῆναι καὶ ²⁴λόγον αὐτὸν ὑποσχεῖν τῶν
τετολμημέ-²⁵νων καὶ εἰς τὸ πέραν ⟨ἀν⟩επ⟨η⟩-
{κ}ρεάστους φυλα-²⁶χθῆναι. (2nd hand) διευ[τυ]-
χεῖτε. (ἔτους) δ Αὐτοκράτορος ²⁷Καίσαρος Λουκίου Σε[πτι]μίο[υ Σε]ουήρου Εὐσεβοῦς Περτίνακος
²⁸Σεβαστοῦ Ἀραβικ(οῦ) Ἀδιαβηνικ[(οῦ) Μεσ]ορὴ
κ̄. (3rd hand) Λούκιος ²⁹[Ο]ὐαλέριος Λ[ο]υκ[ρ]η-
τιανὸς ἐπιδέδοκα ³⁰καὶ ἔγραψα ὑπὲρ Ἑρεννίου μὴ
[εἰ]δότος ³¹γρά[μμα]τα.

11. l. Φιλα[δ]έλφειαν.   14. [ὀφει]λημάτων Ε.-Η.:
[. . .] . . λοτων Wilcken.   29. l. ἐπιδέδωκα.

aware, excellencies, that we [a] were exempted from all compulsory services in other districts by order of the deified Hadrian, founder and colonizer of our city. Seeing therefore that during our presence at the village of Philadelphia in the division of Heraclides in the Arsinoite nome, where we own land, at the time of payment of public dues the village scribe of the aforesaid village, Aphrodas son of Theon, arbitrarily gave in our names for the transport of corn in spite of the edict, we are obliged, gentlemen, to have recourse to you, requesting you, if you approve, to report to his excellency the epistrategus, Calpurnius Concessus, about this matter, in order that in accordance with the rights which we possess he may command that other persons be appointed instead of us and that the offender be called to account for what he has dared to do and that we be protected against further molestation. Farewell. The 4th year of the Emperor Caesar Lucius Septimius Severus Pius Pertinax Augustus Arabicus Adiabenicus, Mesore 20. (Signed) I, Lucius Valerius Lucretianus have presented this, and I wrote for Herennius, as he is illiterate.

[a] That is, all citizens of Antinoe.

SELECT PAPYRI

289. PETITION OF VILLAGERS CONCERNING SHORE-LAND

P. Gen. 16.   A.D. 207.

¹Ἰουλίῳ Ἰουλιανῷ (ἑκατοντάρχῳ) ²π[αρὰ] Ἐρι-
ε[ῦ]τος Στοτοήτεως λαξοῦ καὶ Παβουκᾶτος Παβοῦτος καὶ Ἑριέως Πακύσεως ³κα[ὶ Ἀπύ]γχεως
Ὡρίωνος καὶ Ἐσούρεως Παουιτῆτος καὶ Δημᾶ
Δημᾶ καὶ Ὀρσενούφεως ⁴[Ἑριέ]ω[ς] καὶ Πετεσούχου Σώτου καὶ Ὥρου μητρὸς Θαϊσᾶτος καὶ
Σωτηρίχου ἀπάτορος μητρὸς ⁵Θα[ήσ]εως καὶ Τεικᾶ
Πακύσεως καὶ Πατῆτος Σαταβοῦτος καὶ Παβοῦτος Παβοῦτος καὶ Κάννι-⁶το[ς Π]ατῆτος καὶ
Σώστου Παβοῦτος καὶ Πάιτος Σαταβοῦτος καὶ
Πακύσιος Ψενήσιος ⁷κα[ὶ] Ἀπύγχεως Ἀπύγχεως
καὶ Ἀβοῦτος Σαταβοῦτος καὶ Πακύσεως Ἑριέως
καὶ Ποῦσι ⁸Ματάιτος καὶ Πακύσεως Ἀπύγχεως
καὶ Σαταβοῦτος Πακύσεως καὶ Ἀειτος Κάν-
⁹νη[τος] καὶ Μέλανος Ἀρήυτος, πάντων ἀπὸ κώμης
Σοκνοπαίου Νήσου τῆς Ἡρα-¹⁰κλείδου μερίδος.
[δ]έησίν σοι προσφέρομεν, κύριε, χρῄζουσαν τῆς
σῆς ἐγδι-¹¹κίας, ἥτις ἔχει τὸν τρόπον τοῦτον.
ἔστιν παρ' ἡμῖν αἰγιαλὸς ἀναγραφόμε-¹²νος [π]ερὶ
τὴν ἡμετέραν κώμην, ὃν [[.]] ἐν πλείσταις ἀρούραις,
καὶ ὁπόταν ἡ τοι-¹³αύτη γῆ ἀποκαλυ[φθ]ῇ, μισ-
θοῦται καὶ σπείρεται κατὰ τὴν συνήθεια[ν ἐ]κφορί-
¹⁴ο[υ] κατ' ἄρουραν, καὶ τοῦτο μετρῖται τῷ ἱερωτάτῳ ταμείῳ, καὶ διὰ αὐτὸ ¹⁵τ[ο]ῦτο <τὸ> μέρος
πάντα τὰ ὑποστέλλοντα τῇ κώμῃ πάμπολλα ὄντα
ἀπο-¹⁶δ[ί]δοται ἕνεκ[α] τοῦ μὴ ἔχιν τὴν κώμην

12. l. ὤν.

282

289. PETITION OF VILLAGERS CON-CERNING SHORE-LAND

A.D. 207.

To Julius Julianus, centurion, from Herieus son of Stotoetis, stone-cutter, Paboukas son of Pabous, Herieus son of Pakusis, Apunchis son of Horion, Esouris son of Paouites, Demas son of Demas, Orsenouphis son of Herieus, Petesouchus son of Sotas, Horus whose mother is Thaisas, Soterichus whose father's name is unknown and whose mother is Thaesis, Teikas son of Pakusis, Pates son of Satabous, Pabous son of Pabous, Kannis son of Pates, Sostus son of Pabous, Pais son of Satabous, Pakusis son of Psenesis, Apunchis son of Apunchis, Abous son of Satabous, Pakusis son of Herieus, Pousi son of Matais, Pakusis son of Apunchis, Satabous son of Pakusis, Aeis son of Kannes, Melas son of Areus, all of the village of Socnopaei Nesus in the division of Heraclides. We submit to you, my lord, a complaint which craves for redress at your hands, the matter being as follows. There exists here a stretch of shore registered as part of the area of our village,[a] consisting of a great number of arurae, and whenever the said land is uncovered by the water, it is leased and sown according to custom, paying rent arura by arura, which rent is delivered in kind to the most sacred Treasury ; and it is owing to just this portion of land that all the liabilities of the village, which are very large, are paid, because the village has no

[a] The village in question lay on the north side of Lake Moeris. See No. 282, note *a*.

μήτε ἰδι[ω]τικὴν γῆν [17]μήτε βασ[ιλ]ικὴν μηδὲ ἄλλην
εἰδέαν. ἀλλὰ ὑπὲρ τοῦ πάντας [18]δ[υ]νηθῆναι ἐ[ν]
τῇ ἰδίᾳ συμμένιν, μάλιστα τοῦ λαμπροτάτου [19]ἡγε-
μόνος Σουβατιανῶ Ἀκύλα κελεύσαντος πάν-[20]τας
τοὺς ἀπὸ ξένης ὄντας καλισελθεῖν εἰς τὴν ἰδίαν
[21]ἐχομένους τῶν συνηθῶν ἔργων, ἐπ[εὶ ο]ὖν Ὀρ-
σεύς τις [22]Στοτοήτεως καὶ τοὶ τούτου ἀδελφοὶ
ὄντες τὸν ἀριθμὸν [23]πέντε ἐπῆλθαν ἡμῖν κωλύοντες
τοῦ μὴ σπείρειν τὴν [24]τοιαύτην γῆν, ἀναγκαίως
ἐπιδίδομεν ἀξιοῦντες, [25]ἐάν σοι δόξῃ, κελεῦσαι
αὐτοὺς ἀχθῆναι ἐπὶ σὲ λόγον [26]ἀποδώσοντας περὶ
τούτου. διευτύχει. [27](ἔτους) ιϛ" Φαῶφι ιδ.

290. ATTESTATION OF A COPY OF A PETITION WITH REPLY

P. Oxy. 2131.   A.D. 207.

[1](Ἔτους) ιε Αὐτοκρατόρ[ων] Κα[ι]σάρων Λουκίου
Σεπτιμίου Σεουήρου Εὐσεβοῦς Περτίνακος Ἀρα-
βικοῦ Ἀδιαβηνικοῦ Παρθικοῦ Μεγίστου καὶ Μάρ-
[κου] [2]Αὐρηλίου Ἀντωνείνου Εὐσεβοῦς Σεβαστῶν
καὶ Πουβλίου Σεπτιμίου Γέτα Καίσαρος Σεβαστοῦ
Φαμενὼθ κθ. ἐμαρτύρατο ἑαυτὸν [3]Τοτοῆς χρη-
ματίζ(ων) μητ(ρὸς) Τσενπετσίριος ἀπ' Ὀξυρύγ-
χ(ων) πόλ(εως) διὰ τῶν ὑπογεγραμμένων μαρ-
τύρων ἐξειληφέναι καὶ προσαντιβεβληκέ-[4]ναι ἐκ
τεύχους συνκολλησίμων βιβλειδίων ἐπιδοθήντων
Σουβατιανῷ Ἀκύλα τῷ λαμπρο(τάτῳ) ἡγεμόνι

4. l. ἐπιδοθέντων.

private land or Crown land or any other kind. But in order that all may be able to remain in their own homes, especially as the most illustrious praefect Subatianus Aquila has ordered all persons who are strangers to return home and apply themselves to their customary business, we accordingly, seeing that a certain Orseus son of Stotoetis and his brothers, numbering five persons in all, have descended upon us preventing us from sowing the land described, are forced to present this petition, requesting you, if it please you, to order them to be brought before you to answer for their action. Farewell. Year 16, Phaophi 14.

---

19. *l.* Σουβατιανοῦ.   **20.** *l.* κατεισελθεῖν.   **22.** *l.* οἱ.

290. ATTESTATION OF A COPY OF A PETITION WITH REPLY

A.D. 207.

The 15th year of the Emperors and Caesars Lucius Septimius Severus Pius Pertinax Arabicus Adiabenicus Parthicus Maximus and Marcus Aurelius Antoninus Pius, Augusti, and Publius Septimius Geta Caesar Augustus, Phamenoth 29. Totoes, styled as having Senpetsiris as his mother, of the city of Oxyrhynchus, has testified through the witnesses below written that he has extracted and collated from the roll of conjoined [a] petitions presented to his highness the praefect Subatianus Aquila and displayed at

---

[a] Separate petitions gummed together to form a roll after their examination by the praefect.

προτεθέντων ἐν Ἀντι-⁵νόου πόλ(ει) ἐν τῷ Ἀντι-
νοείῳ ἐν οἷς καὶ τὸ ὑπογεγραμμένον βιβλείδιον
σὺν τῇ ὑπ' αὐτὸ ὑπογραφῇ, ὅπερ οὕτως ἔχει· κολ-
λημ(άτων) Ἀθ. ⁶Σουβατιανῷ Ἀκύλᾳ ἐπάρχῳ
Αἰγύπτου π(αρὰ) Τοτοέως χρηματίζοντος μητρὸς
Σενπετσείρ[ιο]s ἀπ' Ὀξυρύγχων πόλε[ω]s. ⁷τῆς
ἐμφύτου σου, ἡγεμὼν δέσποτα, δικαιοδοσίας δι-
ηκούσης εἰς πάντας ἀνθρώπους καὶ αὐτὸς ἀδικηθεὶς
ἐπὶ σὲ καταφεύ-⁸γ[ω] ἀξιῶν ἐκδικίας τυχεῖν. ἔχει
δὲ οὕτω[ς· ἐν] μητροπόλ(ει) τυγχάνων ἀναγραφό-
μενος ἐπ' ἀμφόδου Παρεμβολῆς ἀεὶ χρη-⁹ματίζων
τῷ προ[ο]κειμένῳ ὀνοματίῳ, ᾧ συμφώνως ἀναδοθεὶς
ἔτι ἄνωθεν εἰς φυλακίαν ταύτην ἀμέμπτως ἐξ[ε]τ[έ-]
¹⁰λεσα, οὐ μόνον ἀλλὰ καὶ τὰ κατ' ἔτος ὀφειλό-
μενα ἐπικεφάλια τελῶ γεωργικὸν [κα]ὶ ἀπράγμονα
βίον ζῶν, ἀνεδόθην οὐ δε-¹¹όντως ὑπὸ Ἡρακλάμ-
μωνος τοῦ νυνὶ ἀμφοδογραμματέως πρώτης φυλῆς
εἰς δημοσίαν ὀνηλασίαν τῆς αὐτῆς πόλεω[s] ¹²πάνυ
βαρυτάτην χρείαν ἑτέρῳ ὀνοματίῳ Σβῖχις Ἀρ-
μιύσιος μητρὸς Τασεῦτος, σωματίσαντός μοι ἀνύπ-
αρκτον πόρον ¹³(δραχμῶν) Ἀσ· ὅθεν, κύριε, βίᾳ
ἀναγκασθεὶς ταύτης τῆς ὀνηλασίας ἀντιλαβέσθαι
ἄπορος παντελῶς ὑπάρχων μηδ' ὅλως ὑπο-¹⁴στέλ-
λων τῷ [ν]υνὶ ἀμφοδογραμματεῖ ἀλλ' εἰς τοὐπίον
τοῦ ἡμετέρου ἀμφόδου Ἱππέως Παρεμβολῆς μέλ-
λοντος λει[το]υ[ρ-]¹⁵γεῖν ἀκολούθως τῷ γενομένῳ
ὑπὸ Γαμεινίου Μοδέστ{ρι}ου τοῦ κρα(τίστου) ἐπι-

14. l. Ἱππέων.   15. l. Γεμεινίου.

---

[a] After being subscribed by the praefect, who evidently
had examined them at Antinoe.

[b] In the nome-capitals, such as Oxyrhynchus, the population was in later times divided territorially into " tribes."

Antinoe [a] in the temple of Antinous, including the petition below written, together with the subscription beneath it, as follows :—No. 1009. To Subatianus Aquila, praefect of Egypt, from Totoes, styled as having Senpetsiris as his mother, of the city of Oxyrhynchus. Since your ingrained justice, my lord praefect, is extended to all men, I too, having been wronged, have recourse to you, begging for redress. The matter is on this wise. I happen to be registered in the metropolis in the Camp quarter and am always styled by the name given above, in accordance with which I was designated some time ago to the duty of guard, which I discharged blamelessly, and I have besides paid my annual personal dues, living a quiet cultivator's life. I have been improperly designated by Heraclammon, the present district-scribe of the first tribe,[b] for the post of public donkey-driver [c] in the said city, a most onerous service, under another name, Sbichis son of Harmiusis and Taseus, and have had booked to me by him property to-the value of 1200 drachmae [d] which I do not possess ; wherefore, my lord, as I have been compelled to take up this post of donkey-driver although I am entirely without means and am not at all subject to the present district-scribe, our quarter on the contrary having presently to serve in accordance with the lot drawn for the districts by his excellency the epistrategus Geminius Modestus, and have been lawlessly and

The tribes and demes of the Greek cities proper, such as Alexandria and Antinoe, were a different kind of organization.

[c] A person who was required to provide donkeys for government services.

[d] See Nos. 341-343. The persons nominated for public services had to possess property of a certain value.

SELECT PAPYRI

στρα(τήγου) τῶν ἀμφόδων κλήρῳ, [το]ῦ Ἡρα-
κλάμμωνος [16]ἀνόμως καὶ ῥειψοκινδύνως ἀναδόντος
μ[ε], ἀξιῶ, ἐὰν σο[ῦ] τῇ εὐμ[εν]εστάτῃ τύχῃ δόξῃ,
διακοῦσαί μου πρὸς αὐτόν, τῆς γ[ὰ]ρ [17]σῆ[ς] μεγα-
λειότητός ἐστιν ἐπεξελθεῖν τοῖς [ἀδίκ]ως καὶ ἀ-
νόμω[ς] τετολμημένοις, ὅπως τυχὼν τῶν δικαίων
δυνηθῶ εἰς [18]ὕστε[ρο]ν τῷ ἐπιβάλλοντι ἔτει ἀντι-
λαβέ[σ]θαι τῆς ἐνχειρισθησομένης ὡς πρόκειται,
ἵν' ὦ εὐεργετημέν[ο]ς.   διευτύχει.   [19](ἔτους ?)
ι[ε . . . . .] μηδε[νὸ]ς ἐπεχομ[έν]ο[υ ὁ κρά(τιστος)
ἐπιστρά(τηγος) εἴ]σεται [ὁποῖ]α [. . .] . [. .] . .
ε . . ι[.] ἡ ἀξίωσις.   πρόθες.

Verso : (3rd hand) [20]. . λλευς . . [.]ιος Φυαν-
[. .] . νησ[ἐσφράγισα].   (4th hand) [21][.]α . [. . .]-
. ς . ε . . τευς ἐ[σφ]ράγισα.   (5th hand) [22]Γάιος
Ἰούλιος Σαραπίων ἐσφράγισα.   (6th hand) [23]. . . .
α . ος Ἡρακλείδης ἐσφράγισα.   (7th hand) [24]Αἴας
[Ο]ὔλπιος Θέων ἐσφράγισα.   (8th hand) [25]Λούκι[ος
Οὐο]λύσιος Δομίττιος Σαλουιανὸς ἐσφράγισα.

291. COMPLAINT OF ASSAULT

P. Graux 4.   A.D. 248.

[1]Αὐρηλίωι Μαρκιανῶι (ἑκατοντάρχωι) [2]παρὰ
Αὐρηλίου Σαραπίωνος Πάσει ἀπὸ κώμης Φιλαδελ-
[3]φείας. ὕβρεως οὐδὲν οὔτε δεινότερον οὔτε χαλεπώ-
[4]τερον. εἰς τοῦτο γὰρ ἡλικίας ἐλθών, ὀγδοηκοστὸν
καὶ [5]πρὸς ἐνιαυτὸν γενόμενος, ἀμέμπτως ὑπηρετῶ
[6]Ἀραβοτοξότης ὤν. χοίρου ὑὸς ἀποπλανηθείσης
[7]τῆς θυγατρός μου ἐν τῇ κώμῃ καὶ ὀνομαζομένης
288

recklessly designated by Heraclammon, I beg you, if it seem good to your most benign fortune, to hear me against him, for it appertains to your power to punish unjust and lawless deeds of daring, in order that I may obtain my rights and be able subsequently in the year allotted to me to take up the service with which I may be entrusted. Farewell. (Subscribed) Year 15, . . . Without prejudice to anything, his excellency the epistrategus shall discover what [rights underlie] this petition. To be displayed. (Signed) I, . . ., have sealed. I, . . ., have sealed. I, Gaius Julius Sarapion, have sealed. I, . . . Heraclides, have sealed. I, Aias Vulpius Theon, have sealed. I, Lucius Volusius Domitius Salvianus, have sealed.

291. COMPLAINT OF ASSAULT

A.D. 248.

To Aurelius Marcianus, centurion, from Aurelius Sarapion son of Pasei, of the village of Philadelphia. There is nothing more dreadful or harder to bear than maltreatment. At the time of life which I have reached, being eighty years old and more, I am serving blamelessly as an Arab archer.[a] A sow having escaped from my daughter in the village and being

a See No. 282, note b.

[8]ὡς παρὰ Ἰουλίωι στρατιώτῃ, προσῆλθον αὐτῷ [9]αἰτήσων ὅρκον περὶ τούτου· ὃς λαβόμενός μου [10]τοῦ πρεσβύτου ἐν τῇ κώμῃ μεσούσης ἡμέρας ὡς [11]οὐκ ὄντων νόμων πληγαῖς με ᾐκίσατο, παρόντων [12]Νεπωτιανοῦ ἐπιτρόπου τοῦ διασημοτάτου Οὐα- λερίου [13]Τιτιανοῦ καὶ Μαύρου καὶ Ἀμμωνίου Ἀραβοτοξοτῶν, [14]ὡς ἀγανακτησάντων αὐτῶν ἐπὶ πλησσομένου μου [15]διαλῦσαι ἡμᾶς καὶ μόλις ἐπι- κερδᾶναι ψυχῆς [16]ἐπιβουλήν. ἀνανκαίως τὴν ἐπί- δοσιν τῶν βιβλιδίων ποι-[17]οῦμαι καὶ ἀξιῶ ἀχθῆναι αὐτὸν πρὸς τὸ τὰ τολμηθέν-[18]τα ἐκδικίας τυχεῖν, καὶ μένη μοι ὁ λόγος. διευτύχει. [19]Σαραπίων ὡς (ἐτῶν) πδ οὐλὴ γόνατι δεξιῷ. [20](ἔτους) ϛ Αὐτο- κρατόρων Καισάρων Μάρκων [21]Ἰουλίων Φιλίππων Εὐσεβῶν Εὐτυχῶν Σεβαστῶν Ἀθὺρ κϛ.

18. *l.* μένει.

292. APPLICATION TO THE BOARD OF GYMNASIARCHS

P. Oxy. 2130.   A.D. 267.

[2]Τῷ τάγματι τῶν γυμνασιάρχων τῆς [3]Ὀξυρυγ- χειτῶν πόλεως διὰ τοῦ διαδεχομέ-[4]νου τὴν πρυτα- νείαν Αὐρηλίου Σαραπίω-[5]νος τοῦ καὶ Φιλοξένου γυμνα(σιαρχήσαντος) [6]παρὰ Αὐρηλίου Σαραπίωνος τοῦ καὶ Σερήνου [7]γυμνα(σιαρχήσαντος) πρυτανεύ- σαντος ἐπὶ τῶν στεμμάτων βου(λευτοῦ) [8]τῆς λαμ- πρᾶς Ἀντινοέων πόλεως καὶ ὡς χρημα(τίζω) [9]διὰ

290

reported to be at the house of the soldier Julius, I went to him to demand his oath about this matter, and he laying hands on me, old as I am, in the village in the middle of the day, as if there were no laws, belaboured me with blows in the presence of Nepotianus, steward of the most eminent Valerius Titanianus, and of Maurus and Ammonius, Arab archers, so that they, being shocked to see me beaten, separated us and I barely overcame his attempt on my life. I am compelled to present this petition and to request that he be arrested in order that his audacious behaviour may receive punishment; and I hold him to account. Farewell. (Identification) Sarapion, aged about 84 years, with a scar on the right knee. (Dated) The 6th year of the Emperors and Caesars Marci Julii Philippi Pii Felices Augusti, Hathur 26.

292. APPLICATION TO THE BOARD OF GYMNASIARCHS

A.D. 267.

To the board of gymnasiarchs of the city of Oxyrhynchus through the deputy-prytanis Aurelius Sarapion also called Philoxenus, ex-gymnasiarch, from Aurelius Sarapion also called Serenus, ex-gymnasiarch, ex-prytanis, superintendent of the *stemmata*,[a] senator of the illustrious city of Antinoe, and however I am styled, through Aurelius Gaianus,

---

[a] The meaning is obscure. Perhaps " municipal guilds." Or the word may refer to the crowning of magistrates on election to office.

Αὐρηλίου Γαϊανοῦ πραγματευτοῦ. πρὸς ὁποί-[10]αν
δήποτε γενομένην ἔκ τινος παρανομίας [11]ἀναγνω-
σθέντος ἐν ὑμῖν ὡς ἔμαθον πιτ-[12]τακίου τῇ δι-
ελθ(ούσῃ) λ βουλῆς οὔσης ὀνομασίαν [13]ἐξ ἐπωνυ-
μίας μου διαφέρουσαν γυμνασιαρχί-[14]ας ἀρχῇ παρ'
αὐτὸ προσήγαγον ὑμῖν [15]ἐκκλήτου βιβλία ἐπὶ τὸν
κράτιστον [16]ἐπιστράτηγον Αἴλιον Φαῦστον δουκη-
[17]νάριον, καὶ μὴ προσεθέντων τούτων [18]ἀνεθέμην ἐν
τῷ αὐτ[ό]θι Σεβαστείῳ [19]πρὸς τοῖς θείοις ἴχνεσι
τοῦ κυρίου ἡμῶν [20]Αὐτοκράτορος Γαλλιηνοῦ Σεβαστοῦ δια-[21]πεμφθησόμενα ὑπὸ τοῦ στατίζοντος
[22]τῷ λαμπροτάτῳ ἡγεμόνι Ἰουουενίου [23]Γενεαλίου
αὐτῷ τε τῷ στατίζοντι τὰ ἴσα [24]ἐπιδούς, καὶ νῦν
δὲ ἀξιῶ κατὰ τὰ κεκε-[25]λευσμένα ἐγδοθῆναί μοι
τὴν ὀπι-[26]νίωνα δηλοῦσαν τὴν αἰτίαν δι' ἣν [27]οὐ
προσήκασθε τὰ τῆς ἐκκλήτου βιβλία, [28]ὅπως δυνηθῇ
τὰ ἀκόλουθα πραχθῆναι. [29](ἔτους) ιδ Αὐτοκράτορος
Καίσαρος Που[π]λίου [30]Λικιννίου Γαλλιηνοῦ Γερμανικοῦ [31]Μεγίστου Περσικοῦ Μεγίστου Εὐσεβοῦς
[32]Εὐτυχ[οῦς] Σεβαστοῦ, Φαμενὼθ κ. [33]Αὐρήλιος
Σαρ[απίω]ν δι' ἐμοῦ [34]Γαϊανοῦ ἐπιδέδωκα.

22-23. l. Ἰουουενίῳ Γενεαλίῳ.

293. PETITION TO THE PRAEFECT

P. Ryl. 114.   About A.D. 280.

[1]- - - λε[.]ίῳ τῷ διασημοτάτῳ ἡγεμόνι [2][παρὰ
Αὐρηλίας] Ἀρτέμιτος Παησίου ἀπὸ κώμης Θρασὼ
[3][τοῦ Ἀρσινοΐτου] νομοῦ. τὸ μετριοφιλές σου

agent. In opposition to the nomination, in which my name was concerned, of whatever kind it might be, pertaining to the office of gymnasiarch, which was made by some illegality in a list read before you, as I learn, on the 30th of last month at a meeting of the senate, I immediately presented to you a petition of appeal to his excellency the epistrategus Aelius Faustus, *ducenarius*,[a] and since it was not accepted I deposited it in the local Sebasteum at the divine feet of our lord the Emperor Gallienus Augustus [b] to be forwarded by the resident officer to his highness the praefect Juvenius Genealis, giving a copy also to the resident officer himself ; and now too I beg that in accordance with orders the legal opinion be issued to me declaring the reason why you have not accepted the petition of appeal, in order that the consequent steps may be taken. The 14th year of the Emperor Caesar Publius Licinnius Gallienus Germanicus Maximus Persicus Maximus Pius Felix Augustus, Phamenoth 20. Presented by me, Aurelius Sarapion, through me, Gaianus.

  [a] " Receiving a salary of 200,000 sestertii," a designation of rank.
  [b] That is, before the statue of the Emperor in the temple of the Caesars.

293. PETITION TO THE PRAEFECT

About A.D. 280.

To . . ., the most illustrious praefect, from Aurelia Artemis daughter of Paesius, of the village of Thraso in the Arsinoite nome.[a] Conscious of your love of

  [a] For the sequel of this affair see No. 262.

αἰσθομένη, [4][δέσποτά μου ἡ]γεμών, καὶ περὶ πάντας
κηδεμονίαν, [5][μάλιστα περὶ γυ]ναῖκας καὶ χήρας,
τὴν προσέλευσιν ποι-[6][οῦμαί σοι ἀξιο]ῦσα τῆς ἀπὸ
σοῦ βοηθείας τυχεῖν. τὸ δὲ [7][πρᾶγμα οὕτως ἔ]χει.
Συρίων γενόμενος δεκάπρωτος [8][τῆς προκειμέν]ης
κώμης Θρασὼ ἀναπίσας μου τὸν ἄν-[9][δρα Γάνιδα
ὀνό]ματι ποιμένιν αὐτοῦ τὰ πρόβατα, ὅστις [10][ἀδίκως
τὰς τοῦ] προκειμένου ἀνδρὸς αἶγας καὶ πρόβατα τὸν
[11][ἀριθμὸν ἑξήκο]ντα συναπέσπασεν αὐτῷ, καὶ ἐφ᾽
ὅσον μὲν [12][περιῆν ὁ προκείμ]ενός μου ἀνὴρ ἕκαστος
τὰ ἑαυτοῦ ἐκαρποῦ-[13][το ὅ τε ἐμὸς ἀνή]ρ τὰ ἴδια
καὶ ὁ προκείμενος τὰ ἑαυτοῦ. ἐπὶ οὖν [14][κατὰ
τρόπον ἀνθ]ρώπων ἐγένετο ὁ προκείμενός μου
ἀνήρ, [15][εἰσεπήδησε βο]υλόμενος ὁ Συρίων καὶ
ἀφαρπάζειν τὰ τῶν [16][νηπίων μου τέ]κνων τῇ
τοπικῇ δυναστείᾳ χρώμενος παρὰ [17][αὐτῆς τῆς (?)
κοί]της τοῦ ἀνδρός μου καὶ τοῦ σώματος κιμένου.
[18][ἐπεὶ δὲ ἐσπού]δασα τὰ ἡμέτερα ἀπολαβεῖν καὶ
περιστεῖλε τὸν [19][ἄνδρα μου, μετ᾽] ἀπιλῆς με
ἀπέπεμψεν καὶ μέχρι τῆς σήμε-[20][ρον κατέχων
τ]υγχάνι τὰ ἡμέτερα ποίμνια. διὸ παρακαλῶ [21][σε,
δέσποτα, πέμ]ψαι μοι βοηθὸν ἐκ τῆς σῆς προς-
τάξεως, ὅ-[22][πως τά τε τῶν νη]πίων μου τέκνων
καὶ τὰ ἐμοῦ τῆς χήρας ἀπο-[23][λάβω καὶ δυνηθ]ῶ
εὐμαρῶς ὑπακούειν τῷ ἀποτάκτῳ, οὐ γὰρ [24][ἐν
περιγραφ]αῖς κατελήμφθη ὁ προκείμενός μου ἀνὴρ
ὑπὲρ [25][τῶν διαφερόντω]ν τῷ ταμίῳ, οἰκίωται δὲ
τῷ προκειμένῳ Συρίω-[26][νι ἐμὲ τὴν χήρα]ν μετὰ
νηπίων τέκνων ἀεὶ ἀποστερεῖν [27][ὥστε τὸν τοῦ
τε]τελευτηκότος μου ἀνδρὸς σῖτον λαβόντα [28][λι-
φθίσης μου ἄνε]υ βοηθοῦ ὑπὲρ τῶν ἐπιβαλλόντων
μετρη-[29][μάτων σύμβο]λον μὴ ἐκδοῦναι, ὅπως τὰ

equity, my lord praefect, and your solicitude for all, especially women and widows, I approach you praying to obtain your aid. The matter is as follows. Syrion, who had become *decemprimus* of the aforesaid village of Thraso, persuaded my husband, Ganis by name, to pasture his sheep, this Syrion who has wrongfully appropriated my aforesaid husband's goats and sheep to the number of sixty ; and so long as my aforesaid husband lived each enjoyed the fruits of his own property, my husband of his private flock and the aforesaid individual of his. Now when my aforesaid husband went the way of men, Syrion rushed in, wishing by means of his local power to carry off the property of my young children from the very bed of my husband and his body lying there. When I endeavoured to rescue our property and prepare my husband for burial, he drove me away with threats, and until this day he remains in possession of our flocks. Wherefore I entreat you, my lord, to send me an assistant by your command, in order that I may recover the property of my young children and of myself the widow and be able to comply comfortably with what is required of me. For my aforesaid husband was not detected in any fraudulent action touching the interests of the Treasury ; but it is in the nature of the aforesaid Syrion to rob me the widow and my young children on every occasion, so that when he took the corn of my deceased husband for the corn-dues devolving upon me, as I was left without a helper, he gave no receipt. I appeal to you

---

9. *l.* ποιμαίνειν.   13. *l.* ἐπεί.   18. *l.* περιστεῖλαι.
20. κατέχων suppl. E.-H. : οἰκειῶν Edd.

ἴδια ἐκ τῆς σῆς ³⁰[τοῦ κυρίου καὶ] πάντων εὐεργέτου
φιλανθρώπου ὑπογραφῆς ³¹[ἀπολάβω καὶ δυνη]θῶ
μετὰ νηπίων τέκνων ἐν τῇ ἰδίᾳ συν-³²[μένειν καὶ
ἀεὶ] τῇ τύχῃ σου χάριτας ὁμολογεῖν δυνηθῶ.
³³διευτύχει. (2nd hand) ³⁴[(ἔτους) . . . .] θ
πρὸς τὸ τοῖς φόροις χρήσιμον ³⁵[. . . . .
. . .] κατὰ τὸ δικαιότατον δοκιμάσει ὁ κράτιστος
³⁶[ἐπιστράτηγο]ς. κόλ(λημα) ξθ τόμ{μ}(ου) α.

294. PETITION TO A STRATEGUS

P. Oxy. 1204.   A.D. 299.

¹'Επὶ ὑπά[τ]ων τῶν κυρίων ἡμῶν Αὐτοκρατόρων
Διοκλητιανοῦ τὸ ζ καὶ Μαξιμιανοῦ τὸ ϛ Σεβαστῶν.
²Αὐρηλίῳ Ζηνογένει στρατηγῷ 'Οξυρυγχείτου ³παρὰ
Αὐρηλίου Πλουτάρχου τοῦ καὶ 'Ατακτίου κρατίστου καὶ ὡς χρηματίζω. οὐ δεόντως καὶ παρὰ
πάντας ⁴τοὺς νόμους ὀνομασθέντος μου ὡς εἰς
δεκαπρωτείαν ὑπὸ Αὐρηλίου Δημητριανοῦ δεκα-
πρώτου ⁵τῆς πρὸς λίβα τοπαρχίας ἔκκλητον πεποίημαι διὰ τοῦ πατρός μου Αὐρηλίου Σαραπάμμωνος
τοῦ καὶ Διονυσίου ⁶καὶ ὡς χρημα(τίζει) τῷ με
κατὰ καιρὸν ἐκεῖνον εἶναι ἐν τῇ Μικρᾷ 'Οάσει πρὸς
ἐκσφούνγευσιν τῶν ἐκεῖσε ⁷διακειμένων στρατιωτῶν ἐκ προστάξεως τοῦ κυρίου μου τοῦ διασημοτάτου ἐπάρχου Αἰγύπτου ⁸Αἰλίου Πουβλίου, καὶ
ποιήσας τὰ ἐπὶ τῇ ἐκκλήτῳ δέοντα κατέφυγον πρὸς
τὸν κύριόν μου τὸν ⁹διασημότατον καθολικὸν Πομ-
πώνιον Δόμνον καὶ ἐνέτυχον αὐτῷ ἐπὶ ὑπομνη-
296

then, in order that by the appended direction of you the lord and kindly benefactor of all I may recover my property and be able to live with my young children in my own home and ever to avow my gratitude to your fortune. Farewell. (Subscribed) The . . . year, . . . 9. With a view to what is expedient for the revenues . . . his excellency the epistrategus shall sift the matter with the utmost equity. The 69th page of the 1st volume.[a]

[a] The page on which the petition was entered in the book of registration.

294. PETITION TO A STRATEGUS

A.D. 299.

In the consulship of our lords the Emperors Diocletianus Augustus for the 7th time and Maximianus Augustus for the 6th time. To Aurelius Zenogenes, strategus of the Oxyrhynchite nome, from Aurelius Plutarchus also called Atactius, excellency, and however I am styled. Having been nominated wrongfully and in contravention of all law for the decemprimate by Aurelius Demetrianus, *decemprimus* of the western toparchy, I brought an action of appeal through my father Aurelius Sarapammon also called Dionysius, and however he is styled, because I was at that time in the Small Oasis for the discharge of the soldiers stationed there, in accordance with the order of my lord the most eminent praefect of Egypt Aelius Publius, and having taken the proper steps for the appeal I had recourse to my lord the most eminent catholicus Pomponius Domnus, and applied to him in a memorandum setting

μάτων αὐτὰ ταῦτα ¹⁰παρατιθέμενος. ἐπεὶ οὖν διὰ
ἀποφάσεως ἐκέλευσεν τὸ μεγαλεῖον αὐτοῦ παρ-
αγγεῖλαί με τῷ. προκειμένῳ, ¹¹ὧν τὸ διαφέρον
μέρος καὶ τῶν ἀποφάσεων οὕτως ἔχει·

Ἐπὶ τῶν κυρίων ἡμῶν Διοκλητιανοῦ Σεβαστοῦ
τὸ ζ καὶ ¹²Μαξιμιανοῦ Σεβαστοῦ τὸ ς ὑπάτων,
πρὸ ιδ καλανδῶν Σεπτεμβρίων, ἐν Ἀλεξανδρείᾳ
ἐν τῷ σηκρήτῳ. ¹³κληθέντος Πλουτάρχου κρατίστου Ἰσίδωρος εἶπ(εν)· ἀπαλλαγὴν εὕρασθαι πειρώ-
μενος ὁ παρεστὼς ¹⁴τῇ σῇ ἀρετῇ Πλούταρχος ὁ
κράτιστος τῶν πολειτικῶν λειτουργιῶν δεδέηται
τῆς θείας τύχης ἔτι ἄνω-¹⁵θεν τῶν δεσποτῶν ἡμῶν
τῶν Σεβαστῶν καὶ τῶν Καισάρων μεταδοῦναι
αὐτῷ τοῦ τῆς κρατιστίας ¹⁶ἀξιώματος, καὶ ἐπένευσεν ἡ θεία τύχη αὐτῶν καὶ μετέδωκεν, καὶ νῦν
ἔστιν ἐν αὐτῷ. διετέλεσεν ¹⁷γοῦν ὑπηρετούμενος
τῇ σῇ τοῦ ἐμοῦ κυρίου τάξει, εἶτα καὶ τοῖς προσ-
τάγμασιν τοῖς ὑμῶν τῶν μειζόνων. ¹⁸πρώην δέ,
ἐπειδὴ κατὰ τὴν Ὄασιν τὴν Μεικρὰν διέτρειβεν
τοῦ κυρίου μου σοῦ δὲ ἀδελφοῦ Πουβλίου ¹⁹τοῦ
διασημοτάτου ἡγουμένου ἀποστείλαντος αὐτὸν
ἐκσφουγγεύειν τοὺς στρατιώτας, Δημητριανός τις
²⁰Ὀξυρυγχείτης τῆς αὐτῆς πόλεως αὐτῷ ὁρμώ-
μενος τετόλμηκεν αὐτὸν ὀνομάζειν εἰς δεκαπρωτείαν ²¹μὴ ἐπιγνοὺς ὡς ἀξιώματος μείζονος
μετείληφεν, ὃ ἀπαλλάττει ἴσως αὐτὸν τῶν λειτουργιῶν τῶν πολει-²²τικῶν. μεθ' ἕτερα, Δόμνος ὁ
διασημότατος καθολικὸς εἶπ(εν)· ἀνάγνωθι τὴν
ἡμέραν τῆς χειροτονίας. Πλού-²³ταρχος εἶπ(εν)·
Παῦνι λ. ἀπήμην ἐν Ὀάσει· ὅτε ἔγνων ἀπήν-
τησα. Δόμνος ὁ διασημότατος καθολικὸς εἶπ(εν)·
καὶ τὸ βιβλίον ²⁴τῆς χειροτονείας παρασχεθήτω
298

these facts before him. Whereas then his highness ordered me by a judgement to give notice to the aforesaid person, the essential part of the proceedings and the judgement being as follows :

In the consulship of our lords Diocletianus Augustus for the 7th time and Maximianus Augustus for the 6th time, August 19, at Alexandria, in court. Plutarchus, an excellency, having been summoned, Isidorus said : " His excellency Plutarchus who has presented himself before your eminence, endeavouring to procure a release from municipal offices, some time ago besought the divine fortune of our masters the Augusti and Caesars to grant him the rank of excellency, and their divine fortune consented and granted it, and he now enjoys it. Now he has continued in obedience to your lordship's department and also to the orders of you magnates. But lately when he was in the Small Oasis, where he had been sent by my lord your colleague Publius the most eminent praefect to discharge the soldiers, a certain Demetrianus, an Oxyrhynchite of the same city as himself, ventured of design to nominate him for the decemprimate, ignoring his acquisition of a superior rank, which presumably releases him from municipal offices." After other evidence Domnus the most eminent catholicus said : " Read the day of his appointment." Plutarchus said : " Pauni 30. I was away in the Oasis ; I came back when I knew." Domnus the most eminent catholicus said : " Let the document concerning the appointment be pro-

καὶ τὰ ἑξῆς ὡς ἐκέλευσα δειξάτω, ἵνα δὲ ἐννομώ-
τερον ἀκουσθείη, παραγγειλά-²⁵τω τῷ ἐλαμέ[νῳ
αὐτὸν (?) εἰ]ς τὴν δεκαπρωτείαν. Γρηγόριος εἶπ(εν)·
τὰ ὑπομνήματα κέλευσον ἐκδοθῆναι. ²⁶Δόμνος ὁ
διασημ[ό]τατο[ς καθ]ολικὸς εἶπ(εν)· ἐ[κ]δοθήσεται.
Ὀλύμπιος κομενταρήσιος ὀφφικιάλιος ἐξέδωκα τὰ
ὑπομνήματα.
²⁷Ὅθεν ἀ[ξιῶ . . . .] ἐάν [σοι
δόξῃ - - -

295. PETITION FROM A DESERTED VILLAGE

P. Thead. 17.   A.D. 332.

¹Φλα{υ}ουί(ῳ) Ὑγίνῳ τῷ διασημοτάτῳ ἐπάρχῳ
Αἰγύπτου ²παρὰ τοῦ κοινοῦ τῶν ἀπὸ κώμης Φιλ-
αδελφίας ὀγδόου πάγου τοῦ Ἀρσινοεί-³του δι' ἡμῶν
Ἥρωνος καὶ Σακάωνος καὶ Καναῦ. τρὶς ἐσμὲν
οἱ προκίμενοι ⁴ἐν τῇ κώμῃ, ἔπαρχε δέσποτα{ι},
οἵτινες εἰσφέρομεν ὑπὲρ ὅλης τῆς κώμης ⁵ἀρουρῶν
πεντακοσίων καὶ μηδὲ συνπροσχιζομένων καὶ τοῦ
κατ' ἄνδρα ⁶σὺν ταμιακοῖς ἀνδράσι εἴκοσι πένται,
ὡς ἐκ τούτου πάνοι τὴν κώμην ἡμῶν ⁷εἰς <σ>τενο-
κομιδὴν ἐλθῖν. πρὸς ἀναζήτησιν δὲ ἐγενόμεθα τῶν
ὁμοκομητῶν ⁸ἐπὶ τῷ Ὀξυρυγκείτῃ καὶ κατελαβό-

2. l. Θεαδελφίας.   3. l. Καναοῦγ as in l. 20.   6. l.
πέντε (so in l. 9), πάνυ.   7. l. ὁμοκομητῶν.

ᵃ In earlier times Theadelphia was a fair-sized village, but
owing to recurrent neglect of the irrigation system, as well as

300

duced, and let him also show the consequent correspondence, as I ordered ; and that he may be heard
in a more regular way, let him give notice to the
person who nominated (?) him for the decemprimate."
Gregorius said : " Give orders for the issue of the
minutes." Domnus the most eminent catholicus
said : " They shall be issued." I, Olympius, official
notary, issued the minutes.

I therefore beg, if it seem good to you, . . .

295. PETITION FROM A DESERTED VILLAGE

A.D. 332.

To his eminence Flavius Hyginus, praefect of
Egypt, from the community of the village of Theadelphia *a* in the 8th *pagus* *b* of the Arsinoite nome,
through us, Heron and Sakaon and Kanaoug. We the
aforesaid, our lord praefect, are a group of three
persons in the village who pay taxes on behalf of all
the village for five hundred arurae which are not even
being ploughed up and for a roll of twenty-five
individuals including the employees of the Treasury,
so that from this state of things our village is reduced
to great straits. Setting out in search of our fellow-
villagers in the Oxyrhynchite nome we discovered at

to oppressive taxation, it had gradually fallen into decay like
many other villages in the Fayum. It was finally abandoned
in the fourth century.

b About the beginning of the Byzantine period the nomes
were divided into districts called *pagi* in place of the earlier
toparchies.

μεθα ἐν ἐποικίῳ Εὐλογίου υἱῷ Νίδα τῶν ἀπὸ
[9]Σερήνου προβόλους ἄνδρας πένται Διονύσιον καὶ
{Σουχ[[είδαν]] καὶ} [5]Ὧρ καὶ Ἄμμω-[10]να καὶ Σου-
χείδαν καὶ Ἀπὸλ καὶ Σαββῆον μετὰ τῶν γενῶν,
καὶ ὁ τούτων γεο-[11][ύ]χος Εὐλόγιο[ς] ἅμα [τῷ]
Ἀρείωνι ἀμπελουργῷ καὶ Σεραπίωνι γεωργῷ οὐκ
ἐπε[τρέ-][12]ψαντο οὐτὲ τῆς [θύ]ρας τοῦ ἐποικίου
ἐνγίσαι μεθ' ὕβρεων· ἔτι δὲ καὶ εὕραμ(εν) [13]ἐν τῷ
[[αὐτῷ]] Κυνοπολίτῳ νομῷ τρῖς παρατὰς Γερόν-
τιον καὶ Παθὰν καὶ Ἥρω-[14]να ἔχοντας ὅλας
βασιλικῆς ἀρούρας ἑκατὸν καὶ πρός. διὰ τοῦτο
δεόμεθα τῆς [15]σῆς ἐξουσίας, ἄνθρωποι μέτριοι
καὶ μονήρεις, προστάξε τῷ τὰ εἰρηνικὰ ἐπ{επ}-
[16]ιστατουμένῳ τοὺς [ὁ]μοκομήτας ἡμῖν προδοῦναι
μετὰ τῶν γενῶν, εἴνα δυ-[17]νηθῶμεν {μετὰ τῶν
γενῶν εἴνα δυνηθῶμεν} διὰ ταύτης τῆς παραμυθίας
[18]στῆν[α]ι ἐν τῇ κώμῃ καὶ διὰ παντὸς τῇ λαμπρᾷ
σου τύχῃ χάριτας ἔχω[μεν]. [19]διευτύχει. (2nd
hand) [20]Αὐρ(ήλιοι) Σακάων καὶ Ἥρων καὶ Καναοῦγ ἐπιδεδώκαμεν. [21]Αὐρήλιος Μάξιμος ἔγρα(ψα)
ὑπὲρ αὐτῶν [γράμμ(ατα)] μὴ εἰ(δότων).

8. *l.* υἱοῦ.   10. *l.* Σαββαῖον.   12. *l.* οὐδέ.   13. *l.*
Κυνοπολίτῃ, περατάς?   15. *l.* προστάξαι.   16. *l.*
ὁμοκωμήτας.

296. PETITION TO THE *RIPARII*

P. Oxy. 1033.   A.D. 392.

[1]Ὑπατίας τοῦ δεσπότου ἡμῶν Ἀρκαδίου αἰωνίου
Αὐγούστου τὸ β καὶ Φλα(ουίου) Ῥουφίνου [2]τοῦ

the farmstead of Eulogius son of Nidas, of the hamlet of Serenus, five nominated [a] (?) men, Dionysius, Hor, Ammon, Soucheidas, Apol, and Sabbaeus, with their families ; and their landlord Eulogius, together with Arion, a vine-dresser, and Serapion, a cultivator, did not allow us even to approach the door of the farmstead, repulsing us with violence. We also found three migrants in the Cynopolite nome, Gerontius, Pathas, and Heron, holding between them a hundred arurae and more of Crown land. Therefore we, humble and solitary men, beseech your excellency to give orders to the superintendent of public security to deliver up to us our fellow-villagers with their families, in order that we may be enabled by this measure of relief to remain in our village and may for ever feel grateful to your illustrious fortune. Farewell. (Signed) We, the Aurelii Sakaon and Heron and Kanaoug, have presented this petition. I, Aurelius Maximus, wrote for them, as they are illiterate.

[a] That is, nominated for public work ; but the meaning is rather doubtful. The names of six, not five, persons are given.

296. PETITION TO THE *RIPARII*

A.D. 392.

In the consulship of our master Arcadius, eternal Augustus, for the 2nd time and of Flavius Rufinus

λαμπροτάτου Φαῶφι κα. ³Σεπτιμίῳ Παύλῳ καὶ
Κλαυδίῳ Τατιανῷ ῥιπαρίοις Ὀξυρυγχίτου ⁴παρὰ
Αὐρηλίων Γαΐου καὶ Θέωνος ἀμφοτέρων νυκτο-
στρατήγων τῆς αὐτῆς ⁵πόλεως. τῶν εἰρηνικῶν
τὴν φροντίδα ἀναδεδοιημένοι καὶ ἀμέμ-⁶πτως
ὑπουργοῦμεν τοῖς δημοσίοις ἐπιτάγμασι ἐπανέχον-
τες δὲ ⁷καὶ τῇ παραφυλακῇ τῆς πόλεως, ἀναγ-
καζόμεθα δὲ συνεχῶς ⁸ἕνεκεν τῆς παραστάσεως
διαφόρων προσώπων κατὰ πρόσταγμα ⁹τῶν κυρίων
μου τῶν μι{ν}ζόνων ἡμῶν ἀρχόντων, καὶ μὴ ἐχόντων ¹⁰ἡμῶν τὴν βοήθειαν εἴτ' οὖν τοὺς δημοσίους
καὶ τοὺς ἐφοδευτὰς ¹¹πολλάκεις σχεδὸν εἰπε‹ῖ›ν
εἰς ψυχὴν ἐκεινδυνεύσαμεν διὰ τὸ ¹²τούτους παρ'
ἡμῶν ἀπεσπᾶσθαι μόνοι περιερχόμενοι ¹³τὴν πόλιν
καὶ κατοπτεύοντες. διὰ τοῦτο ἑαυτοὺς ἀσφαλισ-
ζόμενοι ¹⁴τούσδε τοὺς λιβέλλους ἐπιδίδομεν ἀξιοῦντες ἢ τὴν προσήκουσαν ¹⁵ἡμῖν βοήθιαν τούς τε
δημοσίους καὶ τοὺς ἐφοδευτὰς ὡς προείπαμεν
¹⁶παραδοῦναι ἢ τὸ ἀνενόχλητον ἡμᾶς ἔχειν περί
τε τῆς παραφυλακῆς ¹⁷τῆς πόλεως καὶ περὶ τῆς
παραστάσεως τῶν ζητουμένων προσώ-¹⁸πων, ἵνα
μὴ ὑπαίτιοι γενώμεθα κινδύνῳ.

5. =εἰς τὴν φροντίδα ἀναδεδομένοι.

297. PETITION OF AN INJURED WIFE

P.S.I. 1075.   A.D. 458.

¹Φλαουίῳ Οὐαλερίῳ τῷ λογιωτάτῳ ἐκδίκῳ τῆς
Ὀξυρυγχιτῶν πόλεως ²παρὰ Αὐρηλίας Σοφίας
θυγατρὸς Ἀνουθίου ἀπὸ τῆς αὐτῆς πόλεως. ³τοῦ

the most illustrious, Phaophi 21. To Septimius Paulus and Claudius Tatianus, *riparii* [a] of the Oxyrhynchite nome, from the Aurelii Gaius and Theon, both night-strategi [b] of the metropolis. Being appointed to the care of the peace we execute public orders irreproachably, while also attending to the watching of the city ; but being constantly under the necessity of producing various persons in accordance with the command of our lords the superior magistrates and having no assistance either of public guards or inspectors we often run the risk, one might almost say, of our lives, because these assistants have been taken from us and we go about the city keeping watch all alone. Therefore to safeguard ourselves we present this petition requesting either that we should be given the proper assistance of the public guards and the inspectors as aforesaid or that we should be free from molestation with regard to the watching of the city and the production of persons who are wanted, in order that we may not be held responsible at our peril.

[a] See No. 228.
[b] Although called strategi these were evidently officials of not very high rank.

297. PETITION OF AN INJURED WIFE

A.D. 458.

To Flavius Valerius the most learned *defensor* of the city of Oxyrhynchus from Aurelia Sophia daughter of Anouthius, of the said city. My husband having

ἀνδρός μου ἐκβληθέντος παρὰ τοῦ ἰδίου πατρὸς
⁴ἐπιρίψαντος αὐτῷ καὶ χρέα συντίνοντα εἰς νομίσ-
[μ]ατα ⁵[δ]εκατέσσαρα, ἅπερ ἐδυνήθην ἐπιγνῶναι ἐκ
τῆς διαπράσεως τῶν τε ⁶[πρ]οικώων μο[υ] καὶ τοῦ
φθορίου ἔδνου, καὶ συνκάμνουσα αὐτῷ τῷ ⁷[ἀν]δρί
μου ἐδυνήθην μὲν καὶ οἰκίαν ἑαυτοῖς περιποιήσα-
σθαι· οὗτος δὲ ⁸[διά]θεσιν ἀγαθὴν μὴ διασώζων εἰς
ἐμὲ παρ' ἔκαστα ἐκβάλλει⟦ν⟧ ⁹με οὐδεμιᾶς [α]ἰτίας
εὑρισκομένης κατ' ἐμοῦ. τούτου χάριν προσκυνεῖ
¹⁰τῇ σῇ λογιότητι ἀξιοῦσα κελεῦσαι παραστῆναι
τοῦτον καὶ ἀναγκασθῆναι ¹¹καὶ τὸ ἔδνον καὶ τὴν
προῖκάν μου ἀποκαταστῆσαι, καὶ τύπον ¹²μοι
δοῦναι περὶ τοῦ συνοικεσίου, λογιώτατε ἔκδικε
κύριε. (2nd hand) ¹³Αὐρηλία Σοφία ἐπιδέδωκα.
(3rd hand) ¹⁴ὑπατίᾳ τοῦ δεσπότου ἡμῶν Φλα(ουίου)
Λέοντος αἰωνίου Αὐγούστου τὸ α΄, Μεσορὴ ι.

298. APPLICATION FOR LEAVE

P. Giess. 41.   About A.D. 120.

(Col. 1) ¹['Ραμμίωι Μαρτιάλι τῶι] κρατίστωι
ἡγεμόνι ²['Απολλώνιος στρατηγὸς] 'Απολλωνο-
π[ολ]ίτου ³['Επτακωμίας] χαίρειν. ⁴[ἧς ἤδη γέ-
γραφά σοι, ἡγεμὼ]ν κύριε, περὶ κομεάτου ἐ-⁵[πι-
στολῆς τὸ ἀντίγραφον ⟦σ⟧οι ὑπέταξα, ἵν', ἐάν σου
τῆι τύ-⁶[χηι δόξηι, συγχωρήσηις] μοι ἡμέρας
ἑξήκοντα [ε]ἰς τὴν ⁷[διόρθωσιν τῶν ἡμετέρω]ν, νῦν
μάλιστα ὅτε οἴομαι ἐν ⁸[. . . . .
. . . κα]τεπείγειν. (2nd hand) ἐρρῶσθαί σε εὔχομαι, ⁹ἡγεμὼν κύ[ρι]ε. (3rd hand) ¹⁰[(ἔτους) . .
306

been cast out by his own father and charged by him
with debts amounting to fourteen solidi, these I was
able to honour by selling the articles of my dowry and
the nuptial gift,[a] and toiling together with him my
husband I was able also to procure for ourselves a
home ; but he, failing to preserve a kindly attitude
towards me, seeks on every occasion to cast me out,
though no fault can be found against me. For this
reason I humbly beseech your erudition to command
that he be brought before you and compelled to
restore both the gift and the dowry, and I beg you
to give me an order concerning the marriage, most
learned lord *defensor*. (Signed) I, Aurelia Sophia,
have presented this petition. (Dated) In the consulship of our master Flavius Leon, eternal Augustus,
for the 1st time, Mesore 10.

[a] From the bridegroom to the bride as *pretium pudicitiae*.

4. *l.* συντείνοντα.   9. *l.* προσκυνῶ.

298. APPLICATION FOR LEAVE

About A.D. 120.

To his excellency the praefect Rammius Martialis
from Apollonius, strategus of the Apollonopolite-
Heptacomia nome, greeting. I append a copy of the
letter which I have already written to you, my lord
praefect, concerning leave, in order that, if it please
your fortune, you may grant me sixty days to put
my affairs in order, especially now that I think . . .
I pray for your health, my lord praefect. The . . year

Αὐτοκράτορος Καίσαρος Τραϊανοῦ Ἀδ]ριανοῦ Σεβαστ[ο]ῦ Χ[ο]ίακ β̄.

(4th hand) ¹¹['Ραμμίωι Μαρτιάλι τῶι] κρατίσ-
[τ]ωι ἡγ[εμόνι ¹²'Απολλώνιος στρατηγὸς Ἀπο]λ-
λωνοπολίτου Ἑ[πτακωμίας χα(ίρειν). ¹³ . . . . .
. . . . . .]ων, ἡγ[ε]μὼν [κύριε, . . . ¹⁴ . . . .
. . . . ἅ]παξ κα[. . . . . .
. . . . . - - - (Col. 2) ¹ . . . . . .] συνχρήσα-
σθαι· οὐ γὰρ μόνον ὑ-²πὸ τῆς μακρᾶς ἀποδημίας
τὰ ἡμέτε[ρα] ³πα[ντ]άπασιν ἀμεληθέντα τυγχ[άνει],
⁴ἀλλ[ὰ καὶ] παρὰ τὴν τῶν ἀνοσίων ['Ιου-]⁵δαίω[ν
ἔ]φοδον σχεδὸν πά[ν]τ[α ὅσα] ⁶ἔχ[ω ἔν τε ταῖ]ς
κώμαις τοῦ ['Ερμοπο-]⁷λίτο[υ κ]αὶ ἐν τῆ[ι μη]τρο-
πόλε[ι . . . .] ⁸γεν[όμενα τ]ὴν παρ' ἐμοῦ ἀνά-
[ληψιν] ⁹ἐπιζητεῖ. ἐπινεύσαντος ο[ὖ]ν ‹σου› τῆ[ι
¹⁰δεήσει μου μετὰ τοῦ διορθῶσ[αι] ¹¹κατὰ τὸ
δυνατὸν τὰ ἡμέτερα δυνή-¹²[σο]μαι εὐθυμότερον
προσέρχεσθαι ¹³[τῆι τῆς σ]τρατηγ[ίας] ἐπιμελείαι.

299. APPLICATION FOR ENROLMENT OF
AN EPHEBUS

J.E.A. xiii. p. 219.   About A.D. 186–187.

¹Α[. .] . . . ω Λογγινίω Λογγίνω ²τ[ῷ κα]ὶ 'Απολ-
λωνίω ἱερεῖ ἐξηγη-³τῆ [κ]αὶ πρὸς τῆ ἐπιμελία τῶν
⁴χρ[η]ματιστῶν καὶ τῶν ἄλλων κρι-⁵τη[ρί]ων ⁶παρὰ
'Ισιδώρας τῆς 'Απολλω-⁷νίου ἀστῆς μετὰ κυρίου
τοῦ ⁸ἐπισυμβιώσαντος αὐτῆ ἀν-⁹δ[ρ]ὸς 'Αγαθοῦ
Δαίμονος τοῦ ¹⁰'Α[μ]μωνίου τοῦ Θεοξένου Σω-

of the Emperor Caesar Trajanus Hadrianus Augustus, Choiak 2.

To his excellency the praefect Rammius Martialis from Apollonius, strategus of the Apollonopolite-Heptacomia nome, greeting . . . For not only are my affairs in an utterly neglected condition by reason of my long absence, but also, owing to the rising of the impious Jews,[a] almost all my property in the villages of the Hermopolite nome and in the metropolis has been . . . and requires to be re-established by me. If therefore you accede to my request, having put my affairs in order as far as possible I shall be able to take up my duties as strategus in better heart.

[a] The revolt of the Jews in Egypt and other provinces, which took place in 116 A.D. and was not finally crushed till after the accession of Hadrian.

---

10. Or l. μετὰ τό Meyer.

299. APPLICATION FOR ENROLMENT OF AN EPHEBUS

About A.D. 186–187.

To . . . Longinius Longinus also called Apollonius, priest, exegetes, and superintendent of the chrematistae [a] and the other courts, from Isidora daughter of Apollonius, of civic rank, having with her as guardian her second husband Agathodaemon son of Ammonius son of Theoxenus, of the Sosicosmian

[a] See No. 264. In Roman times the chrematistae were no longer assize judges, but formed an Alexandrian court.

¹¹σι[κ]οσμίου τοῦ καὶ ᾿Αλθαιέ-¹²ω[ς] τῶν τὸ
ὀκτωκεδέκα-¹³τον ἔτος θεοῦ Αἰλίου ᾿Αντω(νίνου)
¹⁴ἐφηβευκότων. βουλομένη ¹⁵ἰσκρῖναι ἰς τοὺς τὸ
ἰσιὸν ἔ-¹⁶βδ[ο]μον καὶ εἰκοστὸν ἔτος ¹⁷[Αὐτο]-
κράτορος Καίσαρος Μάρκο(υ) ¹⁸[Αὐρη]λίο[υ] Κομμόδου ᾿Αντων(ίνου) ¹⁹Ε[ὐ]σεβοῦς Ε[ὐ]τυχοῦς Σεβαστοῦ ²⁰᾿Α[ρμενιακ]οῦ Μηδικοῦ Παρθ(ικοῦ) ²¹[Σαρ-
ματικοῦ Γε]ρμανικοῦ Μεγ(ίστου) ²²Β[ρετανικο]ῦ
ἐφήβους τὸν ²³γε[γο]ν[ότα μο]ι ἐκ Θέωνος ²⁴τ[οῦ]
Θέωνος τοῦ Θέωνος ²⁵Σ[ωσι]κοσμίου τοῦ καὶ
᾿Αλθαιέ-²⁶ω[ς τ]ῶν τὸ τρισκαιδέκατον ²⁷ἔ[τος] θεοῦ
Αἰλίου ᾿Αντωνίνου ²⁸ἐ[φη]βευκότων, ὃς μετήλ-
²⁹λ[α]χεν, υἱὸν Δίδυμον ἀξι-³⁰ῶ σ[υντάξαι] γράψαι
τοῖς πρὸ(ς) ³¹τούτοις οὖσι [λ]αβοῦσί μου χι-³²ρο-
γ[ρ]αφίαν περὶ τοῦ ἀληθῆ ³³εἶν[α]ι τὰ προκίμαινα
ἰ{ι}πῖν ³⁴οἷς [κ]αθήκει χρηματίζιν ³⁵μοι τελιούσῃ τὰ
πρὸς τὴν ³⁶ἴσκρισιν καὶ ἐφηβίαν τοῦ προ-³⁷γεγραμ-
μένου μου υἱοῦ Διδύ-³⁸μου γράμματα, ἔπιτα τῷ
³⁹τε κ[ο]σμητῇ καὶ τῷ γυμνασ[ι-]⁴⁰άρχῳ τοῖς οὖσι
προσδέξα-⁴¹σθαι αὐτ[ὸ]ν ἰς τοὺς ἐφή-⁴²βους, ἵν᾿ ὦ
[π(εφιλανθρωπημένη)].

12. *l.* ὀκτωκαιδέκατον.　　33. *l.* προκείμενα.

300. PETITION CONCERNING AN EPHEBUS

P. Oxy. 1202.　　　　　　　　　　　　　　A.D. 217.

¹Αὐρηλίωι Σεουήρῳ τῷ κρατίστῳ διαδεχομένῳ
²[τ]ὴν ἐπιστρατηγίαν ³[π]αρὰ Αὐρηλίου Πτολεμαίου
Σεμπρωνίου τοῦ Λου-⁴[κίο]υ μητρὸς Θαήσιος ἀπ᾿
᾿Οξυρύγχων πόλεως. ⁵ἔθους ὄντος ἀφ᾿ οὗ ηὐτυχή-
σαμεν ἐκ τῆς τῶν ⁶[κυρί]ων Σεουήρου καὶ μεγάλου

tribe and the Althaean deme,[a] enrolled as an ephebus in the eighteenth year of the deified Aelius Antoninus. Wishing to submit for enrolment among the ephebi of the coming twenty-seventh year of the Emperor Caesar Marcus Aurelius Commodus Antoninus Pius Felix Augustus Armeniacus Medicus Parthicus Sarmaticus Germanicus Maximus Britannicus my son Didymus whose father was Theon son of Theon son of Theon, of the Sosicosmian tribe and the Althaean deme, enrolled as an ephebus in the thirteenth year of the deified Aelius Antoninus, and now deceased, I request you to order a letter to be written to the officials concerned to take my sworn declaration that the foregoing statements are true and to tell the proper persons to deal with my case when I complete the papers required for the enrolment of my aforesaid son Didymus as an ephebus, and then to tell the cosmetes and the gymnasiarch now in office to receive him among the ephebi, that so I may enjoy your benevolence.

[a] In Alexandria. *Cf.* Vol. I. p. 99.

300. PETITION CONCERNING AN EPHEBUS

A.D. 217.

To his excellency Aurelius Severus, deputy - epistrategus, from Aurelius Ptolemaeus son of Sempronius son of Lucius, his mother being Thaesis, of Oxyrhynchus. It has been the custom since the institution of the contest for ephebi which we acquired as a gift from our lords Severus and the great An-

Ἀντωνίνου ᵓ[δω]ρεᾶς τοῦ τῶν ἐφήβων ἀγῶνος τοὺς
κατὰ και-⁸[ρὸ]ν τῆς πόλεως ἀμφοδογραμματέας
ἐνγίζον-⁹τος τοῦ ἑκάστου ἔτους ἀγῶνος ἐπιδοῦναι
καὶ ¹⁰προθεῖναι τὴν τῶν ἐφηβεύειν μελλόντων
¹¹γραφὴν{αι} πρὸς τὸ ἕκαστον ἀφ' οὗ προσήκει
καιροῦ ¹²[τ]ῆς ἐφηβίας ἀντιλαβέσθαι, ἐπεὶ οὖν ὁ
νυνὶ τῆς ¹³[πό]λεως ἀμφοδογραμματεὺς Αὐρήλιος
Σαραπί-¹⁴ων ἐν τῇ ἔναγχος προτεθείσῃ ὑπ' αὐτοῦ
γραφῇ ¹⁵τῶν ἐπ' ἀγαθοῖς ἐφηβεύειν μελλόντων
παρεῖ-¹⁶[κε]ν τὸν ἡμέτερον υἱὸν Αὐρήλιον Πολυ-
δεύ-¹⁷κην καὶ αὐτὸν μελλοέφηβον καὶ ὄντα ἐκ τοῦ
¹⁸τάγματος τοῦ παρ' ἡμεῖν γυμνασίου, προσβάν-
¹⁹τος εἰς τεσσαρεσκαιδεκαετεῖς τῷ κε (ἔτει) καὶ
ἐπικρει-²⁰θέντα κατ' ἀκολουθείαν τῶν ἐτῶν καὶ τοῦ
γέ-²¹νους εἰς τοὺς ἐκ τοῦ γυμνασίου τῷ αὐτῷ κε
(ἔτει), ²²[ἴ]σως ἀγνοήσας, κατὰ τὸ ἀναγκαῖον
προσφεύ-²³γω σοι ἀξιῶν ἐνταγῆναι κἀμοῦ τὸν υἱὸν
²⁴τῇ τῶν ἐφήβων γραφῇ καθ' ὁμοιότητα ²⁵τῶν σὺν
αὐτῷ καὶ ᾧ βεβοηθημένος. ²⁶διευτύχει. (2nd
hand) ²⁷Αὐρήλιος Πτολεμαῖος ἐπιδέδω-²⁸κα.

301. APPLICATION FOR LEAVE TO CHANGE NAME

Archiv IV. p. 123 (= W. Chrest. 52).   A.D. 194.

¹ʽΗφαιστίων ὁ καὶ ['Α]μμωνῖν[ος] βα[σιλ(ικὸς)
γρα(μματεὺς) Νεσὺτ διαδ(εχόμενος)] ²καὶ τὰ κατὰ
τὴν στρα(τηγίαν) ʽΗφ[αιστίων]ι τῷ [καὶ 'Αμ-

toninus [a] that the district-scribes of the city for the time being should, as the contest of each year approaches, submit and publish a list of those about to become ephebi, in order that each should assume the status of ephebus at the proper season. Since therefore the present district-scribe, Aurelius Sarapion, in the list lately published by him of those who are auspiciously about to become ephebi, has, perhaps in ignorance, omitted my son Aurelius Polydeuces who is an incipient ephebus and on the roll of our gymnasium, having reached the age of fourteen years in the 25th year and passed the examination, in accordance with his age and parentage, for admittance to membership of the gymnasium in the same 25th year, I perforce have recourse to you, requesting that my son too may be entered on the list of the ephebi in the same way as his companions, that so I may obtain relief. Farewell. (Signed) I, Aurelius Ptolemaeus, have presented this petition.

[a] The contest was really founded and endowed by a certain Aurelius Horion, the emperors merely giving their sanction.

301. APPLICATION FOR LEAVE TO CHANGE NAME

A.D. 194.

Hephaestion also called Ammoninus, royal scribe of Nesut,[a] acting as strategus, to Hephaestion also

[a] A nome in the north-east of the Delta.

μωνίνῳ βασιλ(ικῷ)] ³γραμματεῖ τοῦ αὐτοῦ νομοῦ
τῷ φ[ιλτάτῳ χαίρειν]. ⁴τοῦ ἐπενεχθέντος μοι
βιβλειδί[ου ὑπὸ Εὐδαίμονος] ⁵Ψόιτος μητρὸς Τιαθρήους ἀπ[ὸ . . ναμφι . . . εως ἐπὶ ὑπο-]⁶γραφῆς
Κλαυδίου Ἀπολλωνίου τοῦ [κρα(τίστου) πρὸς τῷ
ἰδίῳ λόγῳ] ⁷περὶ χρηματισμοῦ ὀνόματος . [. . . .
. . . . τὸ ἀντίγρα(φον)] ⁸ἐπιστέλλεταί σοι, φίλτατε, ἵν᾽ [εἰ]δ[ῇς καὶ τὰ ἴδια μέρη ἀνα-]⁹πληρώσῃς.
[ἔρρωσο.] ¹⁰(ἔτους) γ Αὐτοκράτορος Καίσαρος
Λουκίου Σεπτ[ιμίου Σεουήρου Περτίνακος] ¹¹Σε-
βαστοῦ [Ἀθύ]ρ.

¹²Κλαυδί[ῳ] Ἀπολλωνίῳ τῷ κρατίστῳ πρὸς τ[ῷ
ἰ]δίῳ λόγ[ῳ] ¹³παρ᾽ Εὐδαίμονος Ψόιτος μητρὸς
Τιαθρήους ἀ[πὸ .] . ναμφι . [. .]εως ¹⁴τοῦ Νεσῦτ
νομοῦ. βούλομαι, κύριε, ἀπὸ τοῦ νῦν ἐπιτρ[απῆ]ναι
¹⁵χρηματίζει[ν] Εὐδαίμων Ἥρωνος ἀντὶ τοῦ Ψ[όι]-
τος καὶ [ἀντὶ] τῆς ¹⁶Τιαθρήου[ς μητ]ρὸς Διδύμης,
μηδενὸς δημ[οσίου ἢ ἰδιωτι]κοῦ ¹⁷καταβλαπ[το-
μένο]υ, ἵν᾽ ὦ πεφιλανθρω[π]ημέ[νο]ς. διευτύχει.
¹⁸Εὐδαίμ[ων ἐπι]δέδωκα. ¹⁹(ἔτους) β Αὐτοκράτορος Καίσαρος Λουκίου Σεπτιμίου Σεου[ήρου Περ-
τίνακ]ος Σεβαστοῦ Μεσορὴ ²⁰ἐπαγομένων δ.

²¹Μηδενὸς [δη]μοσίου ἢ ἰδιωτικοῦ καταβλαπ[το]-
μένου ἐφίημι. ²²ἀπόδος.

---

[a] The writer in his capacity of interim strategus addresses
himself as permanent royal scribe. It seems an anomaly,

called Ammoninus,[a] royal scribe of the said nome, most dear friend, greeting. A copy of the application presented to me by Eudaemon son of Psois and of Tiathres, of . . ., and subscribed by his excellency the idiologus [b] Claudius Apollonius, about authorizing a change of name, is herewith forwarded to you, dearest friend, in order that you may take note and perform your part. Goodbye. The 3rd year of the Emperor Caesar Lucius Septimius Severus Pertinax Augustus, Hathur.

To his excellency the idiologus Claudius Apollonius from Eudaemon son of Psois and of Tiathres, of . . . in the nome of Nesut. I desire, my lord, to have permission henceforth to style myself Eudaemon son of Heron [c] instead of Psois, and son of Didyme [c] instead of Tiathres, without detriment to any public or private interests, that so I may experience your kindness. Farewell. I, Eudaemon, have presented this application. The 2nd year of the Emperor Caesar Lucius Septimius Severus Pertinax Augustus, 4th intercalary day of Mesore. (Subscribed) If there is no detriment to any public or private interests, I give permission. Deliver.[d]

but the same practice is not uncommon at the present day when an official is on leave and a subordinate takes his place.

[b] See No. 206.

[c] Greek forms of the parents' Egyptian names.

[d] See No. 284, note d.

SELECT PAPYRI

302. APPLICATION OF A CULTIVATOR
OF STATE LAND FOR SEED

P. Oxy. 1031.   A.D. 228.

¹Αὐρηλίοις Δημητρίῳ τῷ καὶ Ἀλεξάνδρῳ ἀρ-
²χιερατεύσαντι καὶ Διοσκόρῳ ἀγορανόμῳ ³ἀμφο-
τέροις βουλευταῖς τῆς Ὀξυρυγχειτῶν πό-⁴λεως
αἱρεθεῖσι ὑπὸ τῆς κρατίστης βουλῆς ⁵ἐπὶ ἀνα-
δόσεως σπερμάτων τοῦ ἐνεστῶτος ⁶η (ἔτους) ἄνω
τοπ(αρχίας) ⁷παρὰ Αὐρηλίου Βιαίου Βιαίου μητρὸς
Ταϊόλλης ⁸ἀπὸ τοῦ Ἐπισήμου ἐποικίου. αἰτοῦμαι
ἐπιστα-⁹λῆναι εἰς <σ>πέρματα δάνεια ἀπὸ πυροῦ
γενήμα(τος) ¹⁰τοῦ διελθόντος ζ (ἔτους) εἰς κατα-
σπορὰν τοῦ ἐνεστῶ-¹¹τος η (ἔτους) εἰς ἣν γεωργῶ
δημοσίαν γῆν οὐκ ἔλατ-¹²τον διαρτάβου περὶ κώμην
Σκὼ ὄνομα(τι) ¹³Λουκίου Αὐρηλίου Ἀπολλωνίου
καὶ τοῦ υἱοῦ Λου-¹⁴κίου Αὐρηλίου Ματραίου τοῦ
καὶ Ἡραΐσκου ἐκ τ(οῦ) ¹⁵Ὠδέου κλήρου (ἀρουρῶν)
κϛ (ἡμίσους) καὶ ἐκ τ(οῦ) Παιδιέως ¹⁶κλήρου
(ἀρουρῶν) γ (ἡμίσους), γ(ίνονται) ἐπ(ὶ) τὸ αὐτὸ
(ἄρουραι) λ, ἀρτάβας λ, ἅσπερ κοκκολογή-¹⁷σας
ἀπὸ κριθῆς καὶ αἴρης καταθήσω εἰς τὴν ¹⁸γῆν
ὑγιῶς καὶ πιστῶς ἐπακολουθούντων ¹⁹τῶν εἰς
τοῦτο προκεχειρισμένων, καὶ ἐκ νέ-²⁰ων ἀποδώσω
τὰς ἴσας σὺν τοῖς ἑπομένοις ²¹ἅμα τοῖς τῆς γῆς
τοῦ ἐνεστῶτος η (ἔτους) γνη[σ]ίοις ²²τελέσμασι
μέτρῳ δημοσίῳ ἡμιαρτάβῳ ²³μετρήσει τῇ κελευσθείσῃ, καὶ ὀμνύω τὴν ²⁴[Μάρκο]ν Αὐρηλίου
Σεουήρου Ἀλεξάνδρου ²⁵[Καίσα]ρος τοῦ κυρίου
τύχην μὴ ἐψεῦσθαι. ²⁶[(ἔτους) η Αὐ]τοκράτορος
Καίσαρος Μάρκου ²⁷[Αὐ]ρηλίου Σεουήρο[υ] Ἀ[λ]εξ-

302. APPLICATION OF A CULTIVATOR OF STATE LAND FOR SEED

A.D. 228.

To Aurelius Demetrius also called Alexander, ex-chief priest, and Aurelius Dioscorus, agoranomus, both senators of the city of Oxyrhynchus, elected by their excellencies the senate to superintend the distribution of seed for the present 8th year in the upper toparchy, from Aurelius Biaeus son of Biaeus and Taiolle, from the village of Episemus. I request that there be assigned to me, as one of the loans of seed from the wheat crop of the past 7th year for the sowing of the present 8th year, 30 artabae for the public land which I cultivate at a rent of not less than 2 artabae (per arura) in the area of the village of Sko in the name of Lucius Aurelius Apollonius and his son Lucius Aurelius Matraeus also called Heraiscus, comprising in the holding of Odeas 26½ arurae and in the holding of Pedieus 3½ arurae, total 30 arurae. These 30 artabae I will clear of barley and darnel and sow upon the land honestly and in good faith under the cognizance of those appointed for that duty, and I will repay out of the new crop an equal amount with the accompaniments ^{a} at the same time as the regular dues upon the land for the present 8th year by the public half-artaba measure and according to the measurement ordered ; and I swear by the fortune of Marcus Aurelius Severus Alexander Caesar the lord that I have made no false statement. The 8th year of the Emperor Caesar Marcus Aurelius Severus

^{a} It is not clear what these extras were.

317

ἀνδρου Εὐσεβοῦς ²⁸[Εὐ]τυχοῦς Σεβαστοῦ Χοίακ.
(2nd hand) Αὐρήλιος ²⁹[Βίαιο]ς Βιαίου ἐ[π]ιδέ-
δω[κα - - -

303. APPLICATION FOR A BIRTH CERTIFICATE

P.S.I. 1067.   A.D. 235–237.

¹[Τ]ῇ κρ[ατ]ίστῃ βουλῇ ᾿Αντινοέων Νέ[ων] ²ʿΕλ-
λήνων ³[π]αρὰ Μάρκου Αὐρηλίου ᾿Αμμωνᾶ τοῦ
[καὶ ⁴Σ]αραπίωνος ᾿Αγαθοῦ Δαίμονος τοῦ Α[. . . .
⁵. .]ωνος Παυλ[ι]νίου τοῦ καὶ Μεγαλιαν[. . . .
⁶π]αροικοῦντος ἐν τῷ δ γρ(άμματι) πλινθ(είῳ) δ
καὶ τ[ῆς ⁷γυναι]κὸς Αὐρηλίας ῾Ιερακιαίνης Κα .
[. . . ⁸. . . . .]τος ῾Ιέρακος ἀπὸ κώμης Πώεως
[τοῦ ⁹ʿΕρμο]πολίτο[υ] ὡς (ἐτῶν) λδ χωρὶς κυρίου
[χρη-¹⁰ματι]ζ[ούσ]ης δι[κα]ίῳ τέκνων κατὰ τ[ὰ
¹¹ʿΡωμ]αίων ἔθη. βουλόμενοι ἀ[π]αρχὴν ¹²[ῆς]
ἔσχομεν ἐξ ἀλλήλων [θυ]γατρὸς ¹³[Εὐ]δαιμονίδος
ἡμερῶν κε προή[γμε-¹⁴θα] ὑπόμνημα ἐπιδοῦναι
καὶ ἀξιοῦ[μεν ¹⁵συ]ντάξαι τῷ [γ]ραμματεῖ [θ]έσθαι
[τῆς Εὐδαι-¹⁶μον]ίδος ἀπα[ρχ]ὴν ὡς καθήκει.
¹⁷[(ἔτους) ʹ.] Αὐτοκρ[άτ]ορος Καίσαρος Γαΐου ᾿Ιου-
[λίου ¹⁸Οὐή]ρου Μαξιμείνου Γερμανικοῦ Μεγί[στου
¹⁹Εὐ]σεβοῦς Εὐτυχοῦς Σεβαστοῦ καὶ Γαΐου ᾿Ιου-
[λίου ²⁰Οὐή]ρου Μαξίμου τοῦ ἱερωτάτου Καίσαρο[ς
²¹Γερ]μανικοῦ Μεγίστου Σεβαστοῦ υἱοῦ τοῦ Σεβα[στοῦ, ²²ʿΑδ]ριανοῦ ιδ. (2nd hand) Αὐρήλιος
᾿Αμμωνᾶς ²³ὁ καὶ Σαρα[π]ίων ἐπειδέδωκα. (3rd
hand) ²⁴[Αὐρ]ηλία ῾Ιερα[κί]αινα ἐπιδέ[δ]ω[κα.
318

Alexander Pius Felix Augustus, Choiak. (Signed) Presented by me, Aurelius Biaeus son of Biaeus . . .

303. APPLICATION FOR A BIRTH CERTIFICATE [a]

A.D. 235–237.

To their excellencies the senate of the citizens of Antinoe, Neo-Hellenes, from Marcus Aurelius Ammonas also called Sarapion son of Agathodaemon son of . . ., of the Paulinian tribe and the Megalianian (?) deme,[b] residing in the 4th quarter, block 4, and from his wife Aurelia Hieraciaena daughter of . . . son of Hierax, of the village of Pois in the Hermopolite nome, aged about 34 years, acting without a guardian by right of children [c] according to the Roman custom. Desiring a birth certificate for the daughter who has been born to us, Eudaemonis, 25 days old, we have been moved to present an application and we request you to order the secretary to draw up a birth certificate for Eudaemonis as is proper. The [.] year of the Emperor Caesar Gaius Julius Verus Maximinus Germanicus Maximus Pius Felix Augustus and Gaius Julius Verus Maximus the most sacred Caesar Germanicus Maximus Augustus son of the Augustus, 14th day of Hadrianus.[d] (Signed) I, Aurelius Ammonas also called Sarapion, have presented this. I, Aurelia Hieraciaena, have presented

[a] The word ἀπαρχή means here a birth certificate which showed that the parents belonged to a privileged class and served as an official proof of the status of the child.

[b] See No. 288, note a, p. 279.   [c] See No. 305.

[d] = Choiak.

Αὐρ]ήλιος ²⁵[Ξάν]θιππος Θεοτέκνου ᾽Αθηνα[ιε]ὺς
[ὁ καὶ ²⁶Σα]λαμίνιος ἔγραψα ὑπὲρ αὐτῆς μὴ
ἰδ[υίης ²⁷γρά]μματα.

304. APPLICATION FOR A PERMIT TO
LEAVE EGYPT

P. Oxy. 1271.   A.D. 246.

¹Οὐαλερίῳ Φίρμῳ ἐπάρχῳ Αἰγύπτου ²παρὰ
Αὐρηλίας Μαικιανῆς Σιδήτ(ιδος). ³βούλομαι,
κύριε, ἐκπλεῦσαι διὰ Φάρου· ⁴ἀξιῶ γράψαι σε τῷ
ἐπιτρόπῳ τῆς Φά-⁵ρου ἀπολῦσαί με κατὰ τὸ ἔθος.
⁶Π[α]χὼν α. διευτύχει. (2nd hand) ⁷Valerius
Firmus ⁸Asclepiade . . l . . . si ⁹dimitti . . s d . .
[. . .] ¹⁰co . . us d . . [. . . . .]¹¹. . fie[. . . . . . .]
¹²datum xvii K[al(endas) . . . .] ¹³Presenti A[lbino
co(n)s(ulibus) . . .

8. l. Asclepiadae sal(utem) iussi?   9. l. dimittimus de
P[haro]?

305. APPLICATION FOR *IUS TRIUM*
LIBERORUM

P. Oxy. 1467.   A.D. 263.

¹- - - , δ[ιαση-] ²μότατε ἡγεμών, οἵτινες ³ἐξ-
ουσίαν διδόασιν ταῖς γυναι-⁴ξὶν ταῖς τῶν τριῶν
τέκνων ⁵δικαίῳ κεκοσμημένα[ι]ς ἑαυ-⁶τῶν κυριεύειν
καὶ χωρ[ὶς] κυ-⁷ρίου χρηματίζειν ἐν αἷς ποι-⁸οῦν-

this. I, Aurelius Xanthippus son of Theotecnus, of the Athenaean tribe and the Salaminian deme,[a] wrote for her, as she is illiterate.

[a] See No. 288, note *a*, p. 279.

304. APPLICATION FOR A PERMIT TO LEAVE EGYPT

A.D. 246.

To Valerius Firmus, praefect of Egypt, from Aurelia Maeciana of Side.[a] I wish, my lord, to sail out by way of Pharos ; I beg you to write to the procurator of Pharos to allow me to leave according to the usual practice. Pachon 1. Farewell.

(Below, remains of a permit in Latin from the praefect.)

[a] A town in Pamphylia.

305. APPLICATION FOR *IUS TRIUM LIBERORUM*

A.D. 263.

. . . (Laws have been made), most eminent praefect, which empower women who are honoured with the right of three children to be independent and act without a guardian in whatever business they trans-

[τ]αι οἰκονομίαις, πο[λλ]ῷ ⁹δὲ πλέον ταῖς γρά[μ]-
ματα ¹⁰ἐπισταμέναις. καὶ αὐτὴ τοί-¹¹νυν τῷ μὲν
κόσμῳ τῆς εὐ-¹²παιδείας εὐτυχήσασα, ¹³ἐνγράμ-
ματος δὲ κα[ὶ ἐ]ς τὰ ¹⁴μάλιστα γράφειν εὐκόπως
¹⁵δυναμένη, ὑπὸ περισσῆς ¹⁶ἀσφαλείας διὰ τούτων
μου ¹⁷τῶ[ν] βιβλειδίων προσφω<νῶ> ¹⁸τῷ σῷ
μεγέθει πρὸς τὸ δύνα-¹⁹σθαι ἀνεμποδίστως ἃς ἐν-
²⁰τεῦθεν ποιοῦμαι οἰκ[ον]ομία[ς] ²¹διαπράσσεσθαι.
ἀξιῶ ἔχε[ιν] ²²αὐτὰ ἀπροκρίτως το[ῖς δι-]²³καίοις
μ[ο]υ ἐν τῇ σῇ τοῦ [δια-]²⁴σημοτάτου τ[ά]ξι, ἵν'
ὦ β[εβο-]²⁵ηθ[η]μένη κ[α]ὶ εἰ[σ]αεὶ ὁ[μοίας?]
²⁶χάριτας ὁμολογήσω. διευτ[ύ]χει. ²⁷Αὐρηλία
Θαϊσ[ο]ῦς ἡ καὶ Λολλ[ι-]²⁸ανὴ διεπεμψάμην πρὸς
ἐ-²⁹πίδοσιν. ἔτους ι Ἐπεὶφ κα. ³⁰ἔσται σο[ῦ]
τὰ βιβλία ἐν τῇ [τάξι].

---

[a] According to the *Lex Julia et Papia Poppaea* of Augustus,
as applied in Egypt. The petitioner no doubt possessed the
Roman citizenship extended by Caracalla to free-born in-

306. APPLICATION OF AN ATHLETE FOR PAYMENT OF PENSION

C. P. Herm. 52-56, col. iv.   A.D. 267.

¹[Τῇ κ]ρατίστῃ βουλ[ῇ Ἑρμοῦ πόλεως τῆς
μεγάλης ²ἀρχαίας] καὶ σεμνοτάτη[ς καὶ λαμπροτάτης ³πα]ρὰ Αὐρ(ηλίου) Λευκα[δίου Ἑρμοπο-
λίτου] ἱερο[νίκου] ⁴παγκρατιαστ[οῦ διὰ Αὐρηλίου
Ἀππιανοῦ τοῦ] καὶ ⁵Δημητρίου [Ἑρμοπολίτο]υ
ἐπιτρό[που συστ]α-⁶θέντος. [α]ἰτο[ῦμαι ἐπιστ]αλῆ-
ναι [μοι] ἀπὸ πο-⁷λιτικοῦ λό[γου ὑπὲρ ὀ]ψω(νίων)
322

act, especially those who know how to write.[a] Accordingly, as I too enjoy the happy honour of being blessed with children and as I am a literate woman able to write with a high degree of ease, it is with abundant security that I appeal to your highness by this my application with the object of being enabled to accomplish without hindrance whatever business I henceforth transact, and I beg you to keep it without prejudice to my rights in your eminence's office, in order that I may obtain your support and acknowledge my unfailing gratitude. Farewell. I, Aurelia Thaisous also called Lolliana, have sent this for presentation. The 10th year, Epeiph 21. (Annotation) Your application shall be kept in the office.

habitants of the provinces. In Rome the law conferred various privileges on the parents of three children, but in Egypt its most conspicuous benefit was the right enjoyed by women whom it affected of conducting legal transactions without a guardian. See also No. 206, paragraph 28.

306. APPLICATION OF AN ATHLETE FOR PAYMENT OF PENSION

A.D. 267.

To their excellencies the senate of Hermopolis the great, ancient, most august, and most illustrious city, from Aurelius Leucadius, Hermopolitan, victor in the sacred games, pancratiast,[a] through Aurelius Appianus also called Demetrius, Hermopolitan, delegated as his guardian. I request that an order be given to pay me from the municipal account as my

[a] Wrestler and boxer combined.

323

μου ὧν [ἐνί]κη-[8]σα καὶ ἐστεφαν[ώθη]ν ἱερῶν [εἰσ-
ελαστι]κῶν [9]ἀγώνων τῶν [ἀπὸ μηνὸς] Φαμενὼθ ι
(ἔτους) ἕως [10]λ Μεχεὶρ ιδ (ἔτους) [μην]ῶν μη̄ ὡς
τοῦ μη(νὸς) [11](δραχμῶν) ρπ (τάλαντον) α (δραχμὰς)
Ἐχ[μ] καὶ ὑπὲρ ὧν πρώτως [12]ἐνίκησα κ[αὶ ἐστεφ]α-
νώθην ἱεροῦ εἰσελα-[13]στικοῦ οἰκο[υμενικοῦ] περι-
πορ[φύρου] ἰσο-[14]λυμπίου ἐν [κο]λωνία Σιδονίων
πόλει [15]τῶν ἀπὸ ϛ Φαμενὼθ ια (ἔτους) ἕως Μεχεὶρ
[16]καὶ αὐτοῦ ιδ (ἔτους) μη(νῶν) λε ἡμερ(ῶν) κ[ε] ὡς
τοῦ [17]μη(νὸς) (δραχμῶν) ρπ (τάλαντον) α (δραχμὰς)
υν, (γίνεται) ἐπὶ τὸ αὐτὸ τῆς [18]αἰτήσεως ἀργυρίου
τάλαντα δύο [καὶ] δρα-[19]χμαὶ τρισχείλιαι ἐνε-
νήκοντα, [20](γίνεται) ἀργ(υρίου) (τάλαντα) β καὶ
(δραχμαὶ) Ἐγϥ, λόγου φυλ(ασσομένου) τῇ πόλει
[21]καὶ τῇ βουλῇ περὶ οὗ ἔχουσι παντὸς δικαίου.
[22](ἔτους) ιδ Αὐτοκράτορος Καίσαρος Πουπλίου
[23]Λικιννίου Γαλλιηνοῦ Γερμανικοῦ Μεγίστου [24]Περ-
σικοῦ Μεγίστου Εὐσεβοῦς Εὐτυχοῦς [25]Σεβαστοῦ
Φαμενώθ.

307. REQUEST FOR PAYMENT FOR EMBELLISHMENT OF A NEW STREET

P. Oxy. 55.   A.D. 283.

[1]Αὐρηλίῳ Ἀπολλωνίῳ τῷ καὶ Διονυσίῳ γενομένῳ
ὑπομνη-[2]ματογράφῳ κ[αὶ] ὡς χρηματίζει γυμνα-
σιαρχήσαν[τ]ι βουλευτῇ [3]ἐνάρχῳ π[ρ]υτάνι τῆς
λαμπρᾶς καὶ λαμπροτάτ[ης Ὀ]ξ(υρυγχιτῶν) πόλεως
324

pension for the victory for which I was crowned at
the sacred triumphal games for the 48 months from
Phamenoth of the 10th year to Mecheir 30 of the
14th year, at the rate of 180 drachmae per month,
1 talent 2640 drachmae, and for the first victory for
which I was crowned at the sacred triumphal universal
juvenile contest, held as at Olympia, in the colony
of Sidon [a] for the 35 months 25 days from Phamenoth
6 of the 11th year to Mecheir inclusive of the 14th
year, at the rate of 180 drachmae per month, 1 talent
450 drachmae, making the total of the claim two
talents three thousand and ninety drachmae of silver,
total 2 tal. 3090 dr. of silver, without prejudice to any
rights possessed by the city and the senate. The
14th year of the Emperor Caesar Publius Licinius
Gallienus Germanicus Maximus Persicus Maximus
Pius Felix Augustus, Phamenoth.

[a] Sidon possessed the title and privileges of a Roman
colony.

307. REQUEST FOR PAYMENT FOR
EMBELLISHMENT OF A NEW STREET

A.D. 283.

To Aurelius Apollonius also called Dionysius, ex-
hypomnematographus [a] and however he is styled,
ex-gymnasiarch, senator, prytanis in office of the
illustrious and most illustrious city of Oxyrhynchus,

[a] Literally "memorandum - writer," a high magistrate
of Alexandria. The other offices mentioned were held in
Oxyrhynchus.

[4]διέποντι καὶ τὰ πολιτικά, [5]παρὰ Αὐρηλίων Μενε-
σθαίως καὶ Νεμαισιανοῦ ἀμφ[ο]τέρων Δι-[6]ον[υ]σίου
ἀπ[ὸ] τῆ[ς] αὐτῆ[ς] λαμπρᾶς Ὀξ(υρυγχιτῶν) πόλεως
Κασιωδῶν. αἰδούμεθα [7]ἐπισταλῆναι ἐξοδιασθῆναι
ἡμεῖν ἀπὸ τοῦ τῆς πόλεως λόγου, [8]ὑπὲρ μισθῶν ὧν
πεποιήμεθα Κασιωτικῶν ἔργων τῆς κα-[9]τασκευασ-
θείσης ὑπὸ σοῦ πλατίου ἀπὸ ἡκουμένου πυλῶνος
[10]γυμνασίου ἐπὶ ν[ότ]ον μέχρι ῥύμης Ἱερακίου
ἑκατέρωθεν [11]τῶν μερῶν, τὰ συναγόμενα τῶν
μισθῶν τοῦ ὅλου ἔργου [12][ἀ]κολού[θω]ς τοῖς ψυφι-
στῖση ἐν τῇ γρατίστῃ βουλῇ, ἀργυρίου [13]Σεβασ[τ]ῶν
νομίσματος τάλαντα τέσσαρα καὶ δραχμὰς τετρα-
[14]κισχειλίας, (γίνεται) (τάλαντα) δ (δραχμαὶ) Δ, καὶ
ἀξιοῦμεν ἐπιστεῖλέ σαι τῷ ταμίᾳ [15]τῶν πολιτικῶν
χρημάτων τὸν ἐξοδιασμὸν ἡμεῖν ποι-[16]ήσασθαι κατὰ
τὸ ἔθος. (ἔτους) α" Αὐτοκράτορος Καίσαρος
Μάρκου [17]Αὐρηλίου Κάρου καὶ Μάρκου Αὐρηλίου
Καρείνου Γερμανικῶν [18]Μεγίστων καὶ Μάρκου
Αὐρηλίου Νουμεριανο[ῦ] τῶν ἐπιφανεστάτων [19]Και-
σά[ρ]ων Εὐσεβῶν Εὐτυχῶν Σεβαστῶν Φαρμοῦθι ιβ.
(2nd hand) [20][Αὐρήλιος] Μενεσθεὺς ἔσχον σὺν τῷ
ἀδελ-[21][φῷ μου τ]ὰς τοῦ ἀργυρίου τάλαντα τέσσα-
[22][ρα καὶ δρ]αχμὰς τετρακισχειλίας. (3rd hand)
[23][Αὐρήλιος Νέ]μεσις συναπέσχον.

5. l. Μενεσθέως, Νεμεσιανοῦ.   6. l. Κασιωτῶν, αἰτούμεθα.
9. l. πλατείας ἀπὸ ἡγουμένου.   12. l. ψηφισθεῖσι, κρατίστῃ.
14. l. ἐπιστεῖλαί σε.   21. l. τά.

director also of municipal finance, from the Aurelii Menestheus and Nemesianus, both sons of Dionysius, of the said illustrious city of Oxyrhynchus, Casiotic joiners.[a]   We request that an order be given for payment to be made to us from the municipal account, as wages for the Casiotic work done by us on both sides of the street laid down by you from the front gateway of the gymnasium southwards to the lane of Hieracius, of the total amount due for the whole work in accordance with the vote of their excellencies the senate, namely four talents and four thousand drachmae of Imperial silver coin, total 4 tal. 4000 dr., and we beg you to instruct the treasurer of municipal moneys to make the payment to us as is customary. The 1st year of the Emperor Caesar Marcus Aurelius Carus and Marcus Aurelius Carinus, Germanici Maximi, and Marcus Aurelius Numerianus, the most eminent Caesars Pii Felices Augusti, Pharmouthi 12. (Signed) I, Aurelius Menestheus, have received jointly with my brother the four talents and four thousand drachmae of silver, I, Aurelius Nemesis, have received them jointly.

   [a] Casium near Pelusium was famous for a special kind of carpentry, the " Casiotic work " mentioned in the text.

308. APPLICATION FOR ALTERATION IN TAXING-LISTS

P. Oxy. 1887.   A.D. 538.

¹['Υπατείας Φλ(αουίου) 'I]ωάν[ν]ου τοῦ ἐνδοξ(ο-
τάτου) Φαρμοῦθι κ ἰνδ(ικτίον)ο(ς) α ἐν 'Οξυρυγ-
χ(ιτῶν) πόλει. ²[τῇ ἐξακτορικῇ τάξε]ι μ[ε]ρίδος καὶ
οἴκου τοῦ τῆς περιβλέπτου μνήμης Τιμαγένους διὰ
σο[ῦ] τοῦ [ἐ]λ-³[λογίμου . . . .] Θεοδώρου
βοηθοῦ ἐξακτορίας ταύτης τῆς λαμπρᾶς 'Οξυρυγχιτῶν πόλεως ⁴[Φλ(αουία) Εὐήθεια ἡ εὐγεν]εστάτη
θυγάτηρ τοῦ τῆς εὐλαβοῦς μνήμης 'Απολλῶτος
γενομέ[νο]υ περι-⁵[. . . . . ἀπὸ ταύ]της τῆς
λαμπρᾶς 'Οξυρυγχιτῶν πόλεως. ἐκ τῶν παρὰ σοὶ
δημο[σίων ⁶χαρτῶν ἐκ τοῦ ὀνόμα]τος Θεοπρεπείας
τῆς μακαρίας μου μητρὸς δημόσιον τέλεσμα ὑπὲρ
⁷[τῶν ἐμῶν προικιμαί]ων πραγμάτων προσενεχ-
θέντων παρ' ἐμοῦ τῷ ἐμῷ συμβίῳ [τ]ῷ αἰδεσίμῳ
⁸['Ιουλίῳ . . . .] λόγῳ προικὸς ἀκολούθως
τοῖς γεναμένοις μεταξὺ ἡμῶν γαμικοῖς συμβ[ολαίοις
⁹ὑπὲρ μὲν ἐμβολῆ]ς εἰς σίτου καθαροῦ κάνωνος
καγκέλλῳ δημοσίῳ ἀρτάβας [.] . [.] . . [. . . ¹⁰. . . . .
καὶ ὑπὲρ] χρυσικῶν παντοίων αὐτῶν τίτλων χρυσοῦ
κεράτια ὀκτὼ ἥμισυ ὄγδο<ο>ν πλήρα, τὰ ¹¹[δὲ
τελέσματα μ]ετὰ τῶν ἐξ ἔθους αὐτῶν παντοίων
ἀναλωμάτων, θέλησον ἀποκουφίσαι ¹²[καὶ σύμ-
παντα] τ[αῦ]τα τὰ προγεγραμμένα δημόσια τελέσματα ἐνέγκατε καὶ σωματίσατε ¹³[εἰς τὰς προσ]η-
γορίας τοῦ αὐτοῦ μου συμβίου τοῦ αὐτοῦ αἰδεσίμου
'Ιουλίου ἀπὸ ἐμβολῆς [καρ]πῶν ¹⁴[καὶ χρυσικῶν τῆς

10. l. πλήρη.

308. APPLICATION FOR ALTERATION IN TAXING-LISTS

A.D. 538.

In the consulship of the most honourable Flavius John, Pharmouthi 20, 1st indiction, in the city of Oxyrhynchus. To the office of the collection of taxes of the division and estate of Timagenes [a] of noble memory, through you the reputable . . . Theodorus, assistant to the collector of taxes in this illustrious city of Oxyrhynchus, from Flavia Euethia the most noble daughter of Apollos of discreet memory, formerly . . ., of this illustrious city of Oxyrhynchus. From the public lists in your custody remove from the name of Theoprepia my late mother the public impost payable on the property included in my dowry and brought by me to my husband the worshipful Julius . . . as dowry conformably to the marriage contract concluded between us, namely, for corn-tax a total of . . . artabae of cleansed wheat of the canon,[b] by public *cancellus* measure, and for money taxes of all kinds on the property 8⅝ carats, in full, and together with the imposts the customary expenses of all kinds connected with them ; and enter and register all these the above-written public imposts to the name of my said husband the said worshipful Julius, from the corn-tax and money-taxes of

[a] Either a large land-owner responsible for the collection of taxes on his estate or else an official tax-collector whose estates were still accountable after his death for the collection which he had undertaken.

[b] The regulation concerning the provision of wheat for Constantinople.

σ]ὺν θεῷ δευτέρας ἐπινεμήσεως καὶ αὐτῆς καὶ ἐπὶ
τὸν ἀεὶ ἄπαντ[α χ]ρόνον· [15][καὶ πρὸς ἀσφάλει]αν
τῆς σῆς [θαυ]μασι<ό>τ(ητος) καὶ τοῦ δημοσίου
λόγου τούτοις <ἐχρησάμην> τοῖς ἐπιστάλμασιν τοῦ
[16][σωματισμοῦ μεθ' ὑπο]γραφῆς ἐ[μῆς] ὡς πρ[ό-
κ]ε[ιτ]αι.   + (2nd hand) + Φλ(αουία) Εὐήθεια ἡ
εὐγενε-[17][στάτη θυγάτηρ] τοῦ τ[ῆς εὐλ]αβοῦ[ς μνή]-
μης Ἀ[πολ]λῶτος [18][γενομένου περι . . . . ἡ]
προγ[εγρα]μμ[ένη πε]ποίημ[αι] τοῦτο τ[ὸ] ἐπίσ-
[19][ταλμα τοῦ σωματισμοῦ . . . .]ε[.].[. . . .]τ . .
[. . ὡς π]ρόκε[ιται] καὶ ὑπέγρ-[20][αψα - - -

the (D.V.) second indiction inclusive and for ever hereafter. And for the security of your admirableness and of the public account I have made this application for registration with my signature as aforesaid. (Signed) I, the aforesaid Flavia Euethia the most noble daughter of Apollos of discreet memory, formerly . . ., have made this application for registration . . . as above, and have signed . . .

VIII. DECLARATIONS TO OFFICIALS

309. NOTIFICATION OF BIRTH

P. Fay. 28.   A.D. 150–151.

¹Σωκράτῃ καὶ Διδύμῳ τῷ καὶ Τυράννῳ ²γραμ-
ματεῦσι μητροπόλεως ³παρὰ Ἰσχυρᾶτος τοῦ
Πρωτᾶ τοῦ Μύσθου ⁴[μ]ητρὸς Τασουχαρίου τῆς
Διδᾶ ἀπ[ὸ ἀ]μ-⁵φόδου Ἑρμουθιακῆς καὶ τῆς τούτου
γυ-⁶ναικὸς Θαϊσαρίου τῆς Ἀμμωνίου [τ]οῦ ⁷Μύσθου
μητρὸς Θαϊσᾶτος ἀπὸ τοῦ αὐτοῦ ⁸ἀμφόδου Ἑρμουθιακῆς. ἀπογραφόμεθα ⁹τὸν γεννηθέντα ἡμεῖν ἐξ
ἀλλήλων υἱὸν ¹⁰Ἰσχυρᾶ[ν] καὶ ὄντα εἰς τὸ ἐνεστὸς
ιδ (ἔτος) Ἀντωνείνο(υ) ¹¹Κα[ί]σαρος τοῦ κυρίου
(ἔτους) α. διὸ ἐπιδίδωμ[ι] τὸ ¹²τῆς ἐπιγενήσεως
ὑπόμνημα. ¹³[Ἰσχυρ]ᾶς (ἐτῶν) μδ ἄσημος. ¹⁴Θαϊ-
σάριον (ἐτῶν) κδ ἄσημος. ¹⁵ἔγραψ[ε]ν ὑπὲρ αὐτῶν
Ἀμμώνιος νομογ(ράφος).

VIII. DECLARATIONS TO OFFICIALS

309. NOTIFICATION OF BIRTH

A.D. 150–151.

To Socrates and Didymus also called Tyrannus, scribes of the metropolis,[a] from Ischyras son of Protas son of Mysthes, his mother being Tasoucharion daughter of Didas, of the quarter of Hermouthiace, and from his wife Thaisarion daughter of Ammonius son of Mysthes, her mother being Thaisas, of the said quarter of Hermouthiace. We register the son who was born to us, Ischyras, being one year of age in the present 14th year of Antoninus Caesar the lord. I therefore present this notification of subsequent birth.[b] Ischyras, aged 44, without distinguishing marks. Thaisarion, aged 24, without distinguishing marks. Written for them by Ammonius, public scribe.

[a] In this case, metropolis of the Arsinoite nome.
[b] That is, subsequent to the last census.

333

310. NOTIFICATION OF DEATH

P.S.I. 1064, 2-27.   A.D. 129.

²ʿΕ[ρμείνῳ? βασιλικ]ῷ γραμματ(εῖ) Ἀρσι(νοΐτου)
³[Ἡρακλ]είδου μερίδο(ς) ⁴[παρὰ Σαβεί]νου Σαβείνου
γεγ[υμν(ασιαρχηκότος)] ⁵ἀπὸ ἀμφόδου Διονυσίου
Τόπων [ἀπόν-]ᵗτος διὰ Νεμεσιανοῦ τοῦ καὶ Ἀρ-
τεμιδ[(ώρου)]. ὁ υ[ἱ-]ᵗδοῦς μου Σαραπίων ἀνα-
γρα(φόμενος) ἐπὶ τοῦ ⁸αὐτοῦ ἀ[μφόδ]ου Διονυσίου
Τόπων λαογρα(φούμενος) ἐτε-⁹λεύτησ[εν τῷ] Μεχεὶρ μηνὶ τοῦδε τοῦ ¹⁰ἐνεστῶτος ιγ (ἔτους) Ἀδριανοῦ
Καίσαρος ¹¹τοῦ κυρί[ου]. διὸ ἀξιῶι ταγῆναι αὐτὸν
¹²ἐν τῇ τῶν ὁμοίων τάξει. (2nd hand) Σαβεῖνος
¹³Σαβείνου γεγυμνασιαρχηκὼς ¹⁴ἀπὼν διὰ Νεμεσιανοῦ τοῦ καὶ Ἀρτε-¹⁵μιδώρου Σαραπίωνος ἐπιτρόπου ¹⁶ἐπιδέδωκα, καὶ ὀμνύω τὴν ¹⁷Αὐτοκράτορος
Καίσαρος Τραϊανοῦ ¹⁸ʿΑδριανοῦ Σεβαστοῦ τύχην
ἀλη-¹⁹θῆ εἶναι τὰ προγεγραμμένα. ²⁰(ἔτους) ιγ
Αὐτοκράτορος Καίσαρος Τραϊανοῦ ²¹ʿΑδριανοῦ
Σεβαστοῦ Μεχεὶρ κδ. (3rd hand) ²²Γραμματ(εῦσι)
μητροπ(όλεως). εἰ ταῖς ἀληθείαις ²³ὁ προγε-
γραμ[μ]ένος ἐτελ⟨εύ⟩τησεν, τ[ὸ] ²⁴ἀκ[ό]λουθ(ον)
ἐπιτελεῖτε. (ἔτους) ιγ ²⁵Αὐτοκράτορος Καίσαρος
Τραϊανοῦ ʿΑδ[ρια-]²⁶νο[ῦ Σεβ(αστοῦ)] Μεχ[εὶρ] κδ.
(4th hand) Φιλόξενο(ς) γρ(αμματεὺς) [σε]ση)μεί-
ωμαι). (5th hand) ²⁷Διον[υ]σί(ου) Τόπ(ων).

310. NOTIFICATION OF DEATH

A.D. 129.

To Herminus, royal scribe of the division of Heraclides in the Arsinoite nome, from Sabinus son of Sabinus, ex-gymnasiarch, of the quarter of Dionysius's District, acting in my absence through Nemesianus also called Artemidorus. My grandson Sarapion, registered in the said quarter of Dionysius's District, subject to poll-tax, died in the month Mecheir of this present 13th year of Hadrianus Caesar the lord. I therefore request that he be put on the list of the defunct.[a] (Signed) I, Sabinus son of Sabinus, ex-gymnasiarch, acting in my absence through Nemesianus also called Artemidorus son of Sarapion, my representative, have presented (this notification), and I swear by the fortune of the Emperor Caesar Trajanus Hadrianus Augustus that the foregoing is true. The 13th year of the Emperor Caesar Trajanus Hadrianus Augustus, Mecheir 24. (Order of the royal scribe) To the scribes of the metropolis. If the aforesaid is in truth deceased, take the consequent steps. The 13th year of the Emperor Caesar Trajanus Hadrianus Augustus, Mecheir 24. (Acknowledgement) Signed by me, Philoxenus, scribe. (Docketed) Dionysius's District.

[a] Literally " of those in like condition."

SELECT PAPYRI

311. REGISTRATION OF A SLAVE CHILD

Raccolta Lumbroso, p. 49.   A.D. 124.

¹Ἔτους ὀγδόου Αὐτοκράτορος Καίσαρος ²Τραϊανοῦ Ἁδριανοῦ Σεβαστοῦ Παχὼν ³νουμηνίᾳ διὰ
Διοδώρου τοῦ Τρύφω-⁴νος τοῦ ἀσχολουμένου τὸ
γραφῖον ⁵κώμης Τήνεως καὶ Κερκὴ τοῦ ⁶Μεμ-
φείτου. ⁷οἰκογένεια{ν}· Βαιβία Ῥουφίλλα ἐτῶν
⁸τριάκοντα πέντε ἄσημος μετὰ ⁹κυρίου τοῦ τῆς
μητρὸς αὐτῆς ἀδελ-¹⁰φοῦ Πουπλίου Λουκρητίου
Διογέ-¹¹νους ἐτῶν τεσσαράκοντα πέντε ¹²οὐλὴ
ἀντικνημίῳ δεξιῷ ἀπεγρά-¹³ψατο εἰς τὴν οἰκογέ-
νειαν ἀκο-¹⁴λούθως τῷ τε ψηφίσματι καὶ ¹⁵προσ-
τάγματι ὃν ἔφη ἐσχηκέναι ¹⁶ἐκ τῆς ὑπαρχούσης
αὐτῇ δούλης ¹⁷Τύχης δοῦλον ᾧ ὄνομα Φοινει-¹⁸κᾶς
ὄντα ἐτῶν τριῶν οὐλὴ καρπῷ ¹⁹δεξιῷ καὶ ἐτάξατο
τῆς ὑπερθέσ-²⁰μου ἑβδομαίας ἡμέρας θεᾶς ²¹Βερ-
νείκης Εὐ[εργ]έτιδος τὴν κα-²²θήκουσαν ἀπ[α]ρχήν.

Followed by official subscriptions, of which the
reading and import are doubtful.

ᵃ These words probably refer to an act passed by the
governing body of one of the Greek cities in the Ptolemaic
age and to an edict by one of the kings.

312. CENSUS RETURN

P. Bad. 75 (b).   A.D. 147.

¹Ἰουλίῳ Σατουρνείνῳ ²στρ(ατηγῷ) Ἡρακλεο-
πολ(ίτου) ³παρὰ Πετεσού(χου) Πισόϊτιος ⁴μη(τρὸς)
336

311. REGISTRATION OF A SLAVE CHILD

A.D. 124.

The 8th year of the Emperor Caesar Trajanus Hadrianus Augustus, 1st day of Pachon, through Diodorus son of Tryphon, keeper of the record-office of the village of Tenis and Kerke in the Memphite nome. Declaration of home-bred slaves: Baebia Rufilla, aged thirty-five years, without distinguishing mark, having with her as guardian her mother's brother Publius Lucretius Diogenes, aged forty-five years, with a scar on the right shin, has registered as a home-bred slave, in conformity with the enactment and the edict,[a] the male slave whom she said she had acquired as issue of the female slave Tyche belonging to her, named Phoenicas, three years old, with a scar on the right wrist, and she has paid the due offering for the supernumerary seventh day of the goddess Berenice Euergetis.[b] (Followed by official subscriptions of which the meaning is rather obscure.)

[b] The deified Berenice, wife of Ptolemy III. Apparently a seventh day had been added to the festival held in her honour, and the tax on the acquisition of home-bred slaves was nominally devoted to the maintenance of her cult.

312. CENSUS RETURN [a]

A.D. 147.

To Julius Saturninus, strategus of the Heracleopolite nome, from Petesouchus son of Pisoitis and

[a] The census was taken every fourteen years, the owner of each house presenting a return of all the persons who lived there and of the house property of each.

SELECT PAPYRI

Θεναμεννέως τῶν ἀπ[ὸ] ⁵κώμ(ης) Ἀγκυρώνων.
ἀπογρ(άφομαι) ⁶πρὸς τὸ θ (ἔτος) Ἀντωνείνου
Καίσ(αρος) ⁷τοῦ κυρίου κατὰ τὰ κελ(ευσθέντα)
⁸ὑπὸ Οὐαλερίου Πρόκλου τοῦ ⁹ἡγεμ(όνος) εἰς τὸ
ὑπ(άρ)χ(ον) μοι (ἥμισυ) μέρ(ος) ¹⁰οἰκίας καὶ προ-
νησίου. ¹¹εἰμὶ δὲ ¹²ὁ Πετεσοῦχος (ἐτῶν) μβ
ἄση(μος), ¹³γυνή μου Ταϋσῖρις Παρεί-¹⁴τιος (ἐτῶν)
λδ, ¹⁵Πνεφορῶς υἱός μου (ἐτῶν) ιζ, ¹⁶Ψ'εναμοῦνις
ἄλ(λος) υἱός μου ¹⁷(ἐτῶν) ε ἄση(μος) (2nd hand)
¹⁸Πνεφορὸς αὐτ(οῦ) υἱὸς γενόμεν(ος) ιζ (ἔτους)
ἐπ[ὶ ξένης]. (1st hand) ¹⁹ὑπάρχ(ει) δέ μοι ἐν τῇ
(αὐτῇ) κώμ(ῃ) ²⁰ἕτερα οἰκοδ(ομήματα) καὶ τῇ
γυναι-²¹κί μου Ταϋσίρι ἕτερα οἰκοδ(ομήματα).
²²καὶ ὀμνύω τὴν Αὐτοκράτορ(ος) ²³Καίσαρος Τίτου
Αἰλίου ²⁴᾽Αδριανοῦ Ἀντωνείνου ²⁵Σεβαστοῦ Εὐσεβοῦς ²⁶τύχην καὶ τὸν τοῦ νομ(οῦ) ²⁷θεὸν Ἡρακλέα
ἐξ ὑγι(οῦς) καὶ ²⁸ἐπ᾽ ἀλ(ηθείᾳ) ἐπιδ(εδωκέναι) τὴ(ν)
π(ρο)κ(ειμένην) ἀπογρ(αφὴν) ²⁹καὶ μηδ(ὲν) δι-
εψεῦσθ(αι) μηδ(ὲ) ³⁰παραλελοι(πέναι) τινὰ ὀφειλ(ό-
μενον) ³¹ὑπ᾽ ἐμ(οῦ) ἀπογρ(αφῆναι) μηδ(ὲ) ὁμω-
ν(υμίᾳ) ³²κεχρῆ(σθαι) μηδ(ὲ) τινα ἀντιπαρα-³³στῆ-
(σαι) τῇ ἐπικρίσι, ἢ ἔνοχ(ος) ³⁴εἴην τῷ ὅρκῳ.
³⁵(ἔτους) ι Αὐτοκράτορος Καίσαρος ³⁶[Τίτο]υ
[Αἰλ]ίου ᾽Αδριανοῦ ³⁷᾽Αντωνείνου Σεβαστοῦ ³⁸Εὐ-
σεβοῦς Φαμενὼθ ιε. (2nd hand) ³⁹Μαρεῖς δι᾽
᾽Αλφύγχ(ιος) Φιβ( ), Οὐη( ) ⁴⁰᾽Αρψήμιος καὶ
Παχνοῦβις ⁴¹᾽Επ . . . ρος [. .] . ιοσφο . . . .
. . σσιων ⁴²᾽Ισιδώ(ρου) κω(μογραμματεὺς) δι(ὰ)
Πανᾶ(τος) σεση(μειώμεθα).

18. l. Πνεφερῶς.   32-33. Or ἀντιπαραστή(σειν) Henne.
39. διὰ ᾽Αφύγχ(ιος)?   41. [λα]ογράφοι καί?

338

312. DECLARATIONS TO OFFICIALS

Thenamenneus, of the village of Ancyronon.[a] I make my return for the 9th year of Antoninus Caesar the lord, in accordance with the order of Valerius Proclus the praefect, for the half share which I own of a house and forecourt (?).[b] Myself Petesouchus, aged 42, without distinguishing mark, my wife Tausiris daughter of Pareitis, aged 34, Pnephoros my son, aged 17, Psenamounis another son of mine, aged 5, without distinguishing mark. (Interpolated) "His son Pnephoros was away from home in the 17th [c] year." I own other buildings in the said village, and my wife Tausiris owns other buildings there. And I swear by the fortune of the Emperor Caesar Titus Aelius Hadrianus Antoninus Augustus Pius and by Heracles the god of the nome [d] that I have presented the aforesaid return honestly and truthfully and have told no lie nor omitted anyone who ought to have been returned by me nor taken advantage of an identity of names nor presented any person for examination in the character of another,[e] otherwise may I incur the consequences of the oath. The 10th year of the Emperor Caesar Titus Aelius Hadrianus Antoninus Augustus Pius, Phamenoth 15. (Subscribed) We, Mareis, through Aphunchis son of Phib( ), Ve( ) son of Harpsemis, Pachnoubis son of Ep . . . ., registrars (?), and . . . son of Isidorus, village scribe, through Panas, have signed.

[a] The modern Hibeh in Middle Egypt.
[b] The exact meaning of the Greek word is unknown.
[c] The 17th year of Hadrian, the time of the last census. The note was added by an official.
[d] Really an Egyptian god, but identified with Heracles by the Greeks.
[e] At the personal inspection by the local authorities.

SELECT PAPYRI

313. CENSUS RETURN

P. Tebt. 322.   A.D. 189.

¹'Απολλώνιος ὁ καὶ Διογένης σεση(μείωμαι).
(2nd hand) ²['Αμ]μωνίῳ στρατηγῷ 'Αρσι(νοΐτου)
Ἡρακλείδου μερίδος ³[κ]αὶ 'Αρποκρατίωνι τῷ καὶ
Ἱέρακι βασιλ(ικῷ) ⁴γρα(μματεῖ) τῆς αὐτῆς μερίδος
καὶ Μύστῃ καὶ "Η-⁵ρωνι γενομένοις γραμματεῦσι
μητροπόλ(εως) ⁶παρὰ 'Αχιλλέως 'Απολλωνίου τοῦ
Λουρίου τοῦ ⁷καὶ 'Απολλωνίου κατοίκου ἀνα-
γρα(φομένου) καὶ ἀπογεγρα(μμένου) ⁸δι' ἑτέρου
ὑπομνήματος. ὑπάρχει μοι ἐπ' ἀμ-⁹φόδου Μοήρεως
μέρος οἰκίας καὶ αἰθρίου καὶ αὐλ(ῆς) ¹⁰καὶ ἐξέδρας
ἐν ᾧ προσαπογρά(φομαι) τοὺς ὑπο-¹¹γεγρα(μμένους)
ἐνοίκους εἰς τὴν τοῦ διεληλυθότος ¹²κη (ἔτους)
Αὐρηλίου Κομμόδου 'Αντωνείνου ¹³Καίσαρος τοῦ
κυρίου κατ' οἰκίαν ἀπογρα(φὴν) ὄν-¹⁴τας ἀπὸ τῆς
μητροπόλ(εως) ἀναγρα(φομένους) ἐπ' ἀμφόδου
¹⁵Συριακῆς ἐφ' οὗ καὶ τῇ τοῦ ιδ (ἔτους) κατ'
οἰκ(ίαν) ἀπογρα(φῇ) ¹⁶ἀπεγρά(φησαν)· καὶ εἰσὶ
Πασιγένης Θέωνος τοῦ ¹⁷Εὐτύχους λαογρα(φούμενος) ὀνηλ(άτης) (ἐτῶν) ξα, καὶ τὸν τού-¹⁸του
υἱὸν Εὔτυχον μητρὸς 'Απολλωνοῦτος ¹⁹τῆς 'Ηρώ-
δου (ἐτῶν) λ, καὶ τὴν τοῦ Πασιγένους γυναῖ-²⁰κα
'Ηράκλειαν Κρονίωνος ἀπελ(ευθέραν) Διδύμου
"Ηρωνο(ς) ²¹ἀπὸ Ταμείων (ἐτῶν) μ, καὶ ἐξ ἀμ-
φοτ(έρων) θυγ(ατέρα) Θᾶσιν (ἐτῶν) ε, ²²καὶ τὰ τῆς
'Ηρακλείας τέκνα Σαβεῖνον Σαβεί-²³νου τοῦ Κρονίωνος λαογρα(φούμενον) κτενιστ(ὴν) (ἐτῶν) ιη, καὶ
²⁴Σαραπιάδα (ἐτῶν) κβ ἀπογεγρα(μμένην) τῇ προ-

340

313. CENSUS RETURN

A.D. 189.

Signed by me, Apollonius also called Diogenes.

To Ammonius, strategus of the division of Heraclides in the Arsinoite nome, and to Harpocration also called Hierax, royal scribe of the same division, and to Mystes and Heron, ex-scribes of the metropolis, from Achilles son of Apollonius son of Lurius also called Apollonius, registered as a catoecus,[a] and already returned through another memorandum.[b] I own in the Moeris quarter a share of a house and open-air hall and courtyard and exedra, in which I further return the following occupants for the house-to-house census of the past 28th year of Aurelius Commodus Antoninus Caesar the lord, being inhabitants of the metropolis registered in the Syrian quarter, in which they were also returned in the house-to-house census of the 14th year. They are Pasigenes son of Theon son of Eutyches, subject to poll-tax, donkey-driver, aged 61 years, and his son Eutychus by Apollonous daughter of Herodes, aged 30, and the wife of Pasigenes, Heracleia daughter of Cronion, freedwoman of Didymus son of Heron, of the Treasuries' quarter, aged 40, and the daughter of both, Thasis, aged 5, and the children of Heracleia, Sabinus son of Sabinus son of Cronion, subject to poll-tax, wool-carder, aged 18, and Sarapias, aged 22,

[a] In Roman times catoecus means an owner of land originally granted by the Ptolemies to military settlers. The catoeci possessed certain privileges, the most important of which was exemption from the poll-tax.

[b] His personal return would be made for the house in which he actually lived, as in No. 312.

SELECT PAPYRI

τ(έρᾳ) ἀπογρα(φῇ) ἐπὶ ²⁵Ταμείων, καὶ τοῦ Εὐ-
τύχους γυναῖκα οὖσα(ν) ὁμοπ(άτριον) ²⁶ἀδελφὴ ⟨ν⟩
Ταπεσοῦριν μητ(ρὸς) Ἰσιδώρας (ἐτῶν) ιη. διὸ
ἐπ(ιδίδωμι). (3rd hand) ²⁷ὑπάρχει δὲ τῇ Τα-
πεσούρι ἐπ᾽ ἀμφόδ(ου) Μοήρεως μητρικὸν ἔκτον
μέρος οἰκίας. (2nd hand) ²⁸(ἔτους) κθ Αὐρηλίου
Κομμόδου Ἀντωνίνου Καίσαρος ²⁹τοῦ κυρίου
Μεσορὴ ἐπαγο(μένων) δ. (4th hand) ³⁰κατεχω-
(ρίσθη) στρα(τηγῷ) κθ (ἔτει) Μεσορὴ ἐπαγο(μένων)
δ. (5th hand) κατεχ(ωρίσθη) βασιλ(ικῷ) γρα(μματεῖ)
τῇ α(ὐτῇ) ἡ(μέρᾳ). (6th hand) κατεχω(ρίσθη)
γρα(μματεῦσι) πόλ(εως) τῇ αὐτῇ.

314. EPIKRISIS OF BOYS

P. Ryl. 103.   A.D. 134.

¹[Φρ]ονίμωι καὶ Σαβείνωι τῶι κ[αὶ Θ]ρ[α]κιδᾷ
γεγυμ(νασιαρχηκόσι), τῶι δὲ Σαβείνωι τῶι κ(αὶ)
Θρακιδᾷ ²[ἀφήλ(ικι)] δι᾽ ἐπιτρόπου Ε . . . ου
γ[ε]γυμ(νασιαρχηκότος), ἐπικριταῖς ³[παρὰ] Ὠρίω-
[ν]ος τοῦ [Ἡρ]ακλείδου τοῦ Ἡρακλείδου μητρὸς
Λυκαροῦτος τῆς Ἡρακλείδου ⁴[δο]ύλου Ἰσχ[υ-
ρί]ων[ο]ς τοῦ Πάπου τῶν ἀπὸ τῆς μητροπ(όλεως)
ἀναγραφομένω(ν) ἐπ᾽ ἀμφόδο(υ) Βιθ(υνῶν) Ἄλλω(ν)
Τόπ(ων). ⁵[τοῦ ὁ]μοπα[τρί]ου καὶ ὁμομητρίου μου
ἀδελφο(ῦ) Ἡρακλείδου προσβάντος εἰς (τεσσαρα-
καιδεκαετεῖς) τῶι ⁶[ἐνεσ]τῶτι (ιη) (ἔτει) Ἀδ[ρι]ανοῦ

ᵃ An examination of a boy's credentials for the purpose
of deciding whether his birth entitled him to exemption or
partial exemption from the poll-tax, payment of which began

342

returned in the former census in the Treasuries' quarter, and the wife of Eutyches,[a] who is his sister on the father's side, Tapesouris daughter of Isidora, aged 18. I accordingly present this statement. Tapesouris owns in the Moeris quarter a sixth share of a house, inherited from her mother. The 29th year of Aurelius Commodus Antoninus Caesar the lord, 4th intercalary day of Mesore. (Subscribed) Recorded with the strategus, year 29, 4th intercalary day of Mesore. Recorded with the royal scribe on the same day. Recorded with the scribes of the metropolis on the same day.[b]

[a] Above called Eutychus.
[b] Two copies of each return were presented to several different officials, though not always to the same officials as are mentioned here.

314. EPIKRISIS OF BOYS [a]

A.D. 134.

To Phronimus and Sabinus also called Thracidas, ex-gymnasiarchs and examiners, Sabinus also called Thracidas being a minor and acting through his guardian . . ., ex-gymnasiarch, from Horion son of Heraclides son of Heraclides, whose mother was Lycarous daughter of Heraclides slave of Ischyrion son of Papus, inhabitants of the metropolis [b] registered in the quarter of the Bithynians and Neighbourhood. Whereas my full brother Heraclides has reached the age of 14 years in the present 18th year of Hadrianus

at the age of fourteen. There were other kinds of epikrisis for other purposes (see for instance No. 315).
[b] Arsinoe in the Fayum.

343

Καίσαρος τοῦ [κυρίο]υ καὶ ὀφείλοντος ἐπικριθῆναι
κατὰ τὰ ⁷[κελε]υσθέν[τα ὑπ]έταξα τὰ τῶν γονέ[ων]
ἡμῶν δίκαια· ὁ μὲν οὖν προγεγραμμέ(νος) ⁸[ἡμῶν]
πατ[ὴρ Ἡρ]ακλείδης Ἡρακ[λ]είδου το[ῦ Ἡ]ρα-
κλείδου μητρὸ(ς) Τασουχαρίο(υ) ἀδελφῆς πατρ[ὸ(ς)]
⁹ἀπεγ]ράψα[το τῶι] η [(ἔτει)] θεοῦ Οὐεσ[πασιανοῦ]
ἅμα τοῖς γονεῦ[σι] ἐπ' ἀμφόδο(υ) Κιλ[ίκω]ν, τῶι
δὲ θ (ἔτει) Δομιτιανοῦ ¹⁰[καὶ τ]ῶι [ζ (ἔτει)
Τραϊανοῦ ὁμ]οίως ἀ[πεγ]ρ[ά]ψα[το] ἅμα [το]ῖς
γονεῦσι [ἐπ' ἀμ]φόδ(ου) Βιθυνῶ(ν) Ἄλλω(ν) Τόπ(ων)
¹¹[συναπογραψά]μεν[ος] ὅμου καὶ [τ]ὴν γυναῖκα
ἡμῶν δὲ μητέρα Λυκαροῦν καὶ ἐμὲ ¹²[τὸν Ὠρίωνα],
τῇ δὲ [τοῦ] β (ἔτους) Ἀδριανοῦ Καίσαρος τοῦ
κυρίου κατ' οἰκίαν ἀπογραφῇ ἀπε-¹³[γράψαντο
ἀμ]φ[ό]τεροι οἱ γονεῖς ἡμῶ[ν] ἐπὶ τοῦ αὐτοῦ ἀμ-
φόδ[ο(υ)] συναπογραψάμενοι ἡμᾶς ¹⁴[ἀμφοτέρους,
τῇ] δὲ τ[ο]ῦ ις (ἔτους) Ἀδριανοῦ Καίσαρος τοῦ
κυρίου κατ' οἰκίαν ἀπογραφῇ ἀπεγρα-¹⁵[ψάμην
ἐγὼ ἐμαυτὸν σ]ὺν τῇ μη[τ]ρὶ ἡμ[ῶ]ν καὶ τῶι ἐπ[ι]-
κρεινομ[έ]νῳ ἀδελφῷ μου Ἡρα-¹⁶[κλείδῃ διὰ τὸ
τὸ]ν πατέρα ἡμ[ῶ]ν μετ[ὰ] τὴν τοῦ β (ἔτους) ἀπογραφὴν [τ]ετελευτηκέναι. ἡ δὲ ¹⁷[Λυκαροῦς Ἡρα-
κλείδο(υ) δούλου Ἰσχυρίω[ν]ος τοῦ Πάπου μητρὸς
Διδύμης τῆς Ἑρμᾶ ἀπεγρά(φη) ¹⁸[τῷ η (ἔτει)
Οὐεσπ]ασιανοῦ ἅμα τῆι μη[τ]ρὶ κ[α]ὶ ἀδελφοῖς ἐπ'
ἀμφόδο(υ) Σεκν[ε]βτ(υνείου), ἥτις ¹⁹[καὶ αὐτὴ ἐτε-
λεύτησε] μετὰ τ[ὴ]ν τοῦ ι[ϛ] (ἔτους) Ἀδριανο[ῦ]
Κ[αίσ]αρος τοῦ κυ[ρί]ου κατ' οἰκί(αν) ἀπογραφήν.
²⁰[οἱ δὲ γονεῖς ἀπεγ]ράφ[η]σαν τῶι θ (ἔτει) Δ[ομι]-
τιανοῦ ἐπ' ἀμφόδο(υ) Κιλίκων συνόντες ἀλλήλ(οις).
²¹[συνπαρεθέμη]ν δὲ ὑμεῖν καὶ ἐπίκρι[σ]ι[ν] ἐμαυτοῦ κ[αὶ] κ[ό]λλημα ἀπογραφῆς ἐνκτήσεω(ν) ²²[. . .

314. DECLARATIONS TO OFFICIALS

Caesar the lord and is due to be examined, I append the credentials of our parents in accordance with the ordinance. Our aforesaid father Heraclides son of Heraclides son of Heraclides, whose mother was Tasoucharion his father's sister, registered himself [a] in the 8th year of the deified Vespasianus together with his parents in the quarter of the Cilicians ; in the 9th year of Domitianus and in the 7th of Trajanus he likewise registered himself with his parents in the quarter of the Bithynians and Neighbourhood, at the same time registering his wife Lycarous, who was our mother, and myself, Horion ; in the house-to-house census of the 2nd year of Hadrianus Caesar the lord both our parents registered themselves in the said quarter, at the same time registering the two of us ; and in the house-to-house census of the 16th year of Hadrianus Caesar the lord I registered myself together with our mother and my brother Heraclides, now presented for examination, because our father had died after the census of the 2nd year. Lycarous, again, daughter of Heraclides slave of Ischyrion son of Papus, her mother being Didyma daughter of Hermas, was registered in the 8th year of Vespasianus together with her mother and brothers in the quarter of the Temple of Seknebtunis ; she herself died after the house-to-house census of the 16th year of Hadrianus Caesar the lord ; and her parents were registered as living together in the 9th year of Domitianus in the quarter of the Cilicians. I also lay before you the record of my own examination and a page of the property census . . .

[a] See Nos. 312 and 313.

. . . .] . ων ἡμῶν μέρος ο[ἰ]κ[ί]ας [πα]τρι-
κῆς [. .] . ο[. . .] . [.]δι[. . . . . . .] . π . [.]ς
[γ]εγυ(μνασιαρχηκὼς) ²³[. . . . .] διὰ
Ἡροδώ(ρου) σεση(μείωμαι) Ἡρακλε[ί]δην Ἡρα-
κλείδ[ο(υ) τ]οῦ Ἡρακ(λείδου) μ[η(τρὸς) Λ]υκα-
ρουτος. (ἔτους) ιη ²⁴[Αὐτοκράτορος Καίσαρος]
Τραϊανοῦ Ἀδρια[νοῦ Σε]βαστοῦ Παῦ(νι) δ.

315. EPIKRISIS OF A ROMAN VETERAN

Annales xxix, p. 61.   A.D. 188.

¹Ἐκ τόμου ἐπικρίσεων οὗ παρεπιγραφή· ἐπι-
κρίσεις ²Λογγαίου Ῥούφου γενομένου ἡγεμόνος διὰ
Ἀλλίου ³Ἑρμολάου χειλιάρχου λεγιῶνος β̄ Τραϊανῆς
Ἰσχυρᾶς ⁴ἀπὸ Ἐπεὶφκ̄ε̄ ἕως Θὼθ κθ τοῦ κ̄ς̄ (ἔτους)
Αὐρηλίου ⁵Κομμόδου Ἀντωνίνου Καίσαρος τοῦ
κυρίου. ⁶μετʼ ἄλλα, σελίδ(ων) ᾱ. Οὐαλέριος
Κλήμης βουλό-⁷μενος παρεπιδημεῖν πρὸς καιρὸν
<ἐν> νομῷ Ἀρ-⁸σινοείτῃ ἐτῶν . ὁ προγεγραμ-
μένος οὐετρανὸς ⁹δηλώσας ἑαυτὸν ἐστρατεῦσθαι
ἐν σπείρῃ β̄ ¹⁰Ἰτυραίων ἐπέδειξεν Πακτουμηίου
Μάγνου ¹¹τοῦ ἡγεμονεύσαντος ἐπιστολὴν Ῥωμαϊκὴν
διʼ ἧς ¹²ἐδηλοῦτο στρατευσάμενον αὐτὸν ἐν τῇ προ-
γεγραμ-¹³μένῃ σπείρῃ νομίμῃ ἀπολεύσι ἀπολελύ-
σθαι ἀ-¹⁴πὸ τῆς πρὸ ᾱ Καλανδῶν Ἰανουαρίων
Αὐρηλίῳ ¹⁵Κομμόδῳ Ἀντωνόνῳ Σεβαστῷ Εὐσεβεῖ
¹⁶καὶ Κουιντίλλῳ ὑπάτοις. ἔδωκεν καὶ γνωστῆρας
¹⁷Μάρκον Αὐρήλιον Πετεσοῦχον, Σερῆνον Πετρώ-

13. l. ἀπολύσει.   15. l. Ἀντωνίνῳ.

part of a house inherited from my father . . .
(Subscribed) I, . . ., ex-gymnasiarch, . . ., acting
through Herodorus, have signed [a] in respect of
Heraclides son of Heraclides son of Heraclides,
whose mother was Lycarous. The 18th year of
the Emperor Caesar Trajanus Hadrianus Augustus,
Pauni 4.

[a] An approval of the application.

315. EPIKRISIS OF A ROMAN VETERAN

A.D. 188.

Extract from the roll of examination records bearing the outside title : Examinations of Longaeus
Rufus, late praefect, conducted by Allius Hermolaus, tribune of legion ii Trajana Fortis, from
Epeiph 25 to Thoth 29 of the 26th year of Aurelius
Commodus Antoninus Caesar the lord.[a] After other
entries, on page 1 : Valerius Clemens, who wishes
to reside for the time being in the Arsinoite nome,
aged   years.[b] The above-mentioned, a veteran,
declared that he had served in the 2nd cohort of the
Itureans and exhibited a Latin letter from Pactumeius Magnus the former praefect showing that
after serving in the above-mentioned cohort he had
received his official discharge on the 31st of December
in the consulship of Aurelius Commodus Antoninus
Augustus Pius and Quintillus. He also presented as
warrantors Marcus Aurelius Petesouchus, Serenus

[a] The purpose for which a veteran underwent this epikrisis before a delegate of the praefect was to obtain a certificate of his legal status as a Roman citizen, which would be
particularly useful if he intended to change his residence.
[b] The age has not been filled in.

SELECT PAPYRI

¹⁸νιον, Ἰούλιον Γέμελλον, τοὺς γ̄ οὐετρανούς, συν-
¹⁹χειρογραφοῦντας αὐτ[ῷ] μηδενὶ ἀλλοτρίῳ κεχρῆ-
²⁰σθαι. καὶ τῆς Ἀλλίου Ἑρμολάου χειλιάρχου
λεγιῶνος ²¹β̄ Τραϊανῆς Ἰσχυρᾶς σημιώσεως ἐπὶ τοῦ
προκειμένου ὀνόματος ²²Οὐαλερίου Κλήμεντος πεντήκοντα δύο οὐλὴ ²³ὑπὲρ ἀστράγαλον ποδὸς δεξιοῦ.
(2nd hand) ²⁴Ἀούιος Καλλίμαχος βιβλιοφύλαξ· ὑ-
²⁵πάρχει. (ἔτους) κη Αὐρηλίου Κομμόδου ²⁶Ἀν-
τωνίνου Καίσαρος τοῦ κυρίου ²⁷Παῦνι ιζ.
Verso : ²⁸ἐπίκρισις Οὐαλερίου Κλήμεντος ἐπεσ-
²⁹κεμμένη.

18. τρεῖς altered to γ̄.   23. παρά altered to ὑπέρ.

316. RETURN OF HIEROGLYPHIC CARVERS

P. Oxy. 1029.   A.D. 107.

¹Κλαυδίῳ Μενάνδρῳ βασιλικῷ γραμματεῖ ²παρὰ
Τεῶτος νεωτέρου Ὀννώφριος τοῦ Τεῶτος ³μητρὸς
Τασεῦτος καὶ Ἀσκλᾶτος Ὀννώφρι[ο]ς ⁴τοῦ Ὀσ-
μόλχιος μητρὸς Τεσαῦριος ἀμφοτέρων ⁵ἀπ' Ὀξυρύγχων πόλεως ἱερογλύφων τῶν κε-⁶χειρισμένων
ὑπὸ τῶν συνιερογλύφων· γρ[α-]⁷φὴ ἡμῶν τε καὶ τῶν
αὐτῶν συνιερογλύ-⁸φων τοῦ ἐνεστῶτο[ς ἐ]νδεκάτου
ἔτ[ο]υς ⁹Τραϊανοῦ Καίσαρος τοῦ κυρίου. ¹⁰ὧν εἶναι·
¹¹Δεκάτης· ¹²Τεῶς Ὀννώφριος ὁ προγεγραμμένος,
¹³Ὀννώφρις ἀδελφός, ¹⁴Ἀσκλᾶς Ὀννώφρις ὁ
προγεγραμμένος, ¹⁵Ὀσμόλχις ἀδελφὸς ὢν καὶ
ἱερογλύφο[ς] ¹⁶Ὀσείριος θεοῦ μεγίστου. ¹⁷Δρόμου
Θοήριδος· ¹⁸Πτολεμαῖς Πετοσοράπιος τοῦ Πε-
348

Petronius, and Julius Gemellus, all three veterans, who wrote a sworn declaration along with him that he had used no fictitious evidence. And the signature of Allius Hermolaus, tribune of legion ii Trajana Fortis, attached to the aforesaid name, Valerius Clemens, aged 52, with a scar above the ankle of the right foot. (Subscribed) I, Avius Callimachus, keeper of the archives, state that the original is here. The 28th year of Aurelius Commodus Antoninus Caesar the lord, Pauni 17. (Endorsed) Examination record of Valerius Clemens verified.

316. RETURN OF HIEROGLYPHIC CARVERS

A.D. 107.

To Claudius Menander, royal scribe, from Teos, younger son of Onnophris son of Teos, his mother being Taseus, and Asclas son of Onnophris son of Osmolchis, his mother being Tesauris, both of Oxyrhynchus, hieroglyphic carvers who have been delegated by their fellow-carvers : the list of ourselves and the said fellow-carvers of hieroglyphics for the current 11th year of Trajanus Caesar the lord, as follows :—In the quarter of the Tenth, Teos son of Onnophris, the aforesaid, Onnophris his brother, Asclas son of Onnophris, the aforesaid, Osmolchis his brother who is also a hieroglyphic carver of Osiris [a] the most great god. In the quarter of the Avenue of Thoeris, Ptolemaeus son of Petosorapis son of

[a] The meaning is that he was an employee of the temple of Osiris. Many, perhaps all, of the hieroglyphic craftsmen were in the service of the temples.

τοσοράπιος. [19](γίνονται) ἄνδ(ρες) ε. [20]καὶ ὀμνύομεν
Αὐτοκράτορα Καίσαρα [21]Νέρουαν Τραϊανὸν [Σ]ε-
βαστὸν Γερμανικὸν [22]Δακικὸν ἐξ ὑγιοῦς καὶ ἐπ᾽
ἀληθείας ἐπι-[23]δεδωκέναι τὴν προκειμένην γραφὴν
[24]καὶ πλείω τούτων μὴ εἶναι μηδὲ ἔχει[ν] [25]μαθητὰς
ἢ ἐπιξένους χρω{ω}μένους [26]τῇ τέχνῃ εἰς τὴν
ἐνεστῶσαν ἡμέραν, [27]ἢ ἔνοχοι εἴημεν τῷ ὅρκῳ.
(ἔτους) [ι]α Αὐτοκράτορος [28]Καίσαρος Νερούα
Τραϊανοῦ Σεβαστοῦ [29]Γερμανικοῦ Δακικοῦ Φαῶφι
κθ.

317. ANNOUNCEMENT CONCERNING PRAC-
TICE OF A TRADE

P. Oxy. 1263.   A.D. 128–129.

[1]Διογένει τῷ καὶ Ἑρμαίῳ [2]τῶν ἐξηγητ(ευσάντων)
γρα(μματεῖ) πόλ(εως) [3]παρὰ Διοσκόρου ἀπελευ-
[4]θέρου Σαραπίωνος Σα-[5]ραπίωνος τοῦ Διο[. . . . .]
[6]ἀπ᾽ Ὀξυρύγχων π[όλεως] [7]ἀμφόδου Ἑρμαί[ου].
[8]βούλομαι πρώτως [9]ἀπὸ τοῦ ἐνεστῶτος [10]τρισκαι-
δεκάτου [11]ἔτου[ς] Ἁδριανοῦ Καίσαρος [12]τοῦ κυρίου
χρήσα-[13]σθαι τῇ τῶν ἐργ[ατῶν] [14]ποταμοῦ τέχ[νῃ].
[15]διὸ ἐπιδίδ[ωμι τὸ] [16]ὑπόμνημα [ὡς πρό-][17]κ[ιται.
(ἔτους)] τρισκα[ιδεκάτου - - -

350

Petosorapis. Total 5 men. And we swear by the Emperor Caesar Nerva Trajanus Augustus Germanicus Dacicus that we have honestly and truthfully presented the foregoing list, and that there are no more than these, and that we have no apprentices or strangers practising the craft down to the present day, otherwise may we incur the consequences of the oath. The 11th year of the Emperor Caesar Nerva Trajanus Augustus Germanicus Dacicus, Phaophi 29.

317. ANNOUNCEMENT CONCERNING PRACTICE OF A TRADE

A.D. 128–129.

To Diogenes also called Hermaeus, ex-exegetes, scribe of the city, from Dioscorus, freedman of Sarapion son of Sarapion son of . . ., inhabitant of Oxyrhynchus in the quarter of the Hermaeum. I wish, beginning from the current thirteenth year of Hadrianus Caesar the lord, to practise the trade of a river-worker [a] ; wherefore I present this application as above. The thirteenth year . . .

---

[a] That is, as a labourer on the embankments, canals, etc. The declaration was probably required because the trade, like most others, was subject to the tax called χειρωνάξιον, which was really a license to practise a trade.

318. DECLARATION OF PAGAN SACRIFICE

P. Oxy. 1464.   A.D. 250.

¹[Τοῖς] ἐπὶ τῶν θυσιῶν αἱρεθεῖσι τῆς ²['Ο]ξυρυγ-
χειτῶν πόλεως ³[παρ]ὰ Αὐρηλίου Γαΐωνος 'Αμ-
μωνίου ⁴[μη]τρὸς Ταεῦτος. ἀεὶ μὲν θύειν καὶ
⁵[σπέ]νδειν καὶ σέβειν θεοῖς εἰθισμένος ⁶[κατ]ὰ τὰ
κελευσθέντα ὑπὸ τῆς θείας κρίσεως ⁷[καὶ] νῦν
ἐνώπιον ὑμῶν θύων καὶ σπέν-⁸[δω]ν καὶ γευ[σ]ά-
μενος τῶν ἱερείων ἅμα ⁹[Τα?]ῶτι γυναικὶ [κ]αὶ
'Αμμωνίῳ καὶ 'Αμμω-¹⁰[νι]ανῷ υἱοῖς καὶ Θέκλᾳ
θυγατρὶ δι' ἐμοῦ κ[α]ὶ ¹¹[ἀξι]ῶ ὑποσημιώσασθαί
μοι. (ἔτους) α ¹²[Αὐ]τοκράτορος Κ[α]ί[σαρο]ς Γαΐου
Μεσσίου ¹³[Κυί]ντου Τ[ρ]αϊανοῦ Δεκίου Εὐσεβοῦς
¹⁴[Εὐ]τυχοῦς Σεβαστοῦ 'Επεὶφ γ. Αὐρή[λιος
¹⁵Γαΐ]ων ἐπιδέδωκα. Αὐρήλ(ιος) Σαραπίων ¹⁶[ὁ
κ(αὶ)] Χαιρήμων ἔγρ[αψα] ὑπὲρ αὐτοῦ μὴ [εἰδό-
¹⁷τος] γράμματα.

319. CERTIFIED DECLARATION OF PAGAN SACRIFICE

P. Ryl. 12.   A.D. 250.

¹Τ[οῖ]ς ἐπὶ τῶν θυσιῶν ἡρημένοις ²παρὰ Αὐρηλίας
Δημῶτος ἀπάτορος ³μητρὸς 'Ελένης γυνὴ Αὐρηλίου
Εἰρηναίου ⁴ἀπὸ ἀμφόδου 'Ελληνείου. καὶ ἀεὶ
θύουσα τοῖς ⁵θεοῖς διετέλεσα καὶ νῦν ἐπὶ παροῦσι

3. l. γυναικός.

---

318. DECLARATION OF PAGAN SACRIFICE

A.D. 250.

To the commissioners of sacrifices at Oxyrhynchus from Aurelius Gaion son of Ammonius and Taeus. I have always been accustomed to sacrifice and make libations and pay reverence to the gods in accordance with the orders of the divine decree,[a] and now in your presence I have sacrificed and made libation and tasted the offering along with Taos my wife and Ammonius and Ammonianus my sons and Thecla my daughter, acting through me, and I request you to certify my statement. The 1st year of the Emperor Caesar Gaius Messius Quintus Trajanus Decius Pius Felix Augustus, Epeiph 3. I, Aurelius Gaion, have presented this declaration. I, Aurelius Sarapion also called Chaeremon, wrote for him, as he is illiterate.

[a] A decree of the Emperor Decius at the time of the persecution of Christians. A proof of conformity to pagan worship was apparently required from all persons and not merely from suspected Christians. One of the extant declarations is from the priestess of an Egyptian god.

319. CERTIFIED DECLARATION OF PAGAN SACRIFICE

A.D. 250.

To the commissioners of sacrifices from Aurelia Demos, without patronymic, daughter of Helena and wife of Aurelius Irenaeus, of the quarter of the Hellenium.[a] I have always been wont to sacrifice to the gods, and now also in your presence, in

SELECT PAPYRI

ὑμῖν ⁶κατὰ τὰ προστετ[α]γμένα καὶ ἔθυσα καὶ ἔσπι-
⁷σα καὶ τῶν ἱερείων ἐγευσάμην καὶ ἀξιῶ ⁸ὑμᾶς
ὑποσημιώσασθαί μοι. διευτυχεῖται. (2nd hand)
⁹Αὐρηλία Δημῶς ἐπιδέδωκα. Αὐρήλ(ιος) ¹⁰Ἐ[ἰ]ρη-
ναῖος ἔγραψα ὑπὲρ αὐτῆς ἀγρα(μμάτου). (3rd hand)
¹¹Αὐ[ρή]λ(ιος) Σαβεῖνος πρύτ(ανις) ε[ἶ]δ[ό]ν σε
θύουσαν. (1st hand) ¹²(ἔτους) α Αὐτοκράτορος
Καίσαρος Γαΐου Μεσσίου ¹³Κυίντου Τραϊανοῦ
Δεκίου Εὐσεβοῦς Εὐτυχοῦς ¹⁴Σ[ε]βαστοῦ Παῦνι κ.

8. l. διευτυχεῖτε.

320. DECLARATION IN VIEW OF A DISTRIBUTION OF CORN

P. Lond. 955.   A.D. 261.

¹Τῇ [κρ]ατίστῃ βουλῇ Ἑρμοῦ πόλ(εως) τῆς
²μ[εγ]άλ(ης) ἀρχαίας καὶ λαμπρ(οτάτης) καὶ σεμνο-
(τάτης) ³παρὰ Αὐρηλίου Φιβίωνος Πανε-⁴χ[ώτο]ν
Διοσκόρου Ἀχιλλέως τοῦ ⁵καὶ [. . .]νίου Ἑρμο-
πολ(ίτου) ἀπὸ γυ(μνασίου) ἀναγρ(αφομένου) ⁶ἐπ'
[ἀμφό]δου Φρουρίου Λι(βὸς) κδ ἀμ(φοδαρχίας).
⁷[ἀπογρά]φ[ομ]αι [εἰς] τὴν ἐπ' ἀγαθοῖ[ς ⁸ἐσομέν]ην
διάδοσιν τοῦ ἐπὶ ⁹[πλείστοις ἀ]γαθοῖς συνχωρη-
¹⁰[θέντο]ς ἡμῖν σιτηρεσίου ἐκ ¹¹[τῆ]ς μεγαλοδωρίας
τῶν ¹²[κυρί]ων ἡμῶν Μακριανοῦ ¹³[καὶ] Κυ[ή]του
Καισάρων Σεβαστῶν ¹⁴[ἐ]μαυτὸν ¹⁵[Αὐρήλιο]ν Φι-
βίωνα τὸν προ-¹⁶[γεγρ(αμμένον)] Φρουρίου Λιβ(ὸς)
κδ ἀμ(φοδαρχίας) ¹⁷[   ] (ἐτῶν) μβ. ¹⁸[εὐτυχ]εῖτε.
¹⁹[ἔτους α] Αὐτοκρατόρ̣ων ²⁰[Καισάρων Τίτου]
Φ[ο]υλουίου ²¹['Ιουνίου Μακρ]ιανοῦ καὶ ²²[Τίτου
354

accordance with the command, I have made sacrifice and libation and tasted the offering, and I request you to certify my statement. Farewell. (Signed) I, Aurelia Demos, have presented this declaration. I, Aurelius Irenaeus, wrote for her, as she is illiterate. (Attested) I, Aurelius Sabinus, prytanis, saw you sacrificing. (Dated) The 1st year of the Emperor Caesar Gaius Messius Quintus Trajanus Decius Pius Felix Augustus, Pauni 20.

320. DECLARATION IN VIEW OF A DISTRIBUTION OF CORN

A.D. 261.

To their excellencies the senate of Hermopolis the great, ancient, most illustrious and august city from Aurelius Phibion son of Panechotes son of Dioscorus son of Achilles also called . . ., Hermopolitan, member of the gymnasium,[a] registered in the quarter of the Western Guard-house, 24th amphodarchy.[b] I give in my name for the auspiciously coming distribution of the corn allowance most auspiciously accorded to us from the bounty of our lords Macrianus and Quietus Caesars Augusti, being Aurelius Phibion the aforesaid, of the Western Guard-house quarter, 24th amphodarchy, aged 42. Farewell. Year 1 of the Emperors Caesars Titus Fulvius Junius Macrianus

[a] To have been admitted to a gymnasium was a mark of superior standing and conferred certain privileges.
[b] A numbered district under the superintendence of an official called amphodarch.

Φ]ουλουίου Ἰουνίου ²³[Κυῆ]του Εὐσεβῶν Εὐτυχῶν
²⁴[Σεβαστῶν Με]χεὶρ κ̄ᾱ. (2nd hand) ²⁵[Αὐρήλιος
Φιβίων] ἐπιδέδωκα. (3rd hand) ²⁶[- - -] Πρόδικος
σεσημ(είωμαι).

321. PROPERTY-RETURN OF SHEEP

P. Hib. 33, ll. 10-16.   245 B.C.

Written in duplicate; the following is the outer
text, restored from the inner.

¹⁰("Ετους) β Παμενώτ. ἀπογρα-¹¹φὴ λείας εἰς
τὸ τρίτ[ον ἔ-]¹²τος παρὰ Ῥοιμηώτου Θραι-¹³κὸς
ἰδιώτου τῶν Ἀέτου. ¹⁴ὑπάρχει μοι [πρόβατα ἴδια
¹⁵ἔ]ν [κώμη]ι [Ψεπθονέμβη ¹⁶τοῦ Κωείτου ὀγ-
δοήκον]τα.

322. PROPERTY-RETURN OF SHEEP

P. Oxy. 245.   A.D. 26.

²Χαιρέαι στρατηγῶι ³παρὰ Ἡρακλείου τοῦ
⁴Ἀπίωνος καὶ Νάριδος τοῦ Κολλούθου πρ‹ε›σβυ-
⁵τέρου. ἀπογραφόμεθα ⁶εἰς τὸ ἐνεστὸς ιβ (ἔτος)
⁷Τιβερίου Καίσαρος Σεβαστοῦ ⁸τὰ ὑπάρχοντα ἡμεῖν
⁹πρόβ(ατα) ἑκάστῳ ἔξ, ¹⁰πρ(όβατα) ιβ, ἃ νεμήσεται
¹¹σὺν το‹ῖ›ς ἐπακολουθοῦ-¹²σι ἄρνασι περὶ Πέλα τῆς
¹³πρὸς λίβα τοπαρχίας ¹⁴καὶ δι' ὅλου τοῦ νομοῦ
¹⁵ἐπιμεμιγμένα τοῖς ¹⁶Διονυσίου τοῦ Ἱππάλου ¹⁷διὰ
νομέως τούτου ¹⁸υἱοῦ Στράτωνος νεω-¹⁹τέρου
λαογραφουμένο(υ) ²⁰εἰς τὴν αὐτὴν Πέλα· ²¹ὧν καὶ

and Titus Fulvius Junius Quietus Pii Felices Augusti, Mecheir 21. (Signed) Presented by me, Aurelius Phibion. (Subscribed) Signed by me, . . . also called Prodicus.

321. PROPERTY-RETURN OF SHEEP

245 B.C.

Year 2, Phamenoth. Return of a flock *a* for the third year from Roimeotes, Thracian, private of the troop of Aetus. I possess eighty sheep of my own at the village of Psepthonembe in the Koite district.

a The Greek word means properly " plunder," but is used as a general term for sheep and goats. The return was of course required for purposes of taxation.

322. PROPERTY-RETURN OF SHEEP

A.D. 26.

To Chaereas, strategus, from Heraclius son of Apion and Naris son of Colluthus the elder. We return for the current 12th year of Tiberius Caesar Augustus the sheep which we own as six each, or twelve sheep in all. They will pasture, together with the lambs which they may produce, in the neighbourhood of Pela in the western toparchy and throughout the nome,*a* mixed with those of Dionysius son of Hippalus and having for shepherd his son Straton the younger, who is on the poll-tax list of the said Pela.

a The Oxyrhynchite.

357

ταξόμεθα τὸ καθῆ-²²κον τέλος. εὐτ[ύ]χ(ει). (2nd
hand) ²³Σαρα(πίων) τοπ(άρχης) σεση(μείωμαι) πρόβατα ²⁴δέκα δύο, (γίνονται) ιβ. (1st hand ?) ²⁵(ἔτους)
ιβ Τιβερίου Καίσαρος ²⁶Σεβαστοῦ (3rd hand ?)
Μεχ(εὶρ) ε̄.

323. REGISTRATION OF A BOAT

P. Grenf. i. 49.   A.D. 220–221.

¹Αὐρηλίωι Σαβεινιανῷ ²[τῷ κρατί]στῳ ἐπιστρατήγῳ ³παρὰ Αὐρηλίου Πτο-⁴λεμαίου τοῦ καὶ
Σεμ-⁵πρωνίου Ἀπολινα-⁶ρίου Ἀντινοέως. ⁷ἀπο-
γράφομαι κατὰ ⁸τὰ κελευσθέντα ⁹ὑπὸ τοῦ λαμπροτάτου ¹⁰ἡγεμόνος Γεμεινίου ¹¹Χρήστου τὸ ὑπ-
άρ-¹²χον τῷ ἀφήλικί μου ¹³υἱῷ Αὐρηλίῳ Ἀφρο-
¹⁴δ[ισ]ίῳ τῷ καὶ Φιλαντι-¹⁵νόῳ ὁμοίως Ἀντινοεῖ
¹⁶πλοῖον [Ἑλ]ληνικὸν ¹⁷ἀγωγῆς ἀρταβῶν ¹⁸δια-
κοσίων πεντήκον-¹⁹τα, οὗ παράσημον ²⁰παντό-
μορφος, ²¹οὗ εἰμὶ γυβερνήτης. ²²Αὐρήλιος Πτολεμαῖος ὁ καὶ Σεμ-²³πρώνιος ἐ[πιδέ]δωκα ὡς
²⁴πρόκειται. ²⁵(ἔτους) δ Αὐτοκράτορος ²⁶Καίσαρος
Μάρκου ²⁷Αὐρηλίου Ἀντωνείνου ²⁸Εὐσεβοῦς Εὐτυχοῦς ²⁹Σεβαστοῦ . . . .

324. REGISTRATION OF PROPERTY

P. Oxy. 247.   A.D. 90.

²Θέωνι καὶ Ἐπιμάχωι ³βιβλιοφ(ύλαξι) ⁴παρὰ
Πανεχώτου τοῦ ⁵Παυσίριος τοῦ Πανεχώ-⁶του

We will also pay the proper tax upon them. Farewell. (Signed) I, Sarapion, toparch, have signed a return of twelve sheep, total 12. (Dated) The 12th year of Tiberius Caesar Augustus, Mecheir 5.

323. REGISTRATION OF A BOAT

A.D. 220–221.

To his excellency the epistrategus Aurelius Sabinianus from Aurelius Ptolemaeus also called Sempronius son of Apollinarius, of Antinoe. I register in accordance with the orders of the most illustrious praefect Geminius Chrestus the boat belonging to my son, who is a minor, Aurelius Aphrodisius also called Philantinous, likewise of Antinoe, being a Greek boat of 250 artabas' burden having for sign a multiform god, of which I am the pilot. I, Aurelius Ptolemaeus also called Sempronius, have presented this declaration as aforesaid. The 4th year of the Emperor Caesar Marcus Aurelius Antoninus Pius Felix Augustus . . .

---

21. *l. κυβερνήτης.*

324. REGISTRATION OF PROPERTY

A.D. 90.

To Theon and Epimachus, keepers of the archives, from Panechotes son of Pausiris son of Panechotes, his

μητρὸς Τσεναμμω-ʼνᾶτος τῆς Πανεχώτου ⁸τῶν ἀπ᾽
Ὀξυρύγχων πόλ(εως). ⁹ἀπογράφομ[αι τῷ ὁμογν]η-
¹⁰σίῳ μου ἀδελ[φῷ . . . .] ¹¹ἀπὸ τῆς αὐτῆς
πόλεως ¹²προστρέχοντι τῇ ἐννό-¹³μῳ ἡλικίᾳ κατὰ
τὰ ὑπὸ ¹⁴τοῦ κρατίστου ἡγεμόνος ¹⁵Μεττίου Ῥούφου
προσ-¹⁶τεταγμένα τὸ ὑπάρ-¹⁷χον αὐτῷ εἰς τὴν ἐνεσ-
¹⁸τῶσαν ἡμέραν ἐπὶ τοῦ ¹⁹πρὸς Ὀξυρύγχων πόλ(ει)
²⁰Σαραπίου ἐπ᾽ ἀμφόδου ²¹Ἱππέων Παρεμβολῆς
²²[ἐ]ν τῷ Κάμπῳ τρίτον ²³[μέ]ρος οἰκίας διπυργί-
²⁴ας, ἐν ᾗ κατὰ μέσον αἴ-²⁵[θρ]ιον, καὶ τῆς προσ-
οῦ²⁶[σης] αὐλῆς καὶ ἑτέρων ²⁷[χ]ρηστηρίων καὶ εἰσ-
²⁸όδου καὶ ἐξόδου καὶ ²⁹τῶν συνκυρόντων, ³⁰κατην-
τηκὸς εἰς αὐτὸν ³¹ἐξ ὀνόματος τῆς ση-³²μαινομένης
καὶ με-³³τηλλαχυίας ἀμφοτέ-³⁴ρων μητρὸς Τσεναμ-
³⁵μωνᾶτος ἀπὸ τῆς αὐ-³⁶τῆς {α} πόλεως ἀκολού-
³⁷θως οἷς ἔχει δικαίοις. ³⁸(ἔτους) ἐνάτου Αὐτοκράτορος ³⁹Καίσαρος_Δομιτιανοῦ ⁴⁰Σεβαστοῦ Γερμανικοῦ ⁴¹Φαμενὼθ ιδ.

325. DECLARATION OF A PURCHASE OF PROPERTY

P. Hamb. 16.   A.D. 209.

(2nd hand) ¹[- - - σεση(μείωμαι). (ἔτους) ιη
Αὐτο]κρατό[ρων Καισάρων] Λουκίου Σεπτιμίου
Σεουήρου ²Εὐσεβ[οῦς Περτίνακος καὶ] Μάρκου
Αὐρηλίου Ἀντωνίνου Εὐσεβ[ο]ῦς ³Σεβαστῶν καὶ
[Πουβλίου Σε]πτιμίου Γέτα Καίσαρος Σεβαστοῦ
Φαῶφ(ι) ι. (1st hand) ⁴Διδᾷ ἐξηγ(ητεύσαντι) καὶ

mother being Tsenammonas daughter of Panechotes, of the city of Oxyrhynchus. I register for my full brother . . ., of the said city, who is approaching the legal age,[a] in accordance with the commands of his excellency the praefect Mettius Rufus,[b] his property at the present date in the Campus near the Serapeum by the city of Oxyrhynchus in the Cavalry Camp quarter, namely a third part of a double-towered house, in the middle of which is an open-air hall, and of the courtyard attached to it and the other fixtures and the entrance and exit and appurtenances, which has descended to him from the personalty of the deceased mother of us both, the aforesaid Tsenammonas, of the said city, in accordance with his rightful claims. The ninth year of the Emperor Caesar Domitianus Augustus Germanicus, Phamenoth 14.

[a] Probably twenty-five years.
[b] See No. 219, which is the edict referred to, and in which the object of such declarations is explained.

325. DECLARATION OF A PURCHASE OF PROPERTY

A.D. 209.

(Docketed) Signed by me,[a] . . . The 18th year of the Emperors and Caesars Lucius Septimius Severus Pius Pertinax and Marcus Aurelius Antoninus Pius, Augusti, and Publius Septimius Geta Caesar Augustus, Phaophi 10. (Text of declaration) To Didas, ex-exegetes, and Mystes, ex-cosmetes,

[a] The clerk of the archives.

SELECT PAPYRI

[Μύστῃ κο]σ(μητεύσαντι) βουλ(ευταῖς) βιβλ(ιο-
φύλαξιν) ἐνκ(τήσεων) Ἀρσ[ι(νοΐτου)] [5]παρὰ Ἀντωνίας
Θερμουθαρίου χωρὶς κυρίου χρηματιζού-[6]σης κατὰ
τὰ Ῥωμαίων ἔθη τέκνων δικαίῳ. κατὰ δημόσιον
[7]χρηματισμὸν τελιωθέντα τῇ ἐνεστώσῃ ἡμέρᾳ διὰ
ἀρχείου [8]ἐνθάδε ἠγόρασα ἐν κώμῃ Φιλαδελφείᾳ
ἥμισυ πέμπτον δέ-[9]κατον μέρος κοινὸν καὶ ἀδιαί-
ρετον ἕκτου μέρους οἰκίας καὶ [10]χρηστηρίων τιμῆς
ἀργυρίου δραχμῶν ἑκατὸν παρὰ Τιτοληίου [11]τοῦ καὶ
Ἰσιδώρου καὶ Τιτοληίου ἀμφοτέρων Ἀντινοέων
Σα-[12]βεινίων τῶν καὶ Ἁρμονιέων καὶ Κυρίλλης καὶ
Τιτανίας τῶν [13]τεσσάρων Λογγείνου τοῦ καὶ Σαραπίωνος τοῦ Ἰσιδώρου μὴ [14]ἀπογεγραμμένων, τῶν
δὲ γυναικῶν ἑκατέρας μετὰ κυρίου [15]τοῦ ἀνδρός,
τῆς μὲν Κυρίλλης Σωκράτους Θέωνος τοῦ Πτολε-
[16]μαίου ἀπὸ ἀμφόδου Ἀράβων, τῆς δὲ Τιτανίας
Ἀμμωνίου υἱοῦ [17]Κλαυδιανοῦ τοῦ καὶ Πτολεμαίου
ἀρχιερατεύσαντος τῆς Ἀρσινοϊ-[18]τῶν πόλεως. διὸ
ἐπιδίδωμι εἰς τὸ τὴν παράθεσιν γενέσθαι [19]ἀκολού-
θως ᾧ παρεθέμην ἀντιγράφῳ τοῦ χρηματισμοῦ.
[20]ὁπόταν γὰρ τὴν ἀπογραφὴν αὐτοῦ ποιῶμαι,
ἀποδείξω ὡς ὑπάρ-[21]χει καὶ ἔστι καθαρὸν μηδενὶ
κρατούμενον· εἰ δὲ φανείη ἑτέρῳ [22]προσῆκον ἢ
προκατεσχημένον διὰ τοῦ βιβλιοφυλακείου, μὴ
[23]ἔσεσθαι ἐμπόδιον ἐκ τῆσδε τῆς παραθέσεως.
(3rd hand) Διδᾶς ἐξηγ(ητεύσας) [24]βουλ(ευτὴς) κατ-
εχώ(ρισα). (4th hand) Μύστης κοσμητεύσας [25]βουλ-
(ευτὴς) κατεχώρισα. (ἔτους) ιη Λουκίου Σεπ-

---

[a] See No. 305.　　　[b] Compare No. 288, note a, p. 279.

[c] The property being still booked in the register under
the name of their father.

[d] This annotation was to be made beside the registration

362

senators, keepers of archives of the Arsinoite nome, from Antonia Thermoutharion, acting without a guardian by right of children [a] in accordance with the Roman custom. In virtue of a public deed executed on the present day through the record-office here I have bought in the village of Philadelphia the four-fifth part, which was owned in common and undivided, of the sixth part of a house and fixtures for the price of a hundred drachmae from Tituleius also called Isidorus and Tituleius, both of them citizens of Antinoe of the Sabinian tribe and the Harmoniean deme,[b] and Cyrilla and Titania, who are all four children of Longinus also called Sarapion son of Isidorus and have not registered their ownership,[c] each of the women acting with her husband as guardian, Cyrilla with Socrates son of Theon son of Ptolemaeus of the Arabs' quarter, and Titania with Ammonius son of Claudianus also called Ptolemaeus, ex-chief priest of the city of Arsinoe. Wherefore I present this application in order that the annotation [d] may be made in conformity with the copy of the deed which I have deposited. For when I make the declaration of the property, I will show that it belongs to me and is free from any lien; but if another person should be proved to have a right to it or a hold upon it recorded through the archives-office, the present notification shall not stand in the way of his claim. (Subscribed) I, Didas, ex-exegetes, senator, have placed this on record. I, Mystes, ex-cosmetes, senator, have placed this on record. The 18th year

of the property under the name of Longinus. It is known from another document that the property was mortgaged; and until the applicant could show that the mortgage had been paid off, she could not register the property in the regular way under her own name.

τιμίου ²⁶Σεουήρου Εὐσεβοῦς Περτίνακος καὶ Μάρκου ²⁷Αὐρηλίου ᾿Αντωνίνου Εὐσεβοῦς Σεβαστ[ῶ]ν
²⁸καὶ Πουβλίου Σεπτιμίου Γέτα Καίσαρος Σεβαστοῦ ²⁹Φαῶφι ῑ.

326. DECLARATION OF INHERITANCE

P. Oxy. 1114.   A.D. 237.

¹Perpet[uo et Corneliano co(n)s(ulibus) anno iii
Imperatoris Caesaris Gaii Iuli Veri Maximini] ²Pii
A[ug(usti) Germanici Max(imi) Dacici Max(imi) Sar-
m]atici [Max(imi) et Gaii Iuli Veri Maximi Germanici
Max(imi)]³Dacici M[ax(imi) Sarmatici Max(imi) Caesaris
sancti]ssim[i Aug(usti) fili Aug(usti) ⁴ - - - ⁵A]pud
Geminium Vale[ntem - - -] ⁶procurationis. ⁷Marcus
Aurelius Saras fa[ctus] gymnas[iarchus decurio
civ]itat[i]s O[xyri]nchitarum ⁸filius Marci Aureli Dio-
genis q(ui) e(t) Hel[iodori facti euthe]n[ia]rchae . . .
[. . . .] . . [.]s . . . . ae ⁹civitatis Alexandrinorum pro-
f[iteor . . . .] filiabus me[i]s Aureliabus Stra-
¹⁰tonice q(uae) e(t) Sosipatrae et Apolloniae [q(uae) e(t)
Dieuti] h[er]editatem seu bonorum posses-¹¹sionem
Aureliae Ap[o]lloniae filiae Marci Aurel[i] Apolloni
Demetri q(ui) e(t) Psammi-¹²dis facti gymnasiarchi
decurionis civitatis Oxyrinchitarum, matris eorum uxoris
¹³autem suae, intestatae defunctae civitat{a}e Oxyrinchitarum prid(ie) non(as) Iul(ias) q(uae) p(roximae)
f(uerunt) ¹⁴hora diei tertia secundum testation[e]m de hac
re factam cuius exemplum subieci, ¹⁵eamque hereditatem

12. l. earum.   13. l. meae.

of Lucius Septimius Severus Pius Pertinax and Marcus Aurelius Antoninus Pius, Augusti, and Publius Septimius Geta Caesar Augustus, Phaophi 10.

326. DECLARATION OF INHERITANCE

A.D. 237.

In the consulship of Perpetuus and Cornelianus, in the 3rd year of the Emperor Caesar Gaius Julius Verus Maximinus Pius Augustus Germanicus Maximus Dacicus Maximus Sarmaticus Maximus and Gaius Julius Verus Maximus Germanicus Maximus Dacicus Maximus Sarmaticus Maximus the most sacred Caesar Augustus son of the Augustus, . . ., before Geminius Valens . . . of the procuratorship.[a] I, Marcus Aurelius Saras, ex-gymnasiarch, senator of the city of Oxyrhynchus, son of Marcus Aurelius Diogenes also called Heliodorus, ex-eutheniarch of the [most illustrious] city of Alexandria, declare [on behalf of (?)] my two daughters Aurelia Stratonice also called Sosipatra and Aurelia Apollonia also called Dieus the inheritance or possession of the property of Aurelia Apollonia daughter of Marcus Aurelius Apollonius son of Demetrius also called Psammis, ex-gymnasiarch and senator of the city of Oxyrhynchus, their mother and my wife, who died intestate at the city of Oxyrhynchus on the day before the succeeding Nones of July at the third hour of the day according to the affidavit made on this matter, of which I append a copy, and I certify that the in-

---

[a] That is, an employee in the office of the procurator of the 5 per cent tax on inheritances.

esse ducena[*ri*]*am et inmunem a vicensima.* [16]*Exemplum testationis.*

(2nd hand) [17]Ἔτους τρίτου Αὐτοκράτορος Καίσαρος Γαΐου Ἰουλίου Οὐήρου Μαξιμείνου Εὐσεβοῦς Εὐτυχοῦς [18]Σεβαστοῦ Γερμανικοῦ Μεγίστου Δακικοῦ Μεγίστου Σαρματικοῦ Μεγίστου καὶ Γαΐου Ἰουλίου [19]Οὐήρου Μαξίμου Γερμανικοῦ Μεγίστου Δακικοῦ Μεγίστου Σαρματικοῦ Μεγίστου τοῦ [20]ἱερωτάτου Καίσαρος Σεβαστοῦ υἱοῦ τοῦ Σεβαστοῦ Ἐπεὶφ ιβ, ἐν Ὀξυρίνχων πόλει. [21]Μάρκος Αὐρήλιος Σαρᾶς γυμνασιαρχήσας βουλευτὴς τῆς Ὀξυρινχειτῶν πόλεως υἱὸς Μάρ-[22]κου Αὐρηλίου Διογένους τοῦ καὶ Ἡλιοδώρου εὐθηνιαρχήσαντος βουλευτοῦ τῆς λαμπροτά-[23]της πόλεως τῶν Ἀλεξανδρέων καὶ ὡς χρηματίζει ἐμαρτύρατο τοὺς τόδε τὸ μαρτυρο-[24]ποίημα σφραγίζειν μέλλοντας τῇ ἐνεστώσῃ ἡμέρᾳ{ν} περὶ ὥραν τρίτην ἀπευ-[25]κταίως Αὐρηλίαν Ἀπολλωνίαν θυγατέρα Μάρκου Αὐρηλίου Ἀπολλωνίου Δημητρί-[26]ου τοῦ καὶ Ψάμμιδος καὶ ὡς χρηματίζει γυμνασιαρχήσαντος βουλευτοῦ τῆς Ὀξυριν-[27]χειτῶν πόλ[εω]ς γυναῖκα ἑαυτοῦ μητέρα τῶν κοινῶν θυγατέρων Αὐρηλιῶν Στρα-[28]τονείκης τῆς καὶ Σωσιπάτρας καὶ Ἀπολλωνίας τῆς καὶ Διεῦτος ἀφηλίκων ἀδι-[29][άθετον τελευτῆσαι - - - (3rd hand) [30]- - - (4th hand) [31]Σα]ραπίων ὁ κ[α]ὶ [- - -] [32]ἀποδεδειγμέ[νος] ἀρχιερεὺς βουλε[υτὴς] <τῆς> προκειμ[έ]νη[ς πόλ(εως) - - -] (5th hand) [33]Μάρκος Αὐρήλιος Σαρᾶς γυμν[α]σιαρχήσα[ς] βουλ(ευτὴς) τῆς Ὀξυρυ[γ]χειτῶ[ν] [34]πόλ(εως) ἐπιδέδωκα τὴν ἀπογραφήν. (6th hand) [35]*Ivivilinus Aug*(*usti*) *lib*(*ertus*) *tabul*(*arius*) *intestatam dec*[*e*]*ssisse secundum* [36]*adfirmationem insertam pr*(*idie*)

366

heritance is of the value of 200,000 sestertii and free
of the tax of five per cent.[a]

Copy of the affidavit. In the third year of the
Emperor Caesar Gaius Julius Verus Maximinus Pius
Felix Augustus Germanicus Maximus Dacicus Maxi-
mus Sarmaticus Maximus and Gaius Julius Verus
Maximus Germanicus Maximus Dacicus Maximus
Sarmaticus Maximus the most sacred Caesar Augustus
son of the Augustus, Epeiph 12, at the city of
Oxyrhynchus. Marcus Aurelius Saras, ex-gymnasiarch and senator of the city of Oxyrhynchus, son of
Marcus Aurelius Diogenes also called Heliodorus, ex-
eutheniarch and senator of the most illustrious city of
Alexandria, and however he is styled, called to witness
the persons about to seal the present affidavit that
on this day at about the third hour, to the loss of our
hopes, Aurelia Apollonia daughter of Marcus Aurelius
Apollonius son of Demetrius also called Psammis,
and however he is styled, ex-gymnasiarch and senator
of the city of Oxyrhynchus, his wife and the mother
of their daughters Aurelia Stratonice also called
Sosipatra and Aurelia Apollonia also called Dieus,
who are under age, died intestate . . . (Signed)
I, . . ., [witness]. I, Sarapion also called . . .,
appointed chief priest, senator of the aforesaid city
. . . [witness]. I, Marcus Aurelius Saras, ex-
gymnasiarch, senator of the city of Oxyrhynchus,
have presented this declaration. (Subscribed in
Latin) I, Ivivilinus freedman of Augustus, clerk,
have noted that she died intestate according to the
inserted declaration on the 4th of July in the consul-

------

[a] The immunity was due to the fact that the beneficiaries
were near relations of the deceased. Exemption could also
be claimed, though evidently not in the present case, on the
ground of poverty.

non(as) Iul(ias) Perpetuo et [37]*Corneliano co(n)s(ulibus)*
notavi pr(idie) id(us) Iul(ias) co(n)s(ulibus) s(upra)
s(criptis). (7th hand) [38]*act(um) s(   ) . . . [. . . . .]*
I[u]l(ias) Perpetuo et Corneliano co(n)s(ulibus).

38. Perhaps *s(upra) s(cripto) die.*

327. SWORN DECLARATION OF TEMPLE LAMPLIGHTERS

P. Oxy. 1453.   30–29 B.C.

²'Αντί[γ]ρ[α]φον ὅρκου. Θῶ[ν]ις ὃς καὶ ³Πα-
τ[ο]ῖφι{ο}ς [Θ]ώνις καὶ 'Ηρακλείδης ⁴Τοτ[ή?]ου,
ἀμφότεροι λυχνάπτοι ⁵ἱερο[ῦ Σαράπι]δος θεοῦ
μεγίστ[ο]υ καὶ ⁶τοῦ αὐ[τόθ]ι 'Ησίου, <καὶ> Παᾶπις
ὁ Θοώνιος ⁷καὶ Πετ[οσῖ]ρ[ις ὁ] Πατοίφις τοῦ
πρ[ο]γε-⁸γραμμέν[ου], ἀ]μφότεροι λυχνάπτοι ⁹τοῦ
ἐν 'Οξυρύ<γ>γχων πόλει [ἱ]εροῦ Θούριδο[ς] ¹⁰θεᾶς
με[γί]στης, οἱ τέσσαρες ὀμ[ν]ύο-¹¹μεν Καίσαρος
θεὸν ἐκ θεοῦ 'Ηλιοδώρω[ι] ¹²ᶜ'Ηλιοδώρου καὶ
'Ηλιοδώρωι Πτολεμαίου ¹³τοῖς ἐπὶ τῶν ἱερῶν τοῦ
'Οξυρυ<γ>χίτου κ[αὶ] ¹⁴Κυνοπολείτου εἶ μὴν προ-
στατήσ[ειν] ¹⁵τοῦ λύχνου τῶν προδεδηλωμέν[ων]
¹⁶ἱερῶν καθὼς πρόκειται, καὶ χορη[γ]ή-¹⁷σειν τὸ
καθῆκον ἔλαιον εἰς τοὺς καθ' ἡ-¹⁸μέραν λύχνους
καομένους ἐν τοῖς ¹⁹σημαινομένοις ἱεροῖς ἀπὸ Θωὺθ
α ²⁰ἕως Μεσορὴ <ἐπαγομένων?> ε τοῦ ἐνεστῶτος α
(ἔτους) ²¹Καίσαρος ἀν[υπε]ρ[θέτως?] ἀκολού-²²θως
τοῖς ἕως τοῦ κβ τοῦ καὶ ζ (ἔτους) ²³κεχωρηγημένοις,

4. *l.* λυχνάπται; so in l. 8.   6. *l.* 'Ισείον.   11. *l.*
Καίσαρα.   23. *l.* κεχορηγημένους.

ship of Perpetuus and Cornelianus. The 14th of July in the aforesaid consulship. (Docketed in Latin) Done on the said day (?) of July in the consulship of Perpetuus and Cornelianus.

327. SWORN DECLARATION OF TEMPLE LAMPLIGHTERS

30–29 B.C.

Copy of an oath. We, Thonis also called Patoiphis son of Thonis and Heraclides son of Totoes, both lamplighters of the temple of Sarapis, the most great god, and of the Iseum thereby, and Paapis son of Thonis and Petosiris son of the aforesaid Patoiphis, both lamplighters of the temple of Thoeris, the most great goddess, at Oxyrhynchus, swear all four by Caesar, god and son of a god, to Heliodorus son of Heliodorus and Heliodorus son of Ptolemaeus, overseers of the temples of the Oxyrhynchite and Cynopolite nomes, that we will superintend the lamps of the above-mentioned temples, as aforesaid, and will supply the proper oil for the daily lamps burning in the temples specified from Thoth 1 to the 5th intercalary day of Mesore of the present 1st year of Caesar punctually in conformity with the amounts supplied up to the 22nd which was also the 7th year [a] ; and we the aforesaid

[a] The last year of Cleopatra. From 37 B.C. onwards the years of her reign were double-numbered as above, the second number probably representing the year of her reign over Chalcis in Syria. The 1st year of Augustus was reckoned from Thoth 1 (= August 30), 30 B.C.

ὄντων ἡμῶν ²⁴ἀλληλενγύων τῶν προγεγραμμέ-²⁵νων,
τῶν ὑπαρχόντων ἡμεῖν πάν-²⁶των ὄντων ‹κατο-
χίμων ?› ἐπὶ τοῦ ποιή-²⁷{η}σειν κα{ι}τὰ τἀπι-
γεγραμμένα. εὐ-²⁸[ορ]κ[οῦν]τι μέν] μοι εὖ εἴη, ἐφι-
ορ[κοῦν-²⁹τι δὲ τὰ ἐναν]τία. (ἔτους) [α] Καίσαρος
[. . . . .³⁰. . . . . . .] ἀντίγρ[α(φον).] Παᾶπις
Θώνις ³¹[ὀμώμοκα] καὶ ποιήσω καθότ[ι] πρό-
³²[κειται. Θ]ῶνις ʿΑρπ[α]ήσις γέγρα-³³[φα ὑπὲρ]
αὐτοῦ ἀξιωθεὶς τιὰ τὸ ³⁴[μὴ εἰδ]έναι αὐτὸν γράμμα[τ]α. ³⁵[ʿΗρακλεί]δης ὀμώμοκα καὶ πο[ι]ή-³⁶[σω
καθό]τι πρόκειται. ³⁷[Πετοσῖρι]ς ὀμώμοκα καὶ
ποιή[σω ³⁸καθότι πρό]κειται. Ὧρος Τοτοεῦτ[ος
³⁹ἔγραψα ὑπὲρ α]ὐτοῦ ἀξιωθεὶς δ[ιὰ τὸ ⁴⁰μὴ]
εἰδέναι αὐ]τὸν γράμματα. Θ[ῶνι]ς ⁴¹[ὀμώμοκα]
ὁμοίως καθότ[ι πρ]ό-⁴²[κειται].

26. l. ἐπὶ τῷ.   33. l. διά.

328. SWORN DECLARATION OF FLOODGATE GUARDS

Raccolta Lumbroso, p. 46.   A.D. 25.

¹[Μαρεψῆμ]ις ὡς (ἐτῶν) κα οὐλὴ μερῷ (?) ἀρισ-
τερ[ῷ], ²Π[εχεῦς] ὡς (ἐτῶν) με οὐλὴ ἀντίχ(ειρι
ἀριστερῷ, ³Σ[οκονῶ]πις ὡς (ἐτῶν) μ οὐλὴ δακ-
(τύλῳ) χειρὸς ἀριστερᾶς, ⁴Φα[νῆσ]ις ὡς (ἐτῶν) λθ
οὐλὴ γαστροκ(νημίᾳ) ἀριστερᾷ.
⁵Γαΐ[ωι] Ἰουλίωι Φιλήτωι κατασπορεῖ Ἀρσινοείτου ⁶πα[ρ]ὰ Μαρεψήμιος τοῦ Μαρεψήμιος καὶ
Κατύτιος καὶ ⁷{καὶ} Πεχεῦτος τοῦ Ψήφιος φυλασ-
σόντων τὴν ἀπὸ λι-⁸βὸ[ς] τῆς γεφύρης ἄφεσιν
370

are mutual sureties, all our property being security
for the performance of the duties herein stated. If
I swear truly, may it be well with me, if falsely, the
reverse. The 1st year of Caesar, . . . Copy. I,
Paapis son of Thonis, have sworn, and I will do as
stated above. I, Thonis son of Harpaesis, have
written for him by request, because he is illiterate.
I, Heraclides, have sworn, and I will do as stated
above. I, Petosiris, have sworn, and I will do as
stated above. I, Horus son of Totoeus, have written
for him by request, because he is illiterate. I,
Thonis, have sworn likewise as stated above.

328. SWORN DECLARATION OF FLOODGATE
GUARDS

A.D. 25.

Marepsemis, aged about 21 years, with a scar on
the left thigh ; Pecheus, aged about 45 years, with
a scar on the left wrist ; Sokonopis, aged about 40
years, with a scar on a finger of the left hand ;
Phanesis, aged about 39 years, with a scar on the
left calf.

To Gaius Julius Philetus, inspector of sowings in
the Arsinoite nome, from Marepsemis son of Marepsemis also called Katutis and Pecheus son of Psephis,
who guard the priests' outlet on the west of the

---

1. _l._ μηρῷ, but the letters are doubtful.

ἱερέων καὶ παρὰ Σοκονώ-⁹π[ιος] τοῦ Σοκονώπιος
καὶ Φ[αν]ήσιος τοῦ Παστ[ο]ῦτος ¹⁰φυλασσόντων
τὴν ἀπὸ ἀπηλιώτου ἄφεσιν ¹¹ἱερέων. οἱ τέσσαρες
ἱερεῖς τῶν ἀπὸ Τεβτύνεως ¹²τῆς Πολ[έ]μωνος
μερίδος φυλάσσοντες τὰς προκι-¹³μένας ἀφέσεις
δύο ὀμνύομεν Τιβέριον Καίσαρα ¹⁴Σεβαστὸν
Νέον Αὐτοκράτορα θεοῦ Σεβαστοῦ υἱὸν ¹⁵εἶ μὴν
φυλάξειν ἕκαστον τὴν ἰδίαν ἄφεσιν ¹⁶χωρὶς πάσης
δαπάνης καὶ παρεδρεύσειν καθ᾽ ἑ-¹⁷κάστην ὥραν
πρὸς τὸ μηδὲν ἔλαττον ἐπακ⟨ο⟩λου-¹⁸θῆσαι, ἐὰν
δὲ μὴ [. . . . .]θει προστῶμεν ἐκ-¹⁹{χ}ρηγῆς, ὑμεῖς
αὐτοὶ ὑπεύθυνοι ἐσόμεθα ²⁰παντὸς τοῦ ἐσομένου
βλάβο⟨υ⟩ς. εὐορκοῦ[σι] μὲν ²¹ὑμεῖν εὖ εἴη, ἐφι-
ορκοῦσι δὲ [τ]ἀναντία. ²²ἔγραψεν ὑπὲρ αὐτῶν μὴ
εἰδότων γράμματα ²³᾽Απίων ὁ τῆς κ[ώ]μης νομογράφος. (ἔτους) [ι]α ²⁴Τιβερίου Καίσαρος Σεβαστοῦ μ[ηνὸς] Σεβαστ[ο]ῦ ι̅ς̅. (2nd hand) ²⁵Μαρε-
ψῆμις Μαρεψήμις καὶ Κατύτις συνομόμεκα ²⁶τὸ
προκίμενον ὅρκων καὶ φυλάξω καὶ ποι[ήσω κα-]
²⁷θὸς πρόκιται. (ἔτους) ια Τιβερίου Καίσαρος
Σεβαστοῦ μ[ηνὸς] ²⁸Σεβαστοῦ ι̅ς̅.

19. l. ἡμεῖς.   21. l. ἡμῖν.   25. l. συνομώμοκα.
26. l. τὸν . . . ὅρκον.   26-27. l. κα]θώς.

329. SWORN DECLARATION OF FISHERMEN

P.S.I. 901, ll. 7-16.   A.D. 46.

⁷῾Ηρακλείδης Τρύφωνος γραμματεὺς ἁλιέων
α⟨ἰ⟩γιαλοῦ Βερνικίδος Θεσμοφόρου κ(αὶ) ῾Αρμιεῦς
᾽Ανουβᾶτος κ(αὶ) Παπεῖς ᾽Οννόφρεος ⁸κ(αὶ) Πανο-

372

bridge, and from Sokonopis son of Sokonopis and
Phanesis son of Pastous, who guard the priests' outlet
on the east. We four, priests [a] of Tebtunis in the division of Polemon guarding the two aforesaid outlets,
swear by Tiberius Caesar Augustus Novus Imperator,
son of the deified Augustus, that we will each guard
his own outlet without causing any expense and attend
to it at every hour so that no loss may result; and if we
do not . . . superintend the discharge, we ourselves
shall be responsible for all the ensuing damage. If
we swear truly, may it be well with us, if falsely, the
reverse. Apion, public scribe of the village, wrote
for them, as they are illiterate. The 11th year of
Tiberius Caesar Augustus, 16th day of the month
Sebastus.[b] (Signed) I, Marepsemis son of Marepsemis also called Katutis, have sworn with the others
the aforesaid oath, and I will keep guard and do as
stated above. The 11th year of Tiberius Caesar
Augustus, 16th day of the month Sebastus.

[a] The reason why priests were appointed for this compulsory service may have been that the land irrigated by
these outlets was temple property.
[b] = Thoth.

329. SWORN DECLARATION OF FISHERMEN

A.D. 46.

We, Heraclides son of Tryphon, scribe of the fishermen of the shore of Berenicis Thesmophori,[a] and
Harmieus son of Anoubas, Papis son of Onnophris,

[a] A village in the south of the Fayum near a marshy lake.

μιηῦς Ἀκήους κ(αὶ) Σεκονεῦς Πατύνις κ(αὶ) Ἀνχο-
ρίμφις Ὀρσεῦς κ(αὶ) Ἁρπαγάθης Νίλου κ(αὶ) Πανομιεῦς Ἀρμάις κ(αὶ) Νεκχῆς ⁹Ὧπεος κ(αὶ) Ὀρσεῦς
Ὧπεος κ(αὶ) Πατῦνις Ὀρσεῦς κ(αὶ) Ὀρσεῦς Ὀρ-
<σ>εῦτος κ(αὶ) Πατῦνις Σαταβοῦτος κ(αὶ) Πελῶὺς
Πατῦνις, ¹⁰οἱ δεκατρῖς προσβύτεροι ἁλιέων κωμῶν
Ναρμούθεος κ(αὶ) Βερνικίδος Θεσμοφόρου, οἱ δεκα-
τέσσαρος τοῖς ¹¹παρὰ Σα[ρ]απίωνος τοῦ Πτολεμαίου νομάρχου κ(αὶ) ἐπὶ τῶν προσόδων κ(αὶ) ἐπὶ
τοῦ ἐπιδασμοῦ τοῦ Ἀρσινοΐτου ὀμνύωμεν ¹²Τιβέ-
ρι[ο]ν Κλαύδιον Καίσαρα Σεβαστὸν Γερμανικὸν
Αὐτοκράτορα εἶ μὴν μηδὲ ἓν συνεστορηκέναι μηδὲ
συνιστο-¹³ρήσιν ἀ[λ]ιέουσι μηδὲ σαγηνεύσι μηδὲ
ἀμφιβολέουσι κυνηγοῦντες ἴδωλα θεῶν ὀξυρύνχων
κ(αὶ) λεπιδωτῶν ¹⁴ἀκ<ο>λούθως τῇ γεγεν[η]μένηι
ὑφ' ἡμῶν τε κ(αὶ) τῶν ἑτέρων ἁλιέων δημοσίᾳ
χιρογραφίᾳ. εοὐωρκοῦσι μὲν ¹⁵ἡμῖν εοὐ ἤηι, ἐφιορ-
κοῦσι τὰ δ' ἀναντία. ἔτους ς Τιβερίου Κλαυδίου
Καίσαρος Σεβαστοῦ Γερμανικοῦ Αὐτοκράτο-¹⁶ρος,
Φ[αρ]μοῦθι κβ.

8. l. Πανομιεῦς, Ὀρσεῦτος.   9. l. Πατῦνις Ὀρσεῦτος.
10. l. πρεσβύτεροι, δεκατέσσαρες.   11. l. ὀμνύομεν.   12. l. ἦ
συνιστορηκέναι.   13. l. ἁλιεύουσι, σαγηνεύουσι, ἀμφιβολεύ-
ουσι.   14. l. εὐορκοῦσι.   15. l. εὖ εἴη, δὲ τὰ ἐναντία.

330. SWORN DECLARATION CONCERNING
AN EDICT

P. Fay. 24.   A.D. 158.

¹[Ε]ὐδώρῳ στρ(ατηγῷ) Ἀρσι(νοΐτου) Θεμ(ίστου)
²καὶ Πολέμωνος μ[ερίδων παρὰ] ³Πουσείμις Ὀρ-

374

Panomieus son of Akes, Sekoneus son of Patunis, Anchorimphis son of Orseus, Harpagathes son of Nilus, Panomieus son of Harmais, Necches son of Opis, Orseus son of Opis, Patunis son of Orseus, Orseus son of Orseus, Patunis son of Satabous, Pelous son of Patunis, all thirteen being elders of the fishermen of the villages of Narmouthis and Berenicis Thesmophori, swear, all fourteen, to the agents of Sarapion son of Ptolemaeus, nomarch and superintendent of the revenues and the distribution of imposts of the Arsinoite nome, by Tiberius Claudius Caesar Augustus Germanicus Imperator that we never have been or will be privy to fishing or dragging a net or casting a net to catch the images of the divine oxyrhynchi and lepidoti,[a] in conformity with the public engagement signed by us and the other fishermen. If we swear truly, may it be well with us, if falsely, the reverse. The 6th year of Tiberius Claudius Caesar Augustus Germanicus Imperator, Pharmouthi 22.

[a] These fish, which were regarded as sacred animals in certain parts of Egypt, are called images of the deities who assumed their form. In the same way, cats might have been called images of the cat goddess Bastet.

330. SWORN DECLARATION CONCERNING AN EDICT

A.D. 158.

To Eudorus, strategus of the divisions of Themistes and Polemon in the Arsinoite nome, from Pouseimis

σενούφε[ως τοῦ] ⁴Πετεραίπιος ἀρχεφ[όδου ἐποι-]
⁵κίου Δαμᾶ. ὀμ[νύω τὴν] ⁶Αὐτοκράτορος Καίσα[ρος
⁷ᵃΑ]δριανοῦ 'Αντων[ίνου Σεβαστοῦ ⁸Ε]ὐσεβοῦς
τύχην π[ροτεθεικέναι ⁹ἐν] τῷ ἐποικίῳ ἀντίγρ[αφον]
¹⁰ἐπιστολῆς γραφείσης ὑ[πὸ τοῦ ¹¹λα]μπροτάτου
ἡγεμόν[ος] ¹²Σεμπρωνίου Λιβεράλις ¹³περὶ τῶν
ἐπιξένων κατα-¹⁴μενόντων ἐν τῷ ἐποικίῳ ¹⁵ὥστε
αὐτοὺς εἰς τὴν ἰδίαν ἀνέρ-¹⁶χεσθαι, καὶ μηδὲν
διεψεῦσθαι, ¹⁷ἢ ἔνοχος εἴην τῷ ὅρ[κῳ]. ¹⁸Που-
σεῖμις (ἐτῶν) λ οὐλ(ὴ) ποδὶ [ἀ]ριστ(ερῷ). ¹⁹ἐγρ(άφη)
δ(ιὰ) Σα . . . . ς νομο[γ]ρ(άφου) ἐπακο-²⁰λου-
θοῦντος Διοδώρου ὑπηρέ-²¹του, φαμένου μὴ εἰδέναι
γρ(άμματα). ²²(ἔτους) κβ 'Αντωνείνου Καίσαρος
τοῦ ²³κυρίου Φαῶφι λ.

331. SWORN DECLARATION BY AN EGG-SELLER

P. Oxy. 83.   A.D. 327.

¹Φλαουίῳ Θεννύρᾳ λογ(ιστῇ) 'Οξ(υρυγχίτου)
²παρὰ Αὐρηλίου Νίλου Διδύμου ³ἀπὸ τῆς λαμ-
(πρᾶς) καὶ λαμ(προτάτης) 'Οξ(υρυγχιτῶν) πόλεως
⁴ὀπωλοῦ τὴν τέχνην. ⁵ὁμολογῶ ὀμνὺς τὸν σεβάσμιον ⁶θεῖον ὅρκον τῶν δεσποτῶν ⁷ἡμῶν Αὐτο-
κράτορός τε καὶ Καισάρων ⁸τὴν διάπρασίν μοι τῶν
ὀῶν ⁹ποιήσασθαι ἐπὶ τῆς ἀγορᾶς ¹⁰δημοσίᾳ πρὸς
διάπρασιν ¹¹καὶ εὐθενίαν τῆς αὐτῆς ¹²πόλεως
ἡμερησίως ἀδι-¹³αλίπτως καὶ μὴ ἐξῖναί ¹⁴μοι
εἰς τοὐπιὸν κρυβῇ ¹⁵ἢ καὶ ἐν τῇ ἡμετέρᾳ οἰκίᾳ

4. l. ᾠοπώλου.   8. l. με, ᾠῶν.

son of Orsenouphis son of Peteraipis, chief policeman of the hamlet of Damas. I swear by the fortune of the Emperor Caesar Hadrianus Antoninus Augustus Pius that I have set up in the hamlet a copy of the letter written by the most illustrious praefect Sempronius Liberalis [a] ordering strangers staying in the hamlet to return to their own home, and that I have told no falsehood, otherwise may I incur the consequences of the oath. Pouseimis, aged 30, with a scar on the left foot. Written by S . . . ., public scribe, with the concurrence of Diodorus, assistant, Pouseimis professing to be illiterate. The 22nd year of Antoninus Caesar the lord, Phaophi 30.

[a] The edict referred to was issued in A.D. 154, as shown by an extant copy published in B.G.U. 372.

331. SWORN DECLARATION BY AN EGG-SELLER

A.D. 327.

To Flavius Thennyras, logistes of the Oxyrhynchite nome, from Aurelius Nilus son of Didymus, of the illustrious and most illustrious city of Oxyrhynchus, egg-seller by trade. I acknowledge, swearing the august, divine oath by our masters, both Emperor and Caesars, that I am to carry on the retailing of eggs in the market-place publicly, for the supply in retail of the said city, every day without intermission, and that it shall not be lawful for me in the future to sell secretly or in my house. If hereafter I should

377

[16]πωλῖν. εἰ δὲ ὕστερον φα-[17][νε]ίη[ν] ἐν τῇ οἰκίᾳ
μου [18][πωλῶν - - -][24] τῶν λαμ(προτάτων) Τῦβι
κα. (2nd hand) [25][Αὐρ(ήλιος) Ν]ῖλος ὤμοσα τὸν
θῖον [26][ὅρκο]ν ὡς πρόκ(ειται). Αὐρ(ήλιος) Δῖος
[27][ἔγρ(αψα)] ὑπ(ὲρ) αὐτοῦ μὴ εἰδ(ότος) γρ(άμματα).

332. SWORN DECLARATIONS BY GUILDS OF WORKMEN

P. Oxy. 85.   A.D. 338.

(α)

[1]Φλαουίῳ Εὐσεβίῳ λογι-[2]στῇ Ὀξυρυγχείτου
[3]παρὰ τοῦ κοινοῦ τῶν [4]χαλκοκολλητῶν τῆς [5]αὐτῆς
πόλεως (2nd hand) δι᾽ ἐμοῦ [6]Αὐρ(ηλίου) Θωνίου
Μάκρου. (1st hand) [7]προσφωνοῦμεν ἰδίῳ [8]τιμή-
ματι τὴν ἑξῆς [9]ἐγγεγραμμένην τι-[10]μὴν ὧν χιρί-
ζομεν [11]ὠνίων εἶναι ἐπὶ τοῦ-[12]δε τοῦ μηνός, καὶ
ὀμνύ-[13]ομεν τὸν θεῖον ὅρκον [14]μηδὲν διεψεῦσθαι.
[15]ἔστι δέ· [16]χαλκοῦ τοῦ μὲν ἐλα-[17]τοῦ λί(τρας) α
τάλ(αντα) ϛ (δηνάρια) ᾽Α, [18]τοῦ δὲ χυτοῦ λί(τρας)
α τάλ(αντα) δ. [19]ὑπατείας Φλαουίων [20]Οὔρσου
καὶ Πολεμίου [21]τῶν λαμ(προτάτων) ᾽Αθὺρ λ.
(2nd hand) [22]Αὐρήλιος Θώνιος [23]προσφωνῶ ὡς
πρόκιται.

(β)

(1st hand) [1]Φλαουίῳ Εὐσεβίῳ λογι-[2]στῇ [[τ]]
Ὀξυρυγχείτου [3]παρὰ τοῦ κοινοῦ τῶν [4]ζυθοπωλῶν
τῆς α[ὐ-][5]τῆς πόλεως (3rd hand) δι᾽ ἡμ[ῶν] [6]Αὐ-

be detected selling in my house, . . . [In the consulship *a* of . . .] the most illustrious, Tubi 21. (Signed)
I, Aurelius Nilus, have sworn the divine oath as
aforesaid. I, Aurelius Dius, wrote for him, as he is
illiterate.

a With the help of a duplicate copy the names of the consuls may probably be restored as Constantius and Maximus.

332. SWORN DECLARATIONS BY GUILDS
OF WORKMEN

A.D. 338.

(*a*)

To Flavius Eusebius, logistes of the Oxyrhynchite
nome, from the guild of coppersmiths of Oxyrhynchus
through me, Aurelius Thonius son of Macer. We
declare that by our own estimate the price of the
commodities which we handle is as given below for
the present month, and we swear the divine oath that
our statement is correct. The price is : for 1 pound
of malleable copper 6 talents 1000 denarii, and for
1 pound of cast copper 4 talents. In the consulship
of Flavius Ursus and Flavius Polemius the most
illustrious, Hathur 30. I, Aurelius Thonius, make
the foregoing declaration.

(*b*)

To Flavius Eusebius, logistes of the Oxyrhynchite
nome, from the guild of beer-sellers of Oxyrhynchus
through us, Aurelius Salaminus son of Apollo and

379

ρ(ηλίων) Σαλ[α]μῖνος Ἀπολ[λὼ] [7]καὶ [Εὐ]λο[γί]ου
Γελα[. . . .]. (1st hand) [8]προσφωνοῦμ[εν ἰδί-][9]ῳ
τιμ[ή]ματι τ[ὴν ἑξῆς] [10]ἐγγεγραμμ[ένην τι-][11]μὴν
ὧν χιρ[ίζομεν] [12]ὠνίων εἶν[αι ἐπὶ το]ῦ-[13]δε τοῦ
μην[ός, καὶ] ὀ-[14]μνύομεν τὸν [θ]εῖ-[15]ον ὅρκον μηδὲ[ν
δι-][16]εψεῦσθαι. ἔστι [δ]έ· [17]κριθῆς (ἀρτάβης) α
τάλ(αντα) ιγ (δηνάρια) φ. [18]ὑπατείας Φλαουίων
[19]Οὔρσου καὶ Πολεμίου [20]τῶν λαμ(προτάτων) Ἀθὺρ
λ. (3rd hand) [21]Αὐρήλιοι Σαλαμῖν[ος] καὶ [22]Εὐ-
λογίου προσφωνοῦμεν [23]ὡς πρόκ(ειται). Θέων
ἔγρ(αψα) γρ(άμματα) μὴ εἰδ(ότων).

6. *l.* Σαλ[α]μίνου.   22. *l.* Εὐλόγιος.

333. SWORN DECLARATION OF A MARINE SHIPMASTER

P. Oxy. 87.   A.D. 342.

[1]Ὑπατείας τῶν δεσπ[οτῶν ἡμῶν] [2]Κωνσταντίου
τὸ γ̄ καὶ Κώ[νσταντος τὸ β̄] [3]τῶν Αὐγούστων
Φαμενὼ[θ .]. [4]Φλαουίῳ Διονυσαρίῳ λογιστῇ Ὀξ[υ-
ρυγχίτ]ου [5]παρὰ Αὐρηλίου Σαραπίωνος Εὐδαί-
μο[6]νος βουλευτοῦ τῆς αὐτῆς πόλεως ναυ-[7]κλή-
[ρο]υ θαλαττίου ναυκληρίου νυ-[8][ν]ὶ [αἱρ]εθέντος (?).
ἀκολούθως τοῖς κελευ<σ>-[9]θεῖσ[ι ὑ]πὸ τοῦ κυρίου
μου διασημοτάτο(υ) [10]ἡγεμόνος Αὐγουσταμνεικῆς
[11]Φλαουίου Ἰουλίου Αὐσονίου π[ερὶ] [12][τ]οῦ ἡμᾶς
τοὺς ναυκλήρους ἀ[παν-][13]τῆσαι ἐπὶ τὴ[ν] λαμ-
προτ[άτην] [14]Ἀλεξάνδριαν, [κατὰ] ταῦτα νῦν [ὑ]πο-
[15]λόγως ὀμνύω [τὸν] σεβάσμιον [16]θεῖον ὅρκον τῶ[ν]

Aurelius Eulogius son of Gela[. . . .]. We declare that by our own estimate the price of the commodities which we handle is as given below for the present month, and we swear the divine oath that our statement is correct. The price is : for 1 artaba of barley[a] 13 talents 500 denarii. In the consulship of Flavius Ursus and Flavius Polemius the most illustrious, Hathur 30. We, Aurelius Salaminus and Aurelius Eulogius, make the foregoing declaration. Written by me, Theon, as they are illiterate.

[a] The price is probably that of an artaba of barley when brewed. The declarations imply that the prices of various goods were subject to some official control. Compare the Ptolemaic regulations in No. 204.

333. SWORN DECLARATION OF A MARINE SHIPMASTER

A.D. 342.

In the consulship of our masters Constantius Augustus for the 3rd time and Constans Augustus for the 2nd time, Phamenoth . . . To Flavius Dionysarius, logistes of the Oxyrhynchite nome, from Aurelius Sarapion son of Eudaemon, senator of Oxyrhynchus, shipmaster of a sea-going ship now called up (?). In conformity with the command of my lord the most eminent *praeses* of Augustamnica,[a] Flavius Julius Ausonius, to the effect that we shipmasters should present ourselves in the most illustrious city of Alexandria, I now accordingly swear under responsibility the august, divine oath by our masters the

[a] One of the main districts into which Egypt was at this time divided for administrative purposes.

δεσποτῶν ¹⁷ἡμῶν Αὐγούστων ἀπαντῆσαι ¹⁸ἅμα τοῖς
εἰς τοῦτο{ν} ἀποσταλί[σ]ι ¹⁹[ὀ]φ(φικιαλίοις) ὑπα-
κούοντα ἐν πᾶσι τοῖς πρός ²⁰με ζητουμένοις περὶ
τοῦ ναυκλη-²¹ρίου καὶ μηδὲν διεψεῦσθαι. (2nd
hand) ²²[Α]ὐρήλιος Σαραπίων ὤμοσα ²³[τ]ὸν θῖον
ὅρκον ὡς πρόκ(ειται).

334. NOTIFICATION OF A ROBBERY

P. Gurob 8.   210 b.c.

¹(Ἔτους) ιβ Ἐπεὶφ ι. ὑπ(όμνημα) Τεῶι βα-
(σιλικῶι) γρ(αμματεῖ). ²[Ἀ]μῶσις κωμογραμματεὺς Ἀπολλωνιάδος Τεῶι χαίρειν. ³[το]ῦ δοθέν-
τος ἡμῖν προσαγγέλματος παρ' Ἡρακῶντος τοῦ
προεστη[κ]ότο[ς ⁴τ]ῶν Πειθολάου ὑποτέθεικά σοι
τὸ ἀντίγραφον ὅπως εἰδῆς. ⁵ἔρρωσο. ιβ Ἐπεὶφ θ.

⁶[Π]ροσ[ά]γγελμα Ἀμώσει κωμογραμματεῖ κώμης Ἀπολλωνιάδος π[αρὰ ⁷Ἡ]ρακ[ῶ]ντος τοῦ προ-
εστηκότος τῶν Πειθολάου. ἐπελθόντες [τῆι .
⁸το]ῦ Ἐ[π]εὶφ ἐπὶ τὸν παράδεισον τοῦ προγεγραμ-
μένου Πειθολάου ὄ[ντα] ⁹περὶ τὴν προγεγραμ-
μένην κώμην Θεόφιλος Δωσιθέου, Φιλιστίων
[. . . .] ¹⁰καὶ Τιμαῖος Τελούφιος οἱ τρεῖς Ἰουδαῖοι
τῆς ἐπιγονῆς ἐξετρύγησ[αν] ¹¹ἀμ[π]έλους ῑ καὶ
Ὥρου τοῦ φύλακος ἐκδραμόντος ἐπ' αὐτοὺς
κακ[οποή-]¹²σα[ν]τες αὐτὸν ἔτυπτον εἰς ὃ ἔτυχον
μέρος τοῦ σώματος καὶ ἀφεί[λον-]¹³το [ἀμ]πελουρ-
γικὸν δρέπανον. τυγχάνουσι δὲ οἱ προγεγραμ-

---

1. This line is superscribed in a different hand.

Augusti that I will present myself in the company of the attendants who have been sent for this purpose, answering to all the inquiries to which I shall be subjected concerning the ship, and that I have told no falsehood. (Signed) I, Aurelius Sarapion, have sworn the divine oath as aforesaid.

334. NOTIFICATION OF A ROBBERY

210 b.c.

Year 12, Epeiph 10. Memorandum to Teos the royal scribe. Amosis, village scribe of Apollonias,[a] to Teos greeting. I subjoin for your information a copy of the notification presented to me by Heracon the superintendent of the estate of Pitholaus.[b] Goodbye. (Year) 12, Epeiph 9.

Notification to Amosis, scribe of the village of Apollonias, from Heracon, superintendent of the estate of Pitholaus. On the . . . of Epeiph Theophilus son of Dositheus, Philistion son of . . ., and Timaeus son of Telouphis, all three Jews of the Epigone, raided the fruit-garden of the aforesaid Pitholaus, which is in the bounds of the aforesaid village, and stripped the grapes from ten vines ; and when Horus the guard ran out against them, they maltreated him and struck him on any part of the body that offered ; and they carried off a vine-dresser's pruning-hook. The aforesaid robbers are

[a] A village in the Fayum.
[b] Probably the commander of the elephant hunters mentioned in *P. Eleph.* 28. 4, and identified by Rostovtzeff with the Pytholaus of Strabo xvi. 4. 14.

μένοι λῃσ[ταὶ ἐν] ¹⁴Κε[ρ]κεοσίρει κατοικοῦντες.
ἱκάζω δὲ τὰ τετρυγημένα εἰς οἴνου με(τρητὰς) ϛ.
Verso: ¹⁵⁻¹⁶βα(σιλικῶι) γρ(αμματεῖ). (ἔτους) ιβ
Ἐπεὶφ ι. περὶ ἀμ(πελῶνος) Πειθολάου τετρυ-
¹⁷γημένου.

335. POLICE REPORT

P. Tebt. 730, ll. 1-6.   178 or 167 B.C.

¹(Ἔτους) δ ʽΑθὺρ ϛ. ²ʾΟσοροήρει βα(σιλικῶι)
γρ(αμματεῖ). τῆι ε τοῦ ἐνεστῶτος μη(νὸς) ἐφ-
οδεύων ³τὰ περὶ τὴν κώ(μην) πέδια εὗρον ⟦αἵματος⟧
ἔκχυσιν αἵμα[τος] ⁴⟦σῶμα δὲ μὴ ὄν⟧, πυνθάνομαι
δὲ τῶν ἐκ τῆς κώμη[ς] ⁵Θεόδοτον Δωσιθέου ἐξελ-
θόντα ὡς ἐπὶ ταῦτα ⁶μηκέτ᾽ ἐπιστρέψαι. ἀναφέρω.

336. NOTIFICATION OF A SUSPECTED MURDER

P. Tebt. 333.   A.D. 216.

¹Αὐρηλίῳ [ʾΙ]ουλίῳ Μαρκελλίνῳ (ἑκατοντάρ)χ(ῃ)
²παρὰ Αὐρηλίας Τισάιτος μητρὸς ³Τάεως προ-
χρηματισάσης ἀπὸ ⁴κώμης Τεπτύνεως τῆς Πολέμω-
⁵νος μερίδος. τοῦ πατρός μου, κύριε, ⁶Καλα-
βάλεως κυνηγοῦ τυγχάνοντος ⁷ἀποδημήσαντος σὺν
τῷ ἀδελφῷ ⁸μου Νείλῳ ἔτι ἀπὸ τῆς γ τοῦ ὄντος
⁹μηνὸς πρὸς κυνηγίαν λαγῶν ¹⁰μέχρι τούτ[ο]υ οὐκ

384

living in Kerkeosiris. I estimate the grapes gathered as enough to make 6 metretae of wine. (Endorsed) To the royal scribe. Year 12, Epeiph 10. Concerning a vineyard of Pitholaus stripped of its grapes.

335. POLICE REPORT

178 or 167 B.C.

4th year, Hathur 6. To Osoroeris, royal scribe. On the 5th of the present month when patrolling the fields near the village I found an effusion of blood (deleted : but no body), and I learn from the villagers that Theodotus son of Dositheus, having set out in that direction, has not yet returned. I make this report.

336. NOTIFICATION OF A SUSPECTED MURDER

A.D. 216.

To Aurelius Julius Marcellinus, centurion, from Aurelia Tisais, whose mother is Tais, formerly styled as an inhabitant of the village of Tebtunis in the division of Polemon. My father Kalabalis, Sir, who is a hunter, left home with my brother Nilus as long ago as the 3rd of the present month to hunt hares,

ἐπανῆλθαν. ὑφορῶ-[11]μαι οὖν μὴ ἔπαθάν τι ἀν-
θρώπινον. [12]ἐπιδίδωμι αὐτὸ τοῦτο φανερόν σοι
[13]ποιοῦσα πρὸς τὸ ἐὰν ᾖσάν τι παθόντες [14]ἀνθρώ-
π[ι]νον μένιν [μ]οι τὸν λόγον [15][π]ρὸς τοὺ[ς] φανη-
σο[μέ]νους αἰτίους. (2nd hand) [16][τ]υγχάνω δ[ὲ
τ]ούτων τὸ [ἴσον] ἐπιδοῦσα [17]κὲ τῷ στρα(τηγῷ)
[Α]ὐρηλίῳ Ἰδιο[μ]άχῳ (?) πρὸς [18]τὸ ἐν κατα-
χ[ωρ]ισμῷ γενέ[σ]θαι. (1st hand) [19][(ἔτους)] κε
Μάρκου Αὐρηλίου [Σ]εουήρου [20]Ἀντωνείνου Καίσαρος το[ῦ] κυρίου Χύακ [21]κϛ.

17. l. καί.   20. l. Χοίακ.

337. REPORT OF AN ACCIDENT

P. Oxy. 475.   A.D. 182.

[1]Ἱέραξ στρατηγὸς Ὀξυρυγχείτου Κλαυ-[2]δίῳ
Σερήνῳ ὑπηρέτῃ. τῶν δοθέν-[3]των μοι βιβλιδί[ω]ν
ὑ[π]ὸ Λεωνίδου [4]το[ῦ] κ(αὶ) Σερήνου τὸ ἴσον
ἐπεστέλλεταί σοι, [5]ὅπως παραλαβὼν δημόσιον
ἰατρὸν [6]ἐπ[ι]θεωρήσῃς τὸ δηλούμενον νε-[7]κρὸν
σῶμα καὶ παραδοὺς εἰς κηδεί-[8]αν ἐγγράφως ἀπο-
φάσεις προσφω-[9]νήσητε. (2nd hand) σεσ[η]-
μ(είωμαι). (1st hand) [10](ἔτους) κγ [Μ]άρκου
Αὐρηλίου Κομμόδου [11]Ἀντωνίνου Καίσαρος τοῦ
κυρίου [12]Ἀθὺρ ζ.

(3rd hand) [13]Ἱέρακι στρα(τηγῷ) [14]παρὰ Λεωνίδου
τοῦ καὶ [Σερήνου χ]ρη-[15]ματίζοντος μητρὸς Ταύ-
ριο[ς] ἀπὸ Σε-[16]νέπτα. ὀψ[ί]ας τῆς διελθούσ[ης]

4. l. ἐπιστέλλεται.   8. Or ἐγγράφους.

386

and up to this time they have not returned. I therefore suspect that they have come to a fatal end, and I present this statement, making the matter known to you, in order that, if they have come to a fatal end, the persons found guilty may be held accountable to me. I have also presented a copy of this notice to the strategus Aurelius Idiomachus (?) to be placed on record. The 25th year of Marcus Aurelius Severus Antoninus Caesar the lord, Choiak 26.

337. REPORT OF AN ACCIDENT

A.D. 182.

Hierax, strategus of the Oxyrhynchite nome, to Claudius Serenus, assistant. A copy of the application which has been presented to me by Leonidas also called Serenus is herewith sent to you, in order that you may take a public physician and inspect the dead body referred to and after delivering it over for burial make with him a report in writing. Signed by me. The 23rd year of Marcus Aurelius Commodus Antoninus Caesar the lord, Hathur 7.

To Hierax, strategus, from Leonidas also called Serenus, styled as having Tauris for mother, of Senepta.[a] At a late hour of yesterday the sixth,

[a] A village in the Oxyrhynchite nome.

ἔκ‹τ›ης ¹⁷ἑορτῆς οὔσης ἐν τῇ Σενέ[πτα καὶ κρο-]
¹⁸ταλιστρίδων λειτουργου[σῶν κατὰ τὸ] ¹⁹ἔθος πρὸς
οἰκίᾳ Πλουτίωνος τοῦ [γαμ-]²⁰βροῦ μου . . . [.]
. . . . . τοδήμου ²¹’Επαφρόδειτος δοῦλος αὐτοῦ
ὡς ²²(ἐτῶν) η βουληθεὶς ἀπὸ τοῦ δώματος ²³τῆς
αὐτῆς οἰκίας παρακύψαι καὶ ²⁴θεάσασθαι τὰς
[κρο]ταλιστρίδας ²⁵ἔπεσεν καὶ ἐτελε[ύ]τησεν. οὗ
χά-²⁶ριν ἐπιδιδοὺς τὸ βιβλείδιον [ἀξ]ιῶ, ²⁷ἐὰν δόξῃ
σοι, ἀποτάξαι ἕνα τῶν περὶ ²⁸σὲ ὑπηρετῶν εἰς τὴν
Σενέπτα, ²⁹ὅπως τὸ τοῦ ’Επαφροδείτου σῶμα
³⁰τύχῃ τῆς δεούσης περιστολ[ῆς] καὶ ³¹καταθέσεως.
(ἔτους) κγ Αὐτοκράτορος ³²Καίσαρος Μάρκου
Αὐρηλίου Κομμόδου ’Αντωνίνου ³³Σεβαστοῦ ’Αρ-
μενιακοῦ Μηδικοῦ Παρθικοῦ ³⁴Σαρματικοῦ Γερμανικοῦ Μεγίστου ‘Αθὺρ ζ. ³⁵Λεωνίδης ὁ καὶ
Σερῆνος ἐπι[δ]έδωκα.

338. REPORT ON AN APPLICATION FOR CIRCUMCISION

P. Tebt. 293.   About A.D. 187.

¹Παρὰ Κρονίωνος Πακήβκεως τοῦ ‘Αρπο-
²κρατίωνος διαδόχου προφητείας καὶ ³Μάρωνος
Κρονίωνος τοῦ ‘Αρποκρατίωνο[ς] ⁴καὶ Μάρωνος
Μάρωνος τοῦ Μαρεψήμεως ⁵καὶ Πακήβκεως Κρονίωνος τοῦ Ψύφεως ⁶τῶν γ ἱερέων τῶν δ ἱεροῦ
λογίμ[ο]υ ἀπο-⁷λυσίμου κώμης Τεπτύνεως. πρὸς
τὸ ⁸ἐπιδοθέν σοι βιβλείδιον ὑπὸ Μαρεψήμε-⁹ως
Μαρσισούχου τοῦ ‘Αρποκρατίωνος ¹⁰ἱερέως τοῦ

5. l. Ψοίφεως.

while a festival was taking place at Senepta and
castanet-dancers were giving the customary performance at the house of Plution my son-in-law . . .,
his slave Epaphroditus, aged about 8 years, wishing
to lean out from the house-top of the said house and
see the castanet-dancers, fell and was killed. I therefore present this application and request you, if it
please you, to appoint one of your assistants to come
to Senepta, in order that the body of Epaphroditus
may receive the necessary laying out and burial.
The 23rd year of the Emperor Caesar Marcus Aurelius
Commodus Antoninus Augustus Armeniacus Medicus
Parthicus Sarmaticus Germanicus Maximus, Hathur
7. Presented by me, Leonidas also called Serenus.

338. REPORT ON AN APPLICATION FOR
CIRCUMCISION

About A.D. 187.

From Cronion son of Pakebkis son of Harpocration,
deputy prophet,[a] and from Maron son of Cronion son
of Harpocration, and Maron son of Maron son of
Marepsemis, and Pakebkis son of Cronion son of
Psoiphis, all three priests, all four from the famous
exempted temple [b] of the village of Tebtunis. With
regard to the application presented to you by
Marepsemis son of Marsisouchus son of Harpocra-

[a] Acting as prophet, an important member of the priesthood.
[b] That is, the members of the temple were exempt from
the poll-tax and some other burdens.

αὐτοῦ ἱεροῦ ἀξιοῦντος τὸν ¹¹υἱὸν αὐτοῦ Πανῆ[σ]ιν
μητρὸς Θενπα-¹²[κήβ]κεως τῆς Πανή[σ]εως περι-
τμηθῆ-¹³[ναι, ἐ]πιζητοῦντί σοι εἰ ἔστιν ἱ[ερα]τικοῦ
¹⁴[γέ]νους καὶ ὀφείλει{ν} περιτμη[θῆνα]ι προσ-
¹⁵φων[ο]ῦ[με]ν ὀμνύοντες τὴν Μάρκου ¹⁶Αὐρηλίου
Κομμόδου Ἀντωνίνου Σεβαστοῦ ¹⁷[τ]ύχην ἀληθῆ
εἶναι αὐτὸν ἱερατικοῦ ¹⁸[γέ]νους καὶ τὰς παρα-
τεθείσας ὑπὸ αὐτο(ῦ) ¹⁹[ἀσ]φα[λ]είας εἶναι καὶ δεῖν
αὐτὸν περι-²⁰[τμη]θῆναι διὰ [τ]ὸ μὴ δύνασθαι τὰς
ἱε-²¹[ρου]ργίας ἐκτελεῖν εἰ μὴ τοῦτ[ο γενήσε-²²τα]ι,
ἢ ἔνοχοι εἴημ[εν] τῷ ὅρκῳ. Κρονί-²³ων Πακήβ-
κεω[ς] ὤμοσα τὸν προκεί-²⁴μενον ὅρκον κ[α]θὼς
πρόκειται. (2nd hand) Μά-²⁵[ρ]ων Μάρωνος συν-
ομόμεχα ὡς ²⁶[π]ρόκιται. (3rd hand) Μάρων
Κρονίωνος συν-²⁷ομόμεχα ὡ[ς] πρώκιται.

25. l. συνομώμοκα ; so in 26.   27. l. πρόκειται.

tion, priest of the said temple, requesting that his son Panesis by Thenpakebkis daughter of Panesis should be circumcised,[a] in reply to your inquiry whether he is of priestly descent and ought to be circumcised we declare, swearing by the fortune of Marcus Aurelius Commodus Antoninus Augustus, that he is in truth of priestly descent and that the vouchers submitted by him are genuine and that it is necessary for him to be circumcised because he cannot perform the sacred offices unless this is done ; otherwise may we incur the consequences of the oath. I, Cronion son of Pakebkis, have sworn the above oath, as aforesaid. I, Maron son of Maron, have also sworn, as aforesaid. I, Maron son of Cronion, have also sworn, as aforesaid.

[a] Before being admitted to the Egyptian priesthood a candidate had to be circumcised by permission of the high priest, after examination of his credentials. See No. 244.

IX. NOMINATIONS AND APPOINTMENTS

339. APPOINTMENT OF A VILLAGE SCRIBE

P. Tebt. 10.   119 B.C.

¹Ἀσκληπιάδης Μαρρεῖ χαίρειν. Μεγχῆι τῶι ὑπὸ
τοῦ διοικητοῦ ²καθεσταμένωι πρὸς τῆι κωμογραμ-
ματείαι Κερκεοσίρεως ἐφ' ὧι κατεργᾶται ³τοῖς
ἰδίοις ἀνηλώμασιν ἀπὸ τῆς ἀναφερομένης περὶ τὴν
κώμην ⁴ἐν ὑπολόγωι γῆς (ἀρούρας) δέκα (ἀρταβῶν)
πεντήκοντα, ἃς καὶ παραδώσει ⁵ἀπὸ τοῦ νβ (ἔτους)
εἰς τὸ βασιλικὸν κατ' ἐνιαυτὸν ἐκ πλήρους ἢ τὰ
ἀπολείψοντα ⁶ἐκ τοῦ ἰδίου μετρήσει, μετά[δ]ος τὰ
τῆς χρείας γράμματα καὶ φρόντισον ⁷ὡς τὰ τῆς
ὑποσχέσεως ἐκπληρωθήσεται. ⁸ἔρρωσο. (ἔτους)
να Μεσορὴ γ.

Verso: τοπογρ(αμματεῖ) Μαρρεῖ.

IX. NOMINATIONS AND APPOINTMENTS

339. APPOINTMENT OF A VILLAGE SCRIBE

119 B.C.

Asclepiades to Marres greeting. Menches having been appointed by the dioecetes to the village secretaryship of Kerkeosiris on the understanding that he shall cultivate at his own expense ten arurae of the land in the area of the village which has been reported as unproductive at a rent of fifty artabae,[a] which he shall deliver annually from the 52nd year to the Crown in full or else make up the deficiency from his private means, give to him the papers of his office and take care that the terms of his undertaking are fulfilled. Goodbye. Year 51, Mesore 3. (Addressed) To Marres, district secretary.

[a] As the rent was high, this seems to have been a premium for the privilege of holding the office.

340. LETTER OF APPOINTMENT TO OFFICE

B.G.U. 362, col. 5, ll. 1-18.   A.D. 215.

¹Ἀ[γαθῇ τύχῃ. θεοὶ] σωτήριοι. [Πτολεμαι-]
²έω[ν Ἀρσιν]οϊ[τ]ῶν ἄ[ρ]χ[ο]ντες βουλὴ [Αὐρηλίῳ]
³Σ[ερήνῳ τ]ῷ καὶ Ἰσιδώρῳ κοσμ(ητεύσαντι)
βου[λ(ευτῇ) τῷ] φιλ-⁴τά[τῳ] χα[ίρ]ειν. ⁵εἰς ἐπι-
μ[έλεια]ν τῶν προσηκόντων τῷ πα[ρ]' ἡμεῖν
⁶θεῷ Διεὶ Κα[πι]τωλίῳ εἰλάμεθα σέ. ἵν' οὖν
εἰδῇς, ᾿φίλτατε, κα[ὶ] μετὰ πάσης πίστεως καὶ
ἐ[π]ιμελεί-⁸ας ἔχῃ τ[ῶν ἐ]νκεχειρισμένων, πρὸ
ὀφθαλμῶν ⁹θέμενος [τ]ὰ κελευσθέντα ὑπὸ Αὐρη-
[λίου] Ἰταλικοῦ ¹⁰τοῦ κρατίστ[ο]υ ἐπιτρόπου τῶν
οὐσιακῶ[ν] διαδεχομ(ένου) ¹¹[τὴ]ν ἀρχιερ[ωσ]ύνην,
ἐπιστέλλομεν σοί. ¹²ἐρρῶσθαί σε εὐχόμεθα, φίλτατε. ¹³διὰ Αὐρη[λίου] Ἡρακ]λείδου τοῦ καὶ
Ἀγαθοῦ Δαί[μονος ἀρ-]¹⁴χιερατεύσ[αν]τος ἐνάρχου
πρυτάνεως [. . . . .] ¹⁵(ἔτους) κγ″ Α[ὐ]τ[οκρ]ά-
τορος Καίσαρος Μάρκου Αὐρηλ[ίου] ¹⁶Σεουήρου
[Ἀντ]ωνίνου Παρθικοῦ Μεγίστου [Βρεταννικοῦ]
¹⁷Μεγί[στου Γερμα]νικοῦ Μεγίστου Εὐσεβοῦς [Εὐ-
τυχοῦς Σεβ(αστοῦ)] ¹⁸Τῦβι.

1-2. Suppl. Martin.

340. LETTER OF APPOINTMENT TO OFFICE

A.D. 215.

For good fortune. Saviour gods ! The magistrates and senate of the Arsinoite Ptolemais [a] to their dearest Aurelius Serenus also called Isidorus, ex-cosmetes, senator, greeting. We have chosen you to take charge of the interests of our god Jupiter Capitolinus.[b] In order therefore that you may be informed, most dear Sir, and attend with all faithfulness and care to the duties entrusted to you, keeping before your eyes the orders of his excellency Aurelius Italicus, procurator of the Imperial estates and deputy chief priest,[c] we send you this notification. We pray for your health, most dear Sir. Sent through Aurelius Heraclides also called Agathodaemon, formerly chief priest,[d] prytanis in office. The 23rd year of the Emperor Caesar Marcus Aurelius Severus Antoninus Parthicus Maximus Britannicus Maximus Germanicus Maximus Pius Felix Augustus, Tubi.

[a] The city which we usually call Arsinoe, capital of the Arsinoite nome.
[b] The cult of this Roman god is thought to have been introduced into Egypt at the time when Caracalla extended the Roman citizenship to all inhabitants above a certain status.
[c] The Alexandrian chief priest of all Egypt.
[d] Local chief priest of Arsinoe, a municipal magistrate.

SELECT PAPYRI

341. APPOINTMENT OF A DEPUTY-PRYTANIS

P. Oxy. 1662.   A.D. 246.

¹Αὐρήλιος Βίων ὁ καὶ ᾿Αμμώ-²νιος γυμνασίαρχος
βουλευτὴς ³ἔναρχος πρύτανις τῆς ᾿Οξυρυγ-⁴χιτῶν
πόλεως Αὐρηλίῳ ⁵Δίῳ τῷ καὶ Περτίνακι στρα-
⁶τηγῷ τοῦ αὐτοῦ νομοῦ ⁷τῷ φιλτάτῳ χαίρειν.
⁸ἐξιὼν ἅμα ἄλλοις ἐπὶ τὸν ⁹λαμπρότατον ἡμῶν
¹⁰ἡγεμόνα Οὐαλέριον ¹¹Φίρμον ἕνεκεν πρεσβεί[[ς]]-
¹²ας περὶ τῆς ἐπιβληθείσης ¹³ἐπιβολῆς τῷ ἡμετέρῳ
¹⁴νομῷ τοῦ ἱεροῦ ἀποτάκτου, ¹⁵ἐπιστέλλω σοι,
φίλτατε, ¹⁶ὅπως φανερὸν ποιή-¹⁷σῃς Αὐρηλίῳ
᾿Ισιδώρῳ ¹⁸ἀρχιερατεύσαντι βουλευ-¹⁹τῇ εἰρηνάρχῳ
διαδέξα-²⁰σθαί με τὰ τῇ πρυτανίᾳ δια-²¹φέροντα,
ἔστ᾿ ἂν ἐπανέλ-²²θω.   (2nd hand) ²³ἐρρῶσθαί σε
εὔχομαι, φίλ(τατε).   (3rd hand) ²³(ἔτους) γ Αὐτοκράτορος Κα[ίσαρος] ²⁴Μάρκου ᾿Ιουλίου Φιλίπ-
πο[υ] ²⁵Εὐσεβοῦς Εὐτυχοῦς καὶ Μάρκου ²⁶᾿Ιουλίου
Φιλίππου γενναιοτάτ[ο]υ ²⁷καὶ ἐπιφανεστάτου
Καίσαρος ²⁸Σεβαστῶν ᾿Επεὶφ κγ.

342. APPOINTMENT TO A COMPULSORY OFFICE

B.G.U. 18.   A.D. 169.

¹᾿Αντίγραφον προγράμματος.   Σερ[ῆ]νος βα-
σιλ(ικὸς) ²γραμματεὺς ᾿Αρσι(νοΐτου) ῾Ηρακλείδου
μερίδος ³διαδεχόμενος τὰ κατὰ τὴν στρατηγίαν.
⁴εἰς τὸ συντιμήσασθαι τὰ ἐν ἀπράτοις ὑπάρχοντα
396

341. APPOINTMENT OF A DEPUTY-PRYTANIS

A.D. 246.

Aurelius Bion also called Ammonius, gymnasiarch, senator, and prytanis in office of the city of Oxyrhynchus, to his dearest Aurelius Dius also called Pertinax, strategus of the Oxyrhynchite nome, greeting. Since I am leaving with others to meet our most illustrious praefect Valerius Firmus on a deputation concerning the quota of the Imperial assessment imposed upon our nome, I beg you, dearest friend, to inform Aurelius Isidorus, ex-chief priest, senator, and irenarch, that he is to act as my deputy in the office of prytanis, until I return. I pray for your health, most dear friend. The 3rd year of the Emperor Caesar Marcus Julius Philippus Pius Felix and Marcus Julius Philippus the most noble and eminent Caesar, Augusti, Epeiph 23.

342. APPOINTMENT TO A COMPULSORY OFFICE

A.D. 169.

Copy of announcement. Serenus, royal scribe of the division of Heraclides in the Arsinoite nome, acting as strategus. To be assessors of unsold lands,[a]

---

[a] Government land for which no purchaser or lessee had been found.

397

⁵ἀντὶ Γαΐου Ἰουλίου Πτόλλιδος καὶ Ἀμ[α]ράντου
⁶Ἑστιαίου καὶ Ἥρωνος ἐπικαλουμέν[ο]υ Εὐδαίμονος καὶ Διοδώρου Θεογείτον[ο]ς ⁸τῶν δ πε-
πληρωκότων τὸν ὡρισ[μ]ένον ⁹χ[ρ]όνον καὶ Ἀνου-
βίωνος Ἥρωνος καὶ Δημητρίου ¹⁰Σουχάμμωνος
τῶν δύο δηλωθέν[τ]ων τε[τ]ε-¹¹λευτηκέναι ἀνεδό-
θησαν οἱ ὑπογεγραμμέ-¹²νο[ι] ὑπὸ τῶν τῆς πόλεως
γραμματέ[ω]ν ὡς ¹³εὔ[π]οροι καὶ ἐπιτήδιοι [εἰ]ς
δημόσ[ια]. παραγ[γ]έλ‹λ›εται ¹⁴ἀντιλαμβάνεσθαι
τῆς ἐνχιρισθίσης α[ὐ]τοῖς ¹⁵χρε[ία]ς ὑγιῶς καὶ
πιστῶς εἰς τὸ ἐν μηδενὶ ¹⁶με[μ]φθῆναι. σεσημίωμαι.
(ἔτους) θ Αὐρηλί[ο]υ ¹⁷Ἀντωνί{νι}νου Καίσα[ρ]ος
τοῦ κυρί[ο]υ Ἀρμ[εν]ιακοῦ ¹⁸Μηδικοῦ Πα[ρθ]ικοῦ
Μεγίστου [Μ]ε[σορ]ὴ ιζ̅. ¹⁹ἔστι δέ· Γάιος Ἰούλιος
Ἀπολινάριος γεουχῶν ²⁰ἐν Καρανίδι ἔχων πόρον
(δραχμὰς) Ἀ. ²¹Μύσθης Κορνηλίου γεουχῶν ἐν
Πτολεμαΐδι ²²Νέᾳ ἔχων πόρον (τάλαντον) α. ²³Ἀν-
τώ[ν]ιος Ἡρακλιανὸς γεουχῶν ἐν τῷ ²⁴Νέστου
ὁμοίως (δραχμὰς) Ἀ. ²⁵Γάιος Ἰούλιος Σατορνεῖ-
λος γεουχ[ῶν] ἐν Τάνι ²⁶ἔχων πόρον (δραχμὰς) Ἀ.
²⁷Πτολεμαῖος καὶ ὡς χρηματίζει νομογρ(άφος)
Φα[ρ]βαίθων ²⁸ἔχων πόρον (δραχμὰς) Ἀ. ²⁹Πασίων
Πετερμούθεως τοῦ Πετερμούθεως ³⁰ἀ[π]ὸ Ἑλ-
ληνίου ἔχων πόρον (δραχμὰς) Ἀ. ³¹Ἥρων [ὑ]π-
ηρέτης ἀποτα[γεὶ]ς κατεχώ(ρισα) Μ[εσο]ρὴ κ̅.

342. NOMINATIONS AND APPOINTMENTS

in place of Gaius Julius Ptollis, Amarantus son of Hestiaeus, Heron surnamed Eudaemon, and Diodorus son of Theogeiton, who have all four completed the prescribed period, and of Anubion son of Heron and Demetrius son of Souchammon, both stated to be deceased, the underwritten persons have been nominated by the scribes of the city as well-to-do and suitable for public duties. They are ordered to take up the task entrusted to them honestly and faithfully so as not to incur blame in any respect. Signed by me. The 9th year of Aurelius Antoninus Caesar the lord Armeniacus Medicus Parthicus Maximus, Mesore 17. The list is : Gaius Julius Apollinarius owning land at Karanis,[a] having property worth 4000 drachmae ; Mysthes son of Cornelius owning land at Ptolemais Nea, having property worth 1 talent ; Antonius Heraclianus owning land at the hamlet of Nestus, likewise worth 4000 drachmae ; Gaius Julius Saturnilus owning land at Tanis, having property worth 4000 drachmae ; Ptolemaeus, however he is styled, public scribe of Pharbaetha, having property worth 4000 drachmae ; Pasion son of Petermouthis son of Petermouthis, of the Hellenion quarter,[b] having property worth 4000 drachmae. Registered by me, Heron, special assistant, Mesore 20.

[a] This and the other villages mentioned were in the Fayum.
[b] In Arsinoe.

SELECT PAPYRI

343. NOMINATION FOR COMPULSORY SERVICES

P. Ryl. 90, ll. 30-56.   Early 3rd cent. A.D.

³⁰[Δίδομεν καὶ εἰσαγγέλλομεν τοὺ]ς ἑξῆς ³¹[ἐγγε]-
γρ[αμ]μένους χρεία[ς τ]οῦ ἔτους πλη[ρ]ώ[σο]ντας
εὐπόρους ³²[κ]αὶ ἐπιτηδείους τῶν ἡμῶν κινδύνων.
ἔστι δέ· Κυνῶν ³³πόλεως. εἰς δὲ ἀναψ[ησμ]οὺς
διο[ρ]ύχων ³⁴[Γ]ίκων Διοδώρο[υ] ὡς (ἐτῶν) μς ἔχων
πόρων (δραχμὰς) χ. ³⁵καὶ εἰς γενηματοφυλ(ακίαν)
οἱ κα[ὶ] π[ρ]οανα[[..]]τοθέντος ⟨ἐπί⟩ τε λειμνασμοῦ
³⁶καὶ ἀρδείας καὶ κατ[α]σπορᾶς καὶ τῶν ἄ[λλ]ων
δημο[σ]ίων ³⁷πάντων Πάτρων ἀπάτωρ μη(τρὸς)
Προτο[ῦ]τος ὡς (ἐτῶν) λ ἔχων πόρο(ν) (δραχμὰς)
Ἀ, ³⁸Ἀφροδᾶς Νεφερῶτος ὡς (ἐτῶν) με ἔχων
πόρων ἐν οἰ(κοπέδοις) (δραχμὰς) Ἀ. ³⁹καὶ εἰς
ἁλωνοφυλακίαν Ἑκῦσις Σανπᾶτος ὡς (ἐτῶν) κε
ἔχω(ν) [(δραχμὰς) χ], ⁴⁰Λάτρων Ἀνουβᾶ ὁμοίω[ς]
(δραχμὰς) χ. καὶ εἰς τὸ πρόνοιαν {ον} ποιήσασ-
⁴¹θαι τ[οῦ] καθαρὸν εἶναι καὶ ἄδωλον τοῦ μετρου-
μένου δημοσίου ⁴²πυροῦ Ἀνουβᾶς Νεφερῶτος ὡς
(ἐτῶν) μ ἔχων πό(ρον) ἐν οἰ(κοπέδοις) (δραχμὰς)
χ, ⁴³Πετε[[..]]νοῦφις Μαξίμου ὁμοί(ως) (δραχμὰς) χ.
καὶ εἰς τὸ προστῆναι ⁴⁴τοῖς δημοσίοις {δη[μοσ]ί[ο]ις}
⟨θησαυροῖς⟩ καὶ συνσφραγίζιν ἅμα τοῖς ⁴⁵σιτο-
λόγοις Πετενοῦφις Σαραπίωνος ὡς (ἐτῶν) λε ἔχ(ων)
(δραχμὰς) Ἀ, ⁴⁶Ἥρων Ἥρωνος ὡς (ἐτῶν) λε
ὁμοίως (δραχμὰς) Ἀ. καὶ εἰς φυλαγείας τῆς

32. l. τῷ ἡμῶν κινδύνῳ.   33. l. διω[ρ]ύχων.   34. l.
πόρον; so in l. 38.   35. l. π[ρ]οαναδοθέντες.   37. l.
Πρωτο[ῦ]τος.   46. l. φυλακίαν.

343. NOMINATION FOR COMPULSORY
SERVICES

Early 3rd cent. A.D.

We [a] present and report at our own risk the persons
mentioned below, being well-to-do and suitable, for
the performance of the services of the year. They
are as follows. For Cynopolis : for the cleaning of
canals Gikon son of Diodorus, aged about 46 years,
having property worth 600 drachmae ; for the guarding of crops the persons previously nominated to
superintend flooding, watering, sowing, and all other
public works, Patron, without patronymic, his mother
being Protous, aged about 30, having property worth
1000 drachmae, Aphrodas son of Nepheros, aged
about 45, having house-sites worth 1000 drachmae ;
and for the guarding of threshing-floors Hekusis son
of Sanpas, aged about 25, having property worth
600 drachmae, Latron son of Anoubas, having similarly 600 drachmae ; and for taking care that the
government wheat when delivered is pure and unadulterated Anoubas son of Nepheros, aged about
40, having house-sites worth 600 drachmae, Petenouphis son of Maximus, having similarly 600 drachmae ;
and for taking charge of the public granaries and
sealing (receipts ?) along with the sitologi Petenouphis
son of Sarapion, aged about 35, having property
worth 1000 drachmae, Heron son of Heron, aged
about 35, having similarly 1000 drachmae ; and for

[a] The heads of the villages concerned, who presented the
names to the local strategus. Cynopolis and Lysimachis
were villages in the Fayum.

[47]στρατηγείας Ὡρίω[ν] Ἀρεί[ο]υ ὡς (ἐτῶν) κε
ὁμοί(ως) (δραχμὰς) χ. [48]Λυσιμαχίδος ὁμοίως, εἰς
μὲν χ[ωμα]τεκβολ[ί]αν Ἰσχυρᾶς [49]Πακήμεως ἐπ(ι-
καλούμενος) Ἀγῆς ἐν οἰκ(οπέδοις) (δραχμὰς) χ.
εἰς δὲ [ἀν]αψησμοὺς διωρύ-[50]χων Στοτοῆτις Σοκ-
μήνεως. καὶ ε[ἰ]ς γενηματοφυλακίαν ὃν [51]καὶ
π[ρο]ανα[δο]θέντος ἐπί τε λειμνασμοῦ καὶ ἀρδείας
[52][κ]αὶ [κατασπορᾶς] καὶ τῶν ἄλλ[ω]ν δη[μ]οσίων
πάντων [53]Ἐριε[ὺ]ς Ζωΐλ]ου, Ἑρμῆς Ἀπ[ύγ]χεω[ς].
καὶ εἰς ἀλωνοφυλ(ακίαν) [54][Πω]λίων Π[το]λεμαίου,
Ε[ὐ]πορίων Διοσκόρου. καὶ εἰς τὸ πρόνοιαν
[55][πο]ιήσασθα[ι τ]οῦ καθαρὸν εἶναι καὶ ἄδωλων τοῦ
μετρου-[56][μ]έν[ου δη]μοσίο[υ] πυροῦ - - -

50. l. οἱ καὶ π[ρο]ανα[δο]θέντες.

344. NOMINATION TO COMPULSORY OFFICE

P. Oxy. 2124.   A.D. 316.

[1]Αὐρηλίῳ Ἡρᾷ τῷ καὶ Διονυσίῳ πραιπ(οσίτῳ)
[2]η πάγου νομοῦ Ὀξυρυγχείτου [3]παρὰ Αὐρηλίων
Ἡρακλείου Πεκωοῦτος [4]καὶ Ἰακὼβ Ὡρίωνος καὶ
Θῶνις Ἀτρῆτος [5]οἱ γ γενόμενοι ἀπαιτηταὶ σίτου
κώμης [6][Δ]ωσιθέ[ο]υ τοῦ διελθόντος ἔτους ἐννάτου
[7]καὶ ζ (ἔτους). δίδωμεν καὶ εἰσαγγέλλομεν τῷ
ἰδί<ῳ> [8]ἡμῶν κινδύνῳ εἰς ἀπαίτησιν σίτου [9]τῆς
αὐτῆς κώμης γενήμα(τος) ι καὶ η (ἔτους) [10]ἰ[δ]ιω-

5. l. τῶν γ γενομένων ἀπαιτητῶν.   7. l. δίδομεν.

the guard of the strategus Horion son of Arius, aged
about 25, having similarly 600 drachmae. Similarly
for the village of Lysimachis : for the throwing up
of dykes Ischyras son of Pakemis surnamed Ages,
having house-sites worth 600 drachmae ; for the
cleaning of canals Stotoetis son of Sokmenis ; and
for the guarding of crops the persons previously
nominated to superintend flooding, watering, sowing,
and all other public works, Herieus son of Zoilus,
Hermes son of Apunchis ; and for the guarding of
threshing-floors Polion son of Ptolemaeus, Euporion
son of Dioscorus ; and for taking care that the
government wheat when delivered is pure and unadulterated . . .

344. NOMINATION TO COMPULSORY
OFFICE

A.D. 316.

To Aurelius Heras also called Dionysius, *praepositus* of the 8th *pagus* of the Oxyrhynchite nome,
from the Aurelii[a] Heracleius son of Pekoous and Jacob
son of Horion and Thonis son of Hatres, all three
having been collectors of corn at the village of
Dositheou in the past 9th which = the 7th year.[b]
We[c] present and report at our own risk for the office
of collector of corn at the said village of the produce
of the 10th which = the 8th year for the private

[a] The innumerable families who received the Roman citizenship from Caracalla in A.D. 212 took from him the name of
Aurelius.
[b] That is, the 9th of Constantinus and the 7th of Licinius.
[c] Contrary to the usual procedure the nominations are
here made by the outgoing officials.

τικ[ο]ῦ καν[ό]νος τοὺς ἑξῆς ἐνγε[γ]ραμμέν-[11][ους]
ὄντ[α]ς εὐπόρους καὶ ἐπιτηδίους [12]π[ρ]ὸς τὴν χρείαν.
εἰσὶ δὲ {Αὐ[ρ]ήλιοι} [13]Αὐρήλιοι [14]Θε[.] . . . s
[Δ]ι[ο]γᾶτος, [15][. . .] . . [.] Διονυσίου, [16]Α(ὐ)-
ρήλιος Ἡράκλεως Πεκωοῦτος προγεγρα(μμένος)
[17][ἀ]πὸ τῆς αὐτῆς κώμης. [18][ὑπ]ατία[ς Κ]αικ[ι]-
νί[ο]υ Σαβείνου καὶ Οὐεττίου [19]Ῥ[ου]φ[ί]νο[υ] τῶν
λαμπροτάτων. (2nd hand) [20]Αὐρήλιοι Ἡράκλεις
καὶ Θῶνεις καὶ Ἰακὼβ [21]ἐπιδεδώκαμεν. Αὐρήλιος
Θεόδωρος [22]ἔγρα(ψα) ὑπ(ὲρ) αὐτῶν μὴ εἰδότων
γράμματα.

16. l. Ἡράκλειος.

345. NOMINATION OF A DONKEY-DRIVER

P. Oxy. 1425.   A.D. 318.

[1]Ὑπατίας τῶν δεσποτῶν ἡμῶν Λικ[ι]ννίο[υ]
[2]Σεβαστοῦ τὸ ε καὶ Κρίσπου τοῦ ἐπιφανεστάτ[ου]
[3]Καίσαρος τὸ α. [4]Αὐρηλίῳ Ἡρᾷ τῷ καὶ Διονυσίῳ
πραιπ(οσίτῳ) η πάγ(ου) νομ(οῦ) Ὀξ[(υρυγχίτου)]
[5]παρὰ Αὐρηλίου Ἀτρῆτος Ἱερακίωνος τεσσαλαρίου
[6]κώμης Δωσιθέου τοῦ ὑπὸ σοὶ πάγου. δίδομι τῷ
ἰ-[7]δίῳ μου κινδύνῳ πρὸς ἄμιψιν τοῦ ἐν τῷ Πη-
[8]λουσίῳ ὀνηλάτου ἀντὶ τοῦ ἐκῖ ὄντος τὸν ἑξῆς
[9]ἐνγεγραμμένον [ὄ]ντα εὔπορον καὶ ἐπιτή-[10]διον
πρὸς τὴν χρείαν. ἔστι δὲ [11]Αὐρήλιος Ὧρ[ο]ς
Παθώθου ἀπὸ τῆς [12]αὐτῆς κώμ[η]ς. [13]ὑπατίας
τῆς [προκιμ]ένης Φαρμοῦθι ιη. (2nd hand) [14]Αὐ-
ρήλιος Ἀτρ[ῆς ἐπι]δέδωκα. Αὐρήλιος [15]Ἀμμωνᾶς
[ἔγραψα] ὑπ(ὲρ) μὴ εἰδότος γράμματα.

404

impost [a] the persons specified below, being well-to-do and suitable for this service. They are the Aurelii The . . . son of Diogas, . . . son of Dionysius, Aurelius Heracleius son of Pekoous the aforesaid, of the said village. In the consulship of Caecinius Sabinus and Vettius Rufinus the most illustrious. Presented by us the Aurelii Heracleius, Thonis, and Jacob. I, Aurelius Theodorus, wrote for them, as they are illiterate.

[a] An impost on private land.

345. NOMINATION OF A DONKEY-DRIVER

A.D. 318.

In the consulship of our masters Licinius Augustus for the 5th time and Crispus the most illustrious Caesar for the 1st time. To Aurelius Heras also called Dionysius, *praepositus* of the 8th *pagus* of the Oxyrhynchite nome, from Aurelius Hatres son of Hieracion, *tesserarius* [a] of the village of Dositheou in the *pagus* under your charge. I present at my own risk in relief of the donkey-driver at Pelusium in place of the one now there the person specified below, being well-to-do and suitable for the duty. He is Aurelius Horus son of Pathotes, of the said village. In the consulship aforesaid, Pharmouthi 18. I, Aurelius Hatres, have presented this. I, Aurelius Ammonas, wrote for him, as he is illiterate.

[a] An officer of low rank who gave out the watchword ; but perhaps the village *tesserarii* were different from the military ones.

---

5. *l.* τεσσαραρίου.　　6. *l.* δίδωμι.　　11. *l.* Παθώτου.

X. CONTRACTS AND TENDERS

346. TENDER FOR REPAIRING
EMBANKMENTS

P.S.I. 488, ll. 9-19.   257 B.C.

⁹['Α]πολλωνίωι διοικητῆι χαίρειν Ἁρμάις. κατὰ
πόλιν Μέμφεως ἐστὶν τὰ κατὰ μέ[ρος] ¹⁰χώματα
σχοινίων ρ. τούτων Συροπερσικοῦ σχοινίων ιβ,
Πιασὺ ζ, τὰ ἐπάνω τ[ῆς] ¹¹Ἡφαίστου κρηπῖδος
καὶ τὰ ὑποκάτω δ, τὰ κατὰ πόλιν σὺν τοῖς βασιλείοις
κ̄γ̄, Καρικοῦ [. .], ¹²ʿΕλληνίου γ̄, πέρα Μέμφεως
τὰ πρὸς λίβα τοῦ βασιλικοῦ κήπου κ̄ καὶ πρὸς
ἀπηλι[ώτην .] ¹³καὶ πρὸς βορρᾶν ε̄ (πηχῶν) λ. εἰς
δὲ τὴν ἀνάχωσιν τούτων τῶν χωμάτων ἐδόθη ἐν
τ[ῶι κη (ἔτει)] ¹⁴(τάλαντον) α (δραχμαὶ) Ἐφ ἀναβάσεως γενομένης πη(χῶν) ι πα(λαιστῶν) γ δα(κ-
τύλου) ας′, καὶ ἐν τῶι κζ (ἔτει) ἐδόθη (τάλαντον) α
(δραχμαὶ) Ἁτ [τοῦ] ¹⁵ποταμοῦ ἀναβάντος πή(χεις)
ι πα(λαιστὰς) ς̄ δα(κτύλους) ββ′. νυνὶ δὲ ὑφίσταμαί
σοι χώσειν τὰ αὐτὰ χώματα ἐνα[ρχό-]¹⁶μενοι ἀπὸ

13. κη E.H. : κς̄ ? Edd.

ᵃ About 5000 yards, a schoenion being 50 yards approximately.

X. CONTRACTS AND TENDERS

346. TENDER FOR REPAIRING
EMBANKMENTS

257 B.C.

To Apollonius the dioecetes greeting from Harmais.
At the city of Memphis the various embankments
measure 100 schoenia,[a] being as follows : those of the
Syro-Persian quarter 12 schoenia, of Paasu 7, those
above the quay of ·Hephaestus [b] and those below 4,
those about the city together with the palace 23,
those of the Carian quarter . . ., of the Hellenion 3,
beyond Memphis those on the west of the royal
garden 20 and on the east . . . and on the north
5 schoenia 30 cubits. For the heaping up of these
embankments the sum given in the 28th year was
1 talent 5500 drachmae, when the rise of the river
was 10 cubits 3 palms $1\frac{1}{8}$ fingerbreadths,[c] and in the
27th year the sum given was 1 talent 1300 drachmae,
when the river rose 10 cubits 6 palms $2\frac{2}{3}$ fingerbreadths. I now undertake to heap up the same

[b] The landing-place in front of the Egyptian temple of
Ptah.
[c] The rise of the river was always recorded with the utmost
accuracy.

τοῦ θεμελίου τῶν χωμάτων ἕως ἀναβάσεως πη(χῶν)
ιβ, ἀρεστὰ τῶι οἰκονόμ[ωι] ¹⁷καὶ τῶι ἀρχιτέκτονι,
λαμβάνοντες ἐγ βασιλικοῦ (τάλαντον) α. χορη-
γηθήσεται δὲ ἡμῖν ¹⁸κατὰ τὸ εἰωθὸς σκαφεῖα, ἃ
πάλιν ἀποκαταστήσομεν. ¹⁹εὐτύχει.

347. UNDERTAKING TO PAY PHYSICIAN-TAX

P. Hib. 102, 6-10.   249 B.C.

Written in duplicate, the following being the outer
text :
⁶[. . . . . Κυρηναῖο]ς τῶν Ζωίλου ἰδιώτης Εὐ-
κάρπωι ἰατρῶι ⁷[χαίρειν. τέτα]κται σοὶ ἀποδώσειν
ὀλυρῶν ἀρτάβας δέκα ἢ δρα-⁸[χμὰς τέσσαρα]ς τὸ
ἰατρικὸν τοῦ λη (ἔτους), ταύτας δέ σοι ἀπο-
⁹[δώσω ἐμ μηνὶ Δ]αισίωι· ἐὰν δέ σοι μὴ ἀποδῶ,
ἀποτείσω σ[ο]ι ¹⁰[τιμὴν τῆς ἀρτά]βης ἑκάσ(της)
(δραχμὰς) β. ἔρρωσο. (ἔτους) λζ Παῦνι ϛ.

ᵃ As the physician-tax was 2 artabae of wheat (= 5 of olyra)
each year, the writer had apparently obtained a moratorium for
year 37 on condition of paying a double amount in year 38.
The tax was levied on certain classes of the population for the

348. CONTRACT FOR PUBLIC WORKS

From P. Petr. iii. 43 (2).   About 245 B.C.

(Col. 3) ¹¹[Βασιλεύο]ντος Πτολεμαίου ⟨τοῦ
Πτολεμαίου⟩ καὶ Ἀρσινόης [θε]ῶν ¹²[Ἀδελφῶν

embankments beginning from their bases to the height of a rise of 12 cubits,[a] to the satisfaction of the oeconomus and the chief engineer, if I receive 1 talent from the Treasury. And according to the usual practice we shall be furnished with mattocks, which we will return. Farewell.

[a] This was considered to give a sufficient margin of safety for the coming flood of year 29.

347. UNDERTAKING TO PAY PHYSICIAN-TAX

249 B.C.

. . ., Cyrenaean, of the troop of Zoilus, private, to Eucarpus, physician, greeting. It has been ordered that I shall pay you ten artabae of olyra or four drachmae as the physician-tax for the 38th year.[a] These I will pay you in the month of Daesius ; and if I fail to pay you, I will forfeit to you as the value of each artaba 2 drachmae. Goodbye. Year 37, Pauni 6.

maintenance of public physicians, but this is the only case in which we find it paid direct to the physician.

348. CONTRACT FOR PUBLIC WORKS

About 245 B.C.

In the 2nd year of the reign of Ptolemy [a] son of Ptolemy and Arsinoe, gods Adelphi, the priest of

[a] Ptolemy Euergetes, son of Ptolemy Philadelphus and, by adoption, of Arsinoe, who were deified as the gods Adelphi.

409

(ἔτους) β], ἐφ' ἱερείως Τληπολέμου τοῦ Ἀρταπάτου
[13]Ἀλε[ξάν]δρου καὶ θεῶν Ἀδελφῶν, κανηφόρου
Ἀρσινόης [14]Φιλα[δέλφο]υ Πτολεμαΐδος τῆς Θυίω-
ν[ος], [15]μηνὸς [. . . . . .] ., ἐν Κροκοδείλων π[όλει
τοῦ Ἀρσινοΐτου. ἐξ]εδόθ[η] [16]ἐκ τοῦ βασιλικοῦ
ὑπὸ κήρυκα διὰ Ἑρμαφίλου [οἰκονόμου, παρόντος
Θεοδώρ]ου τοῦ [ἀρχ]ι-[17]τέκτ[ον]ος, Λων . . . . . . ς
τοῦ παρὰ Π[ετοσίριος τοῦ] βασιλι[κοῦ] γ[ραμ-]
[18]ματέως· τὰς δύο γεφύρας τὰς ἐν Κερ[. . . . . .
. . . . . .] . ν καθ[ε]λ[εῖν] [19]καὶ παραφρυγανί[σ]αι
κατὰ τὰ ὑποκείμ[ενα καὶ ἐπάνω δι]αζεῦξα[ι] [20]τὸ
πλάτος π(ήχεις) η καὶ παραφρυγανίσαι κατὰ τὴν
. ρ . . . υγ . ν [ἀπὸ το]ῦ [21]ἀγκῶνος ἐπὶ σχοινία λε·
τὰς δύο γεφύρας τὰς ἐν . . . . . [22]καθελεῖν καὶ
πάλιν παραφρυγανίσαι κατὰ τὰ ὑποκείμεν[α] καὶ
[ἐ]πά[νω] [23]διαζεῦξαι τὸ πλάτος π(ήχεις) ιδ· τὴν
γέφυραν τὴν ἐν Ἱερᾶι Νήσωι καθελεῖν [24]καὶ [πάλιν
π]αραφρυγανίσαι κατὰ τὰ ὑποκείμενα καὶ ἐπάν[ω]
δια-[25]ζεῦξαι τὸ πλάτος π(ήχεις) η καὶ παραφρυγανίσαι τὰ ἐγβεβρεγμένα [26]ὑπὸ τοῦ ὕδατος σχοινία
ε· τὸν καθ' Ἱερὰν Νῆσον παραφρυγα-[27]νισμὸν
καθελεῖν καὶ πάλιν παραφρυγανίσαι ἐν τοῖς ἀσθενε-
στάτοις [28]τόποις ἐπὶ σχοινία ιε· τὴν γέφυραν τὴν ἐν
Θμοινέτη καθε-[29]λεῖν καὶ πάλιν παραφρυγανίσαι
καὶ ἐπάνω διαζεῦξαι τὸ πλάτος π(ήχεις) ιδ· [30]τὴν
γέφυραν τὴν ἐν Φνέβγει καὶ τὴν ἄγουσαν εἰς
Χανααναῖν [31]καθελεῖν [καὶ] πάλιν παραφ[ρυ]γ[αν]ίσαι
καὶ ἐπάνω [δι]αζεῦξαι [32]τὸ πλάτος π(ήχεις) η· τὴν

30. Or Φνεβίει (=Φνεβίη)?

---

[a] All the localities mentioned in the text were in the
Fayum.

348. CONTRACTS AND TENDERS

Alexander and the gods Adelphi being Tlepolemus son of Artapates, the canephorus of Arsinoe Philadelphus being Ptolemais daughter of Thyion, on the . . . of the month . . ., at Crocodilopolis in the Arsinoite nome. A contract was given out from the Treasury after public auction through Hermaphilus the oeconomus in the presence of Theodorus the engineer and of Lon . . . the agent of Petosiris the royal scribe for the following work : to take down the two bridges at Ker . . .ᵃ and lay fascines against the underlying parts and make the opening at the top 8 cubits in width,ᵇ and to lay fascines along the . . . for a distance of 35 schoenia from the bend ; to take down the two bridges at . . . and replace the fascines against the underlying parts and make the opening at the top 14 cubits in width ; to take down the bridge at Hiera Nesus and replace the fascines against the underlying parts and make the opening at the top 8 cubits in width, and to fascine the 5 schoenia eaten away by the water ; to take down the fascine work at Hiera Nesus and replace it in the weakest parts for a distance of 15 schoenia ; to take down the bridge at Thmoinete etc. and replace the fascines and make the opening at the top 14 cubits in width ; to take down the bridge at Phnebgis and the one leading to Chanaanais and replace the fascines and make the opening at the top 8 cubits in width ; to treat the bridge at Bou-

ᵇ The fascines, consisting of hurdles of reeds or brushwood, were intended to consolidate the mud banks on which the bridges rested. The bridges themselves were probably constructed, either wholly or mainly, of wood. Smyly explains the opening as a cutting at the top of the bank. Or perhaps it might mean the span of the bridge as it was to be when relaid.

γέφυραν τὴν ἐν τῶι Βουκότωι ἐ[ρ]γάσασθαι ὡσαύ-
³⁸τως· τὴν γέφυραν τὴν ἐν τῆι Φυλακιτικῆι Νήσ[ωι]
καθελεῖν ³⁴[καὶ] πάλιν παραφρυγ[αν]ίσαι κατὰ τὰ
[ὑποκείμενα]· τὴν γέφυραν ³⁵[τὴν ἐ]πὶ τοῦ ὑδραγω-
γοῦ [το]ῦ εἰς τὸ Πτεροφορίωνος ἐποίκιον (Col. 4)
¹ἐργάσασθαι ὡσαύτως· τὰς τρεῖς γω-²νί[ας τὰ]ς ἐπὶ
τῆς διώρυγος τῆς ἀγού-³σης εἰς Λυσιμαχίδα ἐργάσασθαι ὡσ-⁴αύτως· τὴν γέφυραν τὴν πρὸς τῶι
Καλλι-⁵φάνους ἐποικίωι ἐργάσασθαι ὡσαύτως· ⁶τὴν
γέφυραν τὴν ἐπὶ τοῦ ⁷[ὑδρ]αγωγοῦ τὸ διάχωμα
. . . . . . ν . ν ⁸τὴν εἰς Τεβετνόιν ἐργάσασθαι
ὡσαύτως· ⁹τὴν γέφυραν τὴν εἰς τὰς Καμίνους
¹⁰ἐργάσασθαι ὡσαύτως· τὴν γέφυραν ¹¹[τὴν κ]ατὰ
Κυνῶν πόλιν ἐργάσασθαι ὡσαύτως ¹²καὶ καταπῆξαι
καταπῆγας ἰσχύ-¹³οντας τῶι μήκει βαθύτερον τοῦ
θεμε-¹⁴λίου π(ῆχυν) α ἀπέχοντας ἀπ᾽ ἀλλήλων
¹⁵π(ήχεις) . καὶ συστρώσας σχοινίοις παρα-¹⁶[φρυ-
γα]νιεῖ πάντα τὰ ἔργα ἀνοῦχι - - - ²⁵ὕψος π(ήχεις)
β καὶ ἐπάνω διαζεῦξαι τ[ὰς] ²⁶ἀφέσεις πάσας τὸ
πλάτος π(ήχεις) η. ἐγγύ[ους] δὲ ²⁷καταστήσας
ἀξιοχρέους τῶι οἰκονόμωι λ[ήμψε-]²⁸ται τὸ ἥμυσυ
τῆς ἐργολαβίας, ὅταν [δὲ τοῦ] ²⁹δεδομένου ἀργυρίου
ἀπεργ[άσηται], ³⁰λήμψεται τὸ λοιπὸν . .
. . . . . [. . . . .] ³¹δοθήσεται δ᾽ ἐκ τοῦ βασιλικοῦ, ὧν τιμὴ [οὐ προσ-]³²λογισθήσεται, σκαφεῖα τὰ
ἱκανά, ἃ ἀποδώ[σει] ³³ὡς ἂν συντελέσηι τὰ ἔργα
ἄ[γ]οντα τ[ὸν ἴσον] ³⁴σταθμόν, καὶ . . . . .
. . . . [. . . . .] ³⁵ἃ παρακομιεῖ ἑαυτῶι.
ἐὰν δὲ μὴ [ἐργάσηται] ³⁶ἢ μὴ ποιῆι κατὰ τὰ γεγραμμένα, [ἐξέστω τῶι] ³⁷ἐπὶ τούτων τεταγμένωι
ἐπαναπ[ωλεῖν τὰ ἔργα] ³⁸καὶ καθ᾽ ἡμέραν ἐπι-
μι[σθοῦσθαι], ³⁹καὶ ὅσωι ἂν πλεῖον εὕρηι ἀ[ναπω-

koton in the same way ; to take down the bridge at
Phylacitice Nesus and replace the fascines against
the underlying banks ; to treat in the same way the
bridge over the watercourse running to the farmstead of Pterophorion ; to treat in the same way the
three angles of the canal leading to Lysimachis ; to
treat in the same way the bridge by the farmstead of
Calliphanes ; to treat in the same way the bridge
over the watercourse, . . . the cross embankment,
the one leading to Tebetnois ; to treat in the same
way the bridge leading to Camini ; to treat in the
same way the bridge at Cynopolis, and to drive in
strong stakes to a depth of 1 cubit below the founda-
tion at a distance of . . . cubits from each other, and
entwining them with ropes (the contractor) shall
fascine all the works with *anouchi*[a] . . . 2 cubits high
and to make the openings at the top of all the outlets
8 cubits wide. On furnishing substantial sureties to
the oeconomus he shall receive half of the fee for the
contract, and when he has done work up to the value
of the money given he shall receive the remainder. . . .
There shall be supplied from government stores a
sufficient number of mattocks, of which the price
shall not be added to the account and which he shall
return on completion of the work weighing their
original weight, and . . ., which he shall transport
for himself. If he fails to perform the work or to act
in accordance with the stated terms, the official in
charge of these matters shall be empowered to put
up the work to auction again and to hire labour from
day to day ; and whatever additional sum it costs
when resold or whatever is spent in hiring labour from

[a] An Egyptian word meaning some kind of brushwood.

λού-]⁴⁰μενον ἢ ἐπιμισθούμενόν τι καθ' [ἡμέραν
ἀνη-]⁴¹λωθῆι ἀποτείσει ὁ ἐργολάβ[ος τό τε ἀργύ-]
⁴²ριον ὃ ἂν προειληφὼς ἦι π[αρ]α[χρῆμα ἡμιόλιον]
⁴³καὶ τὸ βλάβος καὶ περὶ αὐτοῦ [ὁ] β[ασιλεὺς δια-]
⁴⁴γνώσεται.   ⁴⁵ἐξέλαβεν ˝Ωρος νο(μάρχης).

349. CONTRACT CONCERNING A CROP
OF SESAME

P. Hamb. 24.   222 B.C.

¹[Βασιλεύοντ]ος Πτολεμαίου τοῦ Πτολεμαίου καὶ
Ἀρσινόης θεῶν Ἀδελφῶν ἔτους τετάρ-²[του καὶ
εἰκοστο]ῦ, ἐπὶ ἱερέως Ἀρχέτου τοῦ Ἰασίου Ἀλεξάνδρου καὶ θεῶν Ἀδελφῶν καὶ θεῶν ³[Εὐεργετῶν,
κανη]φόρου Ἀρσινόης Φιλαδέλφου Τιμωνάσσης τῆς
Ζωΐλου, μηνὸς Δίου, ἐν Ἱερᾶι ⁴[Νήσωι Θεῶν
Σωτ]ήρων τοῦ Ἀρσινοΐτου νομοῦ. ὁμολογεῖ
Πτολεμαῖος Μνησίου τῶν ⁵[Πτολεμα]ίου τοῦ
Ἐτεωνέως τῆς δευτέρας ἱππαρχίας ἑκατοντάρουρος
⁶[Πετοσίρει] Σεαρμώτου τοπάρχηι τῶν μεμερισ-
μένων αὐτῶι τῆς Ἡρακλεί-⁷[δου μερίδο]ς καὶ
˝Ωρωι βασιλικῶι γραμματεῖ ἐσπαρκέναι ἐν τῶι
ἰδίωι ⁸[κλήρωι πε]ρὶ Ἱερὰν Νῆσον Θεῶν Σωτήρων
σησάμωι θερινῶι ἀρούρας ⁹[ὀγδοήκον]τα εἰς τὸ
πέμπτον καὶ εἰκοστὸν ἔτος καὶ ἔχειν ἀπὸ τῆς ¹⁰[ἐν
Κροκοδ]ίλων πόλει τραπέζης κάτεργον εἰς ἑκάστην

6. Σεαρμώτου Ε.-Η. : Σε⟨ν⟩αρηώτου Ed.

_____

ᵃ The reigning king and queen, already deified.
ᵇ A village called after Ptolemy Soter and Berenice.

day to day, this the contractor shall straightway forfeit together with the money which he has already
received, increased by one half, and the damages,
and concerning himself the king shall give judgement. (Subscribed) Horus, nomarch,[a] undertook the
contract.

[a] A district official who had various duties in all questions
concerning land. Perhaps it was the failure of private contractors to come forward that caused him to undertake the
work.

349. CONTRACT CONCERNING A CROP OF SESAME

222 B.C.

In the 24th year of the reign of Ptolemy son of
Ptolemy and Arsinoe, gods Adelphi, the priest of
Alexander and of the gods Adelphi and the gods
Euergetae [a] being Archetas son of Iasius, the canephorus of Arsinoe Philadelphus being Timonassa
daughter of Zoilus, in the month of Dius, at Hiera
Nesus of the Gods Soteres [b] in the Arsinoite nome.
Ptolemaeus son of Mnesias, of the troop of Ptolemaeus
son of Eteoneus in the second hipparchy, holder of
100 arurae, acknowledges to Petosiris son of Sear-
motes, toparch of the district assigned to him in the
division of Heraclides, and to Horus, royal scribe,
that he has sown on his own holding in the area of
Hiera Nesus of the Gods Soteres eighty arurae with
summer sesame to be harvested in the 25th year, and
that he has received from the bank in Crocodilopolis
as wages for labour two drachmae of silver for each

415

ἄρουραν ¹¹[ἀργυρίου δρα]χμὰς δύο ὥστ' εἶναι
δραχμὰς ἑκατὸν ἑξήκοντα καὶ ¹²[παραμετρή]σειν τὸ
γενόμενον αὐτῶι σήσαμον πᾶν εἰς τὸ βασιλικὸν ἐν
τῶι ¹³[πέμπτωι] καὶ εἰκοστῶι ἔτει καὶ ἀποδώσειν
τὸ κάτεργον τῶι βασιλεῖ ¹⁴[διὰ τῆς αὐ]τῆς τραπέζης
ἐν τῶι πέμπτωι καὶ εἰκοστῶι ἔτει· ¹⁵[ἐὰν δὲ μὴ
ἀ]ποδῶι, ἀποτεισάτω παραχρῆμα ⟨ἡμιόλιον·⟩ καὶ
ἡ πρᾶξις ἔστω ¹⁶[Πετοσίρει (?) κ]αὶ ἄλλωι τῶι τὴν
συγγραφὴν ἐπιφέροντι ἐκ τῶν Πτο-¹⁷[λεμαίου
ὑ]παρχόντων πάντων καὶ τῶν τοῦ ἐγγύου ὡς πρὸς
βασι-¹⁸[λικά. ἔγγυο]ς Πτολεμαίου εἰς ἔκτεισιν τοῦ
κατέργου Πανεῦις Πάιτο[ς ¹⁹ . . . .]ης. ἡ
δὲ συγγραφὴ ἥδε κυρία ἔστω. μάρτυρες Ἀντιγέ-
νης ²⁰[. . . . ., Ἑρμω]ν Πέρσης οἱ δύο τῶν Πτολεμαίου τοῦ Ἐτεωνέως, Σώστρατος Θρᾶιξ, Διῆς
²¹[. . . . .]νης Ἀχαιὸς οἱ τρεῖς τῶν
Ἱπποκράτους, οἱ πέντε τῆς δευτέρας ²²[ἱππαρχίας
ἑκα]τοντάρουροι, Πολέμων Μενελάου Μακεδὼν
τῆς ἐπιγονῆς.

350. TENDER FOR A BRICK-MAKING CONCESSION

P. Fay. 36.   A.D. 111–112.

²Φίλωνι καὶ Σαβείνωι ἐπιτηρηταῖς ³πλίνθου νομοῦ
⁴παρὰ Σανεσνέως τοῦ Ὀρσεῦτος τῶν ἀπὸ κώ-
⁵μης Ναρμούθεως Πολέμωνος μερίδο(ς). ⁶ἐπι-
χωρηθείσης μοι πρὸς μόνον τὸ ⁷ἐνεστὸς πεντε-
καιδέκατον ἔτος ⁸Αὐτοκράτορος Καίσαρος Νερούα
Τραϊανοῦ ⁹Σεβαστοῦ Γερμανικοῦ Δακικοῦ τῆς πλιν-

arura, making one hundred and sixty drachmae, and that he will deliver his whole crop of sesame to the Crown in the 25th year and will repay the wages for labour to the king through the said bank in the 25th year. If he fails to repay, he shall forthwith forfeit one and a half times (?) the amount, and Petosiris or another person producing the contract shall have the right of execution upon all the property of Ptolemaeus and that of his surety as in the case of debts to the Crown. Surety for Ptolemaeus for the refunding of the wages for labour : Paneuis son of Pais, . . . This contract shall be valid. Witnesses : Antigenes, . . ., Hermon, Persian, both of the troop of Ptolemaeus son of Eteoneus, Sostratus, Thracian, Dies, . . ., . . ., Achaean, all three of the troop of Hippocrates, the whole five belonging to the second hipparchy, holders of 100 arurae, Polemon son of Menelaus, Macedonian of the Epigone.

350. TENDER FOR A BRICK-MAKING CONCESSION

A.D. 111–112.

To Philon and Sabinus, superintendents of brick in the nome,[a] from Sanesneus son of Orseus, of the village of Narmouthis in the division of Polemon. If I am granted, for the duration only of the present 15th year of the Emperor Caesar Nerva Trajanus Augustus Germanicus Dacicus, the concession of

[a] The brick industry was a government monopoly, leased yearly in each locality to the highest bidder.

417

[10]θοποιίας καὶ πλινθοπωλικῆς [11]καὶ ἑτέροις ἐπι-
χωρηθεὶς διδόναι [12]κώμης Κερκεθοήρεως τῆς
[13]αὐτῆς μερίδος καὶ τῶν ταύτης ἐποι-[14]κίων καὶ
πεδίων, ὑφίσταμαι τε-[15]λέσειν φόρον ἀργυρίου
δραχμὰς [16]ὀγδοήκοντα καὶ τῶν τούτων προσ-
[17]διαγραφομένων καὶ ἑκατοστῶν καὶ [18]κηρυκικῶν,
ὧν ἂν καὶ τὴν ἀπόδοσιν [19]ποιήσομαι κατὰ μῆνα
ἀπὸ μηνὸς [20]Σεβαστοῦ ἕως Καισαρείου ἐξ ἴσου,
ἐὰν [21]φαίνηται ἐπιχωρῆσαι. [22]Σανεσνεὺς (ἐτῶν) ξ
ο(ὐλὴ) γόνατι ἀριστ(ερῷ). [23]Κάστωρ νομογράφος
εἰκόνικα [24]φαμένου μὴ εἰδέναι γράμματα.

16. l. τὰ . . . προσδιαγραφόμενα, etc.

351. TENDER FOR A FOWLING CONCESSION

P. Ryl. 98(a).   A.D. 154–155.

[1]Φιλίπ[πω ᾿Αφροδισίου] [2]καὶ μετ[όχ(οις)] ἐπ[ι]-
τη[ρ]ητ(αῖς) νομῶν [3]δρυμοῦ κώμης Θεαδ[ε]λφείας
[4]παρὰ ῞Ηρωνος τοῦ ᾿Απολλωνίου [5]ἀναγρα(φομένου)
ἐπ᾿ ἀμφόδο(υ) Κιλίκων κυνηγο(ῦ) [6]Πέρσου τῆς
ἐπιγονῆς. βούλομαι [7]ἐπιχωρηθῆναι παρ᾿ ὑμῶν θη-
[8]ρεύειν καὶ ἀγριεύειν ἐν τῷ προκ(ειμένῳ) [9]δρυμῷ
πᾶν ὄρν[εο]ν ἐπὶ γῆς [10]πρὸς μόνον τὸ ἐνεστὸς ιη
(ἔτος) [11]᾿Αντωνίνου Καίσαρος τοῦ κυρίου [12]φόρου
τοῦ παντὸς ἀργυρίου δραχμ(ῶν) [13]τεσσαράκοντα
καὶ τὴν ἀπόδοσιν ποιή-[14]σομαι ἐν μηνὶ Φαρμοῦθι
τοῦ [15]αὐτοῦ ἐνεστῶτος ἔτους, ἔξω δὲ [16]σὺν ἐμαυτῷ
ἐργάτας δύο, ἐὰν φαί(νηται) [17]ἐπιχω(ρῆσαι). - - -

making and selling bricks, with liberty to transfer
it to others, for the village of Kerkethoeris in the said
division with its farmsteads and plains, I undertake
to pay as rent 80 drachmae of silver and the additional
charges and one per cent taxes and auction fees,
which sum I will deliver in equal monthly instalments
from Sebastus to Caesareus,[a] if the grant is approved.
Sanesneus, aged 60, with a scar on the left knee. I,
Castor, public scribe, have made the description of
him,[b] as he stated that he was illiterate.

[a] That is, from Thoth to Mesore.
[b] In lieu of his proper signature. The "description" is
given in the preceding line.

351. TENDER FOR A FOWLING
CONCESSION

A.D. 154–155.

To Philippus son of Aphrodisius and his fellow
superintendents of pastures in the marshland of the
village of Theadelphia from Heron son of Apollonius,
registered in the Cilician quarter, huntsman and
Persian of the Epigone. I desire to be granted a
permit by you for hunting and catching in the aforesaid marshland every bird in the locality, for the
present 18th year only of Antoninus Caesar the lord,
at a total rent of forty silver drachmae which I will
pay in the month Pharmouthi of the said present year,
and I shall have with me two assistants, if you agree
to give the concession. . . .

352. TENDER FOR A CONCESSION TO RETAIL OIL

P. Amh. 92.   A.D. 162–163.

¹Κλαυδιανῷ νομάρχῃ ’Αρσι(νοΐτου) ²παρὰ Μάρκου
’Ανθεστίου Καπιτω-³λείνου. βούλομαι ἐπιχωρη-
θῆναι ⁴παρὰ σοῦ πρὸς μόνον τὸ ἐνεστὸς ⁵[τ]ρίτον
ἔτος ’Αντωνίνου καὶ Οὐήρ[ο]υ ⁶τῶν κυρίων Σεβαστῶν κοτυλί-⁷ζειν πᾶν ἔλαιον ἐν ἐργαστηρίῳ
⁸ἑνὶ ἐν κώμῃ ‘Ηρακλείᾳ Θεμίστου ⁹μερίδος καὶ
τελέσιν εἰς τὸν τῆς ὠ-¹⁰ν[ῆς λόγ]ον ὑπὲρ ὅλου τοῦ
ἐν[ιαυτοῦ ¹¹ἀ]ργυρ[ίο]υ δραχμὰς ὀγδοήκον[τα ¹²ὀ]βο-
λ[ο]ὺς ὀγδοήκοντα σύνπα[ν-]¹³τ[ι] λό[γῳ], ὧν καὶ
τὴν δ[ι]αγραφὴν ¹⁴ποι[ήσ]ωι κατ[ὰ] μῆν[α] τ[ὸ]
αἱρ[ο]ῦν ¹⁵ἐξ ἴσου, τῶν ε[ἰ]ς ἑτέρους λό[γους ¹⁶π]ρὸς
διοίκησ[ιν τε]λουμένω[ν] ¹⁷ὄντων πρὸς ἐμὲ τὸν
’Ανθέστιον ¹⁸Καπιτωλεῖνον. οὐχ ἔξω δὲ κ[ο]ινω-
¹⁹νὸν οὐδὲ μίσθιον γεν[ό]μενον ²⁰τῆς ὠνῆς ὑποτελῆ,
δώσω [δ]ὲ ²¹καὶ ὑπὲρ διπλώματος ἵππω[ν] ²²δύο
τ[ὰ] κατὰ συνήθιαν ν[ό]μ[ι-]²³μα, ἐξουσίας σοι
οὔσης ἑτέρο[ις] ²⁴μεταμ[ι]σθοῦν ὁπότε ἐὰν αἱρῇ,
²⁵ἐὰν φαίνηται μισθῶσαι.

353. OFFER TO PURCHASE A PRIESTLY OFFICE

P. Tebt. 294.   A.D. 146.

¹’Αντίγ[ρ]αφον. ²Τιβ[ερίωι] Κλ[α]υδίωι ’Ιούστωι
τῶι πρὸς τῶ[ι] ³ἰδίωι λόγων ⁴πα[ρὰ Πα]κήβκιος

2-3. Revised reading.   3. l. λόγωι.

420

352. TENDER FOR A CONCESSION TO RETAIL OIL

A.D. 162–163.

To Claudianus, nomarch of the Arsinoite nome, from Marcus Anthestius Capitolinus. I wish to be granted by you, for the present third year only of Antoninus and Verus the lords Augusti, the right to retail all the oil in one factory at the village of Heraclea in the division of Themistes, and I undertake to pay to the account of the monopoly for the whole year a total sum of eighty drachmae of silver and eighty obols, payment of which I will make in equal monthly instalments, the fiscal charges [a] payable to other accounts being borne by me, Anthestius Capitolinus. I will have no partner or servant who has worked for the monopoly, and I will give for a licence for two horses [b] the sum prescribed by custom, you having the right to make a fresh lease with other persons whenever you choose, if you agree to let the concession.

[a] It is not definitely known what these charges were; perhaps they included a trade tax (see No. 317).
[b] To be used in the business.

353. OFFER TO PURCHASE A PRIESTLY OFFICE

A.D. 146.

Copy. To Tiberius Claudius Justus, administrator of the private account,[a] from Pakebkis son of Marsi-

[a] See No. 206, note b, p. 43.

Μαρσισούχου [ἱ]ερέως ἀπολυσίμου ⁵ἀ[πὸ] Σοκνε-
πτύνεως τ[ο]ῦ καὶ Κρόνου καὶ τῶν συννάων ⁶[θεῶν
μεγ]ίστων ἱεροῦ λογίμου τοῦ ὄντος ἐν κώμῃ Τε-
⁷[πτύνει τ]ῆς Πολέμωνος μερίδος τοῦ Ἀρσιν[ο]είτου
νομοῦ. ⁸β[ούλομα]ι ὠνήσασθαι τὴν τοῦ προκιμέ-
νου ἱεροῦ προ-⁹φη[τ]εία[ν] εἰς π[ρ]ᾶσιν π[ρ]οκιμέ-
νην ἔτι πάλαι ἐπὶ τῶι κα-¹⁰ταχ[. . . . .]ν καὶ
βαϊοφορε[ῖ]ν με καὶ τὰ ἄλλα τὰ τῇ προφη-¹¹τείᾳ
προ[σ]ήκοντα ἐ[πι]τ[ελ]ε[ῖ]ν καὶ λαμβάνε[ι]ν πάσης
¹²ὑποπιπτούσης τῶι ἱ[ε]ρῶι προσόδου τὸ πέμπτον
κατὰ ¹³τὰ κ[ε]λευ[σ]θέντα τειμῆς ἀντὶ ὧν ὑπέσχετο
ἔτι πάλαι ¹⁴Μαρσ[ι]σοῦχος Πακήβκιος δραχμῶν
ἑξακοσίων τεσσα-¹⁵ράκ[ο]ντ[α] ἐπ[ὶ] ταυτὸ δραχμῶν
δι[σχ]ειλί[ω]ν διακοσίων, ¹⁶ἃς κ[αὶ] διαγράψω κυρωθεὶς ἐπὶ τὴν ἐπὶ τόπων δημοσίαν ¹⁷τράπεζαν ταῖς
συνήθεσι προθεσμίαις, μενεῖ{ν} δ᾽ ἐμοὶ ¹⁸καὶ ἐγ-
γόνοις καὶ τοῖς παρ᾽ ἐμοῦ μεταλημψομένοις ἡ τού-
¹⁹των κυρεί[α] καὶ κράτησ[ις ἐπὶ τ]ὸν ἀεὶ χρόνο[ν]
ἐπὶ τοῖ[ς αὐ-]²⁰τοῖς τιμίοις καὶ δικαίοις πᾶσει,
διαγράφου[σ]ι ὑπὲρ ἰσκριτικ[οῦ] ²¹δραχμὰς δια-
[κ]οσίας. ἐὰν οὖν σοι δόξῃ, κύριε, κυρώσει[ς]
²²μοι ἐνθάδε ἐπὶ τῆς πόλεως ἐπὶ τούτοις μου
[τ]οῖς δικαί-²³οις καὶ γράψῃς τῷ τοῦ νομοῦ στρατηγῶι περὶ τούτου ἵνα ²⁴καὶ αἱ ὀφίλ[ο]υσαι ἱερουργίαι
τῶν σε φιλούντων θεῶν ἐπι-²⁵τελῶνται. ἔστι δὲ
τὸ ἐπιβάλλον μοι ε´ μέρος τῶν ²⁶ἐκ τῶν προσ-
πειπτόντων ὡς πρόκιται μετὰ τὰς γινο-²⁷[μέ]νας
δαπάνας (πυροῦ) (ἀρτάβαι) ν φακοῦ (ἀρτάβαι) θ
(ἥμισυ) (τρίτον) ἀργυρίου (δραχμαὶ) ξ. ²⁸δι-
ευτύχει. ²⁹(ἔτους) ι Αὐτοκράτορος Καίσαρος Τίτου
Αἰλίου Ἁδριανοῦ ³⁰Ἀντωνείνου Σεβαστοῦ Εὐσεβοῦς Τῦβει ι.

souchus, exempted [a] priest of the famous temple of
Soknebtunis [b] also called Cronus and the most great
associated gods, which is situated in the village of
Tebtunis in the division of Polemon in the Arsinoite
nome. I wish to purchase the office of prophet [c] in
the aforesaid temple, which has been offered for sale
for a long time, on the understanding that I shall
. . . and carry the palm-branches and perform the
other functions of the office of prophet and receive
in accordance with the orders the fifth part of all the
revenue which falls to the temple, at the total price
of 2200 drachmae instead of the 640 drachmae offered
long ago by Marsisouchus son of Pakebkis, which
sum I will pay, if my appointment is ratified, into the
local public bank at the customary dates ; and I and
my descendants and successors shall have the permanent ownership and possession of this office for
ever with all the same privileges and rights, on payment (by each one) of 200 drachmae for admission.
If therefore it seem good to you, my lord, you will
ratify my appointment here in the city [d] upon these
terms and write to the strategus of the nome
about this matter, in order that the due services of
the gods who love you may be performed. The 5th
share of the proceeds of the revenues which falls
to me, as aforesaid, after deducting expenses is 50
artabae of wheat, $9\frac{5}{8}$ artabae of lentils, 60 drachmae
of silver. Farewell. The 10th year of the Emperor
Caesar Titus Aelius Hadrianus Antoninus Augustus
Pius, Tubi 10.

[a] See No. 338, note b, p. 389.
[b] One of the crocodile gods of the Fayum.
[c] For the sale of these offices compare Nos. 210, 425.
[d] Alexandria, where the tender was made.

23. l. γράψεις.

SELECT PAPYRI

354. OFFER TO LEASE STATE LANDS AT A REDUCED RATE

P. Giess. 4.   A.D. 118.

¹['Απολλωνίῳ στρατηγῷ 'Απολλωνοπ(ολίτου)
²('Επτα)κωμίας ³π]αρὰ Ψεαθ[ύ]ριος ν[εω(τέρου)
Ψεαθύριος . . . .] ⁴καὶ Σενπαχομψάιτος νεω-
(τέρας) Ψ[εαθύριος τῶν] ⁵ἀπὸ τῆς μητροπόλ(εως).
τοῦ κ[υ]ρ[ίου ἡμ]ῶ[ν] ⁶ʿΑδριανοῦ Καίσαρος ὁμόσ[ε]
ταῖς ἄλλαις ⁷[εὐ]εργεσία[ι]ς στήσαντος τὴ[ν] βασι-
λ(ικὴν) ⁸γῆν καὶ δημοσίαν καὶ οὐσιακὴν γῆν ⁹κα[τ]'
ἀξίαν ἑκάστης καὶ οὐκ ἐκ τοῦ παλαιοῦ ¹⁰π[ρο]στάγ-
ματος γεωργεῖσθαι αὐτοί τε ¹¹βεβαρημένοι πολλῶι
χρόνωι δημοσίοις ¹²[βασιλ(ικῆς)] περὶ γρα(μματείαν)
μητροπόλ(εως), ὁ μὲν [Ψε]αθῦρις ¹³[ν]εώτερο(ς)
ἀν(ὰ) β ι'β' (ἀρουρῶν) η∠, ἀν(ὰ) γ [ι'β' (ἀρούρης) η'
ι'ς' λ']β', ¹⁴ἡ δὲ Σενπαχομψᾶις Ψεαθύριο(ς) ἀν(ὰ)
δ ι'β' α∠ η' ι'ς', ¹⁵(γίνονται) (ἄρουραι) ι δ' η', καὶ
μόλ[ις τ]υχόντες ταύ-¹⁶της τῆς εὐεργεσίας ἐπι-
δίδωμεν ¹⁷τόδε τὸ ἀναφ[ό]ριον ὑπισχνούμενοι ¹⁸τὰς
προκειμέν[ας (ἀρούρας)] ι δ' η' ἀνὰ λόγον ¹⁹ἑκάστης
ἀρούρης (πυροῦ) α κ'δ', παραδεχομέ-²⁰νης ἀβρόχου
καὶ ἡμισείας ἐπηντλ(ημένης) ²¹[κα]τὰ τὸ ἔθος.
²²(ἔτους) β Αὐτοκράτορος Καίσαρος ²³ʿΑδριανοῦ
Σεβαστοῦ Τῦβι ιε. (2nd hand) ²⁴[Ψε]αθ[ύ]ρειος
νεώ(τερος) κ[αὶ] Σενπ[α]χομψᾶεις ο[.] . ²⁵ . . . Σεν-
παχομψάειτος ἐπιδ[έδ]ωκ[α] ὡς [πρ]όκ(ειται) ²⁶διὰ
'Ανταῖς υἱοῦ.

16. l. ἐπιδίδομεν.   24. l. Ψεαθῦρις.   26. l. 'Ανταίου.

354. OFFER TO LEASE STATE LANDS AT A REDUCED RATE

A.D. 118.

To Apollonius, strategus of the Apollonopolite-Heptacomia nome, from Pseathuris the younger, son of Pseathuris . . ., and from Senpachompsais the younger, daughter of Pseathuris, inhabitants of the metropolis. As our lord Hadrianus Caesar among his other indulgences has ordained that Crown land, public land, and domain land [a] shall be cultivated at rents corresponding to their various values and not in accordance with the old order, and as we have been overburdened for a long time with public dues on Crown land in the area of the metropolis, Pseathuris the younger paying on $8\frac{1}{2}$ arurae at the rate of $2\frac{1}{12}$ artabae for each and on $\frac{7}{32}$ of an arura at the rate of $3\frac{1}{12}$, and Senpachompsais daughter of Pseathuris on $1\frac{11}{16}$ arurae at the rate of $4\frac{1}{12}$ artabae, total $10\frac{3}{8}$ arurae, having just now obtained the indulgence mentioned we present this application, undertaking to cultivate the aforesaid $10\frac{3}{8}$ arurae at the rate of $1\frac{1}{24}$ artabae of wheat for each arura, unirrigated land and half of the artificially irrigated land being exempted according to custom. The 2nd year of the Emperor Caesar Hadrianus Augustus, Tubi 15. (Signed) I, Pseathuris the younger, and I, Senpachompsais . . . have presented this application as above, through Antaeus my son.

[a] Of these three sorts the first two were categories of state land and the third was the private property of the emperor inherited from his predecessors.

SELECT PAPYRI

355. OFFER TO PURCHASE STATE LAND

P. Lond. 1157 verso.   A.D. 246.

¹Αὐρηλίῳ Μαικίῳ Ν[ε]μεσ[ι]ανῷ ἀ[πα]ιτητῇ δια-
δεχομένῳ τὴν στρα(τηγίαν) τοῦ Ἑρμοπολ(ίτου)
νομοῦ ²καὶ Αὐρηλίοις Αρα . . ῳ βουλ(ευτῇ) ἐξ[ηγ]η-
τεύσαντι ἐνάρχῳ πρυτάνι Ἑρμοῦ πόλεως τῆς
μεγάλ(ης) ἀρχαίας ³καὶ λαμπρᾶς καὶ σεμνοτάτης
καὶ Ἑ[ρμ]είνῳ βουλευτῇ ἀγορανομήσαντι τῆς
α(ὐτῆς) πόλεως δεκαπρώτ(οις) ⁴τοπαρχείας Πατε-
μίτ(ου) Ἄνω π[αρὰ] Αὐρηλίου Ἀπολλοδώρου υἱοῦ
Σαβείνου βενεφικιαρίου ⁵ἐπάρχου Αἰγύπτου. βιβλιδίων ἐπ[ιδοθ]έντων ὑπ' ἐμοῦ Κλαυδίῳ Μαρκέλλῳ
τῷ διασημοτάτῳ ⁶καθολικῷ καὶ Μαρκίῳ Σαλου-
τ[αρ]ίῳ τῷ κρατίστῳ ἐπιτρόπῳ Σεβαστῶν καὶ ἧς
ἔτυχον ⁷ὑπογραφῆς βουλόμενος ὠνή[σα]σθαι κατὰ
τὰ κελευσθέντα ὑπ' αὐτῶν ἐκ τοῦ δημοσίου ⁸ἀπὸ
ὑπολόγου ἀφόρ[ου] τοῦ εἰς π[ρ]ᾶσιν ἐπιγεγραμμένου
ἐπὶ ἁπλῇ τιμῇ εἰκοσαδράχμῳ ⁹περὶ κωμογραμ-
μ[ατεί]αν Ἀλαβα[στ]ρ[ίν]ης ἐκ τοῦ Ἀδήμαντος καὶ
Ἀπολλωνίου κλήρων (ἀρούρας) ιβ ¹⁰ἐπὶ γειτ(νίαις)
δεδηλωμένα[ις διὰ τῶν βιβλιδί]ων ἐστὶν ἀντίγραφον.

¹¹Κλαυδίῳ Μαρκέλλ[ῳ τῷ διασημοτ]άτῳ καθολικῷ καὶ Μαρκίῳ Σαλουταρίῳ τῷ ¹²κρ[ατίστῳ
ἐπιτρόπῳ] Σεβα[στῶν] παρὰ Αὐρηλίου Ἀπολλοδώρου υἱοῦ Σαβείνου βενε-¹³φικι[αρ]ίου ἐπ[άρ]-
χ[ου] Αἰγύπ[του]. βούλομαι ὠνήσασθαι κατὰ τὰ
κελευσθέντα ὑφ' ὑμῶν ¹⁴ἐκ τοῦ δημοσίου ἀπὸ
ὑπο[λόγου] ἀφόρου τοῦ εἰς πρᾶσιν ἐπιγεγραμμένου

9. l. τῶν; so in l. 16.

ᵃ For this and the other titles see Glossary.

355. CONTRACTS AND TENDERS

355. OFFER TO PURCHASE STATE LAND

A.D. 246.

To Aurelius Maecius Nemesianus, collector, acting as strategus of the Hermopolite nome, and to Aurelius . . ., senator, ex-exegetes, prytanis in office of Hermopolis the great, ancient, illustrious, and most august city, and Aurelius Herminus, senator, ex-agoranomus of the said city, *decemprimi* [a] of the toparchy of Upper Patemites, from Aurelius Apollodorus son of Sabinus, *beneficiarius* of the praefect of Egypt. Below is a copy of the application presented by me to the most eminent catholicus Claudius Marcellus and his excellency the imperial procurator Marcius Salutaris and of the subscribed answer which I received concerning my desire to buy from the state in accordance with their orders, from the unproductive, non-paying land which has been assigned for sale at the fixed price of twenty drachmae the arura in the circumscription of Alabastrine, from the holdings of Ademas and Apollonius [b] 12 arurae, of which the boundaries are as stated in the application. [c]

" To the most eminent catholicus Claudius Marcellus and his excellency the imperial procurator Marcius Salutaris from Aurelius Apollodorus son of Sabinus, *beneficiarius* of the praefect of Egypt. I wish to buy from the state in accordance with your orders, from the unproductive, non-paying land which

[b] The land, though belonging to the state, was still known by the names of the original holders to whom it had been granted.

[c] Applications to purchase this class of land, which required to be reclaimed before it could be of any use, were probably not altogether voluntary.

ἐπὶ ἁπλῇ [15]τιμῇ εἰκοσαδρ[ά]χμ[ῳ πε]ρὶ [κω]μογραμ-
ματείαν Ἀλαβαστρίνης τοῦ Ἑρμοπολείτου [16]νομοῦ
ἐκ τοῦ Ἀδήμαντος καὶ Ἀπολλωνίου κλήρων (ἀρούρας) ιβ, γείτονες νότου ψιλὴ [17]γῆ ἀπὸ [ἀ]μπέλου
πρ[ό]τερ[ο]ν [ἐλ]αιὼν καὶ ἐπί τι μέρος πρὸς τῷ
ἀπηλιώτῃ παρά-[18]δεισος, βορρᾶ πρὸς μὲν [τ]ῷ λιβὶ
παράδεισος καὶ ἰδιωτικὰ ἐδάφη, πρὸς δὲ τῷ [19]ἀπη-
λιώτῃ ἰδιωτικὰ ἐδάφη, ἀπηλιώτου παλαιὸς λάκκος
καὶ χέρσος Ἰσιδώρας [20]Χαιρήμονος, λιβὸς παλαι[ὰ
ῥύ]μη, ἢ οἳ ἐὰν ὦσι γείτονες πάντῃ πάντοθεν,
ἅσ-[21]περ κυρωθεὶς διαγράψω [εἰς τ]ὴν ἐν Ἑρμοῦ
πόλει δημοσίαν τράπεζαν, ἐὰν [22]δὲ μὴ κυρωθῶ, οὐ
κατασχεθήσομαι τῇδε τῇ αἰτήσι.   διευτύχει.
[23](ἔτους) γ´ Παῦνι ιγ.   Αὐρήλιος Ἀπολλόδωρος
[24]Σαβείνου ἐπιδέδωκα.

Καὶ ὑπεγράφη μοι οὕτως· [25]οἱ τῆς τοπαρχείας
δεκάπρωτοι σὺν τῷ στρα(τηγῷ) [26]τὴν παράδοσίν
σοι ποιήσωνται.   προτεθ(ήτω). [27]κόλλημ(α) λγ
τόμ(ος) ᾱ. προτεθ(ήτω) ἐν Ἑρμοῦ πόλ(ει).

[28]Ὅθεν ἀξιῶ τὴν παράδοσίν μοι γενέσθαι [29]ὑφ᾽
ὑμῶν καθὼς ἐκελεύθητε τῆς τι-[30]μῆς ὑπ᾽ ἐμοῦ
διαγραφομένης εἰς τὴ[ν] [31]ἐπὶ τόπων δημοσίαν
τράπεζαν. διευτυχεῖτε. [32](ἔτους) γ´ Αὐτοκράτορος
Καίσαρος Μάρκου Ἰουλίου [33]Φιλίππου Εὐσεβοῦς
Εὐτυχοῦς καὶ Μάρκου [34]Ἰουλίου Φιλίππου γεν-
ναιοτάτου καὶ ἐπιφανεστάτου [35]Καίσαρος Σεβαστῶν.   Αὐρήλιος Ἀπολλόδωρος [36]Σαβείνου ἐπιδέδωκα.

26. l. ποιήσονται.

355. CONTRACTS AND TENDERS

has been assigned for sale at the fixed price of twenty
drachmae the arura in the circumscription of Alabastrine in the Hermopolite nome, from the holdings of
Ademas and Apollonius 12 arurae, of which the
boundaries are : on the south waste land lately
grown with vines and formerly an olive-grove, and
for some distance at the east end an orchard, on the
north at the west end an orchard and private grounds
and at the east end private grounds, on the east an
old pond and dry land belonging to Isidora daughter
of Chaeremon, on the west an old street, or whatever
the boundaries may be all round ; and if my offer is
ratified, I will pay the money to the government bank
in Hermopolis, but if it is not ratified, I shall not be
bound by this application. Farewell. Year 3, Pauni
13. Presented by me, Aurelius Apollodorus son of
Sabinus."

And the subscription to my application was as
follows : " The *decemprimi* of the toparchy in concert
with the strategus shall deliver the land to you. Let
this application be displayed publicly.[a] Page 33,
roll 1.[b] Let the application be displayed publicly
in Hermopolis." [c]

Wherefore I request that you deliver the land to
me as commanded, the price being paid by me to the
local government bank. Farewell. Year 3 of the
Emperor Caesar Marcus Julius Philippus Pius Felix
and Marcus Julius Philippus the most noble and
excellent Caesar, Augusti. Presented by me,
Aurelius Apollodorus son of Sabinus.

[a] Subscription of the catholicus.
[b] See No. 293, note a, p. 297.
[c] Subscription of the procurator.

SELECT PAPYRI

356. PUBLICATION OF AN OFFER FOR LEASE

P. Oxy. 2109.   A.D. 261.

¹Αὐρήλιος Διοσκουρίδης ²ὁ καὶ Σαβῖνος γυ(μ-
νασιαρχήσας) ³βουλ(ευτὴς) καὶ ὡς ⁴χρη(ματίζω),
ἔναρχος πρύτανις ⁴τῆς Ὀξυρυγχιτῶν πόλεως,
⁵διέπων καὶ τὰ πολιτικά. ⁶τῆς δοθείσης αἱρέσεως
⁷ὑπὸ τοῦ δι᾽ αὐτῆς δηλουμέ-⁸νου πολιτικοῦ τόπου
Κα-⁹πιτωλείου ὑπὸ τὴν ἀπηλιω-¹⁰τικὴν στοὰν πρὸς
ἄνοιξιν ¹¹καπηλείου ἡ ἴση δημοσίᾳ ¹²πρόκειται ἵνα
πάντες εἰδῶσι ¹³καὶ οἱ βουλόμενοι ἀμείνους ¹⁴αἱρέ-
σεις διδόναι προσέλθωσι, ¹⁵τηρουμένου λόγου τῇ
πό-¹⁶λει περὶ ὧν ἔχει παντοίων ¹⁷δικαίων. σεση-
μι(είωμαι). ¹⁸(ἔτους) α τῶν κυρίων ἡμῶν Μακριανοῦ
¹⁹καὶ Κυήτου Σεβαστῶν Τῦβι λ. (2nd hand)
²⁰Αὐρηλίῳ Διοσκουρίδῃ τῷ καὶ ²¹Σαβείνῳ γυμ-
νασιαρχήσαντι ²²ἐνάρχῳ πρυτάνει τῆς Ὀξυρυγ-
²³χειτῶν πόλεως, διέποντι ²⁴καὶ τὰ πολιτικά, ²⁵παρὰ
Αὐρηλί[ο]υ Ὡρίωνος Κολ-²⁶λούθου μητρὸς Τερεῦτος
²⁷ἀπ᾽ Ὀξυρύγχων πόλεως. ἑκου-²⁸σίως ἐπιδέχομαι
μισθώσασθαι ²⁹ἐν τῷ τῆς πόλεως Καπιτω-³⁰λείῳ
ὑπὸ τὴν ἀπηλιωτικὴν ³¹στοὰν ἐργαστήριον πρὸς
³²ἄνοιξιν καπηλείου εἰς ἐνιαυ-³³τὸν ἕνα ἀπὸ νεομηνίας τοῦ ³⁴ἑξῆς μηνὸς [Με]χεὶρ τοῦ ἐνε-³⁵στῶτος
α (ἔτους) ἐνοικίου κατὰ μῆ-³⁶να ἕκαστον δραχμῶν
ὀκτώ. ³⁷βεβαιουμένης δέ μοι τῆς ³⁸ἐπιδοχῆς
χρήσομαι τῷ ἐργα-³⁹στηρίῳ σὺν τῇ τούτου εἰσ-
ό-⁴⁰δῳ καὶ ἐξόδῳ ἐπὶ τὸν χρόνον ⁴¹ἀκωλύτως, καὶ
ἀποδώσω τὸ ⁴²ἐνοίκιον κατὰ μῆνα τριακάδι ⁴³ἀν-
υπερθέτως, καὶ ἐπὶ τέλει τοῦ ⁴⁴χρόνου παραδώσω τὸν
430

356. CONTRACTS AND TENDERS

356. PUBLICATION OF AN OFFER FOR LEASE

A.D. 261.

(Notice by) Aurelius Dioscurides also called Sabinus, ex-gymnasiarch, senator, and however I am styled, prytanis in office of the city of Oxyrhynchus, director also of municipal finance. Of the offer made by the person specified therein for a site belonging to the city in the Capitol *a* below the east colonnade, with a view to opening a tavern, a copy is publicly displayed, in order that all may know and those who wish to make better offers may come forward, without prejudice to rights of any kind pertaining to the city. Signed by me. 1st year of our lords Macrianus and Quietus Augusti, Tubi 30.

To Aurelius Dioscurides also called Sabinus, ex-gymnasiarch, prytanis in office of the city of Oxyrhynchus, director also of municipal finance, from Aurelius Horion son of Colluthus and Tereus, of Oxyrhynchus. I voluntarily engage to lease the workshop in the city Capitol below the eastern colonnade, with a view to opening a tavern, for one year from the first day of the next month Mecheir of the present 1st year at a monthly rent of eight drachmae. If my engagement is confirmed I am to use the workshop with its entrance and exit for the term without hindrance, and I will pay the rent on the 30th of each month without delay, and at the end of the term I will deliver the site free from filth and

a Precinct of a temple of Jupiter Capitolinus. See No. 340.

431

SELECT PAPYRI

τόπον ⁴⁵καθαρὸν ἀπὸ κοπρίων καὶ ἀκαθαρ-⁴⁶σίας
πάσης κα[ὶ] ἃς ἐὰν παραλάβω ⁴⁷θύρας καὶ κλεῖδας ἢ
ἀποτείσω ⁴⁸οὗ ἐὰν μὴ [π]αρα[δ]ῶ τὴν ἀξίαν ⁴⁹τιμήν,
τῆς πράξεως οὔσης ⁵⁰ὡς καθήκει. κυρία ἡ ἐπιδοχή,
περὶ ⁵¹ἧς ἐπερωτηθεὶς ὡμολόγησα. ⁵²ἐὰν δὲ μὴ
κυρωθῶ, οὐ κατασχε-⁵³θήσομαι τῇδε τῇ ὑποσχέσει.
⁵⁴(ἔτους) α Αὐτοκρατόρων Καισάρων ⁵⁵Τίτου Φουλ-
ουίου Ἰουνίου Μακριανοῦ ⁵⁶καὶ Τίτου Φουλ[ο]υίου
Ἰουνίου Κυήτου ⁵⁷Εὐσεβῶν Εὐτυχῶν Σεβαστῶν
⁵⁸Τῦβι κη. (3rd hand) Αὐρήλιος Ὡρεί-⁵⁹ων Κολλ-
[ο]ύθου ἐπιδέδω-⁶⁰κα ἐπιδεχόμ[ε]νος μισθῶ-⁶¹σα-
σθαι καὶ ἀποδώσω ⁶²τὸ ἐν[ο]ίκιον ὡς πρόκειται.
⁶³Αὐρήλιος Δίδυμος ἔγρα-⁶⁴ψα ὑπὲρ αὐτοῦ μὴ
εἰδό-⁶⁵τος γράμματα.

357. OFFER FOR A HOUSE

C. P. Herm. 119, col. iv.   A.D. 266.

¹Αὐρήλιος Νεμε[σιαν]ὸς Κρατίστου τ[ῇ] κρατ[ί-
σ]τῃ ²βουλῇ Ἑρμοῦ πόλ[ε]ως τῆς μεγάλης ἀρχαίας
κ[αὶ] λαμ-³πρᾶς καὶ σεμνοτάτης διὰ Μάρκου
Αὐρηλ(ίου) Κορελλίου ⁴'Αλεξάνδρου ἱππικοῦ ἀπὸ
στρατιῶν γυμνα-⁵σιάρχου βουλευτοῦ ἐνάρ[χου] πρυτάνεως τῆς α(ὐτῆς) ⁶πόλεως τοῖς φιλτάτοις χαίρειν.
βούλομαι ⁷ὠνήσασθαι ἀπὸ πολιτικοῦ λόγου οἰκίαν
καὶ τὰ ⁸περὶ αὐτὴν οἰκόπεδα καὶ ψιλοὺς τόπους
ἐν οἷς ⁹κοπρίαι, τὰ πάντα ὄντα ἐν συμπτώσει καὶ
ἐν ἀ-¹⁰χρησίμῳ νῦν διαθέσι, καλούμενα πρότερον
Ὅ-¹¹πλωνος, ἐν Ἑρμοῦ πόλει ἐπ' ἀμφό[δ]ου
Πόλεως ¹²'Απηλιώτου ὑπὸ στοὰν νοτίνην τῆς

all uncleanness, and any doors and keys which I received, or will forfeit the value of whatever I fail to deliver, right of execution duly subsisting. This engagement is valid, and in answer to the formal question concerning it I gave my consent. But if my offer is not accepted, I shall not be bound by this promise. The 1st year of the Emperors Caesars Titus Fulvius Junius Macrianus and Titus Fulvius Junius Quietus Pii Felices Augusti, Tubi 28. (Signed) I, Aurelius Horion son of Colluthus, have presented this, engaging to take the lease, and I will pay the rent as stated above. I, Aurelius Didymus wrote for him, as he is illiterate.

357. OFFER FOR A HOUSE

A.D. 266.

Aurelius Nemesianus son of Cratistus to their excellencies the senate of Hermopolis the great, ancient, illustrious, and most august city, through Marcus Aurelius Corellius son of Alexander, retired officer of equestrian rank, gymnasiarch, senator, prytanis in office of the said city, most affectionate greeting. I wish to purchase from the municipal treasury a house with the surrounding premises and waste grounds containing rubbish-heaps, the whole property being in ruins and for the present in useless condition. It was formerly called Hoplon's and is situated in Hermopolis in the East-end quarter below the south

'Αντινο-¹³ειτικῆς πλατείας, ἀφ' ὧν οὐδὲν περ[ι-
γίνετ]αι ¹⁴τῷ πολιτικῷ λόγῳ διὰ τὸ ἐξ ὁλοκλήρου
βεβλά-¹⁵φθαι ἐν τοῖς πρόσθεν συμβεβηκόσι κατὰ
¹⁶τὴ[ν πό]λειν ἀπευκταίοις τα[ρ]άχοις, ὧν γεί-
¹⁷το[νες] νότου Δομιτιανοῦ π[λα]τεία δι' ἣν ¹⁸εἴσοδος
καὶ ἔξοδος, βορρᾶ 'Αντινοϊτικὴ ¹⁹πλατεία δι' ἧς
ὁμοίως εἴσοδος καὶ ἔξοδος, ²⁰ἀπηλιώτου Ἑρμοῦ
παστοφόρου καὶ μετό-²¹χων, λιβὸς Κλαυδίου Δικαιάρχου ἄρξαν-²²[τος τῆ]ς λαμπρᾶς 'Αντινόου πό-
[λεω]ς, προσ-²³βληθέντα τῇ πόλει ἀκολούθως τοῖς
κελευ-²⁴[σ]θεῖσι ὑπὸ τοῦ τῆς διασημοτάτης μνήμης
²⁵Κλαυδίου Θεοδώρου, τιμῆς ἀργυρίου δρα-²⁶χμῶν
δισχειλίων, γ(ίνονται) ἀργ(υρίου) (δραχμαὶ) 'Β,
ἅσπερ ²⁷κυρωθεὶς διαγρά[ψω τῷ] π[ο]λιτικῷ λόγῳ,
²⁸μενῖ δ' ἐμοὶ καὶ [ἐ]γγόνοις καὶ τοῖς παρ' ἐμοῦ
²⁹με<τα>παραλημ[ψο]μένοις ἡ τούτων κράτησις
³⁰καὶ κυρία βεβαία, [τῆς] πόλεως μοι βεβαιού-³¹σης
διὰ παντὸ[ς] πρὸ[ς π]ᾶσαν βεβαίωσιν. ³²ἐὰν δὲ μὴ
κυρωθῶ, οὐκ ἐνσχεθήσομαι ³³τῇδε τῇ αἱρέσει. ἐρρῶσθαι ὑμᾶς εὔχομαι, ³⁴τιμιώτατοι. ³⁵(ἔτους) ιδ
[Αὐ]τοκράτορος Καίσαρος Πουπ[λί]ου ³⁶Λ[ικινν]ίου
Γ[α]λλιηνοῦ Γερμανι[κοῦ Μεγίστου] ³⁷Π[ερσικοῦ]
Μεγίστου Εὐσεβοῦ[ς Εὐτυχοῦς] ³⁸Σεβ[αστο]ῦ Ἁθὺρ
ιϛ.

358. ENGAGEMENT OF A DELEGATE
BY A TAX-COLLECTOR

P. Lond. 306.   A.D. 145.

¹Ἔτους ὀγδόου Αὐτοκράτορος Καίσαρος Τίτου
Αἰλίου ²ᶜΑδ[ρι]ανοῦ 'Αντωνίνου Σεβαστοῦ Εὐ-

colonnade of the Antinoite street; and no profit is
derived from it by the municipal treasury owing to its
having been completely damaged in the abominable
riots which have formerly taken place in the city.
Its boundaries are : on the south the street of
Domitianus by which there is entrance and exit, on
the north the Antinoite street by which likewise there
is entrance and exit, on the east the house of Hermes
the pastophorus and partners, on the west that of
Claudius Dicaearchus, ex-magistrate of the illustrious Antinoopolis. It was assigned to the city
in accordance with the order of Claudius Theodorus
of most distinguished memory. I am willing to purchase it for the price of two thousand silver drachmae,
total 2000 silver dr., which if my offer is ratified I will
pay to the municipal treasury, and the possession and
ownership of the property shall be permanently
guaranteed to me and my descendants and successors,
the city guaranteeing it to me for ever by every sort
of guarantee ; but if it is not ratified, I shall not be
bound by this offer. I pray for your health, most
honoured Sirs. The 14th year of the Emperor Caesar
Publius Licinius Gallienus Germanicus Maximus
Persicus Maximus Pius Felix Augustus, Hathur 16.

---

17. *l. δι' ἧς.*

358. ENGAGEMENT OF A DELEGATE BY A TAX-COLLECTOR

A.D. 145.

The eighth year of the Emperor Caesar Titus
Aelius Hadrianus Antoninus Augustus Pius, 5th inter-

σεβοῦς μη-³νὸς Καισα[ρε]ίου ἐπαγομένων ε̄ ἐν
Ἡρακλείᾳ τῆς Θεμισ-⁴του μερίδ[ος] τοῦ Ἀρσινοείτου νομοῦ. ὁμολογεῖ Στοτο-⁵ῆτις Στο[τοή]-
τεως τοῦ Ὥρου [πράκ]τωρ ἀργυρικῶν τῆς ⁶προ-
κειμένης κώμης Ἡρακλείας ὡς (ἐτῶν) κ̄ς̄ οὐλ(ὴ)
ἀντικνη-⁷μίῳ ἀριστερῷ Σατορνίλῳ Ἀπίωνος τοῦ
Διδύμου ὡς (ἐτῶν) ν ⁸οὐλὴ μετ[ώ]πω μέσω τὸν
[ὁ]μολογοῦντα συνεστακέ-⁹ναι τὸν Σα[το]ρνῖλον
πρακτορεύοντα ἀπὸ τοῦ ἰσιόντος ¹⁰θ (ἔτους) Ἀν-
τ[ωνίν]ου Καίσαρος τοῦ κυρίου ἐφ' ἔτη δύο ¹¹καὶ
δια[γρά]φοντα εἰς τὸ δημόσιον τὸ ἐπιβάλλον ¹²τῷ
Στοτοήτει τρίτον μέρος τῆς προκειμένης πρακ-
¹³τωρίας, [τ]οῦ Σατορνίλου π[λ]ηροῦντος κατὰ
ἀρίθμη-¹⁴σιν ὁμοίως τὸ ἐπιβάλλον αὐτῷ τρίτον
μέρος, ¹⁵ἔτι δὲ κα[ὶ κ]αταχωρ<ι>εῖ ὁ Σατορνῖλος
τὰ τῆς τά-¹⁶ξεως β[ι]βλία ταῖς ἐξ ἔθους προθεσμίαις, τοῦ ¹⁷Σατορνίλου χορηγοῦντας χάρτας καὶ
τῆς ἄλλης ¹⁸δαπάνης οὔσης πρὸς αὐτόν, αὐτοῦ
λαμβάνοντος ¹⁹παρὰ τοῦ Στοτοήτεως κατ'{ατ} ἔτος
εἰς λόγον ὀψονίου ²⁰ἀργυρίου δραχμὰς διακωσίας
πεντήκοντα δύο, ²¹ὧν καὶ [τὴ]ν ἀπόδωσιν ποιή-
σεται αὐτῷ ἐν προθεσ-²²μίαις τέ[σ]σαρσι διὰ τ[ρι]-
μήνου τὼ αἰροῦν ἐξ ἴσου. ²³συνπρακτωρεύσι δὲ
[αὐ]τῷ ὁ Στοτ[οήτι]ς ὁπότε ἐὰν ²⁴[χρεί]α γένηται
διὰ τὸ ἐπὶ τούτ[οις] τὴν σύσ[τασιν] γεγονέν[αι].
²⁵[Σατο]ρνεῖλος Ἀπ[ίω]νο[ς - - -

10. l. ἐπ' ἔτη δύο.   12-13. l. πρακτορείας.   17. l.
χορηγοῦντος.   19. l. ὀψωνίου.   20. l. διακοσίας, δύο.
21. l. ἀπόδοσιν, αὐτῷ.   22. l. τό.   23. l. συμπρακτορεύσει.

calary day of the month Caesareus,[a] at Heraclea in the division of Themistes in the Arsinoite nome. Stotoetis son of Stotoetis son of Horus, collector [b] of money taxes for the aforesaid village of Heraclea, aged about 26 years, with a scar on the left shin, acknowledges to Saturnilus son of Apion son of Didymus, aged about 50 years, with a scar on the middle of the forehead, that he, the acknowledging party, has appointed Saturnilus to act as collector for two years from the coming 9th year of Antoninus Caesar the lord and to pay to the Treasury the third part, that for which Stotoetis is responsible, of the liabilities of the aforesaid collectorship, Saturnilus having similarly to make good by serial payments the third part for which he is responsible. Saturnilus shall further send in the books of the office at the usual appointed times, and he shall provide writing paper and shall be accountable for the other expenses. For salary he shall receive from Stotoetis two hundred and fifty-two drachmae a year, which the latter shall pay to him on four fixed dates every three months in equal instalments. And Stotoetis shall join in the work of collecting whenever there is need, because the appointment has been made on these terms. I, Saturnilus son of Apion . . .

[a] = Mesore.
[b] It appears from the context that Stotoetis was not the sole collector for the village, but merely one of three.

359. ENGAGEMENT OF PERFORMERS

P. Oxy. 1025.   Late 3rd cent. A.D.

¹Αὐρήλιοι Ἄγαθος γυ(μνασιάρχης) ²ἔναρχος πρύτανις καὶ ³Ἑρμανοβάμμων ἐξηγ(ητὴς) ⁴καὶ Δίδυμος
ἀρχιερεὺς ⁵καὶ Κοπρίας κοσμητὴς ⁶πόλεως Εὐερ-
γέτιδος ⁷Αὐρηλίοις Εὐριπᾷ βιολό-⁸γῳ καὶ Σαραπᾷ
ὁμηριστῇ ⁹χαίρειν. ¹⁰ἐξαυτῆς ἥκετε, καθὼ[ς] ¹¹ἔθος
ὑμῖν ἐστιν συνπα-¹²νηγυρίζειν, συνεορτάσον-¹³τες ἐν
τῇ πατρῴᾳ ἡ[μῶν] ¹⁴ἑορτῇ γενεθλίῳ τοῦ Κρόνου
¹⁵θεοῦ μεγίστου ἀναν . . . . [.] ¹⁶τῶν θεωριῶν
ἅμ' αὔ[ρ]ιον ¹⁷ἥτις ἐστὶν ι ἀγομ[έν]ων ¹⁸ἐπὶ τὰς
ἐξ ἔθους ἡμ[έρ]ας ¹⁹λαμβάνοντες το[ὺς] μισ-²⁰θοὺς
καὶ τὰ τείμια. ²¹σεσημ(είωμαι). (2nd hand)
²²Ἑρμανοβάμμων ἐξηγ(ητὴς) ²³ἐρρῶσθαι ὑμᾶς εὔχο-
μ(αι). (3rd hand) ²⁴Δίδυμος ἀρχιερ(εὺς) ἐρρῶσθ(αι)
ὑμᾶς εὔχομ(αι). (4th hand) ²⁵Κοπρίας ἐρρῶσθαι
ὑμᾶς ²⁶εὔχομαι.

360. A PAINTER'S ESTIMATE

P. Oxy. 896.   A.D. 316.

²Οὐαλερίῳ Ἀμμωνιανῷ τῷ καὶ Γεροντίῳ λ[ογιστῇ
Ὀξ(υρυγχίτου)] ³παρὰ Αὐρηλίου Ἀρτεμιδώρου
Ἀρσινόου ἀπὸ τῆς ⁴λαμπ(ρᾶς) καὶ λαμπ(ροτάτης)
Ὀξυρυγχιτῶν πόλεως ζωγράφου τὴν ⁵ἐπιστήμην.
ἐπιζητούσῃ τῇ σῇ ἐμμελείᾳ τὴν ⁶σύνοψιν τῶν δεο-
μένων τόπων ζωγραφίας ⁷τοῦ εὐτυχῶς ἐπισκευα-

359–360. CONTRACTS AND TENDERS

359. ENGAGEMENT OF PERFORMERS

Late 3rd cent. A.D.

The Aurelii Agathus, gymnasiarch and prytanis in office, Hermanobammon, exegetes, Didymus, chief priest, and Coprias, cosmetes of the city of Euergetis,[a] to the Aurelii Euripas, actor, and Sarapas, Homeric reciter, greeting. Come at once, in accordance with your custom of taking part in the holiday, in order to celebrate with us our traditional festival on the birthday of Cronus [b] the most great god. The spectacles begin to-morrow the 10th and will be held for the regular number of days ; and you will receive the usual payments and presents. Signed by me.[c] I, Hermanobammon, exegetes, pray for your health. I, Didymus, chief priest, pray for your health. I, Coprias, pray for your health.

[a] Ptolemais Euergetis (= Arsinoe) in the Fayum.
[b] An Egyptian god identified with the Greek Cronus. Compare No. 353. [c] That is, by Agathus.

360. A PAINTER'S ESTIMATE

A.D. 316.

To Valerius Ammonianus also called Gerontius, logistes of the Oxyrhynchite nome, from Aurelius Artemidorus son of Arsinous, of the illustrious and most illustrious city of Oxyrhynchus, a painter by profession. In accordance with the request of your grace for an estimate of the places which require painting in the public bath of the said city, now

ζομένου Τραϊανῶν ⁸ʿΑδριανῶν θερμῶν δημοσίου τῆς
ʿαὐτῆς πόλεως βαλανίου κατὰ ταῦτα δηλῶ χρή-
¹⁰ζειν εἰς λόγον ζωγραφίας τῶν τε δεομένων ¹¹τόπων
τῶν δύο ψυχροφόρων καὶ ἐμβατικοῦ ¹²[θ]όλου ἑνὸς
καὶ ἀρδρομηκιαίων ὅλου ξυστοῦ ¹³[εἰ]σόδων καὶ
ἐξόδων καὶ παραθολίων τεσσάρων ¹⁴[τ]οῦ ἐξωτέρου
ξυστοῦ καὶ τῶν ἄλλων τόπων ¹⁵[εἰς μ]ὲν τιμὴν
χρωμάτων ἀργυρίου δηναρίων ¹⁶[μυριάδ . . .] .
[. . . . .] . εου ζωγραφίας ὅλων ἔργων ¹⁷[ἀρ-
γυρίου δηναρίων μυ]ριάδαν μίαν, ὅπερ ¹⁸[προσφωνῶ.
¹⁹ὑπατείας Καικινίου Σαβίνο]υ καὶ Οὐεττίου ʿΡου-
φίνου ²⁰[τῶν λαμπ(ροτάτων) . . . .
(2nd hand) Αὐρή(λιος) ᾽Αρτεμίδωρος ²¹[ἐπιδέδωκα.
Αὐρή(λιος) . . . . .]ων ἔγρα(ψα) ὑπ(ὲρ) αὐτοῦ μ(ὴ)
ἰδ(ότος).

12. l. ἀνδρομηκιαίων.   16. μι]σθοῦ ?

361. CONTRACT CONCERNING A CONVOY OF ANIMALS

P. Oxy. 1626.   A.D. 325.

¹ʿΟμολογο[ῦσ]ι[ν ἀλλή]λοις Αὐρήλιοι ᾽Αλόις Χω-
οῦτος ²καὶ ʿΗρακλῆ[ς] Πούδεντος καὶ οἱ κοινωνοὶ οἱ
πάντες ³δεκανοὶ ἀπὸ κώμη[ς] Πανευεὶ μετ᾽ ἐγγυη-
τοῦ εἰς ⁴ἔκτισιν τῶν φανη[σο]μένων μισθῶν Πτολεμαίου ⁵Πτολεμαίου μείζονος τῆς αὐτῆς κώμης καὶ
Αὐρήλιος ⁶ʿΗρακλείδης Σκυλακίου ἐπιμελητὴς ζώων
⁷ἀποστελλομένω[ν εἰς τ]ὴν Βαβυλῶνα πρὸς ⁸θείαν
ἐπιδημίαν, οἱ μὲν δεκανοὶ συνηλλαχέναι ⁹τῷ ἐπι-

auspiciously under repair, at the warm baths of
Trajanus Hadrianus, I declare that for the painting
of the places which require it, comprising the two
cold baths, and one round bathroom, and the man-
high entrances and exits of the whole colonnade, and
four antechambers in the outer colonnade, and the
other places, I require for the cost of pigments . . .
thousand denarii of silver and as painter's fee for the
whole work ten thousand denarii of silver ; and this
I report.   In the consulship of Caecinius Sabinus and
Vettius Rufinus the most illustrious. . . . (Signed)
I, Aurelius Artemidorus, have presented this report.
I, Aurelius . . ., wrote for him, as he is illiterate.

361. CONTRACT CONCERNING A CONVOY
OF ANIMALS

A.D. 325.

Aurelius Alois son of Choous and Aurelius Heracles
son of Pudens and their associates, all *decani* [a] from
the village of Paneuei, with Ptolemaeus son of
Ptolemaeus, headman of the same village, as surety
for payment of the wages eventually earned, and
Aurelius Heraclides son of Scylacius, superintendent
of animals which are being sent to Babylon [b] for the
Imperial visit,[c] mutually agree, the *decani* that they

  [a] Official overseers of various public services.
  [b] The Roman fortress at Old Cairo.
  [c] There is no evidence that the Emperor Constantine was
in Egypt in the year 325, but a visit may have been projected.
The animals were presumably required for the carriage of
supplies.

SELECT PAPYRI

μελητῇ χώραν μίαν ῥαβδούχου ἑνὸς [10]τῶν αὐτῶν
ζῴων ἀπὸ ὀγδόης τοῦ ὄντος μηνὸς [11]Παῦνι, λαμβάνοντος τοῦ ἐπιμελητοῦ παρὰ τῶν [12]δεκανῶν ὑπὲρ
μισθοῦ ἡμερησίως δραχμὰς [13]δισχιλίας. ἐντεῦθεν
δὲ ὁμολογεῖ ὁ ἐπιμελητὴς [14]ἐσχηκέναι παρὰ τῶν
δεκανῶν ὑπὲρ μισθοῦ [15]μηνῶν δύο ἀπὸ τῆς αὐτῆς
ὀγδόης ἀργυρίου [16]τάλαντα εἴκοσι, τὰ δὲ φανησόμενα ἄχρι συνπληρώ-[17]σεως τῆς ἐπιμελείας ἀπο-
λήμψεται παρὰ τῶν [18]αὐτῶν δεκανῶν, ἐμὲ δὲ τὸν
Πτολεμαῖον παρασχεῖν [19]τὰ φανησόμενα σαλάρια
πρὸς τὸ ἀπαρενοχλή-[20]τους καὶ ἀσκύλτους καὶ
ἀζημίους παρέχειν περὶ τῶν [21]τῇ αὐτῇ ῥαβδουχίᾳ
διαφερόντων. κύριον τὸ συνάλ-[22]λαγμ[α] δισσὸν
γραφέν, καὶ ἐπερωτηθέντες ὡμολόγησαν. [23]ὑπα-
τ[είας Παυ]λίνου καὶ Ἰουλιανοῦ τῶν λαμπροτάτων
Παῦνι α. (2nd hand) [24]Αὐ[ρήλιοι Ἀλό]ις καὶ
Ἡρακλῆς [εὐ]δοκοῦμεν πᾶσι [25]τοῖς προκ(ειμένοις)
καὶ ἐπερωτηθ(έντες) ὡμολ(ογήσαμεν). Αὐρήλ(ιος)
Πτολεμαῖος [26]ἐγ[γυῶμ]αι ὡς π[ρ]όκ(ειται) γρά(ψας)
κ[α]ὶ ὑπὲ[ρ] αὐτῶν μὴ εἰδ(ότων) γρά(μματα).

---

[a] Literally "staff-bearer." In the papyri the word usually
denotes a conductor of requisitioned beasts of burden.

362. CONTRACT CONCERNING A PUBLIC SERVICE

P. Oxy. 1627.   A.D. 342.

[1]Ὑπατίας τῶν δεσποτῶν ἡμῶν Κωνσταντίου τὸ
γ' [2]καὶ Κώνσταντος τὸ β' τῶν Αὐγούστων Μεσορὴ
ιθ. [3]Αὐρήλιος Ἀπφοῦς Παθερμουθίου ἀπὸ τῆς

442

have contracted with the superintendent that he
should take the single post of an attendant[a] of
the said animals from the 8th of the present month
of Pauni, the superintendent receiving from the
decani for wages two thousand drachmae a day.
And the superintendent forthwith acknowledges
that he has received from the *decani* as two
months' wages from the said 8th twenty talents
of silver, and he shall receive from the said *decani*
the amount eventually earned up to the termina-
tion of his duties as superintendent. And it is
acknowledged that I, Ptolemaeus, am to provide
the salary eventually payable, in order to render the
decani free from molestation, annoyance, or loss in
what concerns the said office of attendant. This
contract, written in duplicate, is valid, and in answer
to the formal question they have given their consent.
In the consulship of Paulinus and Julianus the most
illustrious, Pauni 1. (Signed) We, the Aurelii Alois
and Heracles, agree to all the aforesaid, and in
answer to the formal question we have given our
consent. I, Aurelius Ptolemaeus, am surety as aforesaid, and I have written for them also as they are
illiterate.

362. CONTRACT CONCERNING A PUBLIC
SERVICE

A.D. 342.

In the consulship of our masters the Augusti,
Constantius for the 3rd time and Constans for the
2nd, Mesore 19. Aurelius Apphous son of Pather-

⁴λαμ(πρᾶς) καὶ λαμπ(ροτάτης) Ὀξυρυγχειτῶν πόλεως ⁵Αὐρηλίῳ Διογένου Σαραπίωνος συστάτῃ ⁶τῆς
αὐτῆς πόλεως τῆς νυνὶ λειτουργού-⁷σης φυλῆς
χαίρειν. ἐπιδὴ αἱρῖται ⁸ἐμοί τε καὶ τῷ ἡμετέρῳ
υἱῷ Θωνίῳ ⁹ἐν τῷ ἑξῆς ἐνιαυτῷ ὀκταμηνιαῖος
¹⁰χρόνος λιτουργίας, ἠξιώσαμεν δέ σαι εἰσ-¹¹αγγεῖλαι
ἡμᾶς εἰς κουφοτάτην χρίαν, ¹²τουτέστιν εἰς φυλακίαν
ἱεροῦ Θοηρίου, ¹³διὰ τὴν περὶ ἡμᾶς μετριότητα καὶ
¹⁴πίστις συνέθου ἡμεῖν κατὰ ταῦτα, ¹⁵καὶ αὐτοὶ
ὁμολογοῦμεν ἀντὶ ἴσης ἀμοιβῆς ¹⁶καὶ χάριτος
ἐπάναγκες ἡμᾶς ὅλον τὸν ¹⁷ἐνιαύσιον χρόνον πληρῶσαι ἐν τῇ τοῦ ¹⁸αὐτοῦ ἱεροῦ Θοηρίου ἀρχιφύλακος
¹⁹χώρᾳ ἀντὶ τῶν μηνῶν ὀκτώ. πρὸς ²⁰δὲ ἀμεριμνίαν
σου τήνδε τὴν ὁμολογίαν ²¹σοι ἐξεδόμην, ἥτις κυρία
ἔστω, καὶ ἐπερ(ωτηθεὶς) ²²ὡμολόγησα. (2nd hand)
²³[Αὐρ]ήλιος Ἀπφοῦς Πατερμουθίου ²⁴[εὐδ]οκῶ
πᾶσι τοῖς προκειμένοις ²⁵[καὶ ἐπ]ερωτηθεὶς ὡμολόγησα. ²⁶[Αὐρήλ]ιος Ῥουφίων Ἀπολλωνίου
²⁷[. . . .]υ ἔγραψα ὑπὲρ αὐτοῦ μὴ εἰδό(τος) ²⁸[γρά]μ-
ματα. (3rd hand) ²⁹[δι' ἐμο]ῦ Διογένους ἐγρά(φη).

5. l. Διογένει.   10. l. σε.   14. l. πίστεις.

363. CONTRACT WITH AN OFFICIAL IN CON-STANTINOPLE CONCERNING A LAW-SUIT

P. Cairo Masp. 67032.   A.D. 551.

¹[☧ Βα]σιλ[είας τοῦ θ]ειοτά[του καὶ εὐσε]βεστάτου
δεσπότου ἡμῶν Φ[λαυίου ²Ἰου]στινιανοῦ τοῦ αἰω-

mouthius, of the illustrious and most illustrious city of Oxyrhynchus, to Aurelius Diogenes son of Sarapion, delegate of appointments in the said city for the tribe [a] now undertaking public services, greeting. Whereas in the coming year an eight months' term of public service is allotted to me and my son Thonius, and we requested you to nominate us to a very light duty, namely the guarding of the temple of Thoeris,[b] owing to our moderate means, and you gave us a guarantee accordingly, we for our part acknowledge ourselves bound, as an equivalent return and act of gratitude, to complete a whole year's service in the post of chief guard of the said temple of Thoeris in place of the eight months. And for your security I have issued to you this agreement, which shall be valid, and in answer to the formal question I have given my consent. (Signed) I, Aurelius Apphous son of Pathermouthius, agree to all that is stated above, and in answer to the formal question I have given my consent. I, Aurelius Rufion son of Apollonius . . . have written for him, as he is illiterate. (Subscribed) Written by me, Diogenes.

[a] See No. 290, note *b*.　　　[b] The hippopotamus goddess.

363. CONTRACT WITH AN OFFICIAL IN CONSTANTINOPLE CONCERNING A LAWSUIT

A.D. 551.

The 25th year of the reign of our most godlike and pious master Flavius Justinianus the eternal Augustus

[νί]ου Αὐγούστου καὶ Αὐτοκράτορ[ος] [3]ἔτους εἰκοστοῦ πέμπτου, μετὰ τὴ[ν] ὑπατίαν Φλ[α]υίου)
Βασιλίο[υ] [4]τοῦ λαμπρ(οτάτου) ἔτους δεκάτ[ου], τῇ
πρὸ πέντε Εἰδῶν Ἰουλίων ?] [5]ἰνδ(ικτίονος) τεσ-
σαρεισκαιδεκ[άτης], ἐν τῇ λαμπρᾷ καὶ [ἐν]δόξῳ
Φλ(αυίου) Κ[ω]νστ[αν]τί[νου] [6]πόλει Ῥώμῃ. τάσδε
τὰς [ἀν]τισυγγράφου[ς ὁμ]ολογείας καὶ [7]συνθήκας
<τίθενται καὶ ποιοῦνται> [π]ρὸς ἀλλήλους [δ]ίχα
δόλου κα[ὶ] βίας καὶ [ἀπάτ]ης [8]καὶ ἀνάγκης καὶ
πάσης περιγραφῆς, ἑκούσῃ γνώμῃ κα[ὶ] [9]αὐθαιρέτῳ
προαιρ[έ]σει ἐκ μὲν τοῦ ἑνὸς μέρ[ους Διόσκορος]
[10]Ἀπολλῶτος καὶ Καλλί[ν]ικος Βίκτορος καὶ Ἀπολ-
λῶς Ἰωάνν[ου] [11]καὶ Κῦρος Βίκτορος διὰ Σενο[ύ]θου
Ἀπολλῶτος πο[ι]ουμένου τὴ[ν] [12]χώραν αὐτοῦ
ἀπόντος, ὁρμώ[μ]ενοι ἅπαντες ἀπὸ κώμης [13][καλο]υ-
μέν[ης Ἀ]φρ[οδιτ]ῶν το[ῦ] Ἀν[ταιοπ]ολείτου ν[ομοῦ
τῆς Θηβαίων [14]ἐπ]αρχεί[ας], ἐκ [δὲ τοῦ] ἑτέρου
μέρους Φλ(αύιος) Π[αλλάδιος ὁ λαμπρ(ότατος)
[15]κόμης] τοῦ θ[είου] κωνσιστωρίου, υἱὸς Ἰωάνν[ου
τοῦ τῆς μακαρίας] [16]μνήμη[ς, κα]ὶ Ἐπίγονο[ς] ὁ
λαμπρό(τατος) κ[ό]μ(ης), ἀμφό[τεροι . . . . . .]
[17]ὁρμώμενοι ἐκ τῆς Λεοντί(ου) ? [λαμπρ(οτάτης) ?]
π[ό]λεως τ[ῆς πρώτης] [18]Καππαδοκῶν ἐπ[αρ]χεία[ς,
. . . .] νε[ωσ]τὶ δ[ι]άγ[οντες] κ[ατὰ ταύτην] [19]τὴν
βασιλεΐδ[α] π[ό]λιν, καὶ [ὁμολ]ογοῦ[ντ]ε[ς] ἀλλ[ή]λοις
ἐ[πὶ το]ῖς ἑξ[ῆς] [20]δηλουμένοις συμφώνοις. κατα-
λαβόντες ἐνταῦθα ἐπὶ ταύτη[ς] [21]τῆς βασιλευούσης
ἡμεῖς οἱ προγεγραμμένοι Διόσκορος καὶ [22]Ἀπολλῶς
καὶ Καλλίνικος καὶ Κῦρος δι' ἐμ[ο]ῦ Σενούθου

and Imperator, the 10th year after the consulship of
Flavius Basilius the most illustrious, July 11, 14th
indiction, in the illustrious and honourable city Rome
of Flavius Constantinus.[a] The under-mentioned draw
up and make the present reciprocal agreements
and covenants with each other, without guile or
violence or deceit or compulsion or any fraud, of their
own free will and deliberate choice, of the one part
Dioscorus[b] son of Apollos, Callinicus son of Victor,
Apollos son of John, and Cyrus son of Victor acting
through Senouthes son of Apollos who represents him
in his absence, all natives of the village called Aphrodito in the Antaeopolite nome in the eparchy of the
Thebaid,[c] and of the other part Flavius Palladius the
most illustrious count of the sacred consistory,[d] son
of John of blessed memory, and Epigonus the most
illustrious count, both natives of the most illustrious
city of Leontius in the 1st eparchy of Cappadocia, but
of recent years resident in this royal city, agreeing
with each other on the following terms of accord.

We the aforesaid, Dioscorus, Apollos, Callinicus, and
Cyrus, acting through me, Senouthes, as his repre-

[a] That is, Constantinople, the new Rome founded by the
Emperor Constantine.

[b] See No. 218, p. 101, note *a*. Dioscorus and his companions, having a grievance against some of their fellow-
villagers, had gone to Constantinople, presented a petition to
the Emperor, and obtained a rescript giving certain directions.
Being obliged to engage an *exsecutor negotii* to present their
case in the law-court and conduct it to a conclusion, they
made the present contract with Flavius Palladius, who agreed
to come to Egypt and give the required assistance. He also
undertook to secure for the village the right of collecting its
own taxes (see No. 218); but as this part of the contract is
badly mutilated, we have not printed it here.

[c] The province of Upper Egypt.

[d] The Emperor's council.

SELECT PAPYRI

ποιου‹μέ›νου ²³τὴν χώραν αὐτοῦ θείαν ἐπορισάμεθα
κέλευσιν κ[ατὰ] τῶν ²⁴ἀντιδίκων ἡμῶν τὸν περὶ
Ἡράκλειον Ψαΐωτος καὶ λοιπῶν ²⁵ἀπὸ τῆς ἡμετέρας κώμης, ἔτι μὴν καὶ καθ' οἱονδήποτε
²⁶προσώπου ἀποδεικνυμένου ἀκολούθως τῇ θείᾳ
ὑμῶν ²⁷[κε]λεύσει, καὶ δεηθ[έντε]ς κατὰ νόμον
πρα . . . τρος ἐκβιβαστο[ῦ ²⁸τοῦ πρ]άγματος
παρακ[λήσ]εις προσηνενόχ[α]μ[εν] τῇ [ὑμῶν] ²⁹λαμ-
πρότητι ἐπὶ Ἰουνίου μηνὸς τῆς ἀρτίως τεσσαρ[εισ-
καιδεκάτης] ³⁰ἐπινεμήσεως, κατ' Αἰγυπτίους δὲ
πεντεκαιδ[εκάτης], ³¹ὥστε αὐτὴν σὺν θεῷ παρα-
γεινομένην τῇ Θη[βαίων χώρᾳ] ³²λαβεῖν τὴν εἰρη-
μένην θείαν κέλευσιν ἤτοι τ[ὸ φυλαχθὲν ?] ³³παρ'
ἡμῶν θεῖον ὑπομνηστικὸν καὶ ἐμφανίσασθαι τοῖς
³⁴κατὰ χώραν δικαστηρίοις καὶ πᾶσαν εὔνοιαν καὶ
σ . . ρ . . . . ³⁵καὶ ἔπειξιν καὶ ἀγρυπνίαν καὶ
ἐκβιβ[ασ]μὸν θέ[σθαι ? τῷ] ³⁶ἡμετέρῳ πράγματι,
ἕως οὗ πέρατι παραδο[θήσεται ἡ] δίκη ³⁷πρὸ[ς]
πᾶσα[ν] ἀπαλλαγὴν α[ὐ]τοῦ . . . . μι τῆς
αὐτῆς ³⁸θείας κελεύσεως, καὶ π[αρέ]ξαι παρὰ τὸ
δικαστήριον πά[ντ]α ³⁹τὰ ἐντεταγμένα πρόσωπα τῇ
αὐτῇ κελεύσει ὑπὸ ἐγγύα[ς] ⁴⁰ἀσφαλεῖς, οὐ μὴν ἀλλὰ
καὶ πάντα τὰ ἀποδεικνύμενα πρόσωπα ⁴¹κατὰ τὴν
δύναμιν τοῦ εἰρημένου τύπου καὶ ἐκβιβάσ[αι]
⁴²ἄχρει πέρατος δίκης, ἡμῶν μέντοι διδομένων τὰ
ἐμφ[α]νιστικ[ὰ] ⁴³καὶ τὰ ἀναλώματα τῆς τάξεως
καὶ ἀπολαμβανόντων τὸ τέταρτον ⁴⁴μέρος πάντων
τῶν ‹τῶν› ἐναγομένων προσώπων σπορ[τ]ούλ[ων],
⁴⁵τοῦ δὲ ἄλλου ἡμίσεως τετάρτου μέρους τῶν αὐτῶν
σ[πορτούλων] ⁴⁶στελλομένου τῇ ὑμετέρᾳ λαμπρότητι·
τῶν δὲ ἐ[κβησομένων ?] ⁴⁷ἐκ τῆς δίκης ἢ πρὸ δίκης
ἔξεστι ἡμῖν λαβεῖν εἰ[ς] λόγο[ν κέρδους ?] ⁴⁸ὑπὲρ
448

sentative, arriving here in this royal city obtained a
divine order against our adversaries the party of
Heraclius son of Psaios and other people of our village,
furthermore against any person whatsoever indicated
by the purport of our divine order, and requiring by
the law an . . . *exsecutor* [a] of the suit we have presented a request to your excellency in June of the
present 14th indiction, but of the 15th according to
Egyptian reckoning,[b] that by the leave of God you
should come to the Thebaid and take the said divine
order, that is, the divine memorandum held by us,
and lay it before the local courts and devote all goodwill and . . . and expedition and watchfulness and
furtherance to our suit until the case be brought to
an end and completely dispatched (in pursuance ?) of
the said divine order, and produce before the court all
the persons mentioned in the said order under safe
security, and furthermore all the persons indicated
by the import of the said decree, and prosecute the
suit till the end of the case, we paying the charges for
presenting the order and the costs of the *officium* [c] and
receiving one quarter of all the defendants' fees, and
the other three quarters of the said fees being allotted
to your excellency ; and of the sums which will be
forthcoming in consequence of the action or in antici-
pation of it, we again are entitled to receive as com-

[a] See No. 252. It seems strange that an eminent personage should come from Constantinople to undertake this office.
[b] The new indiction had already begun in Egypt, though
not at Constantinople, where its starting-point was later.
[c] *Cf.* Nos. 250-252.

24. *l.* τῶν.   25. *l.* οἰουδήποτε.   26. *l.* ἡμῶν.

ζημιωμάτων ἡμῶν καὶ αὐτῶν τὸ ἥμ[ι]σ[υ τέτα[ρ-
[τον] ⁴⁹μέρος καὶ τῇ ὑμετέρᾳ λαμπρότητι τὸ ἄλλο
τέταρτον, [ὥ]στε εἶ[ναι] ⁵⁰τοῦτο ὑπέρ τε σκυλμοῦ
καὶ κόπου καὶ ἀναλωμάτ[ων] αὐτῆς ⁵¹ἤτοι καὶ τῶν
προσηκόντων αὐτῇ παιδαρίων· καὶ μὴ δύνασθαι
⁵²αὐτὴν ἐν οὐδενεὶ ἀμφιβάλλειν ἢ παραβῆναι τὰ
προκείμ[ενα] ⁵³σύμφωνα, ἀλλ' εἰς πέρας ἄξαι
εὐλόγως καὶ σπουδαίως καὶ δικ[α]ίω[ς] ⁵⁴κατὰ πάντα
ἐντρανῆ τρόπον, δίχα οἱασδήποτε προδοσία[ς] ⁵⁵καὶ
ῥᾳδιουργείας καὶ ὑπερθέσεως καὶ ἀναβολῆς καὶ
μετεωρεισμο[ῦ] ⁵⁶καὶ χλεύης, ἑτοίμως ἔχοντες καὶ
ἡμεῖς ὑπὸ λόγον προσεδρεῦσ[αι] ⁵⁷τοῦ ἐνδοξοτάτου
στρατηλάτου τῆς χώρας καὶ τοῦ α[.........]ου,
⁵⁸ὃν ἂν προλήμψεται ἡμῖν ἀπ' αὐτῶν ἡ ὑμετέρ[α]
λαμ[πρότης], ⁵⁹ἕως ὅτε εἰς πέρας ἀχθῇ ἡ τοῦ καθ'
ἡ[μᾶ]ς πράγματο[ς δίκη, ⁶⁰ἀμ]έμπτως καὶ ἀκατα-
γνώστως κα . ειδ (?) ἐκβιβ[ασμὸν] ⁶¹ποιήσασθαι καὶ
ἐκδοῦναι τοῖς ἐναγομένοις [τὸ βιβλίον ?] ⁶²ἑτοίμως
ἔχομεν κινδύνῳ ἡμῶν καὶ πόρῳ <τῆς> πα[ντοίας
ὑποστάσεως] ⁶³καὶ δίκας λέγειν. ἐγώ τε ὁ προλεχ-
θεὶς λαμπρότατος Π[αλλάδιος] ⁶⁴ἀνθομολογῶ ἑτοίμως ἔχειν ἐμμεῖναι τοῖς προδιορεισθεῖσί μοι παρ'
[ὑμῶ]ν ⁶⁵συμφώνοις καὶ ὁμολογήμασιν καὶ στέρξα[ι
π]άντα καὶ εἰς πέρας ⁶⁶[ἄ]ξαι καθ' οἱονδήποτε
προμνημ[ον]ευθέντα παρ' ὑμῶν ⁶⁷τρόπον . . . . . .
. . . . . πρ . . . . . . αι ἐν τα[ύταις ταῖ[ς δυσὶ]
⁶⁸ὁμολογίαις κ[αὶ] μὴ ἐν οὐδενεὶ π[αρα]βῆναι . . . .
. . . . ταῦτα ⁶⁹κα[τ]ὰ [τ]ὴν δύναμιν τῆς πορει-
σθ[είσ]η[ς ὑμῖν θείας κελεύ]σεως, ⁷⁰ἀλλὰ μᾶλλον
ἐκβιβάσα[ι π]άντας τοὺς [ὑμ]ετέρους [ἀν]τιδίκους
⁷¹τοὺς ἐντεταγμένους καὶ ἀποδεικνυμένους ἐπὶ
παντὶ κεφαλαί[ῳ] ⁷²ἀνήκοντι ὑμῖν κατ' αὐτῶν

pensation for our losses the three quarter part, and your excellency the other quarter, to pay for the journey and trouble and expenses of yourself and the servants attached to you ; and you shall not in any wise vacillate or transgress the aforesaid accord, but execute it fairly and earnestly and justly in a perfectly transparent manner, without any kind of treachery or levity or delay or procrastination or abeyance or mockery ; and we again are ready to appear in court at the summons of the most honourable commander of the province or of the . . ., whichever of them your excellency may prefer, until the action concerning our affair be concluded, and to prosecute it blamelessly and irreproachably and to deliver our complaint to the defendants and to speak in court, at our personal risk and on the resources of our property of every kind.

And I, the aforesaid most illustrious Palladius, acknowledge in return that I am ready to abide by the accords and agreements above formulated to me by you and to accept them all and execute them in whatsoever manner you have set forth . . . in these two agreements and not transgress them in any respect . . . according to the import of the divine order delivered to you, but rather to conduct the case against all your adversaries mentioned or indicated in respect of every

[μ]έχρει τῆς περαιώσεως τοῦ ὑμετέρου ⁷³πράγματος.
καὶ πρόσεπι τούτοις πρὸς σαφεστέραν καὶ ὀχυ[ρω]-
τέραν ⁷⁴ἀσφάλειαν ἐπωμνύμεθα ἀλλήλοις, ἐγὼ μὲν
ὑμῖν, ὑμ[εῖς δὲ ἐμοί], ⁷⁵τὸν θεῖον καὶ σεβάσμιον
ὅρκον, τὴν δὲ ἁγία[ν] καὶ ὁ[μοούσιον] ⁷⁶Τριάδα καὶ
τὴν νίκην καὶ τὴν διαμονὴ[ν] το[ῦ] κ[α]λλι[νίκου]
⁷⁷ἡμῶν δεσπότου Φλ(αυίου) Ἰουστινια[νοῦ τοῦ]
αἰω[νίου Αὐγούστου] ⁷⁸καὶ Α[ὐτο]κ[ράτο]ρ[ος . . .
. . . . ἐμμενε]ῖν τοῖς ὡ[μ]ολογη[θεῖσιν] ⁷⁹παρ'
ἡμῶν ἀμφοτέρων ἐν ταύταις ταῖς ἰσοτύποις δυ[σ]ὶ
⁸⁰ὁμολογίαις. εἰ δὲ μὴ τοῦτο ποιήσομεν, παρέξει
τὸ μὴ ⁸¹ἐμμένον μέρος τῷ ἐμμένοντι χρυσίου λίτρας
δύο ἔργῳ ⁸²καὶ δυνάμει ἀπαιτουμένας, καὶ ἄκον
ἐμμενεῖν πᾶσιν ⁸³τοῖς προγεγραμμένοις συμφώνοις.
καὶ ἐπὶ τούτοις ἅπασιν ⁸⁴ἐπερωτηθέντες παρ'
ἀλλήλων καὶ ἀλλήλους ἐπερωτήσαντες ταῦθ' ⁸⁵οὕτως
ἔχειν δώσειν [π]οιεῖν φ[υλ]άττειν εἰς [πέρα]ς ἄξαι
⁸⁶ὡμολογήσαμεν. - - - ¹⁰⁵☩ Φλ(αυίος) Παλλάδιος
κόμ(ης) ὁ προγεγραμμένος ἐθέμην ταύτην τὴν
ὁμολο-¹⁰⁶γίαν ἐπὶ πᾶσην τοῖς πρ[ο]γεγρ[αμ]μένοις
συμφώνοις καὶ . ρε . . . . ¹⁰⁷ὑπέγραψα
χειρὶ ἐμῇ. + + + ☩ Φλ(αυίος) Φοιβάμμων Ἀθανασίου
ἀπὸ .[. . . . .] ¹⁰⁸τῆς Θηβαίων χώρας μαρτυρῶ [τῇδε τῇ ὁμολογίᾳ ἀκούσας παρὰ τοῦ] ¹⁰⁹θεμέ-
νου. ☩ + Φλ(αυίος) Ἰωάννη[ς Θ]ε[οδ]ώρου ἀπὸ τῆς
Λύκων [πόλεως τῆς ¹¹⁰Θηβαίων χώρας] μαρτυρῶ
[τῇδε τῇ ὁμολογίᾳ ἀκούσα]ς παρὰ [τοῦ θεμένου].
¹¹¹Φλ(αυίος) . ωρ . . ογιος Θεοδοσ[ίου] ε . . πρ . .
. . . . ¹¹²τ]ακτο-
μίσθων ἐπὶ τῆς πρότης τοῦ τα . . . . . . μαρτυρον
τῇ . . ¹¹³ὁμολογίᾳ ἀκούσας παρὰ τοῦ θεμένου.
+ Φλ(αυίος) Θεόδωρος νοτάριος ¹¹⁴τὴν χρείαν

claim which you entertain against them until the conclusion of your suit. And to these terms, for clearer and stronger security, we have sworn to each other, I to you and you to me, the divine and imperial oath, by the holy and consubstantial Trinity and the victory and permanence of our triumphant master Flavius Justinianus the eternal Augustus and Imperator, that . . . we will abide by what we have both agreed to in these two duplicate agreements. If we fail to do so, the party which does not abide by them shall pay to the party which does two pounds of gold to be really and truly exacted, and shall abide against its will by all the foregoing accord. And having formally questioned each other and been questioned by each other on all these terms we have acknowledged that they are correct and that we will give, perform, observe, and complete . . . (Signed) I the aforesaid, Flavius Palladius, count, made this agreement on all the above-mentioned terms of accord and . . . signed it with my hand. (Witnessed) I, Flavius Phoebammon son of Athanasius, of . . . in the Thebaid, witness this agreement, having heard it read by the maker. I, Flavius John son of Theodorus, of Lycopolis in the Thebaid, witness this agreement, having heard it read by the maker. I, Flavius . . . son of Theodosius . . ., *tactomisthus* [a] . . . witness this agreement, having heard it read by the maker. I, Flavius Theodorus, notary, who give my services

---

[a] A word of doubtful meaning, applied to a certain class of soldiers in Ptolemaic documents.

---

75. *l.* τήν τε.   78. *l.* ὁμολογηθεῖσιν.   82. *l.* ἐμμενεῖ.
106. *l.* πᾶσιν.   112. *l.* πρώτης, μαρτυρῶ.

ἐκτελῶν ἅπασιν τοῖς ἐνδεεῖς καὶ τὸ κάθεισμ[α]
¹¹⁵ποι[ού]μενος ἐν τῇ ἁγιωτάτῃ μεγάλῃ ἐκκλησίᾳ
ταύτης ¹¹⁶[τῆς βα]σιλείδος πόλεως μαρτυρῶ τῇδε τῇ
[ἀσφ]αλείᾳ ¹¹⁷τῇ ἐκτεθείσῃ π[αρὰ] Διοσκόρο[υ] καὶ
Καλλινίκου καὶ ¹¹⁸Κύρου διὰ Σενο[ύ]θο[υ] καὶ
['Απολλ]ῶτος εἰς Παλλάδιον ¹¹⁹τὸν - - -

114. *l.* ἐνδεέσι.

364. SURETY FOR A SAUSAGE-MAKER

P. Strassb. 46.   A.D. 566.

¹[Βασιλείας τοῦ θειοτάτου ἡμῶν δεσπότου Φλ(α-
ουίου) ²'Ιουστίνου τοῦ αἰωνίου Αὐγούστου Αὐτοκράτορος ³ἔτους {ε}ἰκοστο[ῦ]} πρώτου {Φ} μετὰ [τὴν
ὑπατείαν] ⁴Φλ(αουίου) Βασιλείου το[ῦ] ἐ[νδο]ξο-
τάτ[ου ἔτ]ου[ς εἰκοστοῦ] ⁵πέμπτου Φαμε[νὼ]θ
κα τρ . [. .] . . [. . . . .] . ⁶τῇ δημοσίᾳ
ἀγορᾷ δ(ιὰ) σοῦ Φιλήμ{μ}ωνος ἀρχιυ[πηρέτ(ου)
⁷'Α]ντι(νοέων πόλεως) Φλ(αούιος) Σαραπάμμων ὁ
<καὶ> Κόλλο[υ]κος ἀπ[ὸ τῆς 'Αντι(νοέων πόλεως).
⁸ὁ]μολογῶ ἑκουσίως καὶ αὐθαιρέτως ἐγ[γ]υ[ᾶσθαι
⁹κ]αὶ ἀναδεδέχθαι παρ' ὑμῖν Αὐρ(ήλιον) Φ . β . .-
ιω[. . . ¹⁰ . . .]θησεψαγαμερ[.] . . ατου ἰσικιά-
ρ(ιον) ἀπὸ [τ]ῆ[ς ¹¹'Αντ]ι(νοέων πόλεως), ἐφ' ᾧ
αὐτοῖς εἶναι ἐνταῦθα ἐπὶ τῆ[ς 'Αντι(νοέων πόλεως)
¹²ἐκτ]ελοῦντα τὴν τῶν ἰσικιαρίω[ν] χρεί[αν ¹³ἀμέ]μ-
πτως καὶ ἀκαταφρονήτως [ποι]εῖσθ[α]ι ¹⁴[ἀπὸ] τῆς

7. *l.* Κόλλουθος.   11. *l.* αὐτόν.

to all who need them and have my place of work
in the most holy great church[a] of this royal city,
witness this deed of surety concluded by Dioscorus,
Callinicus, Cyrus represented by Senouthes, and
Apollos, with Palladius . . .

[a] The newly built St. Sophia. The notary had probably
a booth near the entrance.

364. SURETY FOR A SAUSAGE-MAKER

A.D. 566.

In the 1st year of the reign of our most godlike
master Flavius Justinus the eternal Augustus and
Imperator, the 25th year after the consulship of the
most honourable Flavius Basilius, Phamenoth 21, . . .
To the administration of the market through you,
Philemon, chief assistant at Antinoe, from Flavius
Sarapammon also called Colluthus, of Antinoe. I
acknowledge voluntarily and of my own accord that
I accept at your hands the charge of and responsibility for Aurelius . . ., sausage-maker, of Antinoe,
engaging that he shall remain here in Antinoe pursuing his trade of sausage-making without fault,[a] and
shall devote himself to it from the holy Easter day [b]

[a] Such trades were officially controlled in order to secure
for the town an adequate supply of various comestibles.
Compare No. 331. The tradesmen might even have to provide sureties as in the present case.

[b] Easter fell in this year a little later than the date of the
contract.

ἀγίας ἀναστάσεως τ[ῆ]ς πα[ρούσης ¹⁵τεσσ]αρεσκαι-
δεκάτη[ς ἰ]νδ(ικτίονος) ἕως [τ]ῆς π[αρα]λή[μψεως
¹⁶τῆς σ]ὺν θεῷ πεντεκαιδεκά[της ἰ]νδ(ικτίονος), [καὶ
¹⁷μηδ]αμῶς αὐτὸν ἀπολείπ[εσθαι, ἐὰν δὲ ἀπο-
¹⁸λειφ]θείη καὶ τοῦτον ζητούμ[ενον μὴ παρε-¹⁹νεγ]κῶ
καὶ παραδώσω σοι ἐ[ν] δ[ημοσίῳ τόπῳ ²⁰ἐκτὸς
ἁ]γίων περιβόλων καὶ θείω[ν χαρακτήρων καὶ
²¹ἀγίας] κυριακῆς . . . . ἀπράκ[του ἡμέρας, ἐγὼ
αὐτὸς ²²ὁ τού]του ἐγγυητὴς παρασχεῖ[ν σοι
ὑπὲρ τῆς ²³αὐτοῦ] ἀπολείψεως χρυσοῦ νόμ[ισμ(α)
α. ἡ ἐγγύη ²⁴κ]υρία καὶ βεβαία καὶ εἰς πάν[τα
ἐπερ(ωτηθεὶς) ὡμολ(όγησα) + (2nd hand) + Φλ(α-
ούιος) ²⁵Σα]ραπάμμων ὃς καὶ Κ(όλλ)ουθος [ἐγγυῶμαι
καὶ στοι-²⁶χεῖ] μοι πάντα ὡς πρόκ(ειται). Αὐρ(ή-
λιος) Στέ[φανος Ὥρου . . . . ἀπὸ ²⁷᾽Αν]τι(νοέων
πόλεως) ἀξιωθεὶς ἔγραψα ὑπὲρ αὐτ[οῦ γράμματα
μὴ ²⁸εἰδ]ότος. + (3rd hand) ²⁹δι᾽ ἐμοῦ Κοσμᾶ συμ-
βολαιο[γ]ράφ(ου) [ἐτελειώθη ?].

14. ἀναστάσεως E.-H.: ἁγιοστάσεως Ed.   18-19. μὴ παρ-
ενεγ]κῶ E.-H.   21. ἡ ἄλλης is expected after κυριακῆς.

of the present 14th indiction to the time of taking over [a] in the (D.V.) 15th indiction, and shall in no circumstances leave his work.   If he should leave his work, and I shall fail to bring him when he is wanted and deliver him to you in a public place, debarred from the protection of sacred precincts and sacred images and Sundays and holidays, I as his surety will pay you for his evasion 1 gold solidus.   This deed of surety is valid and guaranteed, and in answer to the formal question I have given my assent on every point. (Signed) I, Flavius Sarapammon also called Colluthus, accept the charge and I agree to everything as aforesaid.   I, Aurelius Stephanus son of Horus . . ., of Antinoe, wrote for him by request, as he is illiterate. (Subscribed) Executed by me, Cosmas, private notary.

  [a] Perhaps the taking over of the contract by another. According to Preisigke " beginning of the indiction," but this is improbable.   (The word is assured by a parallel passage.)

XI. RECEIPTS

365. RECEIPT OF A BOAT-CAPTAIN

P. Hib. 98, ll. 6-21.   252 B.C.

⁶[Βασι]λεύοντος Πτολεμαίου τοῦ Πτολεμαί[ου
⁷Σω]τῆρος (ἔτους) λδ, ἐφ' ἱερέως Νεοπτολέμου
⁸τοῦ Κραίσιος Ἀλεξάνδρου καὶ θεῶν ⁹['Αδελ]φῶν,
κανηφόρου 'Αρσινόης Φιλαδέλ-¹⁰[φο]υ 'Αρσινόης
τῆς Νικολάου, μηνὸς ¹¹Μεσορὴ κδ. [ὁ]μολογεῖ
Διονύσ[ιος] ¹²ναύκληρος ἐμβεβλῆσθα[ι εἰς] κέρ-
(κουρον) ¹³Ξενοδόκου καὶ 'Αλεξάνδρου ἐφ' [οὗ]
κ[υ(βερνήτης)] ¹⁴Ἐκτεῦρις Πάσιτος Μεμφίτης διὰ
¹⁵Νεχθεμβέους τοῦ παρὰ τῶν βασιλικῶν ¹⁶γραμ-
ματέων ὥστε εἰς 'Αλ[εξ]άνδρειαν ¹⁷εἰς τὸ βασιλικὸν
σὺν δείγματι [κριθῶν] ¹⁸ἀρτάβας τετρακισχιλίας
ὀκτ[ακοσίας] ¹⁹σῖτον κα[θαρὸν ἄ]δ[ο]λον κεκο-
σκιν[ευμένον] μέτρωι [καὶ σκυτά-]²⁰ληι οἷς α[ὐτὸς
ἠ]νέγκατο ἐξ 'Αλεξ[ανδρείας] ²¹μετρήσε[ι δικαίαι],
καὶ οὐθ[ὲν ἐγκαλῶ].

458

XI. RECEIPTS

365. RECEIPT OF A BOAT-CAPTAIN

252 B.C.

In the 34th year of the reign of Ptolemy son of Ptolemy Soter, the priest of Alexander and the gods Adelphi being Neoptolemus son of Craesis, the canephorus of Arsinoe Philadelphus being Arsinoe daughter of Nicolaus, the 24th of the month Mesore. Dionysius, boat-captain, acknowledges that he has embarked upon the transport of Xenodocus and Alexander, of which Ekteuris son of Pasis, of Memphis, is pilot, through Nechthembes the agent of the royal scribes, for conveyance to Alexandria to the royal granary, with a sample, 4800 artabae of barley, being pure, unadulterated, and sifted grain, by the measure and smoothing-rod which he himself brought from Alexandria, with just measurement ; and I make no complaint.

366. TWO RECEIPTS FOR WAGES OF GOVERNMENT POSTMEN

B.G.U. 1232.   3rd–2nd cent. B.C.

¹Μηνόφιλος γραμματεὺς ²βυβλιαφόρων Β[ῆ]τι
τῶι παρὰ ³ʿΑρυώτου βασιλικοῦ γραμ[ματ]έως ⁴χαίρειν. [ὁ]μολογῶ μεμετρῆσθαι ⁵διὰ σοῦ παρὰ Πτολεμαίου τοῦ σιτολ(ογοῦντος) ⁶τὴν πρὸ[ς] ἥλιον
τοπαρχίαν τὸ γι-⁷νόμεν[ο]ν μ[έ]τρημα τοῖς ἐν τῶι
⁸ʼΟξυρυγχίτηι βυβλιαφόροις εἰς ⁹Τῦβι καὶ Μεχεὶρ
τοῦ ζ (ἔτους) πυρῶν ¹⁰(ἀρτάβας) ἑβδομήκοντα,
¹¹πυ(ρ.) (ἀρτ.) ο.

¹²Μηνόφιλος γραμματεὺς ¹³βυβλιαφόρων Βῆτι τῶι
¹⁴παρʼ ʼΑρυώτου τοῦ βασιλικοῦ γρ(αμμᾶτέως)
χαίρειν. ὁμολογῶ μεμετρῆσ-¹⁵θαι διὰ σοῦ παρὰ
Πτολεμαίου ¹⁶τοῦ σιτολογ(οῦντος) τὴν πρὸς ἥλιον
¹⁷τοπαρχίαν τὸ γινόμεν[ον] ¹⁸μέτρημα τοῖς ἐν τῶι
ʼΟξυ[ρυγ-]¹⁹χίτηι βυβλιαφόροις εἰς μῆνα[ς] ²⁰Παχὼν
καὶ Παῦνι τοῦ ζ (ἔτους) ²¹τὰς λοιπὰς πυρῶν (ἀρτάβας) ἐξήκοντα πέντε ²²καὶ πρόδομα εἰς ʼΕπεὶφ
²³πυρῶν (ἀρτάβας) εἴκοσι δύο τὰς ²⁴πάσας πυρῶν
(ἀρτάβας) ὀγδοήκοντα ²⁵ἑπτά, (γίνονται) πυ(ρ.)
(ἀρτ.) πζ. Παῦνι ιγ.

367. RECEIPT FOR PAYMENT OF A FINE

P. Amh. 31.   112 B.C.

¹ʼΕτους ϛ Χοίαχ η. τέ(τακται) ἐπὶ τὴν ἐν ʼΕρ-
μ(ώνθει) τρά(πεζαν) ἐφʼ ἧς Διονύσιος εἰς τὸν ἴδιον

366. TWO RECEIPTS FOR WAGES OF GOVERNMENT POSTMEN

3rd–2nd cent. B.C.

Menophilus, scribe of the letter-carriers, to Bes the agent of Haruotes the royal scribe greeting. I acknowledge that I have received through you from Ptolemaeus the sitologus of the eastern toparchy the amount of corn due to the letter-carriers in the Oxyrhynchite nome for Tubi and Mecheir of the 7th year, namely seventy artabae of wheat, 70 art. wheat.

Menophilus, scribe of the letter-carriers, to Bes the agent of Haruotes the royal scribe greeting. I acknowledge that I have received through you from Ptolemaeus the sitologus of the eastern toparchy the amount of corn due to the letter-carriers in the Oxyrhynchite nome for the months Pachon and Pauni of the 7th year, namely the remaining sixty-five artabae of wheat, and in advanced payment for Epeiph twenty-two artabae of wheat, altogether 87 artabae of wheat, total 87 art. wheat. Pauni 13.

367. RECEIPT FOR PAYMENT OF A FINE

112 B.C.

Year 6, Choiach 8. Paid into the bank at Hermonthis [a] of which Dionysius is head, to the private

[a] The modern Erment in Upper Egypt.

461

λόγον τῶν βασιλέων ²κατὰ διαγραφὴν Ἑρμίου τοῦ
ἐπὶ τῶν προσόδων καὶ Φίβιος τοῦ βασιλικοῦ γραμματέως, ἧς καὶ ³τὸ ἀντίγραφον ὑπόκειται, Σενποῆρις Ὀννώφριος προστίμου φοινικῶνος π(ηχῶν)
β χα(λκοῦ) Ἀσ τέλ(η) ρπ. ⁴Διονύ(σιος) τρα-
(πεζίτης).

⁵Ἑρμίας Διονυσίωι χαίρειν. ἐπιβάλλοντες εἰς
τὸν Παθυρίτην διεπεμψάμεθα τοὺς παρ' ἡμῶν
⁶εἰς τὰς τοπαρχίας σχεθησομένους τῆς εἰσαγωγῆς
τῶν ὀφειλομένων πρός τε τὴν σιτικὴν ⁷μίσθωσιν
καὶ τὴν ἀργυρικὴν πρόσοδον, καὶ ἐπὶ τῆς συνστα-
θείσης πρακτορείας ἐν τοῖς ⁸Μεμνονείοις σημαν-
θέντος ὑπάρχειν τόπους περιειλημμένους εἰς φυτείαν φοινίκων ⁹καὶ μεταπεμψάμενος Τοτοῆν τὸν
κωμογραμματέα καὶ ἐπελθόντες ἐπὶ τὸν Σενποῆριος
¹⁰τοῦ Ὀννώφριος τόπον καὶ ἐγμετρήσαντες [ἐ]γ-
βῆναι πήχ(εις) β, καὶ ταύτην μεταπεμψάμενοι
¹¹πειθανάγκης προσαχθείσης περὶ τοῦ καθήκοντος
προστίμου ὡς τῆς (ἀρούρης) διὰ τὸ παρειληφέναι
¹²ἀπὸ χέρσου (ταλάντων) ι τὰς συναγομένας χα(λ-
κοῦ) Ἀσ καὶ ταύτης ἐπιδεξαμένης, κατακολουθήσας καὶ δε-¹³ξάμενος ἐπὶ τῆς ἐν Ἑρμώνθει τρα-
(πέζης), συνυπογρά(φοντος) Φίβιος τοῦ βασιλικοῦ
γραμμα(τέως) τοῦ δὲ τοπογραμματέως ¹⁴ἐντάσ-
σοντος διὰ τῆς ἑαυτοῦ ὑπογρα(φῆς) τά τε μέτρα
καὶ τὰς γειτνίας καὶ προσδιασαφοῦντος μηδὲν ¹⁵ἐν
τούτοις ἠγνοῆσθαι, τὰς τοῦ χα(λκοῦ) πρὸς ἀργύ-
(ριον) Ἀσ ἀνάφερ' ἐν λήμματι εἰς τὸ πρόστιμον

10. *l.* τῆς Ὀννώφριος.

ᵃ That is, for an encroachment of ·2 cubits square measure
(about 50 square yards) on Crown land for the purpose of
planting palms.

account of the sovereigns, in accordance with the note of Hermias the overseer of revenues and Phibis the royal scribe, of which a copy is appended, by Senpoeris daughter of Onnophris as a fine for taking 2 cubits for a palm-grove ^a 1200 copper drachmae and as taxes 180 drachmae. (Signed) Dionysius, banker.

Hermias to Dionysius greeting. On reaching the Pathyrite nome we dispatched our agents to the toparchies to apply themselves to the collection of debts owed on account of both rents in corn and taxes in money, and when the work of collection had started at Memnonea ^b it was reported that certain pieces of land were found to have been enclosed for planting palms, and after sending for Totoes the village scribe I went with him to inspect the land of Senpoeris daughter of Onnophris and measuring it we found that it projected by 2 cubits. We then sent for her, and after forcible persuasion had been applied with regard to the proper fine, it was fixed at the rate of 10 talents the arura, in consideration of the encroachment having been made on dry ground, the total being 1200 drachmae, to which she agreed. Accordingly please receive at the bank at Hermonthis, as Phibis the royal scribe is also subscribing to this and the district scribe is inserting under his own signature the measurements and boundaries and further declares that there has been no oversight in this matter, the 1200 drachmae of copper at a discount,^c and enter them as received in payment of the

---

^b A village near the statues of Memnon opposite Luxor.
^c That is, nominally payable in silver, and therefore, if paid in copper, subject to a premium of about 10 per cent. Actually, almost all payments by common people were at this period made in copper.

SELECT PAPYRI

εἰς τὰ ἀναγεγραμμένα ¹⁶ὑπὸ τῶν παρ' ἡμῶν ὡς
κα[θ]ήκει, ἐφ' ὧι ταξαμένηι ἕξει ἐν φυτείαι τὸν
τόπον φοίνιξι οὐδένα λόγον ¹⁷συνισταμένηι πρὸς
ἡμᾶς περὶ οὐδενὸς ἁπλῶς. προσκόμισαι δὲ καὶ
τὰ καθήκοντα τέλη διπλᾶ ¹⁸καὶ εἴ τι ἄλλο καθήκει.
¹⁹ἔρρωσο. (ἔτους) ς Χοίαχ ϛ̅.

²⁰Δέξαι τὰς τοῦ χα(λκοῦ) πρὸς ἀργύ(ριον) χιλίας
διακοσίας, (γίνονται) Ἀσ, καὶ εἴ τι ἄλλο καθήκει.
(ἔτους) ς Χοίαχ ϛ̅.

²¹Φιβις. ἐὰν ὁ τοπογραμματεὺς ὑπογρά(ψῃ)
ταῦθ' οὕτως ἔχει⟨ν⟩ καὶ μηθὲν ἠγνοῆ(σθαι) καὶ
ἐντάξει τά τε μέτρα καὶ ²²τὰς γειτνίας, δέξαι
τὰ⟨ς⟩ τοῦ χα(λκοῦ) πρὸς ἀργύ(ριον) χιλίας δια-
κοσ(ίας), (γίνονται) Ἀσ, καὶ τἆλλα τὰ προσδια-
γρα(φόμενα). (ἔτους) ς Χοίαχ ϛ̅.

²³Παμώνθης. δέξαι παρὰ τῆς Σενποήριος τιμὴν
τῶν ²⁴δηλουμένων τὰς τοῦ χαλκοῦ πρὸς ἀργύ(ριον)
δραχμὰς χιλίας διακοσ(ίας), ²⁵γίνεται χα(λκοῦ) Ἀσ,
καὶ τἆλλα τὰ καθήκοντα. εἶναι δὲ τὰς γειτνίας
²⁶ἐξ ὧν ἀνενεγκεῖν Τοτοῆν τὸν κωμογραμμα(τέα)
νότου οἰκίαι ²⁷α[ὐ]τῆς Σενποήριος, βορρᾶ περίστασις
τοῦ φρουρίου, ἀπη(λιώτου) οἰκίαι ²⁸Ἀ[. .] . . τος,
λιβὸς ῥύμη. ²⁹(ἔτους) ς Χοίαχ ϛ̅.

**368. RECEIPTS FOR MONEY DEPOSITED
TO THE CREDIT OF RECRUITS**

P.S.I. 1063, 1-14.   A.D. 117.

¹Λονγεῖνος Λόνγ[ος] σημεαφόρ[ο]ς [σπ]είρης ᾱ
²Λουσιτανῶν (ἑκατονταρχίας) Τιτουληίου Λ[ο]ν-
464

fine in the list drawn up by our agents, in the proper way, on the understanding that, having paid this sum, she shall retain the plot for growing palms without incurring any responsibility towards us on any point whatever. Receive also twice the usual taxes and any other charge that is usual. Goodbye. Year 6, Choiach 6.

Receive the thousand two hundred drachmae of copper at a discount, total 1200, and any other charge that is usual. Year 6, Choiach 6.

Phibis. If the district scribe subscribes to the effect that the report is correct and that there has been no oversight, and if he inserts the measurements and boundaries, receive the thousand two hundred drachmae of copper at a discount, total 1200, and the other extra charges. Year 6, Choiach 6.

Pamonthes.[a] Receive from Senpoeris as the price of the said property the thousand two hundred drachmae of copper at a discount, total 1200 copper dr., and the other usual charges. The boundaries are, according to the report of Totoes the village scribe, on the south houses of Senpoeris herself, on the north outskirts of the guard-house, on the east houses of . . ., on the west a street. Year 6, Choiach 6.

[a] The district scribe mentioned in the note of Hermias.

368. RECEIPTS FOR MONEY DEPOSITED TO THE CREDIT OF RECRUITS

A.D. 117.

Longinus Longus, standard-bearer of the 1st Lusitanian cohort, of the *centuria* of Tituleius, to

γείνωι ³Τιτουληίῳ ἰατ[ρῷ] (ἑκατοντάρχῳ) χαίρειν.
ἔλ[αβ]ον παρὰ σοῦ ⁴[δη]νάρια τετρακόσια εἴκοσι
τ[ρί]α ὀβολοὺς κ ⁵ὑπὲρ δηποσίτου τι[ρώνων] ᾿Ασ[ια-
νῶ]ν δισ-⁶τριβούτων ἐν τῇ κεντυρίᾳ ἀνδρῶν ⁷εἴκοσι.
ἔτους εἰκοστοῦ καὶ ἐν [. .]] Τραϊα[νοῦ] ⁸᾿Αρίστου
Καίσαρος τοῦ κυρίου Θὼ[θ] ϛ.

(2nd hand) ⁹Οὐαλέριος ῾Ροῦφος σημεαφόρος
σπείρ(ης) ā Λουσιτανῶν (ἑκατονταρχίας) ¹⁰Κρήσ-
κεντος Λονγείνῳ Τιτουληίῳ (ἑκατοντάρχῳ) χαίρειν.
¹¹ἔλαβον παρὰ σοῦ δηνάρια ἀργυρᾶ διακόσια τριά-
¹²κοντα [[τρία]] δύο ὀβολοὺς τέσσαρες τὰ χωρη-
γ<ηθ>έντα εἰς δη[πό]σιτον τειρώ-¹³νων ᾿Ασιανῶν
ἀριθμῷ δέκ[α] ἑπτά. ἔτους εἰκοστοῦ πρώτου
¹⁴Τραϊανοῦ ᾿Αρίστου Καί[σαρο]ς τοῦ κυρ[ίο]υ
Θὼθ ϛ.

7. For εἰκοστοῦ πρώτου.   12. l. τέσσαρας, χορηγηθέντα.

369. SOLDIERS' RECEIPT FOR FODDER ALLOWANCE

P. Hamb. 39 (33).   A.D. 179.

¹²᾿Ηλιόδωρος Σερήνου ἱππεὺς εἴλης Γαλλικῆς[a]
τούρμης ᾿Αμμωνιανοῦ ¹³καὶ ᾿Ιούλις Σερῆν[ος] ἱππεὺς
εἴλης τῆς αὐτῆς τούρμης τῆς αὐτῆς ¹⁴Σερήνῳ
σ[ούμμῳ] κουράτορι χαίρειν. ἐλάβαμεν παρὰ σοῦ
τὴν ¹⁵γράστιν [ἡμῶν] ἐν προχρείᾳ ἐξερχόμενοι εἰς τὰ
Βο<υ>κόλια ¹⁶ἀνὰ δ[ην]άρια εἴκοσι πέντε ὑπὲρ τοῦ
ιθ (ἔτους) Αὐρηλίων ¹⁷᾿Αντων[ε]ίνου καὶ Κομμόδου

ª A cavalry regiment stationed in Egypt.

Longinus Tituleius, physician, centurion, greeting. I have received from you four hundred and twenty-three denarii 20 obols to be held in deposit for the recruits from Asia allotted to the *centuria*, being twenty men. The 21st year of Trajanus Optimus Caesar the lord, Thoth 6.[a]

Valerius Rufus, standard-bearer of the 1st Lusitanian cohort, of the *centuria* of Crescens, to Longinus Tituleius, centurion, greeting. I have received from you two hundred and thirty-two silver denarii four obols forming the amount supplied as a deposit for the recruits from Asia, seventeen in number. The 21st year of Trajanus Optimus Caesar the lord, Thoth 6.

[a] Trajan had been dead for about a month, but the news had not yet reached the cohort, which was stationed far up the Nile.

369. SOLDIERS' RECEIPT FOR FODDER ALLOWANCE

A.D. 179.

Heliodorus son of Serenus, trooper of the *ala Gallica* [a] in the squadron of Ammonianus, and Julius Serenus, trooper of the same *ala* and the same squadron, to Serenus the chief paymaster greeting. We have received from you our fodder allowance in advance on setting out for the Bucolia,[b] being twenty-five denarii each for the 19th year of Aurelius Antoninus Caesar and Aurelius Commodus Caesar the

[b] The northern part of the Delta, which had lately been the scene of a rebellion.

Καισάρων τῶν κυρίων [18]Τῦβι κγ̄. Ἀχιλλε‹ὺ›ς
Ἀχιλλέως ἱππεὺς εἴλης τῆς αὐτῆς [19]τούρμης Ἡρω-
διανοῦ ἔγραψα ὑπὲρ αὐτῶν ἐρωτηθεὶς [20]διὰ τὸ
βραδέως Ἡλιοδώρου γράφοντος ⟦και⟧. (2nd hand)
[21]Ἡλιόδωρος ἔλαβα ὡς πρόγιται.

20. l. Ἡλιόδωρον γράφειν.   21. l. πρόκειται.

370. RECEIPT CONCERNING A CONSIGNMENT OF ALUM

B.G.U. 697.   A.D. 145.

[1]Ἔτους ἐνάτου Αὐτοκράτορος [2]Καίσαρος Τίτου
Αἰλίου Ἀδριανοῦ [3]Ἀντωνίνου Σεβαστοῦ Εὐσεβοῦς
Τῦβι [4]γ̄ δι(ὰ) τῆς Σαβείνου τραπέζης [5]Ταμείων.
Ἰσχυρίων Ἀφροδ(ισίου) καὶ οἱ [6]σὺν αὐτῷ ἐπι-
τη(ρηταὶ) στυβ(τηρίας) Ἀρσι(νοΐτου) [7]Πανούφι
Τεσενούφεως μη(τρὸς) Στοτοή(τεως) [8]ἀπὸ κώμης
Σοκνο(παίου) Νήσου Ἡρακλ(είδου) [9]μερίδος καμη-
λοτρόφῳ ἀπέχει(ν) αὐτὸ[ν] [10]τέλος ὧν παρεκόμισεν
ἀπὸ Ὀάσεως [11]Μεικρᾶς δι(ὰ) πύλης Νύνπου εἰς
Ἀρσι(νοΐτην) [12]στυπτη[ρίας] ψιλῶν ταλάντων τριά-
κον-[13]τα, ὡς τοῦ (ταλάντου) α (δραχμῆς) α (τριωβόλου), (δραχμὰς) με, τὰ γεινόμε[να] [14]μεταλλικὰ
(τάλαντα) ιβ, φορέτρου αὐτῶν [15]ἐκ (δραχμῶν) ζ
(τριωβόλου) (δραχμὰς) Ϟ, τὰς συναγομ(ένας) ἀργ(υ-
ρίου) (δραχμὰς) ρλε. [16]παρείληφεν δὲ ὁ Ἰσχυρίων
παρ᾽ ἐπιτ(ηρητῶν) [17]Ὀάσεως Μεικ(ρᾶς) δι᾽ οὗ
προγ(έγραπται) καμηλο(τρόφου) [18]τὰ{ς} τῆς στυβ-
(τηρίας) μετα(λλικὰ) (τάλαντα) ιβ . . . .
468

lords, Tubi 23. I, Achilles son of Achilles, trooper of the same *ala* in the squadron of Herodianus, have written for them at their request, because Heliodorus writes with difficulty.[a] (Signed) I, Heliodorus, have received it as aforesaid.

    [a] It is implied that the second trooper was illiterate.

370. RECEIPT CONCERNING A CONSIGNMENT OF ALUM

A.D. 145.

    The ninth year of the Emperor Caesar Titus Aelius Hadrianus Antoninus Augustus Pius, Tubi 3, through the bank of Sabinus in the Treasuries quarter.[a] Ischyrion son of Aphrodisius and his fellow supervisors of the alum monopoly in the Arsinoite nome to Panouphis son of Tesenouphis and of Stotoetis, of the village of Socnopaei Nesus in the division of Heraclides, camel-driver, stating that he has received for the toll (paid by him) on the thirty light talents of alum which he transported from the Little Oasis to the Arsinoite nome through the toll-gate of Nunpou, at the rate of 1 drachma 3 obols per talent, 45 drachmae, and, as the said quantity equals 12 metal talents,[b] for their transport, at the rate of 7 drachmae 3 obols, 90 drachmae, making altogether 135 drachmae. And Ischyrion has received from the supervisors in the Little Oasis through the above-mentioned camel-driver the 12 metal talents of alum

    [a] In Arsinoe, the capital of the nome.
    [b] One metal or heavy talent = $2\frac{1}{2}$ light talents. But what these different talents actually weighed we do not yet know.

[19]εκ . . . τὰς συνήθ(ως) διδομ(ένας) (ἑκατοστὰς)
ἐξ ἥμυ[συ?]. (2nd hand) [20]Ἰσχυρ‹ί›ων ἐπιτηρητὴς
σὺν ἑ-[21]τέροις παρελάβαμεν τὰ{ς} τῆς [22]στυβτηρίας
τάλαντα μετα[λ-][23]λικὰ δέκα δύο, τὰ γεινόμε-[23]να
ψειλὰ τάλαντα τριάκ[ον-][24]τα, ὧν τὸ τέλος καὶ τὰ
φόλε[τρα] [26]ἀποδεδώκαμεν.

24. l. φόρε[τρα].

371. RECEIPT FOR RENT PAID
THROUGH A BANK

P. Fay. 87, ll. 1-13.   A.D. 155.

[1]Ἔτους ιη Αὐτοκράτορος Καίσαρος Τίτου Αἰλί[ο]υ
[2]Ἀδριανοῦ Ἀντωνείνου Σεβαστοῦ Εὐσεβοῦς [3]Με-
χ(εὶρ) κζ. ἐποίησεν ἐπὶ τ(ὴν) Τίτου Φλ(αουίου)
Εὐτυχ(ίδου) τράπ(εζαν) Εὐ-[4]δαίμων Σαραπίωνος
κ(αὶ) μέτοχ(οι) ἐπιτηρηταὶ [5]ὑπαρχόντων οἴκου
πόλεως Ἀλεξανδρέων [6](πρότερον) Ἰουλίου Ἀσκληπιάδου φιλοσόφο(υ) ὄντων περὶ [7]κώμ(ην) Εὐ-
ημερείαν εἰς φόρο(ν) ιζ (ἔτους) τάλαντ[ο]ν [8]ἓν
καὶ δραχ(μὰς) τετρακισχειλίας ἐπὶ τῷ τὸ [9]ἴσον ἐν
Ἀλεξανδρείᾳ δοθῆναι τῷ ἐπὶ τῶν [10]στεμμάτων
προκεχι(ρισμένῳ), (γίνεται) (τάλαντον) α (δραχμαὶ)
Δ. [11]Ἐπεὶφ η, ὁ αὐτ(ὸς) κ(αὶ) μέτοχ(οι) ὁμ(οίως)
εἰς φόρο(ν) ιζ (ἔτους) [12]τάλαντον ἓν κ(αὶ) δραχ(μὰς)
χειλίας τετρα-[13]κοσίας, (γίνεται) ὡς πρόκ(ειται)
(τάλαντον) α (δραχμαὶ) Ἀυ.

. . . the customary 6½ percentage. (Signed) I, Ischyrion, supervisor, and my associates have received the twelve metal talents of alum, equal to thirty light talents, for which we have paid the toll and the cost of transport.

371. RECEIPT FOR RENT PAID THROUGH A BANK

A.D. 155.

The 18th year of the Emperor Caesar Titus Aelius Hadrianus Antoninus Augustus Pius, Mecheir 27. Paid into the bank of Titus Flavius Eutychides by Eudaemon son of Sarapion and partners, overseers of the property belonging to the corporation of the city of Alexandria and formerly to Julius Asclepiades the philosopher,[a] situated in the area of the village of Euhemeria,[b] towards the rent of the 17th year, one talent and four thousand drachmae, on condition that an equivalent amount shall be paid in Alexandria to the superintendent of *stemmata*,[c] total 1 tal. 4000 dr. Epeiph 8, by the same person and his partners, similarly towards the rent of the 17th year, one talent and one thousand four hundred drachmae, total as above written 1 tal. 1400 dr.

[a] Probably the ambassador mentioned in No. 212.
[b] A village in the Fayum.
[c] See No. 292, note *a*, p. 291.

SELECT PAPYRI

372. RECEIPT FOR MONEY PAID FOR THE TRANSPORT OF GOVERNMENT CORN

P. Columbia 1, recto 4, col. 1.   A.D. 155.

¹Σαβείνῳ καὶ τοῖς σὺν αὐτῷ δη(μοσίοις) [τρα]-
π(εζίταις) ²παρὰ τῶν ὑπογεγρα(μμένων) δημοσίων
κτηνοτ(ρόφων) ³κώμη(ς) Μούχ(εως) καὶ Ἐλευσῖνος
διὰ Ἡρακλᾶτο(ς) ⁴ἀποσυσταθέντος. ἀπέχομεν τὰς
ἐπι-⁵σταλείσας ὑμεῖν παρ' ὑμῶν ὑπὲρ φορέτρων
⁶πυροῦ καὶ κριθῆς οὗ ἐδηλώθημεν καταγει-⁷ωχέναι
ἀπὸ θησ(αυρῶν) Πολ(έμωνος) εἰς τοὺς ὅρμους
⁸(πυροῦ ἀρταβῶν) κη (τετάρτου) καὶ κριθῆς β
(τρίτου) (τεσσαρεσκαιεικοστοῦ) ὡς τῆς (ἀρτάβης)
ἐκ(άστης) (δραχμῶν) η ⁹τὰς συναγομ(ένας) (δραχμὰς)
σκς, τῆς δὲ κριθ(ῆς) ὡς τῶν ¹⁰ρ ἀρ(ταβῶν) (δραχμῶν) υ<π> (δραχμὰς) ια (δυοβόλους) (δίχαλκον),
τὰς ἐπὶ τὸ α(ὐτὸ) (δραχμὰς) σλζ (δυοβόλους) (δίχαλκον). ¹¹ἔστι δέ· ¹²Μ[ο]ύχεως· Παχεὺς καὶ Ἑκῦσις
(πυροῦ ἀρτάβαι) ζ (ἥμισυ) (τρίτον), ¹³Παχεὺς καὶ
Ὀννῶφρις (πυροῦ ἀρτάβαι) δ (τρίτον) (ὄγδοον),
¹⁴Χρυσᾶς Παχνούβεως (πυροῦ ἀρτάβαι) ε (τέταρτον),
¹⁵Παχεὺς Παχέως (πυροῦ ἀρτάβαι) ς (ἕκτον) (τεσσαρεσκαιεικοστόν), ¹⁶Χρυσᾶς Παχέως (πυροῦ ἀρτάβαι)
γ (ἥμισυ) (τρίτον) (δωδέκατον). ¹⁷Ἐλευσῖνος·
Πρωτᾶς καὶ Ἀφεὺς ¹⁸(πυροῦ ἀρτάβης) (τρίτον)
(δωδέκατον), κριθῆς (δίμοιρον), ¹⁹Πρωτᾶς Ναα-
βῶτος (πυροῦ ἀρτάβης) (ἕκτον), κριθ(ῆς) α (δίμοιρον) (τεσσαρεσκαιεικοστόν). ²⁰(γίνονται) αἱ
προκ(είμεναι). (2nd hand) ²¹(ἔτους) ιη Ἀντωνίνου
Καίσαρ[ο]ς τοῦ κυρίου ²²Μεχεὶρ κθ. Ἡρακλᾶς ὁ
472

372. RECEIPT FOR MONEY PAID FOR THE TRANSPORT OF GOVERNMENT CORN

A.D. 155.

To Sabinus and his partners, state bankers, from the under-mentioned, state donkey-keepers of the villages of Mouchis and Eleusis, through Heraclas their delegate. We have received from you the money which you were ordered to pay as fees for the transport of wheat and barley which we have carried down, as certified, from the granaries of the division of Polemon to the landing-places, which fees amounted to $28\frac{1}{4}$ artabae of wheat and $2\frac{9}{24}$ artabae of barley,[a] the equivalent of the wheat, at the rate of 8 drachmae for each artaba, being altogether 226 drachmae, and the equivalent of the barley, at the rate of 480 drachmae per 100 artabae, being 11 drachmae 2 obols 2 chalci, making a total of 237 drachmae 2 obols 2 chalci. The list is as follows. For Mouchis : Pacheus and Hekusis $7\frac{5}{6}$ artabae of wheat, Pacheus and Onnophris $4\frac{11}{24}$ artabae of wheat, Chrysas son of Pachnoubis $5\frac{1}{4}$ artabae of wheat, Pacheus son of Pacheus $6\frac{5}{24}$ artabae of wheat, Chrysas son of Pacheus $3\frac{11}{12}$ artabae of wheat. For Eleusis : Protas and Apheus $\frac{5}{12}$ of an artaba of wheat, $\frac{2}{3}$ of an artaba of barley, Protas son of Naabos $\frac{1}{6}$ of an artaba of wheat, $1\frac{17}{24}$ artabae of barley. Total as stated above. Year 18 of Antoninus Caesar the lord, Mecheir 29. I,

---

[a] The fees were computed in wheat and barley and converted into the equivalent in money.

προγεγρα(μμένος) ἀπέχω τὰς ²³προκ(ειμένας) (δραχμὰς) σλζ (δυοβόλους) (δίχαλκον).

373. RECEIPT FOR GOVERNMENT CORN
FOR TRANSPORT

P. Oxy. 2125.   A.D. 220–221.

¹Αὐρήλιος Ἀμμώνι[ο]ς ²ʾΑμμωνίου ναύκληρος
³χειρισμοῦ Νέας πόλεως πλο[ίω]ν ⁴γ ἀγωγῆς (ἀρταβῶν) μ(υριάδος) α ᾽Ε Αὐρηλίῳ ⁵Σαραπίωνι σειτο-
λόγῳ ἄνω τοπ(αρχίας) ⁶Σκὼ τόπ(ων) χαίρειν.
παρέλα-⁷βον καὶ παραμεμέτρημαι παρὰ ⁸σοῦ τὰς
[ἐπ]ισταλείσας μοι ὑπὸ τοῦ ⁹τε στρατη[γοῦ] Αὐρηλίου ῾Αρποκρα-¹⁰τίωνος καὶ Αὐρηλίου Νεμεσί[ω]νος
¹¹τοῦ καὶ Διονυσίου βασιλικοῦ γρα(μματέως), ¹²ἐπ-
ακολουθούντων τῶν ἐπὶ ¹³τῆς ἐμβολῆς τεταγμένων
¹⁴καὶ ὧν ἄλλων δέον ἐστίν, [ἀ]π[ὸ] ¹⁵δημοσίων
θ[η]σαυρῶν τῆς π[ρ]ο-¹⁶κειμένης σειτολογίας εἰς
ὅρ[μ]ον ¹⁷Σατύρου τοῦ μεγάλου ποτα-¹⁸μοῦ πυροῦ
γενήματος τοῦ ¹⁹διελθόντος γ (ἔτους) καθαροῦ
ἀδόλου ²⁰ἀβώλ[ου ἀκρί]θου ἀδιπατήτου ²¹κεκοσ-
κινευμένου μέτρῳ δη-²²μοσίῳ ἡμιαρταβίῳ {δη-
μοσίῳ} ²³μετρήσε[ι] τῇ κελευσθείσῃ σὺν ²⁴(ἑκατοστῇ)
α καὶ ἡμιαρταβίῳ ἀρτάβας ²⁵ἐβδομήκοντα ἑπτά,
γ(ίνονται) (ἀρτάβαι) οζ, ²⁶ἃς καὶ κατάξω εἰς τὴν
᾽Αλεξάν-²⁷δρειαν καὶ παραδώσω εἰς τὸν ἐν ²⁸τῇ
Νέα πόλει χειρισμὸν πλή-²⁹ρη κἀ‹κα›ουργητον
τὸν γόμον. ³⁰κυρία ἡ ἀποχὴ (τρισσὴ) γραφεῖσα,
σοὶ ³¹μὲν τῷ σιτολόγῳ ἁπλῆ τῷ δὲ στρα(τηγῷ)

Heraclas the above-mentioned, have received the aforesaid 237 drachmae 2 obols 2 chalci.

373. RECEIPT FOR GOVERNMENT CORN FOR TRANSPORT

A.D. 220-221.

Aurelius Ammonius son of Ammonius, shipmaster in the administration of Neapolis [a] of 3 boats carrying 15,000 artabae, to Aurelius Sarapion, sitologus of the Sko district of the upper toparchy, greeting. I have received and have had measured out to me from you the amount ordered me by the strategus Aurelius Harpocration and Aurelius Nemesion also called Dionysius, royal scribe, with the concurrence of those placed in charge of the corn tribute and the other officials concerned, from the public granaries of the aforesaid sitologus-district at the harbour of Satyrus on the great river, of wheat from the produce of the past 3rd year, pure, unadulterated, free from earth and barley, not twice-trodden, sifted, by the public half-artaba measure according to the prescribed measurement, with a percentage of $1\frac{1}{2}$ artabae,[b] seventy-seven artabae, total 77 art., which I will carry down to Alexandria and deliver to the administration in Neapolis an entire and undamaged cargo. This receipt is valid and is done in triplicate, one copy for you the sitologus and two for the strategus, and

[a] The government administration of the corn tribute. Neapolis was the part of Alexandria which adjoined the great harbour

[b] The purpose of this percentage is not precisely known.

475

SELECT PAPYRI

³²δισσή, καὶ ἐπ[ε]ρωτηθεὶς ὡμολόγησα. (2nd hand)
³³Αὐρήλιος Ἀμ<μ>ώνιος Ἀμ<μ>ωνίου ³⁴ναύκληρος
χιρισμοῦ Νέας ³⁵πόλεως μεμέτρημε καὶ ἐμ-³⁶βέβλημε
τὰς τ[ο]ῦ [πυ]ροῦ ³⁷σὺν ἡμιαρταβί[ῳ καὶ] ἑκα-
³⁸τοστῇ [μιᾷ ἀρτάβας ἑβδο-³⁹μήκοντα ἑπτά - - -

35-36. l. μεμέτρημαι καὶ ἐμβέβλημαι.

374. RECEIPT FROM IRONSMITHS

P. Oxy. 84.   A.D. 316.

¹Οὐαλερίῳ Ἀμμωνιανῷ τῷ καὶ ²Γ[ε]ροντίῳ
λογιστῇ Ὀξ(υρυγχίτου) ³πα[ρ]ὰ τοῦ κοινοῦ τῶν
σιδηρο-⁴χαλκέων τῆς λαμ(πρᾶς) καὶ λαμ(προτάτης)
Ὀξ(υρυγχιτῶν) πόλεως ⁵δι(ὰ) Αὐρηλίου Σεουήρου
Σαρμάτου ἀπὸ τῆς ⁶αὐ[τ]ῆς πόλεως μηνιάρχου
ἀπὸ τῶν ⁷[αὐτ(ῶν)]. ἠρίθμημε παρ' Αὐρηλίου
⁸Ἀγαθοβούλου Ἀλεξάνδρου δημοσίων ⁹λη[μ]μάτων
τραπ(εζίτου) Ὀξ(υρυγχίτου) πολιτικῆς ¹⁰τραπέζης
ἐξ ἐπιστάλματος τοῦ ¹¹αὐτοῦ ἀξιολογωτάτου λογιστοῦ ¹²ἃ τετάγμεθα ἐπισταλῆνα<ι> ἐξω-¹³διάσθαι
ἡμῖν ὑπὲρ τιμῆς ¹⁴σιδή[ρο]υ ἐνεργοῦ ὁλκῆς κεν-
¹⁵[τ]ηναρ[ί]ου ἑνὸς χωροῦντος εἰς ¹⁶δημόσια πολι-
τικὰ ἔργα ¹⁷ἀργυρί[ου] (τάλαντα) ϛ πλήρη. κυρία
ἡ ἀποχὴ ¹⁸καὶ ἐπ[ε]ρωτητεὶς ὡμ[ολ]όγησα. ¹⁹ὑπα-
τε[ία]ς Καικινίου Σαβίνου ²⁰καὶ Οὐεττ[ίου] Ῥουφίνου τῶν λαμπροτάτων ²¹ʿΑθὺρ ε΄. (2nd hand)
²²Αὐρήλιο[ς] Σεουῆρος ἐρί<θ>μη[μ]αι ²³τὰ τοῦ

7. l. ἠρίθμημαι; so in l. 22.   18. l. ἐπ[ε]ρωτηθείς; so
in ll. 24-25.
476

in answer to the formal question I have given my assent. (Signed) I, Aurelius Ammonius son of Ammonius, shipmaster in the administration of Neapolis, have received and have put on board the seventy-seven artabae of wheat with the percentage of $1\frac{1}{2}$ artabae . . .

374. RECEIPT FROM IRONSMITHS

A.D. 316.

To Valerius Ammonianus also called Gerontius, logistes of the Oxyrhynchite nome, from the guild of ironsmiths of the illustrious and most illustrious city of Oxyrhynchus through Aurelius Severus son of Sarmates, of the said city, monthly president of the said guild. I have received from Aurelius Agathobulus son of Alexander, banker in charge of public receipts in the official bank of Oxyrhynchus, in accordance with an order of the said most estimable logistes, the appointed sum which was to be ordered to be paid to us as the price of one hundredweight of usable iron intended for public works of the city, namely 6 silver talents in full. This receipt is valid and in answer to the formal question I have given my assent. In the consulship of Caecinius Sabinus and Vettius Rufinus the most illustrious, Hathur 5. (Signed) I, Aurelius Severus, have re-

ἀργυρίου τάλαντα ἕξ ²⁴πλήρη ὡς πρόκιτε καὶ
<ἐ>πει-²⁵ρωτητὶς ὡμολόγησα.

24. l. πρόκειται.   25. l. ὡμολόγησα.

375. RECEIPT FOR BEER-TAX

P. Hib. 106.   245 b.c

¹("Ετους) β ʹΑθὺ[ρ λ, (δραχμαὶ)] κ.
²("Ετους) β ʹΑθὺρ λ. πέπτωκεν ³ἐπὶ τὸ ἐμ
Φεβίχι λογευτήριον ⁴τοῦ Κωίτου Πάσωνι τραπε-
⁵ζίτηι καὶ Στοτοήτι δοκι-⁶μαστῆι παρὰ ʹΑρενδώτου
τὸ παρὰ Ταεμβέους ⁷ἐκ Ταλάη ζυτηρᾶς εἰς τὸν
⁸ʹΑθὺρ χα(λκοῦ) εἰς κδ (τέταρτον ?) (δραχμαὶ)
εἴκοσι, (γίνονται) κ. (2nd hand) ⁹[πα]ρόντ[ο]ς
Δωρίωνος.

6. τό E.-H. : το(ῦ) Edd.

376. TAX RECEIPT

O. Tait 49.   165 b.c.

¹"Ετους ε Μεσορὴ ιγ̄. τε(τάχαται) ἐπὶ τὴν ²ἐν
Διὸς πό(λει) τρά(πεζαν) ἐφʼ ἧς ʹΑντιγένης ³εἰς τὸ
ε (ἔτος) ἐννομίου "Αβραμος ⁴καὶ Διοκλῆς ἑκατὸν

ᵃ Great numbers of tax-receipts have been preserved,
mostly written on fragments of pottery, and we can only give
a very small selection of these rather dry documents. The
taxes themselves were exceedingly numerous.

478

ceived the six talents of silver in full as aforesaid, and in answer to the formal question I have given my assent.

375. RECEIPT FOR BEER-TAX

245 B.C.

Year 2, Hathur 30 : 20 drachmae.

Year 2, Hathur 30. Paid into the collecting office of the Koite toparchy at Phebichis, to Pason, banker, and Stotoetis, controller, by Harendotes the amount received from Taembes at Talae for beer-tax [a] on account of Hathur, being twenty drachmae in copper at $24\frac{1}{4}$ obols [b] (per tetradrachm), total 20 (drachmae). In the presence of Dorion.

[a] The manufacture and sale of beer formed one of the government monopolies in the Ptolemaic period (compare No. 3) and were carried on under contract, the main part of the proceeds being payable to the Crown.

[b] The nominal value was 24 obols ; the $\frac{1}{4}$ obol represents a small premium charged for accepting payment in copper.

376. TAX RECEIPT [a]

165 B.C.

Year 5,[b] Mesore 13. Paid into the bank at Diospolis [c] of which Antigenes is the head, as pasture-tax for the 5th year, by Abraham and Diocles one hun-

[b] Of the joint reign of Philometor and Euergetes.

[c] Thebes.

δέκα ⁵ἑπτά, (γίνονται) χα(λκοῦ) οὗ ἀλ(λαγή) ριζ.
᾿Αντιγένης ⁶ρλε.

377. TAX RECEIPT

O. Tait 70.   138 B.C.

¹ʺΕτους λγ ῾Αθὺρ β. ²τε(τάχαται) ἐπὶ τὴν ἐν
Διὸς πό(λει) τῆι με(γάληι) τρά(πεζαν) ³ἐφ᾽ ἧς
῾Ερμόφ(ιλος) ἀπο(μοίρας) ο⟨ἱ⟩ ἱερεῖς τοῦ ⁴ʺΑμ-
μωνος διὰ Πετεμίνιος ⁵τοῦ Παμώνθου τά(λαντα)
δύο, (γίνεται) τά(λ.) β. ⁶῾Ερμ(όφιλος) τρα(πεζίτης).

378. RECEIPT FOR TAX UPON SALES

P. Amh. 53.   114 B.C.

¹ʺΕτους γ Παχὼν γ̄. τέ(τακται) ἐπὶ τὴν ἐν
῾Ερμώ(νθει) τρά(πεζαν) ἐφ᾽ ἧς ᾿Αμμώνιος (δεκάτης)
ἐγκυ(κλίου) ὠνῆς κατὰ διαγρα(φὴν) Μέμνονος ²καὶ
῾Ερμίου τελω(νῶν) ὑφ᾽ ἣν ὑπογρ(άφει) ᾿Ασενώθης
ὁ ἀντιγρα(φεὺς) Σενποῆρις ᾿Οννώφριος τέλος οἴκου
καὶ ³ταμιεῖον καὶ μέρος αὐλῆς ἃ ἠγόρα(σεν) παρὰ
Λολοῦτος τοῦ Πετενεφώτου χα(λκοῦ) (ταλάντων)
ϛ τέ(λος) ᾿Γχ. ⁴᾿Αμμώ(νιος) τρα(πεζίτης).

3. l. ταμιείου καὶ μέρους.

ᵃ The receipt is in the form of a banker's docket affixed
to a demotic deed of sale.   ᵇ See No. 367, note a, p. 461.

dred and seventeen drachmae, total in copper at a discount [a] 117. (Signed) Antigenes. 135.[b]

[a] Literally, copper on which there is a charge for exchange (into silver). See No. 367, note c, p. 463.

[b] This was the sum actually received, the extra 18 drachmae representing the discount at which copper stood in relation to silver and certain additional charges.

377. TAX RECEIPT

138 B.C.

Year 33,[a] Hathur 2. Paid into the bank at Diospolis the Great of which Hermophilus is the head, for *apomoira*,[b] by the priests of Ammon through Peteminis son of Pamonthes two talents, total 2 tal. (Signed) Hermophilus, banker.

[a] Of Euergetes II.   [b] See No. 233, p. 132, note a.

378. RECEIPT FOR TAX UPON SALES [a]

114 B.C.

Year 3, Pachon 3. Paid into the bank at Hermonthis [b] of which Ammonius is head, for the ten per cent tax upon sales, in accordance with the note of Memnon and Hermias, tax-collectors, to which Asenothes the controller subscribes, by Senpoeris daughter of Onnophris [c] upon a house and store and part of a courtyard which she bought from Lolous son of Petenephotes for 6 talents of copper,[d] the tax of 3600 drachmae. (Signed) Ammonius, banker.

[c] See No. 367.   [d] =36,000 drachmae.

SELECT PAPYRI

379. RECEIPT FOR A TITHE FOR
A TEMPLE

P. Tebt. 281.   125 B.C.

¹ʼΈτους με Μεχεὶρ κζ. ²πέπτωκεν Μαρρεῖ
³Σοχώτου ἱερεῖ Σούχου ⁴θεοῦ μεγάλου μεγάλου
⁵καὶ τῶν συννάων θεῶν ⁶τοῦ ἐξειληφότος ἀπὸ τῶν
⁷ἱερῶν προσόδων τοῦ Σούχου ⁸τὴν εἰς τὸ ἱερὸν
καθήκουσαν ⁹δίδοσθαι διδραχμίαν ¹⁰τῶν κ (δραχμῶν) ἥ ἐστιν δεκάτη ¹¹παρὰ τῶν κτωμένων ¹²οἰκίας
ἢ τόπους, παρὰ ¹³Σοκ[ον]ώπιος τοῦ ¹⁴ʼΑχοείους
ἱερέως ¹⁵Σοκνεβτύνιος θεοῦ μεγ(άλου) ¹⁶μεγάλου
τέ(λος) (δίδραχμον) τόπου ¹⁷ψίλου τοῦ ὄντος ἐν
κώμηι ¹⁸Σούχου Τεβτύ(νει) τῆς Πο(λέμωνος)
με(ρίδος) ¹⁹οὗ ἐπρίατο παρὰ ²⁰Φανήσιος τοῦ Πετεαρ-
²¹ψενήσιος, καὶ δέδεγμαι ²²παρὰ σοῦ ἐκ πλήρους
²³ἄνευ παντὸς ²⁴λοιπήματος.

6. l. τῷ ἐξειληφότι.

380. COPY OF TAX-RECEIPTS

P. Oxy. 288, ll. 16-20, 31-34.   A.D. 23–24.

¹⁶ʼΈτους δεκάτου Τιβερίου Καίσαρος Σεβαστοῦ
Μεχεὶρ ιγ ¹⁷διαγέγρα(φεν) διὰ Διογένους [τ]ρα-
(πεζίτου) ἐπικεφαλ(αίου) ʼΙπποδρόμου Τρύφων ¹⁸Διο-
νυσίου σὺν κα(ταγωγίωι) (δραχμὰς) η, καὶ τῆι κδ
τοῦ Φαρμοῦθι ἐπικ(εφαλαίου) ¹⁹ὁ αὐτὸς (δραχμὰς) δ.

ª See Vol. I. No. 13.   ᵇ See No. 223, note d.

482

379. RECEIPT FOR A TITHE FOR A TEMPLE

125 B.C.

Year 45, Mecheir 27. Marres son of Sochotes, priest of the twice great god Souchus and the associated gods, who out of the sacred revenues of Souchus farms the tax of 2 drachmae upon each twenty, making one tenth, due to the temple [a] from those acquiring houses or sites, has been paid by Sokonopis son of Achoes, priest of the twice great god Sokneb-tunis, the two-drachmae tax upon a vacant site in the village of Souchus,[b] Tebtunis in the division of Polemon, which site he bought from Phanesis son of Peteharpsenesis ; and I have received from you the sum in full without any arrearage.

[a] The temple of Souchus at Crocodilopolis, capital of the Arsinoite nome.

[b] The village Tebtunis being part of the god's financial domain.

380. COPY OF TAX-RECEIPTS

A.D. 23–24.

The tenth year of Tiberius Caesar Augustus, Mecheir 13, paid through Diogenes, banker, by Tryphon son of Dionysius [a] for poll-tax in the Hippodrome quarter, including charge for transport,[b] 8 drachmae, and on the 24th of Pharmouthi by the same for poll-tax 4 drachmae. On Pauni 21, *dies Augustus,*

Παῦνι κα Σεβαστῆι ὑικῆς (δραχμὰς) β (ὀβολὸν)
(ἡμιωβέλιον). ²⁰᾽Επεὶφ ιϛ χωμα(τικοῦ) (δραχμὰς) ϛ.
³¹᾽Ετους ι Τιβερίου Καίσαρος ³²Σε[βαστο]ῦ
[Φαῶ]φι Σ[ε]βαστῆι διαγέγρα(φεν) γερδιακοῦ ᾽Ιπ-
ποδ(ρόμου) ³³Τρύφων Δι[ο]νυ[σίου] δ[ιὰ] Παάπιος
(δραχμὰς) γ (τετρώβολον) (ἡμιωβέλιον). ³⁴μηνὸς
Νέ[ο]υ Σεβασ[τοῦ] γ ὁ αὐτὸς (δραχμὰς) γ (τετρώβολον) (ἡμιωβέλιον).

381. TOLL RECEIPT

P. Oxy. 1439.   A.D. 75.

¹Παρέ(σχηκε) Σαραπίων (ἑκατοστὴν) διαπυλίο(υ)
²᾽Οάσ(εως) κριθῆς ὄνον ἕνα καὶ ³σκόρδων ὄνον ἕνα.
(ἔτους) β ⁴Οὐεσπασιανοῦ τοῦ κυρίου ⁵Μ[ε]χεὶρ
ἑβδόμῃ, ζ.

382. TOLL-HOUSE RECEIPT

P. Grenf. ii. 50 (c).   A.D. 147.

¹Τετελ(ώνηται) διὰ πύλ(ης) Φιλαδελ(φίας) ἐρη-
μοφυλ(ακίας) Διωγέν(ης) ²ἐξ(άγων) φοινίκ(ων)χλω -
ρ(ῶν) ὄνο(ν) ἕνα ³καὶ (πυροῦ) ὄνο(ν) ἕνα. (ἔτους)
ἑνδεκάτου ⁴᾽Αντωνείνου Καίσαρος τοῦ κυρίου ⁵Θὼθ
ὀκτωκαιδεκάτῃ, (γίνεται) ιη.

1. l. Διωγέν(ης).

for pig-tax 2 drachmae 1½ obols. On Epeiph 16, for embankment-tax 6 drachmae.

The 10th year of Tiberius Caesar Augustus, Phaophi, *dies Augustus*, paid by Tryphon son of Dionysius through Paapis for weaver's tax in the Hippodrome quarter 3 drachmae 4½ obols. On the 3rd of the month Novus Augustus,[a] by the same 3 drachmae 4½ obols.

<blockquote>
[a] = Hathur.
</blockquote>

381. TOLL RECEIPT

A.D. 75.

Sarapion has paid the one per cent tax for toll dues of the Oasis [a] upon one ass-load of barley and one ass-load of garlic. The 2nd year of Vespasianus the lord, seventh (7th) day of Mecheir.

<blockquote>
[a] The Small Oasis, from which the goods were being exported.
</blockquote>

382. TOLL-HOUSE RECEIPT

A.D. 147.

Paid at the toll-house of Philadelphia [a] the tax for the protection of the desert route by Diogenes, exporting one ass-load of fresh dates and one ass-load of wheat. The eleventh year of Antoninus Caesar the lord, eighteenth (18th) day of Thoth.

<blockquote>
[a] Situated on the edge of the desert on the east side of the Fayum.
</blockquote>

SELECT PAPYRI

383. TOLL-HOUSE RECEIPT

P. Ryl. 197 (a).   A.D. 162.

¹Τετελ(ώνηται) διὰ πύλης Σοκνοπ(αίου) Νήσου
ρ′ ν′ ²Σαραπίων ἐξάγ(ων) ἐπὶ καμήλ(ῳ) α μιᾷ
³λαχανοσπέρμ(ου) ἀρτάβ(ας) ἓξ τελ(ούσας) (δραχμὰς) πέντε ⁴καὶ καμήλῳ ἑνὶ ὄνοις δυσὶ πυρο(ῦ)
(ἀρτάβας) δέ-⁵κα δύο τελ(ούσας) τρεῖς δραχμάς.
(ἔτους) τρίτο(υ) ⁶᾽Αντωνείνο(υ) καὶ Οὐήρου τῶν
κυρίω(ν) ⁷ᾅθὺρ 〚. . . . .〛 τετράδι.

384. RECEIPT FOR *ANABOLICUM*

P. Oxy. 1136.   A.D. 420.

¹᾽Εντάγιον ἐμοῦ ᾽Απφοῦτος δι᾽ ἐμοῦ ²Σαρμάτου
βοη(θοῦ). ἐδεξάμην παρὰ Θέων⟨ος⟩ ³αἰγεωθήτης
ὑπὲρ ἀναβολικοῦ ⁴τετάρτης ἰνδικ[τ]ί(ονος) στιχάριον
τέσσαρες, ⁵γί(νεται) στιχ(άρια) δ μόνα. ⁶(ἔτους) ϙζ
ξϛ Τῦ[β]ι ε. Σαρμάτης ᾽σεσημίωμ(αι).

3. *l.* αἰγοθύτου.   4. *l.* στιχάρια τέσσαρα.

385. RECEIPT FOR TAXES

P. Cairo Masp. 67033.   Before A.D. 535.

¹⳨ Δεδώκασιν οἱ ἀπὸ κώμης ᾽Αφροδίτης τοῦ
᾽Ανταιοπολίτου δ(ιὰ) ᾽Ιωάννου ²ὑποδέκτου εἰς λόγον
486

383. TOLL-HOUSE RECEIPT

A.D. 162.

Paid at the toll-house of Socnopaei Nesus for the taxes of 1 and ½ per cent *a* by Sarapion, exporting on 1 (one) camel six artabae of vegetable seed paying five drachmae and on one camel and two donkeys twelve artabae of wheat paying three drachmae. The third year of Antoninus and Verus the lords, fourth day of Hathur.

a The 1 per cent represented toll dues, the ½ a tax on exports and imports.

384. RECEIPT FOR *ANABOLICUM*

A.D. 420.

Receipt issued by me, Apphous, through me, Sarmates, assistant. I have received from Theon, goat-butcher, for the *anabolicum a* of the fourth indiction four tunics, total 4 tunics only. The 97th which = the 66th year,*b* Tubi 5. Signed by me, Sarmates.

a An imperial tax levied upon certain of the goods manufactured in Egypt, and payable in kind, as here, or in money.
b According to the two local eras of Oxyrhynchus.

385. RECEIPT FOR TAXES

Before A.D. 535.

The inhabitants of the village of Aphrodite in the Antaeopolite nome have paid, through John the

κανονικῶν καὶ παντοίων χρυσικῶν τίτλων ὁμοίως
³πρώτης κα[ταβο]λῆς πρώτης ἰνδ(ικτίον)ο(ς) χρυσοῦ
νομισμάτια εἴκοσι ἑπτὰ κεράτια ⁴δέκα, γί(νεται)
χρ(υσ.) νο(μ.) κζ κ(ερ.) ι'', εὔσταθμα ἁπλᾶ. καὶ
εἰς ὑμῶν ἀσφάλειαν καὶ τοῦ δημοσίου λόγου ⁵πε-
ποίημαι τοῦτο τὸ ἐντάγιον μεθ' ὑπογραφῆς ἐμῆς
ὡς πρόκειται.⊹ ⁶+ Ἡλιόδωρος ἐθνικ(ὸς) χρυ-
σών(ης) ἐπαρχείας Θηβαΐδ(ος) στοιχεῖ μοι ⁷τὸ
ἐντ[ά]γιον τῶν νομισμάτ(ων) εἴκοσι ἑπτὰ κεράτια
δέκα ὡς πρόκ(ειται).

7. l. κερατίων.

386. RECEIPT CONCERNING REVENUES

P. Oxy. 144.   A.D. 580.

- - - ³ὑπεδεξάμην παρὰ τῆς ὑμετέρας ⁴ὑπερφυίας
διὰ Ἰωάννου τοῦ εὐδοκιμωτάτου ἡμῶν ⁵τραπεζίτου
ὑπὲρ προσόδων τρίτης καταβολῆς ⁶τρισκαιδεκάτης
ἐπινεμή(σεως) χρυσοῦ ἐν ὀβρύζῳ χαράγματι ⁷νομίσ-
ματα χείλια τετρακόσια τεσσαράκοντα, καὶ ⁸ἐν
ἀπολύτῳ Αἰγυπτίῳ χαράγματι ζυγῷ Ἀλεξ(αν-
δρείας) νομίσματα ⁹ἑπτακόσια εἴκοσι, καὶ ὑπὲρ
ὀβρύζης καὶ ἀποκαταστατικῶν αὐτῶν ¹⁰νομίσματα
τεσσαράκοντα πέντε, γί(νεται) χρ(υσ.) νο(μ.) ͵βσε·
καὶ ταῦτα ¹¹ἑτοίμως ἔχω καταγαγεῖν ἐν Ἀλεξανδρείᾳ δίχα θεοῦ βίας ¹²καὶ τῶν κατὰ ποταμὸν κινδύνων καὶ ἐπηρειῶν, καὶ καταβαλεῖν ¹³ἐπὶ Ἰωάννην
καὶ Συμεώνιον τοὺς λαμπροτάτους ἀργυροπράτας,

4. l. ὑμῶν.

collector, on account of regular taxes and money taxes of all descriptions likewise, for the first instalment of the first indiction, twenty-seven gold solidi ten carats, total 27 gold sol. 10 car., of correct weight and unalloyed. And for the security of you and of the public account I have made this receipt as above with my signature. (Signed) I, Heliodorus, state banker of the eparchy of the Thebaid, approve the receipt for twenty-seven solidi ten carats as aforesaid.

386. RECEIPT CONCERNING REVENUES

A.D. 580.

. . . I have received from your magnificence through John your most estimable banker for the revenues of the third instalment of the thirteenth indiction one thousand four hundred and forty gold solidi in pure coin and seven hundred and twenty solidi in standard Egyptian coin on the Alexandrian scale, with forty-five solidi to make up their deficiency,[a] total 2205 gold solidi, and this sum I am prepared to carry down to Alexandria, apart from act of God and dangers by river and molestations, and pay to John and Simeonius the most illustrious money-

[a] The Greek words imply that the Egyptian gold solidi were regarded as inferior in purity to the extent of $6\frac{1}{4}$ per cent.

[14]καὶ ἐνεγκεῖν γράμματα τοῦ λαμπροτάτου ἀπο-
κρισιαρίου Θεοδώρου [15]ὡς τὸ εἰρημένον χρυσίον εἰς
πλῆρες κατεβλήθη. καὶ [16]πρὸς ὑμετέραν ἀσφάλειαν
ἤτοι τοῦ αὐτοῦ εὐδοκ(ιμωτάτου) τραπεζίτου [17]πε-
ποίημαι τὴν παροῦσαν παραθηκαρίαν γραφεῖσαν
χειρὶ ἐμῇ [18]μηνὶ Ἀθὺρ κϛ ἰνδ(ικτίονος) ιδ. + βασιλείας τοῦ θειοτάτου καὶ [19]εὐσεβεστάτου ἡμῶν
δεσπότου Φλ(αουίου) Τιβ<ε>ρίου Κωνσταντίνου
[20]τοῦ αἰωνίου Αὐγούστου καὶ Αὐτοκρ(άτορος) ἔτους
ἕκτου, μετὰ τὴν [21]ὑπατίαν τῆς αὐτοῦ δεσποτείας
τὸ δεύτερον. +

387. RECEIPT FOR MILITARY SUPPLIES

P. Amh. 107.   A.D. 185.

[1]Δαμαρίωνι στρατηγῶι Ἑρμοπολ(ίτου) [2]Ἀντώ-
νιος Ἰουστεῖνος δουπλικάριος διαπεμ-[3]φθεὶς ὑπὸ
Οὐαλερίου Φροντείνου ἐπάρχου [4]τῆς ἐν Κόπτῳ
εἴλης Ἡρακλειανῆς. μεμέτρημαι [5]παρὰ πρεσ-
βυτέρων κώμης Τέρτον Ἐπᾶ τοῦ [6]Πατεμί<του>
ἄνω τὰς ἐπιβληθείσας τῇ κώμῃ [7]αὐτῶν ἀ[πὸ] τῶν
κελευσθεισῶν ἀπὸ τοῦ [8]λαμπροτάτου ἡγεμόνος
Λογγαίου Ῥούφου [9]συνωνηθῆναι ἀπὸ γενήματος
τοῦ διελη-[10]λυθότος κδ (ἔτους) κριθῆς ἀρταβῶν
μυριάδων [11]δύο εἰς χρείας τῆς προκειμένης εἴλης
[12]κριθῆς μέτρῳ δημοσίῳ δ[ο]χικῷ μετρήσι [13]τῇ
κελευσθείσῃ ἀρτάβας ἑκατόν, (γίνονται) (ἀρτάβαι) ρ,
[14]ἀκολούθως τῷ γενομένῳ ἐπιμερισμῷ [15][ὑ]πὸ τῶν

7. l. ὑπὸ τοῦ.

changers and bring a receipt from the most illustrious agent Theodorus to the effect that the aforesaid gold has been paid in full. And for your security or that of the said most estimable banker I have drawn up the present acknowledgement of deposit written by my own hand this 26th day of Hathur, 14th indiction. In the sixth year of the reign of our most godlike and pious master Flavius Tiberius Constantinus the eternal Augustus and Imperator, which is the year after the consulship of his said majesty for the second time.

387. RECEIPT FOR MILITARY SUPPLIES

A.D. 185.

To Damarion, strategus of the Hermopolite nome, from Antonius Justinus, *duplicarius*,[a] dispatched by Valerius Frontinus, praefect of the *ala Heracliana* [b] stationed at Coptos.[c] I have had measured out to me by the elders of the village of Terton Epa in the upper Patemite district the proportion imposed upon their village from the twenty thousand artabae of barley which the most illustrious praefect Longaeus Rufus commanded to be bought up from the produce of the past 24th year for the requirements of the aforesaid *ala*, namely one hundred artabae of barley measured by the public receiving standard according to the measurement prescribed, total 100 artabae, in accordance with the division made

[a] Receiving double pay.
[b] A body of auxiliary cavalry ; compare No. 369.
[c] A town in Upper Egypt, not far from Luxor.

τοῦ νομοῦ πραγματικῶν. τὴν ¹⁶[δ' ἀπ]οχὴν ταύτην
τετρασ<σ>ὴν ἐξεδόμην. ¹⁷(ἔτους) κε Αὐτοκράτορος
Καίσα[ρο]ς Μάρκου ¹⁸Αὐρηλίου Κομ[μόδ]ου Ἀντω-
[νίνου Σεβασ]τοῦ ¹⁹Εὐσεβοῦς Ἀρμεν[ιακοῦ Μηδικοῦ
Παρθικοῦ] ²⁰Σαρματικοῦ Γε[ρμανικοῦ Βρεταννικοῦ
²¹Μεγίστου Παῦ[νι . . (2nd hand) Ἀντώνιος
²²Ἰουστῖνος δ[ουπλικάριος με-]²³μέτρημε τὰ[ς τῆς
κριθῆς ἀρτάβας] ²⁴ἑκατόν, (ἀρτάβαι) ρ̄, [ὡς πρό-
κειται].

22. *l.* με]μέτρημαι.

388. RECEIPT FOR PAYMENT ON
ACCOUNT OF MILITARY SUPPLIES

P. Grenf. ii. 95.   A.D. 6th cent.

¹+ Δέδωκεν ἐκκλ(ησία) Ἀπόλλωνος εἰς λόγον
ἀννωνῶν τῶν γενναιοτάτων Σκυθῶν Ἰουστινιανῶν
²ἀγραρευόντων ἐν τῷ μοναστηρίῳ Βαῦ || β̄ || ἐξα-
μήν(ου) κανόνος τεσσαρεσκαιδεκάτης ἰνδ(ικτίονος)
χρυσοῦ νομίσματα ³δύο κεράτια εἴκοσι ἐν{α} ζυγ(ῷ),
γί(νεται) νο(μ.) β κ(ερ.) κα ζυγ(ῷ). Κόλλουθος
διαδότ(ης) δι' ἐμοῦ Βίκτορος ἀδελφοῦ ⁴στοιχεῖ μοι
νομισμάτια δύο καὶ κεράτια εἴκοσι ἐν ζ(υγῷ),
γί(νεται) νο(μ.) β κ(ερ.) κα ζ(υγῷ) ὡς πρόκ(ειται).
+ + +

Verso : ἐκκλησ(ία) Ἀπόλλωνος ιδ ἰνδ(ικτίονος)
νο(μίσματα) β κ(εράτια) κα.

2. Βαῦ || β̄ || revised reading : Βαύλλου Edd.

by the officials of the nome. I have issued four copies of this receipt. The 25th year of the Emperor Caesar Marcus Aurelius Commodus Antoninus Augustus Pius Armeniacus Medicus Parthicus Sarmaticus Germanicus Britannicus Maximus, Pauni... (Signed) I, Antonius Justinus, *duplicarius*, have had measured out to me the hundred artabae of barley, 100 artabae, as aforesaid.

388. RECEIPT FOR PAYMENT ON ACCOUNT OF MILITARY SUPPLIES

A.D. 6th cent.

Paid by the church of Apollonopolis *a* on account of supplies for the most noble Justinian Scythians *b* quartered in the monastery of Bau, being the 2nd half-yearly quota of the fourteenth indiction, two gold solidi twenty-one carats according to the standard, total 2 sol. 21 car. standard. I, Colluthus, distributor,*c* represented by me his brother Victor, agree to having received two solidi twenty-one carats standard, total 2 sol. 21 car. standard, as above. (Endorsed) From the church of Apollonopolis, 14th indiction, 2 solidi 21 carats.

a The modern Edfu.
b A corps which originally consisted of Scythians, called after Justinian.
c A person appointed by a local senate to undertake this compulsory service.

493

SELECT PAPYRI

389. CERTIFICATE OF WORK ON THE EMBANKMENTS

P. Ryl. 210.   A.D. 131.

¹Ἔτους ἑκκαιδε‹κά›του Αὐτοκράτορος Καίσαρος
²Τραϊανοῦ Ἁδριανοῦ Σεβαστ(οῦ).   ³εἴργ(ασται)
ὑπὲρ χωματικῶν ἔργων ⁴τοῦ αὐτοῦ ις (ἔτους)
Φαῶ(φι.) δ η ⁵ἐπ' ὀρινῇ Πατσώ(ντεως) Βακχιάδο(ς)
⁶Ζωίλος Πετεσούχο(υ) το(ῦ) Ἡλείτ(ου) ⁷μη(τρὸς)
Ταορσενο(ύφιος).   (2nd hand) ⁸Διόσκ(ορος) σεση-
μ(είωμαι).

390. RECEIPT FOR LABOUR

P. Thead. 35.   A.D. 325.

¹Αὐρήλιος Καστορίων βουλ(ευτὴς) ²ἐπιμελητὴς
ἐργατῶν τῶν ³[κατ]ὰ τὴν ἀλαβαστρίνην μεγάλ(ην)
⁴Σακάωνι καὶ τ[ῷ] κ[οι]νωνοῦ κωμάρ-⁵χαις Θεαδελ-
φία‹ς› χαίρειν.   ⁶[π]αρέλαβον ἀπὸ σοῦ τὰ ἐροῦντα
⁷ὑ(πὲρ) [τοῦ] ἐργά(του) καὶ τοῦ τέκτονος ⁸ὑ[πὲ]ρ
μηνῶν {ων} τριῶν τῶν ⁹[ἀ]πὸ Παχὼν νεομηνίας
ἕως ¹⁰['Επ]ὶφ τριακάδος.   Καστορίων σεση(μείωμαι).   ¹¹ὑπατείας Παυλίνου καὶ 'Ιουλιανοῦ ¹²τῶν
λαμπροτάτων 'Επὶφ δ'.

4. *l.* κ[οι]νωνῷ.

494

389. CERTIFICATE OF WORK ON THE EMBANKMENTS

A.D. 131.

The 16th year of the Emperor Caesar Trajanus Hadrianus Augustus. Worked on the embanking works of the said 16th year from Phaophi 4 to 8 [a] at the desert canal of Patsontis in Bacchias [b]: Zoilus son of Petesouchus son of Elites, his mother being Taorsenouphis. Signed by me, Dioscorus.

[a] Labour was requisitioned every year for the consolidation of the embankments, each man working 5 days and receiving a certificate at the end of his period.
[b] A village in the Fayum.

390. RECEIPT FOR LABOUR

A.D. 325.

Aurelius Castorion, senator, superintendent of the workmen at the great alabaster quarry, to Sakaon and his colleague, comarchs of Theadelphia,[a] greeting. I have received from you what it falls to you to provide in respect of a workman and a carpenter, for three months from the first day of Pachon to the thirtieth of Epeiph. Signed by me, Castorion. In the consulship of the most illustrious Paulinus and Julianus, Epeiph 4.

[a] See No. 295.

XII. ORDERS FOR PAYMENT

391. ORDER FOR DELIVERY OF A LOAN OF BARLEY

P. Lille i. 41.   End of 251 B.C.

Written in duplicate, the inner text being as follows :

¹Διογένης Θρασυμήδει χαίρειν. ²σύνταξον μετρῆ-
σαι Μένητι (εἰκοσιπενταρούρωι) ³ἐπιγόνωι δάνειον
εἰς κάτεργον ⁴καὶ συναγωγὴν φθινοπωρικοῦ ση-
⁵σάμου ὃ ἀποδώσει ἐγ νέων ἅμα ⁶τοῖς ἐκφορίοις
ἐν τῶι λϛ (ἔτει) ⁷κριθῆς παλαιᾶς ἢ κριθοπύ(ρου)
(ἀρτάβας) ν, καὶ ⁸Βρομένωι ὡσαύτως (ἀρτάβας) ι.
⁹ἔρρωσο. (ἔτους) λε ['Αθ]ὺρ ϛ.
Verso : Θρασυμήδει. (To left) Μένητος κατέρ-
(γου).

392. ORDER FOR PAYMENT OF RENT

P. Petr. iii. 104.   242 B.C.

³'Αχοάπει.ᵃ τοῦ 'Αλκέτου τῶν ἀπὸ τῆς ['Α]σίας
αἰχμαλ[ώ]τωνᵇ κλ(ήρου) ⁴τοῦ ἀνειλημμένου εἰς τὸ

ᵃ A local official in the Fayum.
ᵇ Probably a soldier captured in the Laodicean war who had taken service under Ptolemy III.

496

XII. ORDERS FOR PAYMENT

391. ORDER FOR DELIVERY OF A LOAN OF BARLEY

End of 251 B.C.

Diogenes to Thrasymedes [a] greeting. ' Give instructions to measure out to Menes, *epigonus* [b] with a holding of 25 arurae, as a loan for labour expenses and for gathering in the autumn sesame, to be repaid out of the new crop when the rents are collected in the 36th year, 50 artabae of old barley or barley-wheat,[c] and to Bromenus likewise 10 artabae. Goodbye. Year 35, Hathur 6. (Addressed) To Thrasymedes. (Docketed) Loan to Menes for labour expenses.

[a] Diogenes was a nomarch in the Fayum and Thrasymedes a subordinate.
[b] The *epigoni* were probably soldiers' sons forming a special class of recruits.
[c] A mixture of the two grains.

392. ORDER FOR PAYMENT OF RENT

242 B.C.

To Achoapis.[a] Concerning the holding of Alcetas, one of the prisoners from Asia,[b] in the area of Psinarp-

497

βα(σιλικὸν) μετὰ τὸν σπόρον τοῦ δ (ἔτους) ⁵περὶ
Ψιναρψενῆσιν ἀνενήνοχεν ἐφ᾽ ἡμᾶς ⁶᾽Απολλώνιος
ὁ συγγραφοφύ(λαξ) συγγραφὴν ἣν ἔφη ⁷συγγε-
γράφθαι ᾽Αλκέταν πρὸς ῾Ηλιόδωρον τὸν ⁸γ[ε]ωργὸν
τοῦ κλήρου ἐκφορίου τακτοῦ πυρῶν ⁹(ἀρταβῶν) λ,
καὶ κε[χει]ρογραφήκασι τὸν εἰθισμένον ¹⁰ὅρκον
τοσούτου μεμισθῶσθαι. ἀπομετρηθήτω οὖν ¹¹[εἰς
τὸ β]ασιλικὸν τὸ προγεγραμμένον ἐκφόριον.

393. ORDER FOR PAYMENT OF
SOLDIERS' WAGES

B.G.U. 1749.   63 B.C.

¹[Διονύσιος Πανίσκῳ χαίρειν. τῶν πρὸς ῾Ηρα-
κλείδην τὸν σιτολόγον ²καὶ Φαμῆν τὸν τραπεζίτην
χρηματισμῶν ἀντίγραφα ὑπόκειται. ³ἔρρωσο.
(ἔτους) ιη Μεσορὴ . .

⁴῾Ηρακλείδῃ. τοῦ παρ᾽ ᾽Αθηναίου τοῦ συγ-
γ(ενοῦς) καὶ διοικητοῦ χρηματισμοῦ ἀντί-⁵γραφον
ὑπόκειται. κατακολουθήσας οὖν τοῖς δι᾽ αὐτοῦ
σημαινομένοις ⁶μέτρησον συν]επ[ι]στέ[λλ]οντος [Πα-
νίσκ]ου τ[ο]ῦ βασι[λ]ικ[οῦ γραμματέως ⁷τοῖς ση-
μαινο]μένοις ἀποτετά[χ]θαι εἰς τὸν νομὸν Θηβαίοις
⁸[(πενταρούροις) υη παρα]χρῆμα τὰ μέρη ἑκάστω
(πυροῦ) β, πυροῦ ἀνη(λωτικῷ) ωις, ⁹γίνονται

1-6. Restored from similar texts.

ᵃ Strategus and superintendent of revenues in the Heracleopolite nome.

senesis, which has been confiscated to the Crown after the sowing of the 4th year, Apollonius the keeper of the contract has submitted to us a contract which he said that Alcetas had made with Heliodorus the cultivator of the holding for a fixed rent of 30 artabae of wheat, and they have signed the customary oath that it has been leased for this amount. Therefore let the above-mentioned rent be measured out to the Crown.

393. ORDER FOR PAYMENT OF SOLDIERS' WAGES

63 B.C.

Dionysius [a] to Paniscus greeting. Appended are copies of the orders addressed to Heraclides the sitologus and Phames the banker. Goodbye. Year 18, Mesore . . .

To Heraclides. Appended is a copy of the order from Athenaeus the king's cousin [b] and dioecetes. In conformity therefore with his instructions, which Paniscus the royal scribe is communicating to you at the same time, measure out immediately their portions to the 408 five-arurae Thebans [c] who are declared to have been assigned to our nome, to each man 2 artabae of wheat, making 816 artabae of

[b] An honorary title.
[c] Native soldiers from Thebes holding allotments of 5 arurae.

(πυροῦ) ἀνη(λωτικῷ) ωις, καὶ σύ(μβολα) καὶ ἀ[ν]-
τισύ(μβολα) ποίη(σαι) πρὸς αὐ(τοὺς) ὡς καθή(κει).
¹⁰(ἔτους) ιη Μεσο(ρὴ) ε̄.

¹¹᾽Αθήναιος Διονυσίωι χαίρειν. τοῖς ἀποτεταγ-
μένο<ι>ς σοι ἐν Φάρσεσι ¹²Θηβαίων (πενταρούρων)
ἀνδ(ράσι) υη προοῦ τὸ καθῆκον ἐγλόγισμα εἰς
Μεσορή, ¹³ἑκάστωι χα(λκοῦ) (δραχμὰς) ᾽Γ, πυροῦ
ἀνη(λωτικῷ) (ἀρτάβας) β, τὰ συναγόμενα χα(λκοῦ)
τά(λαντα) σδ, ¹⁴πυροῦ ἀνη(λωτικῷ) ωις, καὶ ἀ(πὸ)
τοῦ ιθ (ἔτους) τιθέσθωσαν αὐτοῖς εἰς δεκάμηνον
¹⁵αἱ σιταρχίαι. (ἔτους) ιη Μεσορὴ ε̄.

¹⁶Φαμῆι τραπεζίτηι. χρημάτισον ὁμοίως χαλκοῦ
τάλαν(τα) διακόσια ¹⁷τέσσαρα, (γίνεται) χα(λκοῦ)
τά(λαντα) σδ.

ᵃ The artaba was not a fixed quantity. According to one
tandard it might contain 40 choenices, according to another
tandard 36; and there were many standards, such as the
'dispensing'' and the ''receiving.'' The fixed unit in

394. PAYMENT ORDER FROM A ROYAL SCRIBE

B.G.U. 1754, ii.   63 B.C.

⁹[῎Ε]ρ[βει (?) ἀντιγραφεῖ θη(σαυροῦ) Πε]ρ[ὶ
Π]ό[λιν]. ¹⁰συμπροοῦ κατὰ τὸν παρὰ ¹¹Διονυσίου
τοῦ συγγενοῦς καὶ ¹²στρατηγοῦ καὶ ἐπὶ τῶν προσόδων ¹³χρημ[ατισ]μὸν ῎Ωρωι Θοτομνᾶτος ¹⁴ἱερακο-
β[οσκ]ῶι τοῦ ἐν τῶι ἐν ῾Ηρακλέους ¹⁵πόλει ἱερῶι
ἱερακεί[ου] εἰς τροφὴν ¹⁶καὶ τὴν ἄλλην ἐπιμέλειαν
500

wheat on the dispensing standard,[a] total 816 artabae of wheat on the dispensing standard, and draw up receipts and counter-receipts with them as is proper. Year 18, Mesore 5.

Athenaeus to Dionysius greeting. To the 408 men of the five-arurae Thebans who have been assigned to you at Pharseis deliver the wages due to them for Mesore as computed, to each man 3000 drachmae of copper and 2 artabae of wheat on the dispensing standard, being altogether 204 talents of copper and 816 artabae of wheat on the dispensing standard, and from the beginning of year 19 let their wages be paid to them for ten months. Year 18, Mesore 5.

To Phames, banker. Pay out in like manner two hundred and four talents of copper, total 204 tal. of copper.

measuring grain was the choenix, which was the same in all the standards.

394. PAYMENT ORDER FROM A ROYAL SCRIBE

63 B.C.

To Erbis (?), controller of the granary of the Suburb. In accordance with the order from Dionysius [a] the king's cousin and strategus and superintendent of revenues, furnish to Horus son of Thotomnas, hawk-tender of the hawk-house in the temple at Heracleopolis,[b] for feeding and otherwise taking care of the

[a] See No. 393.
[b] The hawk being revered as a sacred animal in this and many other localities.

τῶν [17]ἱεράκων [τ]ὰς ὑποκει(μένας) [κα]ὶ ἔω[ς τ]οῦ
ιζ (ἔτους) [18]προειμένας (πυροῦ) δοχ(ικῷ) (ἀρτάβας)
πεντήκοντα, [19]γείνονται (πυροῦ) δοχ(ικῷ) ν, καὶ
σύ(μβολον) καὶ ἀντισύ(μβολον) ποίη(σαι) [20]πρὸς
αὐ(τὸν) ὡς καθήκει.

395. ORDER FOR PAYMENT TO WEAVERS

B.G.U. 1564.   A.D. 138.

[1]Ἀ[ντίγραφ]ον ἐπιστάλ[ματ]ος. Ἀμμ[ώ]ν[ιος]
Πολυδεύκους [κ]αὶ Συρίων Ἡρᾶ καὶ Ἡρακλείδης
Ἡρακλείδου οἱ γ̄ ἱματοπ(αραλήμπται) καὶ Ἑρμῆ(ς)
[2]ἄ[γο]ρα[νομήσας] Ἡρακλείδῃ τρ[απ(εζίτῃ)] χα(ί-
ρειν). χρημάτισον Ἡρακλείδῃ Ὡριγᾶτος καὶ
Ἥρωνι ἀπελευθέρῳ Ποπλίου Μηουίου καὶ Διοσκόρῳ ἀπελ(ευθέρῳ) [3]τοῦ με[γίστου θεο]ῦ Σαράπιδος
γε[ρδί]οις κώμης [Φιλ]αδελφείας ὥστε αὐτοῖς καὶ
τοῖς λοιποῖς γερδίοις τῆς αὐτῆς κώμης ἐξ ἀλλη-
λ(εγγύης) πα . [4]εἰς προχ[ρείαν τι]μῆς ἱματισ[μο]ῦ
ἀπὸ τοῦ κελευσθέντος ὑπὸ Ἀουιδίου Ἡλιοδώρου
τοῦ κρατίστου ἡγεμόνος κατασκευασθῆναι [5]εἰς μὲν
χρ[είας τῶν] ἐν Καππαδοκ[ίᾳ] στρατευμάτων
χιθῶνος λευκοῦ ζωστοῦ ἑνὸς μήκ(ους) πήχ(εων) γ
(ἡμίσους) πλάτους πήχ(εων) β̄ δακ(τύλων) δ [[. . .]]
[6]ὁλκῆς μνῶν γ (ἡμίσους) (τετάρτου) ἐπὶ λόγο(ν)
ἐκ (δραχμῶν) κδ, συριῶν λευκῶν τεσσάρων μήκ-
κ(ους) ἑκάστης πήχ(εων) ς πλάτους πήχ(εων) δ
ὁλκῆ(ς) μνῶ(ν) γ (ἡμίσους) (τετάρτου) [7]ἐπὶ λόγο(ν)

3. Perhaps πᾶσι is meant.

hawks, fifty artabae of wheat on the receiving standard as prescribed and as furnished up to the 17th year, total 50 artabae of wheat on the receiving standard, and draw up a receipt and counter-receipt with him as is proper.

395. ORDER FOR PAYMENT TO WEAVERS

A.D. 138.

Copy of payment order.   Ammonius son of Polydeuces, Syrion son of Heras, Heraclides son of Heraclides, all three receivers of clothing,[a] and Hermes, ex-agoranomus, to Heraclides, banker, greeting. Pay to Heraclides son of Horigas, Heron freedman of Publius Maevius,[b] and Dioscorus freedman of the most great god Sarapis,[c] weavers of the village of Philadelphia, for themselves and the other weavers of the said village on their mutual security the following sums as advanced payment of the price of clothing forming part of that which was ordered by his excellency the praefect Avidius Heliodorus to be manufactured : for the requirements of the troops in Cappadocia, for one white belted tunic 3½ cubits long, 3 cubits 4 fingers broad, weighing 3¾ minae, on account 24 drachmae, and for four white Syrian cloaks, each 6 cubits long, 4 cubits broad, weighing

---

[a] A local board which supervised the provision of clothing ordered by the government for the army.

[b] One of the witnesses in No. 254.

[c] A fictitious purchase by a god, with funds provided by the slave, was a common form of manumission in Greek lands, though this seems to be the only recorded example of the practice in Egypt.

ἑκάστης ἐκ (δραχμῶν) κδ, (γίνονται) (δραχμαὶ) ϙϛ,
(γίνονται) ἐπὶ τὸ α(ὐτὸ) (δραχμαὶ) ρκ, εἰς δὲ χρείας
τοῦ ἐν τῇ Σεβαστῇ παρεμβολ(ῇ) ὑγιαστηρίου
[8]λώδικος λευκῆς ἁπλῆς μιᾶς μήκ(ους) πήχ(εων) ϛ
πλάτους πήχ(εων) δ ὁλκ(ῆς) μνῶ(ν) δ ἐπὶ λόγο(υ)
(δραχμὰς) κη, (γίνονται) ἐπὶ τὸ αὐτὸ τοῦ ἐπιστάλ-
(ματος) [9]ἀργ(υρίου) (δραχμαὶ) ρμη, ἀπὸ δὲ τῶν τῆς
προχρείας τῶν λωδίκων (δραχμῶν) κη ὑπελογήθ(η-
σαν) εἰς τὸν κυριακὸν λόγο(ν) {ρ} (δραχμαὶ) ϛ { . },
[10]ἐφ' ᾧ ποιή[σ]ουσι τὸν ἱματισμὸν ἔκ τε καλῆς καὶ
μαλακῆς καὶ λευκοτάτης ἐρεᾶς χωρὶς παντὸς
ῥύπου εὐυφῆ εὐπαγῆ [11]εὔσημα ἀρεστὰ ἀσινῆ μὴ
ἀποδέοντα τῆς ὑπὲρ αὐτῶν ἐξωδιασθίσης αὐτοῖς εἰς
προχρείαν τιμῆς. ἐὰν δέ τι ἐξ αὐ-[12]τῶν ἐπὶ τῆς
παραδόσεως ἀπολέγῃ ἢ ἐλάσσονος συντιμηθῇ,
ἀποδώσουσι ἐξ ἀλληλ(εγγύης) τῶν μὲν ἀπολεγόν-
τ(ων) τὴν τιμὴν [13]μετὰ καὶ τῶν τελῶν καὶ δαπανῶν,
τῶν δ' ἐλάσσω τὸ ἀποδέον, ἃ καὶ παραδώσουσι ἐν
τάχι ἔχοντα τὰ προκ(είμενα) μέτρα καὶ ὁλκ(ὴν)
[14]χωρὶς ἄλλων ὧν ὀφίλουσι δημοσίων ἱματισμ(ῶν).
ἔτους δευτέρου Αὐτοκράτορος Καίσαρος Τίτου
Αἰλί[ο]υ Ἀδριανοῦ [15]Ἀντωνίνου Σεβαστοῦ Εὐσεβοῦς Θὼθ ιβ̅.

11. *l.* ἐξοδιασθείσης.

396. ORDER FOR MILITARY SUPPLIES

P. Cairo Masp. 67321. A.D. 548 or 563.

(A) [1][☩ Φλαύιος] Θεόδωρος Μηνᾶς Ἰουλιανὸ[ς]
Ἰακκῶβος ὁ μεγαλοπρε(πέστατος) κόμε(ς) καὶ

3¾ minae, on account 24 drachmae apiece, making 96 drachmae, combined total 120 drachmae, and for the requirements of the sanatorium in the Imperial camp, for one plain white blanket 6 cubits long, 4 cubits broad, weighing 4 minae, on account 28 drachmae, total of the payment order 148 drachmae of silver ; but from the advance of 28 drachmae for the blankets 6 drachmae were deducted for the exchequer. It is understood that they will make the clothing of good, soft, pure white wool without any defilement, well woven, firm, well selvaged, satisfactory, undamaged, not worth less than the price paid to them in advance for the garments. If on the delivery any of these is missing or is judged to be of inferior value, they shall repay on their mutual security the price of the missing articles, together with the taxes and expenses, and the deficit of the inferior articles. And they shall deliver them promptly, having the aforesaid measurements and weights, apart from other public clothing which is due from them. The second year of the Emperor Caesar Titus Aelius Hadrianus Antoninus Augustus Pius, Thoth 12.

396. ORDER FOR MILITARY SUPPLIES

A.D. 548 or 563.

Flavius Theodorus Menas Julianus Jacob the most magnificent count and *praeses* of the eparchy of the

ἄρχ(ων) τῆς Θηβ(αίων) ἐπαρχ(είας) τὸ ϛ". ²[πάσας
θεοῦ ἡγο]υμένου τὰς ὑφ' ἡλίῳ πόλεις ἰθύνων
βασιλεὺς ὁ κράτ[ισ]τος ὅπλοις καὶ στρατιωτικοῖς
καταλόγοις εἰς παράταξιν παρεσκευασμένοις τῇ
τῶν τακτικῶν [ἐ]μπειρίᾳ ³[μετὰ τῆς τ]ῶν νόμων
τά[ξε]ως τιχείζει· χαρακτηρίζει τοῦτο τὸ νῦν
[φ]οιτῆσαν εὐτύχημα τῷ Θηβαίων ἔθνει. θεσπίσαι
γὰρ εὐτυχῶς κατηξίωσεν διὰ θείου πραγματικοῦ
τύπου ⁴[ἐνιδρῦσθαι τ]ῇ Ἑρμουπολι[τῶ]ν πόλει
ἀριθμὸν τῶν εὐκαθοσιώτων Νουμίδων Ἰουστινιανῶν, ἀνδρῶν πεντακοσίων ὀκτώ, πρὸς παρα-
φυλακὴν τῆς Θηβαίων ἐπαρχείας καὶ ⁵[πρὸς
ἐκδί]ωξιν πάσης β[α]ρβαρικῆς [ἐπ]ιδρομῆς, καὶ
σιτήσεις αὐ[τ]οῖς χορηγεῖσθαι προσέταξεν. τὴν
γὰρ τοιαύτην ἀγαθὴν καὶ προνοητικὴν διοίκησιν
πέρατι π[α]ραδοῦναι ⁶[προστέτακτα]ι ὁ ἐνδοξότα-
τ[ος] κόμες Πλουτῖνος, ἀνὴρ τῇ εὐσεβεῖ τα[ύτῃ]
πολιτίᾳ χρήσιμος γεγονὼς καὶ ἐν τοῖς κοινοῖς
πράγμασιν εὐδόκιμος φανείς, ὡς καὶ μεμαρτύ-
ρη[τα]ι ⁷[παρὰ τῆς κρα]τούσης τύχη[ς κ]αὶ τῆς
ὑψηλοτάτης καθέδρας, ὅστ[ις ἐ]κ προοιμίων τῆς
αὐτοῦ ἀφίξεως ἔδειξεν τὸ [φύ]σει προσὸν τῇ αὐτοῦ
ἐνδοξότητι πρᾶον τὸ λυ[σι]τελοῦν ⁸[πᾶσιν ἐπι-
σ]κοπῶν. θ[ελήσ]ατε τοίνυν τοῦτο τὸ δικ[ασ]τικὸν
πρό[σταγ]μα δεχ[ό]με[νο]ι χορηγῆσαι τοῖς προδη-
λωθεῖσιν εὐκ[αθ]οσιώτοις Νουμίδοις Ἰουστινιανοῖς,
διὰ Βηρυλλᾶ ⁹[τοῦ καθοσιω]μένου αὐτῷ[ν ὀ]πτίονος,
εἰς ἄνδρας πεντακοσίους [ὀκτ]ὼ τελ[ο]ῦσιν, ὑπὲρ
μηνὸς Σεπτεμβρίου καὶ Ὀκτωμβρί[ο]υ καὶ Νοεμ-
βρίου καὶ Δεκεμβρίου τῆς παρούσης ¹⁰[δωδεκάτης]
ἐπινεμ[ήσε]ως ἀκολ[ούθ]ως τῇ ὑποτ[ετ]αγμένῃ

8. [πᾶσιν ἐπισ]κοπῶν E.-H.

Thebaid for the 6th time. Our most mighty king, ordering with God's guidance all the cities under the sun, is fortifying them with arms and military troops trained for battle by tactical experience, in accord with the ordinance of the laws; and this design characterizes the auspicious event which has now befallen the province of the Thebaid.[a] For he has auspiciously deigned to decree by a divine official order that there shall be quartered in Hermopolis a *numerus* of the loyal Justinian Numidians, five hundred and eight men, to guard the eparchy of the Thebaid and repulse every inroad of barbarians, and he has ordered supplies to be furnished to them. To give effect to this most good and thoughtful measure the most honourable count Plutinus[b] has been appointed, a man who has rendered services to this pious community and gained a good repute in public affairs, as has been recognized by the reigning fortune[c] and by the most lofty magistracy,[d] and who from the first hour of his arrival has shown the gentleness naturally inherent in his nobility, observing the general interest. Be ready therefore on receiving this legal order to furnish supplies, through Beryllas their devoted adjutant, to the above-mentioned loyal Justinian Numidians, amounting to four hundred and eight men, for the months of September, October, November, and December of the present twelfth indiction, in accordance with the appended account,

a The sentence alludes to the military reforms of Justinian.
b The commander of the troops in question.
c That is, the Emperor.
d The praefect of the praetorium in Constantinople.

γν[ώσ]ει, εἰδότες ὡς εἰ κατά τι ῥᾳθυμία τις παρα-
κολουθ[ήσ]ῃ, οὐκ ἐκτὸς ἔσεσθε δικαστικῆς κινή-
σεως. ¹¹[διὰ γὰρ τοῦτ]ο [ἐκ τά]ξεως [ἀ]πέσ[τ]αλ-
τα[ι]. ⳨ Legi. ¹²Legi. ¹³R(ecognovi?) ¹⁴[το]ῖς ἀπὸ
κώ[μης Ἀφροδίτ]ης τοῦ [Ἀν]ται[οπο]λίτου. ⳨

(Β) ¹⳨ Χρὴ ἐκ τῆς ὑμετέρας κώμης τὸ ὑπο-
τεταγμέ(νον) μέτρον ἀπαιτηθῆναι καὶ ²παρασχεθῆναι
τοῖς γενναιοτ(άτοις) Νουμίδοις Ἰουστινιανοῖς διὰ
Βηρυλλᾶ ³τοῦ καθοσιωμέ(νου) αὐτῶν ὀπτί(ονος)
ὑπὲρ μηνὸς Σεπτεμβρίου καὶ Ὀκτωμβρίου καὶ
⁴Νοεμβρίου καὶ Δεκεμβρίου τῆς παρού[σης] ἐπινεμήσεως ⁵ἀποκρίτως ἄχρι κομιδῆς τοῦ εὐτυ-
χ[εστάτ]ου προδηλήγατου τῆς αὐτῆς ⁶δωδεκάτης
ἰνδ(ικτίονος). δηλαδὴ τῆς καταβολ[ῆς] γιγνομέ(νης)
τὰς φορμαρ(ίας) κομίζ(εσθε). ⁷σίτου mo(dii) σμγ
(τρίτον), [οἰ]νοκρ(έου) βϜις, ⁸οὕ(τως)· τῷ ὀπτί(ονι)
σίτου mo(dii) σκ, οἰνοκρ(έου) ͵βχνα· τῷ αὐτ(ῷ)
ὑ(πὲρ) δηπ(ουτάτου) σίτου mo(dii) ζ, οἰνο[κρ(έου)]
πη· τῷ δημοσίῳ σίτου mo(dii) ιϛ (τρίτον), οἰνο-
κρ(έου) ροζ.

knowing that if any slackness is shown on any point, you will not escape the action of the law. Wherefore we have sent this letter from the *officium*. (Signed) Read. Read. Reviewed. (Addressed) To the inhabitants of the village of Aphrodite in the Antaeopolite nome.

(The requisition) The appended quota is required to be collected from your village and supplied to the most noble Justinian Numidians through Beryllas their devoted adjutant for the months of September, October, November, December of the present indiction without prejudice until the receipt of the most auspicious preparatory assignment [a] of the said twelfth indiction, it being understood that you receive the quittance at the time of payment. 243⅓ modii of wheat, 2916 measures of thin wine, divided as follows : to the adjutant, 220 modii of wheat, 2651 measures of wine ; to the same on behalf of the armourer, 7 modii of wheat, 88 measures of wine ; to the officials 16¼ modii of wheat, 177 measures of wine.

[a] The *delegatio* was a yearly order from the praefect of the praetorium fixing the amounts of the various imposts and contributions, the *praedelegatio* an official forecast sent in advance of the final assignment.

XIII. ACCOUNTS AND LISTS

397. POSTAL REGISTER

P. Hib. 110, ll. 51-114.   About 255 B.C.

- - - ^{51}κυλιστοὶ ϛ, (τούτων) βασιλῖ γ κα[ὶ ἐπισ-]
^{52}τολή{ν}, Θευγένι χρηματαγωγ[ῶι ·], ^{53}Ἀπολ-
λωνίω[ι δ]ιοι[κ]η[τῆ]ι [- - - ^{54}]ϛ. [- - - ^{55}Ἀλ]εξ-
άνδρωι ϛ, τ[ο]ύτων [βασι]λεῖ ^{56}Πτο[λ]εμαίωι
κυ(λιστὸς) α, Ἀπολ[λ]ωνί[ωι δ[ιοι-^{57}κη]τῆι κυ(λιστὸς) α, ἐπιστολαὶ δύο πρὸς τῶι ^{58}[κυλ]ιστῶι προσ-
δέδεντ(αι), Ἀντιόχωι Κρητὶ κυ(λιστὸς) α, Μην[ο-]
^{59}δ[ώρω]ι κυ(λιστὸς) α, Χελ[.]ω . [. .]αι ἐν ἄλλωι
κυ(λιστὸς) α, ^{60}Ἀ[λ]έξανδρος δὲ παρέδωκ[εν Ν]ικο-
δήμωι. ^{61}ιζ. ὥρας ἑωθινῆς παρέδωκεν Φοῖνιξ
Ἡρα-^{62}κλείτου ὁ νεώτερος Μακεδὼν ^{63}(ἑκατοντάρουρος) Ἀμίν<ον>ι κυ(λιστὸν) α καὶ τὸ ἄξιον
Φανία[ι], Ἀμ[ί]ν[ω]ν ^{64}δὲ παρέδωκεν Θευχρήστωι.
^{65}ιη. ὥρας πρώτης παρέδωκεν Θεύχρ[η]σ-^{66}τος
ἄνωθεν Δινίαι κυ(λιστοὺς) γ, (τούτων) βασιλῖ
^{67}Πτολεμαίωι κυ(λιστοὶ) β, Ἀπολλωνίωι ^{68}διοικητῆι

---

58. προσδέδεντ(αι) revised reading (Schubart) : προσδεδεγ-
μ(έναι) Edd. The word is added above the line.   59. Or
κ]αὶ Ἐνάλ{λ}ωι Schubart.   66. l. ἄνωθεν : so in ll. 106,
108.

510

XIII. ACCOUNTS AND LISTS

397. POSTAL REGISTER [a]

About 255 B.C.

. . . 6 rolls, of which 3 were for the king together with a letter, [.] for Theogenes the money-carrier, [.] for Apollonius the dioecetes . . . The 16th, . . . delivered to Alexander 6 rolls, of which 1 roll was for King Ptolemy, 1 roll with two letters attached to it for Apollonius the dioecetes, 1 roll for Antiochus the Cretan, 1 roll for Menodorus, 1 roll inside another for Chel . . ., and Alexander delivered them to Nicodemus. The 17th, morning hour, Phoenix the younger, son of Heraclitus, Macedonian, holding 100 arurae, delivered to Aminon 1 roll and the price [b] for Phanias,[c] and Aminon delivered it to Theochrestus. The 18th, 1st hour, Theochrestus delivered to Dinias 3 rolls from the upper country, of which 2 rolls were for King Ptolemy and 1 for

[a] A fragment from the day-book of an intermediate station in the government's express postal service. The rolls and letters were here delivered by mounted postmen to one of the clerks, who transmitted them to the postmen of the next stage after carefully noting all details.

[b] The meaning is obscure.

[c] Perhaps a secretary of the military settlers (see No. 412), but according to Preisigke the postmaster.

κυ(λιστὸς) α, Δινίας δὲ παρέ-[69]δωκεν Ἱππολύσωι.
[70]ιη. παρέδωκεν ὥρας ϛ Φοῖνιξ Ἡρακλείτου [71]ὁ
πρεσβύτερος Μακεδὼν (ἑκατοντάρουρος) [72]Ἡρακλεο-
πολίτου τῶν πρώτων Ἔσοπ[.] . [. .] [73]κυλιστὸν
α Φανίαι, ᾿Αμίνων [δ]ὲ παρέ[δ]ωκ(ε) [74]Τιμοκράτηι.
[75]ιθ. ὥρας ια πα[ρ]έδ[ω]κ[ε Νι]κόδημος [76]κάτοθεν
᾿Αλεξάνδρωι κυ(λιστοὺς) . , παρ[ὰ] [77]βασιλέως
Πτολε<μαί>ου ᾿Αντιόχωι εἰς [78]Ἡρακλεοπολίτην
κυ(λιστὸν) α, Δημητρίω[ι] [79]τῶι πρὸς τῆι χορηγία[ι
τ]ῶν ἐλεφάντω[ν] [80]εἰς τὴν Θηβαΐδα κυ(λιστὸν) α,
Ἱπποτέλ[η]ι [81]τῶι παρ᾿ ᾿Αντιόχου καταλελιμμένωι
[82]ἐν ᾿Απόλλωνος πόλι τῆι μεγάληι [83]κυ(λιστὸν) α,
παρὰ βασιλέως Πτολεμαίο[υ] [84]Θευγένι χρηματ-
α[γω]γῶι κυ(λιστὸν) α, [85]Ἡρακλεοδώρωι εἰς τὴ[ν]
Θηβαΐδα [κυ(λιστὸν) α], [86]Ζωίλωι τραπεζίτηι
Ἑρμοπολίτ[ου] κυ(λιστὸν) [α], [87]Διονυσίωι οἰκο-
ν<όμ>ωι εἰς τὸν ᾿Αρσινοΐτη[ν κυ(λιστὸν)] α, - - -
[91]κ. ὥρας [.] παρέ[δω]κ[εν Λ]υκοκλῆς ᾿Αμ[ίνονι]
[92]κυ(λιστοὺς) γ, (τούτων) [β]α[σι]λῖ [Πτο]λε-
μ[αί]ωι [. . .] τῶν ἐλεφά[ντων] [93]τῶν κα[τ]ὰ Θα-
[. .] . σσου κυ(λιστὸς) α, ᾿Απολλω[νίωι] [94]δι[ο]ικητῆι
κυ(λιστὸς) α, Ἑ[ρ]μίππω[ι] τῶι ἀπ[ὸ τοῦ] [95]πληρώ-
ματος κυ(λιστὸς) α, ᾿Αμίνων δὲ π[αρέδω-][96]κεν
Ἱππολύσωι. [97]κα. ὥρας ϛ παρέδωκεν [·]εναλε
.[. . . . . .] [98]κάτοθεν Φανίαι ἐπιστο[λὰ]ς δύο
[. . . . . . .], [99]Ὧρος δὲ παρέδωκεν Διον[υ]σίωι
. .[. . . . . . .] [100]κβ. ὥρας πρώτης πα[ρ]έδωκεν
Α[. .]ων [Δινίαι] [101]κυ(λιστοὺς) ιϛ, (τούτων) βασιλεῖ
Πτολεμαί[ω]ι κ[υ(λιστοὶ) .] [102]παρὰ τῶν ἐλεφάντων
τῶν κατὰ Θα[. . . σσου], [103]᾿Απολλωνίωι διοικητῆι

76. l. κάτωθεν: so in l. 98.   83. Before παρά an
unknown symbol.

Apollonius the dioecetes, and Dinias delivered them to Hippolysus. The 18th, 6th hour, Phoenix the elder, son of Heraclitus, Macedonian, holding 100 arurae in the Heracleopolite nome, one of the first soldiers [a] in the troop of E . . ., delivered 1 roll for Phanias, and Aminon delivered it to Timocrates. The 19th, 11th hour, Nicodemus delivered to Alexander [.] rolls from the lower country, from King Ptolemy for Antiochus in the Heracleopolite nome 1 roll, for Demetrius the officer in the Thebaid in charge of the supply of elephants [b] 1 roll, for Hippoteles the agent of Antiochus,[c] left in charge at Apollonopolis the Great,[d] 1 roll, from King Ptolemy for Theogenes the money-carrier 1 roll, for Heracleodorus in the Thebaid 1 roll, for Zoilus, banker of the Hermopolite nome, 1 roll, for Dionysius the oeconomus in the Arsinoite nome 1 roll, . . . The 20th, [.] hour, Lycocles delivered to Aminon 3 rolls, of which 1 roll was for King Ptolemy from the elephant-hunters [e] at Th . . ., 1 roll for Apollonius the dioecetes, 1 roll for Hermippus, member of the crew,[f] and Aminon delivered them to Hippolysus. The 21st, 6th hour, . . . delivered two letters from the lower country for Phanias, and Horus delivered them to Dionysius. . . . The 22nd, 1st hour, . . . delivered to Dinias 16 rolls, of which [.] rolls were for King Ptolemy from the elephant-hunters at Th . . ., 4 rolls for Apollonius the dioecetes . . .,

[a] The epithet denotes a certain rank.
[b] Hunting expeditions were sent to the coast of the Red Sea to procure elephants for the Ptolemaic army.
[c] See No. 207, note a.   [d] The modern Edfu.
[e] Literally " from the elephants."
[f] The Greek word may mean crew or a company of workmen ; but we do not know what it refers to here.

κυ(λιστοὶ) δ .[. . . . . . .], ¹⁰⁴Ἀντιόχωι Κρητὶ
κυ(λιστοὶ) δ, Δινίας δὲ [παρέδω-]¹⁰⁵κεν Νικοδήμωι.
κβ. ὥρας ιβ παρέδωκεν Λέων Ἀ[μίνονι] ¹⁰⁶ἄνοθεν
βασιλῖ Πτολεμαίωι [κυ(λιστοὺς) .], ¹⁰⁷Ἀμίνων δὲ
παρέδωκεν ['Ι]ππ[ολύσωι]. ¹⁰⁸κγ. ἑωθινῆς ἄνοθεν
πα[ρέ]δω[κεν . . . . .] ¹⁰⁹Τιμοκράτης κυλιστοῦ[ς .
Ἀλεξάνδρωι], ¹¹⁰(τούτων) βασιλῖ Πτολεμαίωι κ[υ-
(λιστοὶ) ., Ἀπολλωνίωι] ¹¹¹διοικητῆι κυ(λιστὸς) α,
Π[. . . . . χρηματα-]¹¹²γωγῶι κυ(λιστὸς) α, Πα-
ρικ[. . . . . κυ(λιστὸς) α (?)], ¹¹³Ἀλέξανδρος
δὲ πα[ρέδωκεν - - -

398. ACCOUNT OF PAYMENTS IN CORN
TO THE GOVERNMENT

P. Tebt. 89, ll. 1-17, 26-32.　　　　　113 B.C.

¹″Ε[του]ς δ, παρὰ Μεγχείους κωμογραμματέως
²Κ[ερ]κεοσίρεως. προδιαλογισμὸς σιτικὸς ³ἐπι-
κεφαλαίου τοῦ αὐτοῦ (ἔτους), ⁴ὑποκειμένων τῶν
ἐγδιωκημένων ἕως Μεσορὴ λ. ⁵[ἐσπαρ]μέναι
ἦ[σαν] ἐν τῶι αὐτῶι (ἔτει) σὺν νομ[α]ῖς ⁶γῆς (ἄρουραι) Ἀσγ∠δ′ ὧν ἐκφό(ριον) Δχξζ∠γ′ ι′β′, ⁷καὶ
προσγεί(νονται) τῶν ἐπὶ τοῦ διοικητοῦ (ἀρτάβαι) ζ∠,
⁸ὥστ᾽ εἶναι (ἀρούρας) Ἀσγ∠δ′ (ἀρτάβας) Δχοε
γ′ ι′β′, ⁹ὧν (πυροῦ) Ἀχνγ∠, κ(ριθῆς) αῖ (πυροῦ)
Βωοζ δ′, ὀλ(ύρας) αῖ (πυροῦ) ϟζ δ′, χα(λκοῦ) λθ γ′

ᵃ In the Fayum.
ᵇ That is, land of which the rent was subject to a decision
of the dioecetes.

4 rolls for Antiochus the Cretan, and Dinias delivered them to Nicodemus. The 22nd, 12th hour, Leon delivered to Aminon [.] rolls from the upper country for King Ptolemy, and Aminon delivered them to Hippolysus. The 23rd, morning hour, Timocrates delivered to Alexander [.] rolls, of which [.] rolls were for King Ptolemy, 1 roll for Apollonius the dioecetes, 1 roll for P . . . the money-carrier, 1 (?) roll for Par . . ., and Alexander delivered them to . . .

398. ACCOUNT OF PAYMENTS IN CORN TO THE GOVERNMENT

113 B.C.

For year 4, from Menches, village scribe of Kerkeosiris.[a] A preliminary account of the total receipts in corn for the said year, showing below the amounts collected up to Mesore 30. The land sown in the said year, including pastures, comprised $1203\frac{3}{4}$ arurae, of which the rent is $4667\frac{11}{12}$ artabae, with a further $7\frac{1}{2}$ artabae for the land under adjudication of the dioecetes,[b] making a total of $1203\frac{3}{4}$ arurae and $4675\frac{5}{12}$ artabae. These are made up as follows[c] : in wheat $1653\frac{1}{2}$ artabae, in barley the equivalent of $2877\frac{1}{4}$ artabae of wheat,[d] in olyra the equivalent of $97\frac{1}{4}$, in copper the equivalent of $39\frac{5}{12}$; but calculated

---

[c] According to a hypothetical estimate, not based on the actual sowings.

[d] The value of wheat in relation to that of barley and olyra (a kind of spelt) was as 5 : 3 and 5 : 2 respectively.

SELECT PAPYRI

ιβ΄, ¹⁰ἐγ δὲ τοῦ σπόρου (πυροῦ) Γψϙδ γ΄, κ(ριθῆς)
φνϛ∠γ΄ αἱ (πυροῦ) τλδϛ΄, χα(λκοῦ) λθγ΄ ιβ΄,
(2nd hand) φακοῦ φ. (1st hand) ¹¹εἰς ἃς μεμετρῆσθαι ἐν αὑτῆι Ἀμμωνίωι καὶ ¹²ᶜἩρακλείδηι τοῖς
σιτολογοῦσι τὸ περὶ αὐτὴν οἳ καὶ ¹³ἀντιγραφόμενοι·
¹⁴Φαρμοῦθι ἀπὸ α ἕως ι μισ(θοῦ) (πυροῦ) σβ∠,
κρι(θῆς) φγ∠δ΄, ¹⁵καὶ ἀπὸ ια ἕως κ μισ(θοῦ) (πυροῦ)
ψδ∠, κρι(θῆς) νγ, ¹⁶καὶ ἀπὸ κα ἕως λ μισ(θοῦ)
(πυροῦ) ⟦ω ٜ .⟧ ωε∠, ¹⁷(γίνονται) τοῦ μη(νὸς) μισ-
(θοῦ) (πυροῦ) Ἀψιβ∠, κρι(θῆς) φνϛ∠δ΄. - - -
²⁶Με[σο]ρ[ὴ α ἕ]ως ι μισ(θοῦ) φακ(οῦ) ρϙθ∠δ΄.
²⁷τοῦ δὲ μ[εμε]τρη(μένου) (πυροῦ) Γωα∠γ΄, ²⁸κρι-
(θῆς) φνϛ∠δ΄ αἱ (πυροῦ) τλδϛ΄, φακοῦ φ, ²⁹(γίνονται)
εἰς (πυροῦ) Ἀχλϛ. ³⁰καὶ χαλκ[ὸ]ν δια[γ]εγρ(αμμένον) ὦ[ν σ]ῖ(τος) [λθ]γ΄ ιβ΄. ³¹τῶ⟨ν⟩ δ΄ ἐγδιωκη-
μέν[ων ἀπὸ Φαρμοῦθι α] ³²ἕως Μεσορὴ [λ] εἰς
(πυροῦ) Ἀχοε γ΄ ιβ΄.

13. *l.* ἀντιγράφονται, or understand ἐσιτολόγησαν.

ᵃ An artaba of lentils was worth an artaba of wheat.   In

399. MONTHLY RETURN OF REVENUE IN MONEY

P. Oxy. 1283.   A.D. 219.

¹Αὐρηλίῳ Ἁρποκρα-²τίωνι στρα(τηγῷ) Ὀξ(υρυγχίτου) ³π[αρὰ Α]ὐρηλ(ίου) Πατ( ) Εὐτ(υχ) καὶ
τ(ῶν) ⁴σὺν αὐτ(ῷ) πρα(κτόρων) ἀργ(υρικῶν) μη-⁵τρο-
πολ(ιτικῶν) μέσης τοπ(αρχίας) ⁶Πεεννὼ τόπ(ων).
διαστολ(ὴ) ⁷ἀριθ(μήσεως) μη(νὸς) Παῦνι τοῦ ⁸ἐν-
εστ(ῶτος) β (ἔτους) Μάρκου ⁹Αὐρηλίου [Ἀ]ντωνίνου
516

on the sowings the amounts are : in wheat $3794\frac{1}{3}$, in barley $556\frac{5}{6}$ equivalent to $334\frac{1}{6}$ of wheat, in copper the equivalent of $39\frac{5}{12}$, in lentils 500 artabae.[a] Towards this the following amounts have been delivered in the village to Ammonius and Heraclides the sitologi for its area, whose accounts have been countersigned [b] : Pharmouthi 1 to 10, for rent $202\frac{1}{2}$ artabae of wheat, $503\frac{3}{4}$ of barley ; 11 to 20, for rent $704\frac{1}{2}$ of wheat, 53 of barley ; 21 to 30, for rent $805\frac{1}{2}$ of wheat ; total for the month, for rent $1712\frac{1}{2}$ of wheat, $556\frac{3}{4}$ of barley. . . . Mesore 1 to 10, for rent $199\frac{3}{4}$ of lentils. The wheat delivered amounts to $3801\frac{5}{8}$ artabae, barley to $556\frac{3}{4}$ equivalent to $334\frac{1}{6}$ of wheat, lentils to 500, making a total, calculated in wheat, of 4636. And there has been paid in copper the equivalent of $39\frac{5}{12}$. Of the amounts collected from Pharmouthi 1 to Mesore 30 the total, calculated in wheat, is $4675\frac{5}{12}$ artabae.

these calculations the $7\frac{1}{2}$ artabae for the land under adjudication have been omitted.   [b] By the village officials.

399. MONTHLY RETURN OF REVENUE IN MONEY

A.D. 219.

To Aurelius Harpocration, strategus of the Oxyrhynchite nome, from Aurelius Pat . . . son of Eutych . . . and his associates, collectors of money taxes of the metropolis for the middle toparchy in the district of Peenno. The classified list of payments for the month Pauni of the present 2nd year of Marcus Aurelius Antoninus Caesar the lord is as

SELECT PAPYRI

¹⁰Κ[αίσ]αρος τοῦ κυρίου, ¹¹ἔστι δέ· ¹²λημ(μάτων)
τ[ο]ῦ ἐνεστ(ῶτος) β (ἔτους) ¹³ἐπαρο(υρίου) ς΄ (δραχμαὶ) χ, ¹⁴καὶ διεγρά(φησαν) ἐπὶ τ(ὴν) δημ(οσίαν)
τρά(πεζαν) ¹⁵ὑπὸ μὲν Σεπτιμίου ¹⁶Χαιρή(μονος)
ἐπαρο(υρίου) (δραχμαὶ) ρμγ (ἡμιωβέλιον) χ(αλκοῖ)
β, ¹⁷(ὀκταδράχμου) σπονδ(ῆς) Διον(ύσου) (δραχμαὶ)
η (τετρώβολον) χ(αλκοῦς) α, ¹⁸πηχισμ(οῦ) περι-
στ(ερώνων) (δραχμαὶ) ιζ (πεντώβολον), ¹⁹Αὐρήλ(ιος)
Ἀχιλλεὺς ἐπαρο(υρίου) ²⁰(δρ.) ρϙη (πεντώβολον)
(ἡμιωβέλιον), (ὀκταδράχμου) σπονδ(ῆς) ²¹[Δ]ιο-
ν(ύσου) (δρ.) η (τετρώβολον) χ(αλκ.) α, ²²[Α]ὐρήλ(ιος)
Ἀπ[. .]ν[. .] καὶ Τα-²³[. .] . [. . . . . . ἐπαρο(υ-
ρίου) (δρ.)] ρις - - - ²⁶[(ἔτους) β Αὐτοκράτορος
Κ]αίσαρος ²⁷[Μάρκου Αὐρηλίου Ἀντωνίνου ²⁸Εὐσεβοῦς Εὐτυχοῦς Σεβαστοῦ - - -

---

ᵃ These were taxes on vineyards and plantations of olives
and fruit-trees.

400. MONTHLY RETURN OF REVENUE IN CORN

P. Tebt. 339.   A.D. 224.

¹[Α]ὐρηλίωι Σερηνίσκωι τῶι καὶ ²ʿΕρμησίᾳ στρα-
(τηγῷ) Ἀρσι(νοΐτου) Θε(μίστου) καὶ Πολ(έμωνος)
³μερίδων ⁴[π]αρὰ Αὐρηλίου Πωλίωνος ⁵[σι]τολ(όγου)
κώ(μης) Τεπτύ[ν]εως. ⁶[μ]ηνιαῖος ἐν κεφαλαίῳ τοῦ
[Θ]ὼθ ⁷[μ]ηνὸς τοῦ ἐνεστῶτος δ (ἔτους) ⁸[ἀ]πὸ
γενή(ματος) τοῦ αὐτοῦ ἔτους. εἰ-⁹σὶν ἐ μετρη(θεῖ-
σαι) τῷδε τῷ μηνὶ ¹⁰[δ]ιοικήσεως καὶ οὐσιακῶν

9. l. αἱ.

518

follows. Receipts of the present 2nd year : for acreage tax and tax of $\frac{1}{6}$ [a] 600 drachmae ; and paid into the public bank by Septimius Chaeremon for acreage tax 143 drachmae $\frac{1}{2}$ obol 2 chalci, for the eight-drachma libation of Dionysus [b] 8 drachmae 4 obols 1 chalcus, for the cubit-measure of pigeon-houses [c] 17 drachmae 5 obols, by Aurelius Achilles for acreage tax 198 drachmae $5\frac{1}{2}$ obols, for the eight-drachma libation of Dionysus 8 drachmae 4 obols 1 chalcus, by Aurelius Ap . . . and Ta . . . for acreage tax 116 drachmae. . . . The 2nd year of the Emperor Caesar Marcus Aurelius Antoninus Pius Felix Augustus. . . .

[b] A tax on vineyards, nominally for the benefit of the cult of Dionysus.

[c] A tax on pigeon-houses, perhaps graduated in accordance with their size.

400. MONTHLY RETURN OF REVENUE IN CORN

A.D. 224.

To Aurelius Sereniscus also called Hermesias, strategus of the divisions of Themistes and Polemon in the Arsinoite nome, from Aurelius Polion, sitologus of the village of Tebtunis. Monthly summary for the month Thoth of the present 4th year [a] of receipts from the produce of the said year. The amount delivered in this month for the exchequer and the imperial domains is 176 artabae of wheat

[a] Of Severus Alexander.

¹¹[π]υροῦ (ἀρτάβαι) ρος κριθ(ῆς) (ἀρτάβαι) ι, ὧν
¹²[τ]ὰ δη(μόσια) Τε[ππ]ύν[εω]ς (πυροῦ) (ἀρτάβαι)
ρκ[θ] κ[ριθ(ῆς)] (ἀρτάβαι) ι, ¹³κληρούχων (πυροῦ)
(ἀρτάβαι) λζ, ¹⁴ὑπὲρ ἄλλων κωμ[ῶ]ν Πολέμωνος
¹⁵Κερκεσήφεως κλη(ρούχων) (πυροῦ) (ἀρτάβαι) ι,
¹⁶γ(ίνονται) αἱ π(ροκείμεναι). ¹⁷[κα]ὶ ταύταις προσ-
αναλ(αμβάνονται?) ὑπὲρ ποδώ(ματος) ¹⁸(ἑκατοσταὶ)
β (πυροῦ) (ἀρτάβαι) γ∠, ¹⁹(ἑκατοστὴ) α ποδώ(ματος)
πυροῦ (ἀρτάβης) κ'δ', ²⁰[(ἡμι]αρταβίας) ποδώ(ματος)
πυροῦ (ἀρτάβης) μ'η', ²¹[(γίνονται)] ποδώ(ματος) καὶ
ἄλλω(ν) (πυροῦ) (ἀρτάβαι) γ∠κ'δ' μ'η'.

401. REGISTER OF A COHORT

From B.G.U. 696.   A.D. 156.

(Col. 1) ¹Pridianum coh(ortis) i Aug(ustae) Pr(aetoriae)
Lus(itanorum) eq(uitatae) ²mensis Augusti Silvano et
Augurino co(n)s(ulibus), ³quae hibernatur Contrapollo-
⁴nospoli maiore Thebaidis ex viii ⁵Idus Iulias Pontiano et
Rufi[no] co(n)s(ulibus), ⁶praefectus M. Iulius M. f. tribu
⁷Quir(ina) Silvanus, domo Thubursi-⁸ca, militare coepit
ex ix Kal(endas) Ma-⁹ias Commodo et Laterano co(n)s(ulibus) ¹⁰loco Aeli Pudentilli.

¹¹Pridie Kal(endas) Septembres. ¹²summa a[d pr(idie)]
Kal(endas) ¹³Ianuaria[s] D[V], [i]n is (centuriones) vi,
dec(uriones) iii, ¹⁴eq(uites) cxiv, drom(edarii) xviiii,
¹⁵pedites ccclxiii.

(Col. 1) 13. D[V] is in the margin opposite l. 12.

and 10 artabae of barley ; of which the revenues from public land at Tebtunis are 129 artabae of wheat and 10 artabae of barley, from cleruchs 37 artabae of wheat, and on account of other villages in the division of Polemon, from cleruchs at Kerkesephis 10 artabae of wheat, making the aforesaid total. To this are added on account of storage 2 per cent, making $3\frac{1}{2}$ artabae of wheat, 1 per cent upon the charge for storage $\frac{1}{24}$ artaba of wheat, and for the $\frac{1}{2}$ artaba upon the charge for storage $\frac{1}{48}$ artaba of wheat, making the total for storage and other charges $3\frac{9}{16}$ artabae of wheat.

401. REGISTER OF A COHORT

A.D. 156.

Register of cohort i Augusta Praetoria Lusitanorum equitata for the month of August in the consulship of Silvanus and Augurinus,[a] the winter quarters of which cohort have been at Contrapollonopolis Major [b] in the Thebaid since July 7 of the consulship of Pontianus and Rufinus,[c] and the praefect of which is Marcus Julius Silvanus son of Marcus, of the tribe Quirina, from Thubursica,[d] who took up his post on April 23 of the consulship of Commodus and Lateranus [e] in place of Aelius Pudentillus.

August 31. The total strength on December 31 was 505, comprising 6 centurions, 3 decurions, 114 cavalrymen, 19 camel-riders, 363 infantrymen.

[a] A.D. 156.   [b] Facing Apollonopolis Magna (Edfu).
[c] A.D. 131.   [d] In Numidia.   [e] A.D. 154.

¹⁶*Et post Kal(endas) Ianuarias accesser(unt),* ¹⁷*factus
ex p[a]gano a Sempro-*¹⁸*nio Liberale praef(ecto) Aegypt(i)
i* (2nd hand) ¹⁹*Silvano et Augurino co(n)s(ulibus)* ²⁰*Sextus
Sempronius Candidu[s] ex v Kal(endas)* ²¹*Maias,* (1st
hand) ²²*reiectus ab ala{e} i Thrac(um)* ²³*Mauretaniae ad
vircam chor-*²⁴*tis dec(urio) i* (2nd hand) ²⁵*Vibio Varo
co(n)s(ulibus)* ²⁶*A. Flavius Vespasianus ex vi Nonas*
²⁷*Martias,* (1st hand) ²⁸*tirones prob[a]ti volun-*²⁹*tari a
Se[m]pronio Liberalae* ³⁰*praef(ecto) Aeg(ypti) viiii, in is
eq(ues) i drom(edarius) i - - -* (Col. 2) - - - ¹³*accepti ex
leg(ione) ii Tr(aiana) Fort[i]* ¹⁴*dati ab eodem praefect[o]*
¹⁵*Aegypti* (2nd hand) ¹⁶*in (centuria) Lappi Condiano et
Maximo co(n)s(ulibus)* ¹⁷*Valerius Tertius ex viii Ka-
l(endas)* ¹⁸*Apriles,* ¹⁹*in (centuria) Candidi Torquato et
Iuliano co(n)s(ulibus)* ²⁰*Horatius Herennianus ex iv Idus*
²¹*Novembres,* (1st hand) ²²*translatus ex coh(orte) i
Fl(avia) Cil(icum)* (2nd hand) ²³*in (centuria) Candidi
Comm[odo] et Pompeiano co(n)s(ulibus)* ²⁴*Maeviu(s)
Marcellu[s - - -],* (1st hand) ²⁵*item translat[i ex
. . . . . .]* (2nd hand) ²⁶*in (centuria) Lappi Severo
[et Stloga co(n)s(ulibus)]* ²⁷*C. Longinus Apoll[. . . . .
ex . . .]* ²⁸*Idus Feb[ruarias],* - - -

(Col. 1) 18. *i* is in the margin opposite l. 17.   22. *ala{e}*
E.-H.: *ala Ei* Ed.   23. *vircam = virgam.*   24.
dec(urio) i is in the margin opposite l. 22.   29. *l.
Liberale.*

402. ACCOUNT OF PUBLIC GAMES

P. Oxy. 519.   2nd cent. A.D.

- - - ¹(Τούτων) ἀπεδόθη ²Μεχ(εὶρ) κγ ³μίμῳ
(δραχμαὶ) υϛϛ, ⁴ὁμηριστῇ (δραχμαὶ) υμη, ⁵καὶ ὑπὲρ

And since January 1 the following have joined :
1 civilian enrolled by Sempronius Liberalis, praefect
of Egypt, namely Sextus Sempronius Candidus on
April 27 of the consulship of Silvanus and Augurinus ;
1 decurion degraded from the ala i Thracum Mauretaniae to the roll of a cohort,[a] namely Aulus Flavius
Vespasianus on March 2 of the consulship of Vibius
and Varus [b] ; 9 voluntary recruits approved by Sempronius Liberalis, praefect of Egypt, comprising 1
cavalryman, 1 camel-rider, . . . ; received from
legion ii Trajana Fortis by presentation of the said
praefect of Egypt : in the centuria of Lappus, on
April 24 of the consulship of Condianus and Maximus,[c]
Valerius Tertius ; in the centuria of Candidus, on
November 10 of the consulship of Torquatus and
Julianus,[d] Horatius Herennianus ; transferred from
cohort i Flavia Cilicum, in the centuria of Candidus,
on . . . of the consulship of Commodus and Pom-
peianus,[e] Maevius Marcellus ; likewise transferred
from . . ., in the centuria of Lappus, on February . .
of the consulship of Severus and Stloga,[f] Gaius
Longinus Apoll . . .

[a] Literally " to the switch." According to Mommsen's
explanation a soldier degraded from an ala to a cohort
became punishable by flogging with a *virga* instead of the
more honourable *fustis*.　　[b] A.D. 134.　　[c] A.D. 151.
[d] A.D. 148.　　[e] A.D. 136.　　[f] A.D. 141.

402. ACCOUNT OF PUBLIC GAMES

2nd cent. A.D.

. . . Of this sum there were paid on Mecheir 23 :
to an actor 496 drachmae, to a Homeric reciter 448

μου[σ]ι[κῆς (δραχμαὶ) . . ., ⁶ὁ]ρχηστῇ [(δραχμαὶ)]
ρ[.]δ, - - - ⁷ἀπελ[άβ(ομεν)? πα]ρὰ τοῦ ἐξη(γητοῦ)
(δραχμὰς) μβ, ⁸παρὰ τοῦ κοσμητ(οῦ) (δραχμὰς) νγ
(ἡμιωβέλιον), ⁹(γίνονται) (δραχμαὶ) φ (ὀβολός).
¹⁰(τούτων) ἀνηλ(ώθησαν) κωμασταῖς Νείλ(ου) (δραχμαὶ) κ, ¹¹κωμασταῖς θεῶν (δραχμαὶ) νϛ, ¹²ἱπποκόμοις
(δραχμαὶ) ιϛ, ¹³ἱεροδού(λοις) ιδ ὀβ(ολοὶ) πδ, ¹⁴πλοῦ (?)
ἱεροδού(λων) (δραχμαὶ) κ, ¹⁵κήρυκι (δραχμαὶ) η,
¹⁶σαλπικτῇ (δραχμαὶ) δ, ¹⁷παιδίοις ἀρίστου ὀβ(ολοὶ)
ϛ, ¹⁸παλμῶν ὀβ(ολοὶ) ϛ, ¹⁹(γίνονται) (τούτων) (δραχμαὶ) ρκδ ὀβ(ολοὶ) ϛϛ. ²⁰[. .]. α( ) πανκρατ(ιαστῇ)
(δραχμαὶ) . [. . ²¹. .]ανωνι ἀνταγ(ωνιστῇ) (δραχμαὶ)
[. . ²² . .]. νι πύκτῃ μη . ( ) ι[

7. απ . .[. . Edd. : suppl. E.-H.   14. Or an abbreviation πλου( ).   22. μην(ῶν) .[?

403. LIST OF ARTICLES FOR A SACRIFICE

P. Oxy. 1211.   2nd cent. A.D.

¹Στρατηγῷ. τὰ πρὸς τὴν θυ-²σίαν τοῦ ἱερωτάτου
³Νείλου Παῦνι λ· ⁴μόσχος α, οἴνου εὐώ-⁵δη κεράμ(ια)
β, λάγανα ιϛ, ⁶στέφανοι ιϛ, στρόβιλοι ιϛ, ⁷πλα-
κοῦντες ιϛ, ⁸βάις χλωρὰς ιϛ, ⁹κάλαμοι ὁμοί(ως) ιϛ,
¹⁰ἔλεον, μέλι, γάλα, πᾶν ¹¹ἄρωμα χωρὶς λιβάνου.

4-5. l. εὐώδους.   8. l. βάεις χλωραί.   10. l. ἔλαιον.

drachmae, and for music . . . drachmae, to a dancer 1[.]4 drachmae. . . . Received from the exegetes 42 drachmae, from the cosmetes 53 drachmae ½ obol, total 500 drachmae 1 obol. Of this sum there were paid out : to image-bearers of the god Nile 20 drachmae, to image-bearers of the gods 56 drachmae, to grooms 16 drachmae, to 14 temple slaves 84 obols, for the voyage (?) of the temple slaves 20 drachmae, to a crier 8 drachmae, to a trumpeter 4 drachmae, to the boys for breakfast 6 obols, for palms 6 obols, total 124 drachmae 96 obols. To . . ., pancratiast, . . . drachmae, to . . ., competitor, . . . drachmae, to . . ., boxer, . . .

403. LIST OF ARTICLES FOR A SACRIFICE

2nd cent. A.D.

To the strategus. Articles for the sacrifice to the most sacred Nile on Pauni 30 [a] : 1 calf, 2 jars of sweet-smelling wine, 16 wafers, 16 garlands, 16 pine-cones, 16 cakes, 16 green palm-branches, 16 reeds likewise, oil, honey, milk, every spice except frankincense.

[a] For the festival which is still held about the summer solstice when the river begins to rise.

SELECT PAPYRI

404. FROM THE MONTHLY ACCOUNTS OF A TEMPLE OF JUPITER CAPITOLINUS AT ARSINOE

B.G.U. 362, cols. 6-8.   A.D. 215.

(Col. 6) - - - ²ὁμ[οίως παρὰ το]ῦ αὐτοῦ ἀπὸ
τειμῆς σι[δήρου ἀπο-]³λυθέν[τος . .]. . . φ . . ι ἀπὸ
τοῦ κατασκε[υασθέντος] ⁴χαμο[υλκο]ῦ εἰς ὑπηρεσίαν
τοῦ ἀναστ[αθ]έντος ⁵θείου κ[ολοσ]σιαίου ἀνδριάντος
τοῦ κυρ[ίου ἡ]μῶν ⁶Αὐτοκρά[τορ]ος Σεουήρου
Ἀντωνίνου, ὀλ(κῆς) μνῶν ʹν̄β̄ ὡς τ(ῆς) [μ]νᾶς
(δραχμαὶ) ε, αἱ συναγό(μεναι) (δραχμαὶ) σξ. ⁸γ(ί-
νονται) [ἐπ(ὶ τὸ αὐτὸ) λ]ημ(μάτων) (δραχμαὶ) Ἀχε.
⁹καὶ ἐγλόγου τοῦ μηνὸς ἐλοιπογρ(αφήθησαν)
[(δραχμαὶ) κ]δ, ¹⁰γ(ίνονται) ἐπ(ὶ τὸ αὐτὸ) σὺν καὶ
τῇ ἐγλ(όγου) (δραχμαὶ) Ἀχκ[θ]. ¹¹ἐξ ὧν ἀναλώ-
θη(σαν)· ¹²[. ., εἰς δ]ιαγρ(αφὴν) τελ[εσ]μάτων κβ
(ἔτους) τῶν ὑπογεγρ(αμμένων) [κωμῶν]· ¹³Ἀλεξ-
άνδρου [Ν]ήσου ἐπισ(ήμου) [(δραχμαὶ) . .], ¹⁴Πτο-
λεμαΐδος Δρυμ(οῦ) ὁμοί(ως) [(δραχμαὶ) . .]. ¹⁵ε̄,
Τρικωμίας ὁμοί(ως) [(δραχμαὶ) . .]. ¹⁶ϛ̄, εἰς δια-
γρ(αφὴν) [στε]φανικῶν κβ (ἔτους) κώμης [Κερ-]
¹⁷κεσή[φ]εως [(δραχμαὶ) . .], ¹⁸εἰς διαγρ(αφὴν)
τ[ε]λ[εσ]μάτων κώ(μης) Πυρρείας [(δραχμαὶ) . .],
¹⁹στεφανι[κῶν] τῆς αὐτῆς [(δραχμαὶ) . .], ²⁰εἰς
διαγρ(αφὴν) τ[ελ(εσμάτων)] βαλανείου κώμ(ης) Φι-
λαγρί[δος (δραχμαὶ) . .]. ²¹[. ., εἰ]ς διαγρ(αφὴν)
στεφανικῶν κβ (ἔτους) Πυρρείας ἄ[λλαι (δραχμαὶ)
. . ²². . . . . . εἰ]ς ἐπ[ιμέ]λ[ε]ι[α]ν τοῦ πατρῴου
ἡμ[ῶν θεοῦ ²³. . . . . . .]ω . ος Σούχου μεγάλου
μ[εγάλου, ²⁴στέψεως τῶν ἐν [τ]ῷ ἱερῷ ἀσπι[δείων
526

404. FROM THE MONTHLY ACCOUNTS OF A TEMPLE OF JUPITER CAPITOLINUS AT ARSINOE

A.D. 215.

. . . Received likewise from the same as the price of iron removed . . . from the machine constructed to facilitate the erection of the divine colossal statue of our lord the Emperor Severus Antoninus, weighing 52 minae, at 5 drachmae the mina, altogether 260 drachmae. Total of the receipts 1605 drachmae. And there remained from the preceding month a balance of 24 drachmae. Total, including the balance, 1629 drachmae.

Of this have been spent : . . . For payment of dues of the 22nd year at the following villages [a] : at Alexandri Nesus . . drachmae of silver coin, at Ptolemais Drumi likewise . . drachmae. 5th, at Tricomia likewise . . drachmae. 6th, for payment of crown-tax for the 22nd year at the village of Kerkesephis . . drachmae, for payment of dues at the village of Pyrrheia . . drachmae, for crown-tax at the same village . . drachmae, for payment of bath-tax at the village of Philagris . . drachmae, for payment of crown-tax for the 22nd year at Pyrrheia other . . drachmae. . . ., for the service of our ancestral god . . . Souchus [b] the twice great, for crowning all the medallions and statues and

---

[a] The dues were on property owned by the temple in these villages, all of which were in the Fayum.

[b] The crocodile god of Arsinoe (formerly called Crocodilopolis).

(Col. 6) 10. *l.* τῷ or ταῖς ἐγλ(όγου)?

καὶ ἀνδρι-²⁵άντων καὶ ἀγαλμάτων πάν]τ(ων) [(δραχ-
μαί) . ., (Col. 7) ¹[ἐλαίου εἰς λυχνα]ψίαν ἐν τ[ῷ
σηκῷ (δραχμαὶ) . .], ²ναῦ[λον ὄνο]υ ἑνὸς ὑπὸ δένδρα
καὶ β[άις] (δραχμαὶ) δ. ³ῑη, ἱερᾶς [οὔσ]ης καὶ
θεωρίας ὑπὲρ ἀνα[στάσεω]ς ⁴ἀνδ[ρ]ι[ά]ντος τοῦ
κυρίου ἡμῶν Α[ὐτ]οκράτορος ⁵Σεουήρου ᾿Αντω-
νίνου, στέψεως [τῶ]ν ἐν ⁶τῷ ἱερῷ πάντων ὡς
πρόκ(ιται) (δραχμαὶ) ις, ⁷ἐλαίου εἰς λυχναψίαν ἐν
τῷ σηκῷ (δραχμαὶ) δ. ⁸κ̄, ἐπιδημήσαντος τοῦ
λαμπροτάτου ἡγεμόνος ⁹Σεπτιμίου Ἡρακλείτου,
στέψεως τῶν ¹⁰ἐν τῷ ἱερῷ πάντων ὡς πρόκιτ[α]ι
(δραχμαὶ) κδ, ¹¹ἐλαίου εἰς λυχναψίαν ἐν τῷ σηκῷ
(δραχμαὶ) ς, ¹²στροβείλων [κ]αὶ ἀρωμάτων καὶ
ἄλλων [(δραχμαὶ) ιβ], ¹³ναῦλα ὄνω[ν] β ὑπὸ δένδρα
καὶ βάις [(δραχμαὶ) η], ¹⁴ἀλείψεως τῶν ἐν τῷ ἱερῷ
ἀνδριάντων ¹⁵πάντων ἐλαίου (δραχμαὶ) κ, ¹⁶μισθὸς
χα[λκο]υργῷ ἀλείψαντι τοὺς ἀνδριάντ(ας) (δραχμαὶ)
δ, ¹⁷ἐργάταις κ[ωμά]σασι τὸ ξόανον τοῦ θεοῦ πρὸς
[ἀ-]¹⁸πάντη[σιν τοῦ] ἡγεμόνος (δραχμαὶ) λβ, ¹⁹στε-
φάνω[ν τῷ] αὐτῷ ξοάνῳ (δραχμαὶ) δ, ²⁰ῥήτορι
ε[ἰπόν]τι ἐπὶ τοῦ λαμπροτάτου [ἡ]γε-²¹μόνος [Σεπ]-
τιμίου Ἡρακλείτου ἔνεκ[α τῆ]ς ²²ἐπιμερισ[θ]είσης
τοῖς ὑπάρχουσι τοῦ θ[εοῦ] ²³[Ν]είκης [κ]αὶ ἄλλων
(δραχμαὶ) ξ. ²⁴[. ., ἐπιδημήσαν]τος τοῦ κρατίστου
ἐπ[ιτρόπου ²⁵τῶν οὐσιακῶ]ν Αὐρηλίου Ἰταλικοῦ
[διαδεχομ(ένου) ²⁶τὴν ἀρχιερωσύν]ην, στέψεω[ς τῶν
ἐν τῷ ²⁷ἱερῷ πάντων (δραχμαὶ) . ., (Col. 8) ¹ἐλαίου
εἰς λυχναψ]ίαν [ἐν τῷ σηκῷ (δραχμαὶ) . .] ²καὶ
ἀν[αλώθησα]ν εἰς ἐπι[. .]τικὸν [. . . . . .]τος
³πεσό(ντος) . [. . .]ς πρ[ὸ]ς τῷ ἱερῷ τοῦ θεοῦ
μ[ισθὸς ?] οἱ-⁴κοδόμ(οις) γ̄ κατασπῶσι καὶ ἀνοικο-

(Col. 8) 2. ἐπι[σι]τικόν Ed.   3. μ[ισθὸς ?] E.-H.

sacred images in the temple . . drachmae, for oil for lighting lamps in the shrine . . drachmae, charge for one donkey carrying trees and palm branches 4 drachmae. 18th, being a sacred day to celebrate the erection of the statue of our lord the Emperor Severus Antoninus, for crowning all the monuments in the temple as aforesaid 16 drachmae, for oil for lighting lamps in the shrine 4 drachmae. 20th, on the occasion of the visit of the most illustrious praefect Septimius Heraclitus, for crowning all the monuments in the temple as aforesaid 24 drachmae, for oil for lighting lamps in the shrine 6 drachmae, for pine-cones and spices and other things 12 drachmae, charge for two donkeys carrying trees and palm branches 8 drachmae, for polishing all the statues in the temple with oil 20 drachmae, wage of a copper-smith for polishing the statues 4 drachmae, to porters who carried the image of the god in procession to meet the praefect 32 drachmae, for crowns for the said image 4 drachmae, to an orator who made a speech in the presence of the most illustrious praefect Septimius Heraclitus in acknowledgement of the Victory [a] which he contributed to the possessions of the god and of other gifts 60 drachmae . . ., on the occasion of the visit of his excellency the procurator of the Imperial domains Aurelius Italicus, deputy chief priest, for crowning all the monuments in the temple . . drachmae, for oil for lighting lamps in the shrine . . drachmae. Disbursed also for (restoration?), a . . . having collapsed beside the temple of the god, wages of 3 masons demolishing and rebuilding, at

[a] A statue dedicated by the praefect.

SELECT PAPYRI

δόμ(ουσι) ὡς τ(οῦ) (ἑνὸς) ⁵ἑξ (ὀβολῶν) ιη (δραχμαὶ)
ζ (τετρώβολον), ⁶ὁμοίως παιδία ξ̄ ὑπουργοῦσι τοῖς
αὐ-⁷τοῖς οἰκοδόμ(οις) ὡς τ(οῦ) (ἑνὸς) (ὀβολοὶ) ι
(δραχμαὶ) η (δυόβολοι), ⁸μισθὸς πηλοποιῷ (δραχμαὶ) β, ⁹τειμ(ῆς) πλίν[θ]ου ὠμῆς σὺν παραγωγῇ
μετὰ τὰς ¹⁰ἐκβεβηκυίας ἐκ τοῦ κατασπ‹ασμ›οῦ
(δραχμαὶ) ιβ. ¹¹λ, ὀψώνιον Νεμεσιανῷ ναοφύλ(ακι)
ὑπ(ὲρ) Φαμ(ενὼθ) (δραχμαὶ) κη, ¹²Θεωνείνῳ ὁμοίως
[(δραχμαὶ) ιθ], ¹³[Ξ]άνθῳ π[ρ]οαιρέτῃ βιβλ(ιοθήκης)
ὁμοί(ως) [(δραχμαὶ) λ], ¹⁴Βοήθῳ γραμματεῖ ὁμοί(ως)
(δραχμαὶ) [μ], ¹⁵ἐπιτηρητῇ ὑπ(ὲρ) καταπομπῆς
μηνιαί[ου] (δραχμαὶ) ιβ. ¹⁶γ(ίνονται) ἐπ(ὶ τὸ αὐτὸ
τοῦ ἀναλώμ(ατος) (δραχμαὶ) ψλβ (δίχαλκον). ¹⁷λοι-
π(αὶ) εἰς [τὸν] ἑξῆς μῆνα Φαρμ(οῦθι) (δραχμαὶ)
ω[ϛ]ϛ (ὀβολός).

6. *l.* παιδίοις.

405. RETURN OF TEMPLE PROPERTY

P. Oxy. 1449.   A.D. 213–217.

¹Π[α]ρὰ Αὐρ(ηλίων) Ζωίλ(ου) Ἀπολλωνίου μη-
τ(ρὸς) Αὐρ(ηλίας) Ἀχι[λλίδ(ος) καὶ - - - μη]τ(ρὸς)
Αὐρ(ηλίας) Τααφύγχ(ιος) ἀμφοτέρων [. . . . . .
. .] καὶ τῶν σὺν αὐτ(οῖς) ἱερέων Δ[ιὸς καὶ Ἥρας
καὶ Ἀταργάτιδ(ος)] ²καὶ Κόρης καὶ Διονύσου καὶ
Ἀπόλλων[ο]ς [καὶ Νεωτέρας καὶ τῶν συννάων θε]ῶν
καὶ κωμαστῶν προ[τομῶν τοῦ] κυρί[ο]υ Σεβαστοῦ
καὶ Νίκης [αὐτοῦ προαγούσης καὶ] ³Ἰουλίας
Δόμνας Σεβαστῆς καὶ τοῦ θεο[ῦ πατρὸς αὐτοῦ?
Σεουήρου . . . .]νων αὐτῶν ἱερῶν τῶ[ν ὄν-

18 obols each, 7 drachmae 4 obols, likewise of 6 boys
assisting the said masons, at 10 obols each, 8 drachmae
2 obols, wage of a brick-maker 2 drachmae, price of
unbaked bricks including transport, in addition to
those rescued from the demolition, 12 drachmae.
30th, salary of Nemesianus, temple watchman, for
Phamenoth 28 drachmae, of Theoninus likewise 19
drachmae, of Xanthus, keeper of the archives, likewise 30 drachmae, of Boethus, secretary, likewise 40
drachmae, to the official in charge of the dispatch of
the monthly accounts 12 drachmae. Total expenditure 732 drachmae 2 chalci. Left over for the succeeding month of Pharmouthi 896 drachmae 1 obol.

405. RETURN OF TEMPLE PROPERTY

A.D. 213–217.

From Aurelius Zoilus, son of Apollonius and of
Aurelia Achillis, and Aurelius . . ., son of . . . and
of Aurelia Taaphunchis, both . . ., and their associates, priests of Zeus, Hera, Atargatis,[a] Core,
Dionysus, Apollo, Neotera,[b] and the associated gods,
and celebrants of the busts of the lord Augustus and
his advancing Victory[c] and Julia Domna Augusta and
his deified father Severus, at their . . . temples

---

[a] A Syrian goddess.
[b] A Graeco-Egyptian goddess, probably Hathor-Aphro-
dite.
[c] A personification of the victorious rule of the Emperor
Caracalla.

των] ἐν τῇ μητροπόλ(ει), ἐπὶ μὲν το[ῦ Διονύσου
ἐπ' ἀμφόδ(ου)] ⁴Δρόμ(ου) Θοήριδ(ος), τοῦ δὲ ἑτέρου
Ἀπόλλωνος . [- - - θεοῦ μεγ]άλου ἀγαθοῦ δαί-
μ(ονος) καὶ Νεωτ(έρας) [ἐν τοῖς ἀπ]ὸ νότου τῆς
π[ό]λεως ἐπ' ἀ[πη]λ(ιώτην) [μέρεσιν ἐπ' ἀμφόδ(ου)
. . . . ( )], ⁵καὶ ἐν τοῖς ἀπὸ νότου ἐπὶ λίβα μέρεσι
τῆ[ς πόλ(εως) ἐπ' ἀμφόδ(ου) . . . . ( ) Νεω-
τ(έρας)?, καὶ ἐπ' ἀμφόδ(ου) Πλατ(είας) ἐκ νότ(ου)
τοῦ Δημητρ(είου) Διὸς καὶ Ἥ[ρας κ]αὶ Ἀταργάτ[ιδ]ος Βεθεννύν[ιδ(ος)? καὶ Κόρης, καὶ ἐπ' ἀμ-]
⁶φ[ό]δ(ου) Δρόμ(ου) Γυμνα(σίου) Διὸς καὶ Ἥρας
καὶ Ἀταργάτ[ιδ(ος) Βεθεννύνιδ(ος) καὶ Κόρης, καὶ
ἐπ' ἀμφόδ(ου) Ἱ]ππέων Παρεμβολ(ῆς) Πατεμὶτ
λα[ύρα]ς [Δι]ὸς καὶ Ἥρας καὶ Ἀταργάτιδ(ος) κ[αὶ
Κόρης?, καὶ ἐν . . . .] ⁷τοῦ Κυνοπολ(ίτου)
Διὸς καὶ Ἥρας. γρα(φὴ) ἀναθημάτ(ων) [τοῦ κ.
(ἔτους) Μάρκου Αὐρηλίου Σεουήρο]υ Ἀντωνίνου
Παρθικοῦ Μεγίστου Βρεταννικοῦ Μεγίστου Γερμανικοῦ Μεγίστο[υ Εὐσεβοῦς Σεβαστοῦ]. ⁸ἔστι
δέ· τῶν μὲν ἐν τῷ τῆς Νεωτ(έρας) ἱερ[ῷ, εἰκο-
νείδιον τοῦ κυρίου ἡμῶ]ν Αὐτοκράτορος Μάρκου
Αὐρηλί[ο]υ Σεουήρου Ἀντωνίνου Εὐτυχοῦς [Εὐ-
σεβοῦς Σεβαστοῦ] ⁹καὶ Ἰουλίας Δόμνας τῆς κυρίας
Σεβαστῆς [καὶ τοῦ θεοῦ πατρὸς αὐτοῦ Σεουήρου,
ἐπι]κειμέ[ν]ων ἐπί τινων ἀναθημάτ(ων) τὰ ὀνό-
ματ(α) τῶν ἀναθ[έντ(ων) . . . ., ἐπὶ]
¹⁰γὰρ ἄλλων μὴ γεινώσκειν ἡμεῖν τοὺς [ἀναθέντας
διὰ τὸ τὰ ἀναθήματ(α) ἀπὸ ἀρχαί]ων χρόνων ἐν
τῷ ἱερῷ εἶναι, ξόανον Δήμητρος θ[εᾶς μεγίστ(ης),
οὗ ἡ προτομ(ὴ)] ¹¹Παρίνη, τὰ δὲ ἄλλα μέρη τοῦ
σώματ(ος) ξ[ύλινα, - - -]ωνιειου . [. .] . ω[. .]-

situated in the metropolis, in the case of Dionysus in the quarter of the Square of Thoeris,[a] in the other case, that of Apollo . . . the great god and good genius and of Neotera in the south-east part of the city in the quarter of . . ., in the south-west part of the city one of Neotera (?), and in the Broad Street quarter to the south of the shrine of Demeter that of Zeus, Hera, Atargatis Bethennunis,[b] and Core, and in the Gymnasium Square quarter that of Zeus, Hera, Atargatis Bethennunis, and Core, and in the Cavalry Camp quarter, Patemit street, that of Zeus, Hera, Atargatis, and Core, and in . . . of the Cynopolite nome that of Zeus and Hera. List of offerings for the 2[.] year of Marcus Aurelius Severus Antoninus Parthicus Maximus Britannicus Maximus Germanicus Maximus Pius Augustus, as follows. Objects in the temple of Neotera : a small representation of our lord the Emperor Marcus Aurelius Severus Antoninus Felix Pius Augustus and Julia Domna the lady Augusta and his deified father Severus, some of the offerings being inscribed with the names of the dedicators, . . . while in other cases we are ignorant of the dedicators, because the offerings have been in the temple from antiquity ; a statue of Demeter, most great goddess, of which the bust is of Parian marble and the other parts of the body of wood, . . . was

[a] The hippopotamus-shaped goddess of Oxyrhynchus.
[b] Probably an epithet derived from a Semitic place-name.

μ[. .] ἡμεῖν οὐκ ἐπεδείχθ(η). καὶ ἐπὶ [. . . . . . .
τῶν ἐκ τῆς] ¹²ἄνωθ(εν) συνηθ(είας) κατ' εὐχ(ὴν)
καὶ εὐσέβ(ειαν) ἀνιερωθέντ(ων), [- - - ἀ]νατεθ(ε)
ὑπὸ Φρ[α?]γέν[ο]υς Ὡ[ρί]ωνος, (2nd hand) ξό[α]νον
Νεωτ(έρας) χα(λκοῦν) μεικ(ρόν), δακτύλ(ιοι) ε [ἀνα-
τεθ(έντες) ὑπὸ . . . .] ¹³Διδύμ(ου), στολὴ
καλλαΐνη ἀνατεθ(εῖσα) ὑπὸ τ(ῆς) μητ(ρὸς) Ἀν-
[- - - ἀ]νατεθ(ε) ὑπὸ Κάστορος Ἀσκληπ(ιάδου),
[βε?]λένκωτο[ς] μεικ(ρὸς) ἐφ' οὗ ξόανον τῆς Νεω-
τ(έρας) αποθ . [- - -] ¹⁴λιθ(ιν) εὐτόμου λίθ(ου),
πηδάλ(ιον) τῆς [Νεωτ(έρας)?, ξόανον - - - ο]ῦ ἡ
προτομ(ὴ) Π[α]ρίνη, τὰ δὲ περίαπτ[α ἐπί]πλαστ(α),
Τυφῶν τινῶν μερῶν κα[- - -] ¹⁵κατὰ μέ(σον) κεκολ-
(λημεν) καὶ τὰ ἐν γλωσσ[οκόμῳ - - - λύχνοι
χρ(υσοῖ) μεικ(ροὶ) μ]εστ(οὶ) θεί[ου?] β ἀν[ατε]θ(έντες)
ὑπὸ Σαρα[π(ίωνος)] Σαραπ(ίωνος), ἄλ(λος) λ[ύχ-
(νος)] χρ(υσοῦς) [μ]εικ(ρὸς) μεστ(ὸς) θείο(υ?) ἀνα-
τεθ(εὶς) ὑπὸ Σαραε(ῦτος) Ἀχ[ιλλ( ), ἄλ(λος)
λύχ(νος) χρ(υσοῦς) μεικ(ρὸς) μεστ(ὸς) θείο(υ)?] ¹⁶ἀνα-
τεθ(εὶς) ὑπὸ Πτολεμαΐδος γυναι[κὸς - - - ὧν ὁ
στα]θμ(ὸς) δι(ὰ) τῶν κατὰ χρόνο(ν) γρα(φῶν) [δη]-
λοῦτ(αι), πε[ριδέξι]α παιδικ(ὰ) ι καὶ παιδικ(ὸς)
δακτύλ(ιος) α, ἐπὶ [τὸ α(ὐτὸ) χρ(υσοῦ) (τεταρτῶν)? .,
. . . .] ¹⁷μύστ(ρα) χρ(υσᾶ) β, γρ[α]-
φε[ῖο(ν)] χρ(υσοῦν) μεικ(ρὸν) α, ορα[- - - μ]εικ(ρ)
α, πάντ(α) ἐπὶ τὸ α[ὐτὸ] χρ(υσοῦ) [(τεταρτῶν)
. . . .] . χρ(υσ) εὐτο(μο) ἀργυρο-
π(οιητο?) α (τεταρτῶν) β, γραφεῖα ἀργ(υρᾶ) [- - -

15. θείο(υ) E.-H. : θείο(ι) Edd.   17. Or ἀργυρόπ(ους).

not disclosed to us. And with regard to other offerings, which were dedicated in accordance with ancient custom for vows or pious reasons, . . . dedicated by Phragenes (?) son of Horion, a small bronze statue of Neotera, 5 finger-rings dedicated by . . . son of Didymus, a turquoise-coloured robe dedicated by the mother of An . . ., . . . dedicated by Castor son of Asclepiades, a small . . . on which is a statuette of Neotera . . ., a stone . . . of well-cut stone, a rudder of Neotera (?), a statue of . . ., of which the bust is of Parian marble and the ornaments of plaster, a statue of Typhon, part of which . . . joined together in the middle, and the . . . in a casket, 2 small gold lamps, full of brimstone (?), dedicated by Sarapion son of Sarapion, another small gold lamp, full of brimstone (?), dedicated by Saraeus daughter of Achill . . ., another small gold lamp, full of brimstone (?), dedicated by Ptolemais wife of . . ., of which the weight is stated in the periodical lists, 10 armlets for a child and 1 ring for a child, making in all . quarters of gold, . . ., 2 gold spoons, 1 small gold pen, . . . 1 small . . ., making in all . quarters of gold, 1 gold . . . well-cut and decorated with silver, weighing 2 quarters, . silver pens . . .

406. CONCERNING THE WATER SUPPLY OF A MUNICIPALITY

P. Lond. 1177 (extracts from).   A.D. 113.

¹Δημητρίωι γεγυμνασιαρχηκότι ²ἐξεταστῇ ³παρὰ
Κρίσπου τοῦ καὶ Σαραπίωνος ⁴καὶ Μύσθου τοῦ
καὶ Πτολεμ[αί]ου τοῦ ⁵Πτολεμαίου καὶ Μύσθου
διὰ τ[οῦ] πα-⁶τρὸς Διδύμου καὶ Σώτου τοῦ [Ζ]ωίλου
⁷τῶν τεσσάρων φροντιστῶν ἱ[σ]αγωγῆ(ς) ⁸ὑδάτων
καστέλλων καὶ κρηνῶν ⁹μητροπόλεως. ¹⁰λόγος
λημμάτων καὶ ἀναλωμάτ(ων) ¹¹τῶν ἀναλουμένων
εἰς τὴν τῶν ¹²ὑδάτων ἰσαγω[γὴ]ν τῶν ἀπὸ Παχὼν
¹³τοῦ διεληλυθότος ιϛ (ἔτους) Τραϊανο[ῦ] Καίσαρος
¹⁴τοῦ κυρίου ἕως Φαῶφι λ τοῦ ἐνεστῶτο(ς) ¹⁵ιζ
(ἔτους).

¹⁶Λημμάτων· - - - ³⁰χορηγίας ὕδατος βαλανείου
Σευηριανοῦ ἡμερησίω(ν) (ὀβολῶν) ιη· ³¹Παχὼν (δρ.)
οβ (ὀβ.) [ι]η, Παῦνι (δρ.) οβ (ὀβ.) ιη, Ἐπεὶφ (δρ.)
οβ (ὀβ.) ιη, ³²Μεσορὴ ἀπὸ α ἕως ιε διὰ τὸ ἀπὸ ιϛ
ἕως λ μὴ λελουκέναι, ³³ἀντὶ τῶν αἱρου{ρ[ο]υ}σῶν
(δρ.) λϛ (ὀβ.) θ, ὅλαι (δρ.) νβ, ³⁴ἐπαγομένων ἡμερῶν
ε (δρ.) ιβ (τριώβολον), ιζ (ἔτους) Θὼθ (δρ.) οβ
(ὀβ.) ιη, ³⁵Φαῶφι (δρ.) οβ (ὀβ.) ιη, (γίνονται) (δρ.)
υκδ (ὀβ.) ϙγ. ³⁶κρήνης Δρόμου ἡμερ[ησίων] (ὀβ.)
θ· ³⁷Παχὼν (δρ.) λϛ [(ὀβ.) θ, Παῦνι] (δρ.) λϛ [(ὀβ.)
θ, Ἐπεὶφ ἡμερῶν ³⁸κζ αἱ αἱροῦσαι [(δρ.)] λ[γ (ὀβ.)
δ], Μεσορὴ (δρ.) λϛ (ὀβ.) θ, καὶ ³⁹ὑπὲρ ἐπαγομένων

30. ἡμερήσιο(ι) Edd.: corr. E.-H.   32-33. Revised
reading.

ᵃ Arsinoe, the chief town of the Fayum.
ᵇ In Roman times the silver drachma contained nominally

406. CONCERNING THE WATER SUPPLY
OF A MUNICIPALITY

A.D. 113.

To Demetrius, ex-gymnasiarch, auditor, from Crispus also called Sarapion, Mysthes also called Ptolemaeus son of Ptolemaeus, Mysthes son of Didymus acting through his father, and Sotas son of Zoilus, all four overseers of the supply of water for the reservoirs and fountains of the metropolis.[a] Account of receipts and expenses of the water supply from Pachon of the past 16th year of Trajanus Caesar the lord to Phaophi 30 of the current 17th year.

Receipts : . . . For supplying water for the Severian baths at 18 obols per day : Pachon, 72 drachmae 18 obols [b] ; Pauni, 72 drachmae 18 obols, Epeiph, 72 drachmae 18 obols ; Mesore, from the 1st to the 15th, because from the 16th to the 30th there had been no bathing, instead of the normal 36 drachmae 9 obols, a sum of 52 drachmae ; for the 5 intercalary days 12 drachmae 3 obols ; 17th year, Thoth, 72 drachmae 18 obols ; Phaophi, 72 drachmae 18 obols; total 424 drachmae 93 obols. For the Dromos fountain at 9 obols per day : Pachon, 36 drachmae 9 obols ; Pauni 36 drachmae 9 obols ; Epeiph, for 27 days the corresponding 33 drachmae 4 obols ; Mesore, 36 drachmae 9 obols ; and for the 5 inter-

7 obols and the tetradrachm, which was actually the smallest silver coin, 28 obols. But in practice the exchange was subject to slight variations, and in the present case the tetra-drachm is reckoned as equal to 29 obols. At the rate of 18 obols per day the total for 29 days is 72 drachmae, and to facilitate calculation the amount due for the 30th day is added separately, 18 obols.

ε̄ ὀβ(ολ.) με, γ(ίνονται) ἐπὶ τὸ α(ὐτὸ) (δρ.) ρμα (ὀβ.)
οϛ. - - - ⁴⁴κρήνης Κλεοπατρίου ὁμοίως ἡμερησίων
(ὀβ.) θ· ⁴⁵Παχὼν (δρ.) λϛ (ὀβ.) θ, Παῦνι (δρ.) λϛ
(ὀβ.) θ, Ἐπεὶφ (δρ.) λϛ (ὀβ.) θ, ⁴⁶Μεσορὴ (δρ.) κ
καὶ αἱ πλείω βληθεῖσαι βαλανείου Σευηριανοῦ ⁴⁷ἐπὶ
τοῦ α(ὐτοῦ) μηνὸς (δρ.) ιδ (ὀβ.) ε, ⁴⁸ἐπαγομένων
ἡμερῶν δ (δρ.) ε, ⁴⁹ιζ (ἔτους) ἕως Θὼθ ἡμερῶν
κθ (δρ.) λϛ διὰ τὸ τὴν μίαν ⁵⁰ἡμέραν μὴ κεχορη-
γῆσθαι, Φαῶφι (δρ.) λϛ (ὀβ.) θ, (γίνονται) (δρ.)
σε (ὀβ.) λϛ. ⁵¹ζυτοπωλείου Σαραπείου ἡμερησίων
(ὀβ.) ιγ· ⁵²Παχὼν (δρ.) νβ (ὀβ.) ιγ, Παῦνι (δρ.)
νβ (ὀβ.) ιγ, Ἐπεὶφ (δρ.) νβ (ὀβ.) ιγ, Μεσορὴ ἀπὸ
⁵³(δρ.) νβ (ὀβ.) ιγ (δρ.) νβ (πεντώβολον) διὰ τὸ
τοὺς λοιπ(οὺς) ὀβολ(οὺς) ἢ ἐκκεκρουκέναι ⁵⁴ὑπὲρ
ἀργ(ίας) (?) [ἀ]ναφορᾶς ὕδατο{υ}ς ἑαυτῷ χορηγήσαν-
το(ς), ἐπαγομ(ένων) ⁵⁵ὑπὲρ ἡμερῶν ε̄ (δρ.) θ, ιζ
(ἔτους) Θὼθ (δρ.) νβ (ὀβ.) ιγ, Φαῶφι ⁵⁶ημπ( )
χ[. . .] (δρ.) μ̄δ̄ διὰ τὸ τὰς λοιπ(ὰς) μὴ κεχο-
ρηγῆ(σθαι), (γίνονται) (δρ.) τιγ (ὀβ.) ο. ⁵⁷ἀρχόντων
Ἰ[ου]δαίων προσευχῆς Θηβαίων μηνιαίω(ν) (δρ.)
ρκη· ⁵⁸Παχὼν (δρ.) ρκ[η], Παῦνι (δρ.) ρκη, Ἐπεὶφ
(δρ.) ρκη, Μεσορὴ (δρ.) ρκη, ⁵⁹ιζ (ἔτους) Θὼθ
(δρ.) ρκη, Φαῶφι (δρ.) ρκη, (γίνονται) (δρ.) ψ[ξη].
⁶⁰εὐχείου ὁμοίως Παχὼν (δρ.) ρκη, Παῦνι (δρ.)
ρκη, Ἐπεὶφ (δρ.) ρκη, Μεσο(ρὴ) (δρ.) [ρκη], ⁶¹ιζ
(ἔτους) Θὼθ (δρ.) ρκ[η], Φαῶφι (δρ.) ρκη, (γίνονται)
(δρ.) ψξη. ⁶²γίνονται λήμματος ἀπὸ Παχὼν ι

54. ἀργ(ίας)? E.-H.   56. ημπ( ) χ[. . .]: ἡμερῶν κδ is
the phrase required, and does not seem to be excluded by
the facsimile.   62. l. Παχὼν α.

ᵃ A quarter of the town called after the temple of a deified
Cleopatra.

calary days 45 obols ; total 141 drachmae 76 obols.
. . . For the Cleopatreum [a] fountain likewise at 9 obols
per day : Pachon, 36 drachmae 9 obols ; Pauni, 36
drachmae 9 obols ; Epeiph, 36 drachmae 9 obols ;
Mesore, 20 drachmae and the surplus 14 drachmae
5 obols paid for the Severian baths in the same
month [b] ; for 4 intercalary days 5 drachmae ; 17th
year, for only 29 days of Thoth, because on one day
no water was supplied, 36 drachmae ; Phaophi, 36
drachmae 9 obols ; total 205 drachmae 36 obols. For
the Serapeum beer-shop at 13 obols per day: Pachon,
52 drachmae 13 obols ; Pauni, 52 drachmae 13 obols ;
Epeiph, 52 drachmae 13 obols ; Mesore, 52 drachmae
5 obols out of 52 drachmae 13 obols owing to our
having struck out the remaining 8 obols on account of
a stoppage (?) in bringing water, the shop having
provided for itself; for 5 intercalary days, 9 drachmae ;
17th year, Thoth, 52 drachmae 13 obols ; Phaophi,
for 24 days (?), 44 drachmae, because no water
was supplied for the remaining days; total 313
drachmae 70 obols. From the rulers of the syna-
gogue of Theban Jews at 128 drachmae per month :
Pachon, 128 drachmae ; Pauni, 128 drachmae ;
Epeiph, 128 drachmae ; Mesore, 128 drachmae ;
17th year, Thoth, 128 drachmae ; Phaophi, 128
drachmae ; total 768 drachmae. For the place of
prayer [c] likewise : Pachon, 128 drachmae ; Pauni,
128 drachmae ; Epeiph, 128 drachmae ; Mesore,
128 drachmae ; 17th year, Thoth, 128 drachmae ;
Phaophi, 128 drachmae ; total 768 drachmae. Total

[b] See above. The 14 dr. 5 ob. are the difference between
the 36 dr. 9 ob. and the 52 dr. actually paid. Though
entered here a second time, they are not included in the total.

[c] That is, of the Jews.

ἕως Φαῶφι λ [63]Τραϊανοῦ Καίσαρος τοῦ κυρίου
ἀργ(υρίου) (τάλαντον) α (δρ.) ᾿ΕΤ (ὀβ.) ϛ.

[64]᾿Εξ ὧν ἀνηλώθη· [65]καστέλλου ῎Αλσους ἔχοντος
κηλώνεια ιϛ ἀνὰ ἀντλ(ητὰς) α (ἥμισυ) [66]ἀντλούντων
ἀπὸ πρώιας ἕως ὀψέ· [67]ιϛ (ἔτους) Τραϊανοῦ Καίσαρος τοῦ [κ]υρίου Π[α]χὼν ᾿Αφροδισίῳ [68]ἐργοδότῃ
ἀντλητῶν αὐτῷ ὀψώνιον τοῦ Παχὼν (δρ.) μ, [69]καὶ
ὥστε ἀντληταῖς κατὰ μέρος [ἀ]πὸ ᾱ ἕως τριακάδο(ς)
[70]ἀνδρῶν ψϟζ ἐν καστέλ(λῳ) καὶ προβολ(ῇ) διώρυ-
γ(ος) καὶ τῶν διὰ νυκτὸς ἐργασαμένων [71]ὁμοίως τϛ
τῶν [ἐ]πὶ τὸ α(ὐτὸ) ἀνδ(ρῶν) ᾿Αργ ὡς τῶν [72]λ̄
μισθοῦ (δρ.) μ (δρ.) ᾿Αυ[ο], καὶ ὀργανισταῖς ἐργα-
σαμέ(νοις) [73]ἐν κοχλ(ίαις) κατὰ μέρο(ς) ἀνδ(ρῶν) σ
ὡς τοῦ ἑνὸ(ς) (ὀβ.) ι ὀβ(ολ.) ᾿Β, γε(ίνονται) (δρ.)
σοϛ, καὶ [74]τιμῆς ἐλαίου κα[ύ]σεως λύχνων τοῖς διὰ
νυκτὸς ἐργα-[75]ζομένοις (δρ.) ιβ (δυόβολοι), καὶ
τιμῆς κάδ(ων) [ὀστ]ρακ(ίνων) (δρ.) α, (γίνονται) τοῦ
μηνὸ(ς) (δρ.) ᾿Α[ψϟθ (δυόβολοι)]. - - - [112]ὀψώνιον
βοηλατῶν καστέλλου ῎Αλσους ἔχοντος [113]μηχανὰς
β̄ βοηλάτας ϛ· [114]Παχὼν Πετεεῖ Πατύνεως βου-
κόλωι [115]ὀψώνιο(ν) Παχὼ[ν (δρ.)] λβ, καὶ βοηλάταις
ϛ [116]ὁμοίως ὑπὲρ Παχὼ(ν), γ̄ μὲν ἀνὰ (δρ.) ιϛ (δρ.)
μη, ἄλλοις β̄ [117]ἀνὰ (δρ.) ιδ (δρ.) κη, ἑτέρ[ῳ] ᾱ (δρ.)
κδ, (γίνονται) τοῦ μηνὸ(ς) (δρ.) ρλβ. - - -

75. ᾿Α[ωα Edd.

---

[a] Two posts with a cross-bar at the top on which is balanced
a long pole with a bucket at one end and a weight at the other.

of receipts from Pachon 1 to Phaophi 30 (of the 17th year) of Trajanus Caesar the lord 1 talent of silver 5900 drachmae 6 obols.

From this the following sums have been spent. For the reservoir of the Grove, having 16 *shadufs* [a] worked each by 1½ men [b] (per day) who draw up water from morning till evening : 16th year of Trajanus Caesar the lord, Pachon : to Aphrodisius, hirer of the water-drawers, as his own wage for Pachon, 40 drachmae, and to distribute to the water-drawers from the 1st to the 30th, comprising 797 men [c] at the reservoir and the machine (?) of the canal and 320 night-work-men likewise, making altogether 1103 men, at a wage of 40 drachmae for 30 men, 1470 drachmae, and to distribute to the labourers employed on the Archimedean screws, comprising 200 men, at the rate of 10 obols each, 2000 obols, equal to 276 drachmae, and as the price of oil burned in lamps for the night-workmen 12 drachmae 2 obols, and as the price of earthen-ware buckets 1 drachma, total for the month 1799 drachmae 2 obols. . . . Wage of the ox-drivers for the reservoir of the Grove, which employs 2 water-wheels and 6 drivers : Pachon, to Peteeus son of Patunis, herdsman, as wage for Pachon, 32 drachmae, and to 6 ox-drivers likewise for Pachon, 3 at 16 drachmae each, 48 drachmae, other 2 at 14 drachmae each, 28 drachmae, another 1, 24 drachmae, total for the month 132 drachmae. . . .

[b] That is, one full shift and one half shift.
[c] Not 797 different men, but 797 daily shifts.

407. MUNICIPAL ACCOUNT

P. Oxy. 2128.   Late 2nd or early 3rd cent. A.D.

¹Ἡρακλίδῃ Ἀπολλωνίου (τάλαντα ?) . (δραχμαὶ ?) . . ²ὑδροπαρόχοις (δραχμαὶ) Ὑτπγ (δυόβολοι). ³Πουπλίῳ Αἰλίῳ Διογένει καὶ Ἀτρῇ
Ἀκώριος ⁴ἐγλήμπτορσι θυρῶν Καπιτωλείου (δραχμαὶ) Ὑβφ. ⁵Δημητρίῳ καὶ Διογένει ἐπιμελητ(αῖς)
⁶κατασκευῆς πύλης (δραχμαὶ) Ὑβ. ⁷Καλλινίκῳ
Ἐπιμάχου καὶ τοῖς σὺν α(ὐτῷ) ⁸ἐγλήμπτορσι
οὐήλων (δραχμαὶ) Ὑγφ. ⁹διεγράφη εἰς τὴν δημοσίαν
τρά(πεζαν) ¹⁰ὠνῆς πελοχικ(οῦ) καὶ καθαρουργ(ίας)
(τάλαντον) α (δραχμαὶ) Ὑαχνα. ¹¹Ὑπάτῳ Παυλι-
νίου καὶ τοῖς σὺν α(ὐτῷ) ἐπιμελ(ηταῖς) ¹²Ἀντωνι-
νιανῶν θερμῶν (δραχμαὶ) Ὑβ. ¹³Διονυσίῳ τῷ κ(αὶ)
Πετρωνιανῷ ἐπὶ τῶν ¹⁴ν νυκτοφυλάκων (δραχμαὶ)
Ὑβ.

10. l. πελωχικ(οῦ).

408. ACCOUNT OF PAYMENTS TO OFFICIALS

P. Oxy. 1920.   Late 6th cent. A.D.

¹+ Γνῶσις τοῦ δοθ(έντος) ἀναλώμ(ατος) τοῖς
ἀνθρ(ώποις) τοῦ ὑπερφυεστ(άτου) πατρικίου Ἀθανασίου ἐλθ(οῦσιν) ἐνταῦθ(α) ἀπὸ Θηβαείδος ²τῶν ἀπὸ
Μεχεὶρ β ἰνδ(ικτίονος) ια ἕως ιγ, οὕτως· ³τοῖς
μα∠γ′ στρα(τιώταις) τῶν Σκυθῶν τῶν ἀπὸ Μεχεὶρ

ᵃ Probably the *dux et augustalis*, or military commander,
of the Thebaid, who was paying a visit to Oxyrhynchus with

542

407. MUNICIPAL ACCOUNT

Late 2nd or early·3rd cent. A.D.

To Heraclides son of Apollonius . . talents . . drachmae. To the providers of water 3383 drachmae 2 obols. To Publius Aelius Diogenes and Hatres son of Akoris, contractors for the doors of the Capitol, 2500 drachmae. To Demetrius and Diogenes, super-intendents of the construction of the gate, 2000 drachmae. To Callinicus son of Epimachus and his fellow contractors for hangings 3500 drachmae. Paid to the public bank on account of the milling and fine-bread contract 1 talent 1651 drachmae. To Hypatus son of Paulinius and his fellow superintendents of the warm baths of Antoninus 2000 drachmae. To Dionysius also called Petronianus in command of the 50 night-watchmen 2000 drachmae.

408. ACCOUNT OF PAYMENTS TO OFFICIALS

Late 6th cent. A.D.

Account of the rations given out to the retinue of the most magnificent patrician Athanasius[a] on arriving here from the Thebaid, for the days from Mecheir 2 to 13 of the 11th indiction, being as follows. To the 41$\frac{5}{6}$ soldiers [b] of the Scythian corps, for the 12 days

[a] a large number of attendants for whom rations had to be provided.

[b] The fraction means that one of the soldiers received only $\frac{5}{6}$ of the normal allowance.

543

β ἕως ιγ ἡμερ(ῶν) ιβ ἡμερουσί(ως) [4]ἄρ(των) λί(τραι)
ρξζ, κρ(έως) μα∠γ´, ἐλαί(ου) ξ(έσται) εδ´, οἴν(ου)
ξέστ(αι) πγβ´ ἐκ τοῦ ξέστ(ου) αὐτῶν εἰς [5]ξ(έστας)
ρξζγ´, τῶν ξ(εστῶν) η δι(πλοῦ) α δι(πλᾶ) κ∠δ´ η´,
γί(νονται) ὑπὲρ ἡμερ(ῶν) ιβ ἄρ(των) λί(τραι) ͵βδ,
κρ(έως) φβ, ἐλαί(ου) ξ(έσται) ξγ, οἴν(ου) δι(πλᾶ)
σν∠, ξύλ(ου) κεντηνάρ(ια) ιβ. [6]τοῖς νη συμμάχ(οις)
τῶν ἀπὸ Μεχεὶρ γ ἕως ιγ ἡμερ(ῶν) ια ἡμερουσί(ως)
[7]ἄρ(των) λί(τραι) ροδ, κρ(έως) κθ, ἐλαί(ου) ξ(έσται)
ε∠δ´ κ´, οἴν(ου) ξ(έσται) νη εἰς δι(πλᾶ) θβ´, γί(νονται) ὑπ(ὲρ) ἡμερ(ῶν) ια ἄρ(των) λί(τραι) ͵αϡιδ,
κρ(έως) τιθ, ἐλαί(ου) ξ(έσται) ξγ∠δ´ κ´, οἴν(ου)
δι(πλᾶ) ρϛγ´, ξύλ(ου) κεντ(ηνάρια) κβ. [8]τῷ καγ-
κελλαρ(ίῳ) καὶ κούρσορσ(ι) καὶ πραίκο{ρ}σ(ι) καὶ
ἄλλ(οις) ὀνόμ(ασι) κδ τῶν ἀπὸ [9]Μεχεὶρ γ ἕως ιγ
ἡμερ(ῶν) ια ἡμερουσί(ως) ἄρ(των) λί(τραι) ϛϛ,
κρ(έως) κδ, ἐλαί(ου) ξ(έσται) β∠, [10]οἴν(ου) ξ(έσται)
μη εἰς δι(πλᾶ) η, γί(νονται) ὑπὲρ ἡμερ(ῶν) ια
ἄρ(των) λί(τραι) ͵ανϛ, κρ(έως) σξδ, ἐλαί(ου) ξ(έσται) κζ∠, οἴν(ου) δι(πλᾶ) πη, ξύλ(ου) κεντ(ηνάρια)
ια. [11]τοῖς λ συμμάχ(οις) τῶν ῥιπαρ(ίων) τῶν ἀπὸ
Μεχεὶρ δ ἕως Μεχεὶρ ιγ ἡμερ(ῶν) ι [12]ἡμερουσί(ως)
ἄρ(των) λί(τραι) ϛ, κρ(έως) ιε, ἐλαί(ου) ξ(έσται) γ,
οἴν(ου) ξ(έσται) ιε εἰς δι(πλᾶ) β∠, γί(νονται) ὑπ(ὲρ)
ἡμερ(ῶν) ι ἄρ(των) λί(τραι) Ⳛ, κρ(έως) ρν, ἐλαί(ου)
ξ(έσται) λ, οἴν(ου) δι(πλᾶ) κε. [13]γί(νονται) τῶν ἀπὸ
μη(νὸς) Μεχεὶρ β ἰνδ(ικτίονος) ια ἕως ιγ καὶ αὐτ(ῆς)
ἄρ(των) λί(τραι) ͵εωοδ, κρ(έως) ͵ασλε, ἐλαί(ου)
ξ(έσται) ρπδ δ´κ´, οἴν(ου) δι(πλᾶ) υξθ∠γ´, ξύλ(ου)
κεντ(ηνάρια) με, [14]καὶ ἐν χλωρ(οῖς) χόρ(του) (ἄρουραι) ιβ. καὶ ὑπὲρ Μεχεὶρ ιδ ἄρ(των) λί(τραι) φκζ,
κρ(έως) ρθ∠γ´, ἐλαί(ου) ξ(έσται) ιϛ∠κ´, οἴν(ου)

from Mecheir 2 to 13, daily, 167 pounds of loaves, $41\frac{5}{6}$ pounds of meat, $5\frac{1}{4}$ sextarii of oil, $83\frac{2}{3}$ sextarii of wine equal to $167\frac{1}{3}$ of their sextarii or $20\frac{7}{8}$ double jars at the rate of 8 sextarii to 1 double jar, total for 12 days 2004 pounds of loaves, 502 of meat, 63 sextarii of oil, $250\frac{1}{2}$ double jars of wine, 12 hundredweight of wood. To the 58 messengers for the 11 days from Mecheir 3 to 13, daily, 174 pounds of loaves, 29 of meat, $5\frac{4}{5}$ sextarii of oil, 58 sextarii of wine equal to $9\frac{2}{3}$ double jars,[a] total for 11 days 1914 pounds of loaves, 319 of meat, $63\frac{4}{5}$ sextarii of oil, $106\frac{1}{3}$ double jars of wine, 22 hundredweight of wood. To the usher and runners and criers and others, 24 individuals, for the 11 days from Mecheir 3 to 13, daily, 96 pounds of loaves, 24 of meat, $2\frac{1}{2}$ sextarii of oil, 48 sextarii of wine equal to 8 double jars, total for 11 days 1056 pounds of loaves, 264 of meat, $27\frac{1}{2}$ sextarii of oil, 88 double jars of wine, 11 hundredweight of wood. To the 30 messengers of the *riparii* for the 10 days from Mecheir 4 to 13, daily, 90 pounds of loaves, 15 of meat, 3 sextarii of oil, 15 sextarii of wine equal to $2\frac{1}{2}$ double jars, total for 10 days 900 pounds of loaves, 150 of meat, 30 sextarii of oil, 25 double jars of wine. Total for the days from Mecheir 2 to 13 inclusive of the 11th indiction 5874 pounds of loaves, 1235 of meat, $184\frac{3}{10}$ sextarii of oil, $469\frac{5}{6}$ double jars of wine, 45 hundredweight of wood, and in green fodder 12 arurae of grass. And for Mecheir 14, 527 pounds of loaves, $109\frac{5}{6}$ of meat, $16\frac{11}{20}$ sextarii of oil, $41\frac{1}{24}$

---

[a] The double jar is reckoned here as equal to 6 sextarii, which is inconsistent with the preceding entry.

δι(πλᾶ) μα κδ', καὶ ξύλ(ου) κεντ(ηνάρια) δ, καὶ
χόρ(του) (ἄρουρα) α. ¹⁵καὶ ὑπὲρ Μεχεὶρ ιε ἄρ(των)
λί(τραι) φκζ, κρ(έως) ρθ∠γ', ἐλαί(ου) ξ(έσται)
ις∠κ', οἴν(ου) δι(πλᾶ) μα κδ', ξύλ(ου) κεντ(ηνάρια)
δ, καὶ χόρ(του) (ἄρουρα) α. γί(νονται) καὶ τούτων
ἄρ(των) λί(τραι) ,ανδ, κρ(έως) σιθβ', ἐλαί(ου) ξ(έσται)
λγι', δι(πλᾶ) πβ ιβ', ξύλ(ου) κεντ(ηνάρια) η, ¹⁶χόρ-
(του) (ἄρουραι) β. γί(νονται) ὁ(μοῦ) ἄρ(των) λί(τραι)
,ϛ𐅵κη, τῶν λι(τρῶν) π (ἀρτάβης) α (ἀρτάβαι) πϛ∠
χο(ίνικες) δ εἰς νο(μίσματα) ηβ', κρ(έως) ,αυνδβ',
τῶν λι(τρῶν) ρκ νο(μίσματος) α νο(μίσματα) ιβη',
ἐλαί(ου) ξ(έσται) σιζγ' ιβ', τῶν ξ(εστῶν) με νο(μίσματος) α νο(μίσματα) δ∠γ', ¹⁷οἴ(νου) δι(πλᾶ) φνα
[∠γ' ιβ'], τῶν δι(πλῶν) κε νο(μίσματος) α νο(μίσματα)
κβ ιβ', ξύλ(ου) κεντ(ηνάρια) νγ εἰς νό(μισμα) α∠,
χόρ(του) (ἄρουραι) ιδ εἰς νο(μίσματα) ιδ, (γίνεται)
νο(μίσματα) ξγϛ' κδ' ἕως Μεχεὶρ ιε ἰνδ(ικτιόνος) ια.
ὁμοί(ως) Μεχεὶρ ις ἄρ(των) λί(τραι) φκζ, ¹⁸κρ(έως)
ρθ∠γ', [ἐλαί(ου) ξ(έσται) ις]∠κ', [ο]ἴν(ου) δι(πλᾶ)
μα κδ', ξύλ(ου) κεντ(ηνάρια) [δ, καὶ] χόρ(του)
(ἄρουρα) α, Μεχεὶρ ιζ ἄρ(των) λί(τραι) σι, κρ(έως)
νθβ', οἴν(ου) ξ(έσται) οδ∠ εἰς δι(πλᾶ) ιβγ' ιβ',
ἄλλ(α) δι(πλᾶ) ϛδ', (γίνεται) δι(πλᾶ) ιηβ', ἐλαί(ου)
ξ(έσται) ζ, ξύλ(ου) κεντ(ηνάρια) β, χόρ(του) (ἀρούρης) γ'.

double jars of wine, 4 hundredweight of wood, and 1 arura of grass. And for Mecheir 15, 527 pounds of loaves, $109\frac{5}{6}$ of meat, $16\frac{11}{20}$ sextarii of oil, $41\frac{1}{24}$ double jars of wine, 4 hundredweight of wood, and 1 arura of grass. Total for these two days 1054 pounds of loaves, $219\frac{2}{3}$ of meat, $33\frac{1}{10}$ sextarii of oil, $82\frac{1}{12}$ double jars of wine, 8 hundredweight of wood, 2 arurae of grass. Combined total 6928 pounds of loaves, which at the rate of 80 pounds to 1 artaba amount to $86\frac{1}{2}$ artabae 4 choenices costing $8\frac{2}{3}$ solidi, $1454\frac{2}{3}$ pounds of meat, costing at the rate of 120 pounds for 1 solidus $12\frac{1}{8}$ solidi, $217\frac{5}{12}$ sextarii of oil, costing at 45 sextarii the solidus $4\frac{5}{8}$ solidi, $551\frac{11}{12}$ double jars of wine, costing at 25 double jars the solidus $22\frac{1}{12}$ solidi, 53 hundredweight of wood costing $1\frac{1}{2}$ solidi, 14 arurae of grass costing 14 solidi, total cost $63\frac{5}{24}$ solidi to Mecheir 15 of the 11th indiction. Similarly for Mecheir 16, 527 pounds of loaves, $109\frac{5}{6}$ of meat, $16\frac{11}{20}$ sextarii of oil, $41\frac{1}{24}$ double jars of wine, 4 hundredweight of wood, and 1 arura of grass. For Mecheir 17, 210 pounds of loaves, $59\frac{2}{3}$ of meat, $74\frac{1}{2}$ sextarii of wine equal to $12\frac{5}{12}$ double jars, other $6\frac{1}{4}$ double jars, making $18\frac{2}{3}$, 7 sextarii of oil, 2 hundredweight of wood, $\frac{1}{3}$ of an arura of grass.

XIV. CORRESPONDENCE

409. ABOUT THE GOLD COINAGE OF PTOLEMY PHILADELPHUS

P. Cairo Zen. 59021.   258 b.c.

¹ʼΑπολ[λων]ίωι χαίρειν Δημήτριος. ²καλῶς ἔχει
εἰ αὐτός τε ἔρρωσαι καὶ ³τἆλλα σοι κατὰ γνώμην
ἐστίν. ⁴καὶ ἐγὼ δὲ καθάπερ μοι ἔγραψας ⁵προσ-
έχειν ποιῶ αὐτὸ καὶ δέδεγμαι ⁶ἐκ χρ(υσίου) M̅ ʼΖ
καὶ κατεργασάμενος ⁷ἀπέδωκα. ἐδεξάμεθα δ' ἂν
καὶ ⁸πολλαπλάσιον, ἀλλὰ καθά σοι καὶ ⁹πρότερον
ἔγραψα ὅτι οἵ τε ξένοι ¹⁰οἱ εἰσπλέοντες καὶ οἱ
ἔμποροι καὶ οἱ ¹¹ἐγδοχεῖς καὶ ἄλλοι φέρουσιν τό
τε ¹²ἐπιχώριο[ν] νόμισμα τὸ ἀκριβὲς καὶ ¹³τὰ τρί-
χρυσα ἵνα καινὸν αὐτοῖς γέ-¹⁴νηται κατὰ τὸ πρόσταγμα ὃ κε-¹⁵λεύει ἡμᾶς λαμβάνειν καὶ κ[ατ-
ερ-]¹⁶γάζεσ[θα]ι, Φιλαρέτου (?) δέ με οὐκ ἐ-¹⁷ῶντος
δέχεσθαι, οὐκ ἔχον[τ]ες ἐ[πὶ] ¹⁸τίνα τὴν ἀναφορὰν

---

16. Φιλαρέτου δέ Th. Reinach (satisfactory palaeographi-
cally) : φιάλας τοῦδε Ed.

ᵃ The dioecetes.
ᵇ Probably the head of the Alexandrian mint.
ᶜ That is, money struck in the foreign possessions of the
king.

XIV. CORRESPONDENCE

409. ABOUT THE GOLD COINAGE OF PTOLEMY PHILADELPHUS

258 B.C.

To Apollonius [a] greeting from Demetrius.[b] If you are in good health and your affairs are satisfactory, it is well. As for me, I am attending to the work as you wrote to me to do, and I have received in gold 57000 pieces, which I minted and returned. We might have received many times as much, but as I wrote to you once before, the strangers who come here by sea and the merchants and middlemen and others bring both their local money [c] of unalloyed metal and the gold pentadrachms,[d] to be made into new money for them in accordance with the decree which orders us to receive and remint, but as Philaretus [e] does not allow me to accept, not knowing to whom we

[d] Gold coins of the nominal value of 3 gold staters or 60 silver drachmae, but actually worth $66\frac{2}{3}$. They were now being superseded by a new issue of gold tetradrachms and octadrachms.

[e] Owing partly to the condition of the papyrus, the meaning of this passage is obscure. It is difficult to say what sort of gold precisely was being refused by the mint. Perhaps foreign money only, including pentadrachms struck abroad.

ποιησώ[με]θα ¹⁹περὶ τούτων, ἀναγκαζ[όμεθ]α τ[ὰ
²⁰.]. . τα μὴ δέχεσθαι, οἱ δὲ ἄν-²¹θ[ρω]ποι ἀγανακ-
τοῦσιν οὔ[τ]ε τ[ῶν] ²²τραπεζῶν οὔτε εἰς τὰ τ[.].[.-]
²³τα ἡμῶν δεχομ[ένω]ν οὔτε δυνά-²⁴μενοι εἰς τὴν
χώραν ἀποστέλλειν ²⁵ἐπὶ τὰ φορτία, ἀλλὰ ἀργὸν
φάσκουσιν ²⁶ἔχειν τὸ χρυσίον καὶ βλάπτεσθαι
οὐ-²⁷κ ὀλίγα ἔξοθεν μεταπεπεμμένοι ²⁸καὶ οὐδ'
ἄλλοις ἔχοντες ἐλάσσονος τιμῆς διαθέσθαι εὐχερῶς.
²⁹καὶ οἱ κατὰ πόλιν δὲ πάντες τῶι ἀπο-³⁰τετριμ-
μένωι χρυσίωι δυσχερῶς χρῶνται. ³¹οὐδεὶς γὰρ
τούτων ἔχει οὗ τὴν ἀναφο-³²ρὰν ποιησάμενος καὶ
προσθείς τι κο-³³μιεῖται ἢ καλὸν χρυσίον ἢ ἀργύριον
³⁴ἀντ' αὐτοῦ. νῦν μὲν γὰρ τούτων τοι-³⁵ούτων
ὄντων ὁρῶ καὶ τὰς τοῦ βασι-³⁶λέως προσόδους
βλαπτομένας οὐ -³⁷κ ὀλίγα. γέγραφα οὖν σοι
ταῦτα ἵ-³⁸να εἰδῆις καὶ ἐάν σοι φαίνηται τῶι ³⁹βασι-
λεῖ γράψηις περὶ τούτων καὶ ἐμοὶ ⁴⁰ἐπὶ τίνα τὴν
ἀναφορὰν περὶ τούτων ⁴¹ποιῶμαι. συμφέρειν γὰρ
ὑπολαμβάνω ⁴²ἐὰ[ν] καὶ ἐκ τῆς ἔξοθεν χώρας
χρυσίον ⁴³ὅ τι πλεῖστον εἰσάγηται καὶ τὸ νό-⁴⁴μισμα
τ[ὸ] τ[ο]ῦ [β]ασιλέως καλὸν καὶ ⁴⁵καινὸν ἦι διὰ
παντός, ἀνηλώματ[ος] ⁴⁶μηθενὸς γινομένου αὐτῶι.
περὶ μὲν ⁴⁷γάρ τινων ὡς ἡμῖν χρῶνται οὐ καλῶς
⁴⁸εἶχεν γράφειν, ἀλλ' ὡς ἂν παραγένηι ἀ-⁴⁹κούσει[ς
. . . .] γρά-⁵⁰ψον μοι
περὶ τούτων ἵνα οὕτω ποιῶ. ⁵¹ἔρρωσο. ⁵²(ἔτους)
κη Γορπιαίου ιε.

Verso: Ἀπολλωνίωι.   (2nd hand, on left)
Δημητρίου.

can appeal on this subject we are compelled not to accept . . . ; and the men grumble because their gold is not accepted either by the banks or by us for . . ., nor are they able to send it into the country to buy goods, but their gold, they say, is lying idle and they are suffering no little loss, having sent for it from abroad and being unable to dispose of it easily to other persons even at a reduced price. Again, all the residents in the city find it difficult to make use of their worn gold. For none of them knows to what authority he can refer and on paying something extra receive in exchange either good gold or silver. Now things being as they are at present, I see that the revenues of the king are also suffering no little damage. I have therefore written these remarks to you in order that you may be informed and, if you think fit, write to the king about the matter and tell me to whom I am to refer on this subject. For I take it to be an advantage if as much gold as possible be imported from abroad and the king's coinage be always good and new without any expense falling on him. Now as regards the way in which certain persons are treating me it is as well not to write, but as soon as you arrive you will hear . . . And write to me about these matters that I may act accordingly. Goodbye. (Addressed) To Apollonius. (Docketed) From Demetrius.

19-20. τ[ὰ .] . . τα E.-H. : τ[ε τ]αύτας Ed. : τ[ε πάν]τας Reinach.   22. τ[ά]λ[αν]τα Ed. : τ[έ]λ[η αὐ]τά Reinach. 27. l. ἔξωθεν, so too in l. 42.   38. η before τωι erased. 39. και above an erased letter.

410. FROM AN OFFICIAL IN HALICARNASSUS

P. Cairo Zen. 59036.   257 b.c.

¹ʾΑπολλόδοτος Χαρμίδει χαίρειν. ὑπογέγραφά
σοι τῶν πρὸς Ξάνθιππον ²ἐπιστολῶν τὰ ἀντίγραφα.
ἐντυχὼν [ο]ὖν αὐτῶι καὶ περὶ τῶν ʾΒυξε (δραχμῶν)
εἴδησον πῶς ³βούλεται οἰκ[ο]νομῆσαι καί, ἐὰν θέληι
σοι διαγράψαι, λαβὼν παρ᾽ αὐτοῦ διάγραψον
Μηδείωι ⁴ὃ ἐδεδώκει Στράτων ὁ ἐν ʾΑλικαρνασσῶι
γαζοφύλαξ ἀπὸ τῶν ἰατρικῶν ʾΑντιπάτ[ρωι] ⁵τῶι
π[αρὰ] Ξανθίππ[ο]υ εἰς τὴν να[ῦ]ν ἣν τριηραρχεῖ
Ξάνθιππος (δραχμὰς) ʾΒ, τὰς δὲ υξε (δυοβόλους)
[(δίχαλκον)] ⁶διάπεμψον πρὸς ἡμᾶς δούς τινι ἀκίνδυνον, καὶ περὶ τῶν ʾΓ (δραχμῶν) ἐπιμελήθητι
ὅπως ⁷διαγράψηι ʾΑπολλωνίωι καθότι ἐπεστάλ-
καμεν αὐτῶι. ⁸ἔρρωσο. (ἔτους) κη ʾΑπελλαίου
κζ.

⁹ʾΑπολλόδοτος Ξανθίππωι χαίρειν. εἰ τῶι τε
σώματι ἔρρωσαι καὶ τἄλλα σοι κατὰ γνώμη[ν]
¹⁰ἐστίν, εἴη ἂν ὡς ἡμεῖς θέλομεν· ἐρρώμεθα δὲ καὶ
αὐτοί. ἐγράψαμέν σοι πρότερον διότι δεδώ-¹¹καμεν
διὰ Περιγένους εἰς τὴν ναῦν ἣν τριηραρχεῖς ʾΑντι-
πάτρωι τῶι ἐπιπλέοντι ¹²ἐπὶ τῆς νέως (δραχμὰς)
ʾΒ, ὅπως οὖν τοῦτό τε καὶ τὸ δοθὲν ʾΕκατωνύμωι
εἰς τὴν (ἐννήρη) ¹³(δραχμὰς) υξε (δυοβόλους) (δίχαλκον), ἐάν τε φαίνηταί σοι, διαγράψηις Μηδείωι
εἰς τὰ ἰατρικά, ἐάν τε βούλη[ι], ¹⁴γράψηις ʾΙκεσίωι

ᵃ Probably an official in the service of the king.
ᵇ A treasurer in the king's service.
ᶜ The person who paid for the fitting out of the ship.

410. FROM AN OFFICIAL IN HALICARNASSUS

257 B.C.

Apollodotus [a] to Charmides greeting. I have written below for you copies of my letters to Xanthippus. Interview him therefore, and with regard to the 2465 drachmae find out how he wishes to settle, and if he desires to pay the money to you, take it from him and pay to Medeius the sum of 2000 drachmae, which Straton the keeper of the chest [b] at Halicarnassus had given from the proceeds of the medical tax to Antipater the agent of Xanthippus for the ship of which Xanthippus is trierarch,[c] and send over to me the 465 drachmae 2 obols 2 chalci, giving them to someone to carry guaranteed against risk, and with regard to the 3000 drachmae see to it that he pays them to Apollonius [d] as I have sent word to him. Goodbye. Year 28, Apellaeus 27.

Apollodotus to Xanthippus greeting. If you are well in body and other things are satisfactory, it would be as I desire. I myself am well. I wrote to you before that I have given, through Perigenes, for the ship of which you are trierarch 2000 dr. to Antipater who is sailing in charge of the ship, requesting you therefore either, if it so please you, to pay this sum, together with the 465 dr. 2 ob. 2 ch. given to Hecatonymus for the nine-oar,[e] to Medeius to the account of the medical tax or, if you choose, to write

According to Wilcken's view Xanthippus was a rich citizen of Halicarnassus, which was nominally an independent Greek city but was practically in subjection to Egypt.

[d] The dioecetes in Alexandria.

[e] The ship mentioned above, a large war-galley.

553

διορθώσασθαι ἡμῖν ἀπὸ τῶν ἐνηροσίων, οὐθὲν δὲ
σοῦ ἐπεσταλκότ[ος] ¹⁵βέλτιον ὑπελάβομεν εἶναι
πάλιν γράψαι σοι περὶ τούτων. καλῶς ἂν οὖν
ποιήσαις ¹⁶ἐπιστείλας ἡμῖν ὡς βούλει γενέσθαι,
ἵνα καὶ ἡμεῖς οὕτω καταχωρίσωμεν. ἐὰν δὲ
¹⁷φαίνηταί σοι Χαρμίδει τῶι παρ' ἡμῶν τῶι τὴν
ἐπιστολήν σοι ἀποδεδωκότι ¹⁸διαγράψαι, διάγραψον.
¹⁹ἔρρωσο.

²⁰Ἀπολλόδοτος Ξανθίππωι χαίρειν. χωρὶς τῶν
Ἀπολλοδο Β (δραχμῶν) ὧν γεγράφαμέν σοι ἐν τῆι ἑτέ[ρ]αι
²¹ἐπιστολῆι δεδώκαμεν ἄλλας Ἀντιπάτρωι τῶι
παρὰ σοῦ τριηραρχοῦντι τὴν (ἐννήρη) (δραχμὰς)
Γ ²²ἃς δεῖ σε διορθώσασθαι Ἀπολλωνίωι τῶι
διοικητῆι. καλῶς ἂν οὖν ποιήσαις συντάξ[α]ς
²³διαγράψαι αὐτῶι καθότι ὑπογεγράφαμέν σοι.
²⁴ἔρρωσο.

²⁵Ξάνθιππος Ἀπολλωνίωι. ὃ διέγραψεν Ἀπολ-
λόδοτος ἐν Ἁλικαρνασσῶι διὰ τῆς Σωπόλιος
²⁶Ἀντιπάτρωι τῶι ἐπὶ τῆς Ξανθίππου (ἐννήρους),
τὸ πεπτωκὸς (ἔτους) κζ Περιτίου ῆ παρὰ ταμιῶν
²⁷Ἁλικαρνασσέων τῶν ἐπὶ Δημητρίου, ὁ στέφανος
τῶι βασιλεῖ ὃν ἐξεδέξατο Ἀπολλώνιος ²⁸Ἐπικύδει,
ὃ δεήσει Ξάνθιππον διαγράψαι Ἀπολλωνίωι ἐν
Ἀλεξανδρείαι ἀκίνδυνον, (δραχμαὶ) Γ.

Verso : ²⁹Χαρμίδει. (To right) ἀν(τίγραφα) ἐπι-
(στολῶν) τῶν πρὸς ³⁰Ξ[άνθι]ππον.

16. βουλει above an erased δει.   27. Or ὁ στέφανος (Naber).

to Hicesius to refund it to me out of the ship's equipment account (?); but as you have sent no word, I thought it better to write to you again about this affair. You will oblige me therefore by sending word how you wish to make the payment, in order that we may enter it accordingly. If you like to pay the money to Charmides my agent who is delivering this letter to you, do so. Goodbye.

Apollodotus to Xanthippus greeting. Besides the 2000 dr. of which I have written to you in the other letter, I have given to Antipater, who is acting for you as trierarch of the nine-oar, a further 3000 dr., which you have to make good to Apollonius the dioecetes. You will oblige me then by giving an order to pay him in accordance with the following note. Goodbye.

(Owed by) Xanthippus to Apollonius : the sum of 3000 dr. which Apollodotus paid in Halicarnassus through the bank of Sopolis to Antipater who is in charge of the nine-oar of Xanthippus, being the sum paid in on Peritius 8 of year 27 by the treasurers [a] of Halicarnassus in the magistracy of Demetrius and forming the crown [b] for the king, for which Apollonius made himself responsible to Epicydes, which sum Xanthippus shall have to pay to Apollonius in Alexandria guaranteed against risk.

(Addressed) To Charmides. (Docketed) Copies of the letters to Xanthippus.

---

[a] The city treasurers.
[b] The name of a special tribute.

411. FROM THE PRIESTS OF APHRODITE
TO THE DIOECETES

P.S.I. 328.   257 B.C.

¹Οἱ ἱερεῖς τῆς Ἀφροδίτης Ἀπολλωνίωι [τῶι
διοικητ]ῆι χαίρειν. καθάπερ καὶ ὁ βασιλεὺς ²γέγρα-
φέν σοι δοῦναι εἰς τὴν ταφ[ὴν τῆς Ἔσιος] ζμύρνης
τάλαντα ἑκατόν, ³καλῶς ἂν ποιήσαις συντάξας
[δοθῆναι. οὐ γὰ]ρ ἀγνοεῖς ὅτι οὐκ ἀνάγεται ἡ
Ἔσεις ⁴εἰς τὸν νομὸν ἐὰμ μὴ ἕτοιμα ἔ[χωμεν τὰ
δέο]ντα ὅσα ποτὲ χρήαν ἔχουσιν ⁵εἰς τὴν ταφήν,
διὰ τὸ αὐθημερὸν [. . . . .]. γίνωσκε
δὲ εἶναι τὴν Ἔσιν Εἶσιν· ⁶αὕτη δέ σοι δοίη ἐπ-
αφροδισίαν πρ[ὸς τὸν βασι]λέα. ἔρρωσο. (ἔτους)
κη Ἀθὺρ ιε.

1-3. Suppl. M. Norsa.   4. Suppl. E.-H.   l. χρείαν.
5. [ἐνταφιάζειν] ?

412. CORRESPONDENCE ABOUT MILITARY
SETTLERS

P. Freib. 7.   251 B.C.

¹Ἀντίπατρος Πυθοκλεῖ χαίρειν. ὑπογέγραφά
σοι τῆς παρὰ Φανίου γραφείσης μοι ἐπιστολῆς τ[ὸ]
ἀντίγραφον. ὡς ἂν οὖν λάβηις τὴν ἐπιστολήν,
²ἐπελθὼν γεωμέτρησον πάντας τοὺς ἐν τῆι σῆι
ἐπιστατείαι κλήρου[ς], καθότι Φανίας γέγραφεν,

ᵃ The secretary of the cavalrymen.

411. FROM THE PRIESTS OF APHRODITE
TO THE DIOECETES

257 B.C.

The priests of Aphrodite [a] to Apollonius the dioecetes greeting. In accordance with what the king has written to you, to give 100 talents of myrrh for the burial of the Hesis,[b] please order this to be done. For you know that the Hesis is not brought up to the nome [c] unless we have in readiness everything that they require for the burial, because [the embalming is done?] on the day of her death. Know that the Hesis is Isis,[d] and may she give you favour in the eyes of the king. Goodbye. Year 28, Hathur 15.

[a] The Egyptian Hathor at Aphroditopolis, the modern Atfih.
[b] The name of the sacred cow, worshipped as an incarnation of Hathor.
[c] The meaning seems to be that the new Hesis was not installed until everything was ready for her eventual burial.
[d] An assimilation of Hathor and Isis.

412. CORRESPONDENCE ABOUT MILITARY
SETTLERS

251 B.C.

Antipater to Pythocles greeting. I append for you a copy of the letter written to me by Phanias.[a] As soon therefore as you receive my letter, inspect and survey all the holdings under your superintendence, as Phanias has ordered, and after making a list

557

καὶ ἀναγραψάμενος κατὰ γένος ὡς ἐνδέ-[3]χεται
ἀκριβέστατα ἀπόστειλον ἡμῖν ὅπως ἐπὶ Φανίαν
ἀνενέγκωμεν τὴν γεωμετρίαν. οὕτως δὲ ἀκριβολογήθητι πρὸς τὸ πρᾶγμα [4]ὡς χειρογραφή-
σων τὸν βασιλικὸν ὅρκον. ἔρρωσο. (ἔτους) λδ
Χοίαχ ϛ.
   [5][Φα]νίας Ἀντιπάτρωι χαίρειν. πρότερον μέν
σοι ὑποθεὶς τῆς παρὰ Διοτίμου ἐπιστολῆς τὸ ἀντίγραφον ἔγραψα ἐπιμεληθῆναι ἱππέ[ων] [6]ὅσοις
καταμεμέτρηται γῆ δυναμένη σπείρεσθαι εἰς τ[ὸ]
ε̄ καὶ λ (ἔτος) [ἵνα] πᾶσα σπαρῆι κ[α]ὶ δυνηθῶσιν
οἱ ἐν τῆι ἐπιστατείαι ν[εανίσκοι] [7]ἀπὸ τῶν γενομένων καρπῶν χορηγηθέντες καταβαίνειν πρὸς τὸν
βασιλέα ἔφιπποι καὶ τοῖς ἄλλοις ἀναγκαίοις κατ-
εσκευασμένοι. ἐπεὶ δὲ συ[ν]ί[στα-][8]ται ὁ σπόρος
παρ' ὑμῖν, παραλαβών τινα ἔμπειρον γεωμέτρην
ἤδη ἔπελθε πάντας τοὺς ἐν τῆι ἐπιστατείαι κλήρους
καὶ κατ[. . . . . . .] [9]γεωμετρήσας ἀνάγραψον κατὰ
γένος ὡς ἐνδέχεται ἀκριβέστατα τὴν ἐσπαρμένην
ἐν ἑκάστωι κλήρωι ἕως ἂν πάντας ἐπέλθηις.
[10]οὕτως δὲ ἀκριβολογήθητι πρὸς τὸ πρᾶγμα ὡς
μετὰ χειρογραφίας ἀνοίσων ἐπ' ἐμὲ τ[ὴ]ν γεωμετρίαν. διατήρησον ὅπως ἡμῖν ἐπιδῶις. [11]ἔστι
γὰρ ἀναγκαῖον ἕκαστον τῶν νεανίσκων γινώσκεσθαι
πῶς τι ἀπαλλάσσει καὶ ὑμῖν προσῆκον τοῖς ἡγεμονίας αὐτοὺς [12]ἀξιοῦσιν τὰς τοιαύτας χρείας παρ-
έχεσθαι ἕως ἂν καταστῆι τ[ὰ] περὶ τὴν κληρουχίαν,
ἵνα συμπεπονηκότες δικαίως προεδρί-[13]ας τυγ-
χάνητε. ἔρρωσο. (ἔτους) λδ Δίου κβ Ἀθὺρ κθ.

4. Χοίαχ Wilcken : Χοίακ Ed.   6. [ἵνα] E.-H. : [ὡς]
Wilcken. ν[εανίσκοι] W.   7. συ[ν]ί[στα-] W.

as exact as possible according to crops send me the survey to submit to Phanias. Do the work scrupulously in the manner of one prepared to sign the royal oath. Goodbye. Year 34, Choiach 6.

Phanias to Antipater greeting. I wrote to you before, appending a copy of the letter of Diotimus,[a] to look after all the cavalrymen who have been allotted land capable of being sown for the 35th year and see that it is all sown and that the cadets under your superintendence are enabled to provide for themselves out of the produce and to go down to the king [b] mounted and furnished with everything necessary. As sowing has begun in your district, take at once some experienced surveyor and inspect all the holdings under your superintendence and after surveying them make a list according to crops, as exact as possible, of the land sown in each holding, continuing until you have inspected all. Do the work scrupulously in the manner of one prepared to submit the survey to me with a sworn declaration. Take care that you present it to us. For it is essential to know how each of the cadets is acquitting himself and it is proper for you who aspire to a command to render such services until the affairs of the cleruchy are settled, in order that having taken part in the work you may justly obtain promotion. Goodbye. Year 34, Dius 22, Hathur 29.

[a] The sub-dioecetes (see No. 265).
[b] To be reviewed on the occasion of the festival called .τὰ Πτολεμαίεια (cf. No. 267, note e).

413. OFFICIAL CORRESPONDENCE

P. Petr. ii. 12 (1).   241 B.C.

¹Ἀγήνωρ Θεοδώρωι χαίρειν. τῆς παρὰ Ἀφθο-
ν[ήτο]υ γραφείσης μοι ἐπιστολῆς, ὑφ' ἣν καὶ
²[τὸ παρὰ Ἀνδρονίκου Ἀφθον]ήτωι ὑπόμν[ημα
ὑπο]γέγραπται, ἀπέσταλκά σοι τὸ ἀντίγραφον.
‑ ‑ ‑ ‑ ⁶‑ ‑ ‑ τῶν βωμῶν πρὸς τὸ μὴ ἐπισταθμεύεσθαι ⁷[. . . .] γράψον ἡμῖν. ἔρρωσο. (ἔτους)
ϛ Ἀρτεμισίου κβ.

⁸Ἀφθόνητος. τοῦ προσενεγχθέντος ὑπομνήματος
παρὰ Ἀνδρονίκου ἀπέσταλκά σοι τὸ ἀντίγραφο[ν].
⁹ἐπισκεψάμενος οὖν, εἰ ἔστιν ταῦτα οὕτως ἔχοντα,
συντέλεσον κατὰ ταῦτα. (ἔτους) ϛ Ἀρτεμισίου
κ[.].

¹⁰Ὑπόμνημα Ἀφθονήτωι στρατηγῶι παρὰ Ἀνδρονίκου. εὑρίσκομεν ἐν Κροκοδίλων πόλει τ[ινῶν]
¹¹τῶν οἰκιῶν τῶν πρότερον ἐπεσταθμευμένων καθ-
ειρηκότας τὰς στέγας ὑπὸ τῶν κυρίων, ¹²ὡσαύτως
δὲ καὶ ἐνωικοδομηκότας τὰς θύρας τῶν οἰκιῶν
βωμοὺς προσωικοδομήκασιν· τοῦτο δ[ὲ] ¹³πεποιή-
κασιν πρὸς τὸ μὴ ἐπισταθμεύεσθαι. εἰ οὖν σοι
δοκεῖ, ἐπεὶ στενοχωροῦμεν σταθμοῖς, ¹⁴γράψον
Ἀγήνορι ἐπαναγκάζειν τοὺς κυρίους τῶν οἰκιῶν
μεταθεῖναι τοὺς βωμοὺς ἐπὶ ¹⁵τοὺς εὐκαιροτάτους
τόπους καὶ ἐπιφανεστάτους ἐπὶ τῶν δωμάτων καὶ
ἀνοικοδομῆσαι ¹⁶βελτίους τῶν προυπαρχόντων βω-

---

10. τ[ινῶν] E.-H. : τ[ινάς] Edd.   11. l. καθειρημένας.
12. l. ἐνωικοδομηκότες.

ᵃ A strategus at Crocodilopolis.
ᵇ The chief engineer of the district.

413. OFFICIAL CORRESPONDENCE

241 B.C.

Agenor [a] to Theodorus [b] greeting. I have sent you a copy of the letter written to me by Aphthonetus,[c] beneath which the memorandum from Andronicus to Aphthonetus is also appended. . . . the altars, in order that they may not be used for billeting . . . reply to me. Goodbye. Year 6, Artemisius 22.

Aphthonetus. I have sent you a copy of the memorandum submitted to me by Andronicus. Make an inquiry therefore, and if his statements are correct, do as requested. Year 6, Artemisius 2[.].

Memorandum to Aphthonetus, strategus, from Andronicus. We find that several of the houses in Crocodilopolis which had formerly been used for billeting have had their roofs demolished by the owners, who have likewise blocked up the doors of their houses and built altars against them [d] ; and this they have done to prevent them being used for billeting. If therefore you approve, seeing that we are short of quarters, write to Agenor to compel the owners of the houses to transfer the altars to the most convenient and most conspicuous places on the house-tops and to rebuild them better than they were before,[e]

[c] Another strategus, the superior of Agenor.
[d] In order that the authorities might be deterred by religious scruples from opening a passage through the door-way.
[e] The object of this measure was not only to have the obstructive altars removed from the doors, but to ensure that the upper stories were roofed and that more rooms were thus available for accommodation.

μῶν, ὅπως ἂν ἔχωμεν ἀποδιδόναι εἰς τοὺς νῦν
παρα-¹⁷γινομένους ἐπιστάτας τῶν ἔργων.

Verso : ¹⁸[Θεοδώ]ρωι.   (To left in small hand)
(ἔτους) ϛ Χοίαχ θ. ἐκομισάμην ¹⁹παρ᾽ Ἀ[γ]ή-
[νορος.

17. Traces of letters towards end of line, perhaps a date.
18-19. From a revision by Skeat. ἐκομίσαμεν Ed., but -άμην
quite possible.

414. PREPARATIONS FOR THE VISIT OF
A DIOECETES

P. Grenf. ii. 14 (b).   224 B.C. (?)

¹Ἀ[μ]εννε[ὺς] Ἀσκληπιάδει χαίρειν. [κα]θότι
σ[ὺ ἔ]γραψας, ἑτοιμάκαμεν ²ἐπὶ τὴν παρουσίαν τὴν
Χρυσίππου [τοῦ ἀρχισωματο]φύλακος καὶ διοικητοῦ
³λευκομετώπους δέκα, χῆνας ἡμέρους π[έν]τε,
ὄρνιθας πεντήκοντα· ⁴[ἄγ]ρια χῆνες πεντήκοντα,
ὄρνιθες διακόσια[ι], περ[ι]στριδεῖς ἑκατόν· συν-
κεχρή-⁵με[θ]α δὲ ὄνους βαδιστὰς πέντε καὶ τούτων
τὰς .[. . . .]ς, ἑτοιμάκαμεν δὲ ⁶καὶ τοὺς τεσσαράκοντα ὄνους [τοὺς σ]κ[ε]υοφόρους· γινόμ[εθα] δὲ
πρὸς τῆι ὁδοποίαι. ⁷ἔρρω[σο. (ἔτους)] κβ Χοίαχ δ.

Verso : ⁸Ἀσκληπιάδει. (To left) (ἔτους) κβ Χοίαχ
ζ. Ἀμεννεὺς ⁹ξενίων τῶν ἡτοιμασμένων.

4. l. περιστεριδεῖς.

in order that we may have accommodation to give to the overseers of the works who are now arriving. (Addressed) To Theodorus. (Docketed) Year 6, Choiach 9. Received by me from Agenor.

414. PREPARATIONS FOR THE VISIT OF A DIOECETES

224 B.C. (?)

Amenneus to Asclepiades [a] greeting. In accordance with what you wrote we have got ready for the visit [b] of Chrysippus the chief of the bodyguard and dioecetes ten whiteheads,[c] five domestic geese, fifty fowls ; of wild birds there are fifty geese, two hundred fowls, and a hundred pigeons ; we have borrowed five riding donkeys with their . . . and have got ready the forty baggage donkeys ; and we have begun to make the road. Goodbye. Year 22, Choiach 4. (Addressed) To Asclepiades. (Docketed) Year 22, Choiach 7. Amenneus about the gifts prepared.

[a] Probably an oeconomus in the Fayum.
[b] When the king or some other eminent personage travelled through the country, supplies for himself and his retinue were requisitioned from the inhabitants of every district through which he passed.
[c] Some kind of bird.

415. CONCERNING THE REGISTRATION
OF EGYPTIAN CONTRACTS

P. Par. 65.   146 b.c.

¹Πανίσκος [Π]τολεμαίωι χαίρειν. ²ἐκομισά-
[μεθ]α τὴν παρὰ σοῦ ἐπιστολήν, δι' ἧς ³ἐδήλους
[δ]ιασαφῆσαί [σο]ι τὴν γινομένην οἰκονομίαν ⁴ὑπὲρ
τῶ[ν] ἐν τῶι Περὶ Θήβας τιθεμένων ⁵Αἰγυπτί[ω]ν
συναλ<λ>αγμάτων καὶ εἰ, καθάπερ ⁶ἐπέστα[λ]το
ὑπ' 'Αρίστωνος, διὰ τῶν 'κατὰ τόπον προκεχειρισμένων πρὸς ⁸τούτοις ὑπογράφονται, καὶ ἀπὸ τίνος
⁹χρόνου τὸ προκείμενον συνέστηκεν. ¹⁰ἡ μὲν οὖν
οἰκονομία ἐπιτελεῖται καθότι ὑποδέδειχεν ¹¹ὁ 'Αρί-
στων τὸ ἐπενεχθησόμενον ἡμῖν γεγραμμένον ¹²συν-
άλ<λ>αγμα ὑπὸ τοῦ μονογράφου εἰκονίζειν τούς τε
¹³συνηλλαχότας καὶ ἣν πεπόηνται οἰκονομίαν ¹⁴καὶ
τὰ ὀνόματ' αὐτῶν πατρόθεν ἐντάσσειν ¹⁵καὶ ὑπο-
γράφειν ἡμᾶς ἐντεταχέναι εἰς χρηματισμὸν ¹⁶δηλώ-
σαντες τόν τε χρόνον ἐν ὧι ὑπογεγρ[ά]φαμεν
¹⁷ἐπενεχθείσης τῆς συγγραφῆς καὶ τὸν δι' αὐτῆς
¹⁸τῆς συγγραφῆς χρόνον· ἡ τὲ ἐντολὴ ¹⁹ἐγδέδοται
ἡμῖν εἰς τὴν ᾱ τοῦ 'Αθύρ, ²⁰[ὁ] δὲ χρηματισμὸς
συνέσταται ἀπὸ Χ[ο]ίαχ θ. ²¹[ὅ]πως οὖν εἰδῆς,
προσαναφέρομεν. ²²ἔρρωσο. (ἔτους) λς Τῦβι ιγ.

16. l. δηλώσαντας.   18. l. δέ.

ᵃ Head of a record-office.
ᵇ Contracts written in demotic, the later Egyptian script.
ᶜ The district round Thebes.

415. CONCERNING THE REGISTRATION OF EGYPTIAN CONTRACTS

146 b.c.

Paniscus ^a to Ptolemaeus greeting. I have received your letter in which you tell me to inform you of the procedure being followed with regard to Egyptian agreements ^b drawn up in the nome of Perithebas,^c and whether in accordance with the orders given by Ariston they are being subscribed by the persons appointed locally for this duty, and from what date the aforesaid system has been in operation. The procedure then is being conducted in conformity with the instructions given by Ariston to the effect that when an agreement written by the native notary will be submitted to us we shall make a summary ^d of it, stating therein the contracting parties and the settlement which they have made and their patronymics, and that we shall write at the foot of the deed that we have entered it on the records, mentioning the date on which, the contract having been submitted, we wrote the subscription, and the date given in the contract itself. The circular was issued to us on the 1st of Hathur, and the registration has been instituted on Choiak 9. For your information then we submit this report. Goodbye. Year 36, Tubi 13.

^d According to Wilcken, *U.P.Z.* pp. 596 ff., not a summary made in the record-office, but a copy or duplicate prepared by the notary.

416. PREPARATIONS FOR A ROMAN VISITOR

P. Tebt. 33.   112 B.C.

¹'Ερμ(ίας) "Ωρωι χαί(ρειν). τῆς πρὸς 'Ασκλη-
(πιάδην) ἐπισ(τολῆς) ἀντίγρ(αφον) ὑπόκι(ται).
²[φρόν]τισον οὖν ἵνα γένη(ται) ἀκολούθως. ἔρρω(σο).
[(ἔτους)] ε Ξαντικοῦ ιζ Μεχεὶρ ιζ.

³'Ασκλη(πιάδει). Λεύκιος Μέμμιος 'Ρωμαῖος
τῶν ἀπὸ ⁴συνκλήτου ἐν μίζονι ἀξιώματι κα[ὶ] τιμῆι
⁵κείμενος τὸν ἐκ τῆς πό(λεως) ἀνάπλουν ἕως τοῦ
'Αρσι(νοΐτου) νο(μοῦ) ⁶ἐπὶ θεωρίαν ποιούμενος
μεγαλο{υ}πρεπέστερον ⁷ἐγδεχθήτωι, καὶ φρόντισον
ὡς ἐπὶ τῶν ⁸καθηκόντων τόπων αἵ τε αὐλαὶ κατα-
σκευασ-⁹[θ]ήσ[ο]νται καὶ αἱ ἀπὸ τούτων ἐγβα(τηρίαι)
ε[.]ιε[...] ¹⁰π..... συντελεσθήσονται καὶ αὐτῶι
προσ-¹¹ενεχθήσεται ἐπὶ τῆς ἐγβα(τηρίας) τὰ ὑπο-
γεγρ(αμμένα) ξένια, ¹²καὶ τ[ὰ] εἰς τὸν τῆς αὐλῆς
καταρτισμὸν ¹³καὶ τὸ γεινόμενον τῶι Πετεσούχωι
καὶ τοῖς κροκο(δείλοις) ¹⁴ψωμίον καὶ τὰ πρὸς τὴν
τοῦ Λαβυρίνθου θέαν ¹⁵καὶ τὰ . [. .] . [. . σ]ταθη-
σόμενα θύματα καὶ τῆς ¹⁶θυσί[α]ς . . . . . χ . ηκ
. ν[. . .]ται, τὸ δ' ὅλον ἐπὶ πάν[των] ¹⁷τὴν μεγίστην
φροντίδα ποιουμένου τοῦ εὐδοκοῦν[τ]α ¹⁸τὸν ἄνδρα
κατασταθῆ[ναι] τὴν πᾶσαν προσένεγκαι ¹⁹σπου-
δὴ[ν] - - -

17. l. ποιούμενος.

416. PREPARATIONS FOR A ROMAN
VISITOR

112 B.C.

Hermias to Horus greeting. Below is a copy of the letter to Asclepiades. Take care then that its instructions are followed. Goodbye. Year 5, Xandicus 17, Mecheir 17.

To Asclepiades. Lucius Memmius, a Roman senator, who occupies a position of great dignity and honour, is sailing up from Alexandria to the Arsinoite nome to see the sights. Let him be received with special magnificence, and take care that at the proper spots the guest-chambers be prepared and the landing-places to them be completed, and that the gifts mentioned below [a] be presented to him at the landing-place, and that the furniture of the guest-chamber, the titbits for Petesouchus [b] and the crocodiles, the conveniences for viewing the Labyrinth,[c] and the offerings and sacrifices be provided ; in general take the greatest pains in everything to see that the visitor is satisfied, and display the utmost zeal . . .

[a] The gifts, consisting of eatables (*cf.* No. 414), were specified at the end of the letter, which is hopelessly mutilated.
[b] A Fayum god incarnated in a crocodile.
[c] The temple beside the pyramid of Amenemhet III. at Hawara.

417. CONCERNING A REVOLT IN THE THEBAID

Rec. Champ. p. 276 (= P. Lond. 465).   88 B.C.

¹[.Π]λάτω[ν τοῖς ἐν] Παθύρει ²[κ]ατοικ[οῦσι
χαίρει]ν καὶ ³ἐρρῶσθαι. [ἐξωρμη]κότες ⁴[ἐγ] Λάτων
πόλ[εως] ἀντιληψό-⁵[μ]ενοι τῶν ἐν[εστη]κότων
⁶[κα]τὰ τὸ συμφ[έρον] τοῖς ⁷[π]ράγμασι, ἐκρ[ίνα]μεν
σημῆναι ⁸καὶ παρακαλέσαι εὐψυχο-⁹[τ]έρους ὑπ-
άρχοντας ¹⁰ἐφ' ἑαυτῶν εἶνα[ι] καὶ συν-¹¹γίνεσθαι
Νεχθύρει τῶι ¹²ἐφ' ὑμῶν τεταγμένωι ¹³μέχρι τοῦ
[καὶ ἡμᾶ]ς ὅ τι ¹⁴τάχο[ς παρεῖν]αι τοῖς τόπο[ις].
¹⁵ἔρρ(ωσθε). [(ἔτους) κϛ Φα]με(νὼθ) ιϛ.
Verso : ¹⁶τοῖς ἐν Παθύρει ¹⁷[κατοι]κοῦσι.

418. CONCERNING A REVOLT IN THE THEBAID

P. Bour. 12.   88 B.C.

¹Πλάτων τοῖς ἐν Παθύρει ²ἱερεῦσι καὶ τοῖς
ἄλλοις ³τοῖς κατοικοῦσι ⁴χαίρειν. γέγραφεν ⁵ἡμῖν
Φιλόξενος ⁶ὁ ἀδελφὸς δι' ὧν κεκό-⁷μικεν ἡμῖν
Ὄρσης ⁸γραμμάτων περὶ τοῦ ⁹τὸν μέγιστον θεὸν
¹⁰Σωτῆρα βασιλέα ¹¹ἐπιβεβληκέναι ¹²εἰς Μέμφιν,
Ἱέρακα δὲ ¹³προκεχειρίσθαι ¹⁴μετὰ δυνάμεων
¹⁵μυρίων ἐπὶ κατα-¹⁶στολὴν τῆς Θηβαΐδος. ¹⁷ὅπως

ᵃ See No. 417, note a. The present letter was written
seven months later, and in the meantime Ptolemy Alexander
had been expelled and Soter II., to whom Platon had

417. CONCERNING A REVOLT IN THE THEBAID

88 B.C.

Platon [a] to the inhabitants of Pathyris greeting and good health. Having set out from Latopolis to take in hand the present situation in accordance with the interests of the state, I have thought it well to inform you and exhort you to hold together, remaining undaunted, and to assist Nechthuris your appointed governor, until I come to your district with what haste I can. Goodbye. Year 26,[b] Phamenoth 16. (Addressed) To the inhabitants of Pathyris.

[a] Probably the epistrategus of the Thebaid.
[b] Of Ptolemy Alexander, who was still king when the revolt broke out.

418. CONCERNING A REVOLT IN THE THEBAID

88 B.C.

Platon [a] to the priests and other inhabitants of Pathyris greeting. Philoxenus my brother has written to me, in a letter which has been brought to me by Orses, to the effect that King Soter, the most great god, has arrived at Memphis and that Hierax has been appointed commander of a numerous army to subdue the Thebaid. In order therefore that you

promptly transferred his allegiance, had returned to Egypt. The change of kings did not effect the revolt, which was a native rising against foreign rule.

οὖν εἰδότες ¹⁸εὐθαρσεῖς ὑπάρ-¹⁹χητε ἐκρίναμεν
²⁰σημῆναι. ²¹ἔρρ(ωσθε). (ἔτους) λ Φαῶφι ιθ.

Verso : ²²τοῖς ἐν Παθύρει ²³ἱερεῦσι καὶ τοῖς
ἄλλοις.

419. LETTER OF A STRATEGUS

P. Tebt. 289.   A.D. 23.

¹['Α]πολλώνιος στρατηγὸς ᾿Ακοῦτι ²τοπάρχῃ
Τεβτύνεως χαίρειν. ³ἐξαυτῆς πέμπε μοι πρόσ-
γραφον ⁴τῶν μέχρι τῆς σήμερον διαγεγρ(αμμένων)
⁵κατ᾿ εἶδος· οὕτως γὰρ γνώσομαι ⁶πότερον ἐπὶ
τόπων σε ἐάσω ⁷πράττοντά τι ἢ μεταπεμψάμε(νος)
⁸πέμψωι τῶι ἡγεμ[όνι] ὡς ἀ[με-]⁹λοῦντα τῆς εἰσ-
πρά[ξεως]. ¹⁰ἔρρωσο. ¹¹(ἔτους) ἐνάτου Τιβερίου
Καίσαρος Σεβαστοῦ ¹²Μεχ(εὶρ) κα.

Verso : ['Ακοῦτι] τ[ο]π[ά]ρ[χ(ῃ)] Τεβτύν(εως).

420. LETTER FROM A STRATEGUS ABOUT
TAX-FARMERS

P. Oxy. 44.   End of 1st cent. A.D.

¹[Πα]νίσκος [. . . . .]λας στρατηγὸς 'Οξυ-
ρυ[γ]χί(του) ²['Ασ]κληπιάδ[ηι βασιλικῶ]ι γραμ-
μα(τεῖ) τοῦ αὐτοῦ νομοῦ ³χαίρειν. ⁴ἐπὶ τῆς γενομένης διαπράσεως τῶν τελωνι-⁵κῶν ὑπό τε ἐμοῦ
καὶ σοῦ ἐπὶ παρόντων καὶ ⁶τῶν εἰωθότων, δυσ-
πειθούντων τῶν τὸ ἐν-⁷κύκλιον ἀσχολουμένων καὶ

570

may be encouraged by this news, I have thought it well to inform you. Goodbye. Year 30,[a] Phaophi 19. (Addressed) To the priests and other inhabitants of Pathyris.

[a] Of Soter II.

419. LETTER OF A STRATEGUS

A.D. 23.

Apollonius, strategus, to Akous, toparch of Tebtunis, greeting. Send me at once a supplementary classified statement of payments made up to date ; for I shall judge by this whether I shall leave you on duty where you are or summon you and send you to the praefect for neglect of the collecting. Goodbye. The ninth year of Tiberius Caesar Augustus, Mecheir 21. (Addressed) To Akous, toparch of Tebtunis.

420. LETTER FROM A STRATEGUS ABOUT TAX-FARMERS

End of 1st cent. A.D.

Paniscus . . ., strategus of the Oxyrhynchite nome, to Asclepiades, royal scribe of the same nome, greeting. When at the auction of taxes held by me and you in the presence of the customary officials, the farmers of the sales tax [a] and the record-office tax [b]

[a] See No. 378.
[b] Payable by persons making agreements through the record-office.

571

{τοῦ} τὸ ἀγο-⁸ρανόμιον δημοσιωνῶν ὡς ἱκανὰ
βλαπτο-⁹μένων καὶ κινδυνευόντων μεταναστῆ-¹⁰ναι,
δόξαν ἡμεῖν ἔγραψα τῶι κρατίστωι ¹¹ἡγεμόνι περὶ
τοῦ πράγματος. ἀντιγράψαν-¹²τος οὖν αὐτοῦ μοι
περὶ τοῦ ἐφιδόντα τὰς ¹³π[ρο]τέρας μισθώσεις κατὰ
τὸ δυνατὸν ¹⁴[ἀνα]κουφίσαι τοὺς τελώνας ὑπὲρ τοῦ
μὴ ¹⁵φυγ[ά]δας γενέσθαι τ[ο]ὺς πρὸς β[ίαν] ἀ[γο-]
¹⁶μένους, καὶ πρότερόν σοι τὸ ἀντίγ[ραφο]ν ¹⁷τῆς
ἐπιστολῆς μετέδωκα, ἵν᾽ εἰδῇς, καὶ ¹⁸ὅτι ἀποδη-
μοῦντός σου καὶ τῶν ὠνῶν ¹⁹μὴ ἐπιδεδεγμένων ὑπὸ
τῶν τελωνῶν ²⁰μηδὲ μὴν ἄλλων προσερχ[ομ]ένων
αὐ-²¹τοῖς ⟦πολλάκις⟧ πολλάκις προκηρυχθεισῶν
²²ἔλαβον χειρογραφείας τῶν τε τὸ ἐνκύ-²³{κυ}κλιον
καὶ τὸ γραφεῖον ἀσχολουμένων - - -

421. LATIN LETTER FROM THE PRAEFECT
OF EGYPT

P. Oxy. 1022.   A.D. 103.

²[C.] *Minucius Italu[s C]elsiano suo* ³*sal[u]tem.*
⁴*tirones sexs probatos a me in* ⁵*coh(orte) cui praees in*
*nume-*⁶*ros referri iube ex xi* ⁷*kalendas Martias : nomi-*
⁸*na eorum et icon[i]smos* ⁹*huic epistulae subieci.* ¹⁰*vale*
frater karissim[e]. ¹¹*C. Veturium Gemellum* ¹²*an-*
nor(um) xxi sine i(conismo), ¹³*C. Longinum Priscum*
¹⁴*annor(um) xxii, i(conismus) supercil(io) sinistr(o),*
¹⁵*C. Iulium Maximum ann(orum) xxv* ¹⁶*sine i(co-*
nismo), ¹⁷*[.] Lucium Secuñdum* ¹⁸*annor(um) xx sine*
i(conismo), ¹⁹*C. Iulium Saturninum* ²⁰*annor(um) xxiii,*

572

refused to bid, on the ground that they were incurring serious losses, and seemed likely to abscond, I wrote as we decided to his excellency the praefect on the matter. Now he replied to the effect that I should examine the former leases and lighten the burden of the tax-farmers as much as possible in order to avoid a flight of persons engaged by force,[a] and I have already sent you a copy of his letter for your information, adding that in your absence, as the contracts had not been taken up by the tax-farmers nor were any new bidders coming forward in spite of repeated proclamations, I had taken written oaths from the farmers of the sales tax and the record-office tax . . .

[a] The meaning is that, if the tax-farmers were compelled to take up the contracts on very hard terms, they would leave their work and go into hiding.

421. LATIN LETTER FROM THE PRAEFECT OF EGYPT

A.D. 103.

C. Minucius Italus to his dear Celsianus greeting. Give orders that the six recruits who have been approved by me in the cohort under your command be included in the ranks from February 19 : I append to this letter their names and descriptions. Farewell, dearest brother.

C. Veturius Gemellus, aged 21, without description, C. Longinus Priscus, aged 22, a mark on his left eyebrow, C. Julius Maximus, aged 25, without description, [.] Lucius Secundus, aged 20, without description, C. Julius Saturninus, aged 23, a mark on

i(conismus)   manu   sinistr(a),   [21]*Marcum   Antonium
Valentem* [22]*ann(orum) xxii, i(conismus) frontis* [23]*parte
dextr(a).*   (2nd hand) [24]*accepta vi k(alendas) Martias
ann(o) vi* [25]*Imp(eratoris) Traiani n(ostri) per* [26]*Priscum singul(arem).*   [27]*Avidius Arrianus cornicular(ius)*
[28]*coh(ortis)   iii   Ituraeorum*   [29]*scripsi   authenticam*
[30]*epistulam in tabulario* [31]*cohortis esse.*

422. FROM THE PRAEFECT ABOUT A PROPERTY RECORD-OFFICE

Archiv vi. p. 102.   A.D. 103.

[1]'Αντίγραφον ἐπιστολῆς. Μινίκιος ῎Ιταλος [2]Διο-
γένει καὶ Διονυσίωι καὶ ᾿Απολλωνίωι στρατηγοῖς
[3]᾿Αρσινοΐτου χαίρειν. [4]ὁ κράτιστος ἐπίτροπος τοῦ
κυρίου ἡμῶν Κλαστικὸς [5]μετέδωκέν μοι τὴν ἐν
τῷ νομῶι τῶν ἐνκτήσεων [6]βιβλιοθήκην ἀνεπιτήδειον
εἶναι καὶ τὰ ἐν αὐτῇ βιβλία [7]ἀποκείμενα ἀφαν[ί]-
ζεσθαι, τὰ δὲ πλεῖστα καὶ ἀνεύρετα [8]εἶναι. φησὶν
δὲ ἐπιλ[έξαντος π]αρόντων ὑμῶν ἕτερον [9]τόπον ἐπι-
τήδειον τοῦ εἰς τὴν ἀνοικοδομὴν συν-[10]εψηφίσθαι
δραχμὰς τρι[σ]χιλείας διακοσίας ὀγδοήκοντα [11]δύο
τριόβολον. ἵν᾿ οὖν τὰ βιβλία ἀνανκεώτατα [12]ὄντα
μὴ ἀμεληθῇ, βούλομε ὑμᾶς εὐθέως ἐνχιρῆσε [13]τῇ
κατασκευῆι, καὶ ἃ λέγει ἀπὸ τῶν ἀρχεωτέρων
χρόνω(ν) [14]βιβλία ἐκ μέρους διεφθαρμένα ἐσφρα-
γεῖσθαι, ὡς τὴν [15]παράδωσ[ι]ν οὐδεὶς ποιήσασθαι
δύναται, διὰ τὸ τοῦ πολλοῦ [16]χρόνου τοὺς πρὸς

---

4. =Κλασσικός.   8. ἐπιλ[έξαντος E.-H.: ἐπιλ[ελέχθαι
Ed.   11. *l.* ἀναγκαιότατα.   12. *l.*

his left hand, Marcus Antonius Valens, aged 22, a mark on the right side of his forehead.

(Docketed) Received on February 24 in the 6th year of our Emperor Trajanus through Priscus, orderly. I, Avidius Arrianus, adjutant of the 3rd cohort of the Ituraeans, state that the original letter is in the archives of the cohort.

422. FROM THE PRAEFECT ABOUT A PROPERTY RECORD-OFFICE

A.D. 103.

Copy of a letter. Minicius Italus to Diogenes, Dionysius, and Apollonius, strategi of the Arsinoite nome, greeting. His excellency Classicus the procurator of our lord has informed me that the property record-office of the nome is unfit for its purpose and that the documents stored in it are disappearing and are most of them unfindable. He says that he has selected in your presence another site which is suitable and that a computation has been made of the money to be spent on the rebuilding, amounting to three thousand two hundred and eighty-two drachmae three obols. In order therefore that these most necessary documents may not be neglected, I wish you to set to work at once on the construction, and as for those of more ancient date which he says are partly destroyed and have been sealed up, as no one is able to make formal delivery of them, because the persons who were in charge of them have long

βούλομαι, ἐγχειρῆσαι.   13. l. ἀρχαιοτέρων.   15. l.
παράδοσ[ι]ν.

575

αὐτοῖς γεγωνώτας τετελευτηκέναι, [17]μετενενκεῖν
εἰς ἣν νῦν κατασκευάζεσθαι κελεύωι [18]καὶ ἀναγράψασθαι, παρόντων ὧν προσήκει, καὶ τὴν [19]ἀνα-
γραφὴν καταχωρίσῃς. ἐρρῶσθαι ὑμᾶς [20]βούλομαι.
(ἔτους) ἕκτου Αὐτοκράτορος Καίσαρος [21]Νερούα
Τραϊανοῦ Γερμανικοῦ Παχὼν κ̄δ.

16. *l.* γεγονότας.　　17. μετενενκεῖν Skeat: μετενεγκεῖν Ed.
19. *l.* καταχωρίσαι.

423. LETTER FROM A TRANSPORTER
OF GOVERNMENT CORN

P. Giess. 11.　　　　　　　　　　　　　　　A.D. 118.

[1]Παπεῖρεις Ἀπολλωνίῳ στρατη(γῷ) [2]Ἀπολλωνο-
πολείτου (Ἑπτα)κωμίας [3]τῷ τιμιωτάτῳ χαίρειν.
[4]γινώσκειν σε θέλω ὅτι ἐπεστά-[5]λην εἰς τὸν ὑπὸ
σοὶ νομὸν μόνος [6]καὶ πλαιρείδιν ὡς ἀρταβῶν {(ἀρταβῶν)} Ἀ, [7]ἐμοῦ αἰτησαμένου τὸν νομὸν [8]Βησα-
ρίωνος εἴπαντος. ἐπεσταλ{ην}-[9]μένος δὲ κατεσχέ-
την ὑπὸ τοῦ [10]ἐπιτρόπου ὥστε εἱερατεύειν [11]τοῦ
χειρεισμοῦ τῶν κυβερνητ(ῶν). [12]καλῶς οὖν ποι[ή-
σ]ῃς, φίλτατε, σ[υ]ν-[13]λαβόμενος το[ὺ]ς ἐμούς, ἐπὶ
ἐγὼ [14]οὐ πάρειμει προσκυνῆσαί σε τὸν [15]τιμιώ-
τατον, καὶ σύ μοι ἐπείτρε-[16]πε ὡς δυναμένῳ σοι
ἐργασίαν δῶ-[17]ναι· οὐκ ἀγνοεῖς ὅτι ἄλλας ὀκτὸ μυ-
[18]ριάδες ἔχω πλοίων ὧν ἐξουσίαν ἔχω [19]ὥστε σαρω-
θῆναί σου τὸν νομόν. [20]γίνωσ<κε> οὖν, κύριε, ὅτι

6. *l.* πλοιαρίδιον.　　9. *l.* κατεσχέθην.　　12. *l.* ποι[ήσ]εις.
13. *l.* ἐπεί.　　16. *l.* δοῦναι.　　17. *l.* ὀκτὼ μυριάδας.

been dead, I wish you to transfer them to the building which I now order to be constructed and draw up a list in presence of the persons concerned and file the list. I wish you good health. The sixth year of the Emperor Caesar Nerva Trajanus Germanicus, Pachon 24.

423. LETTER FROM A TRANSPORTER OF GOVERNMENT CORN

A.D. 118.

Papiris to his most honoured friend Apollonius, strategus of the Apollonopolite-Heptacomia nome, greeting. I wish you to know that I have been commissioned to go to your nome alone with a boat of about 4000 artabas' burden, having myself asked for your nome and been granted it by Besarion. But after receiving my commission I have been detained by the procurator [a] to act as priest to the pilots' corporation.[b] Be kind enough then, dearest friend, to assist my men, since I have not come in person to do reverence to your most honoured self, and command me in the assurance that I can serve you ; you are aware that I have room for other eighty thousand artabae on the boats at my command, enough to make a clean sweep of your nome. Now you must

[a] The procurator of Neapolis (see No. 373, note *a*).
[b] Probably a corporation, under government control, of pilots or boat-captains employed in government service. The office of priest was a very common one in Egyptian associations of all kinds.

577

SELECT PAPYRI

ἠὰν ε[ἱερα-]²¹τεύῃ τοῦ χειρ[εισμοῦ τῶν κυβερνη-
τ(ῶν)] ²²τῷ ἐπιτρόπῳ σ[. . . . .
. .]. ²³(ἔτους) β̄ Ἀδριανοῦ Κ[αίσαρος Σεβαστοῦ]
²⁴Ἐπε[ὶ]φ ῑϛ. ²⁵ἐρρῶσθαί σε ε[ὔχομαι].
Verso: ²⁶ἀπόδ(ος) Ἀπολλωνίωι στρατη(γῶι)
Ἑπτακωμίας.

20. *l.* ἐάν.

424. REVOCATION OF A WILL

P. Oxy. 106.   A.D. 135.

¹Ἀγορανόμοις Ὀξυρύγ-²χων πόλεως Ἀπολλώνι-
³ος Πτολεμαίου ὑπηρέ-⁴της. ἀπήνγειλα ὑμεῖν ⁵τὸν
τοῦ νομοῦ στρ(ατηγὸν) Δημή-⁶τριον συντεταχέναι
⁷ἀναδοῦναι Πτολέμα ⁸Στράτωνος μητρὸς Διονυ-
⁹σίας ἀπ᾽ Ὀξυρύγχων πό-¹⁰λεως ἣν ἔθετο δι᾽
ὑμῶν ¹¹τῶι θ (ἔτει) θεοῦ Τραϊανοῦ ¹²Μεχεὶρ ἐπὶ
σφραγίδων ¹³διαθήκην, τοῦτο ἀξιω-¹⁴σάσης αὐτῆς,
ἣν καὶ δι᾽ ἐ-¹⁵μοῦ ἀνέλαβεν. ἔτους ¹⁶ἐννεακαιδε-
κάτου ¹⁷Αὐτοκράτορος Καίσαρος ¹⁸Τραϊανοῦ Ἀδριανοῦ ¹⁹Σεβαστοῦ Φαρμοῦθι κ̄ε. (2nd hand) ²⁰Πτο-
λέμα Στράτωνος ἀνέλαβον τὴν ²¹προκειμένην μου
διαθήκην ἐπὶ τῶν ²²αὐτῶν σφραγείδων. Πέδων
Καλλι-²³κόρνου ἐπιγέγραμμαι αὐτῆς κύριος ²⁴καὶ
ἔγραψα ὑπὲρ αὐτῆς μὴ εἰδυίης γράμ(ματα).
²⁵χρόνος ὁ αὐτός.

578

know, my lord, that if one acts as priest to the pilots'
corporation (one must) . . . the procurator . . .
Year 2 of Hadrianus Caesar Augustus, Epeiph 16.
I pray for your health. (Addressed) Deliver to
Apollonius, strategus of Heptacomia.

424. REVOCATION OF A WILL

A.D. 135.

To the agoranomi of Oxyrhynchus from Apollonius
son of Ptolemaeus, assistant.[a] I hereby inform you
that the strategus of the nome, Demetrius, has instructed me to give back to Ptolema daughter of
Straton and Dionysia, of Oxyrhynchus, the will which
she made through you in Mecheir of the 9th year of
the deified Trajanus under seals, in compliance with
her own request, and she has received it back through
me. The 19th year of the Emperor Caesar Trajanus
Hadrianus Augustus, Pharmouthi 25. (Signed) I,
Ptolema daughter of Straton, have received my
aforesaid will under the original seals. I, Pedon son
of Callicornus, have professed myself her guardian,
and wrote for her, as she is illiterate. The same date.

---

[a] Probably an employee of the βιβλιοθήκη ἐγκτήσεων, the
property record-office.

SELECT PAPYRI

425. CONCERNING AN AUCTION OF
PRIESTLY OFFICES

P. Achmim 8, ll. 4-20.   A.D. 197.

⁴Κλαύδιος Διόγνητος ἐπίτροπος Σεβαστοῦ ⁵δια-
δεχόμενος τὴν ἀρχιε[ρ]ωσύνην στρατ(ηγῷ) ⁶Πανο-
πολ(ίτου) χαίρειν. ⁷ἀντίγραφα ἐπιστολῶν δύο
γρ[α]φεισῶν μοι ⁸ὑπὸ Σατουρνίνου ταβουλαρίου
[τ]ῆς ἀρχιερωσύ-⁹νης περὶ Πεκύσιος Ψενθερμού-
θ[ο]υ ἱερέως διαγρά-¹⁰ψαντος τιμὴν στολιστείας ἐν
(δραχμαῖς) ρ καὶ πρὸς καὶ ¹¹Ἀρεμίφιος Σισόιτος
ἱερέως δ[ια]γράψαντος τι-¹²μὴν ἑτέρας στολιστείας
ἐν δραχμαῖς ἑκατὸν καὶ ¹³πρὸς Μητιόχῳ οἰκονόμῳ
τοῦ κυρίου ἡμῶν ¹⁴θειοτάτου Αὐτοκράτορος Σεου[ή]ρου Περτίνακος ¹⁵[τούτο]ις ὑπέταξά μου τοῖς
γράμμασιν. σὺ φρόντισον ¹⁶σὺν τῷ βασιλ(ικῷ)
γρ(αμματεῖ) τὰς τάξεις προκηρῦξαι, κἂν μηδεὶς
¹⁷πλέον δῷ, παραδοῦναι αὐτοῖς, μ[ὴ] μέντοι ἐλάτ-
¹⁸τονος [τ]ῆς συντιμήσεως μηδ[ὲ τ]ῆς ἄλλοτε εἰσ-
¹⁹ενεχθείσ‹ης› ὑπὲρ τῶν τάξεων τιμῆς. ἐρρῶ(σθαί)
σε εὔχομ(αι). ²⁰(ἔτους) εʺ Παχὼ(ν) κθ.

426. REPLY TO A STRATEGUS

P. Oxy. 1115.   A.D. 284.

¹Αὐρηλίῳ Φιλιάρχῳ τῷ καὶ Ὡρίωνι σ[τ]ρατηγῷ
Ὀξυρυγχείτου ²παρὰ Αὐρηλίων Ἰσιδώρου καὶ Ἀ-
σκληπιάδου καὶ Πλουτίνου ἀναπ[ομ-]³πῶν ἄρτου.
580

425. CONCERNING AN AUCTION OF PRIESTLY OFFICES [a]

A.D. 197.

Claudius Diognetus, imperial procurator and deputy-chief-priest, to the strategus of the Panopolite nome greeting. Copies of two letters written to me by Saturninus, secretary of the chief priest, concerning Pekusis son of Psenthermouthus, priest, who has paid the price of an office of stolistes amounting to 100 drachmae and extra charges, and Haremiphis son of Sisois, priest, who has paid the price of another office of stolistes amounting to 100 drachmae and extra charges, in both cases to Metiochus, oeconomus of our most godlike lord the Emperor Severus Pertinax, are appended to my present letter. Take steps on your part along with the royal scribe to put the offices up to auction and, if no one bids higher, to hand them over to them, but not for a price inferior to the valuation or to the sum paid for the offices on other occasions. I pray for your health. Year 5, Pachon 29.

[a] Compare No. 353.

426. REPLY TO A STRATEGUS

A.D. 284.

To Aurelius Philiarchus also called Horion, strategus of the Oxyrhynchite nome, from Aurelius Isidorus, Aurelius Asclepiades, and Aurelius Plutinus, de-

αἰτηθέντες ὑπὸ σοῦ ἐκ τῶν ἐπισταλέντων σοι ὑπὸ
⁴τοῦ διασημοτάτου ἡγεμόνος Πομπωνίου Ἰανουα-
ριανοῦ καὶ τοῦ ⁵δι[α]σημοτάτου διοικητοῦ Αὐρηλίου
[Πρωτέα] ἣν ἔχομεν αὐθεντικὴν ⁶[ἀποχ]ὴν οὗ ἀνη-
νέγκαμεν καὶ δι[αδεδώ]καμεν ἄρτου, ἐπιδίδομέν σοι
⁷τὴ[ν] προκειμένην αὐθεντικὴν ἀποχ[ὴν] καὶ ταύτης
ἀντίγρα[φον ἀξι-]⁸οῦντες ὑποσημιώσασθαί σ[ε] πρὸς
τὸ καὶ ἡμᾶς τὸ ἀ[σ]φ[α]λὲς ἔχειν [τῆς αὐ-]⁹τῆς
αὐθεντικῆς ἀποχῆς. Μίκκαλος ἐπὶ διαδόσεως
ἀννώνης ¹⁰Ἰσιδώρῳ καὶ Ἀσκληπιάδῃ ἐπιμεληταῖς
{ἐ[π]ιμεληταῖς} Ὀξυρυγχείτ[ο]υ. ¹¹παραδ[ε]δώκατε
ἐν τῇ Πανῶν πόλει κατὰ κέλευσιν Αὐρηλίου
Πρ[ω-]¹²τέα τοῦ κρατίστου διοικητοῦ ἀκολούθως
αἷς ἐπηνέγκατε φ[ορ-]¹³μαλείαις χωρήσασι στρ[α-
τιώ]ταις καὶ ναύταις ἄρτου . . [. . . . . -]¹⁴ους
μυριάδας τρῖς καὶ ὀκτακισχιλ[ίους τ]ετρακοσίους
ἐνενή-¹⁵κοντα ἕξ, γί(νονται) μ(υριάδες) γ Ἡϛϟϛ.
¹⁶(ἔτους) ϛ τοῦ κυρίου ἡμῶν Αὐτοκράτορος Καίσαρος
Μάρκου Αὐρηλίου ¹⁷Πρόβου Εὐσεβοῦς Σεβαστοῦ
Τῦβι ἑκκαιδεκάτῃ, Τῦβι ιϛ. (2nd hand) ¹⁸Αὐρήλιος
Φιλίαρχος ὁ καὶ Ὡρίων στρα(τηγὸς) Ὀξυρ[υ]γ-
χ(ίτου) ἔσχον τὴν αὐθεντικὴν ἀποχὴν ¹⁹συμφωνοῦ-
σαν πρὸς τὸ προτεταγμένον ἀντίγρα(φον) ἣν καὶ
κατέπεμψα ²⁰ὡς ἐκελεύσθη. (ἔτους) β Παχὼν κϛ.

12-13. l. φ[ορ]μαρίαις.

---

[a] A town in Upper Egypt.
[b] For the collection of rations for the army compare Nos.
387, 388, 393, 396. The contribution exacted in the present

liverers of bread. Having been asked by you in consequence of letters sent to you by the most eminent praefect Pomponius Januarianus and the most eminent dioecetes Aurelius Proteas for the authentic receipt in our possession for the bread which we have carried up and distributed, we present to you the aforesaid authentic receipt and a copy of it which we beg you to sign in order that we too may have the security of the said authentic receipt. " Miccalus, superintendent of the distribution of the *annona*, to Isidorus and Asclepiades, overseers of the Oxyrhynchite nome. You have delivered in Panopolis [a] in obedience to the order of his excellency the dioecetes Aurelius Proteas, in accordance with the certificates presented by you, to the mobilized soldiers and sailors thirty-eight thousand four hundred and ninety-six modii (?) of bread, total 38,496.[b] The 6th year of our lord the Emperor Caesar Marcus Aurelius Probus Pius Augustus, Tubi sixteenth, Tubi 16." (Signed) I, Aurelius Philiarchus also called Horion, strategus of the Oxyrhynchite nome, have received the authentic receipt, which agrees with the copy above written, and have forwarded it as ordered. Year 2 [c] Pachon 26.

case was the so-called *annona*. In earlier times, as exemplified by No. 387, the required amounts of corn were usually bought, but by compulsory sale and at the government's own price; in later times, as here, the furnishing of supplies was a direct exaction.

    [c] Of Numerianus.

SELECT PAPYRI

427. LETTER OF A STRATEGUS

P. Oxy. 2114.   A.D. 316.

¹Αὐρήλιος ᾿Απολλώνιος ὁ καὶ Εὐδαίμων στρα-
(τηγὸς) ᾿Οξ(υρυγχίτου) δι(ὰ) ²Πλου[. . . . .] διαδόχου ³Αὐρηλίῳ ῾Ηρᾷ πραιπ(οσίτῳ) η πάγου τῷ
φιλτάτῳ χαίρειν. ⁴δι᾿ ὧν ἔγραψεν ἡ ἐμμέλια τοῦ
κυρίου μου ἐπιτρό-⁵που τῆς ῾Επτανομίας Αὐρηλίου
Γρηγορίου ἐκέ-⁶λευσεν τοῦ δηληγατευθέντος οἴνου
τῆς Θη-⁷βαΐδος ἐν τῇ ε ἰνδικτίονι τὴν ἡμίσιαν
⁸ἀποσταλῆναι ἐν παλαιῷ ἢ τιμήματος ἑκά-⁹στου
ξέστου ἐκ (δηναρίων) ξε, ἀπαντησάντων ¹⁰εἰς τοῦτο
ὀπιν{ν}ατόρων ἐρεθέντος τε καὶ ¹¹ἀπὸ βουλῆς
ἐπιμελητοῦ. φρόντισον τοί-¹²νυν δεξάμενος τόδε
τὸ ἐπίσταλμα τὸν ¹³ἐπιβάλλον[τ]α ξεστισμὸν τῷ ὑπὸ
σὲ πάγῳ ¹⁴παραδοῦναι τῷ ἐπιμελητῇ, πρὸς τὸ
μηδε-¹⁵μίαν ἐνδέραν περὶ τὰς στρατιωτικὰς τρο-
¹⁶φὰς γενέσθαι. (2nd hand) ἐρρῶσθαί σε εὔχομαι,
¹⁷φίλτατε. (1st hand) ¹⁸[ὑπατίας Καικι]νίου Σαβίνου καὶ Οὐεττίου ῾Ρουφίνου ¹⁹[τῶν λαμ]προτάτων
Μεσορὴ ιζ. (3rd hand) ²⁰[Αὐρήλιος Διό]σκορος
ὑπ(ηρέτης) [στ]ρα(τηγοῦ) ἐπήνεγκα ²¹[τῇ αὐτῇ
ἡ]μέρᾳ.

428. ABOUT SMUGGLERS OF NATRON

Lond. 231.   Middle of 4th cent. A.D.

¹[Κυρίῳ μου] ἀδελφ[ῷ] ᾿Αμινναί[ῳ] ²Δημήτριος.
³καὶ δεῖ᾿ ἑτέρων γραμμάτων ἐδήλωσα τῇ εὐγενίᾳ
584

427. LETTER OF A STRATEGUS

A.D. 316.

Aurelius Apollonius also called Eudaemon, strategus of the Oxyrhynchite nome, through his deputy Plu . . ., to his dearest Aurelius Heras, *praepositus* of the 8th *pagus*, greeting.   In the letter written by his grace my lord the procurator of the Heptanomia, Aurelius Gregorius, he ordered half the prescribed wine from the Thebaid to be delivered in the 5th indiction in old produce or else at a valuation of 65 denarii for each sextarius, collectors having arrived for this purpose and an overseer having been chosen from the senate.   Accordingly on receipt of this missive take care to deliver to the overseer the quota of sextarii falling to the *pagus* under you, in order that no fraud may occur with regard to the soldiers' victuals.   I pray for your health, dearest friend. The consulship of Caecinius Sabinus and Vettius Rufinus the most illustrious, Mesore 17.   (Docketed) Delivered by me, Aurelius Dioscorus, assistant of the strategus, on the same day.

---

7. *l.* ἡμίσειαν.   10. *l.* αἱρεθέντος.   15. *l.* ἐνέδραν.

428. ABOUT SMUGGLERS OF NATRON

Middle of 4th cent. A.D.

To my lord and brother Aminnaeus [a] from Demetrius. I have already sent word to your nobility in another

[a] Aminnaeus or Abinnaeus was a *praefectus castrorum* at Dionysias in the Fayum.   *Cf.* Vol. I. No. 161.

σου ⁴ὥστε τὰ νίτρα ⟨ἃ⟩ καταλαμβάνεις εἴτε διὰ
Μαρεωτῶν εἴτε ⁵διὰ Αἰγυπτείων κατερχόμενα ἐν
τῇ Ἀρσινοειτῶν ἢ καὶ ⁶ἐν ἑτέροις τόποις ταῦτα
ἐπέχειν καὶ νομίζω μὴ δεδέχθαι ⁷σε τὰ γράμματα,
οὐδὲ γὰρ ἔσχον παρὰ τῆς εὐγενίας σου ⁸περὶ τῆς
ὑποθέσεως ταύτης γράμματα. καὶ νῦν δὲ διὰ ⁹τοῦ
ἡμετέρου παιδὸς Σαραπίωνος ἀνερχομένου ἐν τῇ
Ὀάσει ¹⁰τὰ αὐτὰ δηλῶ, ἵνα μετὰ πάσης ἐπιεικείας
τὴν φρουρὰν ¹¹τῶν ταμειακῶν νίτρων ποιήσῃ καὶ
πάντας ὅσους καταλαμ-¹²βάνεις ἐπίσχῃς μετὰ καὶ
τῶν κτηνῶν αὐτῶν. σπούδαζε ¹³δὲ δηλοῖν ἡμεῖν ἐν
τῇ Τερενούθει τοῖς ἡμετέροις ἢ ¹⁴ἐν τῇ Ἀλεξανδρείᾳ. καὶ αὐτὸς δὲ κέλευε περὶ ὧν ἐὰν βούλει,
¹⁵κύριε ἄδελφε, ἵνα καὶ ἡμεῖς τὰ κελευόμενα παρὰ
τῆς διαθέ-¹⁶σεώς σου μετὰ πάσης προθυμείας
ὑπουργῶμεν. ἐρρῶσθαί ¹⁷σε εὔχομαι πολ-¹⁸λοῖς
χρόνοις, ¹⁹κύριε ἄδελφε. ²⁰Τῦβι α.

Verso: ²¹[κυρίῳ] μου ἀδελφῷ Ἀμινναίῳ πραι-
ποσίτῳ ²²Δημήτριος.

13. = δηλοῦν.

429. REPORT OF A FEUD BETWEEN TWO VILLAGES

B.G.U. 1035.   5th cent. A.D.

¹⁺Τῷ κυρίῳ ἡμῶν καὶ δεσπ[ότ]ῃ τῷ ²μεγαλο-
πρεπεστάτῳ καὶ ἐναρετ(ωτάτῳ) κόμετι ³⁺Ἀνούθιος
ἀρχιυπηρέτης. οἱ ἀπὸ κώμης ⁴Κερκήσις ἦλθαν
ε[ἰ]ς τὸν αἰγιαλὸν ⁵τῶν ἀπὸ Ὀξυρύγχων καὶ ἐδίοξαν

1-2. l. τῷ μεγαλοπρεπεστάτῳ.   5. l. ἐδίωξαν.

letter that the natron which you intercept on its
way to Arsinoe or other places, whether carried by
Mareots *a* or by Egyptians, should be detained by
you, and I think that you have not received my letter,
for I have not had a letter from your nobility concerning this subject. And now again I am sending you
the same message by my servant Sarapion who is
travelling to the Oasis, asking you to keep guard over
the natron of the Treasury with all honesty and to
detain all persons whom you intercept together with
their animals. Be prompt to send me word, either
to my agents at Terenouthis *b* or to Alexandria. And
command me in turn, my lord and brother, in any
matter that you wish, in order that I too may attend
to the commands of your discretion with all zeal. I
pray for your lasting health, my lord brother. Tubi 1.
(Addressed) To my lord and brother Aminnaeus,
praepositus, from Demetrius.

a Inhabitants of the district of Mareotis near Alexandria.
b A town on the west edge of the Delta, the usual starting-
point for a journey to the Natron Lakes.

429. REPORT OF A FEUD BETWEEN TWO VILLAGES

5th cent. A.D.

To our lord and master the most magnificent and
virtuous count from Anouthius, chief assistant. The
people of the village of Kerkesis *a* came to the beach
of the people of Oxyrhyncha *a* and drove away the

a These two villages were in the south of the Fayum beside
a lake. *Cf.* No. 329.

587

SELECT PAPYRI

³τοὺς ἀλιεῖς Ὀξυρύγχ(ων) καὶ ὁ θεὸς ⁷ἐβοήθησεν
καὶ οὐ κέγονεν ⁸σφάλμα. οἱ οὖν ἀπὸ Ὀξυρύγχων
⁹ἠθέλησαν ἀπέρειν καὶ πολεμῆσαι ¹⁰μετὰ τῶν ἀπὸ
Κερκήσις. ¹¹ἐγὼ οὖν οὐκ ἔασα αὐτοὺς πολεμῆσαι.
¹²θεὸς οἶδεν ὁ μόνος, ἢν οὐκ εὐκέ-¹³ρημε εἰς Ὀξυρύγχων, κακὸν εἶχι ¹⁴γενέσθαι. ἰδοὺ γεγράφηκα
τῇ ¹⁵ἐξουσίᾳ σου ἵνα δώσῃς αὐτῶν ¹⁶ὦρον. καὶ σὺν
θεῷ ἔρχομε ¹⁷μετὰ τὴν αὔριον φέρον τὸ ¹⁸χρυσικόν.
¹⁹+δέσποτά μου κύριε.

Verso : ²⁰Τῷ κυρίῳ καὶ δεσπότῃ τῷ μεγαλο-
πρ(επεστάτῳ) κ(αὶ) ἐναρ(ετωτάτῳ) κό[μετ]ι ²¹[παρὰ]
Ἀνουθίῳ ἀρχιυπηρέ[του].

7. l. γέγονεν.   9. l. ἀπαίρειν.   11. l. ἐγώ.   12-13. l.
εὐκαίρημαι.   13. l. εἶχε.   16. l. ὅρον, ἔρχομαι.   17. l.
φέρων.   21. l. Ἀνουθίου.

430. LETTER TO A BYZANTINE DIOECETES

P. Oxy. 1835.   Late 5th or early 6th cent. A.D.

¹+Καθὼς παρεκαλέσαμεν τὴν ὑμετέραν δεσποτίαν
ἵνα, ἄχρη γράφ[ωμεν τῇ ὑ]μετέρᾳ ²μεγαλοπρεπίᾳ,
μὴ ἀπολῆσαι τὰς γενέκας τὸν προτοκομιτὸ[ν,
παρακαλ]ῶμεν ³τὸν ἡμῶν δεσπότην ἀπολῆσαι τὴν
γενέκαν Μηνᾶ τοῦ μίσονος [καὶ τὴν γενέ]καν
⁴Διονησίου τοῦ κωμογραμματέου καὶ τὴν τοῦ
Ἐνὼχ τοῦ μίσονος καὶ τὴν γενέκαν ⁵Πκολίου τοῦ
μεγάλου ἀγροφύλακος καὶ τὴν γενέκαν Φοιβάμ-
μων<ος> τοῦ κωμάρχου καὶ τὴν ⁶τοῦ Π[αμου]θίου
τοῦ ἑτέρου αὐτοῦ κωμάρχου καὶ τὴν τοῦ Ἐνὼχ
τοῦ κωμάρχου, γίνονται ⁷εἰ γενέκες αὐτὸν ἑπτά.

588

fishermen of Oxyrhyncha, and God came to the rescue and there was no mishap. The people of Oxyrhyncha therefore desired to go out and fight with those of Kerkesis. I, however, did not allow them to fight. God only knows, if I had not chanced to come to Oxyrhyncha, something evil might have happened. Behold, I have written to your excellency in order that you may restrain them. And, God permitting, I will come the day after to-morrow bringing the gold-tax. My lord master. (Addressed) To his lord and master the most magnificent and most virtuous count from Anouthius, chief assistant.

430. LETTER TO A BYZANTINE DIOECETES

Late 5th or early 6th cent. A.D.

As we urged your lordship not to release the wives [a] of the village headmen until we wrote to your magnificence, we accordingly urge our master to release the wife of Menas the headman, the wife of Dionysius the village scribe, the wife of Enoch the headman, the wife of Pkolius the chief guard of the fields, the wife of Phoebammon the comarch, the wife of Pamouthius the other comarch, and the wife of Enoch the comarch, making seven of their wives. We urge our

[a] Apparently they had been arrested in lieu of their husbands.

---

1. *l.* ἄχρι.   2. *l.* ἀπολύσῃ τὰς γυναῖκας τῶν πρωτοκω-
μητῶν and παρακαλοῦμεν : so in 7.   3. *l.* ἀπολῦσαι, γυναῖκα,
μείζονος : so in 4 and 5.   4. *l.* Διονυσίου τοῦ κωμογραμματέως.   6. *l.* γίνονται.   7. *l.* αἱ γυναῖκες αὐτῶν.

παρακαλῶμεν τὸν ἡμῶν δεσπότην ταύτας ἀπολυθῆναι καὶ πρὸς ⁸ὑμᾶς αὐτούς, ὅδαν κελεύεις, τὰ
αὐτὰ πρόσωπα ἀποφέρωμεν αὐτοὺς εἰς φυλακήν.
⁹ταῦτα γράφωμεν, προσκυνῶμεν τὰ ὑήχνη τοῦ ἡμῶν
δεσπότου.+

Verso : ¹⁰+ ἰδίῳ [ἡμῶν? εὐφη]μοτάτῳ προστάτ(η)
Μαιαιμάκις σὺν θ(εῷ) διοικ(ητῇ) + Φοιβάμμων (καὶ)
Φίλιππο[ς].

8. *l.* ὅταν κελεύῃς, ἀποφέρομεν.   9. *l.* γράφομεν, προσ-
κυνοῦμεν τὰ ἴχνη.   10. *l.* Μαιαιμάκει?

431. FROM A DIGNITARY IN CONSTANTINOPLE

J.E.A. xv. p. 96.   Middle of 6th cent. A.D.

¹[+ Διόσ]κ[ορο]ς ὁ θαυμάσιος ὁ τήνδε μου τὴν
ἐπιστολὴν ἀποδιδοὺς ²[τῇ ὑμ]ετέρᾳ ἐνδόξῳ ὑπεροχῇ
ὥρμηται μὲν ἐκ τῆς Θηβαίων χώρας, ³[ἀδ]ι[κ]ηθεὶς
δὲ ὡς φησιν παρά τινων αὐτόθι τὴν ἐντεῦθεν βλάβην
⁴ἀ[να]φέρων εἰς τὴν βασιλίδα ταύτην παρεγένετο
πόλιν ἱκέτης τε ⁵γενόμενος τοῦ εὐσεβ(εστάτου)
δεσπότου θείων ἔτυχεν συλλαβῶν πρὸς τὴν ⁶ὑμε-
τέραν φιλανθρωπείαν. μίαν ταύτην αὐτῷ βοήθειαν
ἀσφαλῆ ⁷καλῶς ὑπολαβὼν τὴν ἐκ τῆς ὑμετέρας
δικαιοσύνης ἐπικουρίαν ⁸ταύτης δεῖται τυχεῖν παρ᾽
ὑμῶν καὶ τὴν ἐπιστολὴν ὑπὲρ τούτων ⁹ᾔτησεν πρὸς
ὑμᾶς. οἶδα δὲ ὅτι καὶ τῆς ἐμῆς αἰτήσεως χωρὶς
¹⁰αὐτῷ τε καὶ τοῖς ἄλλοις ἅπασιν τὰ δίκαια δίδωσιν
ἡ ὑμετέρα ¹¹ὑπεροχή. παρακαλῶ δὲ καὶ σπουδήν
τινα πλείω προστεθῆναι Διοσκόρῳ ¹²τῷ θαυμασίῳ

master to let these be released, and whenever you
order we will bring the said persons to you to be
put in prison. We write this kissing the feet of our
master. (Addressed) To our most honoured protector Maiaimakis, by the grace of God dioecetes,[a]
from Phoebammon and Philip.

[a] A local official, quite distinct from the dioecetes of earlier
times.

431. FROM A DIGNITARY IN
CONSTANTINOPLE

Middle of 6th cent. A.D.

The admirable Dioscorus [a] who delivers this letter
of mine to your renowned eminence is a native of
the Thebaid. Being wronged, as he says, by certain
persons there he came to this royal city with a report
of the damage thereby caused, and having made
supplication to our most pious master he obtained a
divine letter addressed to your humanity. Rightly
conceiving that his only sure help lies in the support
of your justice he seeks to obtain this from you and
he has asked for this letter to you about his case.
I know that without any request from me your
eminence deals justice both to him and to all others.
But I beg you to see that some more than usual
attention be bestowed upon the admirable Dioscorus,

[a] See No. 218, note a, p. 101. The recipient of the letter
was probably the *Dux et Augustalis* of the Thebaid and the
writer a high official in Constantinople.

591

ὥστε κἀμὲ χρήσιμον αὐτῷ φανῆναι καὶ ὑμᾶς
πολλῷ ¹³πλείονα τὸν ἀπὸ τοῦ δεσπότου θεοῦ μισθὸν
ἀπολαβεῖν. +

432. LETTER FROM THE ARAB GOVERNOR
OF EGYPT

P. Lond. 1346.   A.D. 710.

¹'Αφροδιτώ. ²[(πε)ρ(ὶ) εἰ]δ(ῶν) (καὶ) δαπ(ανῶν)
τοῦ Κλ(ύσματος) ἰ(νδικτίονος) η. Opposite, another
minute in Arabic. ³'Ε[ν ὀνόμα]τι το[ῦ] θεο[ῦ]
Κορρᾶ [υἱ(ὸς)] Σ]ζερὶχ σύμβο[υ]λ[ος] ⁴Βα[σ]ιλείῳ
διοικητῇ κώ[μ]ης 'Αφροδιτώ. ἦμεν ⁵διαστείλαντες
διὰ τῆς διοικήσεώς σου διάφορα εἴδη ⁶λόγῳ φιλο-
καλείας καὶ ἐξαρτίας πλοίων τοῦ Κλύσμα(τος),
⁷ἔτι μὴν καὶ δαπάνην ναυτῶν πλοίων ὄντων ἐν τῷ
αὐτῷ ⁸Κλύσματι, ἀποστείλαντες πρὸς σὲ καὶ τὰ
τούτων ἐντάγια ⁹πρὸ ἡμερῶν πολλῶν, γράψαντες
ταῦτα διὰ συντομίας ¹⁰ἐκπέμψαι πρὸ τοῦ γένηται
ἀπόβασις τῶν ὑδάτων τοῦ Τραϊανοῦ, ¹¹καὶ μέχρι
τῆς δεῦρο οὐκ ἔπεμψας τί ποτε ἐκ τούτων ἄξιον
λόγου. ¹²δεχόμενος οὖν τὰ παρόντα γράμματα
εὐθέως καὶ κατ' αὐτὴν ¹³τὴν ὥραν πέμψον εἴ τί

ᵃ A town or large village, which was the capital of a
district administered by Basilius, the recipient of the letter.

ᵇ The modern Suez.

ᶜ The Arabic name of Aphrodito.

ᵈ After the Arab conquest (A.D. 639-641) Egypt was administered by a governor who was appointed by the caliph
and resided at Fustat, i.e. Old Cairo. As it was found
necessary to employ many Greek-speaking functionaries,

so that I may appear to have been of service to him and you again may receive a much increased reward from the Lord God.

432. LETTER FROM THE ARAB GOVERNOR OF EGYPT

A.D. 710.

(Superscription) Aphrodito.[a] About materials and provisions for Clysma,[b] 8th indiction. (In Arabic) To the lord of Ashkuh [c] to hasten the supplies for Clysma.

(Text of letter) In the name of God, Kurrah son of Sharik, governor,[d] to Basilius, administrator of the village of Aphrodito. We have requisitioned from your district various materials for the upkeep and equipment of the ships of Clysma, and also provisions for the sailors of the ships at the said Clysma, and we sent you the orders for these many days ago, writing to you to dispatch them promptly before the water subsides in the canal of Trajan,[e] and up till now you have sent nothing of these worth mentioning. On receiving the present letter, therefore, send immediately and on the very instant whatever of these things

such as Basilius, Greek was for a long time retained as an official language alongside of Arabic. The letters reprinted here may be presumed to be Greek adaptations of Arabic originals.

  [e] The canal connecting the Nile with the Red Sea at Suez. It had been restored by Trajan and thereafter bore his name, though at the time of the Arab conquest it was silted up and had to be recut by Amr, the first governor.

ἐστι διὰ τῆς διοικήσεώς σου ¹⁴ἐξ αὐτῶν, μὴ
ὑστερῶν τι τὸ σύνολον μήτε μὴν δεόμενος ¹⁵ἑτέρων
ἡμῶν γραμμάτων περὶ τούτου, ἐὰν μέντοι συνίεις
¹⁶καὶ ἔχεις φρένας. ἔσῃ γὰρ ἐπιστάμενος ὡς, ‹ἐὰν›
ὑστερήσῃ(ς) ¹⁷τὸ ὁτιοῦν ἔκ τε τῶν αὐτῶν εἰδῶν
καὶ δαπανῶν καὶ ¹⁸γένηται ἀπόβασις τῶν ὑδάτων,
μέλλεις ταῦτα διὰ στράτας ¹⁹βαστάξαι ἕως τοῦ
αὐτοῦ Κλύσματος παρέχων τὸ φόρετρον ²⁰αὐτῶν
ἐξ ἰδικῆς σου ὑποστάσεως. ἐγρ(άφη) μη(νὸς)
Τῦ(βι) η ἰ(ν)δ(ικτίονος) η. Below, a round seal
showing a wolf (?) and a star.

Verso : ²¹Κ[ο]ρρ[ᾶ] υἱ(ὸς) Σζερὶχ σύμβουλ(ος)
Βασιλείῳ διοικ(ητῇ) κώμ(ης) Ἀφ[ροδ(ιτώ)].
(Docketed) ²²μ(ηνὸς) Μ(ε)χ(εὶρ) ιε ἰ(ν)δ(ικτίονος) η.
ἠνήχ(θη) δ(ιὰ) Σαεὶδ (πε)ρ(ὶ) ἐκπέμψαι τ(ὰς) δια-
ν(ομὰς) τοῦ Κλύ(σματος).

433. LETTER FROM THE ARAB GOVERNOR OF EGYPT

P. Lond. 1350.   A.D. 710.

At the head of the letter is an Arabic minute, as
in No. 432 ; the Greek minute is lost.

¹[Ἐν ὀνόματι τοῦ θεοῦ Κορρᾶ υἱὸς Σζερὶχ σύμ-
βουλος] ²Βασιλείῳ διοικητῇ κώμης Ἀφροδιτ[ώ.
εὐχαριστοῦμεν] ³τῷ θεῷ· καὶ μετὰ ταῦτα οὐκ
ἔγνωμεν τὴν ποσότητα τῶν ἐπαναλυσάντ[ων] ⁴ναυ-
τῶν ἐν τῇ διοικήσει σου ἐκ τῶν ἐξελθόντων εἰς
τὸ κοῦρ[σον] ⁵Ἀφρικῆς μετὰ Ἀτὰ υἱοῦ Ῥαφέ,
ὧνπερ ἀπέστειλεν Μουσῆ ⁶υἱὸς Νοσαείρ, καὶ τῶν
594

is wanted from your district, without the least deficiency and without requiring another letter from us about this matter, if indeed you are sensible and in possession of your wits. For you will learn that if you fail to send any of the said materials and provisions and the water has subsided, you will have to carry them by road as far as the said Clysma, paying the expense of porterage out of your private substance. Written on Tubi 8, 8th indiction. (Addressed) Kurrah son of Sharik, governor, to Basilius, administrator of the village of Aphrodito. (Docketed) Mecheir 15, 8th indiction. Brought by Said. Concerning the dispatch of the requirements for Clysma.

433. LETTER FROM THE ARAB GOVERNOR OF EGYPT

A.D. 710.

(Arabic superscription) To the lord of Ashkuh, as to that which has happened regarding the sailors of Africa.

(The Greek letter) In the name of God, Kurrah son of Sharik, governor, to Basilius, administrator of the village of Aphrodito. We give thanks to God, and to proceed, we have not learned the number of the sailors who returned to your district out of those who departed to the expedition in Africa *a* with Ata son of Rafi, namely those whom Musa son of Nusair

---

a A naval expedition against Sicily in A.D. 703–704. After plundering the island the fleet was wrecked on the African coast, and the survivors were sent back to Egypt by the local governor, Musa ibn Nusair.

ἀπομεινάντων ἐν αὐτῇ 'Αφρικῇ. ⁷λοιπὸν δεχόμενος τὰ παρόντα γράμματα γράψον πρὸς ἡμᾶς
⁸τὴν ποσότητα τῶν καταλαβό<ν>των ἐν τῇ διοικήσει σο[υ] ⁹ὡς εἴρηται ναυτῶν, καταμανθάν{ι}ων
ἐξ αὐτῶν καὶ ἐρωτῶν ¹⁰χάριν τῶν ἀπομεινάντων
ἐν τῇ αὐτῇ 'Αφρικῇ καὶ δι' ἣν αἰτίαν ¹¹ἐναπέμειναν
ἐκεῖσε, ὡσαύτως καὶ τὴν ποσότητα ¹²τῶν τελευτη-
σάντων ἐν αὐτῇ ὡς λέλεκται καὶ κατὰ στράταν
¹³μετὰ τὸ ἀπολυθῆναι αὐτούς, καὶ ἁπλῶς εἰπεῖν
ἅπασαν φανέρωσιν ¹⁴καὶ εἴδησιν αὐτῶν ἀπαρα-
λείπτως ποιῶν ἀπόστειλον ¹⁵πρὸς ἡμᾶς διὰ πάσης
συντομίας μετὰ τὴν ἀνάγνωσιν ¹⁶τῶν παρόντων
γραμμάτων. ἐγρ(άφη) μη(νὸς) Μ(ε)χ(εὶ)ρ δ ἰνδ(ι-
κτίονος) η.

Verso : [μ(ηνὸς) Μ(ε)χ(εὶρ) ιε ἰ(ν)δ(ικτίονος) η.
ἠνήχ(θη) δ(ιὰ) Σαεὶ]δ (πε)ρ(ὶ) καταγρ(άψαι) αὐτ(ῷ)
ναύ(τας) πεμφθ(έντας) μ(ε)τ(ὰ) 'Ατᾶ υἱ(οῦ) 'Ραφὲ
- - -

434. LETTER FROM THE ARAB GOVERNOR OF EGYPT

P. Lond. 1380.   A.D. 710.

¹['Εν ὀνόματι τοῦ θεοῦ Κορρᾶ β(ὲν) Σζερὶχ σύμ-
βουλος Βασιλείῳ διοικη(τῇ)] ²κώμης 'Αφροδιτ[ώ.
εὐχαρισ]τ[οῦμεν] τ[ῷ θεῷ· καὶ με]τ[ὰ] τ[αῦ]τ[α]
³πολλάκις φ[α]ινόμεθα γράμμασιν ἡμῶν χρησάμενοι
[π]ρ[ὸς σὲ] ⁴περὶ τοῦ διμοιρομέρους τῶν χρυσικῶν
δημοσίων τῆς διοική(σεώς) σο[υ], ⁵καὶ ἐδοκοῦμεν
ὡς ἤδη τοῦτο κατεβάλου. ἡμῶν οὖν ⁶ἐπιτρε-

sent back, and of those who remained there in Africa. Now on receiving the present letter write to us the number of the sailors who have arrived in your district as said, inquiring of them and questioning them concerning those who remained in the said Africa and for what reason they remained there, and likewise the number of those who died in the land as aforesaid and on the journey after they were disbanded, and to speak shortly procure for us without wasting time full enlightenment and information about them and send it to us with all dispatch after reading the present letter. Written on Mecheir 4 of the 8th indiction. (Endorsed) Mecheir 15, 8th indiction. Brought by Said. About making for him a list of the sailors sent with Ata son of Rafi . . .

434. LETTER FROM THE ARAB GOVERNOR OF EGYPT

A.D. 710.

In the name of God, Kurrah ibn Sharik, governor, to Basilius, administrator of the village of Aphrodito. We give thanks to God, and to proceed, we have manifestly written to you many times about the two-thirds part of the gold taxes in your district, and we supposed that you had already paid this. Now when

597

ψάντων τοῖς νοταρίοις ἐγκύψαι εἰς τὰ χαρτία τῆς
σακέλλη[s] ᵗἐφ᾽ ᾧ μαθεῖν τὸ τί κατεβάλου ἐν τῇ
σακέλλῃ, ηὕραμεν τὸ ἔργον σο[υ] ⁸ἀνίκανον καὶ
μηδαμινὸν καὶ σὲ εἰς τοῦτο κακῶς διαπραττόμενον.
⁹καὶ γὰρ οὐκ ἀπεστείλαμέν σε σχολάσαι εἰς τὸ
φαγονῖν, μᾶλλον δὲ ¹⁰ἀπεστείλαμέν σε φοβῖσθαι
τὸν θεὸν καὶ φυλάξαι τὴν πίστιν σου ¹¹καὶ ἀνύσαι
τὸ δίκαιον τοῦ Ἀμιραλμουμνίν. οὔτε γὰρ ἔχεις
ἀφορμὴν ¹²τὴν οἱανοῦν οὔτε οἱ τῆς διοικήσεώς σου·
καλῶς γὰρ ¹³γέγονεν ὁ καρπὸς τῆς γῆς καὶ τοῦτο
ὁ θεὸς εὐλόγησεν καὶ ἐδίπλασεν ¹⁴ὑπὲρ ὃ ἦν πρὸ
τούτου, γέγονεν δὲ καὶ ὁ σῖτος πολ<λ>οῦ καὶ
τοῦτο ¹⁵ἐπράθη παρὰ τῶν τῆς χώρας. λοιπὸν ὡς
εἴρηται οὐκ ἔχεις ¹⁶τὴν οἱανοῦν ἀφορμήν. βλέπε
οὖν τὸ λοιπασθὲν ¹⁷διὰ τῆς διοικήσεώς σου ἐκ τοῦ
διμοιρομέρους τῶν χρυ(σικῶν) ¹⁸δημοσίων αὐτῆς,
μετὰ πάσης συντομίας τοῦτο ἄνυσον ¹⁹μὴ ὑστερῶν
ἐξ αὐτοῦ μυλιαρίσιν καὶ μόνον. γινώσκει γὰρ ²⁰ὁ
θεὸς ὡς οὐκ ἤρεσεν ἡμῖν τὸ πῶς πεποίηκας ²¹εἰς
τὸ πρᾶγμα τῶν τοιούτων δημοσίων· ἐβουλόμεθα
γὰρ δοῦναί σοι ²²ἀνταπόδοσιν τούτου χάριν. ἐὰν
οὖν ἐστι ἐν σοὶ ἀγαθόν, ²³ὡς εἴρηται ἄνυσον μετὰ
πάσης σπουδῆς τὸ λοιπασθὲν ²⁴διὰ τῆς διοικήσεώς
σου ἐκ τοῦ τοιούτου διμοιρομέρου[s] ²⁵τῶν χρυσικῶν
δημοσίων καὶ ἀπόστειλον. ὄφελος γάρ ἐστι ²⁶τοῖς
τῆς χώρας δοῦναι κατὰ πρόσβασιν τὰ δι᾽ αὐτῶν
²⁷καὶ μὴ ἐᾶσαι αὐτοὺς ἄχρις οὗ συναχθῶσιν ἐπάνω
αὐτῶν ²⁸καὶ στενωθῶσιν πληρῶσαι. ἐπιστάμεθα δὲ
ὡς ἀνικανίᾳ καὶ ²⁹ἀχρησιμίᾳ φερόμενος ὁ ὑπουργὸς
ζητεῖ τὰ πρὸς ἀφορμ[ὴν] ³⁰τοῦ ὑστερέσαι τὰ δι᾽
αὐτοῦ. μὴ γένῃ οὖν τοιοῦτος καὶ δώσῃ[s] ³¹κατὰ

19. *l.* μιλιαρίσιον.   30. For ὑστερῆσαι.

we ordered the secretaries to look into the books of
the treasury to learn what you had paid into it, we
found that your performance is inadequate and of
no account and that in this matter you are behaving
badly. For we did not send you to pass your time in
gormandizing, but we sent you rather to fear God
and keep faith and fulfil the claims of the Amir al
Muminin.[a] And neither you nor those in your district
have an excuse of any kind. For the produce of the
fields has been abundant, and God has blessed it and
increased it twofold more than it was before, and the
wheat has fetched a good price and it has been sold
by the inhabitants. Now, as has been said, you
have no excuse of any kind. Look therefore to the
arrears of the two-thirds part of the gold taxes in
your district and complete them with all expedition,
not omitting a single farthing. For God knows that
the way you have acted in the matter of these same
taxes did not please us ; indeed we had a mind to
repay you for this. If therefore there is any good in
you, complete with all haste, as we have said, your
district's arrears of this same two-thirds part of the
gold taxes and dispatch them. For it is to the interest
of the inhabitants to deliver their dues promptly and
not to be left in peace until they are saddled with an
accumulation of claims and are hard put to it to pay.
We know that the official whose conduct is inadequate
and unprofitable seeks excuses for the shortcomings
of his work. Do not therefore act in that way and

---

[a] The commander of the faithful, the caliph.

τῆς ψυχῆς σου πρόφασιν. ἰδοὺ μαρτυρόμεθά σ[ε].
³²ἐγρά(φη) μ(ηνὸς) Π(α)ῦ(νι) ζ ἰ(ν)δ(ικτίονος) θ.

Verso : [+ μ(ηνὸς) . . . ἰ](ν)δ(ικτίονος) θ. ἠνήχ-
(θη) δ(ιὰ) Μουσλὴμ βερ(ε)δ(αρίου) π(ε)ρ(ὶ) ἐκπ(έμ-
ψαι) συμπ(λήρωσιν) διμοιρομέ(ρους) χρυ(σικῶν)
δημοσίων.

give us cause to threaten your life. Behold, we solemnly warn you. Written on Pauni 7 of the 9th indiction. (Docketed) + *a* . . ., 9th indiction. Brought by Muslim, courier. Concerning the dispatch of the complement of the two-thirds part of the gold taxes.

a The scribe of the Christian administrator prefixes the cross to his docket (restored in this case from other texts), but this was not likely to come under the eye of a Mohammedan official.

GLOSSARY OF TECHNICAL TERMS

ADELPHI, see Gods

Agoranomus, a government notary through whom publicly made contracts were usually drawn up

Ala, a body of auxiliary cavalry in the Roman army, recruited from provincials

Amphodarchy, see No. 320, note b

Anabolicum, see No. 384, note a

Annona, see p. 582, note b

Anouchi, see p. 413, note a

Apomoira, see p. 132, note a

Artaba, a measure of capacity, usually equal to about forty litres, but variable according to the standard employed. There were numerous standards, such as the "receiving," the "dispensing," the "half-artaba," the "cancellus"

Arura, an area of land, about 2025 square metres

Aurum coronarium, see p. 95, note a

BENEFICIARIUS, a soldier enjoying a privileged status by favour of his commander

Byssus, fine linen

CAESAREUM, temple of the Caesars, often used as a place of public business

Cancellus, see Artaba

Canephorus, "basket-bearer," title of the eponymous priestess of Arsinoe I

Canon, fixation of a tax, or the tax itself.

Carat, as money $= \frac{1}{24}$ of the normal solidus

Catholicus, the chief financial official in Byzantine Egypt, independent of the praefect

Catoecus, in the Ptolemaic period a soldier holding a grant of land ; in the Roman period an owner of land which had originally been granted to military settlers

Centuria, a military company of nominally 100 men

Centurion, an officer in the Roman army, often employed on police duties

Chalcus, eighth part of an obol

Choenix, a measure of capacity, about 1 litre

Chous, a liquid measure, about 3 litres

Chrematistae, in the Ptolemaic period a board of assize judges (see No. 264); in Roman times a tribunal in Alexandria

Cleruch, nearly the same as catoecus ; a holder of a grant of land, usually, but not necessarily, a soldier

Cleruchy, in the Ptolemaic period a settlement of cleruchs; in the Roman period merely a division of the land of a village

Cnecus, see p. 11, note d

Coemptio, see p. 48, note a

Cohort, a body of auxiliary troops in the Roman army, recruited from provincials

Comarch, a village official

Consistory, council of the Byzantine emperors

Coryphaeus, a certain kind of priest

Cosmetes, holder of one of the municipal offices which in the

602

GLOSSARY OF TECHNICAL TERMS

Roman period the richer men in Graeco - Egyptian towns were obliged to undertake at their personal expense. His special duty was to superintend the ephebi

Cotyla, a liquid measure, about ⅓ litre

Croton, see p. 11, note c

DECANUS, see p. 441, note a

Decemprimus, see No. 225, note a

Decurion, military officer commanding a small section. (May also mean a member of a local senate)

Defensor, a municipal magistrate in the Byzantine period, whose nominal duty was to protect the citizens against oppression

Deme, a subdivision of the tribes into which the citizens of the Greek cities in Egypt were divided

Denarius, a Roman coin, see p. xxxiii

Dies Augustus, anniversary of a birthday or other notable event in the life of the Imperial family

Diocese, see No. 228, note c

Dioecetes, under the Ptolemies the minister of finance; in the Roman period a financial administrator of more restricted scope, subordinate to the praefect; but the title is sometimes given also to minor officials in the provinces

Drachma, a Greek coin, see p. xxxiii; also a small weight for weighing silver as in No. 278

Ducenarius, see p. 293, note a

Duplicarius, see No. 387, note a

EPARCHY, in Byzantine times a district, such as Middle or Upper Egypt, administered by a praeses

Ephebus, a youth of privileged status in a Greek or Graecized city, admission to the roll of ephebi being a proof of his right to local citizenship

Epigone : originally the term "of the Epigone" denoted a son of a foreign soldier, born in

Egypt ; but in later times "Persian of the Epigone" merely signified a certain legal status

Epigonus, a soldier's son enrolled in the Ptolemaic army in a special class

Epikrisis, see p. 342, note a

Epimeletes, superintendent, a title of various officials at various periods

Epistates, president ; in Ptolemaic documents usually the head of a village, or perhaps head of the village police

Epistrategia, sphere of administration of an epistrategus

Epistrategus, governor of a large district, Lower, Middle, or Upper Egypt, but not a military commander

Euergetae, see Gods

Eutheniarch, municipal magistrate (see Cosmetes), responsible for the food supply

Exactor, superintendent of the collection of taxes

Exedra, a reception-hall or lounge

Exegetes, municipal magistrate (see Cosmetes) exercising various functions and regulating questions of civil status

Exsecutor, an official who served a summons and saw to the prosecution of a lawsuit

GODS : Adelphi, Euergetae, Philometores, Soteres, titles of the deified Ptolemy II. and Arsinoe I., Ptolemy III. and Berenice II., Ptolemy VII. and Cleopatra II., and Ptolemy I. and Berenice I. respectively

Gymnasiarch, municipal magistrate (see Cosmetes) having for special charge the gymnasium

HERMAEUM, temple of Hermes

Hipparchy, a regiment of cavalry in the Ptolemaic army

Hypomnematographus, "memorandum - writer," under the Ptolemies one of the royal secretaries, in Roman times usually

GLOSSARY OF TECHNICAL TERMS

an Alexandrian magistrate who assisted the praefect in his judicial functions

IDIOLOGUS, see p. 43, note *b*

Indiction, see p. xxxii

Irenarch, an official responsible for public security in his district

Iseum, temple of Isis

JURIDICUS (=dicaeodotes), an important judge who acted as assessor to the praefect and had either delegated or independent jurisdiction

Jus liberorum, see No. 305, note *a*

LAMPADARCH, see p. 252, note *a*

Laographus, one of the officials who kept the register of persons liable to poll-tax

Libellus, a petition

Liberated land, see p. 61, note *b*

Liturgy, a compulsory public service

Logistes, in Byzantine times a magistrate having financial and administrative authority over a metropolis and the nome which formed its territory

METRETES, a liquid measure, containing usually, but not invariably, 6 choes or about 18 litres. (In No. 203 a metretes of oil contains 12 choes)

Metropolis, capital of a nome

Mina, as a sum of money = 100 drachmae; as a weight about an English pound, but variable according to the standard employed

Modius, a Roman measure of capacity, about ⅔ of an artaba

NEOCORUS, see p. 83, note *d*

Nomarch, an official exercising various functions in a special district

Nomarchy, sphere of a nomarch

Nome, an Egyptian district with local administration

Nomophylax, a village official and kind of policeman

Numerus, in Byzantine documents a military force quartered in one of the large towns

OBOL, see p. xxxiii

Octadrachm, a coin of 8 drachmae (see No. 409, note *d*)

Oeconomus, steward; in Ptolemaic documents a financial administrator of a nome or smaller district; in No. 425 steward of the emperor

Officium, bureau and staff of a *praeses* or other high Byzantine official

Olyra, a grain, probably spelt

PAGARCH, in later Byzantine times the administrator of a district, usually a local landowner, appointed by the emperor

Pagarchy, sphere of a pagarch. See also No. 240, note *c*

Pagus, see No. 295, note *b*

Palaestra, school of wrestling and other exercises

Pancratiast, see No. 306, note *a*

Pastophorus, "shrine-bearer," a temple attendant

Patrician, a title given by Byzantine emperors to distinguished members of the court

Pentadrachm, a coin of 5 drachmae (see No. 409, note *d*)

Philometores, see Gods

Pontifex Maximus, chief priest of Rome

Praefect, governor of Egypt; also a military commander

Praefect of the praetorium, originally commander of the emperor's bodyguard, but in Byzantine times a great magistrate in Constantinople

Praefectus alae, commander of an ala

Praepositus pagi, administrator of a pagus, nominated by the local senate

Praeses, in Byzantine times civil governor of one of the main districts of Egypt

Praetorium, see Praefect

Princeps, see No. 251, note *a*

GLOSSARY OF TECHNICAL TERMS

Procurator, superintendent of some branch of administration

Prophet, priest of a certain rank, nominally an interpreter of oracles and revelations

Prytanis, prytany, in later documents, president, presidentship, of a senate

QUARTER, a weight used in weighing gold, ¼ of a gold stater or about 1¾ grammes

RIPARIUS, see No. 228, note *b*

Royal scribe, an official co-operating at first with the oeconomus and after the 3rd cent. B.C. with the strategus. The name as well as the office survived after the fall of the Ptolemaic kingdom

SCHOENION, a measure of length, about 50 yards

Scribes (or secretaries), village, district, etc., functionaries whose duties were mainly clerical, but who in many cases exercised some administrative authority

Sebasteum, temple of the deified emperors

Senate, for Egyptian senates see No. 226, note *b*

Serapeum, temple of the god Serapis

Sestertius, a Roman coin, worth ¼ of a denarius

Sextarius, as a liquid measure about half a litre

Singularis, an orderly attached to a military commander or to a civil governor

Sitologus, official who received deliveries of corn and kept account of the amounts delivered and measured out

Solidus, a Byzantine gold coin weighing about 4½ grammes ; see p. xxxiii

Soteres, see Gods

Stater, in silver = 4 drachmae, in gold = 2 drachmae ; also a weight

Stemmata, see p. 291, note *a*

Stolistes, temple attendant who clothed the sacred images

Strategus, properly a military commander, but in Egypt the civil governor of a nome or other district

Sword-bearer, an armed attendant

TACTOMISTHUS, see p. 453, note *a*

Talent = 6000 drachmae; as a weight originally = 60 minae, but actually there were talents of different standards

Tesserarius, see No. 345, note *a*

Tetradrachm, a coin of 4 drachmae

Toparch, an official performing various duties in a small district, subordinate to the nomarch

Toparchy, sphere of a toparch

Tribe, a division of citizens in a Greek city ; also a territorial division in a Graeco-Egyptian metropolis (see p. 286, note *b*)

Tribune, military commander

Tribunician Power, a Roman magistracy originally instituted for the protection of the commoners and conferred upon the emperor Augustus and his successors

Trierarch, see p. 552, note *c*

INDEX OF SOURCES

INDEX OF SOURCES

INDEX OF SOURCES